Handbook of Research on Behavioral Finance and Investment Strategies:

Decision Making in the Financial Industry

Zeynep Copur
Hacettepe University, Turkey

A volume in the Advances in Finance, Accounting, and Economics (AFAE) Book Series

BUSINESS SCIENCE Reference
An Imprint of IGI Global

Managing Director:	Lindsay Johnston
Managing Editor:	Austin DeMarco
Director of Intellectual Property & Contracts:	Jan Travers
Acquisitions Editor:	Kayla Wolfe
Production Editor:	Christina Henning
Development Editor:	Erin O'Dea
Typesetter:	Tucker Knerr
Cover Design:	Jason Mull

Published in the United States of America by
Business Science Reference (an imprint of IGI Global)
701 E. Chocolate Avenue
Hershey PA, USA 17033
Tel: 717-533-8845
Fax: 717-533-8661
E-mail: cust@igi-global.com
Web site: http://www.igi-global.com

Library of Congress Cataloging-in-Publication Data

Handbook of research on behavioral finance and investment strategies : decision making in the financial industry / Zeynep Copur, editor.
pages cm
Includes bibliographical references and index.
Summary: "This book presents an interdisciplinary, comparative, and competitive analysis of the thought processes and planning necessary for individual and corporate economic management"-- Provided by publisher.
ISBN 978-1-4666-7484-4 (hardcover : alk. paper) -- ISBN 978-1-4666-7485-1 (ebook) 1. Investments--Psychological aspects. 2. Investments--Decision making. I. Copur, Zeynep, 1968-

HG4515.15.H36 2015
332.01'9--dc23

2014045040

This book is published in the IGI Global book series Advances in Finance, Accounting, and Economics (AFAE) (ISSN: 2327-5677; eISSN: 2327-5685)

British Cataloguing in Publication Data
A Cataloguing in Publication record for this book is available from the British Library.

Advances in Finance, Accounting, and Economics (AFAE) Book Series

Ahmed Driouchi
Al Akhawayn University, Morocco

ISSN: 2327-5677
EISSN: 2327-5685

Mission

In our changing economic and business environment, it is important to consider the financial changes occurring internationally as well as within individual organizations and business environments. Understanding these changes as well as the factors that influence them is crucial in preparing for our financial future and ensuring economic sustainability and growth.

The **Advances in Finance, Accounting, and Economics (AFAE)** book series aims to publish comprehensive and informative titles in all areas of economics and economic theory, finance, and accounting to assist in advancing the available knowledge and providing for further research development in these dynamic fields.

Coverage

- Risk Analysis and Management
- Economics of Natural and Environmental Resources
- Environmental and Social Accounting
- Borrowing and Lending
- Wages and Employment
- Economics of Risks, Uncertainty, Ambiguity, and Insurance
- E-Finance
- Comparative Accounting Systems
- Economic Theory
- Economic Policy

IGI Global is currently accepting manuscripts for publication within this series. To submit a proposal for a volume in this series, please contact our Acquisition Editors at Acquisitions@igi-global.com or visit: http://www.igi-global.com/publish/.

The Advances in Finance, Accounting, and Economics (AFAE) Book Series (ISSN 2327-5677) is published by IGI Global, 701 E. Chocolate Avenue, Hershey, PA 17033-1240, USA, www.igi-global.com. This series is composed of titles available for purchase individually; each title is edited to be contextually exclusive from any other title within the series. For pricing and ordering information please visit http://www.igi-global.com/book-series/advances-finance-accounting-economics/73685. Postmaster: Send all address changes to above address.

Titles in this Series

For a list of additional titles in this series, please visit: www.igi-global.com

Agricultural Management Strategies in a Changing Economy
Gabriel Popescu (Bucharest Academy of Economic Studies, Romania) and Andrei Jean-Vasile (Petroleum - Gas University of Ploiesti, Romania)
Business Science Reference • copyright 2015 • 439pp • H/C (ISBN: 9781466675216) • US $225.00 (our price)

Handbook of Research on In-Country Determinants and Implications of Foreign Land Acquisitions
Evans Osabuohien (Covenant University, Nigeria & German Development Institute, Germany)
Business Science Reference • copyright 2015 • 430pp • H/C (ISBN: 9781466674059) • US $265.00 (our price)

Handbook of Research on Strategic Developments and Regulatory Practice in Global Finance
Özlem Olgu (Koç University, Turkey) Hasan Dinçer (Beykent University, Turkey) and Ümit Hacıoğlu (Beykent University, Turkey)
Business Science Reference • copyright 2015 • 430pp • H/C (ISBN: 9781466672888) • US $235.00 (our price)

Regional Economic Integration and the Global Financial System
Engin Sorhun (Istanbul 29 Mayis University, Turkey) Ümit Hacıoğlu (Beykent University, Turkey) and Hasan Dinçer (Beykent University, Turkey)
Business Science Reference • copyright 2015 • 337pp • H/C (ISBN: 9781466673083) • US $200.00 (our price)

Urbanization and Migration as Factors Affecting Global Economic Development
Denis Ushakov (International College Suan Sunandha Rajabhat University, Thailand & Russian Academy of National Economy and Public Administration–South branch, Russia)
Information Science Reference • copyright 2015 • 317pp • H/C (ISBN: 9781466673281) • US $215.00 (our price)

Handbook of Research on Developing Sustainable Value in Economics, Finance, and Marketing
Ulas Akkucuk (Bogazici University, Turkey)
Business Science Reference • copyright 2015 • 550pp • H/C (ISBN: 9781466666351) • US $345.00 (our price)

Handbook of Research on Economic Growth and Technological Change in Latin America
Bryan Christiansen (PryMarke, LLC, USA)
Business Science Reference • copyright 2014 • 504pp • H/C (ISBN: 9781466662247) • US $295.00 (our price)

Impacts of the Knowledge Society on Economic and Social Growth in Africa
Lloyd G. Adu Amoah (Ashesi University, Ghana & Strategy3, Ghana)
Information Science Reference • copyright 2014 • 336pp • H/C (ISBN: 9781466658448) • US $195.00 (our price)

IGI GLOBAL
DISSEMINATOR OF KNOWLEDGE
www.igi-global.com

701 E. Chocolate Ave., Hershey, PA 17033
Order online at www.igi-global.com or call 717-533-8845 x100
To place a standing order for titles released in this series, contact: cust@igi-global.com
Mon-Fri 8:00 am - 5:00 pm (est) or fax 24 hours a day 717-533-8661

Editorial Advisory Board

List of Reviewers

List of Contributors

Table of Contents

Section 2
Psychological Concepts in Behavioral Finance

Section 3
Behavioral Approach to Financial Issues and Investment

Detailed Table of Contents

This chapter gives an overview of the stochastic models and methods used in financial risk management. Given the random nature of future events on financial markets, the field of stochastic processes obviously plays an important role in quantitative risk management. Random walk, Brownian motion and geometric Brownian motion processes in risk management are explained. Simulations of these processes are provided with some software codes.

Utilizing the lens of Heider's (1958) attribution theory and Grable and Joo's (2004) conceptual framework, this chapter studies the effect of situational and dispositional attributions on changes in financial risk tolerance. Situational factors are assessed through changes in household situation and changes in macroeconomic factors. For dispositional factors, changes upon sensation seeking attitudes are explored. The data employed in this research come from the 1993, 1994, and 2006 National Longitudinal Survey of Youth (N = 5,449). Results from structural equation modeling indicate that changes in internal attributions have a significant and positive effect (coefficient = 0.12, p <0.01) on the change in risk tolerance, as is true for changes in external attributions where a significant effect is seen (coefficient = 0.30, p <0.01). Thus, the findings from this study support the conceptual framework premised on Heider's attribution theory and Grable and Joo's (2004) conceptual model.

The purpose of this study is to identify the levels of financial literacy, money attitude, self-esteem, financial capability and financial well-being of young employees, to explore the differences in financial well-being based on demographic characteristics of young employees and to identify the determinants of financial well-being among young employees. The sample consists of 508 of young employees aged 40 and under in central zone of Malaysia, which selected through multi stage sampling technique. Data were collected through self-administered questionnaires. Financial literacy, domains in money attitude and financial capability had significant influence toward financial well-being whereby financial capability become a major contributing factor to the financial well-being. By understanding more about the determinants of financial well-being, it is hoped to help young employees to become financial prudence and in the long-run could decrease the number of young employees declared bankruptcy.

of coverage has resulted in high levels of out of pocket payments. The implementation of the reforms in financing, service delivery and regulation which are aimed to tackle the inefficiencies and inequalities in the health system has been challenged by the decentralized environment and the presence of private sector, often creating fragmentation and variation in the quality of health services across the country.

Health is described not only as the absence of disease and disability but also as physically, psychologically, and socially general well-being of people. Best practices of individuals and the society from the health services depend on taking the correct decisions on health policies. In addition, the thought that a country spending much on health services must have a perfect status of health should not be perceived as right. Effectiveness of the spending result in the efficient practices of these services. Although there have been many institutions carrying out the health services, it has been observed that the share separated for the health from the gross domestic product in Turkey increased until 2009 but decreased as of the mentioned year and it has been stated as low compared with the other countries. In this chapter the effectiveness of Turkey's health spending between 1999 and 2012 has been analysed from this view.

This chapter investigates the cointegration and causal relationship between financial development and energy consumption in the case of Turkey over the period 1960-2011. In doing so, the ARDL bounds testing and Johansen-Juselius approaches to cointegration and Granger causality test based on vectorerror correction model are employed. The empirical results show that the series are cointegrated. The empirical results also show a positive and statistically significant relationship between financial development and energy consumption in the long run. In addition, a unidirectional causality running from financial development to energy consumption is found in the short and long run. Thus, this chapter provides an empirical evidence that financial development is a determinant of energy consumption in Turkey. This chapter also presents some implications for Turkey's energy policy.

In this chapter, the authors investigate the relationship between investor sentiment and stock returns in an out of sample market, namely Borsa Istanbul. The authors use the Consumer Confidence Index as an investor sentiment proxy, while utilizing BIST Second National Index as a measure of small capitalized

Preface

The world of finance is mostly seen as a sideshow. Even so, finance serves important functions such as payment systems, the pooling and transferring of funds, saving and investing, contract design, organizational architecture, and risk management. Due to the rapid spread of more information, life for decision makers in the financial markets is becoming much more complicated. This is true for both investors and asset managers since it requires increasing use of experience and practical efforts to answer questions or improve performance in financial markets (De Bondt, Muradoglu, Shefrin & Staikouras, 2008).

Modern financial economic theory is based on the assumption that the "representative agent" in the economy is rational in two ways: The representative agent (1) makes decisions according to the axioms of expected utility theory and (2) makes unbiased forecasts about the future. An extreme version of this theory assumes that every agent behaves in accordance with these assumptions. Most economists recognize this extreme version as unrealistic; they concede that many of their relatives and acquaintances-spouses, students, deans, government leaders, and so on-are hope-less decision makers. Still, defenders of the traditional model argue that it is not a problem for some agents in the economy to make suboptimal decisions as long as the "marginal investor," that is, the investor who is making the specific investment decision at hand, is rational (Thaler, 1999).

Today, many people are engaged in behavioral finance, and there is wide disagreement about its boundaries and frontiers. Therefore, behavioral finance is one of the most dynamic, rapidly growing and promising fields of economic research by its scope and size (see, Stracca, 2004; Tirole, 2002; Wachter, 2002).

Definition of behavioral finance supposes two important aspects - individual investors and entire market. In other words behavioral finance in a broad sense is divided to macro behavioral finance and micro behavioral finance (Pompian, 2006). Macro behavioral finance discloses and describes anomalies of efficient market hypothesis that could be explained by models of people behavior. Micro behavioral finance analyses behavior and deviations of individual investors' and this separates them from strictly rational person, acting according to stern mathematical- statistic models (Jureviciene, Bikas, & Gausiene, 2012). As for the definition of behavioral finance in the early Eighteenth century, Adam Smith in *The Theory of Moral Sentiments* determined mental and emotional human interaction and communication basics. The author basing on such behavioral elements as pride, disgrace, insecurity, egoism tried to explain the actions of a man and the pursuit of profit (Smith, 1998). However, from the beginning of the Nineteenth century when economics was dominated by neoclassical theories, psychology was displaced from the factors which have an effect on discourse of economy until the mid of Twentieth century (Bikas, Jureviciene, Dubinskas, & Novickyte, 2012). Goldberg and Von Nitzsch (1999) defined behavioral finance as financial market theory oriented towards behavior; subject which is applied to facts that people behave rationally only within specific limits. Thaler (1999) stated that behavioral finance is an integration of classical economics and financial theories within studies investigating psychology and decision making. Fromlet (2001) explained behavioral finance via individuals' attitude and emotions in investment decision making process and market prices. Ritter (2003) stated that behavioral finance strives to supplement standard financial theories introducing psychological dimension into decision-making process (Bikas, Jureviciene, Dubinskas, &Novickyte, 2013). Stracca (2004) emphasize that the focus of behavioral finance is on a positive description of human behavior especially under risk and uncertainty, rather than on a normative analysis of behavior which is more typical of the mainstream approach. According to Shefrin (2001), behavior finance is the study of how psychology affects financial decision making process and financial markets. Since psychology explores human judgment, behavior and welfare, it can also provide important facts about how human actions differ from traditional economic assumptions. Weber (1990) makes the following observation: "Behavioral finance closely combines individual behavior and market phenomena and uses knowledge taken from both the psychological field and financial theory."

Behavioral finance is a young new field, with its formal beginnings in the 1980s. Now, behavioral finance is poised to replace neoclassical finance as a dominant paradigm of the discipline and it gets much attention for understanding the behavior of investing in public in the current capitalist world. It considers psychological and sociological factors as important input to financial analysis and decisions and gains increasing acceleration in academic research and practical application in the world. Behavioral finance is the study of how psychology impacts financial decisions in households, markets and organizations. The main question is: What do people do and how do they do it? Behavioral finance explains many reactions in financial markets which appear to be contrary to the conventional theory and it makes an important contribution to avoiding from serious mistakes in deciding good investment strategies. Despite some interesting approaches, behavioral finance can also make a contribution to improve assets performance however it can hardly pick single winners from the market (Fromlet 2001; De Bondt, Muradoglu, Shefrin & Staikouras, 2008).

The uniqueness of behavioral finance arises from its integration and foundation of many different schools of thought and fields. Scholars, theorists, and practitioners of behavioral finance have backgrounds from a wide range of disciplines. The foundation of behavioral finance is an area based on an interdisciplinary approach including scholars from the social sciences and business schools. From the liberal arts perspective, includes the fields of psychology, sociology, anthropology, economics and behavioral economics. On the business administration side covers areas such as management, marketing, finance, technology and accounting. This evolutionary process continues to occur because many scholars have such a diverse and wide range of academic and professional specialties. Behavioral finance is the result of the structure of various sciences (Ricciardi & Simon, 2000): Psychology- a science that analyses processes of behavior and mind, how processes are influenced by physical, psychical, and external environment of human being; finances- a system of formation, distribution and use of resources; sociology-systematic science about socio- behavior of human being or a group, emphasizing the influence of social relations on people's attitude and behavior (Bikas, Jureviciene, Dubinskas, & Novickyte, 2013).

Behavioral finance is the paradigm where financial markets are studied using models that are less narrow than those based on Von Neumann–Morgenstern expected utility theory and arbitrage assumptions. Specifically, behavioral finance has two building blocks: cognitive psychology and the limits to arbitrage. Cognitive refers to how people think (Ritter, 2003). Cognitive psychologists have documented many patterns regarding how people behave (Barberis & Thaler, 2003; Ritter, 2003). Some of these patterns are as follows.

Figure 1. The important interdisciplinary relationships that integrate behavioral finance (Ricciardi & Simon, 2000)

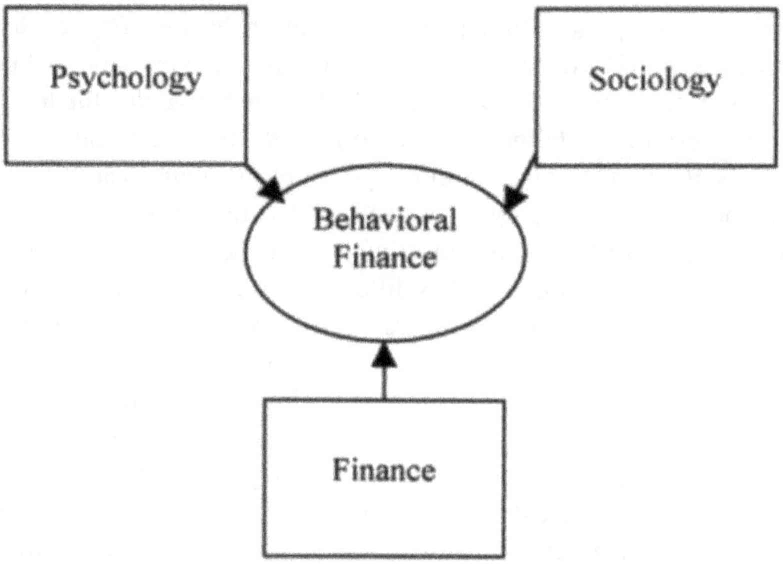

Heuristics, or rules of thumb, make decision making easier. However, they can sometimes lead to biases, especially when things change. These can lead to suboptimal investment decisions. When faced with N choices for how to invest retirement money, many people allocate using the 1/N rule. If there are three funds, one-third goes into each. If two are stock funds, two-thirds goes into equities. If one of the three is a stock fund, one-third goes into equities. Recently, Benartzi and Thaler (2001) have documented that many people follow the 1/N rule (Ritter, 2003).

Overconfidence implies that individuals overvalue their knowledge or abilities (De Bondt, Muradoglu, Shefrin & Staikouras, 2008). Mahajan (1992, p. 330) defines over confidence as "an overestimation of the probabilities for a set of events (Ricciardi & Simon, 2000). Entrepreneurs are especially likely to be overconfident. Overconfidence manifests itself in a number of ways. One example is too little diversification, because of a tendency to invest too much in what one is familiar with. Thus, people invest in local companies, even though this is bad from a diversification view point because their real estate (the house they own) is tied to the company's fortunes. People invest way too much in the stock of the company that they work for. Men tend to be more overconfident than women. This manifests itself in many ways, including trading behavior. Barber and Odean (2001) recently analyzed the trading activities of people with discount brokerage accounts. They found that the more people traded, the worse they did, on average. Additionally, men traded more, and did worse, than women investors (Ritter, 2003).

Mental accounting refers to how people categorize and evaluate financial outcomes (Henderson & Peterson, 1992). Shefrin and Thaler (1988) assume that people categorize wealth in three mental accounts: current income, current wealth, and future income. It is furthermore assumed that the propensity to consume is greatest from the current income account and smallest from the future-income account (De Bondt, Muradoglu, Shefrin & Staikouras, 2008). People sometimes separate decisions that should, in principle, be combined (Ritter, 2003).

Representativeness is overreliance on stereotypes. Investors who regard recent time-series trends as representative of an underlying process are vulnerable to extrapolation bias. The "law of small numbers" is a related bias whereby people behave as if the statistical properties of small samples must conform to the properties of large samples. Investor overreaction is partly rooted in representativeness. The "gambler's fallacy" is also connected to representativeness but leads investors to make unwarranted predictions of reversal (De Bondt, Muradoglu, Shefrin & Staikouras, 2008).

Conservatism; When things change, people tend to be slow to pick up on the changes. In other words, they anchor on the ways things have normally been. The conservatism bias is at war with the representativeness bias. When things change, people might under react because of the conservatism bias. However, if there is a long enough pattern, then they will adjust to it and possibly overreact, underweighting the long-term average (Ritter, 2003).

Disposition effect refers to the pattern that people avoid realizing paper losses and seek to realize paper gains. For example, if someone buys a stock at $30, which then drops to $22 before rising to $28, most people do not want to sell until the stock gets above $30.The disposition effect manifests itself in lots of small gains being realized, and few small losses. In fact, people act as if they are trying to maximize their taxes. The disposition effect shows up in aggregate stock trading volume. During a bull market, trading volume tends to grow. If the market then turns south, trading volume tends to fall. The fact that volume tends to fall in bear markets results in the commission business of brokerage firms having a high level of systematic risk (Ritter, 2003).

Anchoring is a form of bias where beliefs rely heavily on one piece of information, perhaps because it is was available first, and are not sufficiently adjusted afterward. For instance, investor forecasts may anchor on the price at which they bought a security. "Conservatism" is closely related. Investors may place excessive weight on past information relative to new information, i.e., they under react (De Bondt, Muradoglu, Shefrin & Staikouras, 2008).

Availability bias means that investors overweigh information that is easily accessible, e.g., that is easily recalled from memory or that corresponds to a future scenario that is easy to imagine. People are likely to remember events that receive a lot of attention by the media and this influences their behavior (De Bondt, Muradoglu, Shefrin & Staikouras, 2008).

Limits to arbitrage refers to predicting in what circumstances arbitrage forces will be effective, and when they will not be (Ritter, 2003). *Limited arbitrage* plays a crucial role in behavioral asset pricing. A basic tenet of modern finance is that arbitrageurs force prices to converge to their true fundamental values. Yet, research has uncovered a series of financial market phenomena that do not conform to the notion that full arbitrage is always carried out. For this reason, behavioral asset pricing models focus on the limits that arbitrageurs face in attempting to exploit mispricing. Markets are not frictionless because of transaction costs, taxes, margin payments, etc. Therefore, the actions of noise traders (i.e., traders with biased beliefs, not based on fundamental information) may cause prices to be inefficient. As a result, arbitrage can be risky (De Bondt, Muradoglu, Shefrin & Staikouras, 2008).

One of the major criticisms of behavioral finance is that by choosing which bias to emphasize, one can predict either under reaction or overreaction (Ritter, 2003). Additionally, Statman (2008) discussed the many cultural differences that may influence investor behavior and how these differences may influence there commendations of a financial advisor. The author found that people in low-income countries have high aspirations relative to their current income. But it is not that they like risk. Rather, they pay with risk for a chance to move up in life. People in collectivistic countries can afford to take more risk because their in-groups provide down side protection. The propensities for risk, regret, and maximization vary by country of origin. Cultures vary, and culture matters (Statman, 2008).

Over the last few decades, behavioral finance has become a household name in the finance industry and our understanding of finance has increased a great deal, yet there are countless questions begging for answers. On the whole, financial decision making processes in households, markets and organizations remain a grey area waiting for behavioral researchers to shed light on it. Behavioral finance is still a relatively young field which is developing and refining quickly and a lot of behavior needs to be explored further. For example, how do people construct their investment portfolios? Which heuristics do they use to choose between an overload of assets? When do assets draw their attention and what effect does this have on their chosen allocations? How can we help people in improving their allocations? Moreover, when do people become overly optimistic or pessimistic? What effect does this have on market prices? How does this aggregate into market sentiments? Furthermore, how do people respond to sudden increases of fear in markets? What does this do with their expectations and decisions, and how this affects market prices? Over and above, what determines people's personal benchmarks, or reference points? What determines the value they assign to money and consumption? What is the influence of priming? And, how does this aspect affect financial decisions and markets?

Behavioral finance is to be continued...(Baltussen, 2009).

ORGANIZATION OF THE BOOK

The book is organized into twenty six chapters. A brief description of each of the chapters follows:

Chapter 1 explores the evolution of modern behavioral finance theories from the traditional framework. It focuses on three main issues. First, it analyzes the importance of standard finance theories and the situations where they become insufficient i.e. market anomalies. Second, it signifies the role of behavioral finance in narrowing down the gaps between traditional finance theories and actual market conditions. In the end, it provides a synthesis of academic events that substantiate the presence of behavioral biases, their underlying psychology and their impact on financial markets.

Chapter 2 identifies poverty in Turkey. The authors argue that poverty in the light of behavioral finance and game theory. The authors of this chapter contend that each and every situation be approached like a game and claims that it shows the most sensible strategy in such games; in moves falling under the scope of finance, behavioral finance claims to prove that players do not always behave rationally.

Chapter 3 discusses consumer behaviors during periods of economic crises. The author argue that those countries going through tough times like economic crises can predict the change consumers experience so that they could take the necessary precautions brings them competitive advantage and helps them provide solutions accordingly. The author present the studies in Turkey into consumer behavior during periods of economic crises have shown that buying behavior of consumers change, that consumers resort to cheap good and services, and that they limit their spending on food the least.

Chapter 4 determines the relationship between planning retirement financially in middle-age period and some socio-economic variables. The authors planned as a quantitative research with 287 volunteer participants, who live in Nevşehir, Turkey, aged 40-59. They conclude that statistically no significant difference has been found between the responses of women and men about planning the retirement financially. However, it has been verified that men's financial plans for retirement were higher in rates than that of women.

Chapter 5 reviews financial education for child and youth. The author addresses although financial education consists of individuals of all ages, education of young people in the field of finance is more important. They present some applications for financial education.

Chapter 6 introduces the role of psychological factors in behavioral finance, thus explaining the theory of behavioral finance, the application of behavioral finance theory, the experimental work in behavioral finance, the utilization of psychological factors in behavioral finance in terms of beliefs (i.e., overconfidence, too much trading, optimism and wishful thinking, representativeness bias, conservatism bias, belief perseverance, anchoring, and availability bias) and preferences (i.e., prospect theory and ambiguity aversion).

Chapter 7 explores the relationships between financial distress and health. The authors suggest that financial educators and counselors should help financially distressed families so that families better deal with any financial problems or challenges. They present general model of the effect of financial stress on families.

Chapter 8 analyzes the economic, social, and cultural needs of elderly people to determine the poverty thereof in Ankara (the capital city of Turkey). The author reviews different types of vulnerabilities in terms of financial behavior in older age. She concludes that the income of elderly people was not sufficient, and that they could not sufficiently afford electrical power and water invoices, medicine, food, and clothing expenses.

Chapter 9 identifies the goal of investment decision making is to increase the net worth for the investor, through the effective management of money and credit through proper financial planning, savings and credit management. This chapter highlights ten such biases and throws light on how they impact investment behavior both positively and negatively. The author addresses future research directions.

Chapter 10 discusses social exclusion and poverty. The chapter identifies social exclusion, as result of individuals own conditions, and is the situation of being excluded from economic, social and cultural activities. The authors argue that this exclusion could be the consequence of poverty as well as the result of distinctions in age, gender, language, religion and lack of societal support. The authors of this chapter evaluate the 2020 objectives and achievements of the EU concerning social exclusion and poverty. They analyze Turkey's harmony with the EU objectives on social exclusion and poverty issues in the process of its accession to the EU membership.

Chapter 11gives an overview of the stochastic models and methods used in financial risk management. The author reviews the financial markets use stochastic models to represent the seemingly random behavior of assets such as stocks, commodities, relative currency prices such as the price of one currency compared to that of another, such as the price of US Dollar compared to that of the Euro, and interest rates. The author suggests that given the random nature of future events on financial markets, the field of stochastic processes obviously plays an important role in quantitative risk management.

Chapter 12 explores the research question of whether or not changes in circumstantial and internal variables can potentially affect the change in an individual's financial risk tolerance. The authors use the lens of Heider's (1958) attribution theory and Grable and Joo's (2004) conceptual framework that help in achieving this purpose. The chapter sets the background for research conducted by various authors.

Chapter 13 analyses the levels of financial literacy, money attitude, self-esteem, financial capability and financial well-being of young employees, the differences in financial well-being based on demographic characteristics of young employees and the determinants of financial well-being among young employees in Malaysia. The chapter highlights the importance of financial literacy as living skills for the young employees to educate them on how to develop and maintain healthy financial behavior and habits for financial well-being.

Chapter 14 examines the predictors of financial management behavior in family. The authors test the reliability and validity of the Turkish version of the Financial Management Behavior Scale–FMBS developed by Dew and Xiao (2011) to measure individual's saving, investment, expenditure and debt behavior in family. They conclude that demographic characteristics (monthly income of the family, education, employment status of the spouses), saving and investment decision, financial satisfaction and compared financial status was predicted of financial management behavior.

Chapter 15 analyses if even the simplest trading rules could take advantage of the market's inefficiency and lead to profitable trading decisions. For this reason, the author examine the profitability of the simplest trading rules, using only the simple moving averages (SMA) rules that even an amateur investor could apply. The author argue that even if we take into account the most expensive transaction fees the trading rules signal profitable investment decisions; therefore even an amateur trader and/or investor who does not have a significant amount of money to invest (which may lead to reduced transaction costs) could take advantage of the market's inefficiency.

Chapter 16 explores the Philippine health care delivery system and health expenditure. The authors address that the Philippines, compared to most Asian countries, produces more and better human resources for health. It has traditionally been a major source of health professionals to many countries because of their fluent English, skills and training, compassion, humaneness, and patience in caring. The authors contend that the Philippines are challenged by attracting and retaining staff in the under-served areas of the country. The government, as a whole, spent more on personal health care than the public health care each year from 2009 to 2011.

Chapter 17 discusses health care expenses of Turkey between 1990-2012. The authors argue that best practices of individuals and the society from the health services depend on taking the correct decisions on health policies. In addition, the thought that a country spending much on health services must have a perfect status of health should not be perceived as right. Although there have been many institutions carrying out the health services, it has been observed that the share separated for the health from the gross domestic product in Turkey increased until 2009 but decreased as of the mentioned year and it has been stated as low compared with the other countries. The authors present some statistics that help in achieving this purpose.

Chapter 18 investigates the cointegration and causal relation between financial development and energy consumption in the case of Turkey over the period 1960-2011. The authors conclude that a positive and statistically significant relationship between financial development and energy consumption in the long run. The authors provide empirical evidence that financial development is a determinant of energy consumption in Turkey. This chapter presents literature review and some implications for Turkey's energy policy.

Chapter 19 present two major approaches to asset pricing. The first approach suggests that stock prices are determined rationally. This approach clearly maintains that psychology does not play a role in the pricing process of assets. Nevertheless, the second approach asserts the existence of behavioral factors in asset pricing. The authors review several studies contributed to the behavioral finance theory. They contend investor sentiment theory is one of the behavioral finance approaches. This chapter examines the existence of investor sentiment factor in an out of sample market, namely Borsa Istanbul by using consumer confidence index as a proxy of investor sentiment.

Chapter 20 addresses there have been many crises with different degrees of influence since the beginning of 19th century. Among these crises are the 1929 financial crisis, Latin America, East Asia and Russia crisis. Authors analyze the 2008 crisis in this chapter. The overall aim of the chapter is to examine the effects of the global economic crisis on the PIIGS (Portugal, Ireland, Italy, Greece, Spain) countries' budget deficit and debt stock with using Panel Data Analysis over the period 1983-2012.

Chapter 21 reviews the premise of Social Housing Institutions (SHIs) sustainability mechanisms. The authors aim to conduct an audit survey through a critical appraisal and analysis of one of South Africa's social housing projects. The authors systematically review literature and documentation. Based on a survey, the authors report that most tenants currently living in the project earn low incomes; the rate of unemployment is high and the levels of education moderate.

Chapter 22 examines operating performance and capital structure for as well as capital expenditures, working capital and employment management for a reverse leverage buyout sample between 2000 and 2008. The authors argue that the reverse LBO corporations have superior accounting performances compared to their industries exact year of IPO and following years after public offering. The authors conclude that the firms continuously outperform their industry peers for the following four years of initial public offering, while the average debt/capital level decreases in years.

Chapter 23 discusses putting forth the relationship between Emotional Intelligence (EI) and conflict management with theoretical research. The authors reiterated the theoretical studies, state the necessity of having high level of Emotional Intelligence for accomplishing the decision making process and discuss the relationship between Emotional Intelligence, managers and managing conflict. This chapter concludes that managers having high Emotional Intelligence can understand and evaluate the conflicts among employees and encourage their followers in struggling; with comparison to the ones having low Emotional Intelligence.

Chapter 24 discusses in the world of enterprise organizations' financial departments and resulting changes of structures of the financial sector entities, the effects of this structural changes in the operation system with the new business models. The authors present how financial system's agencies and departments can fulfill the requirements of proactive nature revealed. Then they establish future research directions.

Chapter 25 revises definitions and short background of relationship marketing with focusing on components of the concept and relations with customer loyalty, customer value and basic notions. The authors discuss the change from classical marketing concept to the relationship marketing from competitive advantage perspective and probable problems on implication. The authors present financial effect of relationship marketing.

Chapter 26 analyzes the determinants of overconfident CEO appointments and the effect these appointments on competitor stock performance during managerial turnover within the firm. It also analyzes the turnovers that take place in S&P 500 firms and find that an overconfident successor appointed to the firm pertains to a significant positive impact on competitor's stock price. The authors conclude that when the outgoing CEO is overconfident it is more likely for the firm to have an overconfident successor. They suggest that overconfidence should be accounted for in the CEO appointment and contracting practices.

Zeynep Copur
Hacettepe University, Turkey

REFERENCES

Baltussen, G. (2009). *Behavioral finance: An introduction.* Retrieved from http://ssrn.com/abstract=1488110

Barber, B., & Odean, T. (2001). Boys will be boys: Gender, overconfidence, and common stock investment. *The Quarterly Journal of Economics, 116*(1), 261–292. doi:10.1162/003355301556400

Barberis, N., & Thaler, R. (2003). A survey of behavioral finance. In G. M. Constantinidies, M. Harris, & R. Stulz (Eds.), *Handbook of the Economics of Finance* (pp. 1051–1121). Elsevies Science B. V.

Benartzi, S., & Thaler, R. (2001). Naı¨ve diversification strategies in defined contribution savings plans. *The American Economic Review, 91*(1), 79–98. doi:10.1257/aer.91.1.79

Bikas, E., Jureviciene, D., Dubinskas, P., & Novickyte, L. (2012). Behavioural finance: The emergence and development trends. *Procedia: Social and Behavioral Sciences, 82*, 870–876.

De Bondt, W., Muradoglu, G., Shefrin, H., & Staikouras, S. K. (2008). Behavioral finance: Quo vadis? *Journal of Applied Finance (JAF)*, (Fall/Winter): 1–15.

Fromlet, H. (2001). Behavioral finance-theory and practical application. *Business Economics (Cleveland, Ohio), 7*(1), 63–69.

Goldberg, J., & Von Nitzsch, R. (1999). *Behavioural finance*. John Willey & Sons.

Henderson, P., & Peterson, P. (1992). Mental accounting and categorization. *Organizational Behavior and Human Decision Processes, 51*(1), 92–117. doi:10.1016/0749-5978(92)90006-S

Jureviciene, D., Bikas, E., & Gausiene, E. (2012). Behavioural finance during economic downturn in Lithuania. In *The 7th International Scientific Conference Business and Management 2012* (pp. 75-83). Selected Papers. May 10-11, 2012. Vilnius Gediminas Technical University.

Mahajan, J. (1992). The overconfidence effect in marketing management predictions. *JMR, Journal of Marketing Research, 29*(3), 329–342. doi:10.2307/3172743

Pompian, M. M. (2006). *Behavioural finance and wealth management: Building optimal portfolios that account for investor biases*. John Wiley & Sons.

Ricciardi, V., & Simon, H. K. (2000). What is behavioral finance? *Business, Education and Technology Journal*, Fall, 1-9.

Ritter, J. R. (2003). Behavioral finance. *Pacific-Basin Finance Journal, 11*(4), 429–437. doi:10.1016/S0927-538X(03)00048-9

Shefrin, H. (2001). Behavioural corporate finance. *Journal of Applied Corporate Finance, 14*(3), 113–126. doi:10.1111/j.1745-6622.2001.tb00443.x

Shefrin, H., & Thaler, R. H. (1988). The behavioral life-cycle hypothesis. *Economic Inquiry, 26*(4), 609–643. doi:10.1111/j.1465-7295.1988.tb01520.x

Smith, V. L. (1998). The two faces of Adam Smith. *Southern Economic Journal, 65*(1), 1–19. doi:10.2307/1061349

Statman, M. (2008). Countries and culture in behavioral finance. *Wealth Management Conference*, 8-9 April, Atlanta. CFA Institute, cfapubs.org p.38-44.

Stracca, L. (2004). Behavioral finance and asset prices: Where do we stand? *Journal of Economic Psychology*, *25*(3), 373–405. doi:10.1016/S0167-4870(03)00055-2

Thaler, R. H. (1999). The end of behavioral finance. *Financial Analysts Journal*, *55*(6), 12–17. doi:10.2469/faj.v55.n6.2310

Tirole, J. (2002). Rational irrationality: Some economics of self-management. *European Economic Review*, *46*(4-5), 633–655. doi:10.1016/S0014-2921(01)00206-9

Wachter, J. A. (2002). Comment on: Are behavioral asset pricing models structural? *Journal of Monetary Economics*, *49*(1), 229–233. doi:10.1016/S0304-3932(01)00102-7

Weber, M. (1999). *Behavioral finance. Research for Practitioners* (Vol. 0-8). University of Mannheim.

Acknowledgment

The editors would like to acknowledge the help of all the people involved in this project and, more specifically, the authors and reviewers that took part in the review process. Without their support, this book would not have become a reality.

First, the editors would like to thank each one of the authors for their contributions. Our sincere gratitude goes to the chapter's authors who contributed their time and expertise to this book.

Second, the editors wish to acknowledge the valuable contributions of the reviewers regarding the improvement of quality, coherence, and content presentation of chapters. Reviewers of Society for the Study of Business and Finance (SSBFNET) and some of the authors also served as referees; we highly appreciate their task.

Zeynep Copur
Hacettepe University, Turkey

Section 1
Behavioral Finance Theory

Chapter 1
Theory of Behavioral Finance

Jaya M. Prosad
Jaypee Business School, India

Sujata Kapoor
Jaypee Business School, India

Jhumur Sengupta
Management Development Institute, India

ABSTRACT

This chapter explores the evolution of modern behavioral finance theories from the traditional framework. It focuses on three main issues. First, it analyzes the importance of standard finance theories and the situations where they become insufficient i.e. market anomalies. Second, it signifies the role of behavioral finance in narrowing down the gaps between traditional finance theories and actual market conditions. This involves the substitution of standard finance theories with more realistic behavioral theories like the prospect theory (Kahneman & Tversky, 1979). In the end, it provides a synthesis of academic events that substantiate the presence of behavioral biases, their underlying psychology and their impact on financial markets. This chapter also highlights the implications of behavior biases on financial practitioners like market experts, portfolio managers and individual investors. The chapter concludes with providing the limitations and future scope of research in behavioral finance.

INTRODUCTION

… The rage for possessing them soon caught the middle classes of society, and merchants and shopkeepers, even of moderate means, began to vie with each other in the rarity of these flowers and the preposterous prices they paid for them.

One would suppose that there must have been some great virtue in this flower to have made it so valuable in the eyes of so prudent a people as the Dutch; but it has neither the beauty nor the perfume of the rose.- Charles Mackay, on the tulip mania of 1630's, Memoirs of Extraordinary Popular Delusions and the Madness of Crowds (1841)

Investors' irrationality is an inevitable reality as long as the markets themselves have existed. Perhaps its earliest recorded evidence is given by Charles Mackay (1841). In his book *Memoirs of*

DOI: 10.4018/978-1-4666-7484-4.ch001

Extraordinary Popular Delusions and the Madness of Crowds, he mentions three instances that highlight the erratic behavior of crowds. These were the Dutch Tulip bubble (1630's), the South Sea company bubble (1711-1720) and the Mississippi Company bubble (1719-1720). Out of these, the Dutch Tulip bubble, popularly known as tulip mania is one of the most cited accounts. In the Dutch Golden Age, a new flower 'Tulip' was introduced in the Netherlands. The Dutch people became excited about this exotic variety and started investing their money in it. Gradually investments in tulips became a craze which pushed the prices higher and higher. At the peak of tulip mania, a single bulb sold for more than 10 times the annual income of a skilled worker. The market finally collapsed when people sensed they have spent a greater part of their income on a flower bulb. They started to dispose of their tulip stocks as quickly as possible and the price plummeted, leading to heavy losses (Mackay, 1841; Dash, 2001, Shiller, 2005).

Events like the tulip mania makes us ask a very basic question: are investors really rational? This question has been raised by various researchers in the past and it relates to the dilemma that investor behavior does not conform to traditional financial theories. The traditional theories focus on a widely accepted approach of "fully rational agent" where decision making is based solely on available data and mathematically proven concepts. This approach was considered the backbone of financial decision making until its predictions did not confirm with actual market conditions. In an ideal scenario where this approach is applicable, the market is informationally efficient, i.e. the security prices would incorporate all the information available in the market. In this case, all the securities would be fairly priced. However, we do not live in such a utopian world and the markets are largely inefficient. The presence of market anomalies like speculative bubbles, overreaction and underreaction to new information, is a proof that the financial decision making process involves more than a cold, calculative rational agent. Thus, the need for understanding such anomalies and shortcomings of human judgment involved with them became the precursor of behavioral finance.

Behavioral finance is a relatively new school of thought that deals with the influence of psychology on the behavior of financial practitioners and its subsequent impact on stock markets (Sewell, 2007). It signifies the role of psychological biases and their specific behavioral outcome in decision making. Meir Statman (1999) explains its concept in a more straight forward term by stating that "People in standard finance are rational. People in behavioral finance are normal". This field tries to replace the rational *homo economicus* with a more realistic behavioral agent who is ruled by sentiments and is prone to make biased decisions. The knowledge about behavioral biases provides a deeper insight into the underlying psychology of market participants. It enlightens us about the fact that because of our psychology, or more aptly our human nature, we are prone to make certain mistakes. These mistakes can prove to be very costly in financial markets and thus they can't be ignored. Stock market crashes are one of the consequences of such ignorance. This makes behavioral finance an extremely relevant topic in today's times. This field helps the financial practitioners in recognizing their own mistakes along with those of others, understanding the reasons behind these mistakes and avoiding them. It makes the practitioners more aware of the forces that guide them in their decision making, as well as those driving the market. In this chapter we aim to discuss the progression of behavioral finance theories from the traditional framework. We then critically analyze the importance of traditional theories in the field of finance and the situations where they lack, along with the significance of behavioral finance in narrowing down these gaps. We finally provide a synthesis of academic events that substantiate the presence of behavioral biases, their underlying psychology and their impact on financial markets.

TRADITIONAL APPROACH TO INVESTOR BEHAVIOR

Mid eighteenth century is considered to be the onset of the classical period in economics (Pompian, 2011). It is during this time that the concept of utility was introduced which measured the satisfaction of individuals by consuming a good or a service (Bernoulli, 1738). In 1844, John Stuart Mill introduced the concept of rational economic man or *homo economicus* who tries to maximize his economic well being given the constraints he faces. The three underlying assumptions for this agent are; perfect rationality, perfect self- interest and perfect information. These assumptions became the basis of the traditional financial framework that sought equilibrium solutions by maximizing marginal utilities of individuals subject to situational constraint (Pompian, 2011). The behavior of individuals representing this paradigm is uniform as their main focus is on optimizing their marginal gains. As the noted researcher Meir Statman (1999, pp. 19) once quoted that "Standard finance is built on the pillars of the arbitrage principles of Mille r and Modigliani, the portfolio principles of Markowitz, the capital asset pricing theory of Sharpe, Lintner and Black, and the option pricing theory of Black, Scholes and Merton." Standard finance theories have been developed to find mathematical explanations to real life financial problems. Their basic assumption is based on rationality of people. This concept is further elucidated by Barberis and Thaler (2003). According to them rationality has two pronged focus. First, when agents receive new information they update their beliefs correctly according to Bayes' law. Second, given their beliefs, the agents take decisions which would maximize their expected utility. Table 1 provides the summary of these classical researchers that starts with the standard theory of individual choice, i.e. the expected utility theory, followed by the classical models in asset pricing theories that are Markowitz portfolio model and the capital asset pricing model. The discussion concludes with one of the most referred as well as equally criticized theories, the efficient market hypothesis.

Expected Utility Theory (Bernoulli, 1738, 1954; von Neumann & Morgenstern, 1944) states that the market participants make their decisions under risk by comparing the expected utility values of the available alternatives. Rational investors act to maximize their expected utility that is calculated as weighted sums of utility values multiplied by their respective probabilities. It categorizes the decision makers into risk averse, risk neutral and risk loving individuals. Further, it explains that the utility function for a risk averse investor is concave (figure 1a). This implies that, for an increase in expected wealth the utility function of a risk averse person decreases. In other words, for the same amount of utility a risk averse person would like to take lesser risk than a risk loving person. It explains the difference between inves-

Table 1. Traditional financial theories

Author	Year	Finding
John Stuart Mill	1844	Introduced the concept of Economic Man or *homo economicus.*
Bernoulli	1738, 1954	Expected utility theory
Von Neumann and Morgenstern	1944	
Harry Markowitz	1952	Markowitz portfolio theory
Treynor, Sharpe and Lintner	1962,1964, 1965	Capital asset pricing model
Jan Mossin	1966	
Eugene Fama	1970	Efficient market hypothesis

Figure 1. Expected utility functions for three risk attitude types

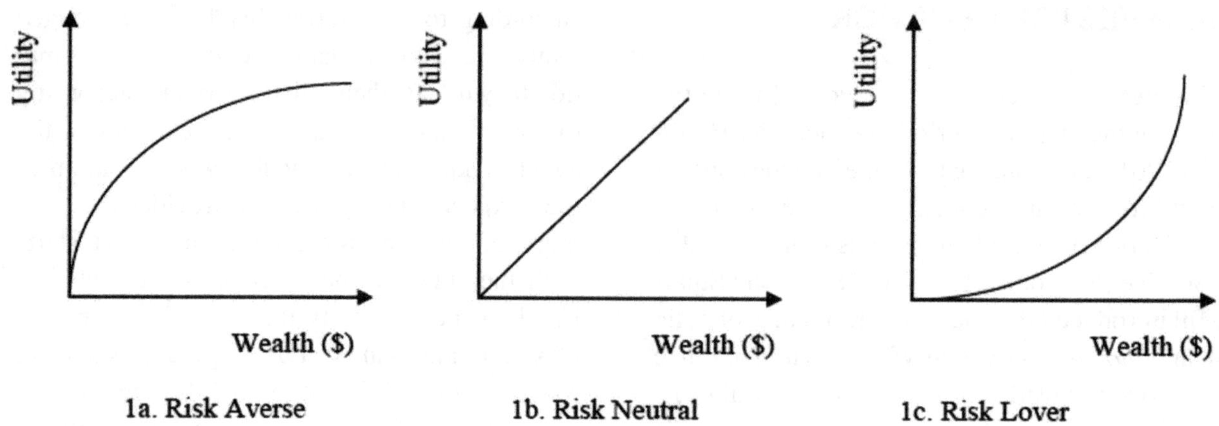

tors' behavior with respect to their risk tolerance. This theory along with its variants like subjective expected utility theory (Savage, 1964) was the most accepted theory for decades in financial literature in decision making under risk.

The rationality of the agents turned out to be the key to unlock the stock market behavior. Alongside this assumption, several corresponding theories developed that established the groundwork of standard finance theories. The predominant theories amongst these were the Markowitz portfolio theory and the capital asset pricing model.

Markowitz (1952) introduces the portfolio selection model. It describes the process of optimal portfolio construction by selecting several risky securities and a risk free asset. It deals with maximizing the expected return of the portfolio for a given amount of risk, or, minimizing the risk for a given amount of expected return. It helps in diversification of portfolio by selecting securities with most optimal risk-return opportunity. Markowitz portfolio theory formed the basis of one of the most central asset pricing models in finance, the capital asset pricing model (CAPM).

CAPM is developed by Sharpe (1964), Lintner (1965) and Mossin (1966). It gives the relationship that should be observed between the risk of the asset and its expected return. The expected return of an asset derived from this model provides an estimate of fair or benchmark return. It also helps the investors to make an educated guess of the expected return of securities that have not yet been traded in the stock market (Bodie et al., 2009). We enlist the basic assumptions of the CAPM. These assumptions, try to ensure the homogeneity (or alikeness) in the behavior of individuals (Bodie et al., 2009).

- It considers that there are many individuals in the market, each with a certain amount of wealth which is small as compared to the total wealth of all investors. Perfect competition prevails in the market where the investors are price-takers and the security prices are not affected by their trades.
- All investors have an identical holding period and their expectations are myopic such that they would ignore everything that might occur at the end of the period.
- The investments are limited only to publicly traded financial assets. The non-traded assets like that of private enterprises are excluded. It is also assumed that investors may borrow or lend any amount at a risk-free rate.
- Investors do not pay any taxes on returns and there are no transaction costs on trading securities.

- All investors are rational and they would try to optimize the risk-return tradeoff of their personal portfolio.
- The investors try to mimic the market portfolio, which is considered to be efficient as it incorporates all the relevant information about the universe of securities. Therefore, all the securities in market portfolio are fairly priced.
- Investors are as alike as possible and they analyze the securities in the same way i.e. they have homogeneous expectations.

The simplicity of CAPM makes it the most widely used asset pricing models. However, traditional theorists abandoned the CAPM in favor of Fama and French's (1992) three-factor model when the CAPM produced anomalies inconsistent with market efficiency (Statman, 1999).

A great deal of asset pricing theories is based on the assumption of market efficiency, which is introduced and explained by Fama (1970). He defines the efficient financial market as one in which security prices always fully reflect available information. It further identifies that in an efficient market all the investors are well informed, rational individuals who aim to maximize their profits. This means that if the efficient market hypothesis (EMH) holds true, then the investors cannot hope to beat the market and no amount of analysis would help in generating abnormal returns. This theory takes the standard finance literature one notch higher by taking into account irrational traders. It notes that the irrational or noise traders can distort the prices, but it is a temporary phenomenon and is quickly eliminated by the arbitrageurs. We illustrate the theoretical and empirical assumptions of EMH as discussed by Shleifer (2000).

The Theoretical Assumptions of the EMH

The Theoretical Assumptions of the EMH

- Investors are assumed to be rational. Therefore, they value the securities rationally, incorporating all the available information.
- Irrational investors, if present, trade randomly; therefore their trades cancel each other out without affecting the prices.
- Further, the effect of irrational investors on prices is also eliminated by the trading activities of arbitrageurs.

The Empirical Assumptions of the EMH

The EMH turned out to be an enormous empirical success in the first decade of its conception. Jensen (1978, pp. 95) stated that, 'there is no other proposition in economics which has more solid empirical evidence supporting it than the Efficient Market Hypothesis'. The empirical focus of the EMH has two aspects. It first considers the impact of new information on security prices. It states that any new information in the market should be incorporated in the security prices quickly and correctly such that price trends or reversals could not exist after the initial impact of the news. Secondly, since the price of a security is equal to its value; therefore it should only move when there is a news about a change in its fundamental value and not otherwise. It is further noted that in an efficient market scenario old information has no monetary value. Fama (1970) categorizes the old information into three types which gives rise to three forms of market efficiencies: weak, semi-strong and strong.

- In the *weak* form of market efficiency, the past prices and returns are taken as old information and here technical or trend analysis cannot yield superior abnormal returns.
- In *semi-strong* form of market efficiency, any publicly available information is considered old and its fundamental analysis also fails to give superior returns. This means that as soon as the information becomes public it gets incorporated into security prices.
- However, investors can still earn abnormal returns by having information that is not made public i.e. insider trading. Here comes the importance of *strong* market efficiency wherein even insider trading cannot provide abnormal return as this information leaks out quickly and gets incorporated into security prices.

For a very long period of time these theories were considered to be the ultimate explanation for investor and market behavior. However, in recent times researchers have been observing that traditional theories get significantly violated in actual market conditions. They have started accepting that these theories are based on the over-simplified assumptions. Its foundations are built on how market participants ought to behave rather than how they actually behave. This led to the emergence of behavioral finance which factors irrationalities and biases of investors.

BEHAVIORAL FINANCE APPROACH

The rationality of investors became debatable from the time standard finance theories could not give sufficient explanation for the stock market anomalies. One of the most apparent example of such an anomaly is the stock market bubble, for instance the dot-com bubble of the 1990's (Cooper et al., 2001) or the recent real estate bubble of 2006 (Zhou & Sornette, 2006). A bubble is created when market participants drive the security prices way above their fair price. During this phase people disregard the fundamental valuation and get attracted to such overpriced securities which strengthen the mispricing even more. However, this 'hot market' situation ends when companies fail to achieve their promised targets or the demand declines. Experts like Mackay (1841) highlight the importance of behavioral biases like herd mentality as the cause of this situation. The existence of such bubbles defies the very core of the "standard finance theories".

The essence of standard finance theories can be captured into four foundation blocks: 1) investors are rational; 2) markets are efficient; 3) investors should design their portfolio according to the rules of mean variance portfolio 4) Expected returns are a function of risk and risk alone (Statman, 2008). Behavioral finance offers an alternative for each of these blocks. It states that investors are "normal" not rational, the markets are not efficient even when they are difficult to beat, investors do not design their portfolio on mean-variance theory and the expected returns are measured by more than just risk (Statman, 2008). We try to examine each of these blocks with the help of suitable behavioral concept in the subsequent section starting with the brief history of the discipline itself.

Behavioral finance emerged as a branch of social psychology that captures the human side of decision making. Research in this field started in the eighteenth century with significant works like *Theory of Moral Sentiments* (1759) and *Wealth of Nations* (1776) by Adam Smith. In these studies Smith suggests the presence of an "invisible hand" or the morality of individuals that guides them in making social, economic and even financial decisions. Smith (1759) emphasizes on the role of sentiments like pride, shame, insecurity and egotism. Another contemporary thinker, Jeremy Bentham (1789) highlights the psychological aspects of utility function. Bentham argues that human concern for happiness makes it impossible for them to make a decision that is entirely devoid of emotions. These researchers stress on the role of psychology on economic behavior, but their consensus was lost over the next century. This work was then reinstated in the twentieth century. Selden (1912) identifies that the stock price movements on the exchanges are dependent on the mental attitude of investors. The role of sentiment is also observed by Keynes (1936) as the "animal spirits" of individuals. Keynes along with many other researchers criticized the concept of *homo economicus* and argued that no human can be completely informed of every situation in order to maximize her expected utility. Instead, they advocate the theory of the bounded rationality given by Simon (1955). This theory assumes that rationality of individuals is constrained by two factors: information they have at their disposal and the cognitive limitations of their minds. Bounded rationality is a more relaxed version of standard expected utility theory. It is also more realistic to its traditional counterpart as it incorporates the limitations of the human judgment. The utility function is further explored by Pratt (1964). The author compares the utility with respect to local risk aversion and global risk aversion and explains that the decision maker will have a greater local risk aversion if he is globally more risk averse. The author also gives a related utility function where risk is measured as a proportion of total assets.

In 1956 the US psychologist Leon Festinger introduces the concept of cognitive dissonance (Festinger, Riecken & Schachter 1956) which occurs when two simultaneously held cognitions are inconsistent. Moreover, this dissonance creates a feeling of unpleasantness or unrest in the people such that they try to avoid it or reduce it by changing their beliefs. The mental processes that are a part of cognitive psychology have been examined by various experts with respect to decision making under uncertainty. One of the significant contributions to this body of literature is by Raiffa (1968). The author analyzes decisions under three approaches that provide a more pragmatic view of an individual's thought process. These approaches are mentioned as follows.

- **Normative Approach:** It is concerned with rational decision making process. It provides ideal solution which a decision making process should strive to achieve.
- **Descriptive Approach:** It deals with the manner in which people actually make decisions in the real life situations.
- **Prescriptive Approach:** It provides the individuals with practical advice and tools that might help them in achieving results that are in close approximation to the normative analysis.

The path-breaking work in behavioral finance is credited to the psychologists Daniel Kahneman and Amos Tversky. They introduced the concept of prospect theory for the analysis of decision making under risk (1979). This theory is considered to be the backbone of behavioral finance. It was developed as an alternative model for expected utility theory. It throws light on how individual evaluate gain or losses. This theory has three key aspects.

- **Key Aspect 1:** People sometimes exhibit risk aversion and sometimes exhibit risk loving behavior depending on the nature of the prospect. This is because people give lower weight age to the outcomes which are probable as compared to those that are certain. This makes them risk averse for choices with sure gains while risk seeker for choices with sure losses. It is also known as certainty effect.
- **Key Aspect 2:** People assign value to losses or gains rather than final assets. Here two thought processes come into play. These are editing and evaluation. During the editing stage, the prospects are ranked as per the rules of thumb (heuristics) and in evaluation stage, some reference point is taken into account that provides a relative basis for determining gain or losses. This reference point is usually their status quo.

- **Key Aspect 3:** The weight age given to losses is higher than given to gains of the same amount. This is because people are averse to losses as they loom larger than gains. This is called *loss aversion.*

The value function in the prospect theory replaces the utility function in the expected utility theory. In addition, instead of using simple probabilities as in the expected utility theory, it uses decision weights which are a function of probability. The value function of the prospect theory is shown below in figure 2.

In this figure the value function of loss is steeper than the gains which corroborate the fact that people overweigh their losses. Another finding is that this function is concave for gains while convex for losses. This leads to the interpretation of four fold pattern of risk attitude in individuals (Tversky & Kahneman, 1992) which is mentioned below.

- Risk seeker for gains with low probability.
- Risk aversion for gains with high probability.
- Risk aversion for losses with low probability.
- Risk seeker for losses with high probability.

Prospect theory is considered to be the seminal work in behavioral finance and it forms the underlying basis of biases like loss aversion, framing and the disposition effect.

It can be seen from the above literature that the work on incorporating behavioral aspects to traditional theories started quite early. This area started gaining the spotlight in late 1970's and 80's. The works of Simon (1955), Pratt (1964), Raiffa (1968) and Kahneman and Tversky (1979) provide an alternative to the expected utility theory. In later years, the expected utility theory wasn't the only theory which faced criticism. Proponents of behavioral finance also found flaws in other standard finance theories like the capital asset pricing model (CAPM), the Markowitz portfolio selection model and the efficient market hypothesis (EMH).

Statman (1999) points that traditional asset pricing models like the CAPM determine the expected return of a security at a given point of time, but do not consider the same over a period of time that could provide an explanation for the stock market bubbles. The author also argues that the rationality in the security prices in the efficient market hypothesis reflects only the utilitarian characteristics like risk and not the value

Figure 2. The value function in the prospect theory (Kahneman & Tversky, 1979)

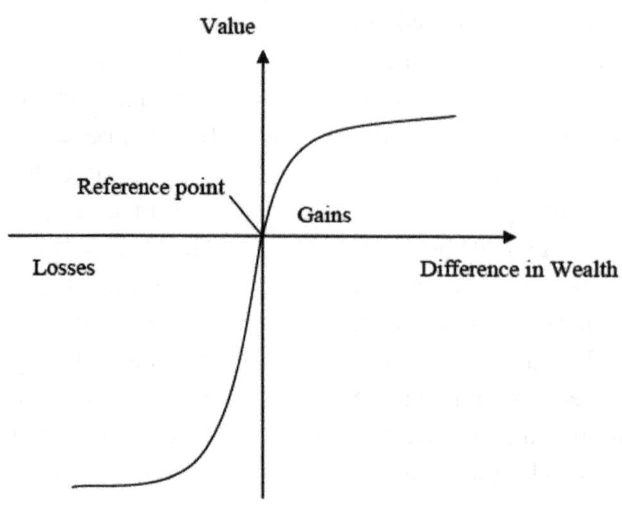

expressive characteristics such as sentiments. He states that both these characteristics influence the risk premium. Further, the author suggests that experts should explore the asset pricing models that reflect both value expressive and utilitarian characteristics.

A similar model is previously developed by Shefrin and Statman (1994) called the behavioral asset pricing model (BAPM). This model explains the market interaction of two groups of traders, i.e. the informational traders and the noise traders. Information traders are the rational traders who follow the CAPM whereas noise traders are the ones who do not follow the CAPM and commit cognitive errors. Here the expected return on securities is determined by their behavioral betas.

Shefrin and Statman (1999) also develop an alternative to the Markowitz portfolio theory, named as the behavioral portfolio theory (BPT). In the Markowitz model, the investors build a mean variance portfolio, thereby trying to optimize their risk-return tradeoff. Here the portfolio is evaluated as a whole and the risk attitude of the investors is also consistent. In contrast, the BPT takes into account the behavioral investors that construct their portfolios as the pyramids of assets, layer by layer, where each layer is associated with its specific goal and risk attitude. This theory tries to explain a part of investor behavior that deals with their differential attitude towards risk.

In 1990's and 2000 the efficient market hypothesis was also challenged by various researchers like Andrei Shleifer (2000) and Robert Shiller (2000). Shleifer (2000) provides an alternative approach to study financial markets with the help of behavioral finance. The author acknowledges the fact the in actual financial markets, irrational investors trade against arbitrageurs whose resources are limited by risk aversion, short horizons, and agency problems. He presents behavioral models that explain various market anomalies such as the superior performance of value stocks, the closed end fund puzzle, the higher returns on stocks included in market indices, the persistence of stock price bubbles, and collapse of several well-known hedge funds in 1998. Some of the key points of Shleifer are enumerated below.

- It is impossible for investors being completely rational. Most of the investors react to irrelevant information or they trade on noise rather than information.
- These investors are prone to various biases like narrow framing, the disposition effect, loss aversion, representativeness and overreaction.
- It counters the assumption of the EMH which states that the irrational investors, if exist, trade randomly such that their trades cancel each other out leaving no impact on stock prices whatsoever. In contrast to this Shleifer argues that trades of irrational investors would not be random, rather they would buy or sell the same securities at the same time.
- The study suggests that, contrary to the EMH, arbitrage in real situations is risky and therefore limited. Since the prerequisite for any arbitrage is the availability of same or essentially similar substitutes, yet in many cases securities might not have such close substitutes. This constraint limits the effectiveness of arbitrage which contributes in making the markets inefficient.

Further contradictions for the EMH are presented by Shiller (1981, 2000). In 1981 the author analyzes the stock market volatility and shows that the stock prices are far more volatile than could be explained by standard financial theories. In his bestselling book *Irrational Exuberance,* Shiller (2000) analyses the ups and downs of Dow Jones industrial average with a behavioral approach of market participants. He stresses on the impact on investor perception, along with psychological and cultural factors in creating the bubble phase of DJIA during late 1990's. In a separate research Jagdeesh and Titman (1993) also provide significant evidence for momentum. They found that individual stock prices over a period of six to twelve months tends to predict the future price movement in the same direction. This finding violates even the weak form of market efficiency.

The aforementioned literature substantiates that the standard finance theories alone cannot explain the anomalies of stock markets. In recent times, the researchers have recognized the importance of incorporating behavioral factors into the traditional theories to get a more realistic insight into the functioning of stock markets. These researches along with various other significant contributions are summarized in Table 2.

In the next section we will unveil some of the behavioral irrationalities identified by eminent psychologists and throw light on how these tendencies can result in anomalies in financial markets.

INTRODUCTION TO BEHAVIORAL BIASES

Behavioral finance captures the role of behavioral biases in investor decision making. Shefrin (2000) broadly classifies these biases into two types: heuristic driven biases and frame dependent biases.

- **Heuristic driven biases:** Shefrin (2000) recognizes that financial practitioners use rules of thumb or heuristics to process data and make decisions. For instance, people believe that future performance of the stock can be best predicted by past performance. The author categorizes such biases under heuristic theme which includes overconfidence, anchoring and adjustment, reinforcement learning, excessive optimism and pessimism.

Table 2. Behavioral finance theories

Researcher Name	Year	Theory/ Concept/ Model
Herbert Simon	1955	Models of bounded rationality
Festinger, Riecken and Schachter	1956	Theory of cognitive dissonance
Tversky and Kahneman	1973,1974	Introduced heuristic biases: availability, representativeness, anchoring and adjustment
Kahneman and Tversky	1979	The prospect theory, introduced loss aversion bias
Tversky and Kahneman	1981	Introduced Framing Bias
Richard Thaler	1985	Introduced mental accounting bias
De Bondt and Thaler	1985	Theory of overreaction in stock markets.
Barberis, Shleifer and Vishny	1998	Investor sentiment model for underreaction and overreaction of stock prices.
Meir Statman	1999	Behavioral asset pricing theory and behavioral portfolio theory
Andrei Shleifer	2000	Linkage of behavioral finance with Efficient market Hypothesis to find that stock markets are inefficient.
Barberis, Huang and Santos	2001	Incorporation of prospect theory in asset prices.
Grinblatt and Keloharju	2001	Role of behavioral factors in determining trading behavior.
Hubert Fromlet	2001	Importance of behavioral finance. Emphasis on departure from '*homo economicus*' or traditional paradigm to more realistic paradigm.
Barberis and Thaler	2003	Survey of Behavioral Finance
Coval and Shumway	2006	Effect of behavioral biases on stock prices. The price reversal for biased investors is quicker than unbiased investors

Figure 3. Categorization of behavioral biases

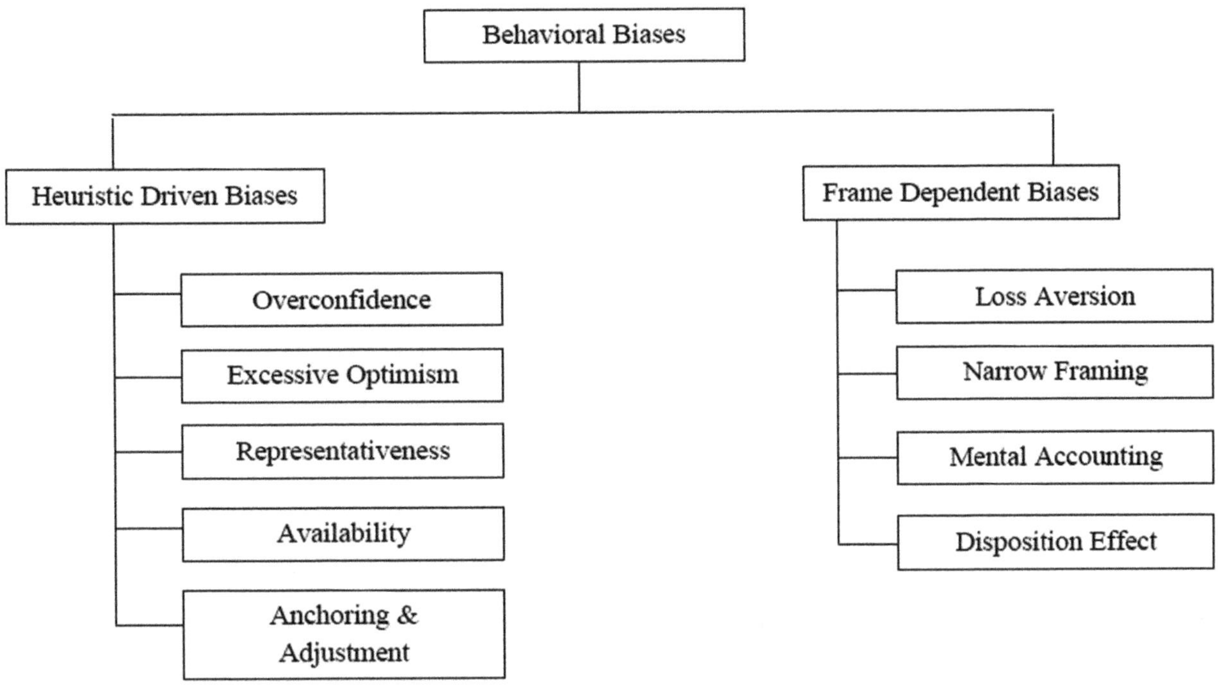

- **Frame dependent biases:** The decision process of financial practitioners is also influenced by the way they frame their options. This theme includes biases like narrow framing, mental accounting and the disposition effect.

Behavioral biases are also categorized by Pompian (2011) into cognitive and emotional biases (Figure 3). The *cognitive* biases include overconfidence, representativeness, anchoring and adjustment, framing, cognitive dissonance, availability, mental accounting, etc. The *emotional* biases include endowment bias, loss aversion, optimism and status quo.

We discuss the presence and impact of some of the prominent biases in this section. These biases are categorized along the lines of Shefrin (2000) into heuristic and frame dependent biases. Table 3 summarizes the findings of the studies on these biases.

Heuristic Driven Biases

Heuristics are introduced by Tversky and Kahneman in 1974. As described earlier, these are the rules of thumb or mental shortcuts that help people in reaching decisions quickly and easily. These shortcuts, although helpful, can lead to erroneous decisions. Three heuristics given by Tversky and Kahneman (1974) that are used for decision making under uncertainty are representativeness, availability, and anchoring and adjustment

Representativeness: It is the tendency of individuals to estimate the likelihood of an event by comparing it to a previous incident that already exists in their minds. This existing incident is generally what they consider to be the most relevant or typical example of the current event. The empirical evidence of representativeness has been given by Dhar and Kumar (2001) who examines the stock price trend for stocks bought by more than 62,000 households at a discount brokerage during a 5-year period. The author finds that investors tend to buy stocks with recent positive abnormal

Table 3. Summary of literature on various behavioral biases

Bias Name	Author	Findings
Representativeness	Tversky and Kahneman (1974)	Tendency of individuals to estimate the likelihood of an event by comparing it to a previous incident that already exists in their minds.
	Kumar (2001)	Past price trend is representative of the future price trend as investors tend to buy stocks with recent positive abnormal returns.
	Kaestner (2005)	Investors extrapolate the recent earnings surprise and hence overreact to subsequent earnings surprise.
Availability	Tversky and Kahneman (1973, 1974)	It is the ease with which relevant issues come to mind. It creates a selection bias in decision making.
	Kliger and Kudryavtsev (2010)	Stock price reaction to recommendation revisions (up or down) is stronger when accompanied by index returns in the same direction.
Anchoring	Tversky and Kahneman (1974)	Tendency of people to estimate an unknown value with the help of an initial value or "anchor".
	Campbell and Sharpe (2009)	Expert forecasts releases are biased (anchored) towards previous months releases.
Overconfidence	Odean (1998a)	Investors' tendency to overestimate the precision of their knowledge about the value of a security.
	Daniel, Hirshleifer and Subrahmanyam (1998)	Overconfidence of investors leads to negative serial correlation in prices (price reversals).
	Barber and Odean (2000)	Overconfidence increases trading activity in investors that in turn depletes their wealth due to higher trading costs.
	Gervais and Odean (2001)	Past successes in trades makes investors overconfident and leads to high trading volume in future periods.
Optimism (Pessimism)	Heifetz and Spiegel (2001)	Investors' tendency to overestimate (underestimate) the expected mean returns of the risky asset.
	Toshino and Suto (2004)	Optimistic investors selectively incorporate only good news in their decision making process.
	Shefrin and Statman (2011)	Excessive optimism creates speculative bubbles in financial markets.
	Hoffman and Post (2011)	Identify the drivers of optimism and pessimism that are return expectations, return tolerance and risk perceptions.
Loss aversion	Kahneman and Tversky (1979)	Loss brings regret and people try to avoid losses in order to avoid subsequent regret.
	Coval and Shumway (2003)	Analyzed loss aversion in intra-day trading. A loss in the morning leads to higher risk taking behavior of market makers in the afternoon.
	Berkelaar and Kouwenberg (2008)	Investors with heterogeneous loss aversion become gradually less risk averse when they experience gains, pushing the security prices up.
	Hwang and Satchell (2010)	Level of loss aversion changes depending on market conditions. Investors become more loss averse in bull markets than bear markets.
Narrow Framing	Shefrin (2000)	Tendency of investors to treat repeated risks as if they were a one-shot deal.
	Barberis and Huang (2005)	People evaluate a new gamble in isolation, separated from their other risks, even if it is just one of many that determine their overall wealth risk.
	Liu and Wang (2010)	Investors could easily become susceptible to narrow framing when trading in the complex derivatives market. Factors like professionalism, sophistication and experience can reduce this bias to a certain extent.
Mental accounting	Thaler (1999)	Investors make mental accounts of their wealth which have an impact on stock selection decisions
	Barberis and Huang (2001)	Comparison between stock accounting by investors to portfolio accounting. Change in investors mental system of accounting affects asset prices.

continued on folllowing page

Table 3. continued.

Bias Name	Author	Findings
Disposition Effect	Shefrin and Statman (1985)	Tendency of investors to sell winning stocks early and holding on to losing stocks
	Odean (1998b)	Using the ratio of proportion of gains realized (PGR) to proportion of loss realized (PLR) show that investors are prone to the disposition effect.
	Grinblatt and Keloharju (2001)	Evidence of the disposition effect in Finnish stock market.
	Shumway and Wu (2006)	The disposition effect drives momentum in Shanghai stock exchange.
	Alok Kumar (2009)	In order to avoid regret investors continue to hold on to loss making stocks in the hope of future gains
Herding behavior	Lakonishok *et al.* (1991)	Developed a model which measures herding by studying a subset of market participants over time.
	Scharfstein and Stein (1990)	Examined herding in money managers. Reputational concerns and 'sharing-the-blame' effect, were some of the factors that could drive managers to herd
	Christie and Huang (1995)	Investigated the presence of herding using cross-sectional standard deviation (CSSD). Analyzed that herding exists in periods of market extremes.
Status quo Bias	Samuelson and Zeckhauser (1988)	Individuals tend to disproportionately stick to their status quo, i.e. maintaining one's current or previous decision.
	Brown and Kagel (2009)	Status quo prevails in an environment in which there are very low costs of identifying better performing stocks.
	Jianbiao	Identified factors affecting the status quo bias as framing, investors' emotion and information structure.

returns. This is consistent with the heuristic that the past price trend is representative of the future price trend. Another instance is presented by Kaestner (2005) who uses the data on current and past earnings for U.S. listed companies for the period of 1983-1999 and suggest that investor overreaction to earnings announcement could be attributed to representativeness bias. The author states that investors initially extrapolate the recent earnings surprise and hence overreact to subsequent earnings surprise.

Availability bias: In this case people evaluate the probability of an outcome based on the familiarity or prevalence of that particular outcome. People prone to availability bias give higher likelihood to the events which they can easily recall as compared to the ones that difficult to remember or comprehend. Kliger and Kudryavtsev (2010) identify this bias in investors' reaction to analysts' recommendation revisions. They use daily market returns as a proxy for information on outcome availability. They find that stock price reaction to recommendation revisions (up or down) is stronger when accompanied by index returns in the same direction.

Anchoring and Adjustment bias: This bias comes into play when people have to estimate an unknown value or magnitude. Here people start their estimation by guessing some initial value or an "anchor". This anchor is then adjusted and refined to arrive at the final estimate. Campbell and Sharpe (2009) investigate the presence of anchoring bias in analysts' forecasts of monthly economic releases for a period of 1991 to 2006. They find that forecasts of any given release were anchored towards the recent months' realized values of that release, thereby giving rise to predictable surprises. This effect is consistent for each of the key releases.

The aforementioned researches substantiate the importance of the representativeness, availability and anchoring bias. It can be observed that representativeness is based on stereotypes and it causes positive earnings surprises to be followed by more positive surprises and negative surprises by more negative surprises (Shefrin, 2000). Representativeness along with availability bias can create overreactions in investors and stock markets. Finally the influence of anchoring and adjustment bias can make the earnings surprises predictable.

Along with representativeness, availability and anchoring bias, the other equally relevant and widely researched heuristic driven biases are overconfidence and optimism.

Overconfidence: It is defined as the investors' tendency to overestimate the precision of their knowledge about the value of a security (Odean, 1998a). Overconfidence is one of the most highly researched biases with abundant empirical findings. Daniel et al. (1998) develop a model based on overconfidence of investors who overestimate the precision of their private signals and show that overconfidence leads to negative serial correlation in prices (price reversals). Gervais and Odean (2001) formulate a multi-period market model to estimate overconfidence. They propose that overconfidence is enhanced in those investors who have experienced high returns; as a result they trade more frequently. Therefore overconfidence leads to increase in trading volume. On the other hand, a loss in the market reduces overconfidence level and subsequently the transaction volume. They assign a positive relationship between volume of transaction and lagged performance of the market. Odean (1999) and Barber and Odean, (2000; 2001) empirically test the theory of overconfidence. They provide evidence that overconfidence leads to greater trading volume in financial markets. Using the data from individual investor accounts held with a large U.S. brokerage firm, they propose that higher trading in turn leads to lower expected utility or poor portfolio performance.

Most of these researches reveal that overconfidence is an illusion of superior knowledge in investors, which is strengthened by their past successes. This tendency makes them trade more as they become sure of the positive outcome. However increase in trading volume comes with high a trading cost which proves to be detrimental to the portfolio performance.

Optimism: In financial context optimism (pessimism) is defined as the propensity of investors to overestimate (underestimate) the expected mean returns of the risky asset (Heifetz & Spiegel, 2001; Germain et al., 2005; Barone Adesi et al., 2012). Researchers have studied this bias with respect to its impact on the stock markets as well as the factors that drive this bias. Toshino and Suto (2004) investigate optimism bias in Japanese institutional investors. They use survey based data and find that the optimistic investors are more sensitive towards positive market news. They selectively incorporate only good news in their decision making process. Further, investors affected by optimism bias tend to undervalue the risk of familiar investment products such that they are more optimistic towards the domestic market than foreign markets. Shefrin and Statman (2011) find that excessive optimism can create speculative bubbles in financial markets by inflating the prices of securities above their intrinsic values. They further state that if bubbles last long enough, some pessimists might become convinced that they are wrong and can convert into optimists and in the process they are likely to intensify this phenomenon. Hoffman and Post (2011) identify the drivers of investors' optimism and fear (pessimism) based on their return expectations, return tolerance and risk perceptions. They use a data set of brokerage records as well as monthly survey measurements to analyze the impact of the past return and past risk on the drivers of optimism (pessimism). They discover that past returns positively impact return expectations, return tolerance and negatively impact risk perceptions. They reason that investors are prone to hot hands fallacy, which means that past returns will continue in future. This makes them more optimistic in return expectations if there past returns are positive. However, past risk has no effect on these parameters.

Optimism (pessimism) is a very influential bias. It is responsible for setting the mood of the financial markets. This bias is driven by past returns that have an impact on return expectations, return tolerance and risk perception of investors. This bias is so potent that it can create stock market bubbles and can convert even pessimists to optimists.

These researches affirm that heuristic driven biases have a fair share of influence on the investors' choices and actions. In the next section we analyze the role of second category given by Shefrin (2000) i.e. the frame dependent biases.

Frame Dependent Biases

The roots of frame dependence trace back to the study by Kahnemann and Tversky (1979). This work is taken forward by Shefrin (2000) who mentions several frame dependent biases, the prominent ones amongst those biases are being discussed here. These are loss aversion, narrow framing, mental accounting and the disposition effect.

Loss aversion: It is introduced by Kahneman and Tversky (1979) and refers to the tendency of individuals to strongly avoid losses as compared obtaining gains. This is because loss brings regret and impact is much greater than that of gains. Several researchers have studied the impact of loss aversion in financial markets. Joshua D. Coval and Tyler Shumway (2005) analyze the effect of loss aversion bias in terms of risk taking in market makers. They show that in intra-day trading, a loss in the morning leads to higher risk taking behavior in the afternoon. Berkelaar and Kouwenberg (2008) examine the impact of heterogeneous loss averse investors on asset prices using annual U.S. consumption data for a period of 1889 to 1985. Their study shows that in a good state loss averse investor gradually become less risk averse as wealth rises above their reference point, pushing equity prices up. On the other hand, when wealth drops below the reference point the investors become risk seeking and demand for stock increases drastically. This eventually leads to forced sell-off and subsequently stock market busts. Hwang and Satchell (2010) investigate loss aversion in financial market using the typical asset allocation model for annual data of U.K. pension funds from 1963 to 2003. Their results reveal that financial markets are more loss averse than assumed in literature. Further, this bias change depending on market conditions, for instance, investors become more loss averse in bull markets than during bear markets indicating the pain of a loss is larger when others are enjoying gains. They also find that investors are more sensitive to changes in loss than in gains.

These studies reveal that there is a differential impact of gains and losses on decision outcome. Further, the pain of loss is described to be greater than pleasure of an equal amount of gain, which makes the investors more sensitive to a change in the loss. These researches also throw light on the risk attitude pattern of individuals. It is seen that people become risk seeker or less risk averse in the prospect experiencing loss of high probability.

Narrow framing: Shefrin (2000) describes narrow framing as the tendency of investors to treat repeated risks as if they were a one-shot deal. Barberis and Huang (2006) elaborate this bias in the context of gambling. They state that, it is the phenomenon wherein people evaluate each new gamble in isolation, separating it from their other risks. In other words, people will ignore all the previous choices that determine their overall wealth risk and directly derive the utility from their current risk. Liu and Wang (2010) document the presence of narrow framing effect in the options trading market. They used the daily trading volume data of Taiwan Futures Exchange for a period of 2001 to 2004. The findings of this study indicate that investors could easily become susceptible to narrow framing when trading in the complex derivatives market. They simplify complicated trading strategies into understandable trading decisions. The study also supports the fact that traders' professionalism, sophistication and experience can reduce this bias to a certain extent.

Mental accounting: Its concept is given by Thaler (1999). It is defined as the tendency of individuals to separate their information into manageable mental accounts. Thaler (1999) explains that mental accounting is a set of cognitive operations used by individuals to organize, evaluate, and keep track of financial activities. Mental accounting comprises of three components. First component captures how outcomes are perceived and experienced, how decisions are made and subsequently evaluated. Second component involves the assignment of activities to specific accounts. The final component focuses on the frequency with which accounts are evaluated and 'choice bracketing'. Barberis and Huang (2001) study investors' mental accounting using simulated data of equilibrium firm-level stock returns. They find that the investors' system of mental accounting affects asset prices. They track the changes in portfolio performance as the individual's decision frame shifts from stock accounting to portfolio accounting. Their results reveal that when this happens, the mean value of individual stock return falls, the stocks become less volatile and more correlated with each other.

Both narrow framing and mental accounting are cognitive processes that simplify the complex decision making problem for investors. In narrow framing, individuals treat their risks in isolation rather than taking a holistic view. This bias can lead to overestimation of risk and make the investors myopic in their investment outlook. On the other hand, during mental accounting people segregate the information into different mental accounts. They evaluate the performance of each account separately instead of evaluating the performance of their portfolio as a whole. So although, this bias helps the investors in managing complex information, it can create distortion in asset prices.

The disposition effect: Shefrin and Statman (1985) introduce the concept of the disposition effect. It is defined as the tendency of investors to hold on to losing stocks and sell winning stocks early. This concept is built on the implications of prospect theory (Kanheman & Tversky, 1979). The possible reasons for this effect as proposed by the authors are loss aversion, seeking pride, mental accounting and regret avoidance. Odean (1998b) documents the presence of the disposition effect using market data on 10000 discount brokerage accounts of individual investors. In his study, the ratio of realized gain over total gains, (i.e. proportion of gains realized or PGR) and the ratio of realized loss over total loss (i.e. proportion of loss realized PLR) are taken as measures to calculate the disposition effect. He finds that a majority of investors are reluctant to realize their losses. Grinblatt and Keloharju (2001) find evidence of the disposition effect in the Finnish stock market using a data set of shareholdings and trades of individual and institutional investors between 1994 and 1997. Shumway and Wu (2006) using a sample of 13,460 Chinese investors note that a majority of these investors exhibit the disposition effect and it drives momentum in the Shanghai stock exchange. Kumar (2009) uses multiple measures of valuation uncertainty and behavioral bias proxies to find that individual investors exhibit stronger disposition effect when stocks are harder to value and when market-level uncertainty is higher.

The above mentioned empirical evidences on the disposition effect show that this bias has an impact on trading volume of stocks. Further, this bias gets intensified in the presence of uncertainty and has the strength to drive momentum in the stock market.

Along with the above mentioned researches, behavioral finance includes several other biases that are equally important. Some of them are discussed below.

Herding: It is the tendency of investors to follow the crowd. One of the pioneer researches on herding is done by Lakonishok *et al.* (1991). They studied the role of herding and positive feedback trading in destabilizing the stock prices. According to them, herding referred to mimicking the investment actions of other fund managers at the same point of time; while positive feedback trading referred to buying winners and selling losers. The data set used in their study comprised of quarterly portfolio holdings of all-equity, pension funds from year 1985 to1989.They developed a model which measures herding by studying a subset of market participants over time. However, they did not find any substantial evidence of herding or positive feedback trading by pension fund managers except in small stocks. Scharfstein and Stein (1990) examine some of the factors that could lead to herd behavior in investment decisions of money managers. They develop a model which separated smart managers from biased (dumb) managers. Smart managers are those who received informative signals about the value of an investment, whereas the biased (dumb) managers receive purely noise signals. They identify that reputational concerns and 'sharing-the-blame' effect, are some of the factors that could drive managers to herd. Christie and Huang (1995) identify herding behavior in the market using cross sectional standard deviation (CSSD) of individual asset returns. CSSD is used to measure the proximity of asset returns to the realized market average. They analyzed that herding exists in periods of market extremes. They argued that when investors follow aggregate market movement, disregarding their own judgment (herding) then individual asset returns will not diverge much from overall market return. Therefore the value of CSSD gets reduced.

Past studies on herding suggest that it is an extremely powerful bias. When people start mimicking each other, the impact of their behavior gets intensified. It can result in bubbles when the demand is high and crashes when people detect overpricing and go on a selling spree (Smith 1991, Smith, 2011). It is not only observed in common investors, but also prevails in market experts like trade analysts, portfolio managers, investment managers, etc. This bias can have a drastic effect on the stock markets, particularly during the periods of extreme i.e. bull and bear phase, when the stock markets are most susceptible.

Status quo bias: Samuelson and Zeckhauser (1988) define the status quo bias as the tendency of individuals to maintain their previous decisions regardless of the changes in their environment. Brown and Kagel (2009) conduct lab experiment on simplified stock market and find that this status quo bias is significant across individuals, over time and is independent of the stock performance. Further, it prevails in an environment in which there are very low costs of identifying better performing stocks. They explain that the underlying factor behind this bias is individuals' reluctance to receive information that might question their own abilities; therefore they choose to restrict their comparisons to their existing choices rather than considering other options that were at their disposal. Li et al. (2009) analyze the presence of status quo bias, its determinants, and its impact on investor decision making using experimental method. Their study reveals the factors affecting the status quo bias are framing, investors' emotion and information structure. They demonstrate that investors' have a lower level of status quo bias under positive emotion, while a higher level under negative emotion. They also explain that people in general try to elude vague options if they have a choice to do so and would rather maintain their original position.

Research work on status quo, shows that individuals succumb to this bias when the existing alternatives are vague or inconsistent with their own beliefs. Further, emotional state of investors also contributes to this bias as the intensity of this bias is higher for negative emotion as compared to positive emotion. These findings emphasize that behavioral biases have far reaching implications on the stock market and its players. Such implications are being pondered upon in the next section.

Implications of Behavioral Biases

It can be seen historically that ignoring the behavior of the decision making process can prove to be quite expensive in the financial markets as it can result in stock market anomalies. For this reason, awareness about behavioral biases is indispensable.

As behavioral biases are unequivocally associated wherever human beings are involved; its implications become very wide. Hence, we narrow down our focus to implications that concern the financial practitioners. It can be suggested that a good grasp of this area will equip the practitioners not just to recognize others mistakes but their own mistakes as well. It facilitates financial advisors to become more effective by understanding their clients' psychology. It aids them in developing behaviorally modified portfolio, which best suits their clients' predisposition. It helps investment bankers in understanding the market sentiments as they make public issues for their companies. It assists the financial strategists in making better forecasts and security analysts for recommending stocks. Finally, the knowledge of behavioral biases is required for individual investors in the pursuit of making sensible and effective financial decisions.

CONCLUSION

The chapter describes the evolution of behavioral finance from standard finance theories. It discusses various traditional theories like expected utility theory, the Markowitz portfolio model, the capital asset pricing model and the efficient market hypothesis. Each of these theories is considered pillars in finance and they have a massive impact on financial researches throughout the history. These theories revolve around some basic assumptions, such as the rationality of individuals and efficiency of the market.

However, the applicability of these theories became questionable in real life scenarios when these rendered insufficient explanations to market anomalies like speculative bubbles, overreaction (underreaction), momentum and reversals, etc. the attention of researchers was then directed towards an alternative explanation that became the discipline: behavioral finance. Behavioral finance relaxes the limitations of traditional finance theories. It starts with accepting the fact that investors are in fact irrational and their decision making biased. This can cause possible inefficiencies in the financial markets. Behavioral finance provided a more realistic view to the researchers and concepts like the prospect theory, the behavioral portfolio theory, the behavioral asset pricing theory and the inefficient markets emerged. These concepts incorporated the psychological aspects of investor thought process and introduced some important behavioral biases that are either heuristic driven like representativeness, availability and anchoring and adjustment or frame dependent like loss aversion and narrow framing.

These biases have a significant impact on the stock market. Previous researches suggest that heuristics like representativeness, availability and anchoring are responsible for overreaction (underreaction) in the stock market. While other heuristics like overconfidence and optimism can create an increase in trading volume and even speculative bubbles. The studies on frame dependent biases reveal that biases like loss aversion can increase investors' risk seeking tendencies when facing the probability of heavy losses. The disposition effect can make investors to sell shares whose price have increased, while holding stocks that have dropped in value. It also has an impact on trading volume of the stocks. Other frame dependent biases are narrow framing and mental accounting. In narrow framing, investors take into account only their current risk and disregard the risks of their previous investments. On the other hand, investors affected by mental accounting segregate their wealth into separate mental accounts based on the different purpose their wealth serves.

Along with the heuristic and frame dependent biases there are other biases that share equal importance, and these are herding and status quo bias. Herd behavior along with optimism is one of the major precursors of speculative bubbles in the stock market. Herding is responsible for stock market crashes as well. Herding tendency in people makes them unsure about their own reasoning and sure about the decision of the masses. This bias exists even in sophisticated and professional market participants like portfolio managers and trade analysts that can make their recommendations and forecasts biased. Another relevant bias is the status quo bias. People with this bias try to maintain their existing position while making a decision instead of choosing the options about which they are unsure.

The previous sections give an account of some of the more researched biases. However, this is by no means an exhaustive account as there are many other significant biases that could not be included in the purview of this study.

As the research in this field progresses, it becomes very clear that these biases are both ubiquitous and germane. Ubiquitous, since they are present wherever investors are involved and germane because the effect of these biases can be very expensive (Shefrin, 2000). Therefore, knowledge of these biases becomes crucial not just for investors, but also for the financial experts like analysts and portfolio managers, so that they can comprehend the market sentiment and advice the investors in a way that they make the most profit out of it.

However, this field is not without its own limitations. It sensitizes people about their psychological errors in decision making, but does not provide any explanation as to how to exploit any irrationality in monetary terms (Statman, 2008). It makes people aware about mispricing in the stock market, but does not give any technique to beat the stock market (Bodie et al., 2009). Additionally, the models that exist in this field do not incorporate all the biases and as such cannot be generalized. All these limitations keep behavioral finance dependent on the traditional theories that it challenges (Harrington, 2010). There are other empirical challenges like in certain countries (for e.g. India) investor specific data is not publicly available which limits the scope of research. Nevertheless, with rapid advances in this field, it is hoped that behavioral theories will become more robust in the near future. Undeniably, this field has already paved the way for a new and improved finance. It has provided an understanding of decision makers that is more intuitive and presents a truer picture as compared to the standard finance.

REFERENCES

Barber, B., & Odean, T. (2000). Trading is hazardous to your wealth: The common stock investment performance of individual investors. *The Journal of Finance*, *55*(2), 773–806. doi:10.1111/0022-1082.00226

Barber, B., & Odean, T. (2001). Boys will be boys: Gender, overconfidence and common stock investment. *The Quarterly Journal of Economics*, *116*(1), 261–292. doi:10.1162/003355301556400

Barberis, N. C., & Huang, M. (2001). Mental Accounting, Loss Aversion and Individual Stock Returns. *The Journal of Finance*, *56*(4), 1247–1292. doi:10.1111/0022-1082.00367

Barberis, N. C., & Huang, M. (2006, July). *The loss aversion/narrow framing approach to the equity premium puzzle* (NBER Working Paper No. 12378).

Barberis, N. C., & Thaler, R. H. (2003). A Survey of Behavioral Finance. In Handbook of the Economics of Finance (pp. 1053-1128). North Holland: Elsevier Science.

Barone-Adesi, G., Mancini, L., & Shefrin, H. (2012, 12 June). *A Tale of two investors: Estimating risk aversion, optimism and overconfidence* (Working Paper).

Bentham, J. (1789). *An Introduction to the Principles of Morals and Legislations*. Oxford: Clarendon Press.

Berkelaar, A., & Kouwenberg, R. (2008, 29 October). *From boom till bust: How loss aversion affects asset prices* (Working Paper).

Bernoulli, D. (1954). *Exposition of a new theory on the measurement of risk.* [Originally published in 1738]. *Econometrica, 22*(1), 23–36. doi:10.2307/1909829

Bodie, Z., Kane, A., Marcus, A. J., & Mohanty, P. (2009). *Investments* (8th ed.). New York: Mc Graw Hill.

Brown, A. L., & Kagel, J. H. (2009). Behavior in a simplified stock market: The status quo bias, the disposition effect and the ostrich effect. *Annals of Finance, 5*(1), 1–14. doi:10.1007/s10436-007-0092-0

Campbell, S., & Sharpe, S. (2007). *Anchoring Bias in Consensus Forecasts and its Effect on Market Prices* (Staff Working Paper). Finance and Economic Discussion Series. Washington, DC: Federal Reserve Board.

Christie, W. G., & Huang, R. D. (1995). Following the Pied Piper: Do individual returns herd around the market? *Financial Analysts Journal, 51*(4), 31–37. doi:10.2469/faj.v51.n4.1918

Cooper, M. J., Dimitrov, O., & Rau, P. R. (2001). A rose.com by any other name. *The Journal of Finance, 56*(6), 2371–2388. doi:10.1111/0022-1082.00408

Coval, J. D., & Shumway, T. (2005). Do behavioral biases affect prices? *The Journal of Finance, 60*(1), 1–34. doi:10.1111/j.1540-6261.2005.00723.x

Dash, M. (2001). *Tulipomania: The story of world's most coveted flower and the extraordinary passions it aroused* (2nd ed.). New York: Three Rivers Press.

Dhar, R., & Kumar, A. (2001, December). *A non-random walk down the main street: Impact of price trends on trading decisions of individual investors* (Working Paper). Yale School of Management.

Fama, E. (1970). Efficient capital markets: A review of theory and empirical work. *The Journal of Finance, 25*(2), 383–417. doi:10.2307/2325486

Fama, E., & French, K. (1992). The cross-section of expected stock returns. *The Journal of Finance, 47*(2), 427–465. doi:10.1111/j.1540-6261.1992.tb04398.x

Festinger, L., Riecken, H. W., & Schachter, S. (1956). *When prophecy fails: A social and psychological study of a modern group that predicted the destruction of the world* (1st ed.). Minneapolis: University Of Minnesota Press. doi:10.1037/10030-000

Germain, L., Rosseau, F., & Vanhems, A. (2005, July). Optimistic and pessimistic trading in financial markets (Working Paper).

Gervais, S., & Odean, T. (2001). Learning to be overconfident. *Review of Financial Studies, 14*(1), 1–27. doi:10.1093/rfs/14.1.1

Grinblatt, M., & Keloharju, M. (2001). What makes investors trade? *The Journal of Finance, 56*(2), 589–616. doi:10.1111/0022-1082.00338

Harrington, B. (2010). *On the limitations of behavioral finance*. Retrieved December 12, 2013, from http://thesocietypages.org/economicsociology/2010/10/31/on-the-limitations-of-behavioral-finanance/

Heifetz, A., & Siegel, Y. (2001, October). *The evolution of biased perceptions* (Working Paper).

Hoffmann, A., & Post, T. (2012, 22 November). *What makes investors optimistic, what makes them afraid.* (Netspar Working Paper Series No. 44).

Hwang, S., & Satchell, S. E. (2010, 19 February). *How loss averse are investors in financial markets?* (Working Paper).

Jegadeesh, N., & Titman, S. (1993). Returns to buying winners and selling losers. *Implications for Stock Market Efficiency, 48*, 65–91.

Jensen, M. (1978). Some anomalous evidence regarding market efficiency. *Journal of Financial Economics*, *6*(2-3), 95–101. doi:10.1016/0304-405X(78)90025-9

Kaestner, M. (2005, March). *Anomalous price behavior following earnings surprises: Does representativeness cause overreaction?* (Working Paper). Université Montpellier II.

Kahneman, D., & Tversky, A. (1979). *Prospect theory: An analysis of decision under risk. Econometrica*, *47*(2), 263–292. doi:10.2307/1914185

Keynes, J. M. (1967). *The General Theory of Employment, Interest, and Money*. London: McMillan. (Originally published 1936)

Kliger, D., & Kudryavtsev, A. (2010). The availability heuristic and investors' reaction to company specific events. *Journal of Behavioral Finance*, *11*(1), 50–65. doi:10.1080/15427561003591116

Kumar, A. (2009). Hard-to-value stocks, behavioral biases, and informed trading. *Journal of Financial and Quantitative Analysis*, *44*(6), 1375–1401. doi:10.1017/S0022109009990342

Lakonishok, J., Shleifer, A., & Vishny, R. W. (1991). *Do institutional investors destabilize stock prices- evidence on herding and feedback trading* (NBER Working paper, no. 3846).

Li, J., Ren, G., Ma, Q., & Liu, L. (2009). An experimental study on investors' status quo bias and its determinants. *Frontiers of Business Research in China*, *3*(4), 543–565. doi:10.1007/s11782-009-0026-y

Lintner, J. (1965). The valuation of risk assets and the selection of risky investments in stock portfolios and capital budgets. *The Review of Economics and Statistics*, *73*(1), 13–37. doi:10.2307/1924119

Liu, J., & Wang, M. C. (2010). Narrow framing: Professions, sophistication and experience. *Journal of Futures Markets*, *30*(3), 203–244.

Mackay, C. (2003). *Memoirs of extraordinary popular delusions and the madness of crowds. original*. Minneapolis, New York: Dover Publication Inc. (Originally published 1841)

Markowitz, H. M. (1952). Portfolio selection. *The Journal of Finance*, *7*(1), 77–91.

Mill, J. S. (1968). *Essays on Some Unsettled Questions of Political Economy*. New York: Augustus M. Kelley. (Original work published 1844)

Mossin, J. (1966). Equilibrium in a capital asset market. *Econometrica*, *34*(4), 768–783. doi:10.2307/1910098

Odean, T. (1998a). Volume, volatility, price and profit when all traders are above average. *The Journal of Finance*, *53*(6), 1887–1934. doi:10.1111/0022-1082.00078

Odean, T. (1998b). Are investors reluctant to realize losses? *The Journal of Finance*, *53*(5), 1775–1798. doi:10.1111/0022-1082.00072

Odean, T. (1999). Do investors trade too much? *The American Economic Review*, *89*(5), 1279–1298. doi:10.1257/aer.89.5.1279

Pompian, M. (2011). *Behavioral Finance and Wealth Management: How to Build Optimal Portfolios That Account for Investor Biases* (2nd ed.). New Jersey: Wiley Finance Publications.

Pratt, J. W. (1964). Risk aversion in the small and in the large. *Econometrica*, *32*(1/2), 122–136. doi:10.2307/1913738

Raiffa, H. (1968). *Decision Analysis: Introductory Lectures on Choices under Uncertainty*. Reading, MA: Addison-Wesley.

Samuelson, W., & Zeckhauser, R. (1988). Status quo bias in decision making. *Journal of Risk and Uncertainty*, *1*(1), 7–59. doi:10.1007/BF00055564

Savage, L. (1964). *The Foundations of Statistics*. New York: Wiley.

Scharfstein, D. S., & Stein, J. C. (1990). Herd behavior and investment. *The American Economic Review*, *80*, 465–479.

Selden, G. C. (1912). *Psychology of the stock market: Human impulses lead to speculative disasters*. New York: Ticker Publishing.

Sewell, M. (2010, April). *Behavioral Finance* (Revised). University of Cambridge

Sharpe, W. (1964). Capital asset prices: A theory of market equilibrium under conditions of risk. *The Journal of Finance*, *19*(3), 425–442.

Shefrin, H. (2000). *Beyond Greed and Fear: Understanding Behavioral Finance and Psychology of Investing*. New York: Oxford University Press.

Shefrin, H., & Statman, M. (1985). The disposition to sell winners too early and ride losers too long: Theory and evidence. *The Journal of Finance*, *40*(3), 777–779. doi:10.1111/j.1540-6261.1985.tb05002.x

Shefrin, H., & Statman, M. (1994). Behavioral capital asset pricing theory. *Journal of Financial and Quantitative Analysis*, *29*(3), 323–349. doi:10.2307/2331334

Shefrin, H., & Statman, M. (2011, November). *Behavioral finance in the financial crisis: Market efficiency, Minsky, and Keynes* (Working Paper). Santa Clara University.

Shiller, R. J. (1981). Do stock prices move too much to be justified by subsequent changes in dividend. *The American Economic Review*, *71*, 457–498.

Shiller, R. J. (2000). *Irrational Exuberance*. Princeton: Princeton University Press.

Shleifer, A. (2000). *Inefficient Markets: An Introduction to Behavioral Finance* (1st ed.). New York: Oxford University Press Inc. doi:10.1093/0198292279.001.0001

Shumway, T., & Wu, G. (2006, May). *Does disposition drive momentum?* (Working paper).

Simon, H. A. (1955). A behavioral model of rational choice. *The Quarterly Journal of Economics*, *69*(1), 99–118. doi:10.2307/1884852

Smith, A. (1759). *The theory of moral sentiments*. London: A. Millar.

Smith, A. (1776). *The Wealth of Nations*. London, W.: Strahan and T. Cadell.

Smith, N. (2011). *Herding and speculation in experimental asset market*. Unpublished dissertation, University of Michigan, Michigan.

Smith, V. L. (1991). Rational choice: The contrast between economics and psychology. *Journal of Political Economy*, *99*(4), 877–897. doi:10.1086/261782

Statman, M. (1999). Behavioral Finance: Past Battles and Future Engagements. *Financial Analysts Journal*, *55*(6), 18–27. doi:10.2469/faj.v55.n6.2311

Statman, M. (2008). What is behavioral finance? In *Handbook of Finance* (Vol. II). New Jersey: John Wiley & Sons, Inc.

Thaler, R. (1999). Mental accounting matters. *Journal of Behavioral Decision Making*, *12*(3), 183–206. doi:10.1002/(SICI)1099-0771(199909)12:3<183::AID-BDM318>3.0.CO;2-F

Toshino, M., & Suto, M. (2004, 25 October). *Cognitive biases of Japanese institutional investors: Consistency with behavioral finance*. (Working Paper Series No. WNIF-04-05). Waseda University Institute of Finance, Japan.

Tversky, A., & Kahneman, D. (1973). Availability: A heuristic for judging frequency and probability. *Cognitive Psychology*, *5*(2), 207–232. doi:10.1016/0010-0285(73)90033-9

Tversky, A., & Kahneman, D. (1974). Judgment under uncertainty: Heuristics and biases. *Science, 185*(4157), 1124–1131. doi:10.1126/science.185.4157.1124 PMID:17835457

von Neumann, J., & Morgenstern, O. (1944). *Theory of Games and Economic Behavior*. Princeton: Princeton University Press.

Zhou, W.-X., & Sornette, D. (2006). Is there a real-estate bubble in the U.S.? *Physica A, 361*(1), 297–308. doi:10.1016/j.physa.2005.06.098

ADDITIONAL READING

Baker, H. K., & Nofsinger, J. R. (2002). Psychological biases of investors. *Financial Services Review, 11*, 97–116.

Barber, B., & Odean, T. (1999). The courage of misguided convictions. *Financial Analysts Journal, 55*(5), 41–55.

Barber, B. M., & Odean, T. (1998). *Too many cooks spoil the profits: The performance of investment clubs* (Working Paper). Davis: University of California.

Belsky, G., & Gelovich, T. (1999). *Why Smart People Make Big Money Mistakes and How to Correct Them*. New York: Simon & Schuster.

Benartzi, S., & Thaler, R. (1995). Myopic loss aversion and the equity premium puzzle. *The Quarterly Journal of Economics, 110*(1), 73–92.

Benartzi, S., & Thaler, R. (2002). How much is investor autonomy worth? *The Journal of Finance, 57*, 1593–1616.

Bernstein, P. L. (1996). *Against the Gods: the Remarkable Story of Risk*. New York: John Wiley and Sons.

Bhandari, G., & Deaves, R. (2006). The demographics of overconfidence. *Journal of Behavioral Finance, 7*(1), 5–11.

Bikhchandani, S., Hirshleifer, D., & Welch, I. (1992). A theory of fads, fashion, custom and cultural change as informational cascades. *Journal of Political Economy, 100*, 992–1036.

De Bondt, W., & Thaler, R. (1985). Does stock market overreact? *The Journal of Finance, 40*(3), 793–808.

Fair, R. (2002). The events that shook the market. *The Journal of Business, 75*(4), 713–731.

Fama, E. (1998). Market efficiency, long term returns, and behavioral finance. *The Journal of Finance, 49*(3), 283–306.

Goetzmann, W., & Peles, N. (1997). Cognitive dissonance and mutual fund investors. *Journal of Financial Research, 20*(2), 145–158.

Hirshleifer, D. (2001). Investor psychology and asset pricing. *The Journal of Finance, 56*(4), 1533–1597.

Langer, E. J. (1975). The illusion of control. *Journal of Personality and Social Psychology, 32*, 311–328.

Miller, M. H. (1986). Behavioral rationality in finance: The case of dividends. *The Journal of Business, 59*(4), S451–S468.

Nofsinger, J. (2001). *Investment Madness*. Upper Saddle River, New Jersey: Financial Times Prentice Hall.

Shefrin, H. (1999). *Irrational exuberance, heterogeneous beliefs and option markets* (Working Paper). Santa Clara University.

Shefrin, H. (1999). *On kernels and sentiment* (Working Paper). Santa Clara University.

Shiller, R. J. (1990). Speculative prices and popular models. *The Journal of Economic Perspectives, 4*(2), 55–65.

Thaler, R., & Shefrin, H. (1981). An economic theory of self-control. *Journal of Political Economy*, *89*(2), 392–410.

KEY TERMS AND DEFINITIONS

Anchoring and Adjustment: A heuristic used to estimate an unknown value by starting with a known figure (anchor) which is then adjusted to arrive at a final value. In this case, people tend to get biased towards the anchor rather than away from it.

Availability Bias: Tendency of individuals to give more weight age to recent information which could be recalled easily.

Behavioral Finance: A field of finance that incorporates the influence of psychology on the behavior of financial practitioners and its role in explaining market anomalies.

Disposition Effect: A tendency of investors to start selling the shares that have gained value early, while, holding the losers for too long.

Efficient Market Hypothesis: A concept given by Fama (1970) that describes an efficient financial market as one in which security prices completely reflect the available information. Further, the investors in this scenario are well informed and make rational choices, such that the mispricing of securities cannot occur.

Herding Bias: It is the propensity of investors to mimic the crowd without taking into consideration their own judgment.

Market Anomalies: (Market Inefficiencies): Aberrations in financial markets that cannot be explained by efficient market hypothesis, for e.g. speculative bubbles, crashes, overreaction and under reaction.

Mental Accounting: Defined as the tendency to segregate complex information into manageable mental accounts. In investment terms, people separate their assets into different categories depending on the purpose each category fulfills.

Narrow Framing Bias: A myopic approach of investors wherein they make investment decisions without considering the context of their entire portfolio. People affected with this bias focus their attention to specific, seemingly attractive investment options while they tend to overlook the full range of options available to them.

Optimism Bias: It causes people to believe that they are less likely to experience negative incidents. In financial terms, it is the tendency of investors to overestimate the expected return of a security.

Overconfidence: Propensity of individuals to overestimate their own knowledge and ability to perform.

Prospect Theory: A concept given by Kahneman and Tversky (1979). This theory analyses the decision making process of individuals under risk. Here the choices are determined in terms of loss and gains. It suggests that same level of joy and pain does not have equal effect on people. An average individual tends to be more sensitive towards losses than gains. This tendency is called loss aversion.

Representativeness: A heuristic driven bias wherein individuals asses their options by comparing its similarity with an existing prototype.

Status Quo Bias: People affected by this bias prefer to maintain their current position, irrespective of the change in their environment.

Chapter 2

A General View of Poverty in Turkey as an Issue for Social Work in the Light of Behavioral Finance and Game Theory

Seher Cesur-Kiliçaslan
İstanbul Arel University, Turkey

Toprak Işik
Independent Scholar, Turkey

ABSTRACT

In this chapter, the authors define poverty in general terms before including statistics for a detailed, Turkey-specific discussion. Once the authors elaborate on the causes of poverty, they introduce behavioural economics and game theory, the fundamental aim of the chapter being to examine how these two theories affect perceptions of poverty and the struggle against poverty. Another issue that enters into the scope of this chapter is to what extent the poor themselves are responsible for their own poverty. On this question, game theory and behavioural economics can potentially be marshalled against the poor. However, we also argue that, by using a different approach, both theories can be interpreted in the poor's favour. We examine the double-sided nature of these two theories in detail and stress how important it is in the study of poverty to consider the disadvantageous position in which the poor find themselves.

INTRODUCTION

Unfortunately, at the present time, poverty is no less widespread than the two extremely up-to-date scientific theories that we shall be using in this study. Poverty is no longer a problem experienced only in the less developed regions of the world. Today, in many developed countries, poverty rates have started to reach alarming levels. For example, although the EU is—generally speaking—a prosperous region, there too poverty is still at a relatively high level: approximately one out of every seven people (seventy-two million people in total) is at risk of poverty or relatively poor, and the poverty rate among disadvantaged groups

DOI: 10.4018/978-1-4666-7484-4.ch002

such as the elderly, the disabled and children is particularly high (Gündoğan, 2008, p. 45).

Poverty has an influence on almost everyone, not only through its actual presence, but also through its prevalence in the world of human emotion. Indeed, those who have never had a direct encounter with poverty in their own life or environment are nonetheless aware of it from portrayals in different media, ranging from stories to films.

According to the calculations of the Turkish Statistical Institute (TÜİK), in Turkey in 2007, approximately 0.54% of the population was living below the starvation line, which only includes food expenses, while 18.56% was living below the poverty line, which includes both food and non-food expenses. When we take the figure of 70 586 000, obtained in the 2007 census, to be the population of Turkey, then according to TÜİK's most recent study on poverty, there are 380 000 people in Turkey living below the starvation line (T.C. Başbakanlık Aile ve Sosyal Araştırmalar Genel Müdürlüğü, 2010, pp. 3-4).

Although they shall be dealt with in more detail below, suffice it to say that both behavioral finance and game theory examine people's decision-making processes. While behavioral finance considers the psychological factors that influence decisions, game theory tries to determine the correct strategies from a logical angle. Based on the assumption that both theories complement each other, they can be dealt with together. At the same time, like all people, the poor, in their roles of making the decisions that influence their own situation, also come within the scope of this joint assessment.

BACKGROUND

Poverty

The first difficulty encountered in a scientific treatment of poverty is that there is no agreed-upon definition. Briefly, it can be described as a state of deprivation wherein the basic needs necessary for survival are not met. If we flesh out the idea of poverty, paying attention to the emotional intensity it contains, then poverty is hunger, poverty is not having a place to shelter, poverty is being ill and not being able to go to the doctor. Poverty is not being able to go to school and not knowing how to read or write. Poverty is not having a job; poverty is looking at the future in fear and living from day to day. Poverty is children dying because there is no clean drinking water. Poverty is weakness; poverty is not having a voice; poverty is not being able to take part in decision-making processes; poverty is not having a representative or having nobody to represent you. It is for these reasons that poverty really does pose a serious threat and a major risk to survival (T.C. Başbakanlık Aile ve Sosyal Araştırmalar Genel Müdürlüğü, 2010, p. 233).

The prevailing theory in the definition and measurement of poverty is the absolute poverty line (threshold) theory, which has roots in studies carried out in England towards the end of the nineteenth century and is based on income/expenditure criteria. According to this theory, poverty is generally defined as "not possessing sufficient resources to meet one's needs" or very similarly, "remaining below the absolute minimum welfare level" and "not being able to meet the need for goods and services necessary in order to stay alive" (Alagh 1992, p. 109).

The Causes of Poverty

We can suggest some very basic explanations for the causes of poverty or about why some people come to need the help of others in order to survive. Just as these causes can be related to personal characteristics, such as skills and abilities, concepts of discipline and responsibility, or levels of frugality, they can also depend on structural factors outside of the individual's own direct control (T.C. Başbakanlık Aile ve Sosyal Araştırmalar Genel Müdürlüğü, 2010, p. 234).

Overpopulation, the unfair distribution of economic resources, inability to afford high standards of living, lack of education and employment possibilities, rapid destruction of the environment, certain economic and demographic trends etc. are among the primary factors that can lead to poverty. In these circumstances, can we blame the poor for their own poverty? Could their poverty not be caused by the development programs that governments follow? Can we gloss over the role of globalization as one of the causes of poverty and inequality? For instance, we certainly cannot ignore that behind the interdependency that, in tandem with globalization, is steadily increasing throughout the world, there are global decisions, policies and practices, generally determined by the rich and powerful. It seems very difficult to bring under control and eradicate the basic factors, such as these, that can be numbered among the causes of poverty. In most cases, the causes of poverty interact with each other and with the consequences of poverty as well. As a result, factors that push people into poverty at the same time also, generally speaking, produce conditions whereby the same people are unable to escape from poverty (T.C. Başbakanlık Aile ve Sosyal Araştırmalar Genel Müdürlüğü, 2010, pp. 1-2).

The Culture of Poverty

Another important concept related to poverty is the "culture of poverty", first formulated in the 1960s by Oscar Lewis(as cited in Theories of Poverty: The culture of poverty, n.d.). Lewis claimed that the culture of poverty was "a way of life handed on from generation to generation along family lines." The people in this culture are marginalized; they consider themselves helpless, powerless and lower class; they live only with an understanding of living from day to day, with no thought of the future. They are fatalistic; there are high divorce rates in their families; women and children are abandoned; the heads of the family are generally women. People who internalize the culture of poverty do not participate in social or political life; they do not join political parties; they have only limited contact with institutions such as banks and hospitals. According to Lewis, the culture of poverty, inasmuch as it affects children, perpetuates poverty. Children in slum areas internalize these behavioral codes when they are six or seven years old and for the rest of their lives do not make the effort to change them (Theories of Poverty: The culture of poverty, n.d.).

Lewis' concept can be summed up as "a subculture of people living in poverty who respond to their lack of resources with a distinct set of negative beliefs, attitudes, and behaviors" (Hill&Gaines, 2007). As for the other basic characteristics of the culture of poverty, they are (Lewis as cited in Erdem, 2003):

- Those living in the culture of poverty do not have a particularly healthy relationship with social institutions.
- The poor are not members of trades unions or political parties. In other words, their cooperative and organizational skills are very weak. Because they are not very familiar with politics, they cannot be used in movements that oppose the system. They have low literacy rates and a low demand for education. They rarely frequent banks, hospitals, department stores, museums or art galleries.
- They live in unhealthy dwellings in slum neighborhoods. Many houses only have one bedroom.

- Their families tend to be large. There is no period of childhood in the family. Children tend to be initiated into sex at an early age. There is a high incidence of cohabitation. Husbands very often abandon their children and spouses.
- On the individual level, there is a high incidence of feelings of exclusion from society, feelings of helplessness, feelings of inferiority, weak ego structure, no impulse control, living for today and not really thinking about tomorrow, resignation and fatalism, and widespread belief in male superiority.

Lewis blamed poverty for creating a subculture within itself and accused the poor of being scathing, reproachful and scornful (Erdoğan, 2011a). However, the attempt to define poverty as a culture or subculture with its own specific psychopathology actually has a result that is tantamount to concealing the structural causes that underlie it (Bilen&Şan as cited in T.C. Başbakanlık Aile ve Sosyal Araştırmalar Genel Müdürlüğü, 2010, p. 14).

Poverty in Turkey

Examining income distribution and the dimensions of poverty in Turkey, we cannot speak of the existence of a balanced income distribution. For 2004-2005, the top 20% of the population received close to half of the total income in the country, while the bottom 20% received only 6%. The top 40% of the population received more than two thirds of total income (T.C. Başbakanlık Aile ve Sosyal Araştırmalar Genel Müdürlüğü, 2010, p. 18).

According to the United Nations Development Programme (UNDP) Human Development Index, considered as one of the indicators of a country's poverty, while Turkey was 69th out of 174 countries in 1995, it had fallen to 86th in 1999 and 84th in 2005 (UNDP, 2007). The concept of human poverty set forth in the UNDP's 1997 Human Development Report is based on the thesis that, in order to meet basic needs, as well as financial opportunities, some economic, social and cultural opportunities are also required. In other words, it takes as its starting point the fact that poverty is multi-dimensional, encompassing more than mere financial needs (T.C. Başbakanlık Aile ve Sosyal Araştırmalar Genel Müdürlüğü, 2010, pp. 18-19). Devised with this idea in mind, the human poverty index measures deprivation arising in human development, such as low life expectancy and lack of educational services or limited access to private and public resources (Aktan&Vural as cited in T.C. Başbakanlık Aile ve Sosyal Araştırmalar Genel Müdürlüğü, 2010, p. 19). According to this, in terms of the indicators measured, we can say that over a ten-year period, Turkey has witnessed a change below the world average and more limited development compared to other countries (T.C. Başbakanlık Aile ve Sosyal Araştırmalar Genel Müdürlüğü, 2010, p. 19). Based the 2012 data and method, Turkey was 90th out of 187 countries on the 2011 Human Development Index (2013 İnsani gelişme raporu. Güney'in yükselişi: Farklılıklar dünyasında insani gelişme. 2013 İnsani gelişme raporu'ndaki muhtelif göstergelerle ilgili açıklama notu, n.d.).

In 2005, there were 623 000 people living below the food poverty line in Turkey. Approximately 20% of the population eked out a living below the food and non-food poverty lines. When we take a poverty line of $2.15 per person per day, the number of poor rises to over one million, while at $4.30, the figure specified for the group of countries that includes Turkey, it is approximately twelve million (T.C. Başbakanlık Aile ve Sosyal Araştırmalar Genel Müdürlüğü, 2010, p. 20).

The latest data used to calculate the Multidimensional Poverty Index (MPI) for Turkey were collected in 2003. While 6.6% of the population lives in multidimensional poverty, a further 7.7% (by the MPI 'reckoning') are at risk of multidimensional poverty. The intensity of deprivation in Turkey, in other words the proportion of indicators in which people living in multidimensional poverty are deprived, is 42% (2013 İnsani gelişme raporu. Güney'in yükselişi: Farklılıklar dünyasında insani gelişme. 2013 İnsani gelişme raporu'ndaki muhtelif göstergelerle ilgili açıklama notu, n.d.).

Taken from a historical perspective, in Turkey, the poor have been helped to a large extent by religious institutions and waqfs and/or by private philanthropy. Until the mid-1980s and even today, successive Turkish governments have tended to deal with the field of welfare, or rather the way in which those in need are cared for, within traditional solidarity mechanisms (Abay as cited in T.C. Başbakanlık Aile ve Sosyal Araştırmalar Genel Müdürlüğü, 2010, p. 20).

Study on the evolution of poverty has intensified in Turkey; this was especially so in the 1990s. One of the most salient reasons for this is that while national income has increased, the income gap between the middle and upper classes, on the one hand, and the lower class, on the other, has broadened in parallel with it. This has made poverty visible in the city. Another reason is that migration from the countryside to the city has increased and the urban poor are losing their organic bonds with their village. While this process induces families to settle in the city, where they can no longer grow their own food, it also results in absolute poverty when the family experiences a loss of income due to unemployment or similar reasons (T.C. Başbakanlık Aile ve Sosyal Araştırmalar Genel Müdürlüğü, 2010, p. 26).

As the result of the evolution in poverty, poor people lack the protective mechanisms that they used to have within the traditional social order. Charity for the poor and the struggle against poverty cannot be sustained on the natural reflexes of present society. The fact that people become grouped according to their incomes in residential areas in big cities has resulted in the poor having social networks, from whom they could have received support in times of need, being composed of people who, like them, are also poor and in need of help. For this reason, there is more need than before for overarching organizations that will identify poverty and make the necessary interventions.

Behavioral Finance

In 1979, in opposition to Expected Utility Theory, Daniel Kahneman and Amos Tversky developed Prospect Theory, which asserts that, due to psychological factors, people assign different probability values to gains and losses. Thus, they made a breakthrough not only in psychology but also in finance. In the same paper, they argue that when studying investment decisions, perceived risk, not expected risk, should be taken into account. Thanks to these findings, traditional finance theories that propose systematic approaches to investor decisions started to be questioned and the groundwork for studies in behavioral finance was laid (Sefil&Çilingiroğlu, 2011, p.253).

Behavioral finance was born as a discipline that points to human psychology as a potential source of the steps in the decision-making process and of market anomalies that cannot be explained by traditional finance theories. Unlike traditional finance theories, the models proposed by behavioral finance methodology make as much use as possible of parameters that feature human behaviors. This incorporates anomalies, representing economic actors' deviations from rational behavior, into the models. Research in the field of behavioral finance is structured around cognitive and emotional tendencies that prevent individuals from behaving rationally. Emotional tendencies are basically guided by desires to avoid loss and regret. Cognitive tendencies are formed as a result of investors seeking to create shortcuts in their decision-making processes (Sefil&Çilingiroğlu, 2011, pp. 252-255).

Among other things, the psychological carriers of value appear to be gains and losses, rather than final wealth, and diminishing sensitivity yields conflicting risk attitudes for losses and gains. People are loss averse (the loss associated with giving up a good is greater than the utility associated with obtaining it), which yields "endowment effects" and a reluctance to depart from the status quo (Kahneman&Tversky, 2000).

Also, contrary to standard fungibility assumptions, people compartmentalize wealth and spending into distinct budget categories, such as savings, rent, and -entertainment, and into separate mental accounts, such as current income, assets, and future income (Thaler, 1999). People typically show different propensities to consume from their current income (where marginal propensity to consume [MPC] is high), current assets (where it is intermediate), and future income (where it is low). In addition, people often fail to ignore sunk costs or to consider opportunity costs and have trouble predicting their future moods and tastes or learning from past experience (Kahneman&Tversky, 2000).

Standard economic-policy thinking attributes to people preferences and motivations that they often lack and ignores psychological factors that can be highly consequential. Deterrence, for example, plays a key role in the legal determination of punishment but appears to be relatively ineffective because those who violate the law often tend not to engage in the presumed cost-benefit analyses. Similarly, policies geared toward the poor are often driven by normative assumptions, rather than empirical facts, in ways that may miss the intended beneficiaries. Standard thinking naturally assumes that big effects are due to big causes and, thus, merit major intervention. If the poor are deeply hurt by their failure to have a bank account, then there must be compelling reasons for that failure. Behavioral research, on the other hand, has shown that highly consequential behaviors often are triggered by what are deemed to be minor causes (Bertrand, Mullainathan&Shafir, 2004, pp. 422-423).

To explain investor irrationality and their decision-making process, behavioral finance uses empirical evidence from cognitive psychology and the types of decision making and prejudices that appear when people form beliefs and preferences (Barberis&Thaler, 2003).

Game Theory

Game theory, which appeared slightly earlier than behavioral finance, has also been crowned with a Nobel Prize, and has received broad acceptance in the academic and intellectual fields. Game theory is based on examining the opposing tactics used by rational actors in "games" and predicting the result.

Game theory is rampant in economics. Having long ago invaded industrial organization, game-theoretic modeling is now commonplace in international, labor, macro and public finance, and it is gathering steam in development and economic history. Nor is economics alone: accounting, finance, law, marketing, political science and sociology are beginning similar experiences. Many modelers use game theory because it allows them to think like an economist when price theory does not apply. That is, game-theoretic models allow economists to study the implications of rationality, self-interest and equilibrium, both in market interactions that are modeled as games (such as where small numbers, hidden information, hidden actions or incomplete contracts are present) and in nonmarket interactions (such as between a regulator and a firm, a boss and a worker, and so on) (Gibbons,1997, p.127). Zhao and Zhang (n.d., p.4) state that game theory can be used in interactions where both sides select profit-maximizing strategies.

Sociologists study games on occasion (e.g., Avery; Puddephatt), but they liken social life to games with abandon. Usually such allusions serve to highlight some property or properties of the setting under study that the author can expect the average reader to already associate with games. Those properties include: that, like games, some areas of social life are rule-governed (Geertz), goal-oriented (Long), and possibly competitive in that there is some coveted reward that not everyone can possess (Bourdieu &Wacquant); that action involves discrete moves (Goffman) and perhaps something approximating alternating turns (Elias); that skilled "play" involves the use of strategies (Bourdieu; Finlay &Coverdill); that with extended play one develops an instinctive "feel for the game" (Lamaison& Bourdieu); that earlier actions constrain subsequent options for oneself and others (Slez& Martin); that a setting may demand that participants ignore external distractions (Goffman); that play is engrossing (Burawoy; Goffman); that roles are differentiated and knowingly coordinated (Mead); that rules are arbitrary, in the sense that they are based on convention rather than physical laws (Kaminski); and that, as a consequence of rules' arbitrariness, many different games are possible (Burawoy) (as cited in DiCicco-Bloom & Gibson, 2010, p. 248).

POVERTY IN THE CONTEXT OF BEHAVIORAL FINANCE AND GAME THEORY

The fact that behavioral finance explains negative situations as incorrect decisions taken by individuals may suggest that also poverty, qua negative situation, can be explained as incorrect behaviorson the part of the poor. As a typical academic example of this approach, Beaulier and Caplan (2007), in their article "Behavioral Economics and Perverse Effects of the Welfare State", have interpreted behavioral economics as a theory showing that we should not help the poor for their own good:

Yes, giving money to the poor reduces their incentive to enter the workforce, acquire experience, and eventually join the middle class through their own efforts. But this hardly shows that it makes the poor worse off! All the transfer program does is make the non-work option more attractive. If it remains less attractive than work, the poor will still opt for work. If, on the other hand, the poor decide to take the government's money and remain idle, it must be because—all things considered—it maximizes their expected lifetime utility. In otherwords, if you were to remindwelfare recipients that they are hurting their future job prospects, they could curtly respond: 'I am well-aware of that, but my welfare checks more than compensate for my loss of future income.'(Beaulier&Caplan, 2007).

The perverse effects frequently attributed to the welfare state are easy to interpret from a behavioral perspective. If people overestimate the magnitude of immediate benefits relative to more distant ones, you can actually—on net—harm them by offering them additional immediate benefits (Beaulier&Caplan, 2007).

One poor family will be better off if it takes government assistance. But its members can be worse off on balance because other families in their area participate in the same program. Their neighborhood becomes a worse place to live as the mix of local activity shifts from productive work to drug use or crime. There could also be intra-family externalities. A father willing to support his family might abandon it if the government will assume his responsibilities. The father is better off as a result of the government program, but his wife and family are worse off if they prefer the presence of a working father to a stream of government checks (Beaulier&Caplan, 2007).

To ascribe the cause of poverty, or—according to the principles of behavioral economics—the mistakes of the poor, to the overt behaviors of individuals contains the error of seeing a social problem as the sum of the independent actions of the individuals that figure within it. Social phenomena are definitely related to the behaviors of individuals, but they are not the sum total of these behaviors. If that were so, it would be possible to solve the problem of poverty by enabling each poor person to act correctly according to the principles of behavioral economics or game theory. Studies on the struggle against poverty clearly show that this is not possible. Even if sometimes the individual mistakes of the poor are enough to explain why they are poor, the number of poor people produced by national conditions would have remained unchanged if these mistakes had not been made. In Turkey, unemployment is one of the major causes of poverty. Individual failings can be posited as the reason why an unemployed person loses his or her job or cannot find work; if the unemployed person in question is freed of these negative qualities and finds work, the employment potential of the country will not be changed: someone else will become unemployed and poor instead.

Moreover, to advocate that the poor forgo benefits because the balance of intra-familial relations will be disrupted is similar to recommending that no medicines be used because of side effects. As in all social work aimed at families, while helping the poor, experts in the field already stress the necessity of paying attention to current family relationships.

The eradication of poverty is not something that will be achieved through individual endeavors alone. It requires an economic and social crusade. For this reason, a multiple-intervention system should be used. For example, while intervening on an individual level in a poor family in areas such as helping a father or mother find work or education, it is also necessary to work with the family as a whole on the mezzo level to improve intra-familial roles and functions that have broken down because of the problem of poverty. Macro interventions can even be planned, for instance,to enable poor individuals and families to participate in social life and make use of their rights, and to bring about the equal distribution of services in society (İçağasıoğlu-Çoban, 2003, p. 201).

Miley, O'Melia, Dubois (as cited in İçağasıoğlu-Çoban, 2003, pp. 202-203) state that generalist social work is carried out in the framework of three interrelated functions: counseling, education and resource management.

As a behavioral economist, Mullainathan (2009), after noting that he is optimistic that behavioral economics can be used in the struggle against poverty, cited the poor in the south of India as an example of what behavioral economics calls "shortsightedness". This example is illuminating about how the principles of behavioral economics can be used in the course satisfying the three functions of social work.

Sugarcane is harvested once a year and paid for in one lump sum. Planting sugarcane, although it's more profitable monetarily, raises an unappealing psychological challenge. Imagine receiving your entire annual salary all at once, at the beginning of the year, and having to dole it out carefully over the course of 12 months. Meanwhile, many who own cows cite the daily income that milk provides as a primary benefit, even though cows are not as profitable as other investments. This is the far more consequential equivalent of someone purchasing the more expensive (per unit) but smaller bag of cookies to avoid the temptation of eating all of them at once. Uncertainty figures in as well: A small-business owner who does not know what she'll earn must have the willpower to save in good weeks to ride out the lean weeks, while a salaried worker knows exactly what is coming, and when(Mullainathan,2009).

Many households seek advice from financial planners and other experts, yet some households make decisions that are hard to reconcile with this advice or with any standard model. One response to this observation is to maintain the assumption that actual and ideal behavior coincide, but to consider nonstandard behavioral models of preferences that incorporate phenomena such as loss aversion and mental accounting. An alternative response is to abandon the framework of revealed preference and to consider the possibility that households may not express their preferences optimally. This response leads to the view that behavioral finance theory describes the choices households currently make, whereas standard finance theory describes the choices that maximize household welfare, and that households can be educated to make (Campbell, 2006, p.1554).

As can be seen, behavioral economics approaches are important in the development of advice designed to help the poor use their scarce resources more efficiently. The poor, as a rule, do not have savings to invest; they can only be steeredtowards being conscious consumers if they are enabledto make effective use of their daily/ weekly/monthly earnings in line with the suggestions of behavioral economics. In Turkey, as in many places in the world, the instruments of consumer-culture propaganda, primarily adverts, drive consumption beyond needs. Even fairly poor homes have televisions. One of the most widespread leisure activities in Turkish households is watching television series, which are interrupted by long commercial breaks, after the evening meal. There is no doubt that the adverts watched along with the series also act on consumer behaviors in the household. This should be taken into account in social work to stop the poor from sinking into the unreasonable consumer behaviorsidentified by behavioral economics.

The fact that the psychological interpretation used in the behavioral finance approach can be readily grasped and that the gains can be seen with simple cost-benefit calculations facilitates the use of behavioral finance in the struggle against poverty. Game theory, in contrast, has a relatively more technical structure and requires a grasp of mathematics; however, there are also approaches aimed at reducing the mathematics contained in the theory. Bernard(as cited in Swedberg, 2001, pp. 304-305), according to Swedberg, has introduced an approach that does limit the mathematical content of game theory,thus enabling it to be widely used: It is of great importance, Bernard stresses, that sociologists learn to translate sociological problems into games. Bernard's treatment is non-mathematical, and she reassures the reader that one can use game theory, just like statistics, without a full understanding of the underlying theorems. Game theory is mainly of help for making predictions, and nothing is said about the problem of verifying the results of game-theoretical analyses with the help of data (Swedberg, 2001, pp. 304-305).

When we look at poverty specifically in Turkey and in the context of game theory, we can see that the game that is the subject of the theory is playedbetween poor people and the government. In the interviews carried out in the study Cases of Poverty in Turkey (Erdoğan, 2011b), a great number of the poor said that they expected the government to help them out of their current situation. This makes it clear that in Turkey, contrary to Lewis'findings, the poor do take an interest in politics, even if this does not amount to an active role. Moreover, due to their voting potential, there is no doubt that political parties do court them.

In Turkey, the current ruling party makes effective use in its political propaganda of the work that it has done to help the poor. In the context of game theory, in such a relationship, the gain to be had by a political party is the votes that it will receive from the poor, while the poor expect their lives to get easier thanks to help that they will receive. The ruling party widely distributes food and fuel aid to the poor.Thus, one of the poor player's constant needsis metas and whenit arises. Should the ruling party lose office, there is a high possibility that this aid will be stopped. In the current state of the game, voting for the ruling party is one profitable strategy for the poor.

According to data from TÜİK's Household Budget Survey Consumption Expenditures 2009 (2011, p. 1), at 28.2%, housing and rent constitutes the biggest slice of household consumer spending. Becoming a homeowner is a major achievement for a poor person and,once acquired, his or her home remains his or hers forever, independently of the existence of a helping hand. The fact that in interviews, poor people who do not own their own homes indicated their wish to do so shows that they thought it more profitable to be a homeowner than to have their other needs met. However, it is understandable that a body that offers help in return for votes will not follow strategies aimed at making homeowners of the poor.After acquiring a home, a poor person is not obliged to take the position that the ruling party should remain in power perpetually.He or she will be able to use his or her power as a voter to make new gains. Nevertheless, to achieve results, it is not possible for players crushed by the pressure of their momentary needs to follow this strategy independently of each other. If the poor act together to ensure that their joint needs, such as housing, are met, it will allow them to take the initiative against a strong player in future games.

CONCLUSION

Game theory recommends that each and every situation be approached like a game and claims that it shows the most sensible strategy in such games; in moves falling under the scope of finance, behavioral finance claims to prove that players do not always behave rationally. When both theories are taken together, it is also possible to assert that when the correct behavioris clear, negative results stem from people not behaving rationally. This approach, if it interprets every bad situation that occurs to be the result of individuals' incorrect behaviors, must not lead to the error of not seeing the distortions created by the economic structure. Game theory and behavioral finance must not acquire the role of absolving the system, especially not with regard to poverty. Otherwise, we might be tempted to see the poor as responsible for, rather than as victims of, the inhuman conditions in which they find themselves, and under the influence of this thought, we might be less willing, or even unwilling, to help them. Yet above all, the children of the poor are also poor and it is certain that they at least are not living in poverty because of their own mistakes. They will have deficiencies in many areas, from the education that they receive to food, and they will make them felt in every game that they will one dayplay as adult individuals. There is a high probability that,as players under the influence not only of the physical but also of the psychological burden of the harsh conditions in which they find themselves,they will make bad moves in life. The poor should definitely be helped to make their living conditions easier and alongside this, strategies in the struggle against poverty should also be formulated in the light of theories such as game theory or behavioral finance.

Close to two thirds of the steel and more than two thirds of the aluminum, copper, lead, nickel and zinc, and three quarters of the energy used in the world is used by industrialized countries and, for example, the demand in developed countries is also behind the destruction of the rainforests (Şenses, 2013, p. 157). These facts also unmask the injustice of seeing the poor as a group that needs help from others while consuming more. The planet that we live on is a joint resource to which future generations are also entitled. The poor have received a much smaller share of this joint resource than the rich have. As the natural result of this, they consume less of the planet. Therefore, it is also possible to think that the rich are indebted to the poor because they consume more natural resources, which are the joint property of humanity.

REFERENCES

Alagh, Y. K. (1992). Growth performance of the Indian economy, 1950-89: Problems of employment and poverty. *The Developing Economies*, *30*(2), 97–116. doi:10.1111/j.1746-1049.1992.tb00007.x

Barberis, N., & Thaler, R. (2003).A survey of behavioral finance. In Handbook of the Economics of Finance, 1 (pp. 1053-1128).

Beaulier, S., & Caplan, B. (2007). Behavioral economics and perverse effects of the welfare state. *Kyklos*, *60*(4), 485–507. doi:10.1111/j.1467-6435.2007.00382.x

Bertrand, M., Mullainathan, S., & Shafir, E. (2004). A behavioral-economics view of poverty. *The American Economic Review*, *94*(2), 419–423. doi:10.1257/0002828041302019

Campbell, J. Y. (2006). Household finance. *The Journal of Finance*, *61*(4), 1553–1604. doi:10.1111/j.1540-6261.2006.00883.x

DiCicco-Bloom, B., & Gibson, D. R. (2010). More than a game: Sociological theory from the theories of games. *Sociological Theory*, *28*(3), 247–271. doi:10.1111/j.1467-9558.2010.01377.x

Erdem, T. (2003).*Ankara kent yoksulları* [The urban poor in Ankara]. Unpublished doctoral dissertation, Hacettepe University, Ankara.

Erdoğan, N. (2011a). Garibanların dünyası: Türkiye'de yoksulların kültürel temsilleri üzerine ilk notlar. [The world of the wretched poor: First notes on the cultural representations of the poor in Turkey] In N. Erdoğan (Ed.), *Yoksulluk halleri: Türkiye'de kent yoksulluğunun toplumsal görünümleri* [Cases of poverty: Social aspects of urban poverty in Turkey]. (pp. 29–46). İstanbul: İletişim Yayınları.

Erdoğan, N. (Ed.). (2011b). *Yoksulluk halleri: Türkiye'de kent yoksulluğunun toplumsal görünümleri* [Cases of poverty: Social aspects of urban poverty in Turkey]. İstanbul: İletişim Yayınları.

Gibbons, R. S. (1997, Winter). An introduction to applicable game theory. *The Journal of Economic Perspectives*, *11*(1), 127–149. doi:10.1257/jep.11.1.127

Gündoğan, N. (2008). Türkiye'de yoksulluk ve yoksullukla mücadele. [Poverty and the struggle against poverty in Turkey]. *Ankara Sanayi Odası. Asodosya.* Ocak-Şubat. 42-56.

Hill, R. P., & Gaines, J. (2007). The consumer culture of poverty: Behavioral research findings and their implications in an ethnographic context. *Journal of American Culture*, *30*(1), 81–95. doi:10.1111/j.1542-734X.2007.00466.x

İçağasıoğlu-Çoban, A. (2006).Yoksulluğun aile sistemi üzerindeki etkileri ve yoksul ailelere ilişkin sosyal hizmet müdahalesi. [The effects of poverty on the family system and social work intervention in poor families].In Ü. Onat (Ed.), *Sosyal Hizmet Sempozyumu 2003: Yoksullukve Sosyal Hizmetler [Social Work Symposium 2003: Poverty and Social Work].* (196-204). Vol.1. Antalya, 9-11 Ekim 2003, Ankara: Hacettepe Üniversitesi Sosyal Hizmetler Yüksekokuluve Sosyal Hizmet Uygulama, Araştırmave Geliştirme Derneği.

2013. İnsani gelişme raporu Güney'in yükselişi Farklılıklar dünyasında insani gelişme. (2013). İnsani gelişme raporu'ndaki muhtelif göstergelerle ilgili açıklama notu. [2013 human development report. The rise of the south: Human progress in a diverse world.explanatory note on 2013 HDR composite indices]. Retrieved January 27, 2014, from http://www.tr.undp.org/content/dam/turkey/docs/Publications/hdr/T%C3%BCrkiye%20De%C4%9Ferlendirmesi.pdf

Kahneman, D., & Tversky, A. (Eds.). (2000). *Choices, values, and frames.* Cambridge, U.K.: Cambridge University Press.

Mullainathan, S. (2009). How behavioral economics can help change the fight against poverty. Retrieved December 9, 2013, fromhttp://seedmagazine.com/content/article/poor_decision_making/

Sefil, S. & Çilingiroğlu, H. K. (2011, Bahar). Davranışsal finansın temelleri: Karar vermenin bilişsel ve duygusal eğilimleri. [The basics of behavioral finance: cognitive and emotional biases in decision making]. *İstanbul Ticaret Üniversitesi Sosyal Bilimler Dergisi. 10*(19), 247-268.

Şenses, F. (2013). *Küreselleşmenin öteki yüzü yoksulluk: Kavramlar, nedenler, politikalar ve temel eğilimler* [Poverty, the other face of globalization: Concepts, causes, policies and basic trends]. İstanbul: İletişimYayınları.

Swedberg, R. (2001). Sociology and game theory: Contemporary and historical perspectives. *Theory and Society*, *30*(3), 301–335. doi:10.1023/A:1017532512350

T.C. Başbakanlık Aile ve Sosyal Araştırmalar Genel Müdürlüğü. (2010). *Sosyal yardım algısı ve yoksulluk kültürü. Türkiye'de kamusal sosyal yardım alanların yardım algısı ve yoksulluk kültürü araştırması* [The perception of social welfare and the culture of poverty.The perception of aid by recipients of public social aid and the study of the culture of poverty in Turkey]. Ankara: Ermat Matbaacılık. [Republic of Turkey, Prime Minister's Office General Directorate of Family and Social Studies]

Thaler, R. H. (1999). Mental accounting matters. *Journal of Behavioral Decision Making*, *12*(3), 183–206. doi:10.1002/(SICI)1099-0771(199909)12:3<183::AID-BDM318>3.0.CO;2-F

Theories of Poverty. The culture of poverty (n.d.). Retrieved January 14, 2014, from http:// www. blacksacademy.net/ content/ 3253.html

Türkiye İstatistik Kurumu (TÜİK). [Turkish Statistical Institute]. (2011). *Hanehalkı bütçe araştırması tüketim harcamaları 2009. [Household Budget Survey Consumption Expenditures 2009].*Ankara: TürkiyeİstatistikKurumuMatbaası.

UNDP. (2007). *Human Development Report 2007/2008.Fighting climate change: Human solidarity in a divided world.* New York: Palgrave Macmillan.

Zhao, J., & Zhang, P. (n.d.).Game analysis on coordinated development in Beijing and Tianjin and poverty-stricken around Beijing and Tianjin. Retrieved December 23, 2013, from http://www.rrojasdatabank.info/zhaojunyan2008.pdf

ADDITIONAL READING SECTION

Adaman, F., & Keyder, Ç. (2006). *Poverty and social exclusion in the slum areas of large cities in Turkey.Report for the European Commission*. Employment, Social Affairs and Equal Oppurtunities.

Alcock, P., & Campling, J. (2006). *Understanding poverty* (pp. 190–198). Palgrave Macmillan.

Barberis, N., & Thaler, R. (2005). A survey of behavioral finance. *Advances in behavioral finance, 2*, 1-75.

Bertrand, M., Mullainathan, S., & Shafir, E. (2004). A behavioral-economics view of poverty. *The American Economic Review*, *94*(2), 419–423. doi:10.1257/0002828041302019

Buğra, A. (2008). *Kapitalizm, yoksulluk ve Türkiye'de sosyal politika* [Capitalism, poverty and social policy in Turkey]. İstanbul: İletisimYayınları.

Buğra, A., & Keyder, Ç. (2005, January).Poverty and social policy in contemporary Turkey. In *Boğaziçi University Social Policy Forum.*

Camerer, C. F., Loewenstein, G., & Rabin, M. (Eds.). (2011).*Advances in behavioral economics*. Princeton University Press.

Cohen, J. (1964). Social work and the culture of poverty. *Social Work*, *9*(1), 3–11.

Craig, G. (2002). Poverty, social work and social justice. *British Journal of Social Work*, *32*(6), 669–682. doi:10.1093/bjsw/32.6.669

Diamond, P., & Vartiainen, H. (Eds.). (2012). *Behavioral economics and its applications*. Princeton University Press.

Jencks, C. (1992). *Rethinking social policy: Race, poverty, and the underclass* (pp. 127–128). Cambridge, MA: Harvard University Press.

Jordan, B. (2008). Social work and world poverty. *International Social Work*, *51*(4), 440–452. doi:10.1177/0020872808090238

Kalaycıoğlu, S. (2006).Dynamics of poverty in Turkey: Gender, rural/urban poverty, social networks and reciprocal survival strategies. *Poverty and social deprivation in the Mediterranean: Trends, policies and welfare prospects in the new millennium*, 218.

Leon, D. A., & Walt, G. (2001). *Poverty, inequality, and health: an international perspective*. Oxford University Press.

Lewis, O. (1966). The culture of poverty. *Scientific American, 215*(4), 19–25. doi:10.1038/scientificamerican1066-19 PMID:5916451

Lewis, O. (1971). The culture of poverty. *Poor Americans: How the white poor live*, 20-26.

Lowe, G. R., & Reid, P. N. (Eds.). (1999). *The professionalization of poverty: Social work and the poor in the twentieth century*. Transaction Publishers.

Mantle, G., & Backwith, D. (2010). Poverty and social work. *British Journal of Social Work, 40*(8), 2380–2397. doi:10.1093/bjsw/bcq068

McLanahan, S. (1985). Family structure and the reproduction of poverty. University of Wisconsin. Madison: Institute for Research on Poverty.

Moulin, H. (1986). *Game theory for the social sciences*. NYU press.

Mullainathan, S., & Thaler, R. H. (2000). *Behavioral economics (No. w7948)*. National Bureau of Economic Research.

Myerson, R. B. (2013). *Game theory*. Harvard university press.

Pogge, T. W. M. (2008). World poverty and human rights. *Polity*.

Polack, R. J. (2004). Social justice and the global economy: New challenges for social work in the 21st century. *Social Work, 49*(2), 281–290. doi:10.1093/sw/49.2.281 PMID:15124969

Ricciardi, V., & Simon, H. (2000). What is behavioral finance? *Business, Education & Technology Journal*, *2*(2), 1–9.

Rogge, M. E., & Darkwa, O. K. (1996). Poverty and the environment: An international perspective for social work. *International Social Work, 39*(4), 395–409. doi:10.1177/002087289603900405

Saleebey, D. (1996). The strengths perspective in social work practice: Extensions and cautions. *Social Work, 41*(3), 296–305. PMID:8936085

Shefrin, H. (2002). *Beyond greed and fear: Understanding behavioral finance and the psychology of investing*. Oxford University Press. doi:10.1093/0195161211.001.0001

Thaler, R. H. (Ed.). (2005). *Advances in behavioral finance* (Vol. 2). Princeton University Press.

KEY TERMS AND DEFINITIONS

Behavioral Finance: A theory, which claims to prove that human does not behave rationally in the financial decision-making process.

Game Theory: A theory, which recommends that each and every situation be approached like a game and claims that it shows the most sensible strategy in such games.

Poverty: A state of deprivation wherein the basic needs necessary for survival are not met.

Poverty Line: The minimum level of income deemed adequate in a given country.

Poverty in Turkey: The situation of poor people in Turkey.

Social Work: A practice-based discipline, which try to improve the quality of life and wellbeing of an individual, group, or community.

Struggle Against Poverty: Fight against poverty.

Chapter 3
An Analysis of the Studies in Turkey into Consumer Behavior During Periods of Economic Crisis

Aybala Demirci Aksoy
Gazi Üniversitesi, Turkey

ABSTRACT

The fact that those countries going through tough times like economic crises can predict the change consumers experience so that they could take the necessary precautions brings them competitive advantage and helps them provide solutions accordingly. With this in mind, the present qualitative study paints a picture of a general overview of consumer behaviors in times of crises. The studies in Turkey into consumer behavior during periods of economic crises have shown that buying behavior of consumers change, that consumers resort to cheap good and services, and that they limit their spending on food the least. The Turkish consumers have started to cut back on their spending and postpone their needs in times of economic crisis. It could be stated that Turkish consumers now avoid hasty decisions when buying.

INTRODUCTION

Consumer behavior refers to a dynamic and very complicated process which is affected by external factors such as economic crisis, and which varies from person to person (Odabaşı & Barış, 2002, p. 30). Estimation of consumer behavior in times of economic crises is especially extremely difficult.

Despite the fact that economic crisis is a popular agenda, studies looking at the process in terms of consumers, families and household are not common. However, previous and prospective research is thought to contribute to the effort to figure out consumer behavior, giving both manufacturers and marketers competitive advantages, as well as giving clues to the policy-makers.

The change which consumers, backbones of economic activities, have been going through needs to be thoroughly identified. Early anticipation of change that consumers go through on the part of those countries undergoing crucial periods like economic crises in order to take the

DOI: 10.4018/978-1-4666-7484-4.ch003

necessary measures in advance not only puts them in an advantageous position but also helps them create effective solutions. With this in mind, this study summarizes the studies examining consumer behavior during economic crises. Analyzing the examples from Turkey, the study is going to help the identification of the shortcomings and hint the necessary precautions.

BACKGROUND

Economic Crisis

Crisis as a term is defined differently in different disciplines. In medicine, it refers to the unexpected physiological disorder in an organ; in psychology, it is defined as a critical turning point resulting from change throughout the life of the individual; and in economics, the focus on this study, crisis is defined as certain developments that cannot be predicted beforehand (Türk Dil Kurumu$_a$, 2013; Karabıçak, 2010, p. 252). Economic crisis can be defined as the wild fluctuations, outside the acceptable limits of change, in the prices or supplies in any markets of commodity or services, or factors of production (Kibritçioğlu, 2001, p. 175). A review of the literature on economic crisis yields globalization as a phenomenon. Globalization can have two basic meanings. In a wider sense, it refers to a process in which a culture of conscious responsiveness or reaction to both positive and negative developments has emerged. In such a process, as the awareness of the international, national and regional political, social, ecological, cultural and even geographical systems of each other has increased, their power of influencing one other has intensified (Zengingönül, 2005, p. 92). In the narrow sense, globalization can be defined as international economic exchange (Albayrak, 2012, p. 166).

Even though there is no commonly agreed definition of globalization, it could be stated that globalization has substantially influenced the economic realm (Öznacar, 2011, p. 16883). With globalization, the area of influence of the monetary markets has widened, which has boosted international trade in particular. This has caused market economies based upon free competition to come into prominence. Such a change in international trade and similar developments has necessarily compelled the countries to turn to privatization. Those countries which have not been able to adapt to this change and been trying to maintain their traditional structures with their inability to manage timely privatization have eventually encountered the problem of economic crisis (Karabıçak, 2002, p. 122). Economic crises can be classified as financial crises and crises in real sector. While the former comes out because of either the wild fluctuations in financial markets or the dramatic increase in the unpaid loans in the banking sector, the latter appears as a result of the decline in employment and production in goods and services (Kibritçioğlu, 2001, p. 175).

During periods of economic crises, businesses experience difficulties on account of such problems as decrease in domestic and external demand, decline in sales, increase in stocks, restricted production, not receiving the debts and hardship in taking loans. The businesses making an effort to save the day struggle to boost consumption through such practices as sales, promotions, and installments. Negatively affected just as the businesses are, consumers develop new behaviors in the way they consider to be for their benefit (Odabaşı, 2009, p. 68).

According to Mishkin (2004, p. 624), if consumers feel they are in financial difficulty, they prefer to hold liquid financial assets. Since durable goods and real estate are not liquid enough, they are likely to be sold off. For instance, when the fall in the price of equities causes a decrease in the value of financial assets, economic units start to worry about financial problems. In such a case, consumer spending on durable goods and real estate goes down. Financial uncertainty leads to decline in the level of consumer expectation and

Figure 1. A conceptual framework of the relationship among the economic environment business and the consumers (Source: Shama, 1981, p. 121).

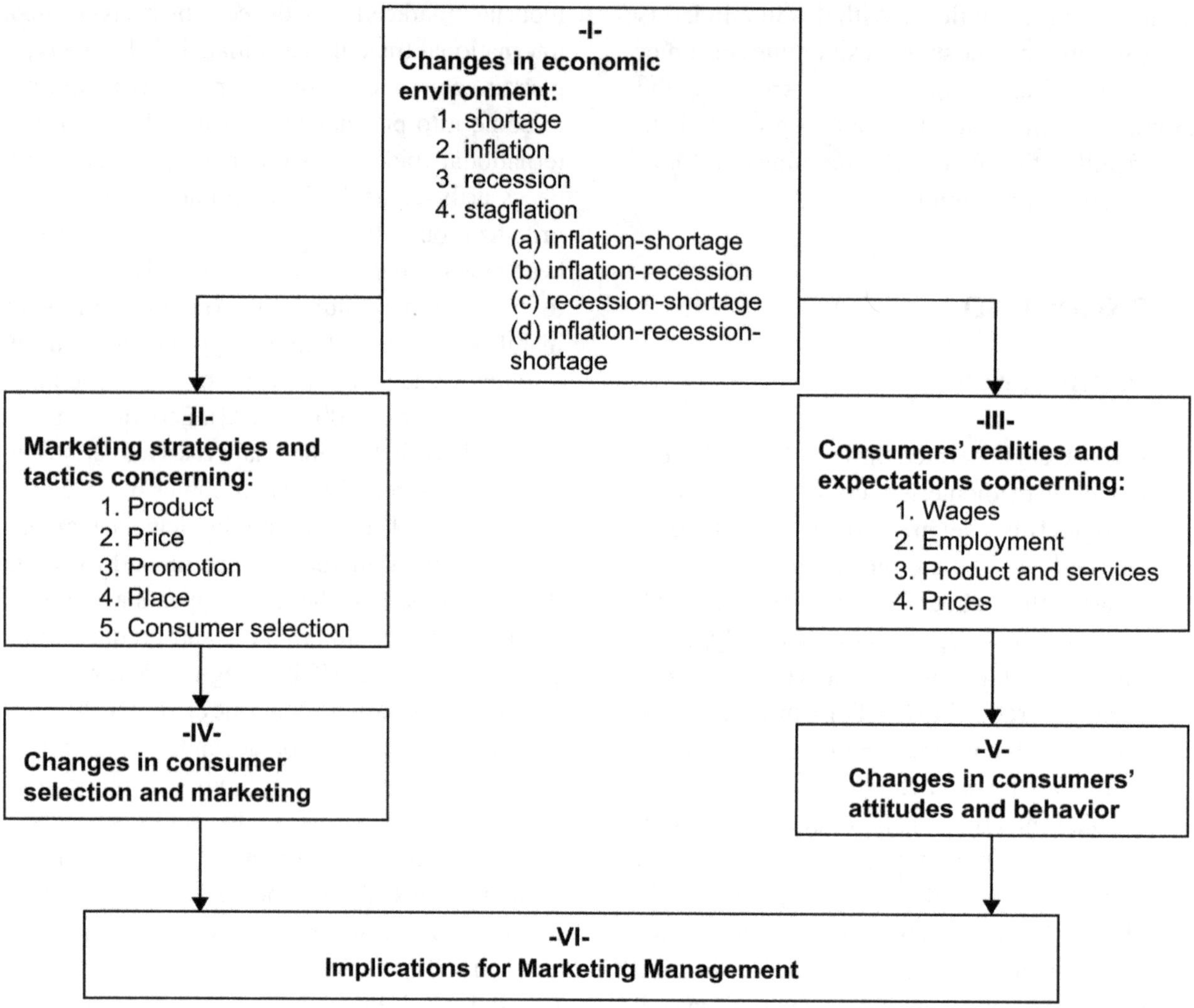

trust. Consumers are influenced by economic crises as much as businesses.

Economic Crises and Consumer Behaviors

Shama (1981, p.121) has developed a conceptual model which illustrates the relationships between and among businesses, consumers, and economic environment (see Figure 1). With reference to this model, consumer behaviors can be summarized within the framework of the changes in the economic environment.

An economic crisis is a period in which certain changes in the conditions of the economic environment, which are one of the most important factors having an impact on the activities of the businesses, take place. The changes in the economic environment are inflation, stagflation, recession, and scarcity (Anonymous, 2013).

Scarcity simply refers to insufficiency in the resources to meet the unlimited demands of the individuals. Further, it also refers to the fact that the demand on the current price level is more than the supply in a given economy (Türk Dil Kurumu$_b$, 2013; Dursun & Nakip, 1997, p. 27).

In a period of scarcity, certain demands of the buyers cannot be met. Consumers will have to wait in long queues for long periods of time and will have to go from this store to that store to find what they are looking for, which leads to unhappiness in consumers. Consumers whose demands and needs are not satisfied may develop a pessimistic view of the future of the economy (Dursun & Nakip, 1997, p. 27).

Another change in the economic environment is inflation. An economic state in which the total demand is more than the total supply, inflation can be defined as increases in the general prices that do not increase the level of employment and real income in an economy (Enç, 1993, p.1). Inflation brings about changes in consumer behavior; thus, it has an effect on the marketing activities of the business. When the purchase power decreases, consumers become more sensitive to inflation and changes in prices. In such a case, three different consumer behaviors may come out. This first one is that "consumers could purchase goods and services in advance for fear that the prices will go up in the future." The second one is that "consumers could reorganize their buying behaviors." For instance, they could start doing the activities on their own which they used to buy as a service, or instead of the brands they used to buy, they could turn to cheaper brands or services, and they could spend cautiously, or cut back on their spending on luxuries. The final one is that consumers may postpone their purchase on a later date (Dursun & Nakip, 1997, p. 12).

Economists define recession as the fall going on for about at least six months in the real GDP, which is measured annually. Recession is a process whereby the demand for goods and services, labor, and raw materials diminishes. In such a process, the demand is low; economic activity slows down and thus economy contracts (Anonymous, 2013). In a period of recession, instead of buying a new product, consumers would suffice to keep what they have, or they could fix or have them fixed. While buying, they would prefer cheaper products. They would also buy from discount stores, turn to cheaper brands, and when buying, pay attention to whether the product is economical or durable (Dursun & Nakip, 1997, p. 24).

Stagflation refers to a period when unemployment, high and continual increase in prices, and unused production capacity come out in combination. Stagflation is derived from "stagnation" and inflation (Altınok, 1999, pp. 59-60). As stagflation is a constituent of the environments where recession and inflation are encountered, the effects of stagflation on society and economy manifest themselves as the combination of these two environments. During stagflation, the national income per capita goes down; prices go up, and unemployment increases. For example, as result of the economic crisis in 1994, national income per capita went down, from $ 3065 in 1993 $2169 in 1994 compared to the previous year (DPT, 2002, p. 6).

In order to minimize the effects of the increasing prices, unemployment as well as income per capita, consumers change their buying habits and preferences during stagflation. They buy products in stores where they could bargain and be offered cheaper products; they buy products and services by comparing more than they used to in the past. Moreover, they cut down on wasting and prefer to continue to use their durable goods by repairing rather than replacing them. In addition, they choose to buy more economical household appliances and more durable goods, and more economical automobiles. Besides changing their buying behavior, they save up less and use more credits so as to lessen the effects of stagflation on their lifestyles (Shama, 1981, p. 123).

Throughout the periods of the global economic crises, a good many changes in consumer behavior have been identified. Consumers have become more responsible, more selective and have started to take more economical decisions (Voinea & Filip, 2011, pp. 16-17).

A Review of Literature

Despite the fact that economic crisis is a popular issue, studies looking at the process in terms of consumers, families, and household are not common. A limited number of studies have been carried out into consumer tendencies in times of economic crises in Turkey, which are chronologically summarized as follows.

Dursun & Nakip (1997) investigated the effects of the Economic Measures and Applications Plan introduced in April 5, 1994 on the consumers and found that 83% of the consumers had changed their buying habits and preferences because of the economic crisis. In addition, they discovered that 88% of the consumers felt more stressed and anxious and that 86% had to work overtime or find a second job. They also revealed that 65% felt less happy and 70% had less optimistic view of the future. The consumers stated that they (26%) avoided having guests in their houses and they (36%) gave few offerings to their visitors. Considering the consumers' spending, thriftiness, and savings, 92% of the consumers spent their money more carefully, and 80% reduced their savings. 68% decided not to buy luxury goods, while 75% bought less then they needed. The consumers limited their spending most on books, newspapers, magazines, and holidays, whereas they limited their spending the least on food and transport. It was found that 91% of Turkish consumers bought more enduring durable goods, and 76% postponed buying furniture. Moreover, 81% of the Turkish consumers were found to look for cheaper products and services and 71% stopped following fashion.

Altunışık, Torlak & Özdemir (2003, pp. 335-341) discovered that transport, food and education were found to be the categories in which spending went up after economic crisis and that clothes, entertainment, toiletries and hygiene products were the categories in which spending went down after economic crisis. Further, the first product categories remaining the same after the economic crisis were seen to be alcohol, healthcare, and cigarettes. It was determined that consumers turned to such financial measures of saving as low prices, promotions, and quantity discount. It was also found that female consumers were more sensitive to prices than male consumers, and that consumers were over middle age valued brands and trust more than younger consumers, and that the value attached to endorsement marketing increased with age. The study also suggested that while the effectiveness of endorsement marketing, price and quantity discounts, the efforts to make a product catch on increased with low income, importance attached to the product, brand, and store went up with high income. Economic crises force consumers to control their spending. Moreover, consumers are more careful about the characteristics of the products in the post-crises periods and they prefer to buy reliable, previously approved and widely known products and brands so that they face no shopping problems. In short, economic crises force consumers to be more selective and to control their shopping behavior.

Çulcuoğlu (2009) investigated how consumers were influenced by the economic crisis, how consumer spending and their habit of consumption changed and what direction this change followed. He concluded that the buying habits of the consumers changed in times of economic crises. It was observed that the consumers, who started to control their shopping behavior with the economic crisis, began to go shopping with their shopping lists, to go after promotions and discounts more carefully, and to have the awareness that they should buy what they needed and would buy when they needed. The consumers who had habitually gone shopping irrespective of whether they needed to buy something started to go shopping less frequently with the economic crisis. The consumers preferred to buy energy saving electrical appliances pre-and-post crisis periods even though these products were always expensive. The consumers started to value the price factor most and increased their frequency to go shopping at street markets, where they could find a good variety of fresh products at reasonable prices. Therefore, these markets were seen to be the new places to go for saving in times of economic crises. With the crises, the consumers went shopping less frequently at shopping malls, where they could find a variety of options for entertainment, shopping and time-out. Such environmental factors as music, interior settings of the stores pushed the consumers to buy. The careful shoppers exhibited this reaction so as not to be trapped by these spending and buying tricks. The consumers started to be more careful about prices, discounts, and promotions. In this way, they had the opportunity to compare and contrast the products and they could have an idea about where to buy the products at the most reasonable prices. The consumers, if they had a permanent income, were tempted by promotions and discounts. However, their brand dependence decreased and because of the crises they ceased to buy brands. The crises changed their habits of consumption concerning food and cleaning products. The consumers started to have a tendency to buy less of the high-priced products. Thus, the consumers cut back on the consumption of the red meat and processed meat products, canned and frozen food, sparkling drinks and fruit juices. They preferred more legumes or light meat to red meat, and more canned and frozen food to seasonal fruit and vegetables. As for the cleaning products, the consumers changed their favorite brands. They started to use second brands in such frequently-consumed products as toilet papers, fabric softeners, and detergents. However, there were no changes in the brands in food items. The consumers cut back on or postponed to buy luxurious products. With the crises, they reduced their spending on some items, changing the structure of their spending habits. For example, they started to spend less money on car care and car cleaning. They saved up by washing their cars themselves. In addition, their holiday expenses went down. In Turkey, most families do not consider going on holiday as something indispensable. With the economic crises, the consumers started to eat out or buy take-away food less frequently. The consumers who postpone or stop buying what they need took out fewer loans. The declining trust in economy and increasing interest rates in loans caused the consumers to avoid taking out loans. However, the crises increased the rate of using credit cards. Further, it also changed the way the consumers made investments. As the rates of foreign currency and gold went up due to the crises, the consumers stared to include them in their investment portfolio.

Marangoz & Uluyol (2010, pp. 90-93) found that the participants stated the economic crises had a negative impact on the family budgets. Investigating the consumer behaviors of the families in Turkey during the periods of economic crises, the study resulted in the following findings:

- The consumer behaviors during the periods of economic crises changed considerably and the tendency to spend went down, whilst tendency to save up increased.
- The spending decreased and the crises had a negative impact on the family budgets significantly
- The most important measure taken to ease the effects of the economic crises was to discontinue the spending on basics or to delay temporarily
- It was possible that the consumers might delay buying durable goods

Odabaşı (2010, pp. 67-84) examined qualitatively consumer behaviors during the times of economic crises and concluded that one of the most profound effects of the global crises was the changes in consumer behaviors and expectations, that uncertainty and lack of trust had affected consumers negatively, and that the consumers developed new behaviors to deal with this negativity. It was indicated that not only demographic variables but also psychological factors needed to be taken into account in the analysis of the data. The most important psychological change caused by the crises was lack of trust and pessimism brought about by uncertainty and unpredictability of the future, which led to undecided and uneasy feelings in consumers, resulting in the intensification of the feelings of hopelessness and unhappiness. He also explained that due to the changes in the psychology of the consumers, permanent changes were observed in the consumer attitudes and behaviors (see Figure 2). The most important of these changes was the tendency of being introvert and avoiding consumption. Thus, the consumers became selective in their demands and turned to products at more reasonable prices and brands creating competitively more values. The consumers started to attach more importance to such values as modesty, simplicity, and spontaneity. In this context, it was shown that the consumers considered fair and ethical trade, sustainable consumption, and green economies significant.

Hüsnüoğlu & Güler (2010, pp. 197-226) conducted a study in provincial Giresun and found that educational expenses of 65% of the consumers remained the same; those of 19% increased; and those of 15% decreased during the economic crises. In the study, 46% of the consumers stated that their frequency of participation in social events went down, 40% remaining the same. 57% of the consumers had less holiday expense, while the holiday expenses of the 38% of the consumers remained the same.

Figure 2. Consumption style and spending model change (Source: Odabaşı, 2009, p. 22).

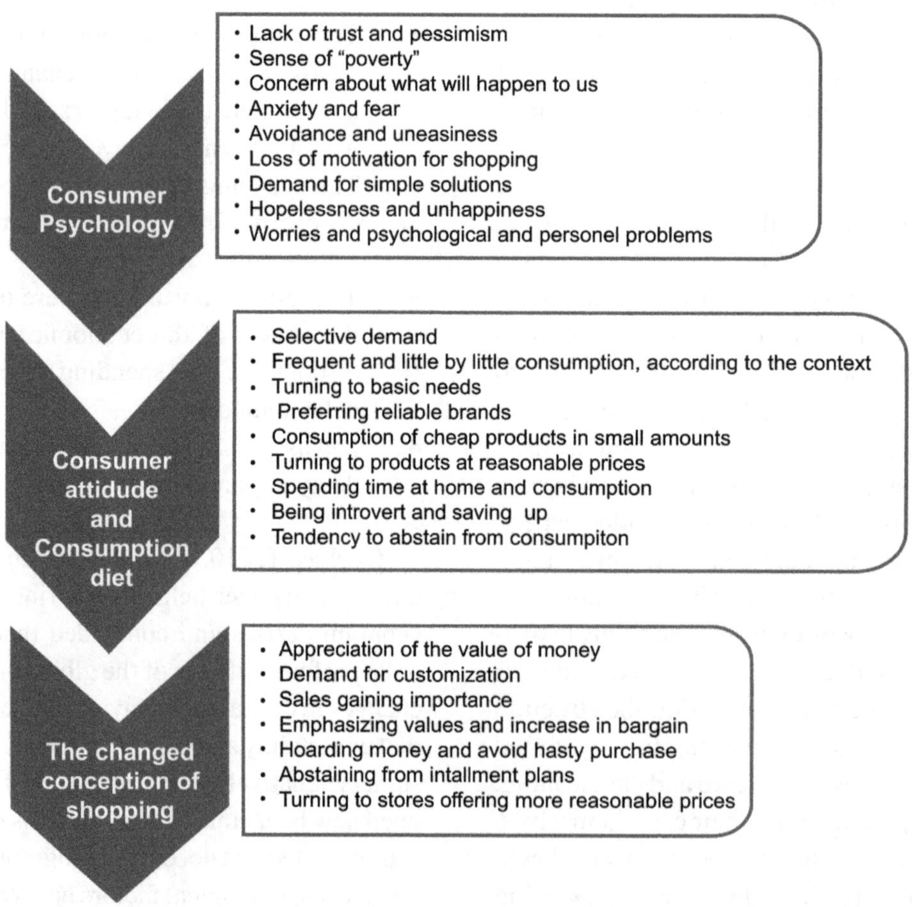

Alimen & Bayraktaroğlu (2011, pp. 193-203) studied the effects of the global economic crises on Turkish consumers in terms of demographic factors and found that According to the results, in the cautious spending and quest for low price dimensions, the factors creating significant differences were occupation, income level, and gender. While age, occupation, and marital status influenced the promotion adjustments, occupation and income affected level of adjustments in the financial anxiety. In general, consumption behavior was adjusted more by females, lower income groups, laborers, teachers, and other occupation groups including doctors, nurses, academics, press members, librarians, government officers, electronic technicians, software specialists, and security personnel. While findings related to females contradict with the general belief that they consume more, 80% of the female respondents had low income, below 2000 Turkish Liras per month. Therefore, greater level of adjustments of the females to the crisis might be related to income as well as gender.

The findings of the study are summarized as follows:

- Consumers could start doing the activities on their own which they used to buy as a service
- Instead of the brands they used to buy, they could turn to cheaper brands or services
- They are more careful with their spending
- They put a limit to buying luxurious and expensive products
- They could delay buying at a later date
- They prefer to continue to use the goods they have by repairing rather than replacing them
- They may opt for cheaper alternatives to the products they usually buy
- They could buy from discount stores
- They turn to cheaper brands
- When buying a product, they value durability and more economical products
- They compare and contrast products and services more in terms of price
- They become more aware of energy consumption like gas, electricity and fuel, and they buy less
- They look for cheaper products and services
- They choose the stores where they could bargain

Özgül & Özgüven (2011, pp. 239-263) analyzed the changes in consumer behavior during economic recessions. 35% of the consumers experienced a decline in personal income, while 42% experienced a decline in family income. In general, almost half of the consumers had no decrease in their incomes, while the rest experienced loss of incomes at various levels. 43.2% of the consumers stated that they had been negatively affected by the recessions at a high level, that 22.3% at a moderate level, 22.8% at a low level. One of the most frequently used economic coping strategies, adaptation strategies included cutting back on the purchase of products barring food, opting for cheaper transportation, buying cheaper alternatives to the food products. Among the most frequently used active coping strategies were using homemade foodstuff, increasing working hours, and getting by with the existing savings. Among the least frequently used adaptation strategies were reducing food consumption and preferring cheaper products. Among the least frequently used active strategies were settling in a cheaper neighborhood and house clearance. It was also found that social networking strategies were the least frequently used strategies, except for receiving financial support from family. Consequently, it was identified that the consumers reduced consumption other than food and limited their spending on basic foods. Instead, they turned to homemade food stuff and cheaper transportation alternatives such as bus, tram, and metro to control their spending. They took such precautions as working overtime to increase their income or to keep the same level of income.

Economic Crises and Turkey

The Republic of Turkey was hit for the first time by the economic crisis in 1929, known as the Great Depression, which has been one of the most serious crises in the history of economics. Turkey's problems with its economy coupled with the first installment of the debts inherited from the Ottoman Empire brought about a serious "foreign exchange" crisis, devaluing the Turkish currency (Turan, 2011, p. 58; ATO, 2005). In this period, some of the banks in European countries suffered and there occurred sudden decrease in the rates of bonds in New York Foreign Exchange, which had a negative impact on US economy. Worse than that, the crisis spread to the other countries in an undulating fashion. Further, a crash in the foreign exchange happened and some banks went bankrupt (Aktan & Şen, 2002).

Between 1929 and 1960, there was no great economic or financial crisis in world economy. However, with globalization as a concept growing more common and due to its "contagious" nature, after 1990, crises got more severe, spread more often, and exhibited their effects accordingly (Bilge, 2009, p. 28). In 1994, Turkey experienced the biggest current deficit and public deficit. The government puts downward pressure on interest rates and attempted to alter the structure of the payment terms of the public debts, which increased liquidity in the economy and the expectancy for devaluation and thus the demand for foreign currency was stimulated. The policies to put pressure on interest rates to finance budget deficits cheaply created a crisis of market confidence; therefore, it caused the interest rates to go up (Işık, Duman & Korkmaz, 2004, p. 62). Certain structural changes were required in the economy so as to set the sustainable grounds for economic development. Hence, a new economic program, known as "April-the-fifth Decisions," was introduced in April, 5, 1994 (Karluk, 2009, p. 421).

Following the "April-the-fifth Decisions," being the biggest financial crises of the republican period, the crises happened in November 2000 (November 22- December 5) and February 2001 (February 19- February 23). The increases in the interest rates and foreign currency rates were the reflections of these crises in monetary markets. The crisis in November emerged as a result of the expansion in the demand for foreign currency caused by the emergencies brought about by the need of the markets for liquidity in Turkey's economy. The country had hardly got over the crisis when it was hit by another crisis in February, which was considered to be the sequel to the crisis in November. While there occurred a 7-billion sale of dollars in a 15-day period during the crisis in November, there occurred a 5 billion 77 million dollars were sold in a 5-hour period during the crisis in February. As a result, the government announced that the country adopted a free exchange policy. In February 22, when this announcement was made, dollar increased from 800.000 Turkish Liras (TL) to more than 1 million Turkish Liras (TL). Subsequently, the economy shrank by 8.5-9%; 19 banks stopped operation, and 1.5 million people became unemployed (Karluk, 2009, pp. 439-442).

In Turkey, estimated from the results of Consumer Tendency Survey, conducted by the cooperative efforts by Turkish Statistical Institute and Central Bank of the Republic of Turkey, Consumer Confidence Index is an indicator used to measure consumers' personal financial positions, their perception as to the current economic conditions and expectations in the coming periods as well as their tendencies to spend and save up in the near future. The index shows consumers' level of trust in economic activity (Turkish Statistical Institute$_a$, 2013). If the index is over 100, it shows optimism in consumer confidence; if the index is below 100, it shows pessimism in consumer confidence; and if the index is 100, it shows neither optimism nor pessimism in consumer confidence.

As seen in Figure 3, the index decreased by 3.5% in January 2014 compared to the previous month; while the index was 75 in December, 2013, it declined to 72.4 in January, 2014.

Figure 3. Consumer confidence index, January 2014 (Source: Turkish Statistical Institute$_b$, 2014).

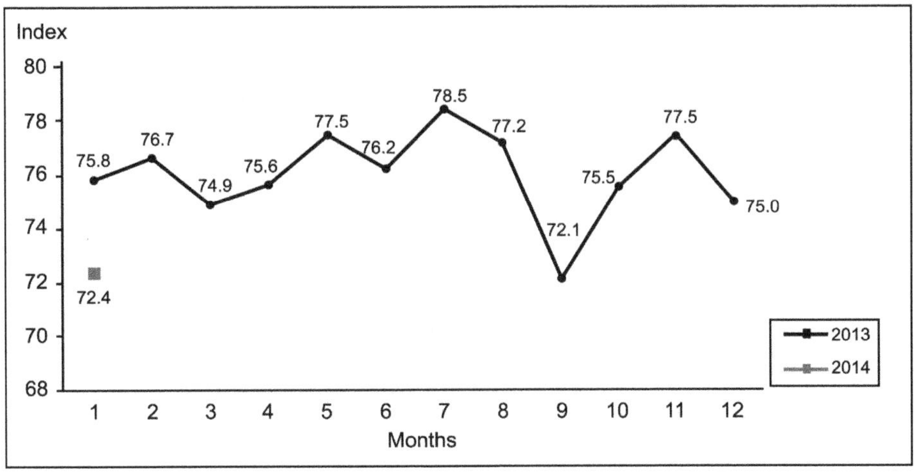

Consumer Confidence Index Decreased by 3.5%

The Consumer Confidence Index calculated from the results of the Consumer Tendency Survey carried out in cooperation with the Turkish Statistical Institute and Central Bank of the Republic of Turkey decreased by 3.5% in January 2014 compared to the previous month; while the index was 75 in December, it declined to 72.4 in January.

General Economic Situation Expectation Decreased by 7.7%

The index of general economic situation expectation in the next 12 months which was 101.9 in December decreased by 7.7% and became 94 in January. This decrease shows that number of consumers expected a better general economic situation in the next 12 months decreased compared to the previous month.

Number of People Unemployed Expectation Decreased by 4.6%

The index of expectation for the number of unemployed persons in the next 12 months which was 81.8 in December decreased by 4.6% and dropped to 78 in January. This drop stemmed from the increase in the ratio of people expecting an increase in the number of unemployed persons.

Financial Situation Expectation Decreased by 1.2%

The index of financial situation expectation of household in the next 12 months period decreased by 1.2% compared to the previous month and became 91.3 in January. This decline arose from the decrease in the ratio of better financial situation expectation of household in the next 12 months period.

Probability of Saving Increased by 9.6%

The index of probability of saving in the next 12 months decreased by 9.6% compared to the previous month and rose from 23.8 in December to 26.1 in January. This increase shows that the possibility of saving of consumers in the next 12 months period increased compared to the previous month (see Figure 4).

Each quarter, the Nielsen Global Consumer Confidence Survey reaches out to more than 25,000 consumers in more than 50 countries

Figure 4. Consumer confidence index, sub-indices and percentages, January 2014 (Source: TUIK$_b$, 2014).

	Index			Percentage change over the previous month (%)	
	11/2013	12/2013	01/2014	12/2013	01/2014
Consumer Confidence Index	77.5	75.0	72.4	-3.3	-3.5
Financial situation expectation of household	92.9	92.4	91.3	-0.5	-1.2
General economic situation expectation	107.3	101.9	94.0	-5.0	-7.7
Number of people unemployed expectation (**)	85.9	81.8	78.0	-4.8	-4.6
The probability of saving	23.9	23.8	26.1	-0.3	9.6

(*) Expectations are examined over the next twelve months.

(**) The increase in number of people unemployed expectation index indicates the decrease of number of people unemployed ecpectation, decrease in number of people unemployed expectation index indicates the increase of number of people unemployed expectation.

throughout Asia Pacific, Europe, Latin America, the Middle East and North America to gauge their economic outlook and confidence in the job market, status of their personal finances and readiness to spend. The sample has quotas based on age and sex for each country based on their Internet users, and is weighted to be representative of Internet consumers. Twice a year, the survey also includes questions related to consumer habits and opinions on a number of topics, ranging from climate change to online shopping to food safety. The Nielsen Global Consumer Confidence Survey (Nielsen 2013$_{a,}$ pp.11-12) 2013 1st quarter shows that Denmark and Finland reach 96% and 76% by 7 points increase, while Turkey goes down to 83% by 8 points decrease. According to the 2013 2nd quarter index, the global consumer trust has increased by 1 point, reaching 94%, in comparison to the 1st quarter. Turkey's score has gone down by 2 points, reaching 81% (Nielsen 2013$_{b,}$ pp. 2-4).

Consumers are influenced by economic crises as much as businesses. Consumer behavior refers to a dynamic and very complicated process which is affected by external factors such as economic crisis, and which varies from person to person (Odabaşı & Barış, 2002, p. 30). Estimation of consumer behavior in times of economic crises is especially extremely difficult. Despite the fact that economic crisis is a popular agenda, studies looking at the process in terms of consumers, families, and household are not common. However, previous and prospective research is thought to contribute to the effort to figure out consumer behavior, giving both manufacturers and marketers competitive advantages, as well as giving clues to the policy-makers. The change which consumers, backbones of economic activities, have been going through needs to be thoroughly identified. Early anticipation of change that consumers go through on the part of those countries undergoing crucial periods like economic crises in order to take the necessary measures in advance not only puts them in an advantageous position but also helps them create effective solutions. With this in mind, this study summarizes the studies examining consumer behavior during economic crises. Analyzing the examples from both Turkey and other countries, the study is going to help the identification of the shortcomings and hint the necessary precautions.

CONCLUSION

The studies into the consumer behavior in Turkey during economic crises have shown that buying habits of consumers change (Dursun & Nakip,

1997; Çulcuoğlu, 2009; Marangoz & Uluyol, 2010; Odabaşı, 2010; Özgül & Özgüven, 2011). Turkish consumers during the periods of economic crises limited least their spending on food, transport, and education (Dursun &Nakip, 1997; Altunışık, Torlak & Özdemir, 2003; Hüsnüoğlu & Güler, 2010; Özgül & Özgüven, 2011). The studies also suggest that consumers start to look for cheaper products and services in times of crises and turn to cheaper alternatives (Dursun & Nakip, 1997; Alimen & Bayraktaroğlu, 2011; Özgül & Özgüven, 2011). It has been observed that during crises Turkish consumers made an effort to adapt to the hard living conditions, that they became more sensitive to prices, and that became more selective in their preferences. They also started to limit and delay their spending. In other words, with economic crises, it can be stated that Turkish consumers became more careful when buying. They developed a more active and demanding consumer profile so that they could get the best with their money. As Odabaşı (2010) indicates, "this crisis caused consumers to be more conscious and aware. Even if it could be expected that the effect of the crisis would soften, the consumers with a new understanding and culture of consumption would become more conscious, more selective, more sensitive to simplicity, and more benefit-oriented." Therefore, it is advisable that marketers develop marketing strategies with these changes in their target consumers during economic crises in mind. On the other hand, it is going to be necessary that those responsible for consumer education inform and educate the consumers in order to protect them against the strategies developed by marketers. Thus, they need to take this point into account.

Prospective research may focus on identifying saving habits of consumers during economic crises and on coping ways and strategies to get over the crises with minimum loss.

REFERENCES

Aktan, C. C., & Şen, H. (2009). Ekonomik Kriz: Nedenler ve Çözüm Önerileri, Yeni Türkiye Dergisi 2002/1. In Bilge, O. (Eds.), Ekonomik krizlerin yoksulluk üzerine etkileri. Sosyal yardım uzmanlık tezi Başbakanlık Sosyal Yardımlaşma ve Dayanışma Genel Müdürlüğü, Ankara.

Albayrak, C. (2012). Küreselleşme ve ekonomik krizin iş hukukuna etkisi. *Türkiye Barolar Birliği Dergisi*, *98*, 166–202.

Alimen, N., & Bayraktaroğlu, G. (2011). Consumption adjustments of Turkish consumers during the global financial crisis. *Ege Academic Review*, *11*(2), 193–203.

Altınok, S. (1999). Stagflasyon ve Stagflasyona Karşı Uygulanan Politikalar. *Selçuk Üniversitesi Sosyal Bilimler Enstitüsü Dergisi*, *4*, 59–72.

Altunışık, R., Torlak, Ö., & Özdemir, Ş. (2003). Ekonomik kriz ve değişen alişveriş alişkanliklari üzerine bir araştirma. *Ulusal Pazarlama Kongresi Bildiri Kitabı*, 16-19.

Anonymous. (2013). *Ekonomik kriz dönemleri; stagflasyon, enflasyon, durgunluk ve kitlik*. Retrieved from http://www.ekodialog.com/Konular/ekonomik-kriz-donemleri.html

ATO. (2005). *Ankara Ticaret Odası, ATO'DAN Krizler Tarihi Raporu, Ankara 17/04/2005*. Retrieved from http://www.atonet. org.tr/yeni/index.php? p=276&l=1

Bilge, O. (2009). Ekonomik krizlerin yoksulluk üzerine etkileri. Sosyal yardım uzmanlık tezi Başbakanlık Sosyal Yardımlaşma ve Dayanışma Genel Müdürlüğü, Ankara.

Çulcuoğlu, C. (2009). *Kriz Dönemlerinde Tüketim Alışkanlıklarındaki Değişim Üzerine Bir Araştırma. Sakarya üniversitesi Sosyal Bilimler Enstitüsü Yayınlanmamış Yüksek Lisans Tezi.* Sakarya.

DPT (Devler Planlama Teşkilatı). (2002). Sayılarla Türkiye Ekonomisi Gelişmeler (1980-2001) Tahminler (2002-2005).

Dursun, Y., & Nakip, M. (1997). 1994 Ekonomik Krizinin İşletmelerin Pazarlama Faaliyetleri ve Tüketiciler Üzerindeki Etkileri. Üniversite-Sanayi Araştırma Birliği Vakfı Yayın No:1, Kayseri.

Enç, E. (1993). ENFLASYON: Tanımı, Ölçümü ve Sorumluları. *Ekonomik Yaklaşım*, *4*(8), 1–8. doi:10.5455/ey.10801

Hüsnüoğlu, N., & Güler, A. (2010). Krizin tüketim harcamalari üzerine etkisi: Giresun ili uygulaması. *Marmara Üniversitesi İİBF Dergisi*, *29*(2), 197–226.

Işık, S., Duman, K., & Korkmaz, A. (2004). Türkiye ekonomisinde finansal krizler: Bir faktör analizi uygulaması. *D.E.Ü. İ.İ.B.F. Dergisi*, *19*(1), 45–69.

Karabıçak, M. (2002). Küreselleşme sürecinde Gelişmekte Olan Ülke Ekonomilerinde Ortaya Çıkan Yönelim ve Tepkiler. *Süleyman Demirel Üniversitesi İktisadi İdari Bilimler Fakültesi Dergisi*, *7*(1), 115–131.

Karabıçak, M. (2010). Küresel Krizleri Tetikleyen Nedenler ve Küresel Krizin Türkiye Boyutu. *Süleyman Demirel Üniversitesi İktisadi ve İdari Bilimler Fakültesi Dergisi*, *15*(3), 251–270.

Karluk, R. (2009). Cumhuriyet'in İlanından Günümüze Türkiye Ekonomisi'nde Yapısal Dönüşüm. Beta yayıncılık. İstanbul.

Kibritçioğlu, A. (2001). Türkiye'de Ekonomik Krizler ve Hükümetler, 1969-2001.*Yeni Türkiye Dergisi, Ekonomik Kriz Özel Sayısı*, 1, *7*(41) (Eylül-Ekim),174-182.

Marangoz, M., & Uluyol, O. (2010). Küresel Ekonomik Krizin Tüketicilerin Harcama ve Tasarruf Eğilimleri Üzerine Etkilerinin Belirlenmesine Yönelik Bir Araştırma. *Muhasebe ve Finansman Dergisi*, *45*, 82–98.

Mishkin, F. S. (2004). *The Economics of Money, Banking and Financial Markets* (7th ed.). New York: Pearson Addison Wesley.

Nielsen (2013a). *Q1 2013 Global Consumer Confidence Report*. Retrieved from https://docs.google.com/file/d/0B05V_TqPz0euN09KMG-dBb2hieTQ/edit?usp=sharing

Nielsen (2013b). *Q2 2013 Global Consumer Confidence Report*. Retrieved from https://docs.google.com/file/d/0B05V_TqPz0euX050VF-9wUHQ5dHM/edit?usp=sharing

Odabaşı, Y. (2009). Küresel Kriz ve Pazarlamanın Yeni Dünyası: Paradigmadan Enigmaya. *Pazarlama ve İletişim (Pİ) Kültürü Dergisi, 8*(28).

Odabaşı, Y. (2010). Küresel kriz ortamında tüketici davranışları. In M. Babaoğul & A. Şener (Eds.), *Tüketici Yazıları-II, Hacettepe Üniversitesi Tüketici - Pazar - Araştırma - Danışma Test ve Eğitim Merkezi. TÜPADEM Yayınları.* Ankara: Comart Kurumsal İletişim Hizmetleri Ltd. Şti.

Odabaşı, Y., & Barış, G. (2002). *Tüketici davranışı*. İstanbul: Mediacat Kitapları.

Özgül, E., & Özgüven, N. (2011). Ekonomik durgunluk dönemlerinde tüketicilerin satin alma davranişinda yaşanan değişimlerin analizi. *ZKÜ Sosyal Bilimler Dergisi*, *7*(13), 239–263.

Öznacar, M. D. (2011). Küreselleşmenin yarattığı etkiler performans görevi. Retrieved from http://websites.ekampus.orav.org.tr/mehmetduranoznacar/2011/3/1/16883/page.aspx

Shama, A. (1981). Coping with Stagflation: Voluntary Simplicity. *Journal of Marketing*, *45*(Summer), 120–134. doi:10.2307/1251547

Turan, Z. (2011). Dünyadaki ve Türkiye'deki Krizlerin Ortaya Çıkış Nedenleri ve Ekonomik Kalkınmaya Etkisi. *Niğde Üniversitesi İİBF Dergisi*, *4*(1), 56–80.

Türk Dil Kurumu (TDK). (2013a). *Kriz*. Retrieved from http://www.tdk.gov.tr/index.php?option=com_gts&arama=gts&guid=TDK.GTS.5294a709bac895.50212827

Türk Dil Kurumu (TDK). (2013b). *Kıtlık* http://www.tdk.gov.tr/index.php?option=com_bts&arama=kelime&guid=TDK.GTS.529dd39ad6b7f7.63149192

Turkish Statistical Institute (TUIK). (2013a). *Tüketici Güven Endeksi Tüketici, EİSBEV Kapsam, Dönem ve Zamanlılık*. Retrieved from http://www.tuik.gov.tr/PreTablo.do?alt_id=1010

Turkish Statistical Institute (TUİK). (2014b). Tüketici Güven Endeksi, Ocak 2014. Türkiye İstatistik Kurumu Haber Bülteni. Sayı: 16093,28 Ocak 2014, Retrieved from http://www.tuik.gov.tr/PreHaberBultenleri.do?id=16093

Voinea, L., & Filip, A. (2011). Analyzing the Main Changes in New Consumer Buying Behavior during Economic Crisis. *International Journal of Economic Practices and Theories*, *1*(1), 14–19.

Zengingönül, O. (2005). Nedir Bu Küreselleşme? Kaçabilir miyiz? Kullanabilir miyiz? *Siyasal*, *1*(1), 85–106.

ADDITIONAL READING

Ang, S. H., Leong, S. M., & Kotler, P. (2000). The Asian Apocalypse: Crisis Marketing for Consumers and Business. *Long Range Planning*, *33*, 97–119.

Aytaç, I. A., & Rankin, B. H. (2009). Economic Crisis and Marital Problems in Turkey: Testing the Family Stress Model. *Journal of Marriage and the Family*, *71*, 756–767.

Berber, Ş. G. (2009). Ekonomik kriz dönemlerinde tüketici satın alma davranışlarındaki değişim üzerine bir araştırma. Marmara Üniversitesi Sosyal Bilimler Enstitüsü İşletme Bölümü Yüksek Lisans tezi.

Bilge, O. (2009). Ekonomik Krizlerin Yoksulluk Üzerine Etkileri. Sosyal Yardım Uzmanlık Tezi. T.C.Sosyal Yardımlaşma ve Dayanışma Genel Müdürlüğü, Ankara.

Bozkuş, S., & Üçdoğruk, Ş. (2007). Hanehalkı Tasarruf Tercihleri- Türkiye Örneği. 8. Türkiye Ekonometri ve İstatistik Kongresi, 24-25 Mayıs, İnönü Üniversitesi, Malatya.

Ceritoğlu, E. (2013). Household Expectations and Household Consumption Expenditures: The Case of Turkey. Türkiye Cumhuriyet Merkez Bankası, Working paper no: 13/10.

Çolak, Ö.F. & Öztürkler, H. (2012). Tasarrufun Belirleyicileri: Küresel Tasarruf Eğiliminde Değişim ve Türkiye'de Hanehalkı Tasarruf Eğiliminin Analizi. Türkiye Bankalar Birliği, Bankacılar Dergisi. Özel araştırma. 23(82),3-43.

Eken, H. (2008). Tüketicilerin Aşırıborçluluk ve Finansal Dışlanma Nedenleri. *Maliye Finans Yazıları*, *22*(79), 61–80.

Eren, A., & Süslü, B. (2001). Finansal Kriz Teorileri Işığında Türkiye'de Yaşanan Krizlerin Genel Bir Değerlendirmesi. *Yeni Türkiye.*, *7*(41), 662–674.

Honkapohja, S., & Koskela, E. (1999). The economic crisis of the 1990s in Finland. *Economic Policy*, *14*(29), 399–436.

Jasiulewicz, A. (2012). Economic Crisis Influence on the Polish Consumer Behavior Overcoming the Crisis: Economic and Financial Developments in Asia and Europe. Retrieved from http://www.hippocampus.si/ISBN/978-961-6832-32-8/contents.pdf

Kanberoğlu, Z., & Kara, O. (2013). Küresel Krizlerin Sosyal Yaşam Üzerindeki Etkisi: Van İli Örneği. *Muğla Sıtkı Koçman Üniversitesi Sosyal Bilimler Enstitüsü Dergisi, 31*, 35–48.

Kang, S. J., & Sawada, Y. (2008). Credit crunch and household welfare, the case of the korean financial crisis. *The Japanese Economic Review, 59*(4), 438–458.

Kaya, K. (2002). Ekonomik Krizin Yaşama Tarzı Üzerindeki Etkileri (Isparta Örneği). *Süleyman Demirel Üniversitesi İktisadi İdari Bilimler Fakültesi Dergisi., 7*(2), 207–226.

Kibritçioğlu, A. (2010). *Effects of Global Financial Crisis on Turkey* (Munich Personal RePEch Archive No.29470). Retrieved from http://mpra.ub.uni-muenchen.de/29470/

Kondawar, D., & Jadhav, P. (2012). Global economic crisis & consumer behaviour. *National Monthly Refereed Journal of Research in Commerce & Management, 1*(12), 82–87.

Kotz, M. D. (2009). The Financial and Economic Crisis of 2008: A Systemic Crisis of Neoliberal Capitalism. *The Review of Radical Political Economics, 41*(3), 305–317.

Mansoor, D., & Jalal, A. (2011). The Global Business Crisis and Consumer Behavior: Kingdom of Bahrain as a Case Study. *International Journal of Business and Management, 6*(1), 104–115.

Martin, R. (2011). The local geographies of the financial crisis: From the housing bubble to economic recession and beyond. *Journal of Economic Geography, 11*, 587–618.

Özdemir, G. Z. (2013).Tüketici Güveninin Tüketim Harcamaları ile İlişkisi ve Öngörü Gücü: Türkiye Örneği Türkiye Cumhuriyet Merkez Bankası İletişim ve Dış İlişkiler Genel Müdürlüğü Uzmanlık Yeterlilik Tezi, Ankara.

Özgüven, N. (2011). Kriz Döneminde Küresel Perakendeci Aktörlerin Performanslarının Topsis Yöntemi ile Değerlendirilmesi. *Atatürk Üniversitesi İktisadi ve İdari Bilimler Dergisi, 25*(2), 151–162.

Pradhan, M., Saadah, F., & Sparrow, R. (2007). Did the health card program ensure access to medical care for the poor during indonesia's economic crisis? *The World Bank Economic Review, 21*(1), 125–150.

Roman, I. (2011). Consumer protection and the role of advice in the market for retail financial services. *Journal of Institutional and Theoretical Economics JITE, 167*(1), 4–21.

Sandıkçı, Ö. & Ger, G. (2005).Contemporary turkish consumptionscape: Polarity and plurality. *New Emerging Economies and Their Culture* (pp. 139-153).

Selçuk, B. (2010). Küresel Krizin Türk Finans Sektörü Üzerindeki Etkileri. *Ekonomi Bilimleri Dergisi, 2*(2), 21–27.

Stillman, S., & Thomas, D. (2008). Nutritional status during an economic crisis: Evidence from Russia. *The Economic Journal, 118*, 1385–1417.

The Effect of Consumer Loans on the Current Account Balance in Turkey. (2005-2011). http://www.opf.slu.cz/kfi/icfb/proc2011/pdf/42_Ozulke.pdf. Access:17.01.2014

Turhan, İ., & Kılınç, Z. (2011). Turkey's Response to the Global Economic Crisis. *Insight Turkey, 13*(1), 37–45.

Wie, K. T. (2000). The impact of the Economic Crisis on Indonesia's Manufacturing Sector. *The Developing Economies, 38*(4), 420–453.

Yaman, Ö. (2010). Finansal Krizler ve Erken Uyarı Sistemleri. Kadir Has Üniversitesi Sosyal Bilimler Enstitüsü Finans ve Bankacılık Ana Bilim Dalı, Yüksek lisans Tezi, İstanbul.

KEY TERMS AND DEFINITIONS

Consumer Behavior: The process by which individuals search for, select, purchase and dispose of goods and services, in satisfaction of their needs and wants.

Economic Crisis: Economic crisis can be defined as the wild fluctuations, outside the acceptable limits of change, in the prices or supplies in any markets of commodity or services, or factors of production.

Global Economic Crisis: A worldwide economic difficulty experienced by markets and consumers.

Globalization: The worldwide movement toward economic, financial, trade and communications integration.

Inflation: Inflation is when the prices of most goods and services continue to creep upward. You have to spend more to get the same goods and services.

Recession: The period of general economic decline, defined as a contraction in the GDP for six months or longer.

Scarcity: Ever-present situation in all markets whereby either less goods are available than the demand for them, or only too little money is available to their potential buyers for making the purchase.

Stagflation: It is an economic anomaly where high unemployment.

Chapter 4
The Relationship between Financial Planning for Retirement and Some Socio-Economic Variables:
A Quantitative Study on Middle-Aged Women and Men

Filiz Yildirim
Ankara University, Turkey

Nuray Akpolat
Nevşehir Provincial National Education Directorate, Turkey

ABSTRACT

The purpose of this study, planned as a quantitative research, is to determine the relationship between planning retirement financially in middle-age period and some socio-economic variables. This study is conducted through 287 participants, who live in Nevşehir, Turkey, aged 40-59, and were reached via the help of some key individuals. As the result of the study, statistically no significant difference has been found between the responses of women and men about planning the retirement financially. However, it has been verified that men's financial plans for retirement were higher in rates than that of women. On the other hand, it was also found that although neither women nor men feel ready for the retirement, it has been determined that for men the factor of being an owner of a house and for women the factor of saving up increases the financial planning for the retirement.

INTRODUCTION

With the increase and aging in the population, planning for the retirement has gained importance in the world. Retirement, generally described as the end of the active working life, starts with middle age period, concurs with transitional period to old ages, and lasts until the end of lives (Günay, 2013). Therefore, retirement is often discussed by the studies on agedness.

DOI: 10.4018/978-1-4666-7484-4.ch004

When people get through one life period to another, different problems and needs emerge simultaneously. Especially, when plans facilitating adaptation to retirement which concurs with transitional period to old ages are not made, this causes psychological, social and financial problems affecting more (İçli, 2008). That is because after leaving the working life, individuals face with more difficulties on meeting their needs especially with increasing costs of health care and decreasing income (Onur, 1995). Similarly, being isolated from the social life with the end of active working life may also cause these individuals to become lonely when old, and to lose their active roles and functions in the society, having some psychological problems. The new social position in the transition to retirement, in a sense, brings about the loss of the previous one, fundamentally changing individuals' lives. In this context, adaptation to retirement means investments not only financially and psycho-socially but also on health and life style in order to lead a happy and active life. It should be also mentioned that planning retirement in a society depends, most of the time, on what financial sources and opportunities individuals have. That is because even if most individuals have certain ideas regarding plans for retirement during their working years, some could realize these ideas while for some others materializing their preparations and plans can be impossible due to financial reasons (Yazıcıoğlu, 2006).

Financial retirement planning is examined in two categories namely formal and informal planning. Formal retirement planning includes financial preparation such as saving up cash, buying a house, stock papers, fund or bond for longer investment, purchasing life insurance or saving insurance policy and buying accident insurance policy (Lee, 2003). Informal retirement plans, which are known to be the other choice in the financial planning, refers to attending educational activities about retirement, talking to others and exchanging ideas about retirement (Noone, 2010).

Some studies on planning retirement financially (Lee, 2003; Yazıcıoğlu, 2006; Noone, 2010) drew attention to the fact that especially women experience inequality of opportunities in planning their retirement financially (especially in working areas) and depending on that, that they have insufficient financial sources. For instance, Yazıcıoğlu (2006) suggested that many women could not participate in the active working life. Likewise, as Lee (2003) mentioned, many women still get caught to retirement unprepared due to economic and social reasons. Similarly, compared to men, more women could be made to work in jobs with no retirement opportunities, or to take responsibility domestically which provides no income owing to gender roles and even in professions, they could be paid less relative to their male colleagues (Lee, 2003). For this reason, chances and opportunities which will enable women to plan their retirement financially get restricted.

Today, on the other hand, as the number of women working in professions increases, worries about not being able to plan retirement also increase among women. That is because as it was previously perceived as women's responsibility to look after family members when they are old, the rates in women's taking responsibility in such work have decreased due to individualization, increasing career opportunities and modernization. Depending on this, the care for especially sick family members has been handed over to hospitals, old pension houses and care institutions. Thus, the requirement to be financially prepared for the care of sick family members for the coming years has also emerged. Additionally, when it is kept in mind that life expectancy of women population in the world is longer than that of men, it is anticipated that retired population will be made up of mostly women (Güleç & Tekbaş, 1997). For this reason, it was suggested that women would be under more health risk and that their life quality would be less when compared to men (Akın, 2012). Therefore, women's planning their retirement financially has become more important to be able to manage their own health care. However, the issue of retirement has been mainly examined men-specifically (Albert, 2006). That is, as Yazıcıoğlu (2006) suggested, since men involved in working life more actively comparing to women, retirement was examined as a men-specific domain in literature for years. In fact, transitional experiences in the retirement were depictured only from men's retirement model (Szinovacz & Washo, 1992). However, with the involvement of more women in the working life, studies on women's planning their retirements have been risen in number (Yazıcıoğlu, 2006).

Considering that retirement plans should be done prior to retirement and taking the cognizance of the studies in literature mentioned below, in this current study, the relationship between financial planning for retirement in middle-aged and the relationship some socio-economic variables will be explored.

LITERATURE REVIEW

The studies on middle-aged women and men in literature (Wiggins & Henderson, 1996; Glass & Kilpatrick, 1998; Joo & Pauwels, 2002; Lee, 2003; Phua, McNally, 2008; Noone, 2010; Wilson & Aggrey, 2012) provided evidence that neither women nor men were ready and that their plans were insufficient for their retirements. For example, in Wiggins and Henderson (1996)'s study conducted on 145 female nurses over 40 years of age, women's financial and health plans before the retirement were surveyed. In this study (Wiggins & Henderson, 1996), it was concluded that the plans of working women, who were formally planning (taking the necessary steps by thinking of the retirement planning) and informal planning (considering plans for the retirement) were insufficient and that knowledge that they should have for their health protection and financial issues would help them plan their retirement beforehand. In some other studies (Glass & Kilpatrick, 1998; Lee, 2003), moreover, it was determined that neither women's nor men's pre-retirement plans were sufficient for their retirement years. For example, Glass and Kilpatrick (1998) compared in their study, conducted on 1287 people, the level of saving and the number of saving instruments used by the women and men of the "baby boomer" (those who were born between post WWII and I960s) generation for retirement. The results (Glass & Kilpatrick, 1998) showed that men had made more investments for the retirement compared to women and that neither women's nor men's investments were sufficient. However, it was found that the gender difference and the level of saving had a significant relationship and that men were more in tendency to save comparing to women. The fact that men used saving instruments more compared to women was among some of the important findings of this study (Glass & Kilpatrick, 1998). The results from Lee (2003)'s study on 1078 working individuals, 40-59 years of age also supported some of Glass and Kilpatrick (1998)'s findings. Accordingly, Lee (2003) compared pre-retirement plans of middle aged women and men in Hong Kong. At the end of the study, Lee (2003) verified that neither women nor men were prepared for the retirement. It was noticed that tendency of financial planning was higher in men than women while women were more inclined to make some health related, life style related and psychological plans for their retirements. As can be seen in the studies of Glass and Kilpatrick (1998) along with Lee (2003), neither women's nor men's preparations for the retirement were adequate, and especially women's financial preparations were lower compared to those of men. Noone (2010)'s study also provided supportive evidence for this finding. This study (Noone, 2010) was conducted on 2227 working women and men between the ages of 55 and 70. This research (Noone, 2010) suggested that there were not any differences between the responses women and men had given about retirement perception and informal retirement planning. In addition, it was again calculated that women in the scope of the study (Noone, 2010) did less financial preparations, had lower life standards and worked in jobs with lower incomes. For this reason, it was emphasized that women were disadvantaged comparing to their partners they lived with. Furthermore, in the study (Noone, 2010), it was also stated that there were differences between women and men's way of preparation for the retirement due to the effects of some social and economic factors. Moreover, the relationship between retirement perception, life standards and financial preparation was indicated among the prominent findings (Noone, 2010).

In Albert (2006)'s study, deductions that health and marital status can be affecting factors on retirement planning can be reached. According to this, it was verified that men with coronary diseases had more tendency to plan their retirements. It was also found that men with hypertension made informal retirement plans while the ones with cardiac problems tended less to make formal planning. When the health related findings are evaluated in terms of women, it was determined that women with stroke history and with psychological problems had less tendency to make formal retirement plans. At the same time, in the study (Albert, 2006), some evidence showing that financial assets had an influence on retirement planning was obtained. This indicated that married men's formal retirement planning was higher than women's and that economic factors such as owning assets had influence on formal and informal retirement planning both in male and female groups.

In Turkey, planning retirement financially has been a subject to studies (Sarım, 1996; Yılmaz, 1996; Salman, 2005; Şahin, 2006; Yazıcıoğlu, 2006; Sevim & Şahin, 2007) conducted rather on retired individuals. Studies on active working retirement nominees (Akçay, 1994; Günay, 2006; Baltacı & Selvitopu, 2012) are quite insufficient. However, just as many studies from different countries (Wiggins and Henderson, 1996; Glass & Kilpatrick, 1998; Joo & Pauwels, 2002; Lee, 2003; Phua, McNally, 2008; Noone, 2010; Wilson & Aggrey, 2012), it was indicated in the studies on retirement nominees that in Turkey women and men were not ready for the retirement and that they had financial worries. For example, in Akçay (1994) conducted a study on retirement nominees who worked as teachers in Çanakkale, Turkey. In his study (Akçay, 1994) he tried to determine the thoughts, worries, expectations and educational needs of retirement nominees about the coming retirement days. The result of this study (Akçay, 1994) it was established that both women and men had worries about the economic problems ahead in the retirement period. Additionally, Akçay (1994) found that gender was influential on thoughts of the nominees who did not feel ready for retirement and its possible problems. The results of Günay (2006)'s study conducted on 393 individuals working under a social security coverage and having at least 3 years to their retirements in the capital city of Turkey, (Ankara) showed similarities with the results of Akçay (1994). In this study (Günay, 2006) again the rates of the women and men who did not have any planning for the retirement was found to be quite high (Günay, 2006). Although both women and men participants indicated that they made rather financial plans and that they applied their plans (especially by purchasing a house), it was seen that the participants needed an expert help especially on financial planning in the study (Günay, 2006). In the study Baltacı and Selvitopu (2012) conducted on 22 teachers, who were about to get retired, and who were entitled to retirement but still continued to work, in Afyonkarahisar city center, Turkey, it was verified that most of the participants did not have any plans or preparations for their retirement. Considering the fact that middle aged women and men are not prepared for their retirements and that planning retirement especially financially depends on what sources (human and financial) these women and men have, the relationship between making financial plans for retirement in middle aged period and some socio-economic variables was tried to be established in this study.

Purpose of the Study

The purpose of this quantitative study is to determine the relationship between planning retirement financially in middle age years and:

- Gender,
- Age,
- Education Level,
- Health Status,
- Having Children,
- Family Income,
- Car Owning,
- House Owning
- Status of Saving Up.

MATERIAL AND METHOD

Data and Sample

The universe of the study is actively working middle aged women and men living in Nevşehir, Turkey. While sampling, it was taken into consideration that

- The beginning of the retirement concurred with middle ages,
- World Health Organization (WHO) had age categories to guide [the ages between 45-59 is middle-aged, 60- 74 is elderly, 75-89 is the aged and, 90 and over is the very old],
- Data collecting instrument to be used, The Process of Financial Planning Scale, which is the sub-scale of The Process of Retirement Planning Scale, had been proven to be valid and reliable in a study conducted on individuals between the ages of 40 and 60 by Günay (2013),
- The retirement eligibility ages in Turkey are 60 for men and 58 for women.

With these criteria, selected by the snowball method, the sample of the study was constituted from 287 participants between the ages of 40 and 59, who lived in Nevşehir, Turkey. %50.2 (144 people) of the sample were female and %49.8 (143) were male. Majority of both females (%91.67) and males (%76.76) were between the ages of 40-50. The age average among females was 44, men was 46. The whole group age average was calculated to be 45.16. The majority of both the women (%97.06) and the men (%96.30) were found to have children.

When the education level of participants were analysed according to their gender, it was found that the rates of both women (%50.69) and men (%32.87) with a university degree were more than the other individuals with other education levels. In addition the percentage of women saying that their health was good was higher (%59.44) than that of men (%56.43). While the rate of women saying that their health status was "not bad not good"(%30.77) was very similar to men (%30.00), the rate of men with "very good" health status (%11.43) was found to be far higher than women's (%4.9).

While the family income and the family expenditures for both women (%65.93) and the men (%50.75) were found to be equal, the rate of the women who indicated that point (%65.93) was higher than that of men. However, the percentage of men saying that their family income was more than their family expenditures (%31.34) was calculated to be nearly twice as many as women who gave the same response (%15.56).

Additionally, it was verified that the rates of men who had a car (%78.32) and/or a house (%70.92) were higher than women who owned a car (%38.46) and/or a house (%60.84). On the other hand, the rate of men who did not save up ("%66.20) was calculated to be higher than women who did not save up (%58.04).

On the issue of feeling prepared for the retirement, the percentage of men who did not feel ready (%65.73) was higher than that of women (%60.42).

Procedure

In order to be able to use the Financial Planning Process Scale, in this study permission from Günay (2013) was taken by the second author. Additionally, in advance, after participants, who had been achieved via key persons, were informed about the aim of the study and that it was conducted on academic purposes, they were specifically assured that any information that can recover their identity would not be shared. Afterwards, the questions from the participants were replied. Collecting the informed consent forms, face to face interviews, each of which lasted about 15 minutes, with the volunteers were conducted in 2014.

Measurements

A sub-scale of The Process of Retirement Planning Scale (PRePS), The Process of Financial Planning Scale, which had been adapted to Turkish (Günay, 2013) and a personal information form were used to collect data in this study.

The Process of Financial Planning Scale

Adapted to Turkish by Günay (2013), the validity and reliability of The Process of Financial Planning Scale, which is a sub-scale of the PRePS, were established (see the validity and reliability studies; Günay, 2013) and consists of 14 items. There are items in the scale aiming to determine the retirement planning thoughts, timing of the retirement planning, retirement planning preparations upon behaviours and upon medical.

The participants were asked to response to the items, which measured their financial plans for their retirements, on a 5 level- Likert-type scale, where 1 referred to "Not true for me at all" 2 referred to "Not true for me", 3= "I am not sure if it is true or not for me", 4= "True for me" and 5 referred to "Definitely true for me" in this scale. Negatively worded items were recoded (1=5, 5=1). Higher scores indicated higher rates of financial planning.

Personal Information Form

Some socio-economic variables including gender, age, having children, education level, health status, family income, owning a car, owning a house, saving up and the state of feeling ready for the retirement were included in the form in order to obtain certain information about the participants. These variables were selected according to the research literature and their potential effects on the results.

Statistical Analyses

The distributions of informative socio-demographic data of participants and their families according to gender were evaluated by using crosstabs. The relationship between financial planning (dependent variable) and some independent variables (gender, age, having children, education level, health status, family income, owning a car, owning a house, status of saving up) was measured by Linear Regression Analysis and Stepwise method (for the coding of the variables see Table 1). Additionally, in order to evaluate the relationship between financial planning for the retirement and the same variables in terms of women and men perspectives, the same analysis (Linear Regression Analysis) and the same method (Stepwise) were reapplied. For the comparison of the scores received from the Process of Financial Retirement Planning Scale according to genders, Mann-Whitney U test was used. The data obtained from this study were analyzed with SPSS 20.0 package program and level of significance was taken as 0.05. On condition that the level of significance was $p<0.05$, there would be a significant difference but if it was $p>0.05$, there would be no significant difference.

Table 1. Dependent and independent variables used in Linear Regression Analysis

Variables	Dependent/ Independent	Measurement Level
The Process of Financial Planning	dependent variable	1.not at all true for me – 5. definitely true for me
Age	independent	Open ended
Education Level	independent	1. illiterate-8.post graduate/PhD
Health Status	independent	1. very bad - 5. very good
Car Owning	independent	0. no-1. Yes
House Owning	independent	0. no-1. Yes
Status of Saving Up	independent	0. no-1. Yes
Having Children	independent	0. no-1. Yes
Family Income	independent	1. income is lower - 2. income and expenditure are equal - 3. income is higher

RESULTS

The Relationship of Some Socio-Economic Variables with Planning Retirement Financially

In order to determine the relationship between financial planning (dependent variable) and some independent variables (gender, age, having children, education level, health status, family income, owning a car, owning a house, status of saving up), Linear Regression Analysis was applied. (see Table 2, Table 3 and Table 4). As can be seen in Table 3, a significant model was formed ($p<0{,}001$). When Table 3 and Table 4 was examined, it was seen that the state of saving up and owning a car made significant contribution to financial planning scores to increase them. In other words, the state of saving up ($p< .001$) and owning a house ($p<.01$) were determined to be in relationship with financial planning (see Table 4).

Predictors: age, having children education level, health status, family income, owning a car, owning a house, status of saving up.

Table 2. The general model of regression analysis related to predictors of financial retirement planning

Model Summary(c)		
Model	R	Durbin-Watson
2	0,299	1,729

Making Financial Plans for Retirement between Women and Men

The women's and men's scores about their making financial plans for retirement were compared in the study. The results of Mann Whitney U test, applied for this purpose, showed that there were not any significant statistical differences in the distribution of women and men's responses about making financial plans for retirement ($p>0.05$). However, it was established that men's scores for making financial plans for retirement (men=42.46) were higher than women's scores for making financial plans for retirement (women=41.15) (Table 5).

Predictors of Making Financial Plans for Retirement Between Women and Men

In order to analyze the relationship between financial planning and some independent variables (age, having children education level, health status,

Table 3. Anova results from predictors of financial retirement planning

ANOVA(c)						
Model		Sum of squares	df	Mean square	F	P
2	Regression	1207.9	2	604.0		
	Residual	12258.5	284	43.2		
	Total	13466.4	286		13.992	0.000

Table 4. Regression analysis results from predictors of financial retirement planning

	B	Std. Error	Beta	T	P
(Constant)	39.1	0.7		55.955	0.000
Can you save up?	3.2	0.8	0.2	3.983	0.000
Do you own a house?	2.3	0.8	0.2	2.845	0.005

Table 5. Comparison of the scores for making financial plans for retirement according to gender and Mann-Whitney U test

		Gender						Mann Whitney U test		
		N	**Mean**	**Median**	**Min**	**Max**	**Std. Deviation**	**Mean Rank**	**U**	**P**
The process of financial planning	Women	144	41.15	41	24	65	7.25	135.59		
	Men	143	42.46	43	28	60	6.41	152.47		
	Total	287	41.80	42	24	65	6.86		9085	0.085

family income, owning a car, owning a house, and saving up), the analyses in Table 2, Table 3 and Table 4 were redone according to gender (Table 6, Table 7, Table 8). As can be seen in Table 7, Anova results of the regression analysis showed that a significant model for women and men emerged ($p<0,001$). Furthermore, it can be seen in Table 7 that the state of saving up and owning a car made significant contribution to financial planning scores both for women ($p< .001$) and men ($p<.01$) and that these variables increased the financial planning for retirement scores. When Table 8 was examined, it was verified that among women, it was saving up that was related to financial planning for retirement ($p< .001$) while among men, owning a house had a relationship with financial planning for the retirement ($p<.01$).

Table 6. The general model of regression analysis related to predictors of financial retirement planning between women and men

Model Summary(c)			
Gender	Model	R	Durbin-Watson
Women	1	0.322	1.640
Men	1	0.228	2.001

Predictors: age, having children, education level, health status, family income, owning a car, owning a house, status of saving up.

Table 7. Anova results from predictors of financial retirement planning between women and men

ANOVA(c)						
Gender		**Sum of Squares**	**df**	**Mean Square**	**F**	**P**
	Regression	780.2	1	780.2	16.4	0.000
	Residual	6741.7	142	47.5		
Women	Total	7521.9	143			
	Regression	300.3	1	300.3	7.7	0.006
	Residual	5496.6	141	39.0		
Men	Total	5796.8	142			

Table 8. Regression analysis results from predictors of financial retirement planning between women and men

		B	**Std. Error**	**Beta**	**t**	**Sig.**
	(Constant)	39.18	0.75		52.113	0.000
Women	Can you save up?	4.72	1.16	0.32	4.054	0.000
	(Constant)	40.33	0.96		41.865	0.000
Men	Do you own a house?	3.18	1.15	0.23	2.775	0.006

DISCUSSION

One of the most remarkable findings of this study aiming to determine the relationship between the financial planning for retirement and some socio-economic variables (which are thought to be have influence on financial sources) is that, even though statistically insignificant, the financial planning for retirement among men is higher in rate than in women group. These results we got in this study show similarities with the results of some other studies (Glass & Kilpatrick, 1998; Günay, 2006; Noone, 2010). In these studies, (Glass & Kilpatrick, 1998; Günay, 2006; Noone, 2010) it was suggested that the financial preparations for retirement rates among women were lower comparing to those of men. In accordance with these studies (Glass & Kilpatrick, 1998; Günay, 2006; Noone, 2010), Lee (2003) also asserted that women spent their time on activities which were not focused on the financial investments when planning for their retirements. In Glass and Kilpatrick (1998)'s study, findings which showed that men had more saving up instruments in rates comparing to women were obtained. In this study, (Glass & Kilpatrick, 1998) it was verified that men not only were more tend to save up but also invested in financial mechanisms more (Glass & Kilpatrick, 1998). In this point, it is suggested that socio-economic variables, the number of assets and the amount of retirement pension play an imminent role on the formal and informal financial planning for retirement among working individuals (Albert, 2006). Sun (2010), supporting Albert (2006), also suggested that people who gained more money had more money to manage, and, therefore, that people with higher level of income would be more interested in financial markets and could get more informed about them through years. Likewise, in our study, it can be maintained that financial sources owned by women and men are of relationship with the financial planning for retirement. It should be emphasized here that in our study, most of the independent variables, which were thought to have effects on financial sources, namely gender, age, having children, education level, health, family income and owning a car were not found to be in relationship with financial planning for retirement when examined on the whole group as well as women and men groups separately. However, in our study, the rate of the men owning assets (a car or/and a house) seems to be higher than that of women. It can be claimed, in a sense that as Albert (2006) suggested, owning these assets could have effects on the fact that the financial plans for retirement of men were higher in rates than those of women. As a matter of fact, in our study, owning a house was found to be in relationship with the financial plans for retirement of men especially in middle age period. In other words, it can be put forward that especially men's owning a house, which means not having to pay rents, enabled them to make financial plans for their retirements.

One of the most important findings of our study worthy to discuss about middle aged women and men is that neither women nor men feel prepared for the retirement. Yet, the rate of the men who did not feel ready was higher than the rate of women who did not feel ready for the retirement. This finding obtained in our study can also be discussed taken Turkey's social structure into consideration. Keeping the degree of the changes in social structure in mind here, it is suggested that both modern and traditional structures can be observed together in Turkey (Arıkan, 1997). When especially roles in the families are taken, while more equalitarian approaches exist in modern part of the society, especially in the more traditional families, domestic roles are generally expected from the women. This means that those working women are supposed to meet the domestic expectations as well as well as working life, which makes it very hard to cope with. That is possibly why they could feel ready for the retirement earlier. As a matter of fact, the reason why they feel more ready comparing to men in this study can also be attributed to this deduction.

Although it was seen in our study that women saved up more than men did, these saving ups were indicated to be insufficient for being ready to retire. However, it was established in our study that as the rate of saving up among women increases, the financial plans for retirement can also increase, which in a sense suggests that financial sources are important for the women who make the financial plans for retirement.

SOLUTIONS AND RECOMMENDATIONS

The importance of (financial) plans prior to retirement for life satisfaction, being happy and peaceful during retirement is eminent. It should be underlined here that having sufficient financial sources also play an important role while working individuals make plan for retirement financially. As a matter of fact, without having adequate financial sources, coping with the retirement or attending the activities and programs that would help prepare to retirement is quite undoable. For this reason, such activities should be offered free of fee to the workers.

Another point is that, when the fact that women live longer generally all through the world is taken into consideration that they will be under health risks more seems more plausible compared to men in coming years. Similarly, when considered that they are more disadvantaged in the access to financial sources and opportunities, it can be easily inferred that women will live with a lower income during their old ages compared to men. In this context, owing to the fact that women need financial planning for their retirement more, they should be informed more especially on issues about planning the retirement.

Moreover, keeping in mind that, as a result of the gender role expectations, women are more forced to run domestic responsibilities and working life together compared to men, therefore, their access to activities about retirement planning can be hard. For this reason, the pre-retirement planning needs including financial needs of all the women who work in public and private sectors should be determined and in line with these needs, employer supported education and consultancy services should be made accessible for women. Yet, employer supported educational services given to working individuals in Turkey are quite inadequate. As Altuntaş (2010) also favored, although there are increasing number of examples which are aimed to prepare actively working individuals to their retirements, a systematically working support model does not still exist in Turkey similar to those which are in many developing countries. As Zastrow (2013) mentioned, Employee Assistance Programs (EAP), serving in the USA, can be shown as an exemplary model in terms of offering consultancy and support services to the workers on many issues including retirement planning. There is a need to establish similar programs in Turkey, within which most of the social services in workplaces is dealt with in the USA. When the fact that neither women nor men feel prepared for the retirement is taken into consideration, it can be said that workers need educational and consultancy services which would enable them, even if indirectly, to plan their retirement financially. In this sense, in Turkey, raising awareness of the workers, helping them raise their financial sources, and enabling them to adapt to retirement can be more achievable through such programs as in the USA. In this point, the responsibilities to support workers and encourage them to plan prior to their retirement should not fall only on the employers' therefore, the institutions', shoulders, nationwide attempts on this matter is also needed.

FUTURE RESEARCH DIRECTIONS

In accordance with the results our study, it is possible to suggest that planning retirement only from financial aspect is not sufficient for being ready for the retirement. In our study, it was verified that although the financial planning for retirement among men is higher in rate than in women group, neither women nor men felt prepared for their retirement. This gives rise to thought that planning retirement does not mean simply financial planning. As a matter of fact, the lack of planning before retirement may not only cause financial crisis in following years, but also health related, psychological and social problems.

When it is regarded that retirement is a whole with its many aspects such as finance, health, psycho-social and life style related factors, especially in Turkey more studies on retirement planning with especially respect to finance, health, psycho-social and life style related aspects can be suggested to scholars.

Moreover, it can also be said that more research is required so as to determine the "gender-based" needs for retirement since, Er (2009) asserted more losses could come into being in retired individuals' roles in new working places (if any), efficiencies and relationships, which are in the center position during their adult life time. For this reason, it is of great importance to define not only needs for financial planning but also prior needs for the retirement. Additionally, scholars can be suggested to conduct more research in order to develop "gender-based" models and solution proposals to meet such needs.

CONCLUSION

As the result of the study, statistically no significant difference has been found between the responses of women and men about planning the retirement financially. However, it has been verified that men's financial plans for retirement were higher in rates than that of women.

On the other hand, it was also established that for the all participants, the state of being an owner of a house and the state of saving up had a correlation with financial retirement planning. It was determined that the factor of being an owner of a house for men and the factor of saving up for women increases the financial planning for the retirement. However, it was also found that neither women nor men in the scope of the study feel ready for the retirement.

ACKNOWLEDGMENT

This study has been achieved based on a term project named "a research on retirement planning behaviours of middle-aged women and men: Nevşehir sample", which was conducted in Ankara University, The Graduate School of Health Sciences, Department of Social Work in 2014.

REFERENCES

Akçay, R. C. (1994). *Çanakkale ilinde görev yapan öğretmenlerin emekliliğe hazırlık eğitimine ihtiyaçları* [The needs of teachers working in Çanakkale for preparation training for retirement]. Unpublished doctoral dissertation, University of Ankara, Turkey.

Akın, A. (2012). Toplumsal cinsiyet ve yaşlılık [Gender and old age]. In D. Aslan, & M. Ertem (Eds.), *Yaşlı Sağlığı: Sorunlar ve Çözümleri* [The Elderly Health: Problems and Their Solutions]. Halk Sağlığı Uzmanları Derneği [Public Health Professionals Associations]. Retrieved May 13, 2014, from http://halksagligiokulu.org/anasayfa/components/com_booklibrary/ebooks/yasl%C4%B1saglgiyeni16.7.2012.pdf.

Albert, L. C. (2006). *A three part study on the relationship between retirement planning and health.* Unpublished doctoral dissertation, University of South Florida, United States of America.

Altuntaş, C. (2010). Çalışan destek programları [Employee assistance programs]. *Dokuz Eylül Üniversitesi Sosyal Bilimler Enstitüsü Dergisi, 12*(1), 57–75.

Arıkan, G. (1997). Ataerkillik kavramıyla ilgili sosyolojik tartışmalar [Sociological debates on the concept of patriarchy]. *H.Ü. Edebiyat Fakültesi Dergisi, 14*(1-2), 1–24.

Baltacı, H. Ş., & Selvitopu, A. (2012). Teacher's view about retirement and pre-retirement training. *Elementary Education Online, 11*(3), 800–812.

Er, D. (2009). Psikososyal açıdan yaşlılık [Elderly from a psychosocial respect]. *Fırat Sağlık Hizmetleri Dergisi, 4*(11), 131–144.

Glass, J. C. Jr, & Kilpatrick, B. B. (1998). Gender comparisons of baby boomers and financial preparation for retirement. *Educational Gerontology, 24*(8), 719–745. doi:10.1080/0360127980240802

Güleç, M., & Tekbaş, Ö. F. (1997). Sağlık perspektifinden yaşlılık [The health of elderly]. *Türkiye Klinikleri Tıp Bilimleri Dergisi, 17*(6), 369–377.

Günay, G. (2006). Bireylerin kişi ve aile olarak emekliliğe hazırlanmalarına ilişkin plan yapma durumlarının incelenmesi [Examination of the status of individuals' planning in preparation for retirement as an individual and a family]. Published doctoral thesis, Hacettepe University, Turkey.

Günay, G. (2013). Emekliliği planlama süreci ölçeğinin Türkçe geçerlilik ve güvenirlilik çalışması: Karabük Üniversitesi örneği. [Turkish reliability and validity study of the process of the retirement planning scale: The Example of Karabük University]. *Türk Geriatri Dergisi, 16*(1), 84–94.

Içli, G. (2008). Yaşlılar ve yetişkin çocuklar [Elderly people and adults]. *Yaşlı Sorunları ve Araştırma Dergisi, 1*, 29–38.

Joo, S. H., & Pauwels, V. W. (2002). Factors affecting workers' retirement confidence: A gender perspective. *Financial Counseling and Planning, 13*(2), 1–10.

Lee, W. K. M. (2003). Women and retirement planning: Towards the "feminization of poverty" in an aging Hong Kong. *Journal of Women & Aging*, *15*(1), 31–53. doi:10.1300/J074v15n01_04 PMID:12678184

Noone, J. H. (2010). *Psychological and socio-economic factors influencing men and women's planning for retirement*. Published doctoral dissertation, Massey University, New Zealand.

Onur, B. (1995). *Gelişim Psikolojisi: Yetişkinlik Yaşlılık Ölüm* [Developmental Psychology, Older Age, Death]. Ankara: İmge Yayınevi.

Phua, V., & Mcnally, J. W. (2008). Men planning for retirement: Changing meanings of preretirement planning. *Journal of Applied Gerontology*, *27*(5), 588–608. doi:10.1177/0733464808321885

Şahin, J. (2006). *Emekliler ve sorunları üzerine sosyolojik bir araştırma: Şanlıurfa örneği* [A sociological research on the retired and their problems: Sample of Şanlıurfa]. Published master's thesis, Fırat University, Turkey.

Salman, S. (2005). *Öğretmenlerin emeklilik dönemine uyumları ve yaşam tatminleri* [Adjustment to retirement and life satisfaction of teacher]. Published doctoral dissertation, Ankara University, Turkey.

Sarım, S. (1996). *Emeklilerin zamanlarını değerlendirme durumlarının incelenmesi* [Analysis on how the retired spend their time]. Unpublished master's thesis, Istanbul University, Turkey.

Sevim, Y., & Şahin, J. (2007). Toplumun yeni yoksulları: Emekliler (Şanlıurfa İli Örneği) [The New Poor Persons of The Society: The Retirements (A Case Study of Şanlıurfa Province)]. *Sosyoloji Araştırma Dergisi*, *10*(1), 195–207.

Sun, R. (2010). *How pre-retirement education in the workplace helps workers to plan for retirement*. Master's thesis, North Carolina State University, United State of America.

Szinovacz, M., & Washo, C. (1992). Gender differences in exposure to life events and adaptation to retirement. *The Journals of Gerontology. Series B, Psychological Sciences and Social Sciences*, *47*(4), 191–196. PMID:1624714

Wiggins, S. D., & Henderson, C. M. (1996). Preretirement planning of female registered nurses. *Western Journal of Nursing Research*, *18*(5), 580–594. doi:10.1177/019394599601800508 PMID:8918209

Wilson, K. N., & Aggrey, M. E. A. (2012). Retirement planning and counseling: Issues and challenges for teachers in public schools in the Sekondi Circuit. *United States-China Education Review A*, *8*, 755–767.

Yazıcıoğlu, A. (2006). *Emekliliğin kadının sosyal yaşamında meydana getirdiği değişmeler üzerine bir grounded theory denemesi* [A grounded theory essay on the changes in woman's social life affected by retirement]. Unpublished master's thesis, Hacettepe University, Turkey.

Yılmaz, S. (1996). *Türkiye'de emeklilik yaşantısı* [The experience of retirement in Turkey]. Unpublished master's thesis, Dokuz Eylül University, Turkey.

Zastrow, C. (2013). *Sosyal hizmete giriş* [Introduction to social work]. Ankara: Nika Yayınevi.

ADDITIONAL READING

Anibueze, A. U. (2013). Effects of gender pre-retirement preparation and adjustment in retirement: A case study of Enugu State, Nigeria. *International Organization of Scientific Research Journal of Humanities and Social Science*, *17*(2), 1–10.

Basu, S. (2005). Age banding: A model for planning retirement needs. *Financial Counseling and Planning*, *16*(1), 29–36.

Brucker, E., & Leppel, K. (2013). Retirement Plans: Planners and non-planners. *Educational Gerontology*, *39*(1), 1–11. doi:10.1080/03601277.2012.660859

Danış, M. Z. (2009). Türkiye'de yaşlı nüfusun yalnızlık ve yoksulluk durumları ve sosyal hizmet uygulamaları açısından bazı çıkarımlar [Loneliness and poverty conditions of the elderly population in Turkey and some inferences about social work interventions] *Toplum ve Sosyal Hizmet Dergisi*, *20*(1), 67–83.

Keele, S., & Albert, P. T. (2013). Retirement financial planning and the RN: An integrative literature review. *The Journal of Nursing Administration*, *43*(11), 574–580. doi:10.1097/01.NNA.0000434508.66749.35 PMID:24153198

Kim, J., Kwon, J., & Anderson, E. A. (2005). Factors related to retirement confidence: Retirement preparation and workplace financial education. *Financial Counseling and Planning*, *16*(2), 77–89.

Kim, J. E., & Moen, P. (2002). Retirement transitions, gender, and psychological well-being: A life -course, ecological model. *The Journals of Gerontology. Series B, Psychological Sciences and Social Sciences*, *57B*(3), 212–222. doi:10.1093/geronb/57.3.P212 PMID:11983732

Kubicek, B., Korunka, C., Hoonakker, P., & Raymo, J. M. (2010). Work and family characteristics as predictors of early retirement in married men and women. *Research on Aging*, *32*(4), 467–498. doi:10.1177/0164027510364120 PMID:21430790

Künemund, H., & Kolland, F. (2007). Work and retirement. In J. Bond, S. M. Peace, F. Dittmann-Kohli, & G. Westerhof (Eds.), *Aging in Society* (pp. 167–186). London: SAGE Publications Ltd.

Loibl, C., & Hira, T. K. (2006). A workplace and gender-related perspective on financial planning information sources and knowledge outcomes. *Financial Services Review*, *15*, 21–42.

Lum, Y. S., & Lightfoot, E. (2003). The effect of health on retirement saving among older workers. *Social Work Research*, *27*(1), 31–44.

Lusardi, A., & Mitchell, O. S. (2011). Financial literacy and retirement planning in the United States. *Journal of Pension Economics and Finance*, *10*(4), 509–525. doi:10.1017/S147474721100045X

Noone, J., Alpass, F., & Stephens, C. (2010). Do men and women differ in their retirement planning? Testing a theoretical model of gendered pathways to retirement preparation. *Research on Aging*, *32*(6), 715–738. doi:10.1177/0164027510383531

Post, C., Schneer, J. A., Reitman, F., & Ogilvie, D. (2013). Pathways to retirement: A career stage analysis of retirement age expectations. *Human Relations*, *66*(1), 87–112. doi:10.1177/0018726712465657

Reitzes, D. C., & Mutran, E. J. (2004). The transition to retirement: Stages and factors that influence retirement adjustment. *International Journal of Aging & Human Development*, *59*(1), 63–84. doi:10.2190/NYPP-RFFP-5RFK-8EB8 PMID:15453412

Sargent, L. D., Lee, M. D., Martin, B., & Zikic, J. (2013). Reinventing retirement: New pathways, new arrangements, new meanings. *Human Relations*, *66*(1), 3–21. doi:10.1177/0018726712465658

Smith, F. L. M., & Dougherty, D. S. (2012). Revealing a master narrative: Discourses of retirement throughout the working life cycle. *Management Communication Quarterly*, *26*(3), 453–478. doi:10.1177/0893318912438687

Szinovacz, M. E., & Davey, A. (2005). Predictors of perceptions of involuntary retirement. *The Gerontologist*, *45*(1), 36–47. doi:10.1093/geront/45.1.36 PMID:15695416

Taylor, M. A., Goldberg, C., Shore, L. M., & Lipka, P. (2008). The effects of retirement expectations and social support on post-retirement adjustment: A longitudinal analysis. *Journal of Managerial Psychology*, *23*(4), 458–470. doi:10.1108/02683940810869051

Topa, G., Moriano, J. A., Depolo, M., Alcover, C. M., & Morales, J. F. (2009). Antecedents and consequences of retirement planning and decision-making: A meta-analysis and model. *Journal of Vocational Behavior*, *75*(1), 38–55. doi:10.1016/j.jvb.2009.03.002

Van Rooij, M. C. J., Lusardi, A., & Alessie, R. J. M. (2011). Financial literacy and retirement planning in the Netherlands. *Journal of Economic Psychology*, *32*(4), 593–608. doi:10.1016/j.joep.2011.02.004

Van Rooij, M. C. J., Lusardi, A., & Alessie, R. J. M. (2012). Financial literacy, retirement planning and household wealth. *The Economic Journal*, *122*(560), 449–478. doi:10.1111/j.1468-0297.2012.02501.x

Wang, W. C., Worsley, A., Cunningham, E., & Hunter, W. (2014). The Heterogeneity of middle-age Australians' retirement plans. *Social Work Research*, *38*(1), 36–46.

Whitaker, E. A., & Bokemeier, J. (2014). Patterns in income source expectations for retirement among preretirees. *Research on Aging*, *36*(4), 467–496. doi:10.1177/0164027513501700 PMID:25651317

Yeung, D. Y. (2013). Is pre-retirement planning always good? An exploratory study of retirement adjustment among Hong Kong Chinese retirees. *Aging & Mental Health*, *17*(3), 386–393. doi:10.1080/13607863.2012.732036 PMID:23072256

KEY TERMS AND DEFINITIONS

Employee Assistance Programs: Programs where consultancy and support services are provided for the actively working individuals on many issues such as retirement, addiction and family consultancy.

Financial Planning for the Retirement: Includes formal retirement plans such as making investments and informal plans such as sharing ideas with others about the retirement.

Gender Roles: The roles imposed to women and men by the society.

Middle-Aged: Used for individuals who are between 45 and 59 years of age acknowledging the World Health Organization's description.

Pre-Retirement Planning: Used to describe the long-term attempts of the individuals for their retirement stage prior to the end of their working life.

Retirement: An important cornerstone in the transition stage towards elderliness with the completion of the active working life.

Retirement Stage: Refers to life period after retirement.

Chapter 5
Financial Education for Children and Youth

Zeynep Tezel
Kırıkkale University, Turkey

ABSTRACT

Although financial education consists of individuals of all ages, education of young people in the field of finance is more important. The young generation faces more financial risks and more complicated financial products than their parents. Besides, young people are introduced to financial services at very early ages owing to cell phones, bank accounts, credit cards. Therefore, it is important that individuals are educated in finance as early as possible.

INTRODUCTION

Today's financial world is highly complex when compared with that of a generation ago (Suwanaphan, 2013). The ability to manage personal finances has become increasingly important in today's world. People must plan for long-term investments for their retirement and children's education (Volpe & Chen, 1998). They must also decide on short term savings and borrowing for a vacation, a down payment for a house, a car loan, and other big ticket items. Additionally, they must manage their own medical and life insurance needs (Chen & Volpe, 1998). Families and schools have continually constructed a shared reality in preparing teens for their financial future (Danes & Haberman, 2007).

Young people are in transition from childhood to adulthood, from financial dependency to independence. Their role in society is changing and they have new economic responsibilities (Shim et al., 2009, Shim et al., 2010). They often find themselves carrying large amounts of student loans or credit card debt, and such early entanglements can hinder their ability to accumulate wealth (Lusardi, Mitchell & Curto, 2010). The capacity to manage personal finances has become increasingly important, particularly for college students (Gutter, Copur & Blanco, 2013).

According to the UN, more than 18% (1.2 billion) of the world's population is comprised of youth, and the combined group of youth and children (those under age 15) makes up fully 40% of the world's population today (Reinsch, 2012).

DOI: 10.4018/978-1-4666-7484-4.ch005

Children and youth are both current and future social and economic actors, whose decisions will influence development of their societies. The recent financial crisis has highlighted the importance of promoting social responsibility and developing skills in financial management for all persons. This is especially true for children and youth, who are particularly vulnerable. Important values of citizenship and skills in managing financial resources at an early age can lessen social and financial vulnerability, thereby reducing the risk of poverty caused by debt (UNICEF, 2012).

In today's age of consumerism and knowledge explosion, young adults seem to be the most highly targeted group by professional marketers and big organizations. Financial prudence paves the way into a bright and safe future among the youth, generating wealth, and avoiding debt and wasteful spending ultimately leading to financial soundness. Financial literacy also helps in building up the skills and confidence of the youth to become more aware of financial opportunities and risks, improve their knowledge of financial markets, concepts and products and assist them in making informed decisions how to generate and maintain a steady balance between their cash inflows and outflows (Pillai, Carlo & D'souza, 2010). Managing money well allows them to distinguish between wants and needs, learn how to save and budget, and make wise spending decisions (Pankow & Brotherson, 2009).

1. FINANCIAL LITERACY

Vitt et al. (2000) defined financial literacy as; the ability to read, analyze, manage, and communicate about the personal financial conditions that affect material well-being. It includes the ability to discern financial choices, discuss money and financial issues without (or despite) discomfort, plan for the future, and respond competently to life events that affect everyday financial decisions, including events in the general economy. Mason & Wilson (2000) defined it as an individual's ability to obtain, understand and evaluate the relevant information necessary to make decisions with an awareness of the likely financial consequences. Hogarth (2002) defined financial literacy as 1) knowledgeable, educated and informed on the issues of managing money and assets; 2) understand the basic concepts underlying the management of money and assets; and 3) use that knowledge and understanding to plan and implement their financial decisions.

Many experts observed the phenomena above and prescribed the same remedy: increased financial literacy and financial education. It is a solution that appeals to all political persuasions and to all geographies. For example, the Second Annual Child and Youth Finance Summit in Istanbul in May of 2013 brought together experts describing initiatives by the US, UK, Turkey, the Philippines, Chile, Nigeria, Egypt, Ghana, Nepal, Macedonia, Spain, and the United Nations to provide financial education to millions. Worldwide, employers, nonprofits, and governments are creating educational interventions that have real costs and create much larger opportunity costs by supplanting some other activities, such as required high school courses that replace other electives (Fernandes, Lynch & Netemeyer, 2014).

Financial literacy defines as the ability to use knowledge and skills to manage financial resources effectively for a life time of financial well-being. The Presidents Advisory Council on Financial Literacy (PACFL) (2008) convened to "improve financial literacy among all Americans," defines financial literacy and financial education as follows;

- **Financial Literacy:** The ability to use knowledge and skills to manage financial resources effectively for a lifetime of financial well-being (Jump$tart, 1997).
- **Financial Education:** The process by which people improve their understanding of financial products, services and con-

Table 1. Conceptual definitions of financial literacy (Hung, Parker & Yoong, 2009)

Source	Conceptual Definitiona
Hilgert, Hogarth & Beverley (2003)	Financial knowledge
FINRA (2003)	"The understanding ordinary investors have of market principles, instruments, organizations and regulations" (p. 2).
Moore (2003)	"Individuals are considered financially literate if they are competent and can demonstrate they have used knowledge they have learned. Financial literacy cannot be measured directly so proxies must be used. Literacy is obtained through practical experience and active integration of knowledge. As people become more literate they become increasingly more financially sophisticated and it is conjectured that this may also mean that an individual may be more competent" (p.29).
National Council on Economic Education (NCEE) (2005) b	"Familiarity with basic economic principles, knowledge about the U.S. economy, and understanding of some key economic terms" (p. 3).
Mandell (2007)	"The ability to evaluate the new and complex financial instruments and make informed judgments in both choice of instruments and extent of use that would be in their own best long-run interests" (pp. 163-164).
Lusardi & Mitchell (2007c)	[Familiarity] with "the most basic economic concepts needed to make sensible saving and investment decisions" (p. 36).
Lusardi & Tufano (2008)	Focus on debt literacy, a component of financial literacy, defining it as "the ability to make simple decisions regarding debt contracts, in particular how one applies basic knowledge about interest compounding, measured in the context of everyday financial choices" (p. 1).
ANZ Bank (2008), drawn from Schagen (2007)	"The ability to make informed judgements and to take effective decisions regarding the use and management of money" (p. 1).
Lusardi (2008a, 2008b)	"Knowledge of basic financial concepts, such as the working of interest compounding, the difference between nominal and real values, and the basics of risk diversification" (p. 2).

cepts, so they are empowered to make informed choices, avoid pitfalls, know where to go for help and take other actions to improve their present and long-term financial well-being (OECD, 2005a).

Table 1 Illustrates the breadth of conceptual definitions, drawn from a number of studies and placed in chronological order (Hung, Parker & Yoong, 2009).

Financial literacy definition largely rests on the ability to use knowledge and skills towards achieving financial well-being, and is hence quite behaviorally based. While practically relevant, such a focus limits insight into mechanisms for impacting financial literacy. Financial knowledge, skills, and behavior, as well as their mutual relationships, should all be considered in an overarching conceptualization of financial literacy. In particular, financial knowledge represents a particularly basic form of financial literacy. Financial knowledge, in turn, is reflected in perceived financial knowledge and influences financial skills that depend on knowledge. Actual financial behavior, in turn, depends on all three (actual knowledge, perceived knowledge, and skills). Figure 1. presents these logical relationships among financial literacy components (Hung, Parker&Yoong, 2009).

Although studying the financial knowledge of teens is not a new phenomenon in the academic literature, it has received increasing attention recently in the public arena, especially in the mass media (Consumer Federation of America, 1991; National Coalition for Consumer Education Inc., 1991; Wang, 1993; Mandell, 1997). Whether the studies evolve from the academic or the public

Figure 1. Conceptual model of financial literacy (Hung, Parker & Yoong, 2009)

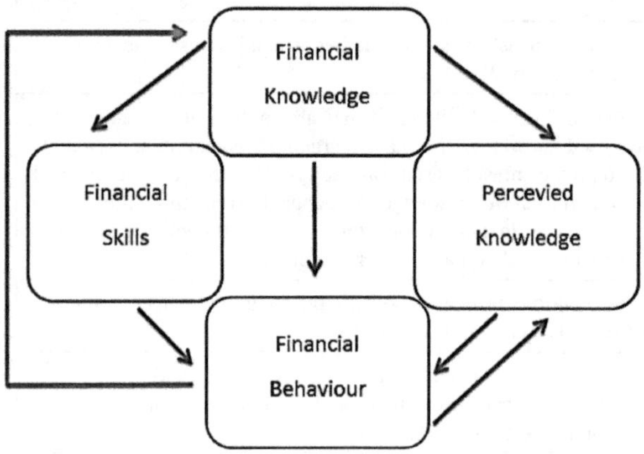

arena or they are historic or recent, they all conclude that teens lack knowledge about personal finance (Bachman, 1983; Danes, Huddleston Casas & Boyce, 1999; Roberts & Jones, 2001; Kasser & Ahuvia, 2002; Bowen, 2002; Anthes, 2004, Godfrey, 2006).

In the 1997-98 school year, the Jump$tart Coalition for Personal Financial Literacy conducted its first Personal Financial Survey, a nationwide survey of 12th grade students to determine the ability of our young people to survive in today's complex economy. The results of this initial "baseline" survey in 1997-98 were not reassuring. Just 10. 2% of the 1,532 high school seniors were able to answer at least three quarters of the basic, age-relevant questions correctly. In fact, the average "grade" on the "exam" was a failing 57. 3% (Mandell, 2008).

Prior studies of high school students consistently find that they are not receiving a good education in personal financial fundamentals and have poor knowledge and they are leaving schools without the ability to make critical decisions affecting their lives (Bakken, 1967; Langrehr, 1979; NAEP, 1979; CFAJAMEX, 1991; HSR, 1993; Chen & Volpe, 1998). According to Danes & Hira (1987) the college students lack knowledge in spesifics. For example, they know credict cards can be used as identification and they know the various costs involved in using credit cards. However they dont know what to do if there are billing errors. In a study of 1,509 high school seniors from 63 schools, Mandell (1997) reports an average correct score of 57% in the areas of income, money management, savings and investment, and spending. His conclusion is that students are not knowledgeable about personal finance.

Concerns about financial preparedness are documented in the past studies demonstrating that both young and older adults lack the basic knowledge needed to make good financial choices (Volpe, Chen & Pavlicko, 1996; Chen & Volpe, 1998; Bianco & Bosco, 2001). These concerns were heightened in a 2005 report by the Organization for Economic Co-operation and Development (OECD) indicating that financial illiteracy is widespread across age groups and geographical areas. (Mandell & Klein, 2009). There is growing concern, across a wide range of countries, about the levels of financial capability of consumers. A large number of initiatives are therefore being developed to address this issue; and countries are increasingly rolling out national strategies on financial capability. To do this effectively requires evidence on the areas where financial capability in the population is low and an identification of the extent to which these should be addressed by financial education and/or consumer protection measures (Kempson, 2011).

Financial literacy is related to education and experience related factors (Chen & Volpe, 2002).

A survey done by Shaari et al. (2013) it shows that five factors including age, spending habit, gender, faculty and year of study are significantly affect the financial literacy level. According to Varcoe, et al., (2002) who suggested that "during school" is the first choice for learning about money topics. Magazines and newsletters delivered to home were the second choice, followed by organizations outside of school and web pages (2002).

2. FINANCIAL EDUCATION

Financial education has always been important for consumers in helping them budget and manage their income, save and invest efficiently. Member countries promote financial education and awareness and in this respect that governments and relevant public and private institutions take due account of and implement the principles and good practices for financial education and awareness (OECD, 2005b).

Financial education programs aim to develop financially literacy and financially capability amongst individuals (Child & Youth Finance International, 2012). According to the Center for Financial Inclusion (2008) financial capability allows for the combination of knowledge, skills, attitudes, and especially behaviors that people need to make sound personal finance decisions, suited to their social and financial circumstances.

Financial education deals with information and learning. It is undeniably essential to help citizens of any country to better manage their financial life and hopefully make favourable choices that will contribute to increasing their well-being too. At the same time, it aims to changing behaviour in the sense that information on financial issues ought to be incorporated into daily life if we mean financial education to be effective (Ferreira, 2011).

Financial education introduces concepts of money and ways to manage it well. It promotes wise spending, regular savings and ways to make the most of one's resources. These skills serve as a foundation for young people as they are in transition from dependent to independent roles in financial management. Youth also need access to affordable and sustainable financial services including credit, savings, and insurance to help them to achieve these goals. Importantly, they need to know how to use these financial services and be able to make informed choices about saving and increasing saving capacity, about borrowing, about protecting themselves against risks.

Financial education can play a role to help young people to:

- Make a plan to achieve short and long term financial goals
- Improve saving capacity by using a budget
- Use financial products and services with confidence
- Develop risk management strategies

These are skills that young people need now and every day of their adult lives. An investment in financial literacy for young people sets the stage for the many changes that are coming. It will increase their ability to manage money, their confidence and their readiness for the challenges and opportunities in their life. Developing positive financial behaviors during the college years increases an individual's chances of attaining a better financial well-being later in life and a better understanding of how college students develop desirable and undesirable financial behaviors, and how these behaviors affect their financial well-being aid those interested in improving their quality of life (Gutter & Copur, 2011).

Financial education supports and enhances the use of behaviourally-motivated products and regulations. Increasing the effectiveness of financial education thus remains a priority for policy makers and practitioners, and integrating future developments in behavioural economics into financial education is a key part of continuing to do so (Yoong, 2011). Research based curricula in personal finance yields positive results. Because teens in general require a different teaching approach, it is important to develop the appropriate pedagogy and settings to ensure learning (Varcoe et al., 2005).

Financial knowledge can open up new opportunities to work, build assets, and save. Access to and control over savings can help to protect against, mitigate, and cope with many risks associated with adolescence by providing resources to draw upon in times of need (International Labour Organization, 2011). A number of theoretical frameworks from a wide range of academic disciplines are currently being used to explain how financial education might be applied so as to facilitate behavior change (Bowen et al., 2008).

2.1.The Principles and Good Practices for Financial Education

The Principles and Good Practices provide solid, but flexible and non-mandatory guidance on strengthening and promoting financial education. The principles and good practices are addressed to governments and all relevant public and private institutions in OECD and non-OECD countries. The Principles are applicable to OECD and non-OECD countries and are used in the context of the International Network on Financial Education (OECD, 2005b).

2.1.1. Principles

1. Financial education can be defined as "the process by which financial consumers / investors improve their understanding of financial products, concepts and risks and, through information, instruction and / or objective advice, develop the skills and confidence to become more aware of financial risks and opportunities, to make informed choices, to know where to go for help, and to take other effective actions to improve their financial well-being." Financial education thus goes beyond the provision of financial information and advice, which should be regulated, as is already often the case, in particular for the protection of financial clients (i.e. consumers in contractual relationships).
2. This financial capacity building, based on proper financial information and instruction, should be promoted. Financial education should be provided in a fair and unbiased manner. Programmes should be co-ordinated and developed with efficiency.
3. Financial education programmes should focus on high priority issues, which, depending on national circumstances, may include important aspects of financial life planning such as basic savings, private debt management or insurance as well as pre-requisites for financial awareness such as elementary financial mathematics and economics. The awareness of future retirees about the need to assess the financial adequacy of their current public or private pensions schemes and to take appropriate action when needed should be encouraged.
4. Financial education should be taken into account in the regulatory and administrative framework and considered as a tool to promote economic growth, confidence and stability, together with regulation of financial institutions and consumer protection (including the regulation of financial information and advice). The promotion of financial education should not be substituted for financial regulation, which is essential to protect consumers (for instance against fraud) and which financial education is expected to complement.
5. Appropriate measures should be taken when financial capacity is essential but deficiencies are observed. Other policy tools to consider are consumer protection and financial institution regulation. Without limiting the freedom to contract, default mechanisms, which take into consideration inadequate financial education or passive/inert behaviour, should be considered.
6. The role of financial institutions in financial education should be promoted and become part of their good governance with respect to their financial clients. Financial institutions' accountability and responsibility should be encouraged not only in providing informa-

tion and advice on financial issues, but also in promoting financial awareness clients, especially for long-term commitments and commitments which represent a substantial proportion of current and future income.

7. Financial education programmes should be designed to meet the needs and the financial literacy level of their target audience, as well as reflect how their target audience prefers to receive financial information. Financial education should be regarded as a life-time, on-going and continuous process, in particular in order to take account of the increased complexity of markets, varying needs at different life stages, and increasingly complex information.

2.1.2. Good Practices

Public Action for Financial Education

8. National campaigns should be encouraged to raise awareness of the population about the need to improve their understanding of financial risks and ways to protect against financial risks through adequate savings, insurance and financial education.
9. Financial education should start at school. People should be educated about financial matters as early as possible in their lives.
10. Consideration should be given to making financial education a part of state welfare assistance programmes.
11. Appropriate specialised structures (possibly embedded within existing authorities) in charge of promoting and coordinating financial education should be encouraged at the national level and regional and local public and private initiatives as close to the population as possible should also be promoted.
12. Specific websites should be promoted to provide relevant, user-friendly financial information to the public. Free information services should be developed. Warning systems by consumer, professional or other organisation on high-risk issues that may be detrimental to the interests of the financial consumers (including cases of fraud) should be promoted.
13. International co-operation on financial education should be promoted, including the use of the OECD as an international forum to exchange information on recent national experiences in financial education.

Role of Financial Institutions in Financial Education

14. Requirements to specify the types of information (including where to find information and the provision of general comparative and objective information on the risks and returns of different kinds of products) that financial institutions need to provide to clients on financial products and services, should be encouraged.
15. Financial institutions should be encouraged to clearly distinguish between financial education and financial information and "commercial" financial advice. Any financial advice for business purposes should be transparent and disclose clearly any commercial nature where it is also being promoted as a financial education initiative. For those financial services that entail long-term commitment or have potentially significant financial consequences, financial institutions should be encouraged to check that the information provided to their clients is read and understood.
16. Financial institutions should be encouraged to provide information at several different levels in order to best meet the needs of consumers. Small print, abstruse documentation should be discouraged.

17. Financial education provided by financial institutions should be regularly assessed to ensure it meets consumer needs. This may be achieved through partnerships with independent, not for profit financial advisory bodies that may have better connection with consumers, particularly those facing disadvantage in their participation in financial markets.
18. Financial institutions should be encouraged to train their staff on financial education and develop codes of conduct for the provision of general advice about investment and borrowing, not linked to the supply of a specific product.

Financial Education for Retirement Savings

19. For individuals in private personal pension plans, the provision by financial institutions of the appropriate financial information and education required for the management of their future retirement savings and income should be promoted.
20. Concerning occupational schemes, (for which the related information and education should be provided in a consistent way across the schemes) financial education and awareness of employees and related policy tools should be further promoted, both for defined contributions and defined benefits schemes.

Financial Education Programmes

21. Financial education programmes that help financial consumers find the facts and understand the pros and cons as well as the risks of different types of financial products and services should be promoted. Further research on behavioural economics should be promoted.
22. The development of methodologies to assess existing financial education programmes should be promoted. Official recognition of financial education programmes which fulfil relevant criteria should be considered.
23. Financial education programmes that develop guidelines on study content and accomplishment level for each financial education programme and for each population sub group should be promoted.
24. In order to achieve a wider coverage and exposure, the use of all available media for the dissemination of education messages should be promoted.
25. In order to take into account the diverse backgrounds of investors/consumers, financial education that creates different programmes for specific sub-groups of investors/consumers (i.e. young people, the less educated, disadvantaged groups) should be promoted. Financial education should be related to the individual circumstance, through financial education seminars and personalised financial counselling programmes.
26. For those programmes which favour use of classrooms, proper education and competence of the educators should be promoted. In this respect, the development of programmes to "train the trainers" and the provision of specific information material and tools for these trainers should be encouraged (OECD, 2005b).

3. SOME APPLICATIONS FOR FINANCIAL EDUCATION

3.1. Global Money Week

Global Money Week is held, as the name implies, one week in March every year. Global Money Week encourages children around the world unite their voices, take action and expand their knowledge and engagement in the financial issues that matter to them most. Through national and global events, youngsters learn about creating livelihoods, gaining employment and even starting their own businesses. Central Banks, Ministries of Finance and Education, NGOs, schools, corporations, professional bodies, the media, all were involved in organizing national Global Money Week events, and participating in the celebrations.

Global Money Week celebrations took place in 80 countries, including Albania, Azerbaijan, Bangladesh, Belarus, Belgium, Bhutan, Botswana, Brazil, Brunei, Bulgaria, Burkina Faso, Cambodia, Canada, Chile, China, Colombia, Congo, Costa Rica, Côte d'Ivoire, Czech Republic, Dominican Republic, Egypt, El Salvador, Estonia, Ethiopia, Finland, France, Gambia, Ghana, Guatemala, Honduras, Hungary, India, Indonesia, Italy, Kazakhstan, Kenya, Kenya, Kuwait, Latvia, Libya, Lithuania, Macedonia, Malaysia, Mexico, Moldova, Mongolia, Montenegro, Morocco, Namibia, Nepal, Nigeria, Pakistan, Palestine, Paraguay, Peru, Philippines, Portugal, Romania, Saudi Arabia, Serbia, South Africa, Sudan, Switzerland, Tanzania, Thailand, The Netherlands, Togo, Turkey, Uganda, Ukraine, United Arab Emirates, United Kingdom, United States, Uruguay, Venezuela, Yemen, Zambia, and Zimbabwe. Over 1 million children participated in Global Money Week celebrations. Global Money Week was globally coordinated by Child and Youth Finance International (Child & Youth Finance International, 2013).

National Activities

- **Visits to the Stock Exchange:** Children and youth visited stock exchanges, where some had the opportunity to ring the opening bell to signal the beginning of trade.
- **Visits to Banks:** Children and youth visited banks and other financial institutions to learn about how they work.
- **Workshops and Lessons:** Young people enjoyed financial education lessons in community centers, schools, and universities.
- **Talking to Central Bank Governors:** Many children shared their recommendations with the governors of their central banks.
- **Debates:** Debates on financial education, employment issues, and entrepreneurship took place in schools.
- **Visit to Money Museums:** Money museums opened their doors to youngsters to teach them about money and its history.
- **Publications:** Resources to educate children about financial issues were made available through libraries and schools.
- **Contests and Competitions:** From poster-making contests to "financial football" competitions, children engaged in fun financial education and financial inclusion contests.
- **Theatre:** Youngsters expressed themselves through theater and the arts.
- **Financial Education Games:** Games were held as a fun way to learn about finance.
- **Radio Talk Shows:** Broadcast media helped spread the Movement's message.
- **Book Bank:** Special book banks were set up to spread financial knowledge to children.
- **Folk Stories:** Storytelling was used to impart financial literacy.
- **Exhibitions:** Youngsters had the opportunity to display their artwork and projects in interactive exhibitions.
- **Cartoons:** Cartoons and comic books helped to engage youngsters.
- **Youth Budget to Parliament:** Children and youth presented their input on the youth budgets of their countries.
- **Learning from the Market:** Young entrepreneurs presented their efforts to central bank governors.
- **Pledge:** Children unified their voices by signing pledge forms showing their commitment to child and youth friendly banking policies.

- **Research and Petition:** Children researched the policies of the banks in their own countries to evaluate the child friendliness of their banking policies. Banks that did not meet the criteria were petitioned to remove the barriers that hinder minors from opening savings accounts.

Global Activities

The Global Activities for Global Money Week are aimed at engaging children, youth and stakeholders at a global level. With the help of video conferencing, webinars, live streaming, the Global Money Week website and social media channels as well as media the activities are elevated to a global level and cross borders to take the celebrations around he globe.

- **Global Theme:** The global theme aims to inspire the celebrations and activities during Global Money Week. The theme of 2014 is the Post 2015 Agenda: What do children and youth want for their future?
- **Connecting the World:** Via online live streaming of the events that are taking place all over the world the national event are able to be shared on a global level to all that are celebrating.
- **Global Web Chat Café:** In the Global Web Chat Café youngsters from different parts of the world are able to connect with one another via web chats and share their stories. It is an opportunity for kids to connect with their peers, share stories, learn about other parts of the world and inspire each other to save, learn about earning a living and much more.
- **VIP Talks:** During the week we will organize live streamed talks by inspiring persons and invite kids to ask questions to them. This is a great opportunity for the youngsters all over the world to be able to connect with the persons that inspire them and ask the questions they care about.
- **Youth and Policy Makers Global Dialogue:** Online chats between youth and policymakers such as govern of central banks and ministers of finance and education.
- **Youth Talks:** Youth talking to youth or inspiring academics talk to youth about entrepreneurship, financial education or financial inclusion at their schools and universities around the world.
- **Global Savings Calculator**: The online calculatoris a fun way for children to share how much they are saving. Children entered how much they saved, converted their currencies, and learned savings rates worldwide.
- **Showcasing and Sharing:** The activities that take place during the celebrations of Global Money Week will be showcased and shared all over the world.

Global Money Week is important because children and youth are the focus of change. They are tomorrow's business leaders, politicians, parents, and teachers. They can unlock their potential when they believe in themselves. They can change lives, their own and others', when they have the right financial tools. They can learn about saving - money and resources. They can learn how to earn a livelihood and gain employment and most of all, Global Money Week provides children and youth with a voice: a voice that can help reshape the future of finance (Child & Youth Finance International, 2013).

3.2. Child Social and Financial Education (CSFE)

Child Social and Financial Education (CSFE) aims to inspire children to be socially and economically empowered citizens by equipping them with the skills and knowledge to become active agents capable of transforming their communities and societies. CSFE provides children with a holistic learning experience that embraces knowledge and skills harnessed from both inside and outside the classroom. Promoting financial education and a positive financial culture in children and youth is essential to ensuring a financially literate population capable of making informed decisions. It offers a design through which children in child-friendly schools can explore their rights and responsibilities in classes or club sessions, take part in saving activities and apply entrepreneurial skills to address social issues that are important to them. The CSFE module allows for maximum flexibility for adaptation to a country's needs.

The CSFE in Schools module is a result of the global partnership between UNICEF and two organizations Aflatoun and Child Savings International that was established to advocate for CSFE through UNICEF education programmes. Much of the material was created in collaboration with Aflatoun and Child and Youth Finance International, an organization that coordinates global efforts to ensure that the human rights (especially economic rights) of children and youth are respected at all times. CSFE comprises three core components: life skills, financial and livelihoods education. Together, the components aim to build life skills, change financial behaviours, stimulate business activity and increase financial literacy and capability. The (CSFE) framework provides a detailed description of the essential attitudes, skills and behaviours at different levels of a child's development. The different levels of the framework are not strictly defined by age parameter, as this might hinder its flexibility, especially with the lack of uniformity of children's ages at different levels of the formal and informal education ladder (UNICEF, 2012).

Financial Literacy Framework: (money and use, planning and budgeting, risk and reward and financial landscape)

"Money And Use"

Working Definitions: Focuses on a broad spectrum of personal financial topics, such as everyday payments, spending, value for money, bank cards, cheques, bank accounts and currencies.

Overall outcomes by theme:

1. Able to appreciate the value of resources, services and products, and how prices can reflect relative value.
2. Recognizes the financial services that are most appropriate for the situation and determines the best option from among options.
3. Able to access and use financial services responsibly to help address needs and wants, while understanding basic symbols and terminology from leading financial service providers.
4. Recognizes how their spending decisions have an impact on their lives, their household, the lives of others and their community.
5. Demonstrates confidence in asking questions before making decisions, in their ability to engage in financial negotiations and in their ability to make smart consumer choices.

"Planning And Budgeting"

Working Definitions: Income and wealth planning and management over the short and long term.

Overall outcomes by theme:

1. Plan and use acquired resources to obtain products and services they need and want today and in the future.
2. Differentiate between needs and wants that will require savings to satisfy. Establish priorities and recognize the need for trade-offs.

Table 2. Child and youth finance international education framework (UNICEF, 2012)

	Social/life Skills Education	Financial Education	Livelihoods Education
Level 1: 0–5 years	Emotions, consequences, health/safety, compassion	Value of money, prices, savings, belongings	Career interests, professions, entrepreneurship, goals, initiative, problem-solving skills, teamwork, taking advice, avoiding hazards
Level 2: 6–9 years	Children's rights, responsibilities, respect for others, rules, listening skills	Needs and wants, savings plan, rewards, recognize banks and financial services	
Level 3: 10–14 years	Express opinions, teamwork, research skills, appreciation for life-long learning	Informed consumer, short vs. long term planning, financial risks, effects of advertising	Vocations,opportunities, action plan, selfdiscipline, perseverance, communication
Level 4: 15+ years	Social justice, time management, relationships, leadership	Negotiation skills, purchasing power, interest rates, financial crimes	Wages, capital needs, marketing, employability, coping with change, management skills

3. Able to set clear financial understands how to track income and expenditures and why this is an important part of being financially responsible.
4. Understands how to make adjustments in personal budgeting in response to financial challenges, opportunities or unplanned expenditures goals and establish a plan in order to achieve them.

"Risk And Reward"

Working Definitions: Incorporates an understanding of the potential for financial gains or losses across a range of financial contexts, and the ability to identify opportunities for achieving rewards and benefits, as well as ways of managing, balancing and covering risks. Two risks are important: 1) financial losses an individual may have to face (loss of income, catastrophic events) and 2) risk inherent in financial products.

Overall outcomes by theme:

1. Compares costs, benefits, and trade-offs before deciding how to use money and resources.
2. Evaluates information about products and services to make informed decisions about spending, saving, borrowing and investing.
3. Invests savings appropriately (considering needs, confronting risk, ability to contend with loss) to help achieve longerterm goals.
4. Understands the risks and opportunities associated with different methods of acquiring money and how different interest, tax and exchange rates have an impact on financial decision-making.
5. Understands the value of diversifying risk and the options for doing so.

"Financial Landscape"

Working Definitions: Relates to the character and features of the financial and economic world, it covers knowing the rights and responsibilities of consumers in the financial marketplace and within the general financial environment, as well as the main implications of financial contracts. It also includes a basic understanding of the economic environment and realities within which financial decisions are made.

Overall outcomes by theme:

1. Able to recognize appropriate financial service providers.
2. Understands basic symbols and terminology from leading financial service providers,

as well as ways in which others may try to influence their financial decisions.

3. Appreciates the basic functions of international markets and commodity chains.
4. Recognizes the role of governments in regulating the financial services industry.
5. Able to identify appropriate, reputable and reliable products and services, able to compare them and make decisions, and knows where they can turn for information on financial services, personal budgeting and smart consumerism.

The learning outcomes described in Levels 1 through 4 of the Child and Youth Finance Education Learning Framework (Table.3 – Table. 6)

A strong monitoring and evaluation system can draw lessons that can help to create a sustainable model that can be rolled out nationally. It can further serve as a replicable approach across countries where child friendly schools are operational. The success of CSFE programming is measured against its core principles and its ability to make a change in children's lives (UNICEF, 2012).

3.3. Money as You Grow

Money As You Grow, developed by Beth Kobliner and the Youth Subcommittee of the President's Advisory Council on Financial Capability, provides 20 essential, age-appropriate financial lessons that kids need to know as they grow. Written in down-to-earth language for children and their families, the lessons in Money as You Grow are based on more than a year of research, drawn from dozens of standards, curricula, and academic studies.

The President's Advisory Council on Financial Capability has developed Money as You Grow, a website creatively highlighting the 20 essential lessons kids need to learn about money. There are four milestones divided in five age groups (3-5, 6-10, 11-13, 14-18, and 18+) with age appropriate activities. It divides up the lessons per age group and includes a downloadable poster (Table. 7).

3.3. Financial Driver's Licence (FLDL) "Fit for Money"

Financial driver's licence "Fit for Money" is financed by local banks and operates solely in the region of Vorarlberg. The basic aim is debt prevention. Depending on their ages, children and young adults have different approaches towards money issues. Hence three workshop curricula have been developed within the programme: "S" for 10-/11-year olds, "M" for 14-/15-year olds and "L" for adolescents from 16 to 18.

The workshops enable kids, adolescents and young adults to get better insight into different topics interlinked to money and private finance. Issues discussed in the workshops are for instance: needs, consumption, credit and debt, risks deriving from the thoughtless handling of financial matters, mobile phones, car, living, spare time, the right use of cash cards, cost of living, debt and possible consequences. In order to better meet the demands of the specific age groups, the Financial Driver Licence Vorarlberg comprises three different curricula:

- **The S (small):** Curriculum for the 11-12 year olds, covering issues like the following: Were does money come from?, wishes and needs, financial resources are limited, pocket money,
- **The M (medium):** Curriculum for the 14-15 year olds, highlighting topics such as: Managing on limited money, saving, current accounts and cash cards, apprenticeship or school and…
- **The L (large):** Curriculum for those who are 16-18 years old with a special emphasis on e.g. majority age, becoming self-employed, life-planning, overindebtedness, credit-institutes (cards, current accounts and credits).

This target group was chosen for the following reasons:

Table 3. Level 1 (5 years old and under): Learning outcomes (UNICEF,2012)

Money & Use	Understands the concept and the value of money
	Able to collect and save things that they find precious or useful.
	Understands where they get money from and what they need it for.
	Appreciates the importance of sharing resources with others.
	Understands the things they can buy and the things they need their parents or caregivers to buy.
Planning & Budgeting	Understands the difference between spending, saving, borrowing and sharing money.
	Understands the different ways in which they can acquire money
	Knows and compares the prices of things that they want to buy
	Understands that choices need to be made regarding things that they can use now and things they want to use, or acquire later.
	Knows how to count their money, buy an item they want and count the change that they may receive.
Risk &Reward	Practices the habit of saving for special things.
	Understands the consequences of being careless with possessions
	Understands the benefits of saving.
	Understands the benefits of sharing.
	Demonstrates appreciation when receiving money or other gifts.
Financial Landscape	Understands how people use money in their community.
	Recognizes that some people have more money and possessions than others.
	Able to differentiate between what belongs to them, what belongs to others and what belongs to the group or community.
	Understands where certain items are sold in their community
	Able and willing to speak with their family about money.

1. According to statistics young people in Austria make their first contact with debt at a very early stage. Many young people don't see the exhaustive use of the overdraft facility of their current accounts as a debt – being not aware that living on credit often has the negative effect that one gets used to a lifestyle which is not affordable with the current income. This often leads to an unbalanced financial situation.
2. The providers of the scheme have also accounted for many young people not having any financial plans for the future. Without substantive savings the purchase of a new car or the first own flat often leads to debt inducing decisions.
3. Labour-market considerations lead to the assumption that young people having to deal with debt are likely to interrupt their studies and earn money at a job that demands only low qualifications and therefore worsens their future perspectives.

The evaluation has also shown that it is crucial for the success of a financial literacy programme that all relevant bodies for financial literacy are both actively involved and support the programme. The content of the Financial driver's licence is adaptable to various target groups due to its comprehensive approach. The content is applicable to students ranging from a low-educational back ground up to better situated groups (Habschick, Seidl & Evers, 2007).

Table 4. Level 2 (6-9 years old): Learning outcomes (UNICEF,2012)

Money& Use	**Understands the relative value of their possessions and uses them responsibly.**
	Understands how prices reflect value of goods in the market.
	Able to use numeracy skills in a practical way with money.
	Sees the importance of donating money to others in need.
	Able to recognize basic symbols and terminology as they relate to money and banks.
Plan& Budgeting	**Appreciates the value of resources and uses them responsibly.**
	Understands the importance of savings and establishing a savings plan.
	Understands the difference between needs and wants.
	Able to classify spending priorities.
	Understands the challenges of saving money.
Risk &Reward	**Understands the concept of living within one's means.**
	Understands how to save for something and why saving may be necessary.
	Appreciates the importance of keeping money and other resources safe.
	Understands how people can experience difficulties if they do not have any savings.
	Appreciates the rewards of sharing or giving resources to others.
Financial Landscape	**Understands that individuals have choices in how they use their money.**
	Able to recognize and identify different financial institutions in their community and what products and services they provide.
	Understands basic 'product trails' and commodity/value chains.
	Understands the different roles of money.
	Understands why people work to earn money.

3.4. I Can Manage My Money

The project conducted with the partnership of Turkish Ministry of Development United Nations Development Program (UNDP) Habitat Center for Development and Governance, Visa Europe and member banks, aims to provide trainings to 20.000 young people, and reach 200,00 people in total since 2009.

The outcome of the project and the results of the impact analysis will be provided to the government as a policy recommendation on financial awareness. The project will serve for the socio - economic empowerment of youth and will significantly contribute to the implementation and realization of UN Youth Policies as well as UN Millennium Development Goals. Members from the Training and Coordination Group of the National Youth Parliament and two representatives of each local youth council will receive trainers' trainings on budgeting; financial-planning and management; personalizing credit cards; loans; good credit standing; the effects of financial awareness on sustainable development. Hence, the project will establish a task force composed of 320 young volunteers in 64 cities from 7 geographical regions. The know-how of Visa and its member banks will be utilized at those trainings (UNDP, 2014a).

This program targets young people aged 15 to 30 and focuses particularly on financial literacy and budget management, through peer education model based on volunteering. The project trainings aim to enable young people to: prepare a payment schedule by focusing on cash flow and budgeting, savings and debt; develop

Table 5. Level 3 (10 -14 years old): Learning outcomes (UNICEF,2012)

Money &Use	Able to recognize the value of money and the value of different denominations.
	Understands the importance of being an informed consumer
	Able to evaluate the results of a financial decision.
	Understands how one's resources and spending decisions can affect their lifestyle and vice versa.
	Knows how money can be used to help others.
Plan& Budgeting	Able to format a personal budget with personal/ household income and expenditures.
	Understands how budgeting can help in making better spending and savings decisions.
	Understands why you might decide to buy one product over another
	Recognizes that families' household budgets change as circumstances change and that a budget should be reviewed from time to time.
	Understands that each money decision made involves a trade-off (giving up something to gain something else) with impact over the short and long term.
Risk &Reward	Able to identify different financial products and recognizes the risks and rewards of each: credit, savings, insurance, etc.
	Appreciates how families and communities cope or prepare themselves against shocks or emergencies.
	Understands the positive and negative consequences of spending decisions
	Understands the rewards of financial responsibility and the risks of financial illiteracy.
	Understands the effects of their spending decisions on others and the environment
Financial Landscape	Understands the different factors that can influence spending decisions.
	Understands that countries have different types, quantities and qualities of resources.
	Understands that the production and delivery of products and services have to abide by regulations and laws protecting consumers
	Knows where to get accurate information to help with financial decisions.
	Understands how advertising tries to influence how consumers spend money.

a budget; differentiate between compulsory and luxury consumption; compare fixed income with compulsory expenditure; prepare a debt repayment schedule; understand the economic role and functioning of finance industry and its products; understand the regulations concerning consumer financial rights and obligations; develop principles for healthy financial behavior for self and family and strengthening financial consumer protection. The program also aims to implement financial awareness courses in the national secondary education curriculum (Child & Youth Finance International, 2014).

A recent research study commissioned by Visa Europe in Turkey came up with some interesting findings. According to this study, 97% of young people make important financial decisions without consulting an expert. 87% of them are not saving for near term financial needs such as education, transportation and housing. And, among those who do save, only a very small minority keep their money in the banking system. This suggests that the level of financial awareness among the youth is very low. "Before the training, 56% of the participants considered themselves to be knowledgeable about personal finances. But, after the training, this figure increased to 84%, which is a good indicator of the programme's positive impact on the perception of its participants (VISA, 2011).

During Global Money Week, an international event between 10 – 17 March, that was initiated by World Economic Forum in 2008 to increase financial literacy, 24 trainings were held where 1287 new young participants met with the 'I can

Table 6. Level 4 (15 +years old): Learning outcomes (UNICEF, 2012)

Money&Use	Able to conduct financial negotiations with confidence.
	Understands factors that affect the purchasing power of money.
	Able to file complaints about particular products and services.
	Understands how to calculate 'after-purchase' costs into the price of a desired item.
	Discovers ways to live an economically and ecologically responsible lifestyle.
Plan& Budgeting	Knows how to manage debt and budgets effectively.
	Knows how to calculate their spending capacity.
	Able to compare income to necessary costs of living.
	Understands when it would be appropriate to borrow or invest money.
	Able to consider financial goals over the short, medium and long term and recognize how they may change over time.
Risk & Reward	Knows the risks of defaulting on payments/ credit commitments.
	Understands the impact of interest rates, Exchange rates, market volatility, taxes and inflation on financial decisions.
	Understands ways to redesign budgets to address changing needs, circumstances or problems.
	Able to distinguish investments with different levels of risk.
	Understands the risks of indulging in gambling or illicit activity to try to get more money
Financial Landscape	Is aware of financial crimes, such as identity theft, frauds and scams, and knows how to take appropriate precautions.
	Able to identify which financial service providers are trustworthy and which products and services are protected through regulation or consumer protection laws.
	Able to recognize factors leading to conditions of poverty and income inequality.
	Able to perform basic financial tasks through Internet or mobile banking safely.
	Understands how governments obtain revenues to provide public goods and services and why taxes are paid.

Manage my Money' Project from 14 different cities attended to. 84% of young people who have attended the trainings are conscious of their monthly spending, 75% of attendees stated that they have adopted a regular budgeting discipline, 87% of these stick to their budgets, 62% list their spending habits regularly. 75% of attendees noted an improvement in their banking transaction knowledge, 84% can now differentiate between luxury and necessities and 74% now understand savings and financial instruments. In this training, illiterate girls were attended to financial literacy course and made a budget work shop which they are now using to manage their households (Child & Youth Finance International, 2014; UNDP, 2014b). According to the 2013 Impact Analysis; 85% percent of young people know how to manage debt and budgets effectively (Paramıyönetebiliyorum, 2014).

CONCLUSION

Financial education is a concept that individuals need to know at every step of their lives and at every aspect of their daily lives. Especially, in today's financial markets, stunningly developing products and services, increasing consumer debts, low financial literacy and changing socio-demographical conditions increase the importance of this education and necessitate the continuity of it.

Therefore, designing and applying a national strategy for financial education seems like a qualified solution suggestion. However, it is impossible to define a single strategy that is suitable for every country. In these circumstances, best results should be expected from solutions that are designed for each country specifically through analyzing examples of countries and international studies.

Table 7. "20 Things kids need to know to live financially smart lives" (Kobliner, 2010)

3-5 years old	1. you need money to buy things
	2. you earn money by working
	3. you may have to wait before you can buy something you want.
	4. there's a difference between things you want and things you need.
6-10 years old	**5.** you need to make choices about how to spend your money
	6. it's good to shop around and compare prices before you buy
	7. it can be costly and dangerous to share information online
	8. there's a difference between things you want and things you need.
11-13 years old	**9.** you should save at least a dime for every dollar you receive.
	10. entering a credit card number online is risky because someone could steal your information.
	11. the earlier you start to save, the faster you'll benefit from compound interest, which means your money earns interest on your interest.
	12. a credit card is a type of loan; if you don't pay your bill in full every month, you'll be charged interest and owe more than you originally spent.
14-18 years old	**13.** it's important to know what a college will cost you before choosing it.
	14. you should avoid using credit cards to buy things you can't afford to pay for with cash
	15. your first paycheck may seem smaller than expected since money is taken out for taxes.
	16. a great place to save and invest money you earn is in a roth ira.
18+ yrs old	**17.** you should use a credit card only if you can pay off the money owed in full each month.
	18. You need health insurance.
	19. Putting all your eggs in one basket can be a risky way to invest; consider a diverse mix of stocks, bonds, and cash.
	20. always consider two factors before investing: the risks and the annual expenses.

REFERENCES

Anthes, W. L. (2004). Financial Illiteracy in America: A Perfect Storm, A Perfect Opportunity. *Journal of Financial Service Professionals*, *58*(6), 49–56.

Bachman, J. G. (1983). Affluence: Do High Schools Students Earn Too Much? *Economic Outlook USA*, *10*(3), 25–60.

Bakken, M. R. (1967). Money Management Understandings of Tenth Grade Students. *National Business Education Quarterly*, *36*, 6.

Bank, A. N. Z. (2008). *ANZ survey of adult financial literacy in Australia*. Retrieved May 25, 2014 from http://www.anz.com/Documents/AU/Aboutanz/AN_5654_Adult_Fin_Lit_Report_08_Web_Report_full.pdf

Bianco, C., & Bosco, S. (2001, October). Financial Illiteracy of College Students. Presentation at the Financial Management Association Conference, Toronto, Canada.

Bowen, C. F. (2002). Financial Knowledge of Teens and Their Parents. *Financial Counseling and Planning*, *13*(2), 93–102.

Bowen, C. F., Laux, S. C., Ratcliffe, J., Staten, M. E., Walstad, W. B., & Willis, L. E. (2008, October). Financial Education and Program Evaluation. *National Research Priorities for Financial Literacy and Education Results of the National Research Symposium on Financial Literacy and Education*, Washington DC (pp.10).

Center for Financial Inclusion. (2008). *Financial inclusion glossary*. Retrieved May 22, 2014, from http://www.centerforfinancialinclusion.org/publications-a-resources/financial-inclusion-glossary

Chen, H., & Volpe, R. P. (1998). An analysis of personal financial literacy among college students. *Financial Services Review*, *7*(2), 107–128. doi:10.1016/S1057-0810(99)80006-7

Chen, H., & Volpe, R. P. (2002). Gender differences in personal financial literacy among college students. *Financial Services Review*, *11*(3), 289–307.

Child & Youth Finance International. (2012). Child and youth finance education. In *An Introduction to Child and Youth Finance Education* (pp. 19–24). Developing Quality Financial Social and Livelihoods Education for Children and Youth.

Child & Youth Finance International. (2013). *Global Money Week Report 2013*, (pp.4-10). Retrieved June 2, 2014, from http://globalmoneyweek.org/resources/2014-GlobalMoneyWeek-Toolkit-sm.pdf

Child & Youth Finance International. (2014). *I Can Manage My Money (Habitat)*. Retrieved May 22, 2014, from http://childfinanceinternational.org/world-programs/europe/turkey-programs/i-can-manage-my-money-harnessing-financial-awareness-among-young-men-and-women

Consumer Federation of America and American Express Company (CFAJAMEX). (1991). Student Consumer Knowledge: Results of a National Test. Washington, D.C.

Consumer Federation of America/American Express. (1991). *Report of Findings: High School Competency Test*. Washington, D.C.: Consumer Federation of America.

Danes, S. M., & Haberman, H. R. (2007). Teen financial knowledge, self-efficacy, and behavior: A gendered view. *Financial Counseling and Planning*, *18*(2), 48–60.

Danes, S. M., & Hira, T. K. (1987). Money management knowledge of college students. *Journal of Student Financial Aid*, *17*(1), 4–16.

Danes, S. M., Huddleston Casas, C., & Boyce, L. (1999). Financial planning curriculum for teens: Impact evaluation. *Financial Counseling and Planning*, *10*(1), 26–39.

Fernandes, D., Lynch, J. G. Jr, & Netemeyer, R. G. (2014). Financial literacy, financial education, and downstream financial behaviors. *Management Science*, 60.

Ferreira, V. R. D. M. (2011, December). Can Economic Psychology and Behavioural Economics Help Improve Financial Education? In *Improving Financial Education Efficiency: OECD-Bank of Italy Symposium on Financial Literacy*. (pp. 104-118).

FINRA. (2003). *NASD Investor Literacy Research: Executive Summary*. Retrieved May 22, 2014, from,http://www.finrafoundation.org/web/groups/foundation/@foundation/documents/foundation/p118411.pdf

Godfrey, N. S. (2006). Making our students smart about money. *Education Digest*, *71*(7), 21–26.

Gutter, M., & Copur, Z. (2011). Financial behaviors and financial well-being of college students: Evidence from a national survey. *Journal of Family and Economic Issues*, *32*(4), 699–714. doi:10.1007/s10834-011-9255-2

Gutter, M. S., Copur, Z., & Blanco, A. (2014). Racial differences in financial socialization and financial behaviors of U.S. college students. In H. Dinçer & Ü. Hacioğlu (Eds.), *Global Strategies in Banking and Finance* (pp. 272–292). Hershey, PA: Business Science Reference; doi:10.4018/978-1-4666-4635-3.ch018

Habschick, M., Seidl, B., & Evers, J. (2007). Survey of financial literacy schemes in the EU27, Hamburg. (pp.24-30).

Harris Scholastic Research (HSR). (1993). *Liberty financial young investor survey*. New York, NY.

Hilgert, M., Hogarth, J., & Beverley, S. (2003). *Household financial management: The connection between knowledge and behavior*. (Technical Report #309-322). Federal Reserve Bulletin.

Hogarth, J. M. (2002). Financial literacy and family and consumer sciences. *Journal of Family and Consumer Sciences*, *94*(1), 14–28.

Hung, A., Parker, A. M., & Yoong, J. K. (2009). *Defining and measuring financial literacy* (Working Paper, WR-708) Rand Corparation.

International Labour Organization (ILO). (2011). *Financial education for youth*. Retrieved May 22, 2014, from http:// www.ilo.org/publns

Kasser, T., & Ahuvia, A. (2002). Materialistic values and well-being in business students. *European Journal of Social Psychology*, *32*(1), 137–146. doi:10.1002/ejsp.85

Kempson, E. (2011,December). A framework for developing international financial literacy surveys. In *Improving Financial Education Efficiency: OECD-Bank Of Italy Symposium on Financial Literacy* (pp.13-41).

Kobliner, B. (2010). *Money as You Grow: 20 Things Kids Need to Know to Live Financially Smart Lives*. Retrieved May 24, 2014, from http:// moneyasyougrow.org

Langrehr, F. W. (1979). Consumer education: Does it change students' competencies and attitudes? *The Journal of Consumer Affairs*, *13*(1), 41–53. doi:10.1111/j.1745-6606.1979.tb00126.x

Lusardi, A. (2008a). *Household saving behavior: The role of financial literacy, information, and financial education programs* (NBER Working Paper 13824).

Lusardi, A. (2008b). Financial literacy: An essential tool for informed consumer choice? (Dartmouth College Working Paper).

Lusardi, A., & Mitchell, O. S. (2007). Financial literacy and retirement preparedness: Evidence and implications for financial education. *Business Economics*, *42*(January), 35–44. doi:10.2145/20070104

Lusardi, A., Mitchell, O. S., & Curto, V. (2010). *Financial literacy among the young: Evidence and implications for consumer policy* (NBER Working Paper Series, Working Paper No. 15352, pp. 3-30). Center for Financial Studies (CFS).

Lusardi, A., & Tufano, P. (2008). *Debt literacy, financial experiences, and over in debtedness* (Dartmouth Working Paper).

Mandell, L. (1997). *Personal Financial Survey of High School Seniors. Jump Start Coalition for Personal Financial Literacy* (p. 7). Washington, D.C.: March/April.

Mandell, L. (2007). Financial Literacy of High School Students. In J. J. Xiao (Ed.), *Handbook of Consumer Finance Research* (pp. 163–183). New York, NY: Springer.

Mandell, L. (2008). Background the 1997-98 Baseline Survey of High School Seniors. The Financial Literacy of Young American Adults Result of the 2008 National Jump$Tart Coalition Survey of High School Seniors and College Students (pp.7-8). Washington, DC: The Jump$Tart Coalition for Personal Financial Literacy.

Mandell, L., & Klein, L. S. (2009). The impact of financial literacy education on subsequent financial behavior. *Journal of Financial Counseling and Planning*, *20*(1), 15–24.

Mason, C., & Wilson, R. (2000). Conceptualizing Financial Literacy (Research Series Paper 2000:7, pp. 4–34). London: Business School, Laughborough University.

Moore, D. (2003). Survey of financial literacy in Washington State: Knowledge, behavior, attitudes, and experiences. (Technical Report Num: 03-39), Social and Economic Sciences Research Center, Washington State University.

National Assessment of Educational Progress (NAEP). (1979). *Teenage Consumers: A Profile*. Denver, CO.

National Council for Economic Education (NCEE). (2005). *What American Teens & Adults Know About Economics*. Retrieved May 22, 2014, from http://www.ncee.net/cel/WhatAmericansKnowAboutEconomics_042605-3.pdf

O'Neil, B. (1992). National Survey, The Status of Consumer Education. In *U.S. Schools K-12*. Chatham, NJ: National Coalition for Consumer Education, Inc.

OECD. (2005a). Improving financial literacy: Analysis of issues and policies. *Financial Market Trends*, *2*, 111–115.

OECD. (2005b).*Recommendation on Principles and Good Practices for Financial Education and Awareness*. Recommendation of the Council, Directorate for Financial and Enterprise Affairs. Retrieved June 2, 2014, from http://www.oecd.org/daf/fin/financial-education/35108560.pdf

PACFL. (2008). Enhancing youth financial education. 2008 Annual Report to the President (pp. 11-19)

Pankow, D. & Brotherson, S. (2009). *Talking to children about money* (NDSU Extension Service, FS-1441).

Paramı Yönetebiliyorum. (2014). *2013 Etki Analizi Sonuçları: Haberler*. Retrieved May 2, 2014, from http://www.paramiyonetebiliyorum.net/bizden-haberler.aspx

Pillai, K. R., Carlo, R., & D'souza, R. (2010). *Financial Prudence among Youth* (MPRA Paper No. 22450, pp. 2-22). Retrieved June 2, 2014, from, http://mpra.ub.uni-muenchen.de/22450/1/MPRA_paper_22450.pdf

Reinsch, M. (2012).Youth financial inclusion: Promising examples for achieving youth economic empowerment. Europan Dialouge, 5, 5-7.

Roberts, J. A., & Jones, E. (2001). Money attitudes, credit card use, and compulsive buying among american college students. *The Journal of Consumer Affairs*, *35*(2), 213–240. doi:10.1111/j.1745-6606.2001.tb00111.x

Shaari, N. A., Hasan, N. A., Mohammed, R. K. M. H., & Sabri, M. A. J. M. (2013). Financial literacy: A study among the university students. *Interdıscıplınary Journal of Contemporary Research in Business*, *5*(2), 279–299.

Shim, S., Barber, B. L., Card, N. A., Xiao, J. J., & Serido, J. (2010). Financial socialization of first-year college students: The roles of parents, work, and education. *Journal of Youth and Adolescence*, *39*(12), 1457–1470. doi:10.1007/s10964-009-9432-x PMID:20938727

Shim, S., Xiao, J. J., Barber, B. L., & Lyons, A. (2009). Pathways to life success: A conceptual model of financial well-being for young adults. *Journal of Applied Developmental Psychology*, *30*(6), 708–723. doi:10.1016/j.appdev.2009.02.003

Suwanaphan, S. (2013, June). Personal Financial Literacy of Academic Support-Employee in Chiang Mai University. In *Proceedings of the Management, Knowledge and Learning International Conference*. (pp.1061-1065). Zadar, Croatia. ToKnowPress.

UNDP. (2014a). *I Can Manage My Money*. Retrieved May 22, 2014, from http://jobs.undp.org/cj_view_job.cfm?cur_job_id=44330

UNDP. (2014b). *Global Money Week Celebrated in Turkey with Financial Literacy Events*. Retrieved May 22, 2014, from http://www.tr.undp.org/content/turkey/en/home/presscenter/news-from-new-horizons/2014/04/_global-money-week-celebrated-in-turkey-with-financial-literacy-/

UNICEF. (2012). Child social and financial education. A Companion to the Child Friendly Schools Manual Unit for Children, (pp. 38-41).

Varcoe, K., Peterson, S., Go, C., Johns, M., Rene Fitch, P., Powell, C., & Costello, C. (2002). Teen financial literacy evaluated to develop outreach materials. *California Agriculture*, *56*(2), 65–68.

Varcoe, K. P., Martin, A., Devitto, Z., & Go, C. (2005). Using a financial education curriculum for teens. *Financial Counseling and Planning*, *16*(1), 63–71.

VISA. (2011). *Financial Awareness* (pp.5-6) Retrieved May 22, 2014, from http://www.fo-der.org/wp-content/uploads/2013/09/Visa-Turkey-Financial-Literacy-Conference-2011-Whitepaper-ENG.pdf

Vitt, L. A., Anderson, C., Kent, J., Lyter, D. M., Siegenthaler, J. K., & Ward, J. (2000). *Personal finance and the rush to competence: Personal financial literacy in the US*. Retrieved May 22, 2014, from http://content.knowledgeplex.org/kp2/kp/report/report/relfiles/ht_pfrc_execsumm.pdf

Volpe, R. P., & Chen, H. (1998). An analysis of personal financial literacy among college students. *Financial Services Review*, *7*(2), 107–128. doi:10.1016/S1057-0810(99)80006-7

Volpe, R. P., Chen, H., & Pavlicko, J. J. (1996). Personal investment literacy among college students: A survey. *Financial Practice and Education*, *6*(2), 86–94.

Wang, P. (1993). Helping your kids become financially independent. *Money*, *22*, 72–78.

Yoong, J. (2011, December). Can behavioural economics be used to make financial education more effective? *Improving Financial Education Efficiency: OECD-Bank of Italy Symposium on Financial Literacy* (pp.66-89).

ADDITIONAL READING

Anderson, J. A., Kerbel, C. M., & Xiao, J. J. (1997). Workplace personal financial education: Program evaluation and needs assessment. In J. J. Xiao (Ed.), *Proceedings of Association for Financial Counseling and Planning Education* (pp. 152–159).

Avard, S., Manton, E., English, D., & Walker, J. (2005). The financial knowledge of college freshmen. *College Student Journal*, *39*(2), 321–338.

Baron-Donovan, C., Wiener, C. R., Gross, K., & Block-Lieb, S. (2005). Financial literacy teacher training: A multiple-measure evaluation. *Financial Counseling and Planning*, *16*, 63–75.

Detweiler, G. (2009). *Talking money with your kids*. Fort Lauderdale, FL.: Consolidated Credit Counseling Services Inc.

Doss, V. S., Marlowe, J., & Godwin, D. D. (2005). Middle-school children's sources and uses of money. *The Journal of Consumer Affairs*, *29*(1), 219–241.

Dotson, M. J., & Hyatt, E. M. (2005). Major influence factors in children's consumer socialization. *Journal of Consumer Marketing*, *1*(22), 35–42.

Gutter, M. S., & Garrison, S. (2008). Perceived norms, financial education, and college student credit card behavior. *Journal of Consumer Education*, *24*, 73–88.

Hancock, A. M., Jorgensen, B. L., & Swanson, M. S. (2013). College students and credit card use: The role of parents, work experience, financial knowledge, and credit card attitudes. *Journal of Family and Economic Issues*, *34*(4), 369–381.

Hathaway, I., & Khatiwada, S. (2008). *Do Financial Education Programs Work?* (Federal Reserve Bank of Cleveland Working Paper No. 08-03). Retrieved from Http://Www.Clevelandfed.Org/Research/Workpaper/2008/Wp0803.Pdf

Huston, S. J. (2010). Measuring financial literacy. *The Journal of Consumer Affairs*, *44*(2), 296–316.

Kim, J., Lataillade, J., & Kim, H. (2011). Family processes and children's financial socialization. *Journal of Family and Economic Issues*, *32*(4), 668–679.

Lawrence, D. (2003). The role of characters in kids marketing. *Journal of Advertisin and Marketing to Children*, *4*(3), 43–48.

Lusardi, A., & Mitchell, O. S. (2007). Baby boomer retirement security: The roles of planning, financial literacy, and housing wealth. *Journal of Monetary Economics*, *54*(1), 205–224.

Mandell, L. (2004). Financial literacy: Are we improving? Washington, DC: Jump$tart Coalition for Personal Financial Literacy.

Masuo, D. M., Malroutu, Y. L., Hanashiro, R., & Kim, J. H. (2004). College students' money beliefs and behaviors: An asian perspective. *Journal of Family and Economic Issues*, *25*, 469–481.

Maurer, T. W., & Lee, S. A. (2011). Financial education with college students: Comparing peer-led and traditional classroom instruction. *Journal of Family and Economic Issues*, *32*(4), 680–689.

Murphy, A. (2005). Money, money, money: An exploratory study on the financial literacy of black college students. *College Student Journal*, *39*, 478–488.

National Endowment for Financial Education. (2001). *Simple Steps to Raising A Money-Smart Child: From Toddlers To Teens*. Greenwood Village, Colo.: National Endowment for Financial Education Press.

National Research Priorities for Financial Literacy and Education. (2008 October). *Results of the National Research Symposium on Financial Literacy and Education, Washington, DC*.

O'Neill, B., & Xiao, J. J. (2012). Financial behaviors before and after the financial crisis: Evidence from an online survey. *Journal of Financial Counseling and Planning*, *23*(1), 33–46.

Peng, T., Bartholomae, M. S., Fox, J. J., & Cravener, G. (2007). The impact of personal finance education delivered in high school and college courses. *Journal of Family and Economic Issues*, *28*, 265–284.

Peterson, N. A. (1992). The high school economics course and its impact on economic knowledge. *The Journal of Economic Education*, *23*, 5–16.

Pliner, P., Freedman, J. L., Abramovitch, R., & Drake, P. (1996). Children as Consumers: In the Laboratory and Beyond. In P. Lunt & A. Furnham (Eds.), *Economic Socialization: The Economic Beliefs and Behaviors of Young People* (pp. 11–34). Cheltenham, UK: Edward Elgar.

Robb, C. A., & Sharpe, D. L. (2009). Effect of personal financial knowledge on college students' credit card behavior. *Journal of Financial Counseling and Planning*, *20*(1), 25–43.

Sabri, M. F., Macdonald, M., Masud, J., Paim, L., Hira, T. K., & Othman, M. A. (2008). Financial behavior and problems among college students in Malaysia: Research and education implication. *Consumer Interests Annual*, *54*, 166–170.

Sasser, D. D., White, R. E., & Neely, R. T. (2000). *Talking With Children about Money. Pub. 2799-P*. Baton Rouge, La: LSU Agricultural Center, Louisiana Cooperative Extension Service.

Schagen, S., & Lines, A. (1996). *Financial Literacy in Adult Life*. Slough: National Foundation for Educational Research.

Stipp, H. H. (1988). Children as consumers. *American Demographics*, *10*(2), 27–32.

Varcoe, K. P., & Fitch, P. R. (2003). Money talks: A program to improve financial literacy of teens. *International Journal of Consumer Studies*, *27*, 225–226.

Xiao, J. J. (2011). Consumer financial behavior, financial education, and well-being. *Economic Research Journal*, *2*, 4–16.

KEY TERMS AND DEFINITIONS

Financial Behavior: Is the capability to capture of understanding overall impacts of financial decisions on one's (ie. person, family, community, country) circumstances and to make the right decisions related to the cash managment, precautions and opportunities for budget planning.

Financial Education: Is the process for the consumers and investors (ie person, family, community) to be developed, informed and taught about financial products and concepts through the financial risks and opportunities. This education aims to help them to be aware and informed about choices that they make and help them to improve their confidence and ability to develop processes for the financial topics.

Financial Knowledge: Is the capability how to manage the money in different usage, including the monitoring of day to day financial matters in the market and make the right choices for "financial literate" people's needs.

Financial Literacy: Is the information for financial consumers (ie person, family, community) increase their awarness about the risks and opportunities within financial products and concepts in order to increase their level of welfare respectively.

Financial Skills: Is the capability to use relevant knowledge and understanding to manage an expected or an unpredictable situation in order to solve a financial problem and convert it to a benefit and opportunity to one's advantage. These skills can be acquired or can be learned through a financial education backround.

Financial Socialization: Is the capability to obtain all relevant technical, commercial, behavioral and emotional information that contribute to one's financial knowledge and skills. The source of financial socialization in the most of the cases is the surrounding social environment, such as family members, parents, relatives, close friends, community organizations and professional financial bodies.

Financial Well-Being: Is the capability to develop decision making ability to have the financial means for the best conditions for saving, investing, using credits and planning for the future. It gives comfortably to the ones (ie, person, family, community) to enjoy a gratifying lifestyle.

Section 2
Psychological Concepts in Behavioral Finance

Chapter 6
The Role of Psychological Factors in Behavioral Finance

Kijpokin Kasemsap
Suan Sunandha Rajabhat University, Thailand

ABSTRACT

This chapter introduces the role of psychological factors in behavioral finance, thus explaining the theory of behavioral finance, the application of behavioral finance theory, the empirical achievement in behavioral finance, the utilization of psychological factors in behavioral finance regarding beliefs (i.e., overconfidence, too much trading, optimism and wishful thinking, representativeness bias, conservatism bias, belief perseverance, anchoring, and availability bias) and preferences (i.e., prospect theory and ambiguity aversion). Behavioral finance is a comparatively new management field that seeks to combine behavioral and cognitive psychological theory with conventional economics and finance to provide descriptions for why people make unreasonable financial decisions. Psychological factors in behavioral finance hold out the expectation of a better understanding of financial market behavior and scope for investors to make better investment decisions. Applying psychological factors in behavioral finance will tremendously enhance financial performance and achieve strategic objectives in global finance.

INTRODUCTION

Behavioral finance studies the psychology of financial decision-making. People in the industry commonly talk about the role greed and fear play in driving stock markets. Behavioral finance extends this psychological analysis to the role of biases in decision making, such as the use of simple rules of thumb for making complex investment decisions. Behavioral finance has been growing over the last twenty years specifically because of the observation that investors rarely behave according to the assumptions made in traditional finance theory. Psychology factors are including in behavioral finance (Brahmana, Hooy, & Ahmad, 2012). The approach of behavioral finance is clustered in functionalism known as behaviorism (Brahmana et al., 2012).

Behavioral finance is reverting back to the original intents of utility theory (Nawrocki & Viole, 2014). Behavioral finance substitutes behavioral portfolio theory for mean-variance portfolio theory, and behavioral asset pricing model for the capital asset pricing model (CAPM)

DOI: 10.4018/978-1-4666-7484-4.ch006

and other models where expected returns are determined only by risk (Statman, 2014). One of the most important factors of behavioral finance is the people's reaction and perception (Bikas, Jureviciene, Dubinskas, & Novickyte, 2014). The finance theory is of limited relevance to practitioners because its quantitative approach requires data about the future that are unavailable (Coleman, 2014). Behavioral finance describes the behavior of people making investment decisions (Sahi, 2012). Behavioral finance suggests that human decision making involves a combination of cognitive and affective dimensions (Olsen, 2010). Behavioral finance holds that human decision making can be explained from cognitive, emotional and social dimensions (DeBondt, Forbes, Hamalainen, & Muragoglu, 2010).

Regarding behavioral finance, the psychological studies are frequently cited in the business and finance literature to bolster claims that various kinds of economic disasters, from the large proportion of start-ups that quickly go out of business to the exaggerated confidence of financial investors, can be attributed to overconfidence (Olsson, 2014). Personal values, emotions, personality traits and societal influence affect investors' subjective perception of reality in financial decision making (Nga & Yien, 2013). In coping with ambiguity and uncertainty, investors often rely on cognitive biases in making financial decisions (Keil, Depledge, & Rai, 2007). Glaser, Noth, and Weber (2004) considered behavioral finance as a sub-discipline of behavioral economics is finance incorporating findings from psychology and sociology into its behavioral finance theories.

The strength of this chapter is on the thorough literature consolidation of psychological factors in behavioral finance. The extant literature of psychological factors in behavioral finance provides a contribution to practitioners and researchers by describing a comprehensive view of the functional applications of psychological factors in behavioral finance to appeal to different segments of psychological factors in behavioral finance in order to maximize the financial impact of psychological factors in behavioral finance.

BACKGROUND

The study of behavioral finance has its roots in cognitive psychology (Sahi, 2012). Cognitive psychology is a branch of psychology that pertains to the understanding of the internal mental processes of thought like visual processing, memory, thinking, learning, feeling, problem solving and decision making, judgment, and language (Sahi, 2012). Cognitive psychology considers emotion to be a product of the cognitive evaluation of an event. Though emotional factors have found to impact the financial decision making in addition to the cognitive limitations that human beings are subject to, these have found to be leading to distortions in cognitions causing biases, that need to be corrected or modified (Pompian, 2006). Behavioral finance models are usually developed to explain investor behavior or market anomalies when rational models provide no sufficient explanations.

People choose between alternatives in a rational manner (Von Neumann & Morgenstern, 1944), and that they know the probability distribution of future states of the world (Arrow & DeBreu, 1954). Modern finance assumes that markets are efficient, and that agents know the probability distribution of future market risk (Markowitz, 1952; Merton, 1969). Interdisciplinary research becomes more widespread and it is likely that greater collaboration between finance and sociology will develop in the future behavioral finance may have started as a multidisciplinary endeavor but it is now an interdisciplinary field with its own learned societies, journals and conferences. In addition, behavioral finance is still developing and continues to borrow methods and ideas from other disciplines.

Bell, Raiffa, and Tversky (1988) stated that it is worth making a conceptual distinction between normative models of decision making that identified optimal ways of making decisions, descriptive models that identified how people actually make decisions under different conditions, and prescriptive models that identified ways of improving decision making when no normative models were available. Slovic (1972) drew the attention of those working within finance to the relevance of research on behavioral decision making to their aspects. Good reviews on the development of the field of behavioral finance include those by Daniel, Hirshleifer, and Teoh (2002), Glaser et al. (2004), Garling, Kirchler, Lewis, and Van Raaij (2009), and DeBondt et al. (2010). Behavioral finance uses the work that demonstrates biases in human judgment and decision making (Kahneman, Slovic, & Tversky, 1982) to explain investor behavior and market anomalies.

THE ROLE OF PSYCHOLOGICAL FACTORS IN BEHAVIORAL FINANCE

This section introduces the theory of behavioral finance, the application of behavioral finance theory, the empirical achievement in behavioral finance, the utilization of psychological factors in behavioral finance correlated with beliefs (i.e., overconfidence, too much trading, optimism and wishful thinking, representativeness bias, conservatism bias, belief perseverance, anchoring, and availability bias) and preferences (i.e., prospect theory and ambiguity aversion).

Theory of Behavioral Finance

The behavioral finance paradigm has emerged in the response to the difficulties faced by the traditional paradigm. The investment choices are not always made on the basis of full rationality, and behavioral finance paradigm attempts to understand the investment market phenomena by relaxing the two doctrines of the traditional paradigm, that is, agents fail to update their beliefs correctly, and there is a systematic deviation from the normative process in making investment choices. Behavioral finance is part of finance that seeks to understand and explain the systematic financial market implications of psychological decision processes (Kishore, 2006).

The financial theory based on Modern Portfolio Theory (Markowitz, 1952) and CAPM (Sharpe, 1964) has long shaped the way in which academics and practitioners analyze investment performance. The theory is based on the notion that investors act rationally and consider all available information in the decision-making process, and thus investment markets are efficient, reflecting all available information in security prices (Kishore, 2006). The field of behavioral finance has evolved that attempts to better understand and explain how emotions and cognitive errors influence investors and the decision-making process. Kahneman and Tversky (1974), Shefrin and Statman (1994), Shiller (1995), and Shleifer (2000) have utilized theory of psychology and other social sciences to shed light on the efficiency of financial markets as well as explain many stock market anomalies, bubbles, and crashes. Financial decision making can be improved by providing decision makers with better quality information presented in an institutional environment conducive to good decisions (Altman, 2012).

Behavioral finance is the study of how psychology affects financial decision making process and financial markets (Shefrin, 2001). Since psychology explores human judgment, behavior and welfare, it can also provide important facts about how human actions differ from traditional economic assumptions (Bikas et al., 2014). Behavioral finance expands the domain of finance beyond portfolios, asset pricing, and market efficiency and is set to continue that expansion while adhering to the scientific rigor introduced by standard finance (Statman, 2014). Behavioral finance is divided into macro behavioral finance and micro behavioral finance (Pompian, 2006). Macro behavioral finance describes anomalies of efficient market hypothesis that can be explained by models of people behavior. Micro behavioral finance recognizes behavior and deviations of investors. Jordan and Miller (2008) studied about behavioral finance through individuals' attitudes and emotions in investment decision making process and market prices.

Ritter (2003) stated that behavioral finance strives to supplement standard financial theories introducing psychological dimension into decision-making process. Levy and Post (2005) defined behavioral finance as theories, able to explain market inefficiency and market anomalies. Bodie, Kane, and Marcus (2007) considered behavioral finance as a set of models of financial markets focusing on potential intervention of psychological factors into investors' behavior. Bikas et al. (2014) examined the five behavioral biases in decision-making process in the stock market and differences of possible individual solutions due to these behavioral deviations (i.e., disposition effect, herd behavior, availability heuristic, gambler's fallacy, and hot hand fallacy).

Application of Behavioral Finance Theory

Behavioral finance is used to make recommendations to finance professionals about how to change their behavior or how to communicate with their clients. Kahneman and Riepe's (1998) list of recommendations includes the following: keep track of instances of your overconfidence; communicate realistic odds of success to your clients; resist the natural urge to be optimistic; ask yourself whether you have real reasons to believe that you know more than the market; make sure the frame chosen has relevance for the client; and assess how risk averse your client is. Behavioral finance encompasses research that drops the traditional assumptions of expected utility maximization with rational investors in efficient markets (Ritter, 2003). The two building blocks of behavioral finance are cognitive psychology (how people think) and the limits to arbitrage. Cognitive psychology refers to how people think. There is an enormous psychology literature documenting that people make systematic errors in the way that they think: they are overconfident, they put too much weight on recent experience. Their preferences may also create distortions. Behavioral finance uses this body of knowledge, rather than taking the arrogant approach that it should be ignored. Limits to arbitrage refer to predicting in what circumstances arbitrage forces will be effective, and when they will not be (Ritter, 2003).

Muradoglu, Altay-Salih, and Mercan (2005) examined the effectiveness of an expectation formation process heuristically based on the subjective forecasts of finance professionals. The portfolio performance of subjective forecasts is superior to that of standard time series modeling. Ricciardi and Simon (2000) stated that behavioral finance enables those who invest in stock and mutual funds to avoid common mental mistakes and errors and develop effective investment strategies. Other researchers have argued that knowledge of behavioral finance should enable investors to become aware of how potential biases can affect investment their decisions and to avoid such errors. Behavioral finance utilizes knowledge of cognitive psychology, social sciences and anthropology to explain irrational investor behavior that is not being captured by the rational-based models. The behavioral finance should act to promote the efficiency of the market (Daniel et al., 2002). An awareness of findings in behavioral finance leads to a change in working practices that improve performance: for example, use of feedback and a change in the way information is presented can improve forecasting performance (Harvey & Bolger, 1996; Onkal & Muradoglu, 1996).

Empirical Achievement in Behavioral Finance

Researchers in behavioral finance have taken the view that financial theory should take account of observed human behavior. Behavioral researchers use research from psychology to develop an understanding of financial decision making, and to create the discipline of behavioral finance. Researchers in behavioral finance have been aware of the potential importance of psychologists' work on cognitive biases for some time. Burns (1985) stated that professionals' financial behavior may differ from non-professionals' financial behavior due to training and reputation. Nonparametric nonlinear statistics are best suited for descriptive and inferential analysis of all possible investor preferences (Nawrocki & Viole, 2014). Katarachia and Konstantinidis (2014) empirically explored whether biases, emotions and overall behavior are likely to deter rational choices and also whether the acquisition of financial knowledge enables generating rational thinking and decisions. Flores and Vieira (2014) empirically revealed a significant difference in the level of debt according to age, gender, marital status, education, religion, religious principles, occupation, family income, credit card, and dependence on credit. Flores and Vieira (2014) further indicated positive influences from the constructs materialism and risk behavior and negative influences from the constructs risk perception, emotion, and value of money.

Jing, Hao, and Xian (2013) explained the influence of the entrepreneurs and venture capitalists psychological and emotional factors on the venture enterprise value and the investment decision-making.

Virlics (2013) stated that risk is an important component of every investment, thus it is necessary to analyze it as both, the objective component of the investment, and as the subjective factor of the investment decision making. Risk taking within the financial domain is often considered to represent a personality trait (Rogers, Viding, & Chamorro-Premuzic, 2013). Li and Yang (2013) developed a general equilibrium model to examine the implications of prospect theory for the disposition effect, asset prices, and trading volume. Diminishing sensitivity predicts a disposition effect, price momentum, a reduced return volatility, and a positive return-volume correlation (Li & Yang, 2013).

Deshmukh, Goel, and Howe (2013) empirically created a model of the dynamic interaction between CEO overconfidence and dividend policy. An overconfident CEO views external financing as costly and builds financial slack for future investment needs by lowering the current dividend payout (Deshmukh et al., 2013). Breuer, Rieger, and Soypak (2014) stated that the relationships among dividends and patience, loss aversion, and ambiguity aversion can be empirically verified. Similar views have been expressed by Christensen-Szalanski and Beach (1984) and Frederick and Libby (1986). Experimenters are increasingly adopting web-based experimentation (Reimers & Harvey, 2011; Lo & Harvey, 2012; Harvey & Reimers, 2013). Daniel, Hirshleifer, and Subramanyam (1998) explained event-related security price anomalies according to the cognitive biases of investors' overconfidence and self-attribution. Dremen and Lufkin (2000) presented evidence that investors' under and overreaction exist and are part of the same psychological process.

Chan (2001) illustrated the price trend reversals often occur when a majority of market agents follow the same investing strategy (buying or selling), unsupported by new information. Schacter, Oulette, Whittle, and Gerin (1987) demonstrated investors' tendencies to reinforce existing price trends and brief price reversals. Chopra, Lakonishok, and Ritter (1992) provided compelling evidence in support of the idea that investors make irrational forecasts of future cash flows. If excessive optimism or pessimism is driving these irrational forecasts, then earnings announcement dates should provide the impetus for correction. Barberis and Thaler (2003) stated that behavioral finance describes anomalous corrective activity following earnings announcements from these companies. However, Shiller (1998) suggested that descriptions of underreaction and overreaction are not likely to be good psychological foundations upon which to organize a general theory of economic behavior. Cognitive biases inadequately identify the behavioral motivations causing price anomalies (Kishore, 2006).

Utilization of Psychological Factors in Behavioral Finance

Behavioral finance states that there is the limits to arbitrage which allows investor irrationality to be substantial and have long-lived impact on prices (Kishore, 2006). The theory of limited arbitrage states that if irrational traders cause deviations from fundamental value, rational traders will often be powerless to do anything about it. In order to explain more about the structure of these deviations, behavioral finance models often assume a specific form of irrationality. There are a number of researchers studying psychological factors on behavioral factor (Rabin, 1998; Kahneman & Tversky, 2000; Gilovich, Griffin, & Kahneman, 2002). Economists turn to the experimental evidence compiled by cognitive psychologists on the systematic biases that arise when people form beliefs and on people's preferences shown in the followings:

1. Beliefs

A crucial component of any model of financial markets is a specification of how agents form expectations (Barberis & Thaler, 2003). Entrepreneur's cognitive biases have emerged as one of the central themes in understanding the performance of entrepreneurial organizations (Gudmundsson & Lechner, 2013). Entrepreneur's overconfidence and optimism bias support organizational creation, but also contribute to organizational failure (Gudmundsson & Lechner, 2013). Beliefs include overconfidence, too much trading, optimism and wishful thinking, representativeness bias, conservatism bias, belief perseverance, anchoring, and availability bias.

1.1 Overconfidence

Established financial theory focuses on the tradeoff between risk and return. However, the behavioral finance suggests investors are overconfident with respect to making gains and oversensitive to losses. As a fundamental part of human nature, these biases affect all types of investors, both professional and private. Psychology has found that humans tend to have unwarranted confidence in their decision making. Overconfidence occurs when individuals develop the illusion of control over certain familiar attributes which leads them to place excess emphasis on their own knowledge and capabilities (Keil et al., 2007; DeBondt et al., 2008). In financial decisions, overconfidence can occur due to familiarity toward a particular company or financial instrument and/or past successes (Barber & Odean, 1999). Overconfident investors, who show a better than average bias, trade more frequently (Abreu & Mendes, 2012). People overestimate the accuracy of their judgments based on observed overconfidence measured as the difference between mean subjective probability and proportion correct (Olsson, 2014). Managers in countries with high level of individualism exhibit strong optimism and overconfidence which cause an upward bias in perception of supportable debt ratios (Antonczyk & Salzmann, 2014).

Jing et al. (2013) stated that overconfidence of entrepreneurs may lead to lower corporate value, but it may also make the venture enterprise with a negative net present value (NPV) get investment, while overconfidence of investors may cause overreaction in investment decision-making. Overconfident individuals tend to ignore negative feedback and/or problems (Keil et al., 2007). Financial researchers have asked people to rate their own abilities, for example in driving, relative to others and found that most people rate themselves in the top third of the population (Barber & Odean, 1999). Alpert and Raiffa (1982) stated that people are poorly calibrated in estimating probabilities and usually overestimate their precision of the knowledge and ability to do well. People show their overconfidence about good things happening in future than bad. People overestimate their confidence to the past positive outcomes and usually recall only their successes than their failures (Kishore, 2006). Nevins (2004) stated that investors overestimate their ability to predict market events, and because of their overconfidence they often take risks without receiving commensurate returns.

Few people rate their own abilities as below average, although obviously 50% of all drivers are below average. Many studies have also found these individuals tend to overrate the accuracy of their views of the future (Barber & Odean, 1999). Human beings tend to view the world in positive terms. While this behavior can be valuable, it can help you recover from life's disappointments more quickly. In addition, this behavior can also cause an ongoing source of bias in money-related decisions. Overconfidence has direct applications in investment, which can be complex and involve forecasts of the future. Overconfident investors may overestimate their ability to identify winning investments. Traditional financial theory suggests holding diversified portfolios so that risk is not concentrated in any particular area.

Overconfidence is linked to the issue of control, with overconfident investors for example believing they exercise more control over their investments than they do. Affluent investors stated that their own stock-picking skills are critical to portfolio performance. Affluent investors are unduly optimistic about the performance of the shares they chose, and underestimated the effect of the overall market on their portfolio's performance (DeBondt, 1998). Investors overestimate their own abilities and overlook broader factors influencing their investments. Extensive evidence shows that people are overconfident in their judgments. This appears in two views. Firstly, the confidence intervals people assign to their estimates of quantities are far too narrow. Their 98% confidence intervals, for example, include the true quantity only about 60% of the time (Alpert & Raiffa, 1982). Secondly, people are poorly calibrated when estimating probabilities (Fischhoff, Slovic, & Lichtenstein, 1977).

Barberis and Thaler (2003) stated that overconfidence is related to self-attribution bias and hindsight bias. Self-attribution bias refers to people's tendency to ascribe any success they have in some activity to their own talents, while blaming failure on bad luck, rather than on their ineptitude. This process will lead people to the pleasing but erroneous conclusion that they are very talented. For example, investors might become overconfident after several quarters of investing success (Gervais & Odean, 2001). Hindsight bias is the tendency of people to believe, after an event has occurred, that they predicted it before it happened. If people think they predicted the past better than they actually did, they may also believe that they can predict the future better than they actually can (Barberis & Thaler, 2003).

1.2 Too Much Trading

Investors with too much confidence in their trading skill often trade too much, with a negative effect on their returns. Barber and Odean (1999) studied US investors with retail brokerage accounts and found that more active traders earned the lowest returns according to the results for the most and least active traders. For the average investor switching from one stock to another, the stock bought underperforms the stock sold by approximately 3.0% over the following year (Barber & Odean, 1999). Whatever insight the traders think they have, they appear to be overestimating its value in investment decisions (Barber & Odean, 1999).

1.3 Optimism and Wishful Thinking

Optimism bias and distrust are conflicting cognitive biases influencing overconfidence, but showing a directly opposite influence on organizational survival (Gudmundsson & Lechner, 2013). Many people display unrealistically rosy views of their abilities and prospects (Weinstein, 1980). In addition, over 90% of those surveyed think people are above average in such aspects as driving skill, ability to get along with people and sense of humor. People also display a systematic planning fallacy: they predict that tasks will be completed much sooner than they actually are (Buehler, Griffin, & Ross, 1994).

1.4 Representativeness Bias

The notion of representativeness bias reflects the case where decisions are made based on a situation's superficial characteristics rather than a detailed evaluation of the reality. Another way of putting this would be saying that decisions are made based on financial stereotypes. A common financial example is for investors to assume that shares in a high-profile, well-managed company will automatically be a good investment. This idea sounds reasonable, but ignores the possibility that the share price already reflects the quality of the company and thus future return prospects may be moderate. Another example would be assuming that the past performance of an investment is an indication of its future performance. Investors also suffer from representativeness bias when they evaluate fund managers. Investors are often drawn to a manager with a short track record of beating market averages over a few years.

Kahneman and Tversky (1974) stated that when people try to determine the probability that a data set A was generated by a model B, or that an object A belongs to a class B, they often use the representativeness heuristic. This means that they evaluate the probability by the degree to which A reflects the essential characteristics of B (Kahneman & Tversky, 1974). Representativeness bias also leads to another bias, sample size neglect. When judging the likelihood that a data set was generated by a particular model, people often fail to take the size of the sample into account: after all, a small sample can be just as representative as a large one. Six tosses of a coin resulting in three heads and three tails are as representative of a fair coin as 500 heads and 500 tails are in a total of 1000 tosses. Representativeness bias implies that people will find the two sets of tosses equally informative about the fairness of the coin, even though the second set is much more so (Barberis & Thaler, 2003).

Sample size neglect means that in cases where people do not initially know the data generating process, they will tend to infer it too quickly on the basis of too few data points (Barberis & Thaler, 2003). For instance, they will come to believe that a financial analyst with four good stock picks is talented because four successes are not representative of a bad or mediocre analyst. It also generates a "hot hand" phenomenon, whereby sports fans become convinced that a basketball player who has made three shots in a row is on a hot streak and will score again, even though there is no evidence of a hot hand in the data (Gilovich, Vallone, & Tversky, 1985). This belief that even small samples will reflect the properties of the parent population is sometimes known as the "law of small numbers" (Rabin, 2002).

1.5 Conservatism Bias

Conservatism bias describes the idea the decision maker adheres to an initial judgment despite new contradictory information. Investors who buy shares in a high-profile company may be slow to adjust their view of the company's prospects even after the company's profitability deteriorates. Jing et al. (2013) indicated that the entrepreneurs' negative and conservative psychology may result in the reduction of organizational value, and the venture enterprise with positive net revenue may face the refusal to invest. The venture capitalists negative and conservative psychology may result in under reaction in the decision-making process (Jing et al., 2013). While representativeness bias leads to an underweighting of base rates, there are situations where base rates are over-emphasized relative to sample evidence.

In an experiment run by Edwards (1968), there are two urns, one containing 3 blue balls and 7 red ones, and the other containing 7 blue balls and 3 red ones. A random draw of 12 balls, with replacement, from one of the urns yields 8 reds and 4 blues. What is the probability the draw was made from the first urn? While the correct answer is 0.97, most people estimate a number around 0.7, apparently overweighting the base rate of 0.5 (Edwards, 1968). In addition, the evidence of conservatism bias appears at odds with representativeness bias (Barberis & Thaler, 2003). However, there may be a natural way in which they fit together. It appears that if a data sample is representative of an underlying model, then people overweight the data. However, if the data is not representative of any salient model, people react too little to the data and rely too much on their priors (Barberis & Thaler, 2003).

1.6 Belief Perseverance

There is much evidence that once people have formed an opinion, they cling to it too tightly and for too long (Lord, Ross, & Lepper, 1979). At least two effects appear to be at work. Firstly, people are reluctant to search for evidence that contradicts their beliefs. Secondly, even if they find such evidence, they treat it with excessive skepticism. Some studies have found an even stronger effect, known as confirmation bias, whereby people misinterpret evidence that goes against their hypothesis as actually being in their favor. In the context of academic finance, belief perseverance predicts that if people start out believing in the Efficient Markets Hypothesis, they may continue to believe in it long after compelling evidence to the contrary has emerged (Barberis & Thaler, 2003).

1.7 Anchoring

Decisions can be anchored by the way information is presented. In the financial scheme, values such as market index levels can act as anchors. Round numbers such as 5,000 points on the FTSE 100 Index, seem to attract disproportionate interest, despite them being numbers like any other. Kahneman and Tversky (1974) stated that when forming estimates, people often start with some initial, possibly arbitrary value, and then adjust away from it. Experimental evidence shows that the adjustment is often insufficient. In addition, people anchor too much on the initial value. In one experiment, subjects were asked to estimate the percentage of United Nations' countries that are African. In addition, before giving a percentage, they are asked whether their guess is higher or lower than a randomly generated number between 0 and 100. Their subsequent estimates are significantly affected by the initial random number. Those who are asked to compare their estimate to 10, subsequently estimated 25%, while those who compared to 60, estimated 45% (Barberis & Thaler, 2003).

1.8 Availability Bias

Research in psychology has documented a range of decision-making behaviors called biases. These biases can affect all types of decision-making, but have particular implications in relation to money and investing. Some evidence suggests that the experienced events strongly influence decisions. Psychologists refer to this as the availability bias. To give a financial example, investors are more likely to be fearful of a stock market crash when one has occurred in the recent past. Kahneman and Tversky (1974) stated that while this is a perfectly sensible procedure, it can produce biased estimates because not all memories are equally retrievable or available.

Economists are sometimes wary of this body of experimental evidence because they believe that people, through repetition, will learn their way out of biases; experts in a field, such as traders in an investment bank, will make fewer errors; and the effects with more powerful incentives will disappear (Barberis & Thaler, 2003). While all these availability biases factors can reduce biases to some extent, there is little evidence that they wipe them out altogether. The effect of learning is often muted by errors of application: when the bias is explained, people often understand it, but proceed to violate it again in specific applications. Expertise is a hindrance rather than a help: experts, armed with their sophisticated models, have been found to exhibit more overconfidence than laymen, particularly when they receive only limited feedback about their predictions (Barberis & Thaler, 2003). Camerer and Hogarth (1999) stated that while incentives can sometimes reduce the biases people display, no replicated study has made rationality violations disappear by raising incentives.

2. Preferences

Preferences in this section focus on the prospect theory and ambiguity aversion. Ambiguity aversion involves attitudes to risk and reward, fear of loss, and disposition effect.

2.1 Prospect Theory

Prospect theory preferences and speculative motives are the important drivers of trading in relation to capital gains at the stock level (Lei, Zhou, & Zhu, 2014). Tversky and Kahneman (1974) showed how people manage risk and uncertainty. Prospect theory explains the apparent regularity in human behaviors when assessing risk under uncertainty. Human beings are not consistently risk-averse; and they are risk-averse in gains but risk-takers in losses. According to Tversky and Kanheman (1974), people place much more weight on the outcomes that are perceived more certain than that are considered mere probable, a feature known as the certainty effect. People choices are also affected by framing effect. Framing refers to the way a problem is posed to the decision maker and their mental accounting of that problem (Kishore, 2006). An essential ingredient of any model trying to understand asset prices or trading behavior is an assumption about investor preferences, or about how investors evaluate risky gambles (Barberis & Thaler, 2003).

The vast majority of models assume that investors evaluate gambles according to the expected utility (EU) framework (Barberis & Thaler, 2003). Nicholson and Snyder (2008) stated that EU theory is the behavior of agents is having concave utility function and risk aversion, meaning that the asset pricing is a set by investor's rationality. In economics, the expected utility theory (EUT) operates on the premise that individuals are rational utility maximizes (Nga & Yien, 2013). The EUT assumes that individual preference toward risk remains constant regardless of the current wealth endowment (Kahneman, 2003). Von Neumann and Morgenstern (1944) stated that if preferences satisfy a number of plausible axioms (i.e., completeness, transitivity, continuity, and independence) then they can be represented by the expectation of a utility function. People systematically violate EU theory when choosing among risky gambles. There has been an explosion of work on so-called non-EU theories, all of them trying to do a better job of matching the experimental evidence.

Some of the better known models include weighted-utility theory (Chew, 1983), implicit EU (Dekel, 1986; Chew, 1989), disappointment aversion (Gul, 1991), regret theory (Bell, 1982; Loomes & Sugden, 1982), rank-dependent utility theories (Quiggin, 1982; Yaari, 1987; Segal, 1989), and prospect theory (Kahneman & Tversky, 1979; Tversky & Kahneman, 1992). EU theory is a good approximation to how people evaluate a risky gamble like the stock market, even if it does not explain attitudes to the kinds of gambles studied in experimental settings (Barberis & Thaler, 2003). The difficulty the EU approach has encountered in trying to explain basic facts about the stock market suggests that it may be worth taking a closer look at the experimental evidence.

There is a nontrivial range of preference parameters for prospect theory to simultaneously explain the disposition effect, the momentum effect, and the equity premium puzzle (Li & Yang, 2013). Of all the non-EU theories, prospect theory may be the most promising for financial applications. The difficulty with such models is that in trying to achieve two goals (i.e., normative and descriptive grounds) they end up doing an unsatisfactory job at both. In contrast, prospect theory has no aspirations as a normative theory: it simply tries to capture people's attitudes to risky gambles as parsimoniously as possible (Barberis & Thaler, 2003). Tversky and Kahneman (1986) stated that normative approaches are doomed to failure, because people routinely make choices that are simply impossible to justify on normative grounds, in that they violate dominance or invariance.

2.2 Ambiguity Aversion

This subsection explains the overview of ambiguity aversion and the factors concerning ambiguity aversion such as attitudes to risk and reward, fear of loss, and disposition effect.

Overview of Ambiguity Aversion: Savage (1964) developed a counterpart to expected utility known as subjective expected utility (SEU). Under certain axioms, preferences can be represented by the expectation of a utility function, this time weighted by the individual's subjective probability assessment. According to SEU, people do not like situations where they are uncertain about the probability distribution of a gamble. Such situations are known as situations of ambiguity, and the general dislike for them, as ambiguity aversion. SEU does not allow agents to express their degree of confidence about a probability distribution and therefore cannot capture such ambiguity aversion. Ambiguity aversion appears in a wide variety of contexts (Barberis & Thaler, 2003). For example, a researcher might ask a subject for his or her estimate of the probability that a certain team will win its upcoming football match, to which the subject might respond 0.4. The researcher then asks the subject to imagine a chance machine, which will display 1 with probability 0.4 and 0 otherwise, and asks whether the subject would prefer to bet on the football game. People prefer to bet on the machine, illustrating aversion to ambiguity.

Heath and Tversky (1991) stated that in the real world, ambiguity aversion has much to do with how competent an individual feels he or she is at assessing the relevant distribution. Ambiguity aversion over a bet can be strengthened by highlighting subjects' feelings of incompetence, either by showing them other bets in which they have more expertise, or by mentioning other people who are more qualified to evaluate the bet. Further evidence that supports the competence hypothesis is that in situations where people feel especially competent in evaluating a gamble, the opposite of ambiguity aversion, namely a "preference for the familiar", has been observed. In the example above, people chosen to be especially knowledgeable about football often prefer to bet on the outcome of the game than on the chance machine (Barberis & Thaler, 2003). Ambiguity aversion includes factors (i.e., attitudes to risk and reward, fear of loss, and the disposition effect):

Attitudes to Risk and Reward: Established financial theory focuses on the trade-off between risk and return. Campos-Vazquez and Cuilty (2014) measured the risk and loss aversion using Prospect Theory and examined the impact of emotions on the risk and loss aversion. The risk attitude in losses, together with wishful thinking and misperception of the price process may attribute to the observed disposition effect (Talpsepp, Vlcek, & Wang, 2014). Risk from this perspective means variability of outcomes and riskier investments should, broadly speaking, offer higher rates of return as compensation for higher risk. The theory assumes that investors seek the highest return for the level of risk they are willing and able to bear. Financial advisers often ask clients to complete a risk attitude questionnaire to establish their attitude to risk, and consider issues such as investment time horizon and wealth levels to establish risk tolerance. Risk tolerance drives the types of investments they recommend for the investor.

Fear of Loss: In the current economic downturn, people are fearful, uncertain, and preoccupied about how the recession affects them, their loved ones, and their collective futures (Marjanovic, Greenglass, Fiksenbaum, & Bell, 2013). Behavioral finance suggests investors are more sensitive to loss than to risk and return. Some estimates suggest people weigh losses more than twice as heavily as potential gains. For example, most people require an even (50/50) chance of a gain of £2,500 in a gamble to offset an even chance of a loss of £1,000 before they find it attractive (Montier, 2002). The idea of loss aversion states that people try to avoid locking in a loss (Barber & Odean, 1999). In case of considering an investment bought for £1,000, which rises quickly to £1,500, the investor would be tempted to sell it in order to lock-in the profit. In contrast, if the investment dropped to £500, the investor would tend to hold it to avoid locking in the loss. The idea of a loss is so painful that people tend to delay recognizing it. Investors with losing positions show a strong desire to get back to break even. This means the investor shows highly risk-averse behavior when facing a profit (selling and locking in the sure gain) and more risk tolerant or risk seeking behavior when facing a loss (continuing to hold the investment and hoping its price rises again) (Kahneman & Tversky, 1979).

Disposition Effect: Disposition effect, which refers to investors' being reluctant to realize losses, is very common in financial markets (Li, Shang, Li, Huo, & Xu, 2014). Proper level of disposition effect can avoid some loss in investment, and make chartist get relative higher return than usual (Li et al., 2014). Disposition effect is an occasion where investors have a tendency to sell winners stocks too early and ride losers stocks too long (Shefrin & Statman, 1985). This disposition effect can explain the seasonality (Brahmana et al., 2012). The disposition effect weakens in December (Odean, 1998; Grinblatt & Keloharju, 2001; Grinblatt & Hahn, 2005; Brahmana et al., 2012). The returns of January revert to normal positive as the disposition effect starts diminishing. The regret of investor can be used to explain the seasonality (Brahmana et al., 2012).

The disposition effect refers to the finding that investors are likely to sell shares that have increased in price but tend to keep those that have dropped in price (Shefrin & Statman, 1985). Shefrin and Statman (1985) developed the idea of loss aversion into a theory called the disposition effect which indicates that individuals tend to sell winners and hold losers. Barber and Odean (1999) tested this idea using data from the US retail brokerage. Barber and Odean (1999) found that investors are roughly 50% more likely to sell a winning position than a losing position, despite the fact that US tax regulations make it beneficial to defer locking in gains for as long as possible, while crystallizing tax losses as early as possible. Barber and Odean (1999) also found that the tendency to sell winners and hold losers harmed investment returns.

FUTURE RESEARCH DIRECTIONS

The strength of this chapter is on the thorough literature consolidation of psychological factors in behavioral finance. The extant literature of psychological factors in behavioral finance provides a contribution to practitioners and researchers by describing a comprehensive view of the functional applications of psychological factors in behavioral finance to appeal to different segments of psychological factors in behavioral finance in order to maximize the financial impact of psychological factors in behavioral finance. The classification of the extant literature in the domain of psychological factors in behavioral finance will provide the potential opportunities for future research. Future research direction should broaden the perspectives in the application of psychological factors in behavioral finance in the knowledge-based organizations.

Practitioners and researchers should consider the applicability of a more multidisciplinary approach toward research activities in promoting psychological factors in behavioral finance with knowledge management-related variables (i.e., knowledge-sharing behavior, knowledge creation, organizational learning, learning orientation, and motivation to learn). It will be useful to bring additional disciplines together (i.e., strategic management, information technology, marketing, and human resources) to support a more holistic examination of psychological factors in behavioral finance in order to combine or transfer existing theories and approaches to inquiry in this area. An examination of linkages between psychological factors in behavioral finance and cloud computing would seem to be viable for future research efforts.

CONCLUSION

This chapter introduced the role of psychological factors in behavioral finance, thus explaining the theory of behavioral finance, the application of behavioral finance theory, the empirical achievement in behavioral finance, the utilization of psychological factors in behavioral finance concerning beliefs (i.e., overconfidence, too much trading, optimism and wishful thinking, representativeness bias, conservatism bias, belief perseverance, anchoring, and availability bias) and preferences (i.e., prospect theory and ambiguity aversion). Ambiguity aversion includes factors (i.e., attitudes to risk and reward, fear of loss, and the disposition effect) explained in this chapter. This chapter aimed to provide a practical introduction to general tenants of behavioral finance and highlights the potential lessons for successful investing. The primary input to behavioral finance has been from experimental psychology. Methods developed within sociology such as surveys, interviews, participant observation, focus groups have not had the same degree of influence.

Behavioral finance expands the domain of finance beyond portfolios, asset pricing, and market efficiency. Behavioral finance explores the behavior of investors and managers in direct and indirect ways. The training of finance academics leads them to prefer methodologies that permit greater control and a clearer causal interpretation. Entrepreneurs should balance their organizations, for instance through hiring policies, to prevent extreme overconfidence, optimism or distrust becoming a predominant organizational culture (Gudmundsson & Lechner, 2013). Interdisciplinary research is becoming more widespread and it is likely that greater collaboration between finance and sociology will develop in the future. Researchers and practitioners often cross disciplinary boundaries, thus borrowing a single idea or concept from another discipline. Both of these are examples of multidisciplinary research (Klein, 1990). However, in interdisciplinary research, disciplines or research methods are integrated into a new field of study (Mitchell, 1995). Applying psychological factors in behavioral finance will vastly improve financial performance and reach sustainable competitive advantage in the social media age.

REFERENCES

Abreu, M., & Mendes, V. (2012). Information, overconfidence and trading: Do the sources of information matter? *Journal of Economic Psychology*, *33*(4), 868–881. doi:10.1016/j.joep.2012.04.003

Alpert, M., & Raiffa, H. (1982). A progress report on the training of probability assessors. In D. Kahneman, P. Slovic, & A. Tversky (Eds.), *Judgment under uncertainty: Heuristics and biases* (pp. 294–305). Cambridge, UK: Cambridge University Press. doi:10.1017/CBO9780511809477.022

Altman, M. (2012). Implications of behavioural economics for financial literacy and public policy. *Journal of Socio-Economics*, *41*(5), 677–690. doi:10.1016/j.socec.2012.06.002

Antonczyk, R. C., & Salzmann, A. J. (2014). Overconfidence and optimism: The effect of national culture on capital structure. *Research in International Business and Finance*, *31*, 132–151. doi:10.1016/j.ribaf.2013.06.005

Arrow, K. J., & Debreu, G. (1954). The existence of an equilibrium for a competitive economy. *Econometrica*, *23*(3), 265–290. doi:10.2307/1907353

Barber, B. M., & Odean, T. (1999). The courage of misguided convictions. *Financial Analysts*, *55*(6), 41–55. doi:10.2469/faj.v55.n6.2313

Barberis, N., & Thaler, R. (2003). A survey of behavioral finance. In G. M. Constantinides, M. Harris, & R. Stulz (Eds.), *Handbook of the economics of finance* (pp. 1051–1121). Amsterdam, The Netherlands: Elsevier.

Bell, D. (1982). Regret in decision making under uncertainty. *Operations Research*, *30*(5), 961–981. doi:10.1287/opre.30.5.961

Bell, D. E., Raiffa, H., & Tversky, A. (1988). Descriptive, normative, and prescriptive interactions in decision making. In D. E. Bell, H. Raiffa, & A. Tversky (Eds.), *Decision making: Descriptive, normative, and prescriptive interactions* (pp. 9–30). Cambridge, UK: Cambridge University Press. doi:10.1017/CBO9780511598951.003

Bikas, E., Jureviciene, D., Dubinskas, P., & Novickyte, L. (2014). Behavioural finance: The emergence and development trends. *Procedia: Social and Behavioral Sciences*, *82*, 870–876. doi:10.1016/j.sbspro.2013.06.363

Bodie, Z., Kane, A., & Marcus, A. (2007). *Investments*. New York, NY: McGraw-Hill.

Brahmana, R. K., Hooy, W. W., & Ahmad, Z. (2012). Psychological factors on irrational financial decision making: Case of day-of-the week anomaly. *Humanomics*, *28*(4), 236–257. doi:10.1108/08288661211277317

Breuer, W., Rieger, M. O., & Soypak, K. C. (2014). The behavioral foundations of corporate dividend policy a cross-country analysis. *Journal of Banking & Finance*, *42*, 247–265. doi:10.1016/j.jbankfin.2014.02.001

Buehler, R., Griffin, D., & Ross, M. (1994). Exploring the planning fallacy: Why people underestimate their task completion times. *Journal of Personality and Social Psychology*, *67*(3), 366–381. doi:10.1037/0022-3514.67.3.366

Burns, P. (1985). Experience in decision making: A comparison of students and businessmen in a simulated progressive auction. In V. L. Smith (Ed.), *Research in experimental economics* (pp. 1–43). Greenwich, CT: JAI Press.

Camerer, C., & Hogarth, R. (1999). The effects of financial incentives in experiments: A review and capital-labor production framework. *Journal of Risk and Uncertainty*, *19*(1-3), 7–42. doi:10.1023/A:1007850605129

Campos-Vazquez, R. M., & Cuilty, E. (2014). The role of emotions on risk aversion: A prospect theory experiment. *Journal of Behavioral and Experimental Economics*, *50*, 1–9. doi:10.1016/j.socec.2014.01.001

Chan, W. S. (2001). Stock price reaction to news and no-news: Drift and reversal after headlines. *NBER Working Paper Series*. Retrieved August 23, 2014, from http://www.nber.org/~confer/2001/bfs01/chan.pdf

Chew, S. (1983). A generalization of the quasilinear mean with applications to the measurement of income inequality and decision theory resolving the Allais Paradox. *Econometrica*, *51*(4), 1065–1092. doi:10.2307/1912052

Chew, S. (1989). Axiomatic utility theories with the betweenness property. *Annals of Operations Research*, *19*(1-4), 273–298. doi:10.1007/BF02283525

Chopra, N., Lakonishok, J., & Ritter, J. (1992). Measuring abnormal performance: Do stocks overreact? *Journal of Financial Economics*, *31*(2), 235–268. doi:10.1016/0304-405X(92)90005-I

Christensen-Szalanski, J. J., & Beach, L. R. (1984). The citation bias: Fad and fashion in the judgment and decision literature. *The American Psychologist*, *39*(1), 75–78. doi:10.1037/0003-066X.39.1.75

Coleman, L. (2014). Why finance theory fails to survive contact with the real world: A fund manager perspective. *Critical Perspectives on Accounting*, *25*(3), 226–236. doi:10.1016/j.cpa.2013.02.001

Daniel, K., Hirshleifer, D., & Subrahmanyam, A. (1998). Investor psychology and security market under-and overreactions. *The Journal of Finance*, *53*(5), 1839–1886. doi:10.1111/0022-1082.00077

Daniel, K., Hirshleifer, D., & Teoh, S. H. (2002). Investor psychology in capital markets: Evidence and policy implications. *Journal of Monetary Economics*, *49*(1), 139–209. doi:10.1016/S0304-3932(01)00091-5

DeBondt, W., Forbes, W., Hamalainen, P., & Muragoglu, Y. G. (2010). What can behavioural finance teach us about finance? *Qualitative Research in Financial Markets*, *2*(1), 29–36. doi:10.1108/17554171011042371

DeBondt, W., Muradoglu, G., Shefrin, H., & Staikouras, S. K. (2008). Behavioural finance: Quo vadis? *Journal of Applied Finance (JAF)*, *18*(2), 7–21.

DeBondt, W. F. M. (1998). A portrait of the individual investor. *European Economic Review*, *42*(3), 831–844. doi:10.1016/S0014-2921(98)00009-9

Dekel, E. (1986). An axiomatic characterization of preferences under uncertainty: Weakening the independence axiom. *Journal of Economic Theory*, *40*(2), 304–318. doi:10.1016/0022-0531(86)90076-1

Deshmukh, S., Goel, A. M., & Howe, K. M. (2013). CEO overconfidence and dividend policy. *Journal of Financial Intermediation*, *22*(3), 440–463. doi:10.1016/j.jfi.2013.02.003

Dremen, D., & Lufkin, E. (2000). Investor overreaction: Evidence that its basis is psychological. *The Journal of Psychology and Financial Markets*, *1*(1), 61–75. doi:10.1207/S15327760JPFM0101_06

Edwards, W. (1968). Conservatism in human information processing. In B. Kleinmutz (Ed.), *Formal representation of human judgment* (pp. 17–52). New York, NY: John Wiley & Sons.

Fischhoff, B., Slovic, P., & Lichtenstein, S. (1977). Knowing with certainty: The appropriateness of extreme confidence. *Journal of Experimental Psychology. Human Perception and Performance*, *3*(4), 552–564. doi:10.1037/0096-1523.3.4.552

Flores, S. A. M., & Vieira, K. M. (2014). Propensity toward indebtedness: An analysis using behavioral factors. *Journal of Behavioral and Experimental Finance*, *3*, 1–10. doi:10.1016/j.jbef.2014.05.001

Frederick, D., & Libby, R. (1986). Expertise and auditor's judgments of conjunctive events. *Journal of Accounting Research*, *24*(3), 270–290. doi:10.2307/2491134

Garling, T., Kirchler, E., Lewis, A., & Van Raaij, F. (2009). Psychology, financial decision making, and financial crises. *Psychological Science in the Public Interest*, *10*(1), 1–47. doi:10.1177/1529100610378437

Gervais, S., & Odean, T. (2001). Learning to be overconfident. *Review of Financial Studies*, *14*(1), 1–27. doi:10.1093/rfs/14.1.1

Gilovich, T., Griffin, D., & Kahneman, D. (2002). *Heuristics and biases: The psychology of intuitive judgment*. Cambridge, UK: Cambridge University Press. doi:10.1017/CBO9780511808098

Gilovich, T., Vallone, R., & Tversky, A. (1985). The hot hand in basketball: On the misperception of random sequences. *Cognitive Psychology*, *17*(3), 295–314. doi:10.1016/0010-0285(85)90010-6

Glaser, M., Noth, M., & Weber, M. (2004). Behavioral finance. In D. J. Koehler & N. Harvey (Eds.), *Blackwell handbook of judgment and decision making* (pp. 527–546). Oxford, UK: Blackwell. doi:10.1002/9780470752937.ch26

Grinblatt, M., & Hahn, B. (2005). Prospect theory, mental accounting, and momentum. *Journal of Financial Economics*, *78*(2), 311–339. doi:10.1016/j.jfineco.2004.10.006

Grinblatt, M., & Keloharju, M. (2001). What makes investors trade? *The Journal of Finance*, *56*(2), 589–616. doi:10.1111/0022-1082.00338

Gul, F. (1991). A theory of disappointment in decision making under uncertainty. *Econometrica*, *59*(3), 667–686. doi:10.2307/2938223

Harvey, N., & Bolger, F. (1996). Graphs versus tables: Effects of data presentation format on judgmental forecasting. *International Journal of Forecasting*, *12*(1), 119–137. doi:10.1016/0169-2070(95)00634-6

Harvey, N., & Reimers, S. (2013). Trend damping: Under-adjustment, experimental artifact, or adaptation to features of the natural environment? *Journal of Experimental Psychology. Learning, Memory, and Cognition*, *39*(2), 589–607. doi:10.1037/a0029179 PMID:22774857

Heath, C., & Tversky, A. (1991). Preference and belief: Ambiguity and competence in choice under uncertainty. *Journal of Risk and Uncertainty*, *4*(1), 5–28. doi:10.1007/BF00057884

Hoffmann, A. O. I., & Post, T. (2014). Self-attribution bias in consumer financial decision-making: How investment returns affect individuals' belief in skill. *Journal of Behavioral and Experimental*, *52*, 23–28. doi:10.1016/j.socec.2014.05.005

Jing, G., Hao, C., & Xian, Z. (2013). Influence of psychological and emotional factors on the venture enterprise value and the investment decision-making. *Procedia Computer Science*, *17*, 919–929. doi:10.1016/j.procs.2013.05.117

Jordan, B., & Miller, T. (2008). *Fundamentals of investments*. New York, NY: McGraw-Hill.

Kahneman, D. (2003). A psychological perspective on economics. *The American Economic Review*, *93*(2), 162–168. doi:10.1257/000282803321946985

Kahneman, D., & Riepe, M. W. (1998). Aspects of investor psychology. *Journal of Portfolio Management*, *24*(1), 52–65. doi:10.3905/jpm.1998.409643

Kahneman, D., Slovic, P., & Tversky, A. (1982). *Judgment under uncertainty: Heuristics and biases*. Cambridge, UK: Cambridge University Press. doi:10.1017/CBO9780511809477

Kahneman, D., & Tversky, A. (1974). Judgment under uncertainty: Heuristics and biases. *Science*, *185*(4157), 1124–1131. doi:10.1126/science.185.4157.1124 PMID:17835457

Kahneman, D., & Tversky, A. (1979). Prospect theory: An analysis of decision under risk. *Econometrica*, *47*(2), 263–291. doi:10.2307/1914185

Kahneman, D., & Tversky, A. (2000). *Choices, values and frames*. Cambridge, UK: Cambridge University Press.

Katarachia, A., & Konstantinidis, A. (2014). Financial education and decision making processes. *Procedia Economics and Finance*, *9*, 142–152. doi:10.1016/S2212-5671(14)00015-X

Keil, M., Depledge, G., & Rai, A. (2007). Escalation: The role of problem recognition and cognitive bias. *Decision Sciences*, *38*(3), 391–421. doi:10.1111/j.1540-5915.2007.00164.x

Kishore, R. (2006). *Theory of behavioural finance and its application to property market: A change in paradigm*. Paper presented at the Twelfth Annual Pacific Rim Real Estate Society Conference, Auckland, New Zealand.

Klein, J. T. (1990). *Interdisciplinarity: History, theory, and practice*. Detroit, MI: Wayne State University Press.

Levy, H., & Post, T. (2005). *Investments*. New York, NY: Prentice-Hall.

Li, B., Shang, W., Li, H., Huo, L., & Xu, S. (2014). Disposition effect in an agent-based financial market model. *Procedia Computer Science*, *31*, 680–690. doi:10.1016/j.procs.2014.05.316

Li, Y., & Yang, L. (2013). Prospect theory, the disposition effect, and asset prices. *Journal of Financial Economics*, *107*(3), 715–739. doi:10.1016/j.jfineco.2012.11.002

Lo, H. Y., & Harvey, N. (2012). Effects of shopping addiction on consumer decision making: Web-based studies in real time. *Journal of Behavioral Addictions*, *1*(4), 162–170. doi:10.1556/JBA.1.2012.006

Loomes, G., & Sugden, R. (1982). Regret theory: An alternative theory of rational choice under uncertainty. *The Economic Journal*, *92*(368), 805–824. doi:10.2307/2232669

Lord, C., Ross, L., & Lepper, M. (1979). Biased assimilation and attitude polarization: The effects of prior theories on subsequently considered evidence. *Journal of Personality and Social Psychology*, *37*(11), 2098–2109. doi:10.1037/0022-3514.37.11.2098

Marjanovic, Z., Greenglass, E. R., Fiksenbaum, L., & Bell, C. M. (2013). Psychometric evaluation of the Financial Threat Scale (FTS) in the context of the great recession. *Journal of Economic Psychology*, *36*, 1–10. doi:10.1016/j.joep.2013.02.005

Markowitz, H. M. (1952). Portfolio selection. *The Journal of Finance*, *7*(1), 77–91.

Merton, R. C. (1969). Lifetime portfolio selection under uncertainty: The continuous-time case. *The Review of Economics and Statistics*, *51*(3), 247–257. doi:10.2307/1926560

Mitchell, W. J. T. (1995). Interdisciplinary and visual culture. *The Art Bulletin*, *77*(4), 540–544.

Montier, J. (2002). *Behavioural finance: Insights into irrational minds and markets*. Hoboken, NJ: John Wiley & Sons.

Muradoglu, G., Altay-Salih, A., & Mercan, M. (2005). A behavioral approach to efficient portfolio formation. *Journal of Behavioral Finance*, *6*(5), 202–212. doi:10.1207/s15427579jpfm0604_4

Nawrocki, D., & Viole, F. (2014). Behavioral finance in financial market theory, utility theory, portfolio theory and the necessary statistics: A review. *Journal of Behavioral and Experimental Finance*, *2*, 10–17. doi:10.1016/j.jbef.2014.02.005

Nevins, D. (2004). Goals-based investing integrating traditional and behavioral finance. *The Journal of Wealth Management*, *6*(4), 8–23. doi:10.3905/jwm.2004.391053

Nga, J. K. H., & Yien, L. K. (2013). The influence of personality trait and demographics on financial decision making among Generation Y. *Young Consumers*, *14*(3), 230–243. doi:10.1108/YC-11-2012-00325

Nicholson, W., & Snyder, C. M. (2008). *Microeconomic theory: Basic principles and extensions*. Stamford, CT: Thomson Publishing.

Odean, T. (1998). Are investors reluctant to realize their losses? *The Journal of Finance*, *53*(5), 1775–1798. doi:10.1111/0022-1082.00072

Olsen, R. A. (2010). Toward a theory of behavioural finance: Implications from the natural sciences. *Qualitative Research in Financial Markets*, *2*(2), 100–128. doi:10.1108/17554171080000383

Olsson, H. (2014). Measuring overconfidence: Methodological problems and statistical artifacts. *Journal of Business Research*, *67*(8), 1766–1770. doi:10.1016/j.jbusres.2014.03.002

Onkal, D., & Muradoglu, G. (1996). Effects of task format on probabilistic forecasting of stock prices. *International Journal of Forecasting*, *12*(1), 9–24. doi:10.1016/0169-2070(95)00633-8

Pompian, M. M. (2006). *Behavioral finance and wealth management: How to build optimal portfolios that account for investor biases*. New York, NY: John Wiley & Sons.

Quiggin, J. (1982). A theory of anticipated utility. *Journal of Economic Behavior & Organization*, *3*(4), 323–343. doi:10.1016/0167-2681(82)90008-7

Rabin, M. (1998). Psychology and economics. *Journal of Economic Literature*, *36*(1), 11–46.

Rabin, M. (2002). Inference by believers in the law of small numbers. *The Quarterly Journal of Economics*, *117*(3), 775–816. doi:10.1162/003355302760193896

Reimers, S., & Harvey, N. (2011). Sensitivity to autocorrelation in judgmental time series forecasting. *International Journal of Forecasting*, *27*(4), 1196–1214. doi:10.1016/j.ijforecast.2010.08.004

Ricciardi, V., & Simon, H. (2000). What is behavioral finance? *The Business. Education and Technology Journal*, *2*(1), 26–34.

Ritter, J. R. (2003). Behavioral finance. *Pacific-Basin Finance Journal*, *11*(4), 429–437. doi:10.1016/S0927-538X(03)00048-9

Rogers, J., Viding, E., & Chamorro-Premuzic, T. (2013). Instrumental and disinhibited financial risk taking: Personality and behavioural correlates. *Personality and Individual Differences*, *55*(6), 645–649. doi:10.1016/j.paid.2013.05.011

Sahi, S. K. (2012). Neurofinance and investment behaviour. *Studies in Economics and Finance*, *29*(4), 246–267. doi:10.1108/10867371211266900

Savage, L. (1964). *The foundations of statistics*. New York, NY: John Wiley & Sons.

Schacter, S., Oulette, R., Whittle, B., & Gerin, W. (1987). Effects of trend and of profit or loss on the tendency to sell stock. *Basic and Applied Social Psychology*, *8*(4), 259–271. doi:10.1207/s15324834basp0804_1

Scheinkman, J. A., & Xiong, W. (2003). Overconfidence and speculative bubbles. *Journal of Political Economy*, *111*(6), 1183–1219. doi:10.1086/378531

Segal, U. (1989). Anticipated utility: A measure representation approach. *Annals of Operations Research*, *19*(1-4), 359–373. doi:10.1007/BF02283529

Sharpe, W. (1964). Capital asset prices: A theory of market equilibrium under conditions of risk. *The Journal of Finance*, *19*(3), 425–442.

Shefrin, H. (2001). *Behavioural corporate finance*. Retrieved August 23, 2014, from http://bbs.cenet.org.cn/UploadImages/20055612105669608.pdf

Shefrin, H., & Statman, M. (1985). The disposition to sell winners too early and ride losers too long: Theory and evidence. *The Journal of Finance*, *40*(3), 777–790. doi:10.1111/j.1540-6261.1985.tb05002.x

Shefrin, H., & Statman, M. (1994). Behavioural capital asset pricing model. *Journal of Financial and Quantitative Analysis*, *29*(3), 323–349. doi:10.2307/2331334

Shiller, R. (1995). Conversation, information and herd behaviour. *The American Economic Review*, *85*(2), 181–185.

Shiller, R. (1998). Human behavior and the efficiency of the financial system. *NBER Working Paper Series*. Retrieved August 23, 2014, from: http://www.nber.org/papers/w6375

Shleifer, A. (2000). *Inefficient markets: An introduction to behavioural finance*. Oxford, UK: Oxford University Press. doi:10.1093/0198292279.001.0001

Slovic, P. (1972). Psychological study of human judgment: Implications for investment decision making. *The Journal of Finance*, *27*(4), 779–799. doi:10.1111/j.1540-6261.1972.tb01311.x

Statman, M. (2014). Behavioral finance: Finance with normal people. *Borsa Istanbul Review*, *14*(2), 65–73. doi:10.1016/j.bir.2014.03.001

Talpsepp, T., Vlcek, M., & Wang, M. (2014). Speculating in gains, waiting in losses: A closer look at the disposition effect. *Journal of Behavioral and Experimental Finance*, *2*, 31–43. doi:10.1016/j.jbef.2014.04.001

Tversky, A., & Kahneman, D. (1974). Judgment under uncertainty: Heuristics and biases. *Science*. *New Series*, *185*(4157), 1124–1131.

Tversky, A., & Kahneman, D. (1986). Rational choice and the framing of decisions. *The Journal of Business*, *59*(4), 251–278. doi:10.1086/296365

Tversky, A., & Kahneman, D. (1992). Advances in prospect theory: Cumulative representation of uncertainty. *Journal of Risk and Uncertainty*, *5*(4), 297–323. doi:10.1007/BF00122574

Von Neumann, J., & Morgenstern, O. (1944). *Theory of games and economic behavior*. Princeton, NJ: Princeton University Press.

Weinstein, N. (1980). Unrealistic optimism about future life events. *Journal of Personality and Social Psychology*, *39*(5), 806–820. doi:10.1037/0022-3514.39.5.806

Yaari, M. (1987). The dual theory of choice under risk. *Econometrica*, *55*(1), 95–115. doi:10.2307/1911158

ADDITIONAL READING

Aggarwal, R. (2014). Animal spirits in financial economics: A review of deviations from economic rationality. *International Review of Financial Analysis*, *32*(1), 179–187. doi:10.1016/j.irfa.2013.07.018

Aggarwal, R., & Goodell, J. W. (2014). National cultural dimensions in finance and accounting scholarship: An important gap in the literatures? *Journal of Behavioral and Experimental Finance*, *1*, 1–12. doi:10.1016/j.jbef.2013.11.002

Alghalith, M., Floros, C., & Dukharan, M. (2012). Testing dominant theories and assumptions in behavioral finance. *The Journal of Risk Finance*, *13*(3), 262–268. doi:10.1108/15265941211229262

Baker, M. P., Wurgler, J., & Yuan, Y. (2012). Global, local, and contagious investor sentiment. *Journal of Financial Economics*, *104*(2), 272–287. doi:10.1016/j.jfineco.2011.11.002

Ben-Rephael, A., Kandel, S., & Wohl, A. (2012). Measuring investor sentiment with mutual fund flows. *Journal of Financial Economics*, *104*(2), 363–382. doi:10.1016/j.jfineco.2010.08.018

Borio, C. (2014). The financial cycle and macroeconomics: What have we learnt? *Journal of Banking & Finance*, *45*, 182–198. doi:10.1016/j.jbankfin.2013.07.031

Branch, B. (2014). Institutional economics and behavioral finance. *Journal of Behavioral and Experimental Finance*, *1*, 13–16. doi:10.1016/j.jbef.2013.11.001

Broihanne, M. H., Merli, M., & Roger, P. (2014). Overconfidence, risk perception and the risk taking behavior of finance professionals. *Finance Research Letters*, *11*(2), 64–73. doi:10.1016/j.frl.2013.11.002

Bruce, J. R. (2014). Risky business: How social psychology can help improve corporate risk management. *Business Horizons*, *57*(4), 551–557. doi:10.1016/j.bushor.2014.03.002

Buzatu, C. (2013). The influence of behavioral factors on insurance decision: A Romanian approach. *Procedia Economics and Finance*, *6*, 31–40. doi:10.1016/S2212-5671(13)00110-X

Chiarella, C., He, X. Z., & Zwinkels, R. C. J. (2014). Heterogeneous expectations in asset pricing: Empirical evidence from the S&P500. *Journal of Economic Behavior & Organization*, *105*, 1–16. doi:10.1016/j.jebo.2014.03.003

Corredor, P., Ferrer, E., & Santamaria, R. (2014). Is cognitive bias really present in analyst forecasts? The role of investor sentiment. *International Business Review*, *23*(4), 824–837. doi:10.1016/j.ibusrev.2014.01.001

Deakin, S. (2013). The legal theory of finance: Implications for methodology and empirical research. *Journal of Comparative Economics*, *41*(2), 338–342. doi:10.1016/j.jce.2013.03.005

Driscoll, J. C., & Holden, S. (2014). Behavioral economics and macroeconomic models. *Journal of Macroeconomics*, *41*, 133–147. doi:10.1016/j.jmacro.2014.05.004

Du, D. (2012). Momentum and behavioral finance. *Managerial Finance*, *38*(4), 364–379. doi:10.1108/03074351211207527

Finter, P., Niessen-Ruenzi, A., & Ruenzi, S. (2012). The impact of investor sentiment on the German stock market. *Journal of Business Economics*, *82*(2), 132–163. doi:10.1007/s11573-011-0536-x

Gigerenzer, G., & Gaissmaier, W. (2011). Heuristic decision making. *Annual Review of Psychology*, *62*(45), 451–482. doi:10.1146/annurev-psych-120709-145346 PMID:21126183

Huang, W., & Chen, Z. (2014). Modeling regional linkage of financial markets. *Journal of Economic Behavior & Organization*, *99*, 18–31. doi:10.1016/j.jebo.2013.12.009

Karpavičius, S. (2014). The cost of capital and optimal financing policy in a dynamic setting. *Journal of Banking & Finance*, *48*, 42–56. doi:10.1016/j.jbankfin.2014.07.008

Kearney, C., & Liu, S. (2014). Textual sentiment in finance: A survey of methods and models. *International Review of Financial Analysis*, *33*, 171–185. doi:10.1016/j.irfa.2014.02.006

Kopaneli, A. (2014). Finance, marketing, management and strategy planning. A qualitative research method analysis of case studies in business hotels in Patras and in Athens. *Procedia Economics and Finance*, *9*, 472–487. doi:10.1016/S2212-5671(14)00049-5

Kuhnen, C. M., & Knutson, B. (2011). The influence of affect on beliefs, preferences and financial decisions. *Journal of Financial and Quantitative Analysis*, *46*(3), 605–626. doi:10.1017/S0022109011000123

Kukacka, J., & Barunik, J. (2013). Behavioural breaks in the heterogeneous agent model: The impact of herding, overconfidence, and market sentiment. *Physica A: Statistical Mechanics and its Applications, 392*(23), *5920-5938.*

Lansing, K. J., & LeRoy, S. F. (2014). Risk aversion, investor information and stock market volatility. *European Economic Review*, *70*, 88–107. doi:10.1016/j.euroecorev.2014.03.009

Larkin, C. J. (2014). Rediscovering the human and forgetting the natural in economics and finance. *Journal of Behavioral and Experimental Finance*, *1*, 99–108. doi:10.1016/j.jbef.2014.02.002

Lau, C. M., & Roopnarain, K. (2014). The effect of financial and nonfinancial measures on employee motivation to participate in target setting. *The British Accounting Review*, *46*(3), 228–247. doi:10.1016/j.bar.2014.02.006

Levinthal, D. A. (2011). A behavioral approach to strategy: What's the alternative? *Strategic Management Journal*, *32*(13), 1517–1523. doi:10.1002/smj.963

Liu, Y., Fan, Z. P., & Zhang, Y. (2014). Risk decision analysis in emergency response: A method based on cumulative prospect theory. *Computers & Operations Research*, *42*, 75–82. doi:10.1016/j.cor.2012.08.008

Lo, H. Y., & Harvey, N. (2011). Shopping without pain: Compulsive buying and the effects of credit card availability in Europe and the Far East. *Journal of Economic Psychology*, *32*(1), 79–92. doi:10.1016/j.joep.2010.12.002

Lo, H. Y., Thomson, M., & Harvey, N. (2012). Information search and product knowledge: Differences between shopaholics and general shoppers in Britain and Taiwan. *Journal of Customer Behaviour*, *11*(4), 348–370. doi:10.1362/147539212X13546197910019

Mokhova, N., & Zinecker, M. (2014). Macroeconomic factors and corporate capital structure. *Procedia: Social and Behavioral Sciences*, *110*, 530–540. doi:10.1016/j.sbspro.2013.12.897

Pan, X., & Zuo, Z. (2014). A stochastic user equilibrium model and optimal congestion pricing with prospect theory. *Procedia: Social and Behavioral Sciences*, *138*, 127–136. doi:10.1016/j.sbspro.2014.07.188

Park, B. J. (2014). Time-varying, heterogeneous risk aversion and dynamics of asset prices among boundedly rational agents. *Journal of Banking & Finance*, *43*, 150–159. doi:10.1016/j.jbankfin.2014.03.009

Pasquariello, P. (2014). Prospect theory and market quality. *Journal of Economic Theory*, *149*, 276–310. doi:10.1016/j.jet.2013.09.010

Pepper, A., & Gore, J. (2014). The economic psychology of incentives: An international psychology of top managers. *Journal of World Business*, *49*(3), 350–361. doi:10.1016/j.jwb.2013.07.002

Pinnuck, M., & Shekhar, C. (2013). The profit versus loss heuristic and firm financing decisions. *Accounting, Organizations and Society*, *38*(6-7), 420–439. doi:10.1016/j.aos.2013.09.003

Plotnicki, M., & Szyszka, A. (2014). IPO market timing. The evidence of the disposition effect among corporate managers. *Global Finance Journal*, *25*(1), 48–55. doi:10.1016/j.gfj.2014.03.005

Rieger, M. O. (2014). Evolutionary stability of prospect theory preferences. *Journal of Mathematical Economics*, *50*, 1–11. doi:10.1016/j.jmateco.2013.11.002

Sadi, R., Asl, H. G., Rostami, M. R., Gholipour, F., & Gholipour, F. (2011). Behavioural finance: The explanation of investors' personality and perceptual biases effects on financial decisions. *International Journal of Economics and Finance*, *3*(5), 234–241. doi:10.5539/ijef.v3n5p234

Santoro, E., Petrella, I., Pfajfar, D., & Gaffeo, E. (2014). Loss aversion and the asymmetric transmission of monetary policy. *Journal of Monetary Economics*, *68*, 19–36. doi:10.1016/j.jmoneco.2014.07.009

Sapienza, P., & Zingales, L. (2013). Economic experts versus average Americans. *The American Economic Review*, *103*(3), 636–642. doi:10.1257/aer.103.3.636

Schicks, J. (2014). Over-indebtedness in microfinance: An empirical analysis of related factors on the borrower level. *World Development*, *54*, 301–324. doi:10.1016/j.worlddev.2013.08.009

Shefrin, H., & Nicols, C. M. (2014). Credit card behavior, financial styles, and heuristics. *Journal of Business Research*, *67*(8), 1679–1687. doi:10.1016/j.jbusres.2014.02.014

Smith, A. L., & Harvey, T. W. (2011). Test of a theory: An empirical examination of the changing nature of investor behavior. *Journal of Management Policy and Practice*, *12*(3), 49–68.

Toma, S. G., Grigore, A. M., & Marinescu, P. (2014). Economic development and entrepreneurship. *Procedia Economics and Finance*, *8*, 436–443. doi:10.1016/S2212-5671(14)00111-7

Vermaelen, T., & Xu, M. (2014). Acquisition finance and market timing. *Journal of Corporate Finance*, *25*, 73–91. doi:10.1016/j.jcorpfin.2013.11.004

Wigniolle, B. (2014). Optimism, pessimism and financial bubbles. *Journal of Economic Dynamics & Control*, *41*, 188–208. doi:10.1016/j.jedc.2014.01.022

Xu, Z. Q. (2014). A new characterization of comonotonicity and its application in behavioral finance. *Journal of Mathematical Analysis and Applications*, *418*(2), 612–625. doi:10.1016/j.jmaa.2014.03.053

Yang, C., & Zhang, R. (2014). Dynamic sentiment asset pricing model. *Economic Modelling*, *37*, 362–367. doi:10.1016/j.econmod.2013.11.041

KEY TERMS AND DEFINITIONS

Behavioral Finance: A theory stating that there are psychological and behavioral variables involved in investing in the stock market that provide opportunities for smart investors to profit.

Behavioral Psychology: A school of psychology that explains all mental and physical activities in terms of response by glands and muscles to external factors.

Finance: A branch of economics concerned with resource allocation as well as resource management, acquisition, and investment.

Financial Industry: The part of an overall economy that is primarily made up of money markets, banking institutions, and brokers.

Financial Market: A market for the exchange of capital and credit, including the money markets and the capital market.

Investment Strategy: An investor's plan of distributing assets among various investments, taking into consideration such factors as individual goals and risk tolerance.

Investor: An individual who commits money to investment products with the expectation of financial return.

Resource Allocation: The process of allocating resources among the various projects or business units.

Stock Market: The general term for the organized trading of stocks.

Chapter 7
Financial Distress and Health

Hande Şahin
Kırıkkale University, Turkey

Sibel Erkal
Hacettepe University, Turkey

ABSTRACT

The fundamental socio-economic effects of economic crises on societies are decreasing income, unemployment and hence, negative progress of living standards, increasing income inequality and poverty. According to the Commission on Social Determinants of Health Report of World Health Organization, crises adversely affect many social determinants of health and thus threat health in many aspects. An important part of overall psychological well-being is satisfaction with various aspects of life. One of those domains is one's financial situation. Financial distress has been described as judgments about and responses to one's financial condition. Financial distress is a subjective phenomenon. Two individuals with the same levels of income and economic resources may have different levels of perceived financial distress. Financial distress can result in or result from poor health, or both. The purpose of the study was to explore the relationships between financial distress and health.

INTRODUCTION

The fundamental socio-economic effects of economic crises on societies are decreasing income, unemployment and hence, negative progress of living standards, increasing income inequality and poverty (Caman Karadag & Cilingiroğlu, 2009). According to the Commission on Social Determinants of Health Report of World Health Organization (WHO), crises adversely affect many social determinants of health and thus threat health in many aspects (WHO, 2009).

An important part of overall psychological well-being is satisfaction with various aspects of life. One of those domains is one's financial situation. Researchers over the past 30 years have examined both objective and subjective measures in an attempt to describe the financial condition of individuals and families (Prawitz and et al., 2006).

The research have revealed that unemployment and poverty can lead to mental health problems such as stress disorders, depression, despair, introversion, loss of self-respect, anxiety disorders and behavioral disorders in addition to physical

DOI: 10.4018/978-1-4666-7484-4.ch007

diseases and bodily complaints (Çaman Karadağ & Çilingiroğlu, 2009).

It is also known that the increasing unemployment brings along the increase in unregistered employment rates. In a research conducted on the effect of unregistered employment on mental health; insured employees, unregistered employees and unemployed people were evaluated in terms of mental disorders and it was found that the frequency of mental disorder was two times more in both unregistered employees and unemployed people than in insured employees (Ulaş & Kaya, 2009).

For the last five decades the term stress has enjoyed increasing popularity in the behavioral and health sciences. It first was used in physics in order to analyze the problem of how manmade structures must be designed to carry heavy loads and resist deformation by external focus (Krohne, 2002)Stress occurs when an individual perceives that the demands of an external situation are beyond his or her perceived ability to cope with them (Lazarus, 1966). Stress is an unavoidable accompaniment of everyday life (Skinner, Zautra & Reich, 2004). Stress can cause numerous deleterious changes in health. Stress appears to accelerate the aging process by shortening the lifespan of cells, thereby opening the door to disease (Epel et al., 2004). Some examples of stress-related illnesses are tension headaches, nervous colitis, nausea, irritable bowel syndrome, anxiety, low self-esteem, depression, hives, insomnia, compulsive eating, fatigue, low back pain, stiff neck and shoulders, chest pains, and irritability (Koesten, 2005; Tangri, 2003; Weisman, 2002).

Stress from personal finances is perceived to be one of the most influential sources of stress because many basic life activities are associated with personal financial resources and their management (Peirce et al., 1996). Financial stress is something that many adults experience. Prolonged financial stress over credit problems, for example, can have negative effects on physical and mental health (Kim, Garman & Sorhaindo, 2003). Lyons and Yilmazer (2005) found financial stress to be a predictor of illness-based absenteeism from the workplace. And also they found that poor health significantly increased the probability of financial strain, but there was little evidence that financial strain contributes to poor health. Kim and Garman (2004) examined financial stress and performance in the workplace and found that employee financial stress was related to negative attitudes and behaviors at work. They suggested that employers should offer financial education programs and counseling to their employees as a way of increasing satisfaction with pay, and worker productivity. Financial distress/Financial well-being has also been described as one's feelings about and reactions to one's personal financial condition (Prawitz et al., 2006). Garman, Sorhaindo, Bailey, Kim, & Xiao (2004a) describe financial distress as an intense physical or mental strain that includes concerns and worries about financial matters. Financial distress can be temporary but it is also can turn into and become a persistent state of being illustrative events that could contribute to financial distress are receiving overdue notices from creditors and collection agencies, writing checks with insufficient funds, and experiencing feelings of insecurity about one's financial preparedness a for retirement. A common cause of financial distress is recognizing that one has too much debt. Distress about financial matters, much like distress about poor family relationships or unemployed, can have deleterious effects one's physical and mental health (Garman et al., 2004b). Drentea and Lavrakas (2000) used data from a representative sample of more than 900 adults in Ohio, they found that a high debt-to- income ratio was significantly related to worse physical health and health status, noting that the financial strain associated with this financial condition clearly constituted a stressor that affected health. They also explained that both credit card debt and stress regarding debt are associated with health. Having more stress about overall debt also was associated with worse health, prompting concern

Figure 1. General model of the effect of financial stress on families (Conger et al., 1993)

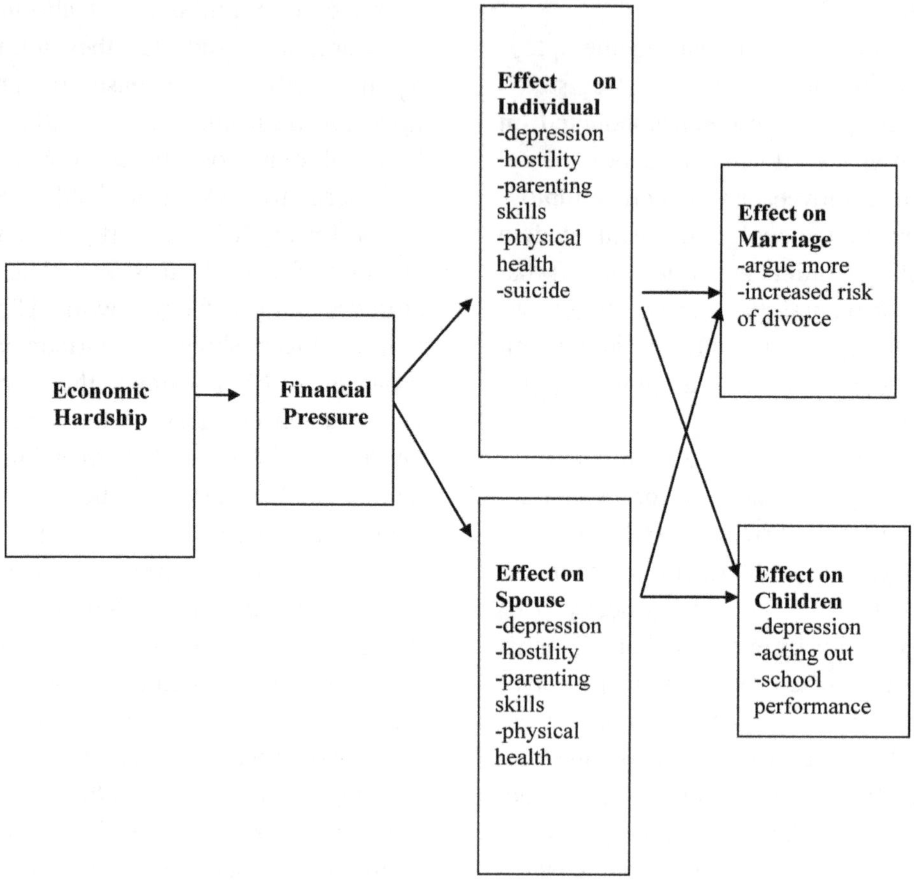

that indebtedness may provide a source chronic strain on financial well-being.

Conger at al. (1993) propose a family systems model that suggests that financial stress has direct on the primary income earner, and then indirectly has an impact on the material relationship, which in turn has an effect on children. A simplified version of this model is given schematically in Figure 1.

Financial strain/stress/distress is subjective reactions. Measuring these reactions can help researchers understand individuals' perceptions about and reactions to their financial condition. Although objective measures of an individual's financial state (household income and / or debt-to-income ratio) provide evidence of where one stands financially, two individuals with the same levels of income and economic resources may have different levels of perceived financial distress and financial well-being (O'Neill et al., 2006a). Two individuals with the same levels of income and economic resources may have different levels of perceived financial distress. Financial distress can last a short time, or it can become a persistent state for families at all income levels. Occurrence of stressors events, sometimes called negative financial events, can contribute to financial distress (O'Neill, et al., 2006b).

Financial distress is different from negative financial events, sometimes referred to as negative stressor events. Occurrence of negative financial events can contribute to financial distress. Financially distressed consumers often report no or low savings and high household debt (O'Neill et al., 2006 a,b). O'Neil, Sorhaindo, Xiao & Garman

(2005a), in a study of financially distressed consumers, found that positive changes in financial practices also reported improved health.

Distress about financial matters is real and increasingly prevalent in society. Most people who contact a consumer credit counseling agency to seek assistance have serious debt problems that create substantial stress in their lives. For these people there likely are negative spillover effects from their distress about financial issues on their health and family relationships as well as on their effectiveness at their place of employment, for those who are employed (Garman et al., 2004a).

Financial distress can result in or result from poor health, or both. Distress and worry about the family's financial situation may also contribute to negative health outcomes and losses beyond the boundaries of the family system. For example, limited finances have been known to negatively affect health, but one's health may have negatively affected one's financial state (Prawitz et al., 2006). Personal finance can negatively affect health because overdue medical debt can result in delayed or inadequate treatment and resulting anxiety. Personal finances can also be negatively affected by health as when increased medical expenses result in lower lifetime asset accumulation and a poor credit history from unpaid medical bills (O'Neill et al., 2005a). Persons experiencing financial distress may also be unable to follow recommended health maintenance practices such as eating a healthy diet and receiving periodic screening exams (O'Neill et al., 2005b).

Common response of financial distress include:

- Anxiety
- Depression
- Post-traumatic stress
- Severe grief
- Alcohol or drug abuse
- Nightmares
- Panic
- Overwhelming levels of stress
- Confusion
- Feelings of detachment
- Feeling surreal
- Over or under eating
- Inability to sleep (or excess sleep)
- Diarrhea
- Nausea
- Upset stomach
- And other physical and mental symptoms of stress and depression (AAMFT, 2014).

Some self-reported health effects of financial problems included worrying, and tension; insomnia, headaches and migraines, high blood pressure, hypertension, stomach problems, ulcers and possible ulcers, weight gain or loss, fatigue and feeling tired/weak, drug, alcohol or cigarette use, and inability to afford or access recommended health maintenance practices (O'Neill et al., 2005a,b).

Financial stress is a sadly widespread experience. *Anxiety* over money can negatively affect health in several ways:

- **Unhealthy Coping Behaviors:** People experiencing financial stress can be more likely to numb their anxiety by drinking, smoking, overeating and practicing other *unhealthy coping behaviors*. This in turn leads to more stress.
- **Less Money for Self-Care:** With less money in the budget, people who are already under financial stress tend to cut corners in areas like health care to pay for basic necessities like food. Small problems can go unchecked and turn into larger problems. This also leads to more stress.
- **Lost Sleep:** When under financial stress, people often experience *trouble sleeping*, which can add up to a sleep deficit, impairing immune functioning and cognitive abilities, causing additional moodiness, and more.
- **Unhealthy Emotions:** Credit card debt can cause unhealthy emotions that can take a toll on health. People can experience anxiety, frustration and a sense of hopelessness

> as the debt piles up and increasing amounts of money are needed just to pay the interest. This causes additional stress, which compounds with the stress from poor coping and self-neglect, to become a menacing amount of stress (Scott, 2011).

Sociological research data indicate that four factors strongly predict happiness and overall well-being in most cultures: health, economic status, employment, and family relationships. People are happier when they are healthy, employed, married or in a committed relationship, and financially secure (O'Neill et al, 2005b). Health and personal finance issues, individually and in combination with each other. Major societal trends that have been widely reported in recent years include an increasing incidence of obesity and diabetes, low household savings rates, and high household debt. There is evidence of many parallels between factors such as environmental controls that affect good health and foster financial success. Health and wealth are also related on a macro level. Modest reductions in the death rate from common killers, such as cancer and heart disease, can lead to trillions of dollars in economic benefits (O'Neill et al., 2005ba).

A number of researchers have examined factors contributing to psychological well-being and found economic distress to be a good predictor of lower levels of well-being (Blumstein & Schwartz, 1983; Mills, Grasmick, Morgan, & Wenk, 1992; Mirowsky & Ross, 2003; Pittman & Lloyd, 1988; Ross & Huber, 1985). Further, Colledge (1982) cautioned that the effect of economic conditions on mental health will be mitigated by socioeconomic status, with the mental health of poorer individuals being negatively affected to a greater extent. Thus, it can be seen that although there is clearly a relation between economic conditions and psychological difficulties, several factors seem to mitigate the magnitude of the effect and the exact nature of the relationship remains largely unknown (Lea, Tarpy & Webley, 1987).

O'Neill et al. (2005a) found that those individuals who had the highest level of financial distress reported being in poorer health while individuals who reported they were in better health had a lower level of financial stress. Copur, Gutter & Erkal (2014) examined the relationship between financial distress and health and financial behaviors among families in Ankara, they found a significant differences in financial distress levels by socioeconomic factors and financial behaviors. In addition, regression analysis showed that saving and self-reported health status was significantly related distress when controlling other factors.

The Garman, Junk et al. (2005) study was released five conclusions. The five conclusions were:

1. Thirty million workers–about a quarter of working adults–are seriously financially distressed.
2. People who are financially distressed often live paycheck-to-paycheck and are dissatisfied with their financial situation.
3. Poor health and financial distress are related.
4. Personal financial problems negatively impact workers' productivity.
5. Financial problems are not confined to lower income levels.

Krause, Jay & Liang (1991) developed a model that attempts to make a more precise accounting of the relationship between financial distress and feelings of psychological wellbeing. Based on concepts developed by Caplan (1981) to account for the manner in which stressful life events erode individuals' feelings of self-worth and control, the model of Krause et al. (Figure 2) basically shows perception of chronic financial stress erodes both individuals' feelings of personal control over their economic life as well their feelings of self-esteem. Further, the weakening of these two personal characteristics is associated with a decrease in well-being as measured by tests of depression and somatic symptoms. Krause et al., however, cau-

Figure 2. Model of the relationship between financial strain and psychological well-being in the elderly proposed by Krause, Jay & Liang (1991)

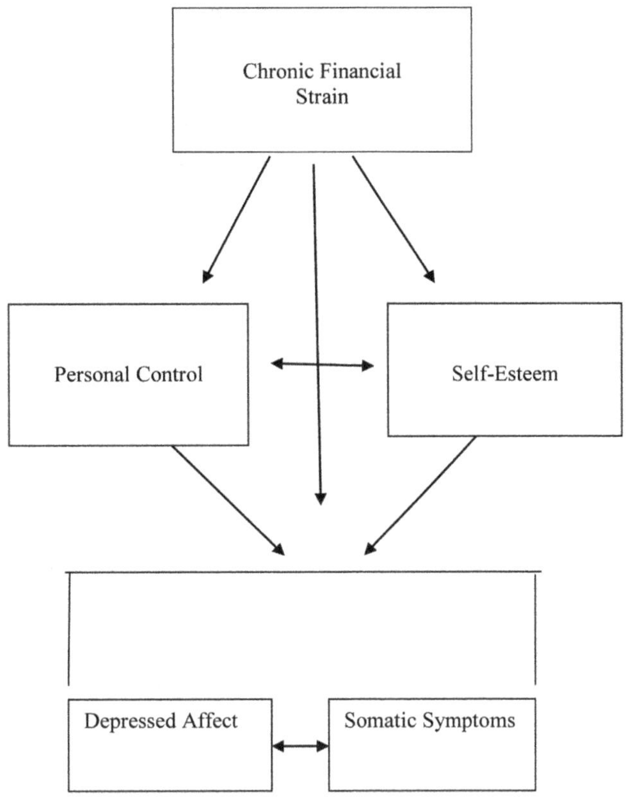

tioned this model was a tentative one and needed further testing to define the relationship between individuals' perceptions of economic distress and psychological health (Lange & Byrd, 1998).

Despite the overall negative effects of financial distress on health reported in the literature, individuals and families varied in their reactions to financial distress. Stress theory has been used to account for differential responses to stressors by examining the process and factors that affect relationships between a stressor and individual and family outcomes. Research on the effects of life events on health has examined several additive and interactive models to determine the influence of coping resources and behaviors including social support (Vaydonoff & Donnely, 1989: 139).

CONCLUSION

Some individually used strategies play important roles in dealing with financial stress. The common aspect of approximately all of these strategies is that they anticipate for taking physical, psychological and behavioral structures under control. So, very hazardous stress response starting in the body is tried to be prevented from by taking counter measures (Pehlivan, 1995). It is necessary to efficiently deal with financial stress (Güçlü, 2001). The individuals should be informed on the finance management they possess to prevent from stress. It is also important that the training programs on this subject are prepared and the individuals are informed by also benefiting from the mass media within the scope of formal education and informal education. Financial educators and counselors should help financially distressed families so that families better deal with any financial problems or challenges.

REFERENCES

American Association for Marriage and Family Therapy. (2014). *Financial Stress & the Family* Retrieved May 22, 2014 from http://www.aamft.org/imis15/Content/Consumer_Updates/Financial_Distress.aspx

Blumstein, P. W., & Schwartz, P. (1983). *American couples: money, work, sex*. New York: William Morrow.

Caman Karadağ & Cilingiroğlu. (2009). Ekonomik krizler ve sağlığa etkisi. *Toplum Hekimliği Bülteni*, *28*(2), 1–11.

Caplan, G. (1981). Mastery of stress: Psychological aspects. *The American Journal of Psychiatry*, *138*(4), 413–420. doi:10.1176/ajp.138.4.413 PMID:7212098

Colledge, M. (1982). Economic cycles and health: Towards a sociological understanding of the impact of the recession on health and illness. *Social Science & Medicine*, *16*(22), 1919–1927. doi:10.1016/0277-9536(82)90391-4 PMID:7157025

Conger, R., Conger, K., Elder, G., Lorenz, F., Simons, R., & Whitbeck, L. (1993). Family economic status and adjustment of early adolescent girls. *Developmental Psychology*, *29*(2), 206–219. doi:10.1037/0012-1649.29.2.206

Copur, Z., Gutter, S. M., & Erkal, S. (2014). Behavioral approach to financial distress and health: Globalization of financial institutions. In Dinçer, H., Hacioğlu (Ed.), A Competitive Approach of Finance and Banking, (pp: 217-233). Switzerland: Springer International Publishing. doi:10.1007/978-3-319-01125-7_16

Drentea, P., & Lavrakas, P. J. (2000). Over the limit: The association among health status, race and debt. *Social Science & Medicine*, *50*(4), 517–529. doi:10.1016/S0277-9536(99)00298-1 PMID:10641804

Epel, E. S., Blackburn, E. H., Lin, J., Dhabhar, F. S., Adler, N. E., Morrow, J. D., & Cawthon, R. M. (2004). Accelerated telomere shortening in response to life stress. *Proceedings of the National Academy of Sciences of the United States of America*, *101*(49), 17312–17315. www.pnas.org/cgi/doi/10.1073/pnas.0407162101 Retrieved January 27, 2005

Garman, E. T., Junk, V. W., Kim, J., O'Neill, B. J., Prochaska-Cue, K., Prawitz, A. D., ... (2005). *Financial stress among American workers, Final report*. Retrieved March, 23, 2005, from http://www.personalfinancefoundation.org/features/Financial-Distress-Among-American-Workers-Final-Report-full.html

Garman, E. T., Sorhaindo, B., Bailey, W., Kim, J., & Xiao, J. J. (2004a). Financially Distressed Credit Counseling Clients and the InCharge Financial Distress Scale, *Proceedings of the Eastern Regional Family Economics and Resource Management Association* (pp.71-81).

Garman, E. T., Sorhaindo, B., Kim, J., Xiao, J. J., Bailey, W., & Prawitz, A. (2004b). The evaluation of the beta version of the ıncharge financial distress scale. *Consumer Interests Annual*, *50*, 134–144.

Güçlü, N. (2001). Stres yönetimi. *G.Ü. Gazi Eğitim Fakültesi Dergisi*, *21*(1), 91–109.

Kim, J., Garman, T., & Sorhaindo, B. (2003). Relationship among credit counseling clients' financial well-being, financial behaviors, financial stressor events, and health. *Financial Counseling and Planning*, *14*(2), 75–87.

Koesten, J. (2005). Reducing stress and burnout for financial planners. *Journal of Financial Planning*, *18*(10), 64–74.

Krause, N., Jay, G., & Liang, J. (1991). Financial strain and psychological wellbeing among the American and Japanese elderly. *Psychology and Aging*, *6*(2), 170–181. doi:10.1037/0882-7974.6.2.170 PMID:1863386

Krohne, H. W. (2002). *Stress and coping theories*. Retrieved March 10, 2014, from http://userpage.fu-berlin.de/schuez/folien/Krohne_Stress.pdf

Lange, C., & Byrd, M. (1998). The relationship between perception of financial distress and feelings of psychological well-being in New Zeland university students. *International Journal of Adolescence and Youth*, *7*(3), 193–209. doi:10.1080/02673843.1998.9747824

Lazarus, R. S. (1966). *Psychological Stress and the coping process*. New York: McGraw-Hill.

Lea, S. E. G., Tarpy, R. M., & Webiey, P. (1987). *The individual in the economy*. Cambridge: Cambridge University Press.

Lyons, A. C., & Yılmazer, T. (2005). Health and financial strain: Evidence from the survey of consumer finances. *Southern Economic Journal*, *71*(4), 873–890. doi:10.2307/20062085

Mills, R. J., Grasmick, H. G., Morgan, C. S., & Wenk, D. (1992). The effects of gender, family satisfaction, and economic strain on psychological well-being. *Family Relations*, *41*(4), 440–446. doi:10.2307/585588

Mirowsky, J., & Ross, C. (2003). *Social causes of psychological distress* (2nd ed.). New York: Aldine de Gruyter.

O'Neill, B., Prawitz, A. D., Sorhaindo, B., Kim, J., & Garman, E. T. (2006a). Financial distress: Definition, effects and measurement. *Consumer Interests Annual*, *52*, 458–465.

O'Neill, B., Prawitz, A. D., Sorhaindo, B., Kim, J., & Garman, E. T. (2006b). Changes in health, negative financial events, and financial distress/financial well-being for debt management program clients. *Financial Counseling and Planning*, *17*(2), 46–63.

O'Neill, B., Sorhaindo, B., Xiao, J. J., & Garman, E. T. (2005b). Negative health effects of financial stress. *Consumer Interests Annual*, *51*(3). Retrieved from URL: www.consumerinterests.org/i4a/pages/Index.cfm?pageid=4077

O'Neill, B., Xiao, J. J., Sorhaindo, B., & Garman, E. T. (2005a). Financially distressed consumers: Their financial practices, financial well-being, and health. *Financial Counseling and Planning*, *16*(1), 71–85.

Pehlivan, İ. (1995). *Yönetimde stres kaynakları*. Ankara: Pegem Yayınları.

Peirce, R. S., Frone, M. R., Russell, M., & Cooper, M. L. (1996). Financial stress, social support, and alcohol involvement: A longitudinal test of the buffering hypothesis in a general population survey. *Health Psychology*, *15*(1), 38–47.

Pittman, J. F., & Lloyd, S. A. (1988). Quality of family life, social support, and stress. *Journal of Marriage and the Family*, *50*(1), 53–67. doi:10.2307/352427

Prawitz, A. D., Garman, E. T., Sorhaindo, B., O'Neill, B., Kim, J., & Drentea, P. (2006). InCharge financial distress /financial well-being scale: Development, administration and score interpretation. *Journal of Financial Counseling & Planning*, *1*, 34–50.

Ross, C., & Huber, J. (1985). Hardship and depression. *Journal of Health and Social Behavior*, *26*(4), 312–327. doi:10.2307/2136655 PMID:4086755

Scott, E. (2011). *Financial stress: How it affects you and what you can do*. Retrieved May, 16, 2011, from http://stress.about.com/od/financialstress/a/financialstress.htm

Skinner, M. A., Zautra, A. J., & Reich, J. W. (2004). Financial stress predictors and the emotional and physical health of chronic pain patients. *Cognitive Therapy and Research*, *28*(5), 695–713.

Tangri, R. (2003). *Stress costs stress-cures: How to recover productivity lost to stress*. Retrieved January 22, 2013, from www.Stress-Cures.com

Ulas, H., & Kaya, B. (2009). Ekonomik krizin ruh sağlığına etkileri ve çözüm önerileri. *TPD Bülteni*, *12*(1), 59–62.

Vaydonoff, P., & Donnely, B. W. (1989). Economic distress and mental health: The role of family coping resources and behaviors. *Lifestyles*, *10*(2), 139–162. doi:10.1007/BF00988534

Weisman, R. (2002). Personal financial stress, depression, and workplace performance. In E. T. Garman, F. Williams, R. Weisman, H. Fried, W. A. Kelly, & W. W. Sayles (Eds.), *Financial stress and workplace performance: Developing employer-credit union partnerships*. Madison, WI: Center for Credit Union Innovation and Filene Research Institute.

World Health Organization (WHO). (2009). *The financial crisis and global health, report on a high-level consultation* (pp. 1–6). Geneva: WHO.

ADDITIONAL READING

Choi, L. (2009). Financial Stress and its physical effects on individuals and communities. *Community Development and Investment Review*, 120-122. Retrieved from www.frbsf.org/community.../files/choi.pdf

Clark-Lempers, D., Lempers, J. D., & Netusil, A. J. (1990). Family financial stress, parental support, and young adolescents' academic achievement and depressive symptoms. *The Journal of Early Adolescence*, *10*(1), 21–36. doi:10.1177/0272431690101002

Conger, R. D., Ge, X. J., & Lorenz, F. O. (1994). Economic stress and marital relations. In R. Conger, (Eds.), *Families in troubled times: Adapting to change in rural America. Social institutions and social change* (pp. 187–203). Hawthorne, NY: Aldine de Gruyter.

Drentea, P. (2000). Age, debt and anxiety. *Journal of Health and Social Behavior*, *41*(4), 437–450. doi:10.2307/2676296 PMID:11198567

Ettner, S. L. (1996). New evidence on the relationship between income and health. *Journal of Health Economics*, *15*(1), 67–85. doi:10.1016/0167-6296(95)00032-1 PMID:10157429

Fox, G. L., & Chancey, D. (1998). Sources of economic distress: Individual and family outcomes. *Journal of Family Issues*, *19*(6), 725–749. doi:10.1177/019251398019006004

Frydman, H., Altman, E. I., & Kao, D. (1985). Introducing Recursive Partitioning for Financial Classification: The Case of Financial Distress. *The Journal of Finance*, *60*(1), 269–291. doi:10.1111/j.1540-6261.1985.tb04949.x

Garman, E. T., Leech, I. E., & Grable, J. E. (1996). The negative impact of employee poor personal financial behaviors on employers. *Financial Counseling and Planning*, *7*, 157–168.

Ge, X., Conger, R. D., Lorenz, F. O., Elder, G. H. Jr, Montague, R. B., & Simons, R. L. (1992). Linking family economic hardship to adolescent distress. *Journal of Research on Adolescence*, *2*(4), 351–378. doi:10.1207/s15327795jra0204_4

Hagquist, C. E. I. (1998). Economic stress and perceived health among adolescents in Sweden. *The Journal of Adolescent Health*, *22*(3), 250–257. doi:10.1016/S1054-139X(97)00168-7 PMID:9502015

Hobfall, S. E., & Spielberger, C. D. (1992). Family stress: Integrating theory and measurement. *Journal of Family Psychology*, *6*(2), 99–112. doi:10.1037/0893-3200.6.2.99

Kessler, R. C., Turner, J. B., & House, J. S. (1989). Unemployment, reemployment, and emotional functioning in a community sample. *American Sociological Review*, *54*(4), 648–657. doi:10.2307/2095885

Kim, J., & Garman, E. T. (2003). Financial stress and absenteeism: An empirically derived model. *Financial Counseling and Planning*, *14*(1), 31–42.

Kokko, K., & Pulkkinen, L. (1998). Unemployment and psychological distress: Mediator effects. *Journal of Adult Development*, *5*(4), 205–217. doi:10.1023/A:1021450208639

Lau, A. H. (1987). A Five-State Financial Distress Prediction Model. *Journal of Accounting Research*, *25*(Spring), 127–138. doi:10.2307/2491262

Lempers, J. D., Clark-Lempers, D., & Simons, R. L. (1989). Economic hardship, parenting, and distress in adolescence. *Child Development*, *60*(1), 25–39. doi:10.2307/1131068 PMID:2702872

Liker, J. K., & Elder, G. H. (1983). Economic hardship and marital relations in the 1930s. *American Sociological Review*, *48*(3), 343–359. doi:10.2307/2095227 PMID:6614668

Porter, N. M., & Garman, E. T. (1993). Testing a conceptual model of financial well-being. *Financial Counseling and Planning*, *4*, 135–164.

Rantakeisu, U., Starrin, B., & Hagquist, C. (1999). Financial hardship and shame: A tentative model to understand the social and health effects of unemployment. *British Journal of Social Work*, *29*(6), 877–901. doi:10.1093/bjsw/29.6.877

Regnier, P. (2003, Fall). Health and money. *Money*, *32*(11), 14–19.

Schipper, K. (1977). Financial Distress in Private Colleges. *Journal of Accounting Research*, *15*(Supplement), 1–40. doi:10.2307/2490628

Starkey, A. J. (2011). *Financial Distress and Depressive Symptoms among African American Women: Exploring the Role of Religious Coping and Social Support.* Doctoral Dissertation, University of Pittsburgh.

Viet, C. T., & Ware, J. E. (1983). The structure of psychological distress and well-being in general populations. *Journal of Consulting and Clinical Psychology*, *51*(5), 730–742. doi:10.1037/0022-006X.51.5.730 PMID:6630688

Vinokur, A. D., Price, R. H., & Caplan, R. D. (1996). Hard times and hurtful partners: How financial strain affects depression and relationship satisfaction of unemployed persons and their spouses. *Journal of Personality and Social Psychology*, *71*(1), 166–179. doi:10.1037/0022-3514.71.1.166 PMID:8708998

Zmijewski, M. E. (1984). Methodological Issues Related to the Estimation of Financial Distress Prediction Models. *Journal of Accounting Research*, *22*(Suppl.), 59–86. doi:10.2307/2490859

KEY TERMS AND DEFINITIONS

Finance: The science that describes the management, creation and study of money, banking, credit, investments, assets and liabilities. Finance can also be defined as the science of money management.

Financial Distress: Financial distress is a term in corporate finance used to indicate a condition when promises to creditors of a company are broken or honored with difficulty.

Financial Problems: A financial problem is a situation in which you are not able to meet your bills on time or afford necessary basic needs.

Financial Well-Being: Informed decision making and learning how to save, invest, use credit wisely, and plan for the future.

Health: Health is a state of complete physical, mental and social well-being and not merely the absence of disease or infirmity.

Chapter 8
Measuring the Poverty of Elderly People with Needs Analysis in Turkey

Emine Özmete
Ankara University, Turkey

ABSTRACT

This study aimed to analyze the economic, social, and cultural needs of elderly people to determine the poverty thereof in Ankara (the capital city of Turkey).The economic, social, and cultural needs of individuals, which are among the indicators taken into consideration by United Nations Development Programme (UNDP) in measurement of human poverty index, were subject to research in measurement of poverty of elderly people. Face-to-face surveys were conducted with individuals over 65 years of age in the study, with 2.522 surveys qualified for evaluation. It was seen that the majority of elderly people were covered by social security. The elderly people reported their health to be good. They stated satisfaction regarding interindividual relationships with regard to social needs. However, it was concluded that the income of elderly people was not sufficient, and that they could not sufficiently afford electrical power and water invoices, medicine, food, and clothing expenses.

INTRODUCTION

In the old age, retirement results in a decrease in income, loss of usual social status, and an alteration in the relations and interactions. Besides, overlapping of losses that are manifest with such original problems as cognitive and physical recession, decline in productive role, change in social position, decrease in interpersonal support, and loss of health that emerge in this period results in poverty. As a notion, which is difficult to define and to determine the limits thereof, poverty has various aspects. Poverty is reflected to the lives of elderly people primarily "in the form of lack of income and productive resources sufficient to ensure sustainable livelihoods," along with "hunger and malnutrition; ill health; limited or lack of access to education and other basic services; increased morbidity and mortality from illness; homelessness and inadequate housing; unsafe environments; and social discrimination and exclusion. It is also characterized by a lack

DOI: 10.4018/978-1-4666-7484-4.ch008

of participation in decision-making and in civil, social and cultural life" (World Summit for Social Development Programme of Action, UN). This study was inspired by both the limited number of scientific studies on poverty of elderly people, and by the fact that having foreseen the number of individuals over 65 years of age, who constitute the dependent population, would also increase in Turkey as it was the case throughout the world, the national and international institutions and organizations focused on initiatives to ensure healthy and successful aging by determining economic, social, and cultural needs of elderly people.

According to the Address Based Population Registration System (ADNKS) by the Turkish Statistical Institute (TUIK), the total population of Turkey is 76 million 667 thousand people (2013), composed of 50.2% (n=38.473.360) male, and 49.8% (n=38.194.504) female citizens. The median age in Turkey, which was 30.1 in 2012, increased to 30.4 in 2013. The median age of men and women were 29.8, and 31 respectively. The ratio of elderly people aging65 years and over was 7.3% in 2011 (n=5.490.715). The same ratio was 7.5%in 2012, and increased to 7.7% in 2013. Pursuant to the population projections, it is predicted that this ratio will increase to 10.2% in 2023, 20.8% in 2050, and 27.7% in 2075. In line with these ratios it can be asserted that Turkey has completed the mature population period and passed to elderly population period.

In this section, the level of ability of elderly people to meet economic, social, and cultural needs, which is among the indicators taken into consideration by United Nations Development Programme (UNDP) in measurement of human poverty index, will be analyzed. The scope of economic, social, and cultural needs can be explained as follows:

In the scope of the *economic needs*, the level of ability of elderly people to meet basic needs and life standards thereof will be determined so as to obtain information and measure awareness with regard to having economic/material resources along with their use and control.

In the scope of the *social needs*, data will be collected concerning the quality of relations and communication of elderly individuals with other family members, their permanent network of relations, also including friends, neighbors, and relatives, their interaction with this network of relations, intergeneration solidarity, social support systems, and confidence.

Finally, educational background, cultural values, habits, and whether the totality of the foregoing reflected concretely and objectively in the form of such documentation as diplomas etc., certain indicators regarding their lives in connection with the culture inherited from the family (age of marriage, last school of graduation etc.), social participation, and the ways of recreation will be determined in the scope of the *cultural needs*.

BACKGROUND

Having existed since the day human beings started to live together, poverty has been subject to a more intense debate especially after growth stalled in developed countries, people steered by the market, and increase underemployment during the foregoing process. Poverty at global and international level has macro reasons along with micro reasons specific to individual, family, and society (Oktik, 2008). The most important society-specific reason is inequality due to income distribution in a given country. Income differences between individuals, regions, and families living in the same city are considered the most important reason of poverty. Economic crises, inflation, and accordingly decrease in the purchasing power of individuals, difficulty or failure in meeting basic needs results in the fact that low-income individuals and families feel poverty deeply (Jehoel-Gijsbers & Vrooman, 2007). However, meeting basic needs at a sufficient level in accordance with the geographical location, the current conditions, and the standards of the social environment based on one's own opportunities are considered the purpose and a condition to subsist for each social individual.

Meeting basic needs in accordance with the current condition and the standard of the society is a must for individuals to sustain a humane life (Yunus, 1999). At this point, in its simplest form, poverty is defined as the status of the inability to meet one's basic needs for a humane life by one's own means. Nevertheless, it is argued that having focused only on meeting basic needs, this definition is not sufficient to explain poverty. This is because of the fact that poverty also brings deprivation (Devicienti & Poggi, 2007; Özmete, 2011). Therefore there emerge two different approaches with regard to the definition of poverty adopted especially by social scientists: Absolute poverty and relative poverty.

"Absolute poverty is a condition characterized by severe deprivation of basic human needs, including food, safe drinking water, sanitation facilities, health, shelter, education and information" (World Summit for Social Development Programme of Action, UN). Absolute poverty definition is based on the basic conditions that should be sustained in order to subsist, i.e. to reinforce a physically healthy existence. In other words absolute poverty is defined as having little or no income in kind or in cash necessary for individual or household members to meet minimum basic needs to survive. In most developing countries, caloric intake and minimum calorie thresholds are used to assess hunger and nutrition and to construct poverty lines.

Relative poverty; each household's income, adjusted for family size, is compared to median income (The median is the "middle" income: half of people have more than the median and half have less). Those with less than 60 per cent of median income are classified as poor. This 'poverty line' is the agreed international measure used throughout the European Union (Zastrow, 2008). Absolute poverty is the complete lack of resources to sustain life, while relative poverty refers to the inadequate lack of income when compared to the average standards living. As such, relative poverty implies that the individual has the ability to sustain his or her basic needs, but may lack the resources to engage in various social activities. The World Development Report on Poverty by the World Bank, published in 1990, defined poverty as "the inability to attain a minimal standard of living" and considered poverty as the relation of a part of individuals in the society with life standard (World Bank, 1990, pp. 24-39). World Bank defines poverty as the inability of individuals and households to attain even the lowest life standards (World Bank, 2000).

In Turkey, Article 4 of the Regulation on Assistance in Cash and in Kind, by the Ministry of Family and Social Policies defined poverty as "the status of deprivation of insufficiency of income, riches, or revenue necessary to sustain one's own life, one's spouse and children, and parents, which the individual is obliged to look after, at a minimum level according to the current life conditions" (Ministry of Family and Social Policies). There are difficulties with explaining both the absolute and relative poverty. This is because of the fact that there are determinants especially of relative poverty, which varies from one individual to another, one family to another and one society to another. Standard considered necessary needs in a society may be perceived as luxury in another society. For instance, city water supply (usable clean water), regular vegetable and fruit consumption are considered basic need for a healthy life and those who cannot access the foregoing are defined as impoverished in the developed countries. However in many underdeveloped or developing countries, these details are not considered standards and poverty is not determined with respect to the existence or non-existence thereof. This is because of the fact that, while the societies develop and their life standards rise, the relative poverty understanding is also subject to change. Despite at the beginning of the industrialization process such items as refrigerators, washing machines, and telephones were perceived as luxury goods, today they are seen as necessities to actively engage with the life especially in the developed societies (Maxwell, 1999; Soyak, 2004; Şahin, 2010).

The increasing life expectancy phenomenon forces the people to have enough money to meet their needs in old age. Therefore the finance matter is vital for the elderly. With increasing life expectancy, people have to seek continuing wealth throughout their extended old age (DeVaney, 1995; Hogarth, 1991). This is because living longer will increase the chances of experiencing poverty and outliving available income and assets. Changes in work, health status, independence to dependence, and all these changes cannot be carried out without money. Thus, finance is vital for this group of older persons. The term "finance" refers to, how an individual manage his/her personal resources. It does mean that one knows what his financial resources are, and understand how the resources can best manage for him now and in the future. As elderly, individuals seek to improve the management of their economic resources and develop plans for strengthening their financial position in the future; a logical first step is to determine their present financial position. Financial status of elderly is able to picture the financial situations of an individual, how wealthy are they? How much money do they make? How much are their spending? What are their spending it on? To survive financially, they have to know whole of financial pictures. Financial behavior refers to the process people use in managing their financial resources to achieve financial success in the areas of retirement plans, financial planning, credit, and money management. Older persons are unable to sustain themselves and keep up with inflationary costs without depending on children and other family members. At the same time in older age some cultural, social and economic factors affect financial behavior of elderly people (Parsa, 2008).

The following items provide an overview of the different types of vulnerabilities faced by individuals at different points in older age, focusing on employment-related risks and vulnerabilities in terms of financial behavior (Bird, 2007).

- Loss of income when work is lost due to age discrimination frailty/illness etc.
- Work in informal sector throughout life means that there is no contributory pension provision.
- Poor health in later life due to poor nutrition, multiple childbirth, poor working environment and lack of health care.
- Continuing to work to support self and dependents in low-income earning and often physically disabled jobs.
- Widow's loss of access to late husband's family resources.
- Increased childcare responsibilities where middle age adults have been lost to HIV and AIDS leaving dependent children in the care of grandparents.
- Increased likelihood of age-related disability and chronic illness.

The argumentation above suggest that absolute poverty is not sufficient to define poverty, that relative deprivation should also be explained, and that poverty should be measured by more comprehensive components thereof. The generally used components of poverty are:

1. Income and consumption-based measures.

These could be any one or all of the following variables: Household or individual incomes and/or consumption; in total and/or per capita terms; unweighted and/or normalized for household demographics (equivalence scale adjusted)

2. 'Human development' linked measures: The more commonly used indicators in this class relate to:

    a. **Health:** Life Expectancy; other mortality based indicators (age-specific mortality such as infant and child mortality, maternal mortality etc.); morbidity based indicators (such as

Disability Adjusted Life Expectancy, incidence of chronic ailments etc.); health infrastructure based indicators (doctors/hospitals per 100,000 populations by location etc.).

b. **Education:** Literacy rates, school enrolment ratio, and related indicators
c. **Wages and Income-Earning Opportunities:** Household and individual incomes, nature and extent of labour market participation etc.
d. **Infrastructure:** Community and household based; Physical (road, waterways, telecommunication networks per capita or per unit of land area); environmental (air and water pollution levels, availability of safe drinking water and sanitation, forest cover etc.); social (social capital, kinship network etc.), institutional (legal system, governance structures etc.) (Mukhopadyay & Shambhu, 2011).

Numerous studies analyzed poverty among the elderly (see Engelhardt & Gruber, 2004, Weir, Willis, & Sevak, 2004, McGarry & Schoeni, 2005, and Zaidi et al., 2006, for only a few recent examples). Most of these studies make use of income or expenditure data at the household level to count the number of individuals in poverty. As Deaton and Paxson (1998) indicate, this transition from households to individuals requires assumptions about the intra-household allocation of resources, about differences in needs and about the importance of economies of scale. Most of the analyses of elderly poverty ignore the issue of the intra-household distribution of resources by assuming that all individuals in a household are equally well off. The literature on intra-household allocation, though, convincingly demonstrated that resources are not equally shared within households (Cherchye, De Rock, & Vermeulen, 2008).

Taking into consideration measurements by income and consumption, one of the indicators to explain poverty in a society is without a doubt the income distribution. The issue of how to share the created values is related to distribution of equality, social justice, and freedom in society (Soyak, 2004). Despite it is observed that income distribution is more equitable and the range of inequality is narrower in governing processes, which put importance on social welfare and social justice, such factors as the unfair income distribution, decrease in national product per capita, consecutive economic crises, and failure of social and economic policies made poverty one of the prioritized issues both in the world and in Turkey (Buğra et al., 2003). The Human Development Report 2010 underlines the gap between women and men and the multidimensional poverty in South Asia and Africa based on long-term human development index. UNDP Coordinator Helen Clark stated on the basis of human development reports having been prepared each year since 1970 that; "There is much that countries can do to improve the quality of people's lives even under adverse circumstances. Many countries have made great gains in health and education despite only modest growth in income. Improvements are never automatic—they require political will, courageous leadership and the continuing commitment of the international community." (UNDP, 2010) Despite the improvements above, the report emphasized that about 1.75 billion people in the 104 countries were living in multidimensional poverty and that 1.44 billion people had to live on $1.25 a day or less (UNDP, 2010).

In Turkey the poverty rate was found to be 18.08% based on the poverty survey by TUIK in 2009. According to 2009 data, 0.48% of individuals, i.e. 339 thousand people, live under the hunger threshold based only on food expenses, and 18.8%, i.e. 12 million 751 thousand, live under poverty threshold based on food and non-food expenses.

It was estimated that the rate of individuals living under the poverty threshold as defined to be $2.15 a day was 0.22%, and the rate of impoverished individuals is 4.35%, provided that the poverty threshold was defined to be $4.3. While the poverty rate in rural population increased from 34.62% in 2008 to 38.69% in 2009, the same rate in urban population decreased from 9.38% to 8.86% in the same period (TUIK, 2011a).

Here an important emphasis should be placed on the deprivations arising from poverty. Most commentators consider that it is when material and social deprivation arise from lack of financial resources that we observe poverty. 'Deprivation' implies that people have unmet needs. 'Needs' must be defined and agreed upon in some way, and as will be seen throughout this report, this is an element of poverty measurement that is controversial and often overlooked. 'Deprivation' too must be defined and measured – to what extent must a need remain unfulfilled to comprise 'deprivation'? For example we may all agree that food is a basic human need, but would a person living in the country on a diet of only bread and water, or just chick peas and rice, be deprived? Deprivation is a continuum it is the combination of all resources that determines whether a person's needs are fulfilled or whether they are deprived. One type of resource (eg help from adult children, or excellent money management skills) may substitute for lack of another (eg low income). Two people might have the same amount of money (income, assets and access to credit), and the same amount of money over time, but through differences in for example personal histories, knowledge and skills, family support, social or charitable support networks, ability to access help from the state, housing conditions or local costs of living, one might be materially and socially deprived and the other not (Price, 2008).

Taking into consideration the measurements regarding the human development, the report published by the General Directorate on the Status of Women (2008) provide significant data. Accordingly it was stated that UNDP measured human poverty in developing countries based on three criteria: Life expectancy at birth, depriving of a long life, is considered the first indication of poverty. In UNDP measurements, the reference life expectancy at birth value is 40 years, and a value below that is considered an element of human poverty. Illiteracy, or depriving of educational opportunities, constitutes the second indicator of human poverty index. The illiteracy rate among adults is another criterion of human poverty in measurements. Economic and social opportunities, i.e. deprivation of individual of economic and social means are other indicators of human poverty index (General Directorate on the Status of Women /KSGM, 2008). UNDP explains the level of having economic and social means in terms of the percentage of population without access to healthy drinking water, percentage of population without access to basic healthcare, and percentage of undernourished population under 5 years of age. "Human poverty index value" is calculated by an average of life expectancy, education, and economic and social means. In accordance therewith, In Turkey the life expectancy of citizens less than 40 years is 5.7% (2005-2010), percentage of illiterate population over 15 years of age is 11.3% (1999-2007), percentage of population without access to clean water supply is 3% (2006), and the percentage of children under 5 years of age, who are below normal weight is 4% (2000-2006) (Human Development Report/HDR, 2009). According to a research by the World Bank in 2001, especially the rural single parent families, with the spouse, on whose income the family relied to live on, was dead, multi-child families (especially those having girl children) with disabled or dead (during military service) spouse were under threat of extreme poverty. Other groups under risk or fit to category of in need of care included those recently migrated to cities and lived in squatter settlements and the elderly people without any social security (World Bank, 2000).

On the other hand, poverty affects women more than men, and aggravates the already existed gender problems. Despite legal and institutional protection, sexual inequality cannot be overcome and that women have gradually become the face of the poverty in the world. The reason for the foregoing is that women are employed in low status and low-wage jobs and that the free work they conduct at home as family labor is not included in the national income calculations (Daly, 1992; Fukuda-Parr, 1999; Bora, 2007). In order to measure the sexual inequality in terms of human development, UNDP developed the Gender Related Development Index based on three basic criteria: (i) average life expectancy, (ii) education (literacy in men and women, schooling rates in men and women), and (iii) average income level (share of women and men in the income). The aim of this index is primarily to reveal the sexual inequality in terms of human poverty along with human development. According to the said index, such countries as Canada, Norway, Australia, USA, Iceland, Switzerland, and Belgium rank the top among 143 countries in terms of sexual inequality. In these countries the sexual inequality is far lower compared to others in terms of human development. The countries with the worse sexual inequality rates are listed as Niger, Burkina Faso, and Ethiopia. Turkey ranks 68th in the list comprised of 143 countries (UNDP, 2011).

It is known that poverty is a result of income inequality. The fact that a large portion of the added value goes to a few people as a result of unequal distribution of income both in domestic and international scale, accounts for the inevitable poverty of those who can have only a quite low portion of the said value added. In fact, welfare in terms of abundance, development, and freedom, and extreme poverty and the phenomena of deprivation as a result thereof coexist today (Maxwell, 1999). The United Nations National Security Strategy Statement emphasized the prevention of poverty and that wealth was a right that should be accessed by everyone, through the statement that "a world, in which some live in comfort and prosperity, while others have to live on less than $2 a day is neither fair, nor balanced. It is an ethical responsibility to have the impoverished people in the world benefited from the developments and opportunities' (UNDP, 2011).

Elderly people constitute a group, which is closely affected by economic developments at micro and macro levels. Changes in money/income resources of elderly people also result in changes in their life styles (Hablemitoğlu & Özmete, 2010; Turaman, 2007). Economic aging underscores these changes in the life of the individual. Especially retirement results in a decrease in income, loss of usual social status, and change in relations and interactions (Gönen & Hablemitoğlu, 1997). On the other hand, overlapping of losses that are manifest with such original problems as cognitive and physical recession, decline in productive role, change in social position, decrease in interpersonal support, and loss of health that emerge in this period results in poverty (Turaman, 2007). As a notion, which is difficult to define and to determine the limits thereof, poverty has various aspects. Poverty is reflected to the lives of elderly people primarily "in the form of lack of income and productive resources sufficient to ensure sustainable livelihoods," along with "hunger and malnutrition; ill health; limited or lack of access to education and other basic services; increased morbidity and mortality from illness; homelessness and inadequate housing; unsafe environments; and social discrimination and exclusion. It is also characterized by a lack of participation in decision-making and in civil, social and cultural life" (World Summit for Social Development Programme of Action, UN). This leads the way for massive poverty in many developing countries, and as poverty compared to the prosperous part of the society in developed countries. Income poverty is measured by the minimum income necessary to sustain one's life and means the lack of purchasing power. Income needed to buy a certain amount of food is defined as "poverty threshold." UNDP developed a new criterion of poverty, namely human poverty. Human poverty means that some individuals lack the opportunities to survive a humane life (UNDP, 2011). At this point, the need for measuring the poverty of elderly people becomes more prominent in order to make plans and conduct programs aiming prevention of elderly people.

The poverty report by the World Bank (2005) examined the rates of poverty by age in Turkey, where the percentage of elderly people aging 65 years and above was 7% (World Bank, 2005). While the dependency rate of elderly people was 6.8% in 1990, it increased to 8.8% in 2010 (European Commission, 2012). The elderly people think that they have become burdens for others due to their retirement, sufficient economic conditions, and decrease in productivity, which translates into a major psychological pressure for them. Especially the old men would describe themselves as "the old and tired workers" of life (Gratton, 1996). Furthermore, for those elderly people, who are not covered with any social security and live alone, this situation results in their isolation from the society, or even "dying silently" without being noticed by anybody.

"To revise the absolute poverty indicators, based on consumption expenditures published since 2002, Turkish Statistical Institution has started evaluation studies in collaboration with local and international experts in order to reveal the socio-economic situation of Turkey and enable the international comparisons. Within this scope; studies on feasible data sources and new estimation methods and works on calculation of new indicators are ongoing. Until the end up these studies, poverty rates in terms of dollars per day according to personal purchasing parity" (TurkStat Poverty Study, 2010). The TUIK poverty study 2012 results indicated that the poverty lines in terms of dollars per person/day according to personal purchasing parity were decreased. "Based on the $2.15-a-day poverty lines in current personal purchasing parity, percentage of poor in 2009 is 0.22% while it is 0.21% in 2010. Based on the $4.3-a-day poverty lines in current personal purchasing parity, percentage of poor in 2009 is 4.35% and it decreased to 3.66% in 2010." "Based on the $4.3-a-day poverty lines in current PPPs, percentage of poor in rural areas in 2009 is 11.92% and it decreases to 9.61% in 2010. Based on the $4.3-a-day poverty lines in current PPPs, percentage of poor in urban areas in 2009 is 0.96% while it is 0.97% in 2010" (TurkStat Poverty Study, 2010).

METHOD

The study was conducted in Ankara. According to the Address Based Population Registration System (ADNKS) by the Turkish Statistical Institute, the total population of Ankara is 4,550,662, with 2,268,598 male and 2,282,064 female residents.4,762,116 persons live in the Centrum, whereas 128,777 live in town and villages. According to TUIK (2011b) data 191,864 persons migrated to Ankara, and 137,385 migrated out of Ankara. The median age in Ankara is 34.2, and the same is 33.3 for men, and 35.2 for women. The numbers of married men and women in Ankara is 1,229,058 and 1,228,492 respectively (TUIK, 2011b).

Three-fourth of Ankara population is employed in the service sector, which has the largest share in the gross product of the city. The fact that service sector developed to such an extent can be attributed to the lack industry large enough to employ migrated population. Ankara holds 9% of the gross national product of Turkey. 12% of the tax income of the country and 12.3% of budget income is collected in Ankara; whereas the share of the city in the country budget is only 6.4%. In general, 60% of land in Ankara is used for agricultural purposes. Livestock sector gradually lose its previously important place in the city economy.

The study population is comprised of a total of 276,608 elderly individual aging between 65 and 89, living in the central districts of Ankara (Altındağ, Çankaya, Etimesgut, Keçiören, Mamak, Sincan, and Yenimahalle). In this process, the number of elderly individuals to be enrolled in the study in the scope of the central districts of Ankara was forecasted to be 2380, taking into consideration a confidence level of 95%, and a confidence interval of 2%.

The data collection tool enabling to determine the poverty of elderly people in terms of social, economic, and cultural needs was prepared in the form of a questionnaire based on open-ended and multiple-choice items. The questionnaire form was comprised of three basic sections. The first section included items introduced with an aim to obtain data on the household, where the elderly people lived in. The second section included questions to obtain information about the elderly individuals, such as sex, age, and marital status etc., and questions regarding the residence. The third section is consisted of open-ended and multiple-choice items to determine to what degree the economic, social and cultural needs of the elderly people were met/not met. Therefore the third section was analyzed under three titles of:

1. Economic Needs
2. Social Needs
3. Cultural Needs.

The first subsection included open-ended and multiple-choice questions regarding the economic needs of the elderly people in relation to money and income. The second subsection included open-ended and multiple-choice questions to reveal the social needs in the context of relations and communications such as the level of elderly people's contentedness about their relations with household members, the frequency to meet with children, grandchildren, friends, and neighbors. The third subsection was designed with open-ended and multiple-choice questions that enable measurement of cultural needs such as reading books and newspapers, daily average TV watching duration, and level of interest in actual events and social issues.

Having been developed as a data collection tool for the study, the questionnaire was tested before its application to elderly individuals in order to determine probable mistakes, and be sure about its reliability and validity. In the scope of the tests the questionnaire was applied to 50 voluntary elderly individuals, within the scope of study population, picked up by simple random sampling method. Serving also as a preliminary application, the approximate time needed to fill in the form was also determined in the course thereof, and the questionnaire was revised upon the opinions of the elderly individuals.

Despite the fact that the study population was determined to include 2,380 elderly individuals at the onset of the study, in practice the questionnaire was applied on one-to-one basis to 2,527 elderly individuals, and 5 questionnaires were excluded due to incomplete and inaccurate filling of the forms. Therefore, a total of 2,522 elderly individuals were included in the scope of the study. The study data were transferred to computer environment via statistical package software (SPSS 20), where filtering and control of the data conducted in electronic media.

RESULTS

In the study hereof, which focused on the elderly poverty, and the analysis of economic, social, and cultural needs, the finding were categorized under below titles:

1. General Information on Elderly People
2. Information on the Residence of Elderly People
3. Self-perception of the Elderly People regarding Aging
4. Poverty Analysis by the Economic, Social, and Cultural Needs of Elderly People

General Information on Elderly People

The percentages of elderly men and women participated in the study were 69.9%, and 30.1%, respectively. The percentage of elderly people in 65-74, 75-84, and 85-94 age groups were 63%, 31.4%, and 5.6%, respectively. 64.5% of the elderly people were married, where 32.0% lost their spouses, and 1.8% was divorced. 68.5% of the elderly people were married for 26-51 years. It was seen that 87.6% had both civil and religious marriage, 97.1% had children, and 93% had grandchildren. It was observed that nearly half (49%) of the elderly people were graduated from a primary education institution, and 20.7% were illiterate. 95.2% of the elderly people were retired and currently not employed in any job. 91% of the elderly people were covered by Social Security. 90.9% of the elderly people considered their health "good."

Information on the Residence of Elderly People and the Inventory of Durables Therein

The majority (75.9%) of elderly people resided at apartment houses. 90.9% of elderly people held the property of their residence. The residences mostly (91.7%) had three-four rooms, and the elderly people had their won room (90.9%). The inventory of durables in the residences of elderly people was listed as below:

- 79.5% had a telephone in the residence;
- 99.2% had a television in the residence;
- 99.0% had a refrigerator in the residence;
- 95% had a washing machine in the residence;
- 71.9% had a computer in the residence;
- 94.9% had an air-conditioner in the residence;
- 65.6% had cell phones in the residence;
- 87.9% did not have a digital camera/camera in the residence;
- 86.9% did not have a video/DVD player in the residence;
- 78% were contented with the comfort of their residence in general.

Self-Perception of Elderly People Regarding Aging

For 63.8% of the elderly people, aging started at below 65 years of age. 57.6% of the elderly people enrolled in the scope of the study felt themselves aged. 79.9% were contented with their physical look. 74.9% of the elderly people did not consider staying at nursing homes. 96.4% of the elderly people consider education of girls as important. 84.6% of the elderly people did not think then that they could make money based on their skills. A great majority (97.1%) of the elderly people consider themselves as religiously faithful-.

Poverty Analysis by the Economic, Social, and Cultural Needs of Elderly People

This section below provides the findings regarding the poverty of elderly people in terms of economic, social, and cultural needs, respectively.

Results of Poverty Analysis by Economic Needs of Elderly People

- The rental price charged for 35.5% of the elderly people in the scope of the study was TL250 ($120) or less. Where the same was TL351-450 ($150-220) for 24%, TL251-350 ($120-150) for 19.2%, TL451-550 ($225-250) for 12.5%, TL551-650 ($275-320) for 3.1%, and TL651-750 ($320-375) for 2.2%.
- It was seen that 85.1% of the elderly people did not possess a car, where 14.6% had their own automobiles.

- It was examined whether the income of the elderly people was sufficient to readily afford necessary food needs for balanced nutrition. In accordance therewith, 51.9% of the elderly people had sufficient income, whereas 47.7% did not.
- It was seen that 52.3% of the elderly people had sufficient income to cover health expenses, such as for medical doctors and medicine, however 46.4% did not have sufficient income to meet health needs including doctors and medicine etc.
- Approximately half of the elderly people (49.8%) stated that their income was not sufficient to afford such needs as clothing, shoes etc., whereas the other half (49.4%) declared that their income was sufficient for the purpose thereof.
- Approximately half of the elderly people (53.5%) had sufficient income to readily pay the water, electricity, and telephone bills etc. However, 45.7% of the elderly people did not have sufficient income to pay water, electricity, and telephone bills etc.
- It was seen that 79.1% of the elderly people could not allocate sufficient budget for such activities as excursions and travels; however 17.6% of the elderly people could have allocated sufficient budget for such activities as excursions and travels. 3.3% of the elderly people declined to answer this question.
- Upon examination of whether the elderly people enrolled in the study ever lent assistance to any person or institution during the previous year, it was seen that 59.3% of the elderly people did not lend any assistance to any person or institution, whereas 39.7% lent assistance to some persons or institutions.
- The elderly people enrolled in the study were asked to evaluate their economic status. Accordingly, 51.7% evaluated the same as "fair," 27.0% found their economic conditions as "poor," and that only 20.8% of the elderly people evaluated their economic status as "good."

Poverty Analysis by Social Needs of Elderly People

- It was found that 93.6% of the elderly people were contented with their relations with the household members residing with them. 2.7% were uncertain, 2% did not reply this question, and 1.7% was not contented with their relations with the household members.
- It was seen that 68.1% of the elderly people stated that their children consulted them while making a decision, whereas 30.9% said they were not consulted by their children, when they made decisions.
- In the context the satisfaction of social needs, the frequency of meeting of elderly people with children was examined. Accordingly, 77.8% of the elderly people stated they were meeting their children frequently, every day to once a week, where 20.7% said they were meeting with their children occasionally, once a month, or at festivals and holidays.
- The level of contentedness of elderly people of their relation with their children was assessed in the scope of social needs. It was seen that 99.3% of the elderly people living in Ankara were contented with their relations with their children, where 5.5% were not pleased thereof.
- In the scope of the study the whether the elderly people enrolled in the study lent social and economic assistance to their children was assessed. It was seen that slightly higher than half of the elderly people (54.1%) lent social and economic assistance to their children, where 44.3% did

not /could not lend social and economic assistance to their children.

- It was seen that 68.4% of the elderly people frequently met their grandchildren (every day to one a week), where 29% met occasionally.
- In the scope of the study, whether the elderly people enrolled in the study take the care of their grandchildren for any reason was assessed in the context of satisfaction of social needs. It was understood that more than half of the elderly people (52.9%) did not have to take care of their grandchildren for any reason, and that 46.5% took care of their grandchildren.
- In the scope of the social needs, it was examined whether the children or grandchildren provided economic or social support to the elderly people. It was understood that 59.9% of the elderly people were provided with economic or social support by their children or grandchildren, where 38.7% did not receive any economic or social support from their children or grandchildren.
- It was found that 82.8% of the elderly people frequently met with their friends or neighbors, every day to once a week, where 12.5% of the elderly people occasionally met with their friends or neighbors.
- It was seen that 91.4% of the elderly people were contented with their relations with friends or neighbors, and that 5.5% were not contented with their relation with friends or neighbors, and that 3.1% did not reply the question.
- It was seen that majority of the elderly people (74.7%) paid occasional visits to their relatives. It was observed that the percentage of those elderly people paid frequent visits (every day to once a week) to their relatives (11.1%) was higher than that of those, who did not pay any visits to relatives (7.6%) and those, who did not have any relatives (5.1%).
- The status of greenery areas in the districts, where the elderly people enrolled in the study, was examined. Accordingly, the majority of elderly people (80.4%) stated they had parks/greenery areas in their districts, where 19.6% said there was no parks/ greenery areas in their districts. 81.7% of the elderly people were benefited from the greenery areas in their districts.
- It was seen that 76% of the elderly people had parks in their district, where 23.4% had no park in their district. It was observed that more than a half of the elderly people (55.1%) were benefited from the park in their district, where 44.9% did not benefit from the park in their district.
- As for the available social facilities in the districts of the elderly people, it was found that more than a half of the elderly people (56.3%) stated there was no social facility in their district, where 43.7% said that they had social facilities in their districts.
- As for the available sports facilities in the districts of the elderly people, it was found that more than a half of the elderly people (55.7%) stated that there was no sports facility in their district, where 44.3% said they had. However, it was also seen that 62.8% of the elderly people did not benefit from the social facility in their districts, where only 37.2% were benefited there from.
- As for the available markets in the districts of the elderly people, it was found that the majority of the elderly people (87.8%) stated they had a market in their district, where 12.2% stated they had no market in their district.78.4% of the elderly people were benefited from the markets in their district.
- As for the available coffeehouses in the districts of the elderly people, it was found that 78.2% of the elderly people stated that there were coffeehouses in their district, where 21.8% said they had no coffeehouses

in their district. 67.3% of those, who had a coffeehouse in their district, were found not to have benefited from these coffeehouses.

- As for the available parking lots in the districts of the elderly people, it was found that 64.6% of the elderly people stated they had no parking lot in their district, where 35.4% said they had parking lots in their district. 77.6% of the elderly people were not benefited from the parking lots in their district. The main reason for the foregoing is that the percentage of elderly people possessing a car was low.
- As for the available primary healthcare centers in the districts of the elderly people, it was found that 96.6% of the elderly people stated that they had a primary healthcare center in their district, where 3.4% did not have any. It was seen that 93.6% of the elderly people were benefited from the primary healthcare center in their district, where 6.4% did not.

Poverty Analysis by Cultural Needs of Elderly People

- As for the status of reading newspapers or magazines, it was seen that 59.6% of the elderly people read newspapers or magazines, and that 43.4% did not read newspapers or magazines.
- It was examined whether the elderly people share newly acquired information with their friends or relatives. It was seen that 80.5% of the elderly people shared newly acquired information with their friends or relatives, where 19.5% did not share newly acquired information with their friends or relative.
- The daily average TV watching durations of the elderly people were assessed. It was found that 79.1% of the elderly people watched TV for an average period of 0-5 hours, 18% for 6-10 hours, and 2.6% for 1o hours and more.
- 78.9% of the elderly people thought that the TV programs they watched were helpful for their lives. Whereas, 19.3% believed these programs were not helpful, and 1.8% did not provide a reply.
- It was observed that 79.7% of the elderly people were interested in actual events and social issues, where 18.8% were not interested in actual events and social issues.
- It was seen that 86.2% of the elderly people were not members of any foundation, association, club, chamber, union, or political party, where 13.2% were members of a foundation, association, club, chamber, union, or political party, and that 0.6% did not provide a reply.
- In the scope of the cultural needs, it was examined whether the elderly people went for a domestic travel for sightseeing. Accordingly, 65.3% of the elderly people stated they did not go for a domestic travel for sightseeing, where 34.2% said they went for a domestic travel, and that 0.5% did not provide a reply.
- It was observed that the majority of the elderly people did not go for an international travel for sightseeing, where 9.2% went for an international travel, and that 0.8% did not reply this item.
- It was examined whether the elderly people could go wherever and whenever they want to in their city. It was seen that 62.6% of the elderly people could go wherever and whenever they want to, that 37.1% could not go wherever and whenever they want to, and that 0.2% did not reply this question.
- The elderly people were asked if there was a place in the country they wanted to see. Accordingly 51.7% of the elderly people said that there was a place they wanted to see, and 48.3% stated there was no place in the country that they wanted to see.

- It was examined, whether the elderly wanted to see a place outside the country. It was found that 72.6% of the elderly people said that there was no place they wanted to see outside the country, and 27.4% stated there was a place outside the country that they wanted to see.

FUTURE RESEARCH DIRECTIONS

In pointing to key future research directions we can identify two separate sets of issues. Firstly a set of thematic concerns which are likely to need particular attention over the coming decade (the what) – and secondly two major priorities in taking forward these concerns in the commissioning and execution of elderly poverty research (the how).

The what: some of these things are already on the radar (for example, politics, or gender) and have been for a long time. However, all are connected with how elderly poverty distribution and dynamics are likely to change over the coming decade. Politics about redistribution, poverty measurement methods for elderly, social differentiation, exclusion and poverty will be important issues for next research.

The how: in order to generate policy relevant elderly poverty diagnostics in parallel to the innovations in 'growth diagnostics', and opportunities for stronger policy evaluation. There are two sets of issues which won't happen automatically, and where long-term investment needs to be made. Firstly longitudinal quantitative and qualitative research is an important new basis for improved poverty diagnostics. Secondly in-country capacity building, stronger in-country networks including not only research institutes but research users, research analysts, statistical offices and citizens are needed. There should be a particular focus on the capacity to do longitudinal mixed methods, policy relevant, research; and an active effort to identify opportunities that information and communications technology provides to leap-frog conventional approaches to data collection, checking and analysis, with potential for gains in cost, speed, frequency and granularity of elderly poverty research.

CONCLUSION

Today the aged population of the world has increased and continues to increase as a result of the social, economic, medical, scientific, and technological changes. It is estimated that the number individual aging over 60 years will be 1.2 billion in 2025, 1.3 billion in 2040, and 2 billion in 2050, with 80% of the developed countries. As of 2002, the number of individuals aging 60 years and over in the developing countries were approximately 400 million. It is forecasted that the same figure will rise to an approximate amount of 840 million as from 2025. Therefore almost all developed countries will be witnessing the aging of their population in the forthcoming decades.

Old age is not a new notion in the globalized world. However, day by day this phenomenon manifests itself through new problematic and the need for new service models. All countries had to face with increased economic and social demands during the aging process. Old age and issues related to old age have become to determine the agenda of the services together with the changing world conditions, developing healthcare system, and cultural and social changes. The elderly people are no more living in the extended family model, but in a world where nucleus family model has become widespread. On the other hand the advancements in technology and healthcare services increase average life expectancy. Due to the changes in needs and consumption habits during the old age period, difficulties in meeting economic and social needs, and prevalence of such conditions as dementia and Alzheimer's disease, this period may become quite challenging for relevant individuals.

The US Population Institute emphasized in its report published in September 2011, that the world population increased from 6 billion to 7 billion since 1999, and that one billion people were added to the global population in the said 12-year period. At this point, the report questions the implications of population increase for the future of the world and for ensuring the welfare of the entire humanity, and especially of disadvantaged, vulnerable groups such as children, elderly people, and women. In the context thereof, the report underscores the importance of such issues as the exhaustion of resources, fight against poverty, reinforcing disadvantaged groups such as children, elderly people, and women, and restructuring of population policies (Population Institute, 2011).

While percentage of employed population decreases in the aging societies the number of retired people increases. As with the increase in the number of retired people, the burden on the social security system and public finance increases. Moreover it seen, due to aging, that the healthcare expenses of the elderly people increase, that the elderly people need to benefit from healthcare services more frequently and for longer periods due to chronic diseases, and that the number of medicines and the administration period thereof is higher in the elderly people. One of the most important issues with regard to the economic cost of aging is the poverty of elderly people.

This study examined the poverty of elderly people upon analysis of economic, social, and cultural needs. Therefore, it was aimed to determine the deprivations accompanying the poverty. In this study, which researched the poverty of elderly people in Ankara, it was found that 64.5% of the elderly people were married, nearly half (49%) were graduated from a primary education institution, and 20.7% were illiterate. 95.2% of the elderly people were retired and were not employed in any job. 91% of the elderly people were covered by social security. 90.9% of the elderly people considered their health status to be "good."

Despite the fact that the residences of the majority of the elderly people were their own property, the percentage of possessing one's own residence and a car was lower in elderly people at low-income level. The percentage of having such durables as TV, air-conditioner, refrigerator, washing machine, telephone, and cell phone at home were lower in low-income elderly people. Therefore the level of dissatisfaction with their residence was higher in low-income elderly people.

It was found that the elderly people were in general not contented with the level of their income, that they found it insufficient, and that they could not sufficiently afford such expenses as food, clothing, electricity and water bills, and medicine. They could not make travel and excursion plans and allocate budget for such activities. Furthermore, the elderly people were economically supported by their children or grandchildren due to the insufficiency of their income. Due to poverty, the elderly people experienced deprivations deeper as well. For instance, it was understood that impoverished elderly people used telephone less frequently due to its cost and visited their children less frequently. It was seen in the scope of the social needs that the elderly people were generally contented with the interpersonal relations and relations with their children, yet the low-income elderly people stated that they were not consulted by their children, when a decision to be made in the family. Moreover, the frequency of meeting with children and grandchildren was lower in such individuals. This suggests the fact that poverty is transferred to next generations. In a metropolitan city long distances increase the transportation cost and that usually the children, also poor themselves, experience difficulty in paying a visit to their poor elderly parents. On the other hand it was found that the elderly people mostly watched TV to meet their cultural needs, and met their need to read newspapers and books at lower degrees. Also despite available urban facilities as parks, sports facilities etc. the level of benefiting from these opportunities was low. Most elderly people did not make plans to see a place inside or outside the country due to poverty and inability to allocate budget there for.

Although the level of meeting the cultural needs is associated with poverty, educational status and intellectual capital also influence the motivation and expectations to meet the cultural needs. Taking into consideration that approximately one-fifth of the elderly people enrolled in this study were illiterate, it was concluded that the motivation to meet cultural needs was low.

While on the one hand the income decreases with old age, the prevalence of diseases rises and the healthcare expenses such as medicine and doctor increases. There are ongoing social assistance programs in cash and in kind for poor elderly people in Turkey, in the scope of social warfare state practices, such as home care giving fee, old age pension for 65 and over age group, and free or discounted transportation opportunity. However it is seen that alleviating poverty is one of the most important issues for the elderly people, as it is with the generality of the population. Therefore it is obvious that effective social policies and intervention methods are required to implement in micro and macro levels.

REFERENCES

Bird, K. (2007). *The intergenerational transmission of poverty: An overview* (Working Paper 99) Manchester, IDPM/Chronic Poverty Research Centre (CPRC). Retrieved from www.chronicpoverty.org/resources/cp99.htm

Bora, A. (2007). D*osya: Yoksulluk ve sosyal dışlanma*. Retrieved from http://www.tes-is.org.tr/TR/tesis_dergi/2007

Buğra, A., Keyder, Ç., Balaban, U., & Yakut, B. (2003). *New poverty and changing welfare regime of Turkey*. UNDP.

Cherchye, L., De Rock, B., & Vermeulen, F. (2008). *Economic well-being and poverty among the elderly: an analysis based on a collective consumption model* (Discussion Paper, IZA DP No. 3349) Bonn, Germany: Institute for the Study of Labor.

Daly, M. (1992). Europe's poor women? Gender in research on poverty. *European Sociological Review*, *8*(1), 1–12.

Deaton, A., & Paxson, C. (1998). *Inquiries in the Economics of Aging* (D. Wise, Ed.). Chicago: Chicago University Press.

Devaney, S. A. (1995). Retirement preparation of older and younger Baby Boomers. *Financial Counseling and Planning*, *6*, 25–33.

Devicienti, F., & Poggi, A. (2007). *Poverty and social exclusion: Two sides of the same coin or dynamically interrelated processes?* Laboratorio R. Revelli: Collegio Carlo Alberto.

Engelhardt, G., & Gruber, J. (2004). *Social security and the evolution of elderly poverty* (NBER Working Paper, WP 10466). National Bureau of Economic Research.

European Commission. (2012). *The 2012 Ageing Report: Economic and Budgetary Projections for The EU 27 Member States (2010-2060)*.European Commission, Brussels. Retrieved from http://ec.europa.eu/economy_finance/publications/european_economy/2012/pdf/ee-2012-2_en.pdf

Fukuda-Parr, S. (1999). What does feminization of poverty mean? It isn't just lack of income. *Feminist Economics*, *5*(2), 99–103. doi:10.1080/135457099337996

General Directorate on the Status of Women. (2008). *Kadın ve Yoksulluk* (pp. 1–20). Ankara.

Gönen, E., Hablemitoğlu, Ş., & Özmete, E. (1997). *Değişen Türkiye'de İnsan Hakları Açısından Sosyal Hizmetler* (K. Karataş, Ed.). Ankara: Sosyal Hizmet Uzmanları Derneği Genel Merkezi.

Gratton, B. (1996). The poverty of impoverishment theory: The economic well-being of the elderly. *The Journal of Economic History*, *56*(1), 39–61. doi:10.1017/S0022050700016016

Hablemitoğlu, Ş., & Özmete, E. (2010). *Yaşlı refahı: Yaşlılar için sosyal hizmet*. Ankara: Kilit Yayınları.

Hogarth, J. M. (1991). Assest management and retired households: Savers, dissavers and alternators. *Financial Counseling and Planning*, *2*, 97–122.

Human Development Report. (2009). *Community-based care*. Retrieved from http://hdr.undp.org/en/content/human-development-report-2009

Jehoel-Gijsbers, G., & Vrooman, C. (2007). *Explaining social exclusion: A theoretical model tested in the Netherlands*. The Hague: The Netherlands Institute for Social Research.

Maxwell, S. (1999). The meaning and measurement of poverty (Poverty briefing: 3). Overseas Development Institute.

McGarry, K., & Schoeni, R. (2005). Widow(er) poverty and out-of-pocket medical expenditures near the end of the life. *Journal of Gerontology*, *60*(3), 160–168. doi:10.1093/geronb/60.3.S160 PMID:15860793

Ministry of Family and Social Policies. (n.d.). *Mevzuat*. Retrieved from http://www.aile.gov.tr/mevzuat/mevzuat

Mukhopadyay, S., & Shambhu, S. (2011). *Analyzing linkages between gender and poverty: A methodological note*. Retrieved from http://www.isst-india.org/PDF/Gender%20and%20Poverty-Methodological%20Note%20GN%20II.pdf

Oktik, N. (2008). *Türkiye'de yoksulluk çalışmaları*. İzmir: Yakın Kitabevi.

Özmete, E. (2011). *Sosyal dışlanma ve aile: Sosyal hizmet müdahalelerinde güçlendirme yaklaşımı*. Ankara: Maya Akademi Yayını.

Parsa, B. (2008). *Financial status among the Malaysian elderly*. Unpublished Master's Dissertation, University Putra Malaysia, Malaysia.

Population Institute. (2011). *From 6 Billion to 7 Billion: How Population Growth is Changing and Challenging Our World*. Retrieved from https://www.populationinstitute.org/external/files/reports/from-6b-to-7b.pdf

Şahin, T. (2010). Sosyal dışlanma ve yoksulluk ilişkisi. *Yardım ve Dayanışma*, *2*(1), 71–80.

Soyak, A. (2004). Yapısal uyum programları ve yoksulluk ilişkisi üzerine bir değerlendirme. *Bilim ve Ütopya Dergisi*, *125*, 36–45.

TUIK. (2011a). *2009 yoksulluk çalışması sonuçları*. Ankara: T.C. Başbakanlık Türkiye İstatistik Kurumu. Retrieved from: http:www.tuik.gov.tr

TUIK. (2011b). *Adrese dayalı nüfus kayıt sistemi (ADNKS)*. Ankara: Türkiye İstatistik Kurumu Matbaası.

TUIK, (2012). 2010 yoksulluk çalışması sonuçları. *TUIK Haber Bülteni*, 58.

Turaman, C. (2007). Yaşlı sağlığı hizmetlerinin birinci basamakta planlanması. *Geriatri*, *4*(1), 22–27.

TurkStat Poverty Study. (2010). Retrieved from http://www.turkstat.gov.tr/PreHaberBultenleri.do?id=8642

UNDP. (2010). *Human development report 2010: The real wealth of nations: pathways to human development (20th ed.)*. Retrieved from http://hdr.undp.org/sites/default/files/reports/270/hdr_2010_en_complete_reprint.pdf

UNDP. (2011). 2010 *Human development report: 40-year trends analysis shows poor countries making faster development gains*. Retrieved from http: www.undp.org

Weir, D., Willis, R., & Sevak, P. (2004). The economic consequences of a husband' death: Evidence from the HRS and AHEAD. *Social Security Bulletin*, *65*, 31–44.

World Bank. (1990). *World Development Report 1990*. Oxford University Press.

World Bank. (2000). *World Development Report 2000/2001: Attacking poverty*. New York: Oxford University Press. Retrieved from http://www.worldbank.org/poverty/wdrpoverty/report/index

World Bank. (2005). *World Bank/WB, Turkey joint poverty assessment report*. Human Development Sector Unit, Europe and Central Asia Region, State Institute of Statistics Turkey. Volume 1: Main Report, Report No: 296-19-TU. World Summit for Social Development Programme of Action, UN. Chapter 2: Eradication of Poverty. Retrieved from: http://www.un.org/esa/socdev/wssd/text-version/agreements/poach2.htm

Yunus, M. (1999). *Yoksulluğun bulunmadığı bir dünyaya doğru (Çev:G. Şen)*. Doğan Kitap Yayınevi.

Zaidi, A., Makovec, M., Fuchs, M., Lipszyc, B., Lelkes, O., Rummel, M., & De Vos, K. (2006). *Poverty of elderly people in EU25 Report*. European Centre for Social Welfare Policy and Research.

Zastrow, C. (2008). *Introduction to social work and social welfare: empowering people*. United States: Thomson Brooks Cole.

ADDITIONAL READING

Anand, S., & Ravallion, M. (1992). *Human development in poor countries: Do incomes matter?* Washington, DC: World Bank.

Charles, K., Danziger, S., Pounder, L., & Schoeni, R. (2006). *Consumption, in-come, and well-being among the mature population* (Working paper). National Poverty Center: University of Michigan.

Cherchye, L., De Rock, B., & Vermeulen, F. (2007). The collective model of house-hold consumption: A nonparametric characterization. *Econometrica*, *75*(2), 553–574. doi:10.1111/j.1468-0262.2006.00757.x

Chiappori, P. A. (1988). Rational household labor supply. *Econometrica*, *56*(1), 63–89. doi:10.2307/1911842

Chiappori, P. A. (1992). Collective labor supply and welfare. *Journal of Political Economy*, *100*(3), 437–467. doi:10.1086/261825

Coder, J., Rainwater, L., & Smeeding, T. (1989). Inequality among children and elderly in ten modern nations: The United States in an international context. *The American Economic Review*, *79*, 320–324.

Doyal, L., & Gough, I. (1991). *A theory of human need*. London: Macmillan.

Glewwe, P., & van der Gaag, J. (1988). *Confronting poverty in developing countries: Definitions, information and policies, living standards measurement study* (Working Paper 48). Washington, DC: World Bank.

Greeley, M., Kabeer, N., Davies, S., & Hussein, K. (1992). *Measuring the poverty reduction impact of development interventions*. Brighton: IDS.

Hagenaars, A. J. M. (1986). *The perception of poverty: Contributions to economic analysis*. Oxford: North-Holland.

Hurd, M. (1990). Research on the elderly: Economic status, retirement, and consumption and saving. *Journal of Economic Literature*, *28*, 565–637.

Hurd, M., & Rohwedder, S. (2006). Economic well-being at older ages: income and consumption based poverty measures in the HRS (NBER Working Paper, WP12680). National Bureau of Economic Research.

Johnson, D., & Smeeding, T. (2000). *Who are the poor elderly? An examination using alternative poverty measures* (Working Paper, 2000-2014). Boston College, Center for Retirement Research.

Lal, D. (1983). *The poverty of development economics*. London: The Institute of Economic Affairs.

Lewbel, A. (2003). Calculating compensation in cases of wrongful death. *Journal of Econometrics*, *113*(1), 115–128. doi:10.1016/S0304-4076(02)00169-0

Lewbel, A. (2003). *Household behavior, equivalence scales, welfare and poverty* (C. Dagum & G. Ferrari, Eds.). New York: Physica Verlag.

Lipton, M. (1983). *Poverty, under nutrition and hunger* (World Bank Staff Working Paper 597). Washington, DC: World Bank.

Little, I. M., & Mirrlees, D. (1974). *Project appraisal and planning for developing countries*. London: Heinemann Educational Books.

Little, I. M. D. (1970). *A critique of welfare economics* (2nd ed.). Oxford: Oxford University Press.

Patton, M. Q. (1990). *Qualitative evaluation and research methods*. London: Sage Pub.

Ravallion, M. (1992). *Poverty comparisons: a guide to concepts and methods, living standards measurement study* (Working Paper 88). Washington, DC: World Bank.

Seers, D. (1972). What are we trying to measure? *The Journal of Development Studies*, *8*(3), 21–36. doi:10.1080/00220387208421410

Sen, A. (1973). *On economic inequality*. Oxford: Clarendon Press. doi:10.1093/0198281935.001.0001

Sen, A. (1985). *Commodities and capabilities*. The Netherlands: Elsevier.

Zia, B. (2009). *Valuing financial literacy: Evidence from Indonesia*. Retrieved from: http://econ.worldbank.org/external/default/main?theSitePK=477894&contentMDK=22183420&menuPK=546584&pagePK=64168182&piPK=64168060

KEY TERMS AND DEFINITIONS

Absolute Poverty: This is a term used in various different ways to denote a poverty level that does not change over time, in terms of the living standard that it refers to. It stays the same even if society is becoming more prosperous. An absolute poverty line thus represents a certain basic level of goods and services, and only rises with inflation to show how much it would cost to buy that package.

Deprivation: Deprivation is the consequence of a lack of income and other resources, which cumulatively can be seen as living in poverty. The relative deprivation approach to poverty examines the indicators of deprivation, which are then related back to income levels and resources.

Elderly People: Most developed world countries have accepted the chronological age of 65 years as a definition of 'elderly' or older person, but like many westernized concepts, this does not adapt well to the situation in Africa. While this definition is somewhat arbitrary, it is many times associated with the age at which one can begin to receive pension benefits. At the moment, there is no United Nations standard numerical criterion, but the UN agreed cutoff is 60+ years to refer to the older population.

Financial Behavior: It can be defined as any human behavior that is relevant to money management. Common financial behaviors include cash, credit and saving behavior.

Life Expectancy: Life expectancy is the expected (in the statistical sense) number of years of life remaining at a given age.

Need Analysis: Requirements analysis focuses on the elements needed to be represented in the system, needs analysis focuses on the requirements related to the goals, aspirations and needs of the users and/or the user community and feeds them into the system requirement analysis process. The main purpose of needs analysis is the user's satisfaction.

Poverty: Poverty is general scarcity or dearth, or the state of one who lacks a certain amount of material possessions or money.

Relative Poverty: Poverty can be defined and measured in various ways. The most commonly used approach is relative income poverty. Each household's income, adjusted for family size, is compared to median income. (The median is the "middle" income: half of people have more than the median and half have less.). Those with less than 60 per cent of median income are classified as poor. This 'poverty line' is the agreed international measure used throughout the European Union.

Chapter 9
Investor Biases in Financial Decisions

Shalini Kalra Sahi
Management Development Institute, India

ABSTRACT

Financial Decisions involve making choices between various investment alternatives, with the aim of increasing the individual's net worth. The investor today is exposed to various investment options, but does not have the knowledge and capability of evaluating all the options and making a rational decision. Due to the limitation in the information processing capacities of the individuals, their beliefs and preferences, the investment decision-making process, gets biased. This chapter highlights ten such biases and throws light on how they impact investment behaviour, both positively and negatively. This understanding of investor psychology will generate insights that will benefit the financial advisory relationship. Further for Individuals, recognizing how the biases impact their financial decisions, can help create self-awareness and an understanding that would help them in better financial management, in case these tendencies are leading them to make unsatisfactory investments.

INTRODUCTION

When it comes to financial decision making, the thought that one comes across is that the process should follow a planned approach, since these decisions will have long term financial and emotional consequences. The long term impacts of financial decisions would enable an individual to successfully fulfill the financial goals that they have set for themselves and their family, and the fulfillment of which bring a sense of peace and well-being to the individual.

The process of financial planning could be based on the individual as the key information gatherer and decision maker, or as a facilitator of decisions that are based on information that is presented to him/her. In either of these cases, it is the individual who has the choice to take the decisions himself/ herself or to allow others to take on their behalf. This choice could be self-imposed or arise on account of the inability of the individual to make the financial decisions themselves.

With the tremendous growth in the financial markets the world over, an individual is exposed to a gamut of information, on which to base their

DOI: 10.4018/978-1-4666-7484-4.ch009

decisions. This is certainly good from the point of view of making investment decisions, but is the individual actually able to make sense of this information? Can the individual take in all the information available in the market, process it, and come out with a decision that is going to maximize their utility? An answer to that would be, 'No'.

If the maximization of utility was so easy, we would not have a problem. However, in reality the situation is not so easy. The limitations that are imposed on the ability of the human mind to process such large chunk of information, in short time, forces people to make decisions based on certain heuristics. These heuristics help to process the information quickly and take decisions. But at times these heuristics can also bias the decisions. Not just heuristics, the individual is also driven by various emotions and sentiments that also bias them towards certain choices. In addition, individual may have certain motives that lead them to choose a particular course of action. Such heuristic driven behaviour, emotions and motives, bias investment decision making. The traditional finance theorists would say that these behaviours lead to suboptimal decisions as these behaviors are irrational. Unfortunately, people are not as rational as the traditional finance theorists claimed them to be. Hence the 'rational man' is in fact the homosapien who by the design of the human mind, is prone to biases. Much literature from evolutionary psychology gives evidence of biases as essential for human existence.

Amos Tversky and Daniel Kahneman (1974) were among the first to identify the presence of psychological biases in decision making under uncertainty and risk. Some examples of behavioural biases are Illusion of control, Illusion of validity, Overconfidence Bias, Anchoring Bias, Self-Control bias, Cognitive dissonance, Framing, Representativeness, Hindsight Bias, Loss Aversion Bias, Status Quo Bias, Regret Aversion, Ambiguity aversion, etc (Tversky & Kahneman, 1974; Kahneman & Tversky, 1979; Thaler, 1980; Kahneman & Riepe, 1998; Barber & Odean, 1999; Hilton, 2001; Shefrin, 2000; Barberis & Thaler, 2003; Pompian, 2008; Szyszka, 2013).

Individual investors are prone to various biases that influence their investment decisions. The literature on finance tells us that biases need to be corrected as these lead to sub-optimal decisions. But biases are actually designs of the human mind and enable people to make sense of their environment and give a sense of wellbeing. The purpose of the chapter is to understand based on the literature in the area of behavioural finance, how the various biases manifest in financial decision making; to try and understand the positive and negative dimensions of the various biases and what ways are there to enable people to overcome the negative aspects of the biases.

BACKGROUND

The volume of research in the field of Behavioural Finance has grown over the recent years. The field predominantly merges the concepts of finance, economics, psychology and sociology, to understand the human behaviour in the financial markets. Decision making under standard finance and economics is based on the theory of expected utility and describes how a rational individual should behave. It is driven by the fact that investment decisions are solely driven by the aim of maximizing the expected utility of returns (El Sehity, Haumer, Helmenstein, Kirchler & Maciejovsky, 2002; Szyszka, 2013). However, the insights from psychology have showed that how people should behave and how they actually behave, is quite different (Kahneman & Riepe, 1998). What are the causes of these deviations in behaviours and what impact these deviations have on the decision choices in the investment decision making domain, is of substantial relevance and interest to the proponents of the Behavioural Finance and Behavioural Economics research.

The application of psychology to investor behaviour has helped in understanding the systematic deviations from the rational behaviour that seemed to be unexplained earlier (Slovic, 1972; Baker & Nofsinger, 2002). Behavioural finance contends that there are various ways in which people behave that are inconsistent with the rational assumptions model (Kahneman & Tversky, 1979), and these behaviours are not chance phenomenon but are occurring frequently and often in a systematic fashion (Odean, 1999; Shefrin, 2000; Barber & Odean, 2001).

Van der Sar (2004) stated that Herbert Simon's work on Satisficing criteria and Bounded Rationality, has played a major role towards the development of behavioural finance. Simon's proposition was that people have a tendency to satisfice rather than optimize when it came to decision making, meaning thereby that the decision path chosen is one that satisfies the individual's most important needs, irrespective of the fact that the choice may not be the ideal or the optimal one (Plous. 1993). Simon (1955; 1956; 1957) stated that the ability of an economic man to be rational is dependent upon and is bounded by the information that he has access to and the computational capacities he possess. If the human brain were a computer, then it could be programmed to analyze huge chunk of information and come out with a decision in a split second. However, the human brain works differently than a computer; it frequently processes information through shortcuts and emotional filters to cut down on analysis time (Nofsinger, 2001). The use of these shortcuts time and again, biases the decision maker towards certain actions or behaviours.

INDIVIDUAL INVESTOR BIASES

Bias: Meaning

Wolman (1973) defined a Bias as a "tendency towards a certain disposition or conclusion" (pp.44).

Psychological Biases in the Behavioural finance literature are referred to as Systematic Errors in Judgment (Kahneman & Riepe, 1998; Szyszka, 2013); Heuristics (rules of thumb) (Tversky & Kahneman, 1974; Shefrin, 2000; Baker & Nofsinger, 2002; Prast, 2004; Pompian, 2006; Szyszka, 2013); Beliefs, judgments or preferences (Tversky & Kahneman, 1974; Pompian, 2006; Szyszka, 2013).

Evolution of Bias

"Evolutionary psychology seeks to explore the ways in which our minds have been formed by the process of evolution" (Montier, 2002; pp.4) and hence gives insights as to why we think the way we do. Most literature in Behavioural Finance considers 'Bias' as an error; a mistake; an anomaly; which needs to be corrected. This meaning holds true when we are comparing the decisions to the standards laid out by the traditional finance theory. If the biases are seen independent of the standard theory, they in reality reflect the designs of the human mind. According to Haselton and Nettle (2006), "one of the curiosities of human cognition—the fact that it seems riddled with biases—may be a functional feature of mechanisms for making judgments and decisions" (p.47).

Haselton, Nettle & Andrews (2005) state that, "biases reveal the intricacy of the mind's design" and "because they depart from standards of logic and accuracy; they appear to be design flaws instead of examples of good engineering" (p.725). They further state that cognitive biases can arise on account of three reasons: heuristics, error management biases and artifact. Heuristics would pertain to the use of shortcuts, when the task presented is not something that the mind has experience of. The use of artifacts also biases the decision (an example would be the confirmation bias-which is tendency to look for confirmatory information). Haselton and Buss (2003) state that, "biases can also emerge as a consequence of trade-offs."(p.30). The Error management biases arise since "many real-world tasks of judgment are probabilistic and, therefore, include an irreducible amount of uncertainty" (Haselton, Nettle & Andrews, 2005).

Decision making in order to be good, must attempt to minimize the errors of decision. However, it is not always possible to reduce both the Type I error and Type II error and hence the endeavor is to reach to a compromise solution. This solution in circumstances of judgment under uncertainty calls for making the less costly error (Type I), over the most costly errors (Type II), as this way thought the error rate may increase but by keeping the Type II error less, the overall costs are less (Haselton & Nettle, 2006). These cost-benefit tradeoffs can lead to certain reasoning that can predispose the individual to act in a systematic way (Haselton & Buss, 2003). Some examples of such biases would be loss aversion tendency, regret aversion tendency, Optimism Bias, Illusion of control and Overconfidence Bias.

Hence, the design features of the human mind that seem like flaws when seen from one perspective are actually human adaptations shaped by the evolutionary forces, for the purpose of ensuring well-being of an individual (Taylor & brown, 1988; Cummins & Nistico, 2002; Haselton, Nettle & Andrews, 2005; Johnson & Fowler, 2009). These design features help to explain that in some situations like those of uncertainty and risk, a biased reasoning is actually more preferred than an unbiased one (Johnson & Fowler, 2009).

Causes of Investor Biases

Due to the presence of uncertainty and the inherent risk associated with Financial Investment Decisions, the individual investor behaviour is likely to be biased (Slovic, 1972; Thaler, 1999). Making an investment decision is a complex process, wherein the investor has to deal with a number of positive and negative emotions pertaining to the parting of the money and the outcome of the decision. Further, making a choice from the plethora of investment opportunities that are available, requires an innate mental ability of the investor to analyze the data available, in order to make the informed decision. Had the number of alternatives been limited and the future more predictable, the human mind could have easily analyzed all the information and made a decision. But with the gamut of information, in the face of risk and uncertainty, decision making, in order to be quick, has to rely on some beliefs and judgments. These judgments can at times be overpowered by the emotions that the individual has with regard to the investment decision. While at times the biases can act in a positive way for the wellbeing of the individual investor, at other instances these very biases can lead to negative results and prevent the investor to achieve their financial goals.

There could be a number of reasons that could lead to a biased behaviour. Some reasons are outlined below:

Cognitive Limitations, i.e. the limitations of the human mind to process huge information, can lead to biased behaviour where the individual's choices are based on simplified procedures or heuristics (Tversky & Kahneman, 1974; Kahneman & Tversky, 1979; Shefrin, 2000; Keren & Teigen, 2004; Van der Sar, 2004; Haselton, Nettle & Andrews, 2005) Further the biases are also on account of *Affective Influences and Emotions* (Montier, 2002; Keren & Teigen, 2004; Haselton, Nettle & Andrews, 2005; Kahler, 2007; Seo & Barrett, 2007); *Psychological Motives* such as Fear, Greed, need for security, need for achievement, conformity, safety also impact the decisions choices and tend to bias an individual's choices (Haselton, Nettle & Andrews, 2005; Roszkowski & Grable, 2007). Biases have also been found to be on account of trying to commit errors that are less costly (Haselton, Nettle & Andrews, 2005)

Thus, Individual investors are prone to various biases that prevent them from making rational investment decisions. As we have seen in the above sections, biases are a normal aspect of 'being human'. At times these biases can help us in decision making by enabling mitigation of risks, while at other times we could be losing out on possible investment rewards, on account of our biases. Olsen (2007) stated that a "bias is not necessarily bad as long as it leads to the results that the decision maker wishes" (p.53).

There are umpteen number of biases that have been mentioned in the literature. In the next section we present 10 such biases that have been well documented in the literature and see how the biases can play a positive and a negative role in our investment decisions. Further, some suggestions have been given on how the negative influences of the biases can be reduced.

Investor Biases: An Insight into the Positive and Negative Aspects

1. Overconfidence Bias

Overconfidence has been defined as: Unwarranted faith in one's intuitive reasoning, judgment and cognitive abilities (*Pompian, 2006*, pp.51)

A. Manifestation of Overconfidence Bias

Odean (1999) found that the individual investors either overestimate the quality of their information or their ability to interpret that information. Overconfidence manifests through excessively positive self-perceptions, wherein the individual can be overconfident with respect to his abilities, knowledge, and accuracy of predictions (Friedman, 2007). Overconfident individuals hold high views of their personal beliefs and abilities (Barber & Odean, 1999; Grinblatt & Keloharju, 2006; Friedman, 2007), and this leads to positive expectations about their endeavors. Overconfidence can be on account of factors like, self-deception, illusion of knowledge, miscalibration, unrealistic optimism, better-than-average-effect and illusion of control (Langer, 1975; Hirshleifer, 2001; Baker & Nofsinger, 2002; Goetzmann & Kumar, 2007; Skala, 2008). Barber and Odean (2001) found that overconfident investors who are men trade more frequently and had lower returns as compared to women.

B. Positive Aspects of Overconfidence Bias

According to Taylor & Brown (1988) "positive self-evaluations, exaggerated perceptions of control or mastery, and unrealistic optimism are characteristic of normal human thought" (p.193). These positive illusions are adaptive and beneficial and create a sense of well-being (Taylor & Brown, 1988; Kinney, 2000; Fenton-O-Creevy, et, al., 2003; Skala, 2008). Nelson and Quick (2008) argued that this faith and trust in one's own judgment gives a sense of satisfaction and contentment to the individual. Johnson and Fowler (2009) added that overconfidence is advantageous because it serves to increase ambition, resolve, morale and persistence. Overconfident behaviour has been related to high self-esteem. Further, it has been seen that "people with high self-esteem perform better and are more satisfied with their jobs" (Nelson & Quick. 2008, pp.72). Cummins & Nistico (2002) in their review of studies from the quality of life literature found that self-esteem was highly correlated with life satisfaction. Confidence with regard to investment decisions would enable people to feel good about their investment decisions and thus feel more financially satisfied.

C. Negative Aspects of Overconfidence Bias

An overconfident investor would ignore negative information about the investment decisions and may end up with a bad decision. Pompian (2006) believed that overconfidence would lead the individual investors to be not well prepared for their future (since they would ignore negative information) and thus they would not reach their financial goals and hence would be unhappy and discouraged. Barber and Odean (2001) found that overconfidence leads to more trading behaviour and lower overall returns. Overconfidence also leads investors to hold under-diversified portfolios, as they feel that the select investments that they have made, would be giving them the required returns that they want. Overconfidence investors also take more risks, which at times can be detrimental to their portfolio, especially if the downside risk of the investment has not been considered (Pompian, 2006).

D. Overcoming Negative Aspects of Overconfidence Bias

Overconfidence being a cognitive bias (Pompian, 2006) can be reduced by collecting important factual information (both positive and negative). This way the investor's assumption and opinions can be corrected/ checked for any signs of overconfident behaviour.

2. Conservatism Tendency

Clinging on to the view or anchor and finding it hard to move away from this view when things change is referred to as the Conservatism Bias (Montier, 2002; Pompain, 2006).

A. Manifestation of Conservatism Tendency

The tendency of the people to be slow to pick up on the changes makes them prefer to keep their anchor on the ways things have normally been (Ritter, 2003). When things change, people might underreact to events, because of the conservatism bias (Ritter, 2003). Hirshleifer (2001) stated that this bias manifests as people feel that it is cognitively costly to process new information and update beliefs. Self-deception can also lead to being conservative (Hirshleifer, 2001). Barberis, Schleifer, and Vishny (1996) formulated a model of investor sentiment to security price over and under-reaction, to information when investor judgment is biased by conservatism and the representativeness heuristic. Their study has yielded a prediction that stock market prices over react to consistent patterns of good or bad news and underreact to earnings announcements.

B. Positive Aspects of Conservatism Tendency

According to Oakeshott, M. (1991) a conservative person takes delight in what is there at present, rather than focusing on the past that was or in the future what may be. Hence, a person who is conservative may handle their finances well. They would prefer to budget their expenses and would prefer safe avenues for investing their money. When people have only limited income, to take care of their basic expenses, then being conservative can actually be a good practice. Being conservative would lead a person to evaluate the consequences of a decision and make appropriate adjustment, even if they are slow (Oakeshott, 1991). Conservative investors would also avoid taking risks with their hard earned money.

C. Negative Aspects of Conservatism Tendency

Not being able to change a view in the light of new information can make people commit investment mistakes. And even if they do change (for example deciding to sell a stock), they do so very slowly, causing them to lose money in the meanwhile (Pompian, 2006). For a well balanced portfolio, it would be essential that an investor diversifies into multiple investment avenues, however a conservative investor would cling on to the old tried and tested avenues, even at the expense of getting more returns for the same amount of risk (that they are presently taking).

D. Overcoming Negative Aspects of Conservatism Tendency

Conservative people enjoy what is available because they are familiar with the same and thus become attached to it, and this tendency is more if there is a risk of losing that thing (Oakeshott, 1991). Oakeshott (1991) further explained that people who are conservative are able to tolerate small and slow changes, but when it comes to large and sudden changes, they can become a little more resistant.

Hence, when it comes to conservatism tendency as an investor bias, it would be essential that the people who exhibit this bias, should not be rushed or pushed into investment decisions that are radically different from the ones that these people are used to. Slow changes in the investment portfolio may go down well with these people in the long term.

3. Regret Aversion Tendency

According to Fisher and Statman (2000), "Regret is the pain we feel when we find, too late, that other choices would have led to better outcomes" (p.7). An aversion to this pain is called regret aversion.

A. Manifestation of Regret Aversion Tendency

Coricelli, Dolan and Sirigu (2007) stated that, "regret is an emotion associated with a decision that turns out badly" (p.258). In order to minimize the pain associated with regret, people avoid taking certain investment decisions, "because they fear that, in hindsight, whatever course they select will be less than optimal" (p.227). People who exhibit regret may also exhibit hindsight bias (Shefrin, 2000). Many a times in order to avoid the feeling of regret on account of having made decisions which have not been successful, the regret aversion bias sets in. This causes the investors to avoid taking a decision for fear that they may regret it later (Shefrin, 2000; Pompian, 2006). Shefrin and Statman (1985) stated that regret is an emotional feeling which is associated with the feeling that if the past decision had been different, it could have been better than the one chosen. Baber and Odean (1999) suggested that investors want to avoid regret as was observed when investors holding the stock in which they have made paper gains, worry that the stock price will fall, so they sell the paper gains stock and make it realized gains. On the other hand, when investors have paper losses on a stock investment, they expect that the stock price will go up in the future, so they continue to hold the stock in which they have losses. Szyszka (2013) stated that the feeling of regret will be more, if the decision that was taken was an exception (something that the investor has never done before), and it went wrong.

B. Positive Aspects of Regret Aversion Tendency

In order to avoid feeling regret, investors tend to be more cautious, thoughtful and prefer investments that are more secure and creditworthy, thereby leading to better decision making (Connolly & Zeelenberg, 2002). Bailey & Kinerson (2005) stated that anticipatory regret could have a positive impact on the retirement saving behaviors of the investors. This would mean that people would end up saving more for their retirement, because they would not want to regret at a later date. This would be useful for the individual's financial well-being.

C. Negative Aspects of Regret Aversion Tendency

Aversion to regret may make people too conservative while investing. Since risk is an inherent part of financial investments, being too conservative may make people miss out on investment opportunities that could be beneficial for them in the long term. To avoid the feeling of regret, people may continue to hold on to investments that are going into losses, causing them to allow erosion of their wealth (Pompian, 2006).

D. Overcoming Negative Aspects of Regret Aversion Tendency

A person may experience regret on account of an action that they took that they should not have taken or their failure to act, when they should have. A person who is prone to this tendency will avoid any action that makes them feel that they should not have done the same, at a later point in time.

The feeling of regret on account of an incorrect decision made earlier tends to make people avoid the same scenario in the future (Szyszka, 2013). It is essential therefore to help people understand the reasons for the investment moving in the opposite direction and the assumptions that were considered at the time of making the original decision. This would help to understand that an informed choice may not have been made in the initial case. Since regret is an emotional phenomenon, it may not be overcome too quickly and hence the investor would need to build themselves mentally and emotionally before venturing in the same investment scenario again, this time taking an informed decision.

Hence, in order to overcome this aspect of behavior, it would be important for the person to collect all the relevant information so as to make an informed judgment. When the judgment is made based on objectively analyzed data, the choice made would not lead to regret or to a lesser degree of regret.

4. Status Quo Bias

Leads an investor to prefer the default choice of holding on to the investments that they already have, and not act with an intention of changing the investment (Baker & Nofsinger, 2002)

A. Manifestation of Status Quo Bias

Samuelson and Zeckhauser (1988) performed a series of decision-making experiments and found evidence of the presence of status quo bias. They stated that the possible explanations for this bias could be on account of three factors, namely rational decision making in the presence of uncertainty, cognitive misperceptions, and psychological commitment stemming from misperceived sunk costs, regret avoidance, or a drive for consistency. Fernandez and Rodrik (1991) stated that due to the uncertainty regarding the distribution of gains and losses from reform, governments tend to avoid policies, which may lead to efficiency enhancement, thereby leading to status-quo bias. With regard to Investment decision making, Baker & Nofsinger (2002) stated that the status quo bias leads an investor to prefer the default choice of holding on to the investments that they already have, and not act with an intention of changing the investment, even if the action is in investors' best interest.

B. Positive Aspects of Status Quo Bias

Status quo tendency has been shown to help people minimize the cognitive effort and cope with the negative emotions that may arise (Luce, 1998). Samuelson & Zeckhauser (1988) explained that "the act of choosing an alternative raises its value to some degree. Other things equal, this induces a bias toward retaining the choice in subsequent decisions even under changed conditions" (p.40). Emotional focused coping behaviour has been shown to lead people to avoidance behaviour or changing the meaning of the situation (Folkman & Lazarus, 1980; Luce, 1998). Further and Luce (1998) explained that people prefer to choose the avoidant options (maintaining the status quo) as it gives them satisfaction that they could minimize the "explicit confrontation of negative potential decision consequences and difficult trade- offs" (p.409).

C. Negative Aspects of Status Quo Bias

Status quo bias can lead to investors holding on to investments which are not always beneficial for their investment profile. People who are conservative and want to invest in familiar avenues also prefer to maintain the status quo, even if the market conditions showed potential for greater returns for their level of risks. This bias is more prominent when the investment alternatives in the market are numerous (Kempf & Ruenzi, 2006). The presence of this bias would cause the investor to not make any changes to their investment portfolio even if doing so would lead them to higher gains (Baker & Nofsinger, 2002)

D. Overcoming Negative Aspects of Status Quo Bias

When the investor feels negative emotions with regard to the investment options available for them, there is a tendency to maintain the status quo. The fear and negative emotions could be stemming from the limited knowledge of the investor. Hence it is important that the investor understands whether maintaining the status quo is helping him/her to achieve the financial goals that they have set for themselves. This way if the person feels that his/her financial goals may not be achieved in the present scenario, they may make an effort to move away from the status quo.

5. Familiarity Bias

According to Foad (2010), the "revealed preference for familiar assets in the presence of higher returns and lower risks from less familiar assets is known as familiarity bias" (p.277). People prefer to play safe and would choose the familiar to the unfamiliar on account of the fear of unknown (Shefrin, 2000).

A. Manifestation of Familiarity Bias

Investors tend to put too much faith on familiar stock as they believe that these stocks are less risky than other companies and at times they consider them even safer than a diversified portfolio (Baker & Nofsinger, 2002; Goetzmann & Kumar, 2005). Familiarity gives an illusion of control as investors tend to feel that more knowledge (i.e. being familiar with the object), does mean control on the outcome (Goetzmann & Kumar, 2005). Familiarity is also related to the Home Bias. The presence of Home Bias (French & Poterba, 1991) leads people to buy more securities from their home country than overseas. This bias is on account of the familiarity of the companies from their own country that investors feel they have, as compared with the foreign companies (Baker & Nofsinger, 2002). Baltzer, Stolper, and Walter (2014) found that investors prefer to take their money out of unfamiliar foreign stocks and put their money into familiar local stocks during times of increased market uncertainty. Huberman (2001) found evidence that people have a propensity to invest in the familiar, while often ignoring the principles of portfolio theory.

B. Positive Aspects of Familiarity Bias

Choosing options that one is familiar with is a self-coping mechanism that allows people to reduce their fears when it comes to investment decisions. In case of decision making under uncertainty, familiarity bias helps the investor to manage their fears (Chew, Ebstein, & Zhong, 2012). This helps to increase their wellbeing.

C. Negative Aspects of Familiarity Bias

Studies as done by Huberman (2001) and Coval and Moskowitz (1999) showed that investors tend to buy stocks of companies that have a local or regional business presence, leading to an under-diversified portfolio.

D. Overcoming Negative Aspects of Familiarity Bias

It is possible that initially when an individual is venturing out into new investment avenues, investing based on familiarity bias can help them test the new grounds. Once they are comfortable they can slowly move into other products in that investment segment, thereby removing the negative aspects of this bias. Massa and Simonov (2002) found that "familiarity is more based on information constraints than on behavioural heuristics" (p. 2). Hence, providing more information both positive and negative about the investment options will help people to make an informed decision and not get entangled in the web of familiarity.

6. Representativeness Bias

According to Taffler (2010), "representativeness refers to the way people make subjective probability judgments based on similarity to stereotypes" (p.259).

A. Manifestation of Representativeness Bias

Representativeness refers to the tendency to evaluate how likely something is with reference to how closely it resembles something rather than using probabilities (Tversky & Kahneman, 1974; Montier, 2002). Representativeness is judgment based on stereotypes (Brabazon, 2000; Baker & Nofsinger, 2002). This bias leads people to underweight long-term averages and put too much weight on recent experience (Ritter, 2003). This is sometimes known as the "law of small numbers." (Brabazon, 2000) When dealing with earnings data, it has been noted that when an investor sees many periods of good earnings, then the law of small numbers leads him to believe that the firm has high earnings growth and this growth is likely to continue. (Montier, 2002; Ritter, 2003). This bias also makes people overreact to new information. (Pompian, 2006)

B. Positive Aspects of Representativeness Bias

Due to the limitation posed by the human mind to analyze huge amounts of data, people tend to form decisions based on limited information. This helps the person to make quick decisions.

C. Negative Aspects of Representativeness Bias

Baker and Nofsinger (2002) elucidated that when investors classify firms which have provided consistent earnings growth as good stocks, they ignore the fact that many of these companies won't be able to sustain the high growth rates in the future also. Eventually, "the popularity of these firms drives prices higher until the stock becomes overpriced. Over time investors become aware that they have been too optimistic in predicting future growth and the stock price falls" (Baker & Nofsinger, 2002, p.100). Chen, Kim, Nofsinger and Rui (2007) in their study on the trading behaviour of Chinese investors found that Chinese investors appeared to believe that that past returns are indicative of future returns. This may not be true if the proper analysis of the company data and performance is done.

D. Overcoming Negative Aspects of Representativeness Bias

Since representativeness is a cognitive bias (Pompian, 2006), investment decisions made after analyzing various parameters over a longer period of time, with regard to the subject matter, will be able to overcome the negative aspects of the representativeness bias.

7. Self-Control Bias

"the relative dominance of will power, over desire as a decision motivator" (Perry, 2000, p.19).

A. Manifestation of Self-Control Bias

Antonides (1996) stated that "people appear to restrict their own behaviour in order to protect themselves against future negative consequences. People save a part of their money to protect themselves against later poverty" (p.261). Shefrin and Thaler (1988) propounded the behavioural life cycle hypothesis, wherein they state that self-control is important as consuming today is always an attractive choice compared to saving for the future.

B. Positive Aspects of Self-Control Bias

To have self-control means that you could control your emotions, since the natural tendency of people is to be impulsive and consume today. "The lack of control over one's finances exposes adults to financial risk in retirement, which can have adverse and long-term consequences" (Zurlo, 2009). Hence, a person who has self-control is able to plan well for his/her retirement years and for other contingencies that may arise.

C. Negative Aspects of Self-Control Bias

Many people are very frugal when it comes to spending money on their living, even when they have a substantial amount of income. Dunn, Aknin and Norton (2008) stated that, "how people spend their money may be at least as important as how much money they earn" (p.1687). Their study found that spending money on other people has a more positive impact on happiness than spending money on oneself (Dunn, Aknin & Norton, 2008). If a person has too much of self-control then they won't be able to spend money, either on oneself or on others. Further from an investment perspective, too much self-control can also prevent you from achieving you financial goals, as you don't diversify your portfolio enough.

D. Overcoming Negative Aspects of Self-Control Bias

It is essential to understand whether this bias is working in your favor or not. Self-control is important if an individual is very consumption oriented and doesn't save enough for the achievement of their financial goals. However, for those who are putting too much control on their spending habits, it is essential to understand whether this behaviour, is making people happy or not. Also the person who has too much of self-control should not miss out on the correct investment avenues for increasing their future wealth. Since, self-control is an emotional bias; hence it is essential to understand the emotions that the person has, associated with, letting go of self-control. Many a times the fear of not having enough in the future may the reason for high self-control. These fears can be reduced by giving proper information about the future financial position of the investor, under different scenarios. If the person feels secure that he/she would have sufficient resources in the future, even if he/she spends a certain percentage of income today, then the negative aspects of the self-control bias can be reduced.

8. Hindsight Bias

Hindsight Bias refers to:

- Person regards the events that happened as much more inevitable than they looked before the fact (Shefrin, 2000)
- Hindsight Bias is the tendency of people to believe, after an event has occurred, that they predicted it before it happened (Barberis & Thaler, 2003)

A. Manifestation of Hindsight Bias

Evidence has shown that some individuals claim to have known the outcome information all along, after receiving such information (Fischhoff, 1975; El-Sehity, Haumer, Helmenstein, Kirchler & Maciejovsky, 2002). Hindsight bias is a phenomenon in which people tend to exaggerate the predictability of an event after it has taken place. It makes people claim that their prediction was very significant. It makes people view the world as more predictable than it actually is (Shiller, 2000). This tendency gives a sense of security to the people (Pompian, 2006). Two ways in which hindsight bias may operate:

- Positive developments as predictable: Rewriting own memory; it leads to excessive risk taking, as people feel that they have "superior predictive powers" (Pompian, 2006; p.202). According to Roese and Vohs (2012), hindsight bias could be on account of memory distortion, beliefs about events' objective likelihoods, or subjective beliefs about one's own prediction abilities.

- Negative Developments: Rewriting History; "block out recollections of prior, incorrect forecasts to alleviate embarrassments" (Pompian, 2006; p.202). So this person rewrites history and "ignores irrelevant information so as to avoid psychological conflict" (Pompian, 2006; p.84).

Consider a decision maker who has been caught unprepared by some turn of events and who tries to see where he went wrong by recreating his pre outcome knowledge state of mind. If, in retrospect, the event appears to have seemed relatively likely, he can do little more than berate himself for not taking the action which his knowledge seems to have dictated. He might be said to add the insult of regret to the injury inflicted by the event itself. When second guessed by a hindsightful observer, his misfortune appears to have been incompetence, folly, or worse. (Fischhoff, 1975, p.299)

B. Positive Aspects of Hindsight Bias

According to Monti and Legrenzi (2009). "hindsightful judge possesses final knowledge, that is, he or she knows what has really happened" (p.768). Hence, once an event is part of history, there is a tendency to see the sequence that led to it as inevitable, as if uncertainty and chance were banished (Fisher & Statman, 2000). This at times can be good as it would enable the individual to understand the way the events took place and what was the information that supported that event taking place. This may make him/her more cautious of the information that needs to be collected, next time when a similar decision needs to be taken.

C. Negative Aspects of Hindsight Bias

Pompian (2006) argued that Hindsight bias "leads investors to believe that they have better predictive powers than they actually do" (p.201). This gives them a false sense of security and they may end up taking more risk than their can tolerate (Pompian, 2006). Commenting on the work of Fischhoff, Fisher & Statman (2000) stated that "in general, people overestimate the quality of their initial knowledge and forget their initial errors" (p. 7).

D. Overcoming Negative Aspects of Hindsight Bias

Helping people understand that there could have been multiple factors that caused the event to have taken place can help to eliminate the hindsight bias to some extent. Also showing people the circumstances in which the factors (which seemed to work in line with the investors' expectation), could have been different and led to varying results.

9. Illusion of Control

"The illusion of control (IC) refers to the belief that one can manipulate, influence, and control outcomes of chance events" (Budescu & Bruderman, 1995, p.109).

A. Manifestation of Illusion of Control

The illusion of control (Langer, 1975; Mckenna, 1993) pertains to greater confidence in one's predictive ability or in a favorable outcome when one has a higher degree of personal involvement (Charness & Gneezy, 2003). Langer (1975) defined illusion of control as "an expectancy of a personal success probability inappropriately higher than the objective probability would warrant" (p.311). Langer (1975) in his work on Illusion of Control found that choice, task familiarity, competition, and active involvement all lead to increase in confidence of the individual with regard to the situation.

Antonides (1996) stated that illusion of control manifests when people believe that exercising their skill will have an effect on the outcome. When an individual "perceives that the event is contingent upon her own behaviour" (p.33), it is called a belief in internal control. An Internal economic locus of control is the perception of personal control over financial affairs (Furnham, 1986; Sumarwan & Hira, 1993).

B. Positive Aspects of Illusion of Control

Illusion of control arises when an individual is familiar with the investments, has choice and is actively involved in the investment process (Zaleskiewicz, 2006). Further positive illusions have shown to be lead to increased motivation and are advantageous (Taylor & Brown, 1988; Bandura, 1989; Fenton-O-Creevy et al., 2003). A person with an internal locus of control believes that his acting in a particular way will result in the desired or positive outcome (Rotter, 1954; Tennen & Sharp, 1983). Further, it has been seen that people with internal locus of control adopt innovations and new practices (Pfeiffer, 1996).

C. Negative Aspects of Illusion of Control

Illusion of control leads to at times overconfidence bias and this would make people feel that they have the ability to always make the profitable investment decisions. This may lead to people ignoring some relevant and important information, which in turn could lead to investment mistakes. On account of Illusion of Control investors may end up trading more frequently and maintaining under diversified portfolios. (Pompain, 2006)

D. Overcoming Negative Aspects of Illusion of Control

Investors need to understand all the possible outcomes of their investment decisions. This way they would know that there are probabilities attached to the various outcomes- both positive and negative. Seeking various points of view would also help in minimizing the negative effects of illusion of control.

10. Loss Aversion Tendency

The tendency of the people to be more sensitive to losses than to gains is referred to as loss aversion (Kahneman & Tversky, 1979) According to Barberis and Huang (2001), the degree of loss aversion that a person experiences would depend upon prior gains and losses. They further stated that, "a loss that comes after prior gains is less painful than usual, because it is cushioned by those earlier gains. On the other hand, a loss that comes after other losses is more painful than usual" (p. 1248). This is because once people have experienced a loss, they "become more sensitive to additional setbacks" (Barberis & Huang, 2001, p. 1248).

A. Manifestation of Loss Aversion Tendency

Loss aversion in case of behavioural finance is based on the observation that when it comes to losses, investors feel more pain, as compared to the pleasure that they feel in the event of a gain, of an equivalent amount (Kahneman & Tversky, 1979). According to Godoi, Marcon and Da Silva (2005), loss aversion is characterized as not, "an investment distance, but as a deep connection, although being negative with the investment object" (p. 48). Kahneman and Tversky (1979) observed in their experiments, that on account of loss aversion, people are impacted by a loss 2.5 times that of a gain of the same value. Godoi, Marcon and Da Silva (2005) linked the loss aversion tendency to the primordial fear in the childhood and noted that these childhood experiences, impact future experiences and this comes in the way of an investor's ability to evaluate an investment decision systematically, as the decision is made in the backdrop of the past experiences. Camerer (2005) stated that loss aversion is rooted in fear and is "an exaggerated emotional reaction of fear, an adapted response to the prospect of genuine, damaging, survival – threatening loss" (p.132).

B. Positive Aspects of Loss Aversion Tendency

Samanez-Larkin, Hollon, Carstensen, and Knutson (2008) stated that "detecting and avoiding threats arguably are the most basic of survival skills" (p.320). A potential loss is like a threat in the mind of the investor who prefers to minimize the same. People who are loss aversive are guided by fear and are less risk taking (Tom, Fox, Trepel, & Poldrack, 2007). It has been seen that risk seeking behaviour doesn't necessarily lead to higher financial satisfaction levels. Avoiding losses is a natural human tendency and this makes a person feel secure. Loss brings with it pain and avoidance of pain is a natural human behaviour. It helps people maintain a sense of well-being.

C. Negative Aspects of Loss Aversion Tendency

"The loss starts to represent a threat to identity, a loss in the life style" (Godoi, Marcon & Da Silva, 2005, p. 49). Hence, investors cope with the pain associated with the loss, by avoiding, the investment choices that show a possibility of negative change in their investment position. "If investors are loss adverse, they may be reluctant to realize losses" and would thereby "play safe when protecting gains but are willing to take chances in an attempt to escape from a losing position" (Brabazon, 2000, p.4). Baker and Nofsinger (2002) stated that a large loss may cause the investor to react in two ways, either avoiding taking any risk by not owning any stocks at all, on account of a fear of losses or taking on more risk in an attempt to recoup the loss, with the intention to get even.

D. Overcoming Negative Aspects of Loss Aversion Tendency

A person who wants to avoid the pain of loss is coming from an emotional perspective. In the attempt to help people overcome the negative aspects of loss aversion, which is on account of them holding on to losing investment, they should be given substantial evidence to understand that pain that they are avoiding in giving up a losing investment would become worse if they were to hold on to it for long.

Further, those people who are loss averse since they have experienced losses in the past can be, through slow effort, made to understand the gaps in the initial decision that could have lead to the loss, so that they understand that the experience of loss was on account of a not well planned portfolio strategy and with portfolio diversification they could have reduced the impact of the loss. Hence, important cues that help the person shift from the emotional domain to the cognitive domain would help people to overcome this bias.

FUTURE RESEARCH DIRECTIONS

Investment decisions are made in very complex and uncertain situations (Ackert & Church, 2006), that it is not possible before hand to rely on fixed rules and thus the decision maker is compelled to rely on intuition. Intuitive judgment makes use of heuristics and lead to biases and cognitive illusions that affect investment decisions. (Pines, 1983; Kahneman & Riepe, 1998). Individuals process information in order to arrive at probabilities and judgments which is further used in the evaluation of the most appropriate decision amongst the various courses of actions, which ultimately depends on their subjective analysis (Pines, 1983). Pines (1983) has stated two kinds of judgmental inconsistencies that an investor ought to understand, random inconsistencies and systematic inconsistencies. He defined random inconsistencies as random judgments of the same event usually arising on account of transitory conditions like that of boredom, fatigue, distraction etc. which tend to cancel out each other over time, whereas the systematic inconsistencies wherein some systematic biases that make we have makes us think in a particular way about the event, tends to lead logically inconsistent choices.

Though insights from evolutionary psychology present the fact that biases are natural designs of the human mind, and are essential for the individual to make sense of the environment, yet at times these biases can work in a detrimental way and reduce the wellbeing of the individual. Most people start associating themselves with their biases, either consciously or unconsciously even if they experience the negative results of the same.

While there may be ways for overcoming the negative dimensions of the biases, it is first and foremost essential to identify the biases and how they are impacting the investor- positively or negatively. Once this diagnosis has been made, the need for correcting would be looked at. However, if the biases are working in a way that they are enabling the individual to be financially satisfied, then an effort to remove the bias/ or to reduce the bias, may lead the investor to be dissatisfied with their changed scenario.

A great potential exists for future research in this area. This chapter looks at ten biases that impact investor behaviour. There are many more such biases, which need to be looked into. Further, finding out ways to understand the predominant biases that impact behavior, also needs to be developed. Further, in case those behavioural dispositions are leading to unsatisfactory results for the investor, the understanding of such biases would help to moderate them in the future.

Further, an understanding of the investor biases and their effect on the investment choices of the individual would help in making better policies and products that suit the needs of the investor. For example an investor who is conservative when it comes to investing in equities, may be suggested an investment product wherein the initial principal is in low risk instruments, but a part of the interest earned at subsequent periods, is invested in dividend paying, low risk stocks. This way since a conservative investor who may be slow to adapt to changes, would be able to venture into equities, through an initial debt investment. Once the investor has tested the market and adapted to the same, he/she can experiment with more investment in equities and diversify his/her portfolio.

CONCLUSION

Traditional Finance theories have taken the assumption that the decision maker is a rational human being whose sole aim is to maximize his/her expected utility. However with the advent of the behavioral finance proponents claiming that it is the irrationality in the decision makers' behaviour that guides most decisions, the study of investor behaviour has taken a different perspective. A bias may be an irrational behaviour from the perspective of traditional finance, but the evidence from evolutionary psychology shows that biases are actually designs of the human mind and help in decision making. Hence, to see investor biases only from the lens of how they must be corrected may not give a complete picture of the phenomenon. It is essential to understand that the while sometimes the bias can be helpful to the decision maker, yet at other times, can harm their investment goals.

There is a need to identify and comprehend the nature of various cognitive and emotional factors that determine the investors' attitude towards the investments. While much has been said about the negative aspects of various investor biases, this chapter looks into what are the positive aspects that lead people to continue to have these biases, in spite of them leading to sometimes incorrect or suboptimal decisions.

An understanding of the various biases and how they impact the portfolio choices both positively and negatively would enable a more comprehensive understanding of individual investor. How one investor is able to use the bias in the positive aspect while another is only facing the negative results of the bias, would help in better financial advisory practices and increased portfolio management. This would in the long term help the investor to meet their financial goals and increase their financial well-being. Further an understanding of the biases and how they vary across investors would also help in better financial advisory practice, by giving more insight to the financial advisors on how investors behave. Researches and Policy makers can also find these insights useful as these would enable them to make better designed policies, practices and products, which would match with the investment needs of the individual.

REFERENCES

Ackert, L. F., & Church, B. K. (2006). Firm image and individual investment decisions. *Journal of Behavioral Finance*, *7*(3), 155–167. doi:10.1207/s15427579jpfm0703_4

Antonides, G. (1996). *Psychology in economics and business: an introduction to economic psychology*. Springer. doi:10.1007/978-94-009-1710-1

Arkes, H. R., Faust, D., Guilmette, T. J., & Hart, K. (1988). Eliminating the hindsight bias. *The Journal of Applied Psychology*, *73*(2), 305–307. doi:10.1037/0021-9010.73.2.305

Bailey, J. J., & Kinerson, C. (2005). Regret avoidance and risk tolerance. *Financial Counseling and Planning*, *16*(1), 23–28.

Baker, H. K., & Nofsinger, J. R. (2002). Psychological biases of investors. *Financial Services Review*, *11*(2), 97–116.

Baltzer, M., Stolper, O., & Walter, A. (2014, in press). Home-field advantage or a matter of ambiguity aversion? Local bias among German individual investors. *The European Journal of Finance*, 1-21.

Bandura, A. (1989). Human agency in social cognitive theory. *The American Psychologist*, *44*(9), 1175–1184. doi:10.1037/0003-066X.44.9.1175 PMID:2782727

Barber, B. M., & Odean, T. (2001). Boys will be boys: Gender, overconfidence, and common stock investment. *The Quarterly Journal of Economics*, *116*(1), 261–292. doi:10.1162/003355301556400

Barberis, N., & Huang, M. (2001). Mental accounting, loss aversion, and individual stock returns. *The Journal of Finance*, *56*(4), 1247–1292. doi:10.1111/0022-1082.00367

Barberis, N., Shleifer, A., & Vishny, R. (1998). A model of investor sentiment. *Journal of Financial Economics*, *49*(3), 307–343. doi:10.1016/S0304-405X(98)00027-0

Barberis, N., & Thaler, R. (2003). A survey of behavioral finance. Handbook of the Economics of Finance, 1, 1053-1128.

Brabazon, T. (2000). *Behavioural Finance: A new sunrise or a false dawn*? Retrieved from http://introduction.behaviouralfinance.net/Brab00.pdf

Budescu, D. V., & Bruderman, M. (1995). The relationship between the illusion of control and the desirability bias. *Journal of Behavioral Decision Making*, *8*(2), 109–125. doi:10.1002/bdm.3960080204

Camerer, C. (2005). Three cheers—psychological, theoretical, empirical—for loss aversion. *JMR, Journal of Marketing Research*, *42*(2), 129–133. doi:10.1509/jmkr.42.2.129.62286

Charness, G., & Gneezy, U. (2003) '*Portfolio Choice and Risk Attitudes: An Experiment*' (February 20, 2003). Retrieved from http://ssrn.com/abstract=397300 or doi:10.2139/ssrn.397300

Chen, G., Kim, K. A., Nofsinger, J. R., & Rui, O. M. (2007). Trading performance, disposition effect, overconfidence, representativeness bias, and experience of emerging market investors. *Journal of Behavioral Decision Making*, *20*(4), 425–451. doi:10.1002/bdm.561

Chew, S. H., Ebstein, R. P., & Zhong, S. (2012). Ambiguity aversion and familiarity bias: Evidence from behavioral and gene association studies. *Journal of Risk and Uncertainty*, *44*(1), 1–18. doi:10.1007/s11166-011-9134-0

Connolly, T., & Zeelenberg, M. (2002). 'Regret in Decision Making'. *Current Directions in Psychological Science*, *11*(6), 212–216. doi:10.1111/1467-8721.00203

Coricelli, G., Dolan, R. J., & Sirigu, A. (2007). Brain, emotion and decision making: The paradigmatic example of regret. *Trends in Cognitive Sciences*, *11*(6), 258–265. doi:10.1016/j.tics.2007.04.003 PMID:17475537

Coval, J., & Moskowitz, T. (1999). 'Home Bias at home: Local equity preference in domestic portfolios'. *The Journal of Finance*, *54*(6), 2045–2073. doi:10.1111/0022-1082.00181

Cummins, R. A., & Nistico, H. (2002). Maintaining life satisfaction: The role of positive cognitive bias. *Journal of Happiness Studies*, *3*(1), 37–69. doi:10.1023/A:1015678915305

Dunn, E. W., Aknin, L. B., & Norton, M. I. (2008). Spending money on others promotes happiness. *Science*, *319*(5870), 1687–1688. doi:10.1126/science.1150952 PMID:18356530

El-Sehity, T., Haumer, H., Helmenstein, C., Kirchler, E., & Maciejovsky, B. (2002). Hindsight bias and individual risk attitude within the context of experimental asset markets. *The Journal of Psychology and Financial Markets*, *3*(4), 227–235. doi:10.1207/S15327760JPFM0304_04

Fenton-O'Creevy, M., Nicholson, N., Soane, E., & Willman, P. (2003). Trading on illusions: Unrealistic perceptions of control and trading performance. *Journal of Occupational and Organizational Psychology*, *76*(1), 53–68. doi:10.1348/096317903321208880

Fernandez, R., & Rodrik, D. (1991). 'Resistance to Reform: Status Quo Bias in the Presence of Individual-Specific Uncertainty', American *Economic Review* [December]. *American Economic Association*, *81*(5), 1146–1155.

Fischoff, B. (1975). 'Hindsight =/ Foresight:The Effect of Outcome Knowledge on Judgment Under Uncertainty'. *Journal of Experimental Psychology. Human Perception and Performance*, *1*(3), 288–299. doi:10.1037/0096-1523.1.3.288

Fisher, K. L., & Statman, M. (2000). Investor sentiment and stock returns. *Financial Analysts Journal*, *56*(2), 16–23. doi:10.2469/faj.v56.n2.2340

Foad, H. (2010). Familiarity Bias. In *Behavioral finance: Investors, corporations, and markets.* Wiley.

Folkman, S., & Lazarus, R. S. (1980). An analysis of coping in a middle- aged community sample. *Journal of Personality and Social Psychology*, *21*, 219–239. PMID:7410799

French, K., & Poterba, J. (1991). Investor Diversification and International Equity Markets. *The American Economic Review*, *81*(2), 222–226.

Friedman, H. (2007). Does Overconfidence Affect Entrepreneurial Investment? *Wharton Research Scholars Journal. University of Pennsylvania.* Retrieved from http://repository.upenn.edu/wharton research scholars/42

Furnham, A. (1986). Economic Lotus of Control. *Human Relations*, *39*(1), 29–43. doi:10.1177/001872678603900102

Godoi, C. K., Marcon, R., & Barbosa da Silva, A. (2005). Loss Aversion: A Qualitative Study In Behavioural Finance. *Managerial Finance*, *31*(4), 46–56. doi:10.1108/03074350510769613

Goetzmann, W. N., & Kumar, A. (2005). *Why Do Individual Investors Hold Under-Diversified Portfolios?* Yale School of Management.

Gonzalez, C., Dana, J., Koshino, H., & Just, M. (2005). The framing effect and risky decisions: Examining cognitive functions with fMRI. *Journal of Economic Psychology*, *26*(1), 1–20. doi:10.1016/j.joep.2004.08.004

Grinblatt, M., & Keloharju, M. (2001). How distance, language, and culture influence stockholdings and trades. *The Journal of Finance*, *56*(3), 1053–1073. doi:10.1111/0022-1082.00355

Haselton, M. G., & Buss, D. M. (2000). Error management theory: A new perspective on biases in cross-sex mind reading. *Journal of Personality and Social Psychology*, *78*(1), 81–91. doi:10.1037/0022-3514.78.1.81 PMID:10653507

Haselton, M. G., & Buss, D. M. (2003). Design Flaws or Design Features? *Social judgments: Implicit and explicit processes, 5*, 23.

Haselton, M. G., & Nettle, D. (2006). The paranoid optimist: An integrative evolutionary model of cognitive biases. *Personality and Social Psychology Review*, *10*(1), 47–66. doi:10.1207/s15327957pspr1001_3 PMID:16430328

Haselton, M. G., Nettle, D., & Andrews, P. W. (2005). The evolution of cognitive bias. The handbook of evolutionary psychology, 724-746.

Hilton, D. J. (2001). The psychology of financial decision-making: Applications to trading, dealing, and investment analysis. *The Journal of Psychology and Financial Markets*, *2*(1), 37–53. doi:10.1207/S15327760JPFM0201_4

Hirshleifer, D. (2001). Investor psychology and asset pricing. *The Journal of Finance*, *56*(4), 1533–1597. doi:10.1111/0022-1082.00379

Huberman, G. (2001). Familiarity breeds investment. *Review of Financial Studies*, *14*(3), 659–680. doi:10.1093/rfs/14.3.659

Kahler, R. (2007). 'Beyond the Numbers'. *Financial Planning*. May

Kahneman, D., & Riepe, M. W. (1998). Aspects of investor psychology. *Journal of Portfolio Management*, *24*(4), 52–65. doi:10.3905/jpm.1998.409643

Kahneman, D., & Tversky, A. (1979). Prospect theory: An analysis of decision under risk. *Econometrica*, *47*(2), 263–291. doi:10.2307/1914185

Kempf, A., & Ruenzi, S. (2006). Status Quo Bias and the Number of Alternatives: An Empirical Illustration from the Mutual Fund Industry. *Journal of Behavioral Finance*, *7*(4), 204–213. doi:10.1207/s15427579jpfm0704_3

Keren, G., & Teigen, K. H. (2004). Yet another look at the heuristics and biases approach. Blackwell handbook of judgment and decision making, 89.

Kinney, A. (2000). Positive Illusions of Well-Being and Irrationality: Implications for Rational-Emotive Behaviour Therapy. *Journal of Contemporary Psychotherapy*, *30*(4), 401–415. doi:10.1023/A:1010235620775

Klein, C., & Gotti, R. (1992). *Overcoming Regret: Lessons from the Roads Not Taken*. Bantam Books.

Kuhnen, C. M., & Knutson, B. (2005). The neural basis of financial risk taking. *Neuron*, *47*(5), 763–770. doi:10.1016/j.neuron.2005.08.008 PMID:16129404

Langer, E. J. (1975). The illusion of control. *Journal of Personality and Social Psychology*, *32*(2), 311–328. doi:10.1037/0022-3514.32.2.311

Lovric, M., Kaymak, U., & Spronk, J. (2008). *A Conceptual Model of Investor Behaviour* (ERIM Report Series Reference No. ERS-2008-030-F&A). Retrieved from http://ssrn.com/abstract=1144293

Luce, M. F. (1998). Choosing to Avoid: Coping with Negatively. Emotion-Laden Consumer Decisions. *The Journal of Consumer Research*, *24*(4), 409–433. doi:10.1086/209518

Marshall, J. A., Trimmer, P. C., Houston, A. I., & McNamara, J. M. (2013). On evolutionary explanations of cognitive biases. *Trends in Ecology & Evolution*, *28*(8), 469–473. doi:10.1016/j.tree.2013.05.013 PMID:23790393

Massa, M., & Simonov, A. (2005). Behavioral biases and investment. *Review of Finance*, *9*(4), 483–507. doi:10.1007/s10679-005-4998-y

Mckenna, F. P. (1993). It won't happen to me-unrealistic optimism or illusion of control. *British Journal of Psychology*, *84*(1), 39–50. doi:10.1111/j.2044-8295.1993.tb02461.x

Monti, M., & Legrenzi, P. (2009). *Investment Decision-Making and Hindsight Bias*. Retrieved on 15th September 2009 from http://141.14.165.6/CogSci09/papers/135/paper135.pdf

Montier, J. (2002). *Darwin's Mind: The Evolutionary Foundations of Heuristics and Biases*. Retrieved from http://papers.ssrn.com/sol3/papers.cfm?abstract_id=373321

Nelson, D. L., & Quick, J. C. (2008). *Understanding Organizational Behaviour* (3rd ed.). Canada: Thompson South Western.

Nofsinger, J. R. (2001). *Investment Madness: How Psychology Affects Your Investing--and what to Do about it*. Financial Times Prentice Hall.

Nosic, A., & Weber, M. (2007). *Determinants of Risk Taking Behavior: The role of Risk Attitudes, Risk Perceptions and Beliefs*. Sonderforschungsbereich 504, Universität Mannheim & Sonderforschungsbereich 504, University of Mannheim. No 07-56. Retrieved from http://www.sfb504.uni-mannheim.de/publications/dp07-56.pdf

Oakeshott, M. (1991). On being conservative. *Rationalism in politics and other essays*, 168-96.

Odean, T. (1999). Do Investors Trade Too Much? *The American Economic Review*, *89*(5), 1279–1298. doi:10.1257/aer.89.5.1279

Odean, T., & Barber, B. (1999). The courage of misguided convictions: The trading behavior of individual investors. *Financial Analysts Journal*, *55*(6), 41–55. doi:10.2469/faj.v55.n6.2313

Olsen, R., A. (2007). Investors' Predisposition for Annuities: A Psychological Perspective. *Journal of Financial Service Professionals*. September

Perry, V. G. (2000). Antecedents of consumer financing decisions: A mental accounting model of revolving credit usage (Ph.D. dissertation, The University of North Carolina at Chapel Hill). *ABI/INFORM Global Publication No. AAT 9979480*.

Pfeiffer, J. W. (1996). *Theories and Models in Applied Behavioural Science: Individual* (Vol. 1). New Delhi: Pfeiffer & Company.

Pines, H. A. (1996). The Psychology of Investor Decision Making. In S. Lofthouse (Ed.), *Readings in Investments*. Wiley Publishers.

Plous, S. (1993). *The psychology of judgment and decision making*. Mcgraw-Hill Book Company.

Pompian, M. M. (2006). *Behavioral finance and wealth management*. New Jersey: How to Build Optimal Portfolios That Account for Investor Biases.

Pompian, M. M. (2008). Using behavioral investor types to build better relationships with your clients. *Journal of Financial Planning*, *21*(10), 64–76.

Prast, H. (2004). Investor Psychology: A Behavioural Explanation of Six Financial Puzzles. *Research Series of De nederlandsche Bank*

Ritter, J. R. (2003). Behavioral finance. *Pacific-Basin Finance Journal*, *11*(4), 429–437. doi:10.1016/S0927-538X(03)00048-9

Roese, N. J., & Vohs, K. D. (2012). Hindsight bias. *Perspectives on Psychological Science*, *7*(5), 411–426. doi:10.1177/1745691612454303

Roszkowski, M. J., & Grable, J. (2007). How are income and net worth related to happiness? *Journal of Financial Service Professionals, 61*(1).

Rotter, J. B. (1954). *Social learning and clinical psychology*. New York: Prentice-Hall. doi:10.1037/10788-000

Rubaltelli, E., Rubichi, S., Savadori, L., Tedeschi, M., & Ferretti, R. (2005). Numerical information format and investment decisions: Implications for the disposition effect and the status quo bias. *Journal of Behavioral Finance, 6*(1), 19–26. doi:10.1207/s15427579jpfm0601_4

Samanez-Larkin, G. R., Hollon, N. G., Carstensen, L. L., & Knutson, B. (2008). Individual differences in insular sensitivity during loss anticipation predict avoidance learning. *Psychological Science, 19*(4), 320–323. doi:10.1111/j.1467-9280.2008.02087.x PMID:18399882

Samuelson, W., & Zeckhauser, R. (1988). Status quo bias in decision making. *Journal of Risk and Uncertainty, 1*(1), 7–59. doi:10.1007/BF00055564

Seo, M., & Barrett, L. F. (2007). Being emotional during decision making—Good or bad? An empirical investigation. *Academy of Management Journal, 50*(4), 923–940. doi:10.5465/AMJ.2007.26279217 PMID:18449361

Shefrin, H. (2000). *Beyond greed and fear: Understanding behavioral finance and the psychology of investing*. Oxford University Press.

Shiller, R. J. (2000). *Irrational Exuberance*. Princeton: Princeton University Press.

Simon, H. (1957). A Behavioural Model of Rational Choice. In *Models of Man, Social and Rational: Mathematical Essays on Rational Human Behaviour in a Social Setting*. New York: Wiley.

Simon, H. A. (1955). A Behavioural Model of Rational Choice. *The Quarterly Journal of Economics*, 69.

Simon, H. A. (1956). Rational Choice and the Structure of Environments. *Psychological Review, 6*(2), 129–138. doi:10.1037/h0042769 PMID:13310708

Skala, D. (2008). *Overconfidence in Psychology and Finance - An Interdisciplinary Literature Review (September 1, 2008). Bank i Kredyt, No. 4* (pp. 33–50). Available at SSRN; http://ssrn.com/abstract=1261907

Slovic, P. (1972). Psychological study of human judgment: Implications for investment decision making. *The Journal of Finance, 27*(4), 779–799. doi:10.1111/j.1540-6261.1972.tb01311.x

Sumarwan, U., & Hira, T. K. (1993). The effects of perceived locus of control and perceived income adequacy on satisfaction with financial status of rural households. *Journal of Family and Economic Issues, 14*(4), 343–364. doi:10.1007/BF01013984

Szyszka, A. (2013). *Behavioral Finance and Capital Markets: How Psychology Influences Investors and Corporations*. Palgrave Macmillan. doi:10.1057/9781137366290

Taffler, R. J.(2010). The Representativeness Heuristic. *Behavioral Finance: Investors, Corporations, and Markets*, 259-276.

Taylor, S. E., & Brown, J. D. (1988). Illusion and well-being: A social psychological perspective on mental health. *Psychological Bulletin, 103*(2), 193–210. doi:10.1037/0033-2909.103.2.193 PMID:3283814

Tennen, H., & Sharp, J. P. (1983). Control orientation and the illusion of control. *Journal of Personality Assessment, 47*(4), 369–374. doi:10.1207/s15327752jpa4704_6 PMID:16367577

Thaler, R. (1980). Toward a positive theory of consumer choice. *Journal of Economic Behavior & Organization, 1*(1), 39–60. doi:10.1016/0167-2681(80)90051-7

Thaler, R. H. (1999). Mental accounting matters. *Journal of Behavioral Decision Making*, *12*(3), 183–206. doi:10.1002/(SICI)1099-0771(199909)12:3<183::AID-BDM318>3.0.CO;2-F

Tom, S. M., Fox, C. R., Trepel, C., & Poldrack, R. A. (2007). The neural basis of loss aversion in decision-making under risk. *Science*, *315*(5811), 515–518. doi:10.1126/science.1134239 PMID:17255512

Tversky, A., & Kahneman, D. (1974). Judgment under uncertainty: Heuristics and biases. *Science*, *185*(4157), 1124–1131. doi:10.1126/science.185.4157.1124 PMID:17835457

Van der Sar, N. L. (2004). Behavioral finance: How matters stand. *Journal of Economic Psychology*, *25*(3), 425–444. doi:10.1016/j.joep.2004.02.001

Wolman, B. B. (1973). *Dictionary of Behavioural Science*. Van Nostrand Reinhold Company.

Zaleskiewicz, T. (2006). Behavioural Finance. In M. Altman (Ed.), *Handbook of Contemporary Behavioural Economics* (pp. 706–728). New York: M.E. Sharpe.

Zurlo, K. A. (2009). Personal attributes and the financial well-being of older adults: the effects of control beliefs (PARC Working Papers, 27).

ADDITIONAL READING

Baker, M., & Wurgler, J. (2006). Investor sentiment and the cross-section of stock returns. *The Journal of Finance*, *61*(4), 1645–1680. doi:10.1111/j.1540-6261.2006.00885.x

Barber, B. M., & Odean, T. (2002). Online investors: Do the slow die first? *Review of Financial Studies*, *15*(2), 455–488. doi:10.1093/rfs/15.2.455

Chou, R. K., & Wang, Y. Y. (2011). A test of the different implications of the overconfidence and disposition hypotheses. *Journal of Banking & Finance*, *35*(8), 2037–2046. doi:10.1016/j.jbankfin.2011.01.018

De Bondt, W. F. (1998). A portrait of the individual investor. *European Economic Review*, *42*(3), 831–844. doi:10.1016/S0014-2921(98)00009-9

Fellner, G. (2009). Illusion of control as a source of poor diversification: Experimental evidence. *Journal of Behavioral Finance*, *10*(1), 55–67. doi:10.1080/15427560902740006

Fujita, K. (2011). On conceptualizing self-control as more than the effortful inhibition of impulses. *Personality and Social Psychology Review*, 1088868311411165. PMID:21685152

Gächter, S., Johnson, E. J., & Herrmann, A. (2010). *Individual-level loss aversion in riskless and risky choices* (No. 2010-20). CeDEx discussion paper series.

Gervais, S., & Odean, T. (2001). Learning to be overconfident. *Review of Financial Studies*, *14*(1), 1–27. doi:10.1093/rfs/14.1.1

Glaser, M., & Weber, M. (2007). Overconfidence and trading volume. *The Geneva Risk and Insurance Review*, *32*(1), 1–36. doi:10.1007/s10713-007-0003-3

Goetzmann, W. N., & Kumar, A. (2008). Equity portfolio diversification*. *Review of Finance*, *12*(3), 433–463. doi:10.1093/rof/rfn005

Graham, J. R., Harvey, C. R., & Huang, H. (2009). Investor competence, trading frequency, and home bias. *Management Science*, *55*(7), 1094–1106. doi:10.1287/mnsc.1090.1009

Grou, B., & Tabak, B. M. (2008). Ambiguity aversion and illusion of control: Experimental evidence in an emerging market. *Journal of Behavioral Finance*, *9*(1), 22–29. doi:10.1080/15427560801897162

Hoppe, E. I., & Kusterer, D. J. (2011). Behavioral biases and cognitive reflection. *Economics Letters*, *110*(2), 97–100. doi:10.1016/j.econlet.2010.11.015

Karlsson, A., & Nordén, L. (2007). Home sweet home: Home bias and international diversification among individual investors. *Journal of Banking & Finance*, *31*(2), 317–333. doi:10.1016/j.jbankfin.2006.04.005

Kudryavtsev, A., & Cohen, G. (2011). Behavioral biases in economic and financial knowledge: Are they the same for men and women? *Advances in Management & Applied Economics*, *1*(1), 15–52.

Kumar, A., & Lee, C. (2006). Retail investor sentiment and return comovements. *The Journal of Finance*, *61*(5), 2451–2486. doi:10.1111/j.1540-6261.2006.01063.x

Li, S., Zhou, K., Sun, Y., Rao, L. L., Zheng, R., & Liang, Z. Y. (2010). Anticipated regret, risk perception, or both: Which is most likely responsible for our intention to gamble? *Journal of Gambling Studies*, *26*(1), 105–116. doi:10.1007/s10899-009-9149-5 PMID:19728049

Liu, Y. J., Tsai, C. L., Wang, M. C., & Zhu, N. (2010). Prior consequences and subsequent risk taking: New field evidence from the Taiwan Futures Exchange. *Management Science*, *56*(4), 606–620. doi:10.1287/mnsc.1090.1131

Massa, M., & Simonov, A. (2006). Hedging, familiarity and portfolio choice. *Review of Financial Studies*, *19*(2), 633–685. doi:10.1093/rfs/hhj013

Merkle, C. (2013, August). Financial Overconfidence over Time-Foresight, Hindsight, and Insight of Investors. In AFA 2013 San Diego Meetings Paper.

Mitchell, O., & Utkus, S. (2004forthcoming). *Lessons from behavioral finance for retirement plan design. Pension design and structure: New Lessons from behavioral finance*. Oxford, UK: Oxford University Press.

Nofsinger, J. R. (2011). *The psychology of investing*. Prentice Hall.

Nofsinger, J. R., & Sias, R. W. (1999). Herding and feedback trading by institutional and individual investors. *The Journal of Finance*, *54*(6), 2263–2295. doi:10.1111/0022-1082.00188

Portes, R., & Rey, H. (2005). The determinants of cross-border equity flows. *Journal of International Economics*, *65*(2), 269–296. doi:10.1016/j.jinteco.2004.05.002

Seasholes, M. S., & Zhu, N. (2010). Individual investors and local bias. *The Journal of Finance*, *65*(5), 1987–2010. doi:10.1111/j.1540-6261.2010.01600.x

Shefrin, H. M., & Statman, M. (1984). Explaining investor preference for cash dividends. *Journal of Financial Economics*, *13*(2), 253–282. doi:10.1016/0304-405X(84)90025-4

Stotz, O., & von Nitzsch, R. (2005). The perception of control and the level of overconfidence: Evidence from analyst earnings estimates and price targets. *Journal of Behavioral Finance*, *6*(3), 121–128. doi:10.1207/s15427579jpfm0603_2

Thaler, R. (2012). *The winner's curse: Paradoxes and anomalies of economic life*. Simon and Schuster.

Tversky, A., & Kahneman, D. (1971). Belief in the law of small numbers. *Psychological Bulletin*, *76*(2), 105–110. doi:10.1037/h0031322

Watson, J., & McNaughton, M. (2007). Gender differences in risk aversion and expected retirement benefits. *Financial Analysts Journal*, *63*(4), 52–62. doi:10.2469/faj.v63.n4.4749

KEY TERMS AND DEFINITIONS

Familiarity Bias: The tendency to make investment decisions based on the lens of: being familiar with the investment option.

Hindsight Bias: The tendency to see past events as being predictable (when analyzed at a later point in time).

Illusion of Control: The tendency to feel that one can influence the outcome of the decisions (which may be driven by chance).

Investor Bias: The tendency towards a certain disposition that guides the investor's decisions pertaining to saving and investments.

Overconfidence Bias: A tendency to overestimate ones capabilities with regard to investment decision making.

Regret Aversion Tendency: The tendency to avoid taking an action due to a fear that it may turn out to be less than optimal.

Status Quo Bias: The tendency of a person to want to stick to the investment portfolio and the investment opinion and not make any changes to it very quickly.

Chapter 10
Social Exclusion and Poverty: EU 2020 Objectives and Turkey

Davuthan Günaydin
Namık Kemal University, Turkey

Hakan Cavlak
Namık Kemal University, Turkey

Neslihan Cavlak
Namık Kemal University, Turkey

ABSTRACT

In this chapter The EU's 2020 Objectives concerning social exclusion and poverty and Turkey's vision on social exclusion and poverty based on tenth development plan and Justice and Development Party's 2023 vision is dealt. The EU has developed a growth strategy named "EU 2020" in 2010. The objective concerning social exclusion and poverty of this strategy is to rescue as much EU citizens as possible from social exclusion and poverty and decreasing the number of EU citizens who live under poverty line by 20%. Although Turkey is not officially obliged to follow goals stated in EU 2020 objectives, it is integral for Turkey to pursue those principles in order to be harmony with the EU and reach her final aim of being a member of the EU.

INTRODUCTION

Poverty, which can be summarized as an individual's struggle with meeting the basic needs resulting from being a human, is a notion as old as the history of humanity. On the other hand, poverty, as a social phenomenon, is evaluated as a product of the industrial revolution. Oppressive wage policies brought by the industrialization process pushed the laborers, who have no income but their labor, and their families into poverty. Individuals became dependent on the "affection" granted by the capitalist system in this period where the social solidarity weakened and alienation process got faster. This also brought about a new type of poverty, social exclusion, which causes class conflicts and causes the social order to be disturbed as it has never been before.

Issues of poverty and social exclusion in European Union are matters evaluated within the framework of European Social Charter. All the

DOI: 10.4018/978-1-4666-7484-4.ch010

citizens have the right to be protected against social exclusion and poverty. This right is not only evaluated on the basis of employment but also on the basis of citizenship. Within this framework, many decisions have been made towards prevention of social exclusion and poverty in European Union since the beginning of 1990s. In 2000, major advancements were aimed within ten years in the issues of poverty and social exclusion in the Lisbon Council. However the evaluation made in 2010 showed that the objectives were not met as a result of the economic crises. In light of these developments, EU decided to bring the EU 2020 Strategy into action to solve negativities to be seen within the next ten years with sensible, sustainable and inclusive growth strategies. This strategy, bringing new developments in the issues of poverty and social exclusion, tacitly imposes responsibilities to candidate countries like Turkey.

Turkey has worse indicators in the issues of poverty and social exclusion than EU member countries. It is inextricable that Turkey which is on course of full membership to EU primarily catches on similar objectives with member countries to go through a smooth integration process The opposite would cause Turkey's membership to either be delayed or problematical. Justice and Development Party's 2023 vision and particularly 10th Five-Year Development Plan come to the forefront as the most concrete objectives put forward in the issues of poverty and social exclusion in Turkey where the anticipation that economic growth will eliminate poverty is dominant.

POVERTY AS A SOCIAL PHENOMENON

It is possible to mention about poverty in every period of the history. Poverty which is caused by individual or social circumstances can be evaluated as the inadequacies or difficulties faced in meeting the needs of an individual stemming from being a human. But poverty, as a social phenomenon, can be accepted as a product of the industrial revolution. It characterizes the struggles of masses in factories flooding to cities from rural areas with the thought of a better life and more freedom. Individuals earning their keep as agricultural laborers have become unsuccessful in meeting their basic needs against the competitive wage systems of the factories. This situation not only causes absolute poverty for individuals but also makes social life change as it has never changed before. Loss of the culture of solidarity and support of traditional society created the need to take institutional precautions and caused poverty to become more structural.

In modern world, however, the causes of poverty are based on many economic and social reasons. Even if the short income is always a leading reason among these, the poverty of the modern world together with the weakness sensation against the state and the society has become a social issue containing the insufficiency in dealing with these and the vulnerability for negative situations.

The first studies towards understanding the poverty are seen in the sixteenth century. Vives's "The Relief of the Poor" published in 1526, Paine's "Agrarian Justice" published in 1796 and Mill's studies in which he foresaw relief to the poor draw attention as the first studies to try to explain the notion of poverty (Bugra, 2007, p. 77). Many studies were made in the following days towards evaluating the poverty. Poverty was attempted to be evaluated within the frame of different definitions in these studies. However in present day, it is generally researched in three groups as relative and human poverty, approximation poverty and absolute poverty.

Absolute poverty is the case in which an individual can only meet his basic needs simply to go on living. It can be compared between countries and people with global standards. Per capita income is the most useful measure for this comparison. Individuals who have an income below one Dollar per day are accepted as an absolute poor. In the definition of the United Nations, absolute poverty is defined as the severe poverty in meeting the basic human needs like food, safe drinking water, sanitation, health, shelter and education. This definition evaluates poverty not only in terms of income but also access to other services (Ingstad & Eide, 2011, p. 1). Relative poverty is an approach which evaluates the individual as a social asset and conceptualizes in that whether the individual has the minimum level of living within the society he belongs to. It is related to the division of income and welfare (Gundogan, 2008, p. 43). Human Poverty is focused on income poverty and more extensive human values like education, health and access to safe drinking water. It estimates poverty within the frame of "Human Poverty Index". According to this, while evaluating the data of lifetime, education and a fair living standard for developing countries, social exclusion is added to these parameters for the developed countries (UNDP, 1997, p. 18).

A NEW ASPECT IN POVERTY: SOCIAL EXCLUSION

The industrial society that emerged as a result of the industrial revolution in the nineteenth century brought together a new type of poverty which includes interclass conflicts of interest and causes the social order to be disturbed. This new type of poverty even got worse with the problems resulting from the inability of the proletariat to be represented in the politic institutions and to access full citizenship rights. And with this, it caused the revenue gap between those on top of the scale and those on the bottom to rise and thus starting the social polarization.

Social exclusion is the opposite of the social integration that reflects the importance of being a part of the society. It is an economic, politic, social and a multi-dimensional notion focusing on the mechanisms related to the processes that excludes people. Social exclusion is the situation in which an individual has less chance in accessing financial resources, dwelling, employment, education, health services that rise the level of welfare and accessing social institutions when compared to the rest of the population and the long continuation of this disadvantageous situation (Robilac, 2006, p. 87).

The term of social exclusion started to be used by French sociologists to define social problems emerging in relation with the socio-economic transformation in the 1970s. The term defines the lack of social adaptation caused by the increasing inequalities and massive, social and economic security gap for an increasing part of the population. In this period, an increasing number of individuals were not able to access a proper job and the masses with disadvantages in income, shelter, health and education were growing. This situation caused the social exclusion to be not only about the lack of materialistic wealth but also the formation of deprivation (Bhalla & Frederic, 2004, p. 2).

In fact, social pressures and struggles were reduced in particularly the industrialized countries with the welfare state practices that reached up to the end of 1960s after the Second World War. The social integration was increased with the rising full employment conditions and improvements in the living conditions of the laborers in the welfare atmosphere created by the economic growth achieved in this period. But the crises that started in the late 1970s caused the socio-economic structure in the industrialized countries to transform. New supra-national strategies, new types of social and economic regulations came along with reorganization in the labor market and globalization. This process started to harm the growth and social justice mechanisms that were harmonizing in the Fordist production organization. At the same time, sweeping ideological changes in this period like privatization, liberalization, reduction of public services and deregulation of labor market caused this process to speed up. These circumstances revealed poverty problems of individuals that were integrated well in the society once. This situation not only affected the poor, the handicapped and the marginal groups outside the social norms but it also caused the population to be exposed to an increasing long-term unemployment, loss of the social status and weakening of family and non-family bonds. Thus the notion of social exclusion is more related to the socio-economic structural changes than individual behaviors or characteristics (Bhalla & Frederic, 2004, pp. 3-4).

The notion of social exclusion brings poverty into minds first. In fact, poverty is not the sole determinant of the social exclusion while it is an important element of it. To understand the social exclusion, one must study democratic participation processes, labor market, welfare state practices supporting economic and social integration and domestic and social sub-systems (Kaya, 2009, p. 16). Poverty aspect of the social exclusion is generally a result of the exclusion from labor market, from opportunities of welfare state and from family and society. The faults resulting from wrong fictionalizing in democratic and legal systems reflect the situation of exclusion from citizenship integration (Martin, 1998, p. 43). We can say that there are two basic determinants of the notion of social exclusion. These are economic exclusion meaning the exclusion of people from employment, earnings, property, shelter and education and social exclusion preventing social integration (Haan, 2000, p. 26). Groups that are prone to exclusion are generally ethnic or religious minorities. These groups are perceived as "the others" by the rest of the society because of their different cultural practices (WB, 2011, pp. 2-3).

THE NOTION OF POVERTY AND SOCIAL EXCLUSION IN THE EU

Poverty in EU is a notion mention together with the notions of social exclusion and social inclusion. The notion of social inclusion are the public regulations to make individuals who have less income than most of the society, different ethnicities and religions and whose gender, education and abilities are lower take advantage of equal civil rights in the social level. The content of these regulations is not employment activities towards eliminating absolute poverty but all the practices towards being an equal citizen (Bugra, 2007, p. 77). Poverty, in this sense, is perceived differently by EU than many developing regions of the world. Absolute poverty is an issue that is not accepted in the Union and comes up less for the member states than the developing countries. This is because the main goal of the Union is not only providing basic needs of the citizens as opposed to other countries but also aiming to provide a high level of welfare and the opinion that the acceptable minimum living standard is, as a necessity of the socio-economic development, is enough to keep up living in a developed country (EAPN, 2009, p. 8).

The first definitions in the UN for poverty are based on the studies on the report for fighting the poverty made in 1975. In the report, the poverty is defined as the inability of the country to provide the acceptable living standards that are cash income, property, access to public and private services in family and individual life (European Communities, 1975, p. 2). Based on this definition, it was estimated that there were nearly 10 million poor families in the mid-1970s which corresponds to 11,4 percent of the population. Being unemployed for various reasons, having only one income in the family, belonging to various ethnic groups like immigrants and Romans are seen as the main reasons for poverty (European Communities, 1982, p. 7).

However in the report published in 2004, the notion of poverty became very different than the notion of poverty that was accepted in many regions of the world and a wider definition of poverty was made in parallel with European Social Model. Hereunder, the poverty is defined as the lack of income and sources of an individual as to levels preventing him from accessing the living standards of the society he lives in, unemployment resulting from poverty, low income, poor sheltering, inadequate health services, obstacles in front of the lifelong education, cultural and sportive activities, isolation from social, economic and cultural activities and limitation of basic rights that are standard for other individuals (Council of the European Union, 2004, p. 8).

It is seen that the notion of social exclusion is evaluated together with the notion of isolation mentioned together with the poverty and the notion of poverty of the EU in the report. Social exclusion is defined as the process which drifts some individuals out of the society as a result of the discrimination and keeps them back from the advantages of lifelong education and basic abilities and prevents them from taking part in social activities. As a result of this whole process, individuals are getting away from having a job, education, income and social network and activities and power and a decision mechanism (Council of the European Union, 2004, p. 8).

The individuals who live in European Union countries have a different perception of poverty. In a study made in 2010, 26 percent of the people define poverty as the resources being as limited as to prevent them from participating in the social and economic activities of the society they live in. 17 percent of them define poverty as not having the basic materials needed to keep living. 24 percent define poverty as charity or dependence on the public relief. Nearly 75 percent of the people who participated in the same study state that the poverty is common in their countries. Unemployment (%56) and old age (%42) are seen as the most important reasons of the poverty. These are followed by low education and skill level, disability and long-termed illnesses. Financial and social exclusion are seen as results of the poverty (European Commission, 2010, pp. 9-35).

EU POLICIES FOR POVERTY AND SOCIAL EXCLUSION

Issues of poverty and social exclusion in the EU which predicts an integration founded on economic basics are not among Union's primary and common issues but were seen among social politics practices. Thus particularly in the first days of the Union, the anticipation that a successful economic growth and integration would bring the solution to many social problems like social exclusion and poverty was prevalence. Although a common policy was not determined, the understanding to implement independent practices in the national level was prevalence. However, increasing unemployment and the problems it brought together caused to understand that the practices implemented in the national level on the issues of social exclusion and poverty which were important fields of social policy would not be enough (Sapancali, 2005, p. 60). It is seen in the Treaty of Rome with which the foundation of the Union was formed that social policy arrangements towards adaptation of immigrant laborers and laborer movements that could only evaluate social policy practices as a tool of economic integration were made. Poverty and social exclusion only came up in the European Union with the European Social Charter published in 1961. The article stating that all the individuals have the right to be protected against poverty and social exclusion was added to the European Social Charter which was republished with some amendments in 1996. With this, the aim was to take precautions for individuals and their families who live in the condition of social exclusion and poverty against particularly sheltering, vocational training, education, access to social and cultural activities and health services (Council of Europe, 1996, p. 17).

But the precautions were evaluated within the frame of primarily the issue of unemployment as a product of the welfare understanding based on employment rather than social relief that would directly eliminate the negativities the individual experience. Within this scope, the importance of struggling with social exclusion was emphasized in the Community Charter of Fundamental Social Rights of Workers published in 1989 pursuant to European Social Model (Community Charter of Fundamental, 1989, p. 1).

European Commission started to take an important part in spreading the notion of social exclusion and poverty after late 1980s. Struggling with poverty and social exclusion has become a fundamental goal in national policies and European Social Policy. Social exclusion and poverty started to be evaluated as one of the important issues among the research programs of Europe in this period. "Combating Social Exclusion" report was published in 1989-1994 as a result of the researches made in this context. With this report, it was emphasized that poverty was not only materialistic neediness but also exclusion from rights, benefits and opportunities accepted as a standard for modern society (Harveys, 1994, p. 6).

However major practices were not put into use during 1980s. The issues of poverty and social exclusion started to have an important priority among social policy practices after early 1990s in the EU. It was emphasized with the Maastricht Treaty signed in 1992 that member countries needed to determine their objectives to struggle with social exclusion and social exclusion took place in the official documents of the Union (Maastricht Treaty, 1992, p. 37). Within this scope, the importance of the phenomenon of social exclusion in the social policy was presented in the Green Paper published by European Commission in 1993. It is emphasized in this paper that an individual can isolate himself from the society as a result of the condition he is in because of the injustices in terms of sharing the welfare by touching on social injustice and that this situation could lead to racist ideologies, ethnocentrism and politic and social extremism. The reduction of inequalities in struggling with social exclusion and encouraging participation in labor market were touched on in the White Paper named "Growth, Competitiveness and Employment" which was published at the same period (Bildirici, 2011, p. 30). The struggle against social exclusion and poverty took place as one of the main objectives of the EU in the Amsterdam Treaty which was signed on 1997. In order to struggle with social exclusion, modernist approaches, information exchange, taking advantage of good examples and for encouraging the policies of member states, the tasks of EU institutions were extended (Treaty of Amsterdam, 1997, p. 35).

It is possible to say that after 2000s there has been a turning point in the social policies of the EU. It was emphasized in the Lisbon European Council organized in 2000 that it was inevitable to compromise on new objectives and programs for the Union to experience a healthy transformation in the direction of improvements in information technologies and globalization. One of the most important problems to emerge at this point was reconstruction of European Social Model within the frame of this transformation in a way to react to problems that emerge at this point and moreover the social exclusion (Cakar, 2007, p. 90). It was emphasized within this scope that it was unacceptable for many people in the Union to live below the poverty line and in social exclusion conditions and that the most important protection against Social exclusion was employment. In was decided in the Lisbon European Council to take measures to make welfare state practices applicable in order to improve social exclusion and poverty understanding in the context of Europe, to modernize the European Social Model within the next decade by struggling social exclusion and investing in humans (European Council, 2000).

The struggle with social exclusion was determined as one of the six objectives of the social agenda of EU in the Nice European Council organized in 2000. It was decided that the advantages of the active welfare state practices accepted in Lisbon to struggle with poverty and social exclusion would continue to be taken. It was decided that National Action Plan on Social Exclusion be presented to be implemented in order to struggle with social exclusion and poverty by setting specific objectives out and having regard to local, regional and national differences in the Council (www.consilium.europa.eu).

Despite all these improvements, one of the most substantial practices put forth in the struggle with social exclusion and poverty in the EU is the European Anti-Poverty Network (EAPN). EAPN was put into practice as a reflection of the sensitiveness shown in social rapprochement by non-governmental organizations (NGOs) in early 1990s when issues of poverty and social exclusion started to be on the agenda of EU. It was established in 1990 with the decision taken in Anti-Poverty Conference in 1989. This network created by 200 NGOs gathering together included anti-poverty networks of 11 countries. Today, it is the biggest organization of Europe that struggles against poverty and social exclusion and covers 29 national networks and 18 European Organizations. The mission of the organization is to encourage and support practices towards eliminating poverty and social exclusion, to create awareness about poverty and social exclusion, to support individuals who live in poverty and social exclusion and to carry out lobby activities (www.eapn.eu).

EU 2020 OBJECTIVES AND SOCIAL EXCLUSION

EU 2020 Strategy was shaped under the shadow of failure of the objectives to healthily transform the Union in the direction of improvements in information technologies and globalization set forth for the next decade in the Treaty of Lisbon as a result of the economic crisis recently experienced. It was hoped that the damage the crisis made on the social and economic life would be repaired by setting forth a new decade and that it would be an opportunity for a strong economy.

Despite many decisions on the issues of poverty and social exclusion, it was revealed in the Evaluation Document in the Lisbon Treaty published in 2010 that the EU could not reach the desired level. It is emphasized that increasing employment rate is not successful enough in preventing poverty, and it is stated that some groups are devoid of services that provide opportunities of equality and in some member countries women and children poverty rate is too high (European Commission, 2010b, pp. 3-6) The fact that over 80 million people living in this rich geography live below the poverty line and they cannot access to employment, education, shelter, social and economic services creates an opposite image to principles of solidarity and integration among member nations, gender equality, high living standards which are regarded as basic responsibilities of the Union by the European Social Charter (Parlak & Aykac, 2004, p. 2).

It is seen in 2010, with the effects of the economic crisis that nearly 80 million people, %16,5 percent of the total population in the EU, are living below the poverty line in 2010. More than half of these comprise of women and children. On the other hand, the young, immigrants and those who have low skill levels generally work in temporary and low-wage jobs, thus they are the most affected one from an increase in unemployment. In particular 1 in 5 young is unemployed. The unemployment rate in the Union is more than %11. Also, 10 percent of the working young is living in poverty and 8 percent of all workers are materially poor. This rate is rising up to 30 percent in relatively poorer countries. The risk of poverty for the unemployed multiplied by eight by rising to 44 percent from 33 in proportion to employed since the 2005. This also triggers social exclusion, and poverty and social exclusion go head to head (European Commission, 2010c, pp. 2-4).

This major unemployment and poverty resulting from the economic crisis was accepted as a turning point in that they set forth the important problems within the Union. In this direction, EU 2020 Objectives were explained under topics of "European Strategy for Smart, Sustainable and Inclusive Growth" in the opening speech in March 3rd, by the President of the European Commission in 2010. In this report, it was stated that the economic crisis reversed the positive improvements achieved in the previous years in employment and growth with its results. In this scope, it is stated that GDP decreased by 4 percent averagely within the Union countries, that debt ratio increased to 80 percent of the GDP from 60 percent, that nearly 23 million people are unemployed and unemployment rate increased from 7,1 percent to 10 percent, that a major decline was seen in industrial production and it reached to levels of 1990s. On the other hand, it is assessed that this situation affects the growth potential of the Union adversely and budget deficit reached to 6,5 percent in EU overall (European Commission, 2014, pp. 5-7).

These objectives were set out in the EU 2020 Strategy in order to eliminate all these negativities within the next decade,

- Increasing employment rate to 75 percent from 69 in the active population of 20-64 age range,
- Sparing 3 percent of GDP for R&D,
- Reducing greenhouse gas emission by 20 percent based on 1990, increasing the rate of renewable energy in the total energy consumption to 20 percent, saving 20 percent energy,
- Reducing the rate of dropping out early from 15 percent to 10, increasing 30-34 age college graduate rate in the total population from 31 to 40 percent,
- Reducing the rate of those living below the poverty line in EU by 25 percent by saving 20 million people from social exclusion and poverty.

In fact, the objectives aimed by the report on social exclusion, poverty and employment issues are problems that were aimed since the Lisbon Strategy but not solved and got even worse after the economic crisis. Approximately 116 million individuals representing 23 percent of the total population in the EU are known to be facing the risk of social exclusion. Most of these compose of children, old persons, lonely women, lonely parents, low-skilled persons, the unemployed, inactive individuals of working age, those living in rural areas, immigrants and some ethnic minorities like Romans. The report aims to save 20 million citizens within the Union from the risk of poverty and social exclusion within ten years (European Commission, 2013, p. 5).

In order to achieve this objective, five practices are foreseen to be implemented. These are, ensuring that practices in such issues as labor market, minimum income support, health, education and sheltering spread to all politic practices, utilizing Union funds in a better way to support social inclusion, basing new practices in social policy on strong evidences as to whether they will be useful or not before bringing them into action, increasing cooperation with non-governmental organizations and politic coordination among member nations of the Union. (http://ec.europa.eu).

In order to reach the unemployment target, increasing reliability and flexibility of the labor market (covered flexibility), equipping individuals with accurate skills for the job and ensuring that this is continuous, providing better working conditions and increasing business quality and improving employment conditions are anticipated (http://ec.europa.eu).

It is actually known that individuals who are reckoned to be in the risk of poverty and social exclusion are also facing the risk of unemployment. For this reason, the most concrete steps in objectives of eliminating poverty and social exclusion of the EU 2020 Strategy are the objectives towards reducing unemployment. Approximately 26 million of the population that is in the working age and lives in EU countries is unemployed. Targeted practices to struggle with unemployment in the direction of EU 2020 objectives are supporting the free movement of workers and their families in EU countries, prevention of gender discrimination, increasing measures of occupational health and safety in the workplaces and ensuring that workers are well informed and counseled by their employers (European Commission, 2013, p. 3).

A target was determined for each one of the member states with the EU 2020 Strategy and member countries are expected to report the progress they make in policy priorities. Thus, it is targeted that EU has information about the overall situation and decides on necessary actions to be taken. (Table 1)

THE NOTION OF POVERTY AND SOCIAL EXCLUSION IN TURKEY

Poverty was not seen as a responsibility of the state in Turkey for many years and was evaluated as a phenomenon that could be overcome by be-

Table 1. EU 2020 targets employment and poverty and social exclusion.

	Employment Rate 20-64%					People at Risk of Poverty or Social Exclusion (1000)				
	2010	2011	2012	2013	Target	2010	2011	2012	2013	Target
EU 28					75	118085	121543	124232		20000
Belgium	67.6	67.3	67.2	67.2	73,2	2235	2271	2356		380
Bulgaria	65.4	62.9	63.0	63.5	76	3719	3693	3621		260
Czech Republic	70.4	70.9	71.5	72.5	75	1495	1598	1580		30
Denmark	75.8	75.7	75.4	75.6	80	1007	1039	1057		22
Germany	74.9	76.3	76.7	77.1	77	15962	16074	15909		330
Estonia	66.7	70.4	72.1	73.3	76	289	307	311		49,5
Ireland	64.6	63.8	63.7	65.5	69	1220	1319	1319		186
Greece	64.0	59.9	55.3	53.2	70	3031	3403	3795		450
Spain	62.5	61.6	59.3	58.2	74	12316	12791	13090		1500
France	69.2	69.2	69.4	69.5	75	11712	11840	11760		1600
Croatia	58.7	57.0	55.4	53.9	59	1304	1372	1370		-
Italy	61.1	61.2	61.0	59.8	67	14757	17112	18194		2200
Cyprus	75.0	73.4	70.2	67.1	75	202	207	234		27
Latvia	65.0	66.3	68.1	69.7	73	798	821	731	702	121
Lithuania	64.3	66.9	68.5	69.9	72.8	1068	1011	975		170
Luxembourg	70.7	70.1	71.4	71.1	73	83	84	95		-
Hungary	60.4	60.7	62.1	63.2	75	2948	3051	3188	3285	450
Malta	60.1	61.5	63.1	64.9	62.9	86	90	94		6,56
Netherlands	76.8	77.0	77.2	76.5	80	2483	2598	2492		100
Austria	74.9	75.2	75.6	75.5	77	1373	1407	1542[b]		235
Poland	64.3	64.5	64.7	64.9	71	10409	10196	10128		1500
Portugal	70.5	69.1	66.5	65.6	75	2693	2601	2665		200
Romania	63.3	62.8	63.8	63.9	70	8890	8630	8907		580
Slovenia	70.3	68.4	68.3	67.2	75	366	386	392		40
Slovakia	64.6	65.0	65.1	65.0	72	1118	1112	1109		170
Finland	73.0	73.8	74.0	73.3	78	890	949	916	854	150
Sweden	78.1	79.4	79.4	79.8	80	1418	1538	1519		-
United Kingdom	73.6	73.6	74.2	74.9	-	14211	14044	15078		-
Turkey	50	52,0	52,8	53,4	-	48934 (2006)				-

Reference: Eurostat

ing in traditional solidarity. Nominal social aids were made via various institutions in a limited way and social solidarity was brought into the forefront rather than an institutional understanding of struggling with poverty. In this context, it is hard to talk about a policy to struggle with poverty stipulated by governments until 1980s. Social damages resulting from economic crises experienced after the late 1980s made poverty more apparent to governments and non-governmental organizations. However the effect of mass communication should not be ignored in the improvement of appearance (Gundogan, 2008, p. 52).

The issue of social exclusion is a matter for Turkey which was only recognized within the context of EU adaptation process. In this context, in the Ninth Five-Year Development Plan, the notion of social inclusion is mentioned, it is stated that the preparations started for Social Inclusion Document within the scope of Community Action Plan to Combat Social Exclusion within the EU adaptation process and it is targeted that measures which will contribute to the participation of risk groups to economic and social life for struggling with social exclusion are taken.

Poverty estimations in Turkey are based on studies made by Turkish Statistical Institute. Turkish Statistical Institute studies poverty under two categories as "absolute" and "relative" poverty. Absolute poverty is defined as *"the minimum consumption level needed by an individual or a family to keep on living physically"*. Absolute poverty estimation is made by dividing the monthly consumption expenditures by the equivalent adults living inside the family. If the consumption expenditure per capita in the family is lower than the hunger limit, that family and its individuals are reckoned as "too poor". Households that have lower consumption expenditure per capita than the poverty line which composes of components other than food are reckoned as "poor". Relative poverty is defined as the situation in which the individuals are below the average welfare level of the society. 50 percent of the median household consumption expenditure per capita forms the relative poverty line. Turkish Statistical Institute, to be used in international comparisons, defines those who have lower consumption expenditure per capita than 1 Dollar, 2,15 Dollars and 4 Dollars daily per person according to the purchasing power parity as poor (TUIK, 2008: 34-38). Within this framework, as of 2011, relative poverty rate in Turkey is 22,6 percent and 2,8 percent has lower income than 4,3 Dollar per day.

The notion of struggling with poverty and social exclusion in Turkey was patronized by an understanding that an economic development process which will increase employment will eliminate this problem by itself. However it did not take long to understand that poverty could not be eliminated with this just like economic development alone would not solve the unemployment problem that special regulations had to be made in order to struggle with poverty just like the employment policies.

TENTH FIVE-YEAR DEVELOPMENT PLAN AND 2023 VISION IN THE CONTEXT OF EU 2020 STRATEGY

Turkey's determination to be a full member of the EU has been going on for many years. It is known that many adjustment policies in the perspective of being a full member were brought into action with this in mind. This situation is a result of the fact that full membership is only possible with substantial similitude to member states in politic, social and legal aspects. It is assessed that if this similitude is not achieved Turkey could not be a full member of the Union, or even if it becomes one, the membership would be a painful one within the Union. Thus, it is inevitable that the improvements anticipated by the Union for member states within the context of EU 2020 strategy would apply to Turkey, too. Adaptation to the determined objectives is one of the major milestones of the membership process for Turkey.

In this context, the determination of how similar Turkey is to the member states of the Union is crucial in determining the measures to be taken. The first important data in the self-evaluation of Turkey's own condition of poverty and social exclusion are Laeken Indicators which were set down in 2001 with the decision of Stockholm European Council with the aim of watching objectives determined as part of Lisbon 2010 Strategy.

In order to make comparisons between Turkey and member states, it is primarily needed to determine to which member states Turkey has similarities. It was established in the studies made in this direction that Turkey has similar socio-economic characteristics with member states like Greece, Portugal, Spain, Hungary, Romania, Poland and Czech Republic. (Aykin & Korkmaz, 2014, p. 8; Cakar, 2007, p. 90).

When Turkey's poverty and social exclusion risks are evaluated within the scope of Laeken Indicators, first of all it is seen that the poverty average of Turkey is 26 percent which is 16 percent in the Union. This rate is 21 percent in Greece, 20 percent in Portugal and Italy. While in member states 42 percent of the unemployed are under the risk of poverty, this rate is 31 percent in Turkey. When examined from a point of working poverty, Turkey, with its 23 percent, is far more above 8 percent which is the EU average. This rate is 14 percent in Greece and Romania and 12 percent in Portugal. On the other hand, social protection systems within the scope of the European Social Model need to be protective for individuals against the risks they are under. When considered from this point of view, poverty rate which was 30 percent before the social transfers scales down, almost by not changing at all, to 26 percent after the social transfers. This rate scales down from 40 percent in EU overall to 18 percent, from 41 percent to 21 percent in Greece, from 37 percent to 13 percent in Bulgaria and from 41 percent to 18 percent in Romania. It can be said that the most important cause of this is the fact that the social protection system is largely dependent on employment and that there is no systematical structure. When the data related to the income distribution is reviewed, it is seen that the situation is not so bright for Turkey. While the rate of total income of the population's 20 percent who have the highest income to the total income of the population's 20 percent who have the least income is 4,5 times in EU, it is 10 times in Turkey (Cakar, 2007, pp. 93-94).

Another study showing the adaptation status of Turkey to member states is the study that aims to determine the situation of Turkey and member states, as part of clustering analysis, in reaching EU 2020 Strategy (Aykin & Korkmaz, 2014, p. 8). In this study, Turkey, Malta, Cyprus, Portugal and Spain are in the same cluster. As a result of the analysis made, it was determined that Turkey is mostly similar to Malta in regard to the EU 2020 objectives and it is also close to the other members in the cluster. Therefore, it is evaluated that the recommended resolutions of the Council for Malta could shed light for Turkey.

EU 2020 objectives are crucial for Turkey to achieve Although it is not in the scope of membership negotiations, it is inevitable to achieve these objectives for Turkey to be a full member. In this context, political will set forth by Turkey in the last decade is crucial for achieving these objectives. The most important objectives set forth in this direction are present in Tenth Five-Year Development Plan (TFDP) and 2023 Vision of Justice and Development Party.

Crucial objectives are set forth in the TFDP in the issues of poverty and social exclusion. Resolution of absolute poverty problem is the most important goal among these objectives. Economic growth and increasing employment are put forth as the resolution method. Thus, it is aimed to focus solely on relative poverty just like in the developed countries. On the other hand, it is aimed to boost the living standards of those living under the risk of poverty and social exclusion by removing the barriers in front of their participation in social and economic life, to enhance income distribution and thus reducing poverty. In order to do this, it is aimed to support the families receiving social services and aid with an understanding focused on employment. In this context, it is aimed to reduce relative poverty to 19 percent, reduce population who have income below 4,3 Dollars per day per capita to 1 percent and reduce Gini coefficient to 0,36 percent until 2018. In order to achieve all these objectives, the policy implementations were determined to increase the effect of social transfers and taxes in reducing poverty and inequality of income distribution, to increase opportunity equality in accessing public resources like education, ad hoc to increase the participation of civil society and local government and to increase employment of the poor (Ministry of Development, 2013, pp. 46-48).

It is aimed, in the plan, to achieve 5,5 percent annual growth, to reduce unemployment to 7,2 percent by providing employment to 4 million people and 16 thousand dollars income per capita with the anticipation that poverty and social exclusion will be eliminated with economic growth.

The other crucial goal set forth in struggling with poverty and social exclusion is the 2020 Vision by Justice and Development purporting the objectives which are wanted to be achieved in economic and social life by 100th anniversary of the foundation of Turkish Republic. This strategy is concurrently one of the most prolonged and assertive projects of development set forth so far in Turkey. It is aimed for Turkey to be one of the most improved economies with this project. Main goal of 2023 Vision project in struggling with poverty and social exclusion is solving this problem by means of increasing employment depending on economic growth. When objectives set forth with this aim are examined, it is aimed to reduce the unemployment rate to 5 percent by increasing employment of women and participation of them into workforce. In order to achieve this, it is aimed to strengthen the relation of employment and education, to support policies towards starting a business, to make career plans towards acquiring a profession by favor of vocational and job counselors and to elasticated labor market (Table 2).

It is also seen that objectives that can be reckoned as other than to increase employment in struggling with social exclusion and poverty were determined. The most important one of these objectives is to reduce the population rate below poverty line to 10 percent. It is also aimed to not have any individual who has income below 2,5 Dollars per day until 2015 and 4,3 Dollars until 2019. It is also aimed to provide minimum income support to poor families, to provide employment to the disabled who can work, to take measures in reducing social exclusion and poverty in issues of sheltering and education.

However both the TFDP and 2023 Vision are criticized for the feasibility of their objectives. These criticisms intersect at whether the growth will bring development as well as the feasibility of the economic growth figures targeted. According to those who criticize, economy policies alone will not be enough to put Turkey in the league of developed economies. *The individuals need to improve their welfare, freedom, health, education, to provide equality of opportunities and for these, to make social and politic reforms required* (Aydinonat, 2012, p. 1). From this aspect, it is claimed that economic growth will not occur without averting social exclusion and poverty.

Therefore, the issue which is as important as economic reforms is the need to make reforms in issues of education and employment, especially employment of women. As a matter of fact, it is claimed that the goal to increase women employment to 38 percent until 2023 need to be revised to 50 percent, otherwise the expected growth will not occur (ISO, 2014, p. 2). What's more important is the fact that educated workforce is playing a key role for economic growth, that the developed countries have advanced technologies in manufacturing industry and thus that the developing countries need to have a well-educated workforce to adapt these technologies. It is claimed that economic growth achieved by shifting the

Table 2. 2023 Vision objectives towards eliminating poverty and social exclusion.

Re-determining vocational schools and vocational education centers according to the needs of the industry to prevent unemployment.
Providing employment to every disabled person who is able to work.
Not taking the social security support contribution for three years in first employments to increase employment.
Promoting policies for the young to start a business to increase youth employment.
Not having any individual who has income below 2,5 Dollars per day until 2015 and below 4,3 Dollars per day until 2019.
Making career studies for the unemployed to provide them with a profession by favor of vocational and job counselors.
Reducing population who are below poverty line which includes food and non-food expenditures to 10 percent until 2023.
Supporting poor families enough to save them from poverty .
Reducing unemployment rate to 5 percent and increasing employment rate to 50 percent.
Achieving an economic growth of 2 trillion Dollars.
Providing 25 thousand Dollars income per capita.
Increasing woman workforce to 40 percent and employment of them to 38 percent.
Encouraging girls' attendance to schools to provide equality of opportunities in education.
To combat unemployment, strengthening the relation between education and employment, elasticizing the labor market, strengthening the relation between employment and social protection.
Providing employment for 200 thousand people annually for five years.
Providing minimum income support to every family having regard to criteria such as population, poverty state, old age and disabled state and number of children.
Building 100.000 dwelling houses for the poor and disadvantageous groups.

References: Prepared by writer from Justice and Development Party's 2023 Vision, Politics, Society, World.

employment from agriculture to manufacturing like in most of the developing countries could only be achieved by investing in human capital from now on (Aydinonat, 2012, p. 1).

On the other hand, the fact that TFDP and 2023 Vision set forth parallel and inter compatible objectives is evaluated as a positive politic improvement in contradistinction to other plans in terms of feasibility of the objectives (Caglar & Acar, 2013, p. 6).

CONCLUSION

It is seen that Turkey achieved a major economic growth particularly in the last ten years. However it is hard to say that this growth increased social welfare evenly. This, being a result of the inequality of the income distribution, is also one of the main reasons of poverty and social exclusion. It is also important in that it shows that the notion that economic growth will reduce poverty is groundless. Struggling with social exclusion and poverty requires policies to be implemented in this direction. Turkey needs to carry into effect much more substantial practices towards bringing individuals and communities who are exposed to social exclusion in social and economic life and especially policies towards improving income distribution.

It is also a requirement of social and economic integration to struggle with social exclusion and poverty in the perspective of full membership of Turkey to EU. When compared to member states of the EU in this context, it is seen that Turkey needs to move much more forward. It is seen that Turkey falls much behind in especially poverty, inequality of income distribution and effects of the social transfers to reduce poverty than member states of the EU which have similar socio-economic indicators. In this context, although achieving EU 2020 Strategy objectives does not bring obligations for Turkey, it is important in providing the welfare its citizens deserve from the economic growth and in smooth integration of Turkey. At this point, Turkey needs to carry out policy practices towards achieving EU 2020 Strategy objectives which were determined for countries which have similar socio-economic development level like Malta, Greece and Spain.

In this context, TFDP and Vision 2023 are important in that they are the most important political objectives set forth so far by Turkey. However it should not be ignored that these plans alone cannot achieve the economic growth anticipated to reduce poverty and social exclusion. Therefore, substantial practices towards reducing inequalities of income distribution and social aids and increasing the employment foremost need to be put into practice. In this context, EU 2020 Strategy is evaluated to be a good guiding light.

REFERENCES

AK Parti 2023 Siyasi Vizyonu. (2012). *Siyaset, toplum dünya*

Aydınonat, N. E. (2012). *Değerlendirme Notu.* TEPAV.

Aykın, S., & Mehter, A. (2014). Türkiye ve üye ülkelerin AB-2020 stratejisi göstergeleri açisindan kümelenmesi. *Eskişehir Osmangazi Üniversitesi İİBF Dergisi*, *9*(1), 7–20.

Bhallaand, A. S., & Frederic, L. (2004). *Poverty and exclusion in a global world* (2nd ed.). Palgrave Macmillan. doi:10.1057/9780230005624

Bildirici, Z. (2011). *Avrupa Birliği'nde yoksullukla mücadele ve Türkiye'nin uyum sürecindeki yeni uygulamalar.* unpublished master thesis, University of Istanbul, Institute of Social Sciences, Istanbul.

Buğra, A. (2007).Yoksulluk ve sosyal haklar. *TES-İŞ Dergisi,* June.

Çağlar, E., & Acar, O. (2013). *Değerlendirme notu.* TEPAV.

Çakar, B. Y. (2007).Yoksulluk ve sosyal dişlanmaya genel bakiş: Leaken göstergeleri ile Avrupa Birliği'nde durum. *TES-İŞ Dergisi,* June.

Council of Europe. (1996). *European Social Charter.*

Council of the European Union. (2004). *Joint report by the commission and the council on social inclusion.* Brussels.

de Haan, A. (2000). Social exclusion: enriching the understanding of deprivation, Retrieved March 11, 2014, from http://www.socialinclusion.org.np/userfiles/file/Arjan_de_Haan.pdf

DPT. (2006). *Ninth Five Year Development Plan*

EAPN.(2009). *Poverty and inequality in the EU.*

European Commission. (2010a). *Special Eurobarometer poverty and social exclusion report.* Belgium.

European Commission. (2010b). *Lisbon strategy evaluation document.* Brussels.

European Commission. (2010c). *The European platform against poverty and social exclusion: A European framework for social and territorial cohesion.* Brussels.

European Commission. (2013). *Employment and social affairs.* Brussels.

European Commission. (2014). *Taking stock of the Europe 2020 strategy of smart, sustainable and inclusive growth.* Brussels.

European Commission website on Employment, Social Affairs & Inclusion (n.d.) Retrieved March 12, 2014, from http://ec.europa.eu/social/main.jsp?catId=961&langId=en

European Communities. (1975). *Pilot schemes and studies to combat poverty approved.* Brussels.

European Communities. (1982). *Europe against poverty*. Brussels.

Gundogan, N. (2008). Türkiye'de yoksullukla mücadele, Ankara. *Sanayi Odası Dergisi,* January/February.

Harveys, B. (1994). *Combating exclusion 1989-1994 lessons from the third EU poverty programme in Ireland*. Retrieved March 18, 2014, from http://www.combatpoverty.ie/publications/Combating-Exclusion_1994.pdf

Ingstad, B., & Eide, A. H. (2011). *Disability and poverty: a global challenge*. USA: The Policy Press.

ISO. (2014). *Kadın sanayiciler platformu*. Retrieved March 18, 2014, from file:///C:/Users/davuthang%C3%BCnayd%C4%B1n/Downloads/8_MART_MANIFEST OSU-ek-363%20 (1).pdf

Kaya, E. (2009). *Yoksullukla mücadelede Avrupa'nın ve Türkiye'nin sosyal modeli*. Directorate of Social Assistance and Solidarity.

Lisbon European Council. (2000). Retrieved February 20, 2014, from http://www.europarl.europa.eu/summits/lis1_en.htm

Maastricht Treaty. (1992). Retrieved April 1, 2014, from http://www.eurotreaties.com/maastrichtprotocols.pdf

Martin, E. (1998). Behind the rhetoric: The institutional basis of social exclusion and poverty. *IDS Bulletin*, *29*(1), 42–49. doi:10.1111/j.1759-5436.1998.mp29001005.x

Parlak, Z., & Aykaç, M. (2004). *AB sosyal politikasi: refah devletinden Avrupa sosyal modeline*. Retrieved March 15, 2014, from http://web.sakarya.edu.tr/~kaymakci/makale/absosyal.pdf

Robila, M. (2006). Economic pressure and social exclusion in Europe. *The Social Science Journal*, *43*(1), 85–97. doi:10.1016/j.soscij.2005.12.009

Sapancalı, F. (2005). Avrupa Birliği'nde sosyal dışlanma sorunu ve mücadele yöntemleri. *Çalışma ve Toplum,* 2005/3.

The European Anti-poverty Network. (n.d.) Retrieved March 13, 2014, from http://www.eapn.eu/news-publications/events?view=events&lang=en

Treaty of Amsterdam. (1997). Retrieved March 12, 2014, from http://www.eurotreaties.com/amsterdamtreaty.pdf

TÜİK. (2008). Tüketim harcamaları, yoksulluk ve gelir dağılımı. *Sorularla Resmi İstatistikler Dizisi*– 6.

Turkish Ministry of Development. (2013). Tenth Five Year Development Plan 2014-2018.

UNDP. (1997). Human Development Report. Retrieved March 25, 2014, from http://hdr.undp.org/sites/default/files/reports/258/hdr_1997_en_complete_nostats.pdf

WB. (2011). *Poverty and social exclusion in India*. Washington.

ADDITIONAL READING

Akbağ, G., & Altan, P. (2010). *Avrupa 2020 stratejisi: akilli, sürdürülebilir ve kapsayıcı büyüme için Avrupa stratejisi özet bilgi notu*. Ankara: Secretary General of European Union.

Atik, H. (2012). *AB 2020 derinleşme stratejisi ve Türkiye*. Retrieved March 25, 2014, from http://www.ankarastrateji.org/yazar/prof-dr-hayriye-atik/ab-2020-derinlesme-stratejisi-ve-turkiye/

Atkinson, T., Marlier, E., & Nolan, B. (2004). Indicators and targets for social inclusion in the European Union. *Journal of Common Market Studies*, *42*(1), 47–75. doi:10.1111/j.0021-9886.2004.00476.x

Council of the European Union. (2010). *Europe 2020 strategy for jobs and growth: the Council adopts broad economic policy guidelines*. Brussels.

Council of the European Union. (2010). *Recommendation for a council recommendation on broad guidelines for the economic policies of the Member States and of the Union*, 7 July 2010 (11646/10).

Council of the European Union. (2011.), *Council decision of 19 May 2011 on guidelines for the employment policies of the Member States*, O.J. L 138/56 of 26.5.2011 (2011/308/EU).

DPT. (2007). *Report of Special Expert Commission on Ninth Development Plan concerning income distribution and alleviating poverty.*

Ekin, B. (2007). Sosyal dışlanma ile mücadelede hak temelli yaklaşım: Avrupa yoksulluk ile mücadele aği. *TES-İŞ Dergisi,* June.

Ercan, D. (2003). *Yoksullukla mücadelede kurumsal kapasitenin geliştirilmesi, Yoksulluk Sempozyumu*. İstanbul: Deniz Feneri Derneği.

Erkekoğlu, H. (2007). AB'ye tam üyelik sürecinde Türkiye'nin üye ülkeler karşısındaki göreli gelişme düzeyi: çok değişkenli istatistiksel bir analiz. *Kocaeli Üniversitesi Sosyal Bilimler Enstitüsü Dergisi, 14*(2007/2), 28-50.

European Commission. (2010). *A strategy for smart, sustainable and inclusive growth*. Europe 2020 Strategy, Brussels.

European Commission. (2010). A resource-efficient Europe–Flagship initiative under the Europe 2020 Strategy. Brussels.

European Commission. (2010). *Poverty and social exclusion report*. Brussels.

European Commission. (2014). Employment: Commission welcomes Council adoption of posting of workers enforcement directive. Brussels.

European Union. (2013). *Union Committee of the Regions Poverty and Social Exclusion. What role for regions and cities?* Brussels.

Işık, O., & Pınarcıoğlu, M. (2005). *Nöbetleşe yoksulluk gecekondulaşma ve kent yoksulları: Sultanbeyli örneği. 5.* Basım İletişim Yayınları.

Lelkes, O. & Gasior, K. (2012). *Income poverty and social exclusion in the EU, situation in 2008 and trends* (based on EU-SILC 2005-2009), European Centre Policy Brief. January 2012.

O'Brien, D., Wilkes, J., De Haan, A., & Maxwell, S. (2000). *Poverty and social exclusion in north and nouth* (IDS Working Paper, No. 55).

Peace, R. (2001). Social exclusion: a concept in need of definition ? *Social Policy Journal of New Zealand, 16*.

Sandal, E. K., Karabulut, M., & Gürbüz, M. (2005). Sosyo-ekonomik kriterler bakımından Türkiye'nin konumu v eAvrupa Birliği. *Fırat Üniversitesi Sosyal Bilimler Dergisi, 15*(1), 1–14.

Silver, H. (1994). Social exclusion and social solidarity: Three paradigms. *International Labour Review, 133*(5-6), 531–578.

Toygur, İlke. (2010). *Economic Development Foundation assessment note No. 8*.

United Nations Development Program. (2006). *Human development report 2006*. New York: UNDP.

WHO. (2010). *Poverty, social exclusion and health systems in the WHO European Region?* Copenhagen.

KEY TERMS AND DEFINITIONS

Absolute Poverty: The case in which an individual can only meet his basic needs simply to go on living.

European Social Charter: The European Social Charter is a Council of Europe treaty which guarantees social and economic human rights. It was adopted in 1961 and revised in 1996.

Gender: Refers to the socially constructed roles, behaviors, activities, and attributes that a given society considers appropriate for men and women.

Poverty Line: A level of personal or family income below which one is classified as poor according to governmental standards.

Social Inclusion: The provision of certain rights to all individuals and groups in society, such as employment, adequate housing, health care, education and training, etc.

Social Integration: The set of arrangements adopted by the society and the group to accept a new member among them, and to facilitate this acceptance process.

Welfare State: A concept of government in which the state plays a key role in the protection and promotion of the economic and social well-being of its citizens.

Section 3

Behavioral Approach to Financial Issues and Investment

Chapter 11
Stochastic Processes for the Risk Management

Gamze Özel
Hacettepe University, Turkey

ABSTRACT

The financial markets use stochastic models to represent the seemingly random behavior of assets such as stocks, commodities, relative currency prices such as the price of one currency compared to that of another, such as the price of US Dollar compared to that of the Euro, and interest rates. These models are then used by quantitative analysts to value options on stock prices, bond prices, and on interest rates. This chapter gives an overview of the stochastic models and methods used in financial risk management. Given the random nature of future events on financial markets, the field of stochastic processes obviously plays an important role in quantitative risk management. Random walk, Brownian motion and geometric Brownian motion processes in risk management are explained. Simulations of these processes are provided with some software codes.

INTRODUCTION

Risk is an inherent ingredient of financial business in the sense of the possibility of losses. Financial business is becoming more and more complicated, resulting in greater risks due to the development of financial services and financial products. In addition, the financial industry is getting more involved in the economy, both nationally and globally. The financial market has an influence on economy to a certain extent, e.g. the gloom of the financial market could lead to an economic recession.

The measurement of risk has become a competitive factor for the financial institutions. How can we quantify risk? Risk management deals with this problem. Risk management can be defined as a discipline for "Living with the possibility that future events may cause adverse effects" (Kloman, 1999). In the context of risk management in financial institutions such as banks or insurance companies these adverse effects usually correspond to large losses on a portfolio of assets. Risk management can be seen as a core competence of an insurance company or a bank. Specific examples include losses on a portfolio

DOI: 10.4018/978-1-4666-7484-4.ch011

of market-traded securities such as stocks and bonds due to falling market prices; losses on a pool of bonds or loans, caused by the default of some issuers or borrowers (credit risk); losses on a portfolio of insurance contracts due to the occurrence of large claims (Eberlein et al., 2007). A financial institution can take on risks and manage them by various techniques such as diversification, hedging, or repackaging risks and transferring them back to markets etc.

It is important to understand the character of stochastic process that underlines the dynamic of financial variables for successful modeling of the financial series. To give some insights into the financial market, we present finance as a stochastic process, where psychology of people is the most important element. To define the stochastic process first, we would say that a stochastic process is a variable that evolves over time in a way that is at least partly random. Weather is a stochastic process. Namely, variation in temperatures is partly deterministic and predictable, we can expect to have warm summers and cold winters and that temperatures rise during the day and fall at night, and partly random and unpredictable.

However, if we can predict what the temperature of the January 1 will be over the next two years or even what temperature we will have tomorrow, it is impossible to predict the price of a stock of Google over the next two years. Why is that? This is because weather is a (weakly) stationary process, which means that statistical properties of the variable are constant over time, while asset prices are non-stationary, meaning that the expected value can grow, or fall, without bounds. Precisely this stochastic nature of asset prices is what makes opportunities to individuals for increasing their wealth, but also threats of losing it. Therefore, individuals are taking risks.

In this chapter an introduction to some of the stochastic aspects of financial risk management is given. Firstly, random walk process is explained for the risk management. Random walk process is used in many fields including finance and economics for modeling fluctuations in the stock market. It says that any shock to stock price is permanent and there is no tendency for the price level to return to a trend path over time. Secondly, Brownian motion process is introduced. In the modeling of financial market, especially stock market, Brownian motion plays a significant role in building a statistical model. Finally, we focus on the geometric Brownian motion process. Geometric Brownian motion is a employed to analyze risk for stocks and other financial assets. It is also the model that underpins the famous Black-Scholes option pricing formula.

BACKGROUND

Definitions of risk vary based on context. The International Organization for Standardization (ISO) in the ISO Guide 73 defines risk as the "effect of uncertainty on objectives" (ISO, 2009). The reason for a risk is uncertainty. Uncertainty is "the state of being uncertain." Uncertain means "not able to be relied on; not known or definite." Imagine that you would like to purchase a property in San Francisco, which is known for its susceptibility to earthquakes. We know that there is a risk of an earthquake occurring at any time, but we cannot say if there will be an earthquake during the next three years or not. It is uncertain.

Risk can be negative or positive. Earthquakes and diseases are classic examples of negative risk. In contrast, when somebody plays roulette in a casino, he or she hopes for a positive risk. In a way, this is counterintuitive to the manner in which the word risk is used in our everyday language. We often talk about risk as something inherently bad, for example, health risks (e.g., smoking increases the risk of cancer), natural disasters like earthquakes and floods, and sudden economic downturns. But, in fact, the basis of our market economy is actually taking risks. A merger or takeover of a company is often pursued because the acquiring party expects that it is worth the price of acquisition because it anticipates that future financial returns will be favorable—this is positive risk taking.

Risk can be measured, depending on its nature, using either a statistical approach that uses historical data or a subjective probability approach in an informed decision. Both approaches are frequently used in practice. When assessing risk, one has to keep in mind that risk is context-dependent since it reshapes when the system changes. Measuring risk can be rather difficult when it is difficult to define risk or to capture all of its characteristics. One perspective on the risk of an investment is that it is the uncertainty associated with investment returns or cash flows. However, uncertainty is a complex quality. Analysts often attempt to quantify risk with absolute measures such as variance or relative risk measures.

The ISO Guide defines risk management as "coordinated activities to direct and control an organization with regard to risk" (ISO, 2009). Risk management in an organization often has multiple objectives (e.g., high safety and low costs), which requires adequate modeling and optimization techniques that can take multiple objectives into account. A risk management process is a systematic process to assess and treat risks. Many different risk management processes have been proposed in the literature, which typically contain steps like:

1. Identification of risks,
2. Assessment/measurement of risks,
3. Evaluation, choice, and implementation of risk mitigation options,
4. Monitoring of risk mitigation.

Risk management is concerned with ensuring that an organization recognizes and understands where weaknesses exist and/or where they might arise, and is proactive in addressing those to ensure that there is no adverse interruption to business continuity and/or damage to its reputation. An integral part is therefore the assessment of risk (ISO, 2009):

Given the random nature of future events on financial markets, the field of stochastics (probability theory, statistics and the theory of stochastic processes) obviously plays an important role in quantitative risk management. In addition, techniques from convex analysis and optimization and numerical methods are frequently being used. In fact, part of the challenge in quantitative risk management stems from the fact that techniques from several existing quantitative disciplines are drawn together. The ideal skill-set of a quantitative risk manager includes concepts and techniques from such fields as mathematical finance and stochastic process theory, statistics, actuarial mathematics, econometrics and financial economics, combined of course with non-mathematical skills such as a sound understanding of financial markets and the ability to interact with colleagues with diverse training and background.

Stochastic processes have an important place in the risk management. A continuous-time stochastic process is one where the value of the price can change at any point in time. The theory is very complex and actually this differential notation is just short-hand for an integral equation. A discrete-time stochastic process on the other hand is one where the price of the financial asset can only change at certain fixed times. In practice, discrete behavior is usually observed, but continuous time processes prove to be useful to analyze the properties of the model, besides being paramount in valuation where the assumption of continuous trading is at the basis of the Black and Scholes theory and its extensions. Continuous-time price movements cannot be modeled using a tree and requires the introduction of stochastic calculus and Brownian motion processes.

It has been shown that both statistical and dynamical properties of market price fluctuations can be well described by a random walk in a deforming potential function that moves its center given by the moving average of the market price (Tayakasu et al., 2005). Tayakasu et al. (2005) predicted that the near future market price behaviors by applying random walk process and proposed a novel risk management strategy for financial markets. Recently, Mishra et al. (2014) has been investigated the random walk hypothesis on the Indian stock market.

MAIN FOCUS OF THE CHAPTER

This section provides an introduction to modelling through stochastic processes in the risk management. All the concepts will be introduced using the fundamental process for financial modelling, random walks, Brownian motion, geometric Brownian motion with constant drift and constant volatility.

Random Walk Processes in Risk Management

The behavior of the stock market returns is a central issue to the theory and practice of asset pricing, asset allocation, and risk management. Fama (1965) described the behavior of financial price series as having "… no memory, that is, the past cannot be used to predict the future in any meaningful way." In this regard, the only relevant information about a future outcome of a variable is the current value. Campell et al. (1997) wrote that "… the best forecast of tomorrow's price is simply today's price". Fama (1965), Mandelbrot (1963), Lo and Mackinlay (1988), amongst the many others use the random walk process to describe the dynamics of financial prices. Random walk process says that stocks take a random and unpredictable path. The chance of a stock's future price going up is the same as it going down. This suggests that future returns are unpredictable based on historical observations. The random walk property also implies that the volatility of stock price can grow without bound in the long run. These properties are not only of interest by themselves but also have important implications for asset pricing (Chaudhuri and Wu, 2003).

A random walk is a classic example of a non-stationary stochastic process. Asset prices such as stock prices or exchange rates follow a random walk, thus are non-stationary (Gujarati, 2004). There are mainly two types of random walk processes namely; random walk without adrift (i.e. no constant or intercept term) and random walk with a drift (i.e. a constant term is present).

A time series (P_t) is a random walk process with no drift if it satisfies the following equation

$$P_t = P_{t-1} + \mu_t$$

where P_t is the price at time t and μ is the drift term.

The random walk implies that the value of P at time t is equal to its value at time $(t-1)$ plus a random shock (μ_t). The sequence (μ_t) is white noise error terms with mean zero and variance σ^2. It is easy to see that $E(P_t) = P_0$, $V(P_t) = \sigma^2 t$. The mean of P_t is constant for a random walk without drift but the variance increases with time t. The increasing variance violates a condition of weak stationary. Thus, the random walk model without drift is a non-stationary stochastic process. This random walk process remembers the shocks (random errors) forever and is said to have an infinite memory (Gujarati, 2004).

If the probability of moving up a step and down a step is equal to 0.5, then the process is called a symmetric random walk. Furthermore, if the up-step size and the down-step size are equal, then the process is called a simple random walk. The algorithm, which can easily be implemented and plotted in R, for a simple random walk is as follows in Box 1.

Figure 1 shows that a sample plot of 10 random walks. Random walk process with a drift can be written as

$$P_t = \alpha + P_{t-1} + \mu_t$$

Box 1.

```
# Generate k random walks across time {0, 1, ..., T}
T <- 100
k <- 10
initial.value <- 10
GetRandomWalk <- function() {
# Add a standard normal at each step
initial.value + c(0, cumsum(rnorm(T)))
}
# Matrix of random walks
values <- replicate(k, GetRandomWalk())
# Create an empty plot
dev.new(height=8, width=12)
plot(0:T, rep(NA, T + 1), main=sprintf("%s Random Walks", k),
xlab="time", ylab="value",
ylim=10 + 4.5 * c(-1, 1) * sqrt(T))
mtext(sprintf("%s%s} with initial value of %s",
"Across time {0, 1, ..., ", T, initial.value))
for (i in 1:k) {
lines(0:T, values[, i], lwd=0.25)
}
for (sign in c(-1, 1)) {
curve(initial.value + sign * 1.96 * sqrt(x), from=0, to=T,
n=2*T, col="darkred", lty=2, lwd=1.5, add=TRUE)
}
legend("topright", "1.96 * sqrt(t)",
bty="n", lwd=1.5, lty=2, col="darkred")
savePlot("random_walks.png")
```

where α is the drift parameter. With drift refers to the fact that changes in stock prices are not entirely random. There is a systematic component due to the fact that stock prices tend to increase over time.

The expected value and variance of asset price at time t are given by $E(P_t) = P_0 + \alpha t$, $V(P_t) = t\sigma^2$, respectively. Thus the mean and variance of the random walk process with a drift increases with time t, again violating the conditions of weak stationary.

Brownian Motion Process in Risk Management

Brownian motion is one of the most famous and fundamental of stochastic processes. The formulation of this process was inspired by the physical phenomenon of Brownian motion, which is the irregular jiggling sort of movement exhibited by a small particle suspended in a fluid, named after the botanist Robert Brown (1828) who observed and studied it in 1827. A physical explanation of Brownian motion was given by Einstein (1905), who analyzed Brownian motion as the cumulative effect of innumerable collisions of the suspended particle with the molecules of the fluid. Einstein's analysis provided historically important support for the atomic theory of matter, which was still a matter of controversy at the time shortly after 1900. The mathematical theory of Brownian motion was given arm foundation by Wiener (1923); the mathematical model we will study is also known as the Wiener process.

The Brownian motion models for financial markets are based on the work of Robert C. Merton and Paul A. Samuelson, as extensions to the one-period market models of Harold Markowitz and William Sharpe. The Brownian motion models for financial markets are concerned with defining the concepts of financial assets and markets, portfolios, gains and wealth in terms of continuous time stochastic processes. Under the Brownian motion process, the assets have continuous prices evolving continuously in time and are driven by Brownian motion processes. This model requires an assumption of perfectly divisible assets and a frictionless market (i.e. that no transaction costs occur either for buying or selling). Another assumption is that asset prices have no jumps, there are no surprises in the market.

The standard Brownian motion process is a stochastic process $\{B_t, t \geq 0\}$, with the following properties:

- Every increment $B_t - B_s$ over an interval of length $t - s$ is normal distributed with mean 0 and variance $t - s$, that is $B_t - B_s \sim N(0, t - s)$.
- For every pair of disjoint time intervals $[t_1, t_2]$ and $[t_3, t_4]$, with $t_1 \leq t_2 \leq t_3 \leq t_4$ the increments $B(t_4) - B(t_3)$ and $B(t_2) - B(t_1)$ are independent random variables.
- $B_0 = 0$
- B_t is continuous for all t.

Figure 1. Sample plot of 10 random walks

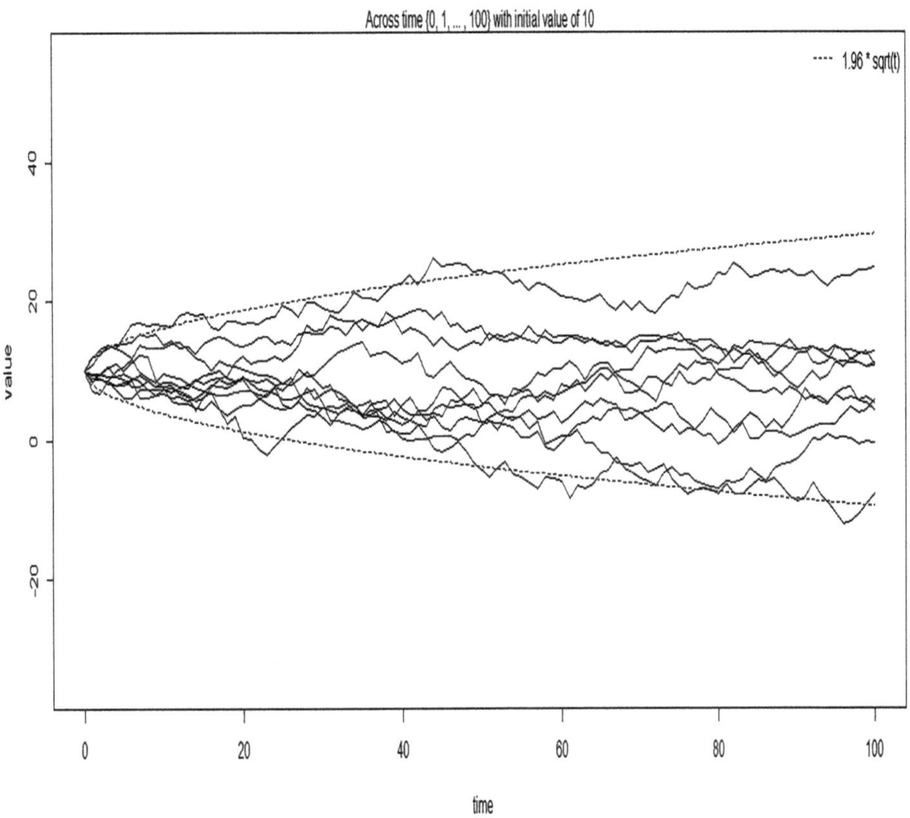

If we were to use Brownian motion to model security prices, we would need to verify that security prices have the four properties of Brownian motion given above. Then, R code is given in Box 2. for the simulation of a standard Brownian motion process:

Using R code, a sample path of standard Brownian motion is presented in Figure 2.

Box 2.

```
t <- 0:500 # time
sig2 <- 0.3
## first, simulate a set of random deviates
x <- rnorm(n = length(t) - 1, sd = sqrt(sig2))
## now compute their cumulative sum
x <- c(0, cumsum(x))
plot(t, x, type = "l", ylim = c(-2, 10))
```

A Brownian motion with drift X_t is the solution of a stochastic differential equation with constant drift and diffusion coefficients

$$dX_t = \mu dt + \sigma dW_t$$

with initial value $X_0 = x_0$. By direct integration

$$X_t = x_0 + \mu t + \sigma W_t$$

and hence X_t is normally distributed, with mean $x_0 + \mu t$ and variance $\sigma^2 t$. Its density function is given by

$$f(t) = \frac{1}{\sigma\sqrt{2\pi t}} e^{-(x-x_0-\mu t)^2/2\sigma^2 t}.$$

Figure 2. Sample path of standard Brownian motion process

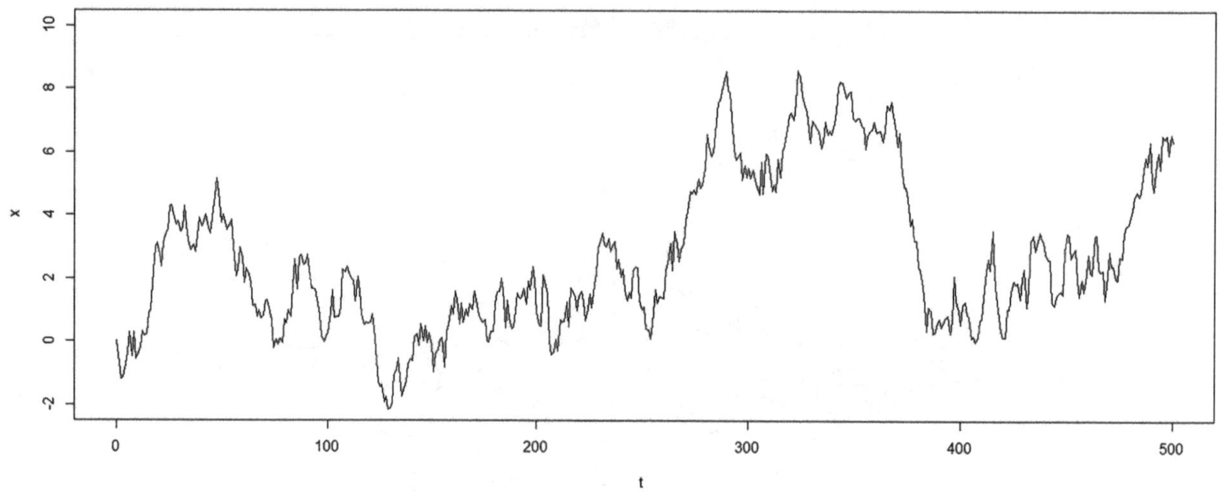

Geometric Brownian Motion Process in Risk Management

The Brownian motion cannot appropriate for modeling stock prices since this process can take on negative values. Instead, we introduce here a non-negative variation of Brownian motion called geometric Brownian motion. The geometric Brownian motion is ubiquitous in finance, being the process underlying the Black and Scholes formula for pricing European options. A standard assumption when valuing financial derivatives on market-traded assets is that the underlying market price is a geometric Brownian motion (Brandão et al., 2005). Two arguments favoring geometric Brownian motion are that prices modeled this way do not become negative, and that investors' responses to price changes will follow a form of Weber's Law, outlined for instance in Blaug (1962). Responses will depend on proportional changes and thus an appropriate stochastic model is the multiplicative random walk of geometric Brownian motion rather than an additive model.

The geometric Brownian motion describes the random behavior of the asset price level S_t over time, which is defined by

$$dS_t = \mu S_t dt + \sigma S_t dW_t$$

Here, W_t is a standard Brownian motion (Wiener process) that is characterized by independent identically distributed (iid) increments that are normally (or Gaussian) distributed with zero mean and a standard deviation equal to the square root of the time step. Independence in the increments implies that the model is a Markov Process, which is a particular type of process for which only the current asset price is relevant for computing probabilities of events involving future asset prices. In other terms, to compute probabilities involving future asset prices, knowledge of the whole past does not add anything to knowledge of the present.

The d terms indicate that the equation is given in its continuous time version. The property of independent identically distributed increments is very important and will be exploited in the calibration as well as in the simulation of the random behavior of asset prices.

Let's first understand this definition, normally, μ is called the percentage drift and σ is called the percentage volatility. So, consider a Brownian motion trajectory that satisfy this differential equation, the right hand side term $\mu S_t dt$ controls the "trend" of this trajectory and the term $\sigma S_t dW_t$ controls the "random noise" effect in the trajectory.

A solution is needed to be finding since it is a differential equation. The technique of separation of variables is applied, then the equation becomes:

$$\frac{dS_t}{S_t} = \mu dt + \sigma dW_t$$

Then taking the integration of both side we have

$$\int \frac{dS_t}{S_t} = \int \left(\mu dt + \sigma dW_t\right) dt$$

Since $\frac{dS_t}{S_t}$ relates to derivative of $\ln S_t$, using Ito calculus, following equation is obtained

$$\ln\left(\frac{dS_t}{S_t}\right) = \left(\mu - \frac{1}{2}\sigma^2\right)t + \sigma W_t.$$

This equation can be rewritten as follows:

$$d \log S_t = \left(\mu - \frac{1}{2}\sigma^2\right)dt + \sigma dW_t$$

where log denotes the standard natural logarithm. The process followed by the log is called an arithmetic Brownian motion. The increments in the logarithm of the asset value are normally distributed.

Taking the exponential of both side and plugging the initial condition S_0, the solution is obtained. The analytical solution of this geometric Brownian motion is given by

$$S_t = S_0 \exp\left(\mu - \frac{1}{2}\sigma^2\right)t + \sigma dW_t$$

This equation shows that the asset price in the geometric Brownian motion follows a log-normal distribution, while the logarithmic returns $\log(S_{t+\Delta t} / S_t)$ are normally distributed.

The moments of S_t are easily found using the above solution, the fact that W_t is Gaussian with mean zero and variance t, and finally the moment generating function of a standard normal random variable Z given by:

$$E[\exp(aZ)] = \exp\left(\frac{1}{2}a^2\right)$$

Hence the first two moments (mean and variance) of S_t are:

$$E(S_t) = S_0 \exp\left(\mu t\right)$$

$$V(S_t) = S_0^2 \exp\left(2\mu t\right)[\exp(\sigma^2 t - 1)]$$

The Matlab code shown in Box 2 simulates sample paths of the geometric Brownian motion.

Unlike the standard Brownian motion, geometric Brownian motion is controlled by the "trend". That is if hundreds of simulation of Geometric Brownian Motion sis done, most of the graph will "heading toward a direction" with some deviation. To verify this, let's plot several graph of Geometric Brownian motion with the same constant in a same graph. Sample paths of geometric Brownian motion processes are shown in Figure 3. As seen from the graph, the trend of those geometric Brownian motions is roughly matches. A numerical example is also provided. Let's assume that initial portfolio value is $S_0 = \$10,000$ and it is being traded over 252 days. We allow the underlying process to have a

Box 3.

```
function S= GBM_simulation (N_Sim, T, dt, mu, sigma, S0)
mean =(mu -0.5* sigma ^2)* dt ;
S= S0 * ones (N_Sim, T +1);
BM = sigma * sqrt (dt)* normrnd (0, 1, N_Sim, T);
S (:, 2: end)= S0 * exp (cumsum (mean + BM, 2));
end
```

drift of $\mu_t = 0.05$ and the overall volatility of $\sigma_t = 5$ constant over time. Since the simulation in every of 252 steps depends on ε drawn from the normal distribution N(0,1), we can obtain any number of possible realizations of the simulated portfolio value path. Coding quickly the above model in R, (See Box 4.)

A sample path of this example is given in Figure 3.

The visual inspection of the path suggests no major drawbacks and low volatility, therefore pretty good trading decisions made by portfolio manager or trading algorithm. Of course, the simulation does not tell us anything about the model, the strategy involved, etc. but the result we obtained is sufficient for further discussion on portfolio key metrics.

Box 4.

```
mu=0.05; % drift
sigma=0.05; % std dev over total inverval
S0=10000; % initial capital ($)
N=252; % number of time steps (trading days)
K=1; % nubber of simulations

dt=sigma/sqrt(N); % local volatility

St=[S1];
for k=1:K
St=[S1];
for i=2:N
eps=randn;
S=St(i-1)+St(i-1)*(mu*dt+sigma*eps*sqrt(dt));
St=[St; S];
end
hold on; plot(St);
end
xlim([1 N]);
xlabel('Trading Days')
ylabel('Simulated Portfolio Value ($)');
```

Stochastic Volatility in Risk Management

The key idea using stochastic volatility in risk management is to devolatilize the observed return series and to revolatilize with an appropriate forecast value. This idea has been applied in several papers (Hull and White (1998), Barone-Adesi et al. (1998, 1999), McNeil and Frey (2000), and, more recently, Venter and de Jongh (2002), Guermat and Harris (2002)).

A univariate price process

$$\{S_t, t \geq 0\},$$

typically a stock price or stock index. Then,

$$\{X_t, t \geq 0\}$$

is defined by,

$$S_t = S_0 \exp(X_t)$$

and is usually termed the return process of S . We assume that the increments of X, i.e., the daily returns, $\Delta X_t = X_t - X_{t-1}$, are the form

$$\Delta X_t = \sigma_t \Delta L_t$$

where denotes a sequence of i.i.d. random variables drawn from an infinitely divisible distribution and σ denotes a randomly changing predictable process, which we call volatility process.

This general set-up may be interpreted as the restriction of the continuous-time model

$$dX_t = \sigma_t dL_t$$

to discrete time, where L denotes a process with stationary, independent increments starting at 0 and the volatility process σ stays piecewise constant between integer time points.

By volatility one usually refers to the standard deviation of the return series, or more precisely, to the standard deviation given all past observations. We do not necessarily take this point of view here. We call the process σ above volatil-

Figure 3. A sample path of geometric Brownian motion process

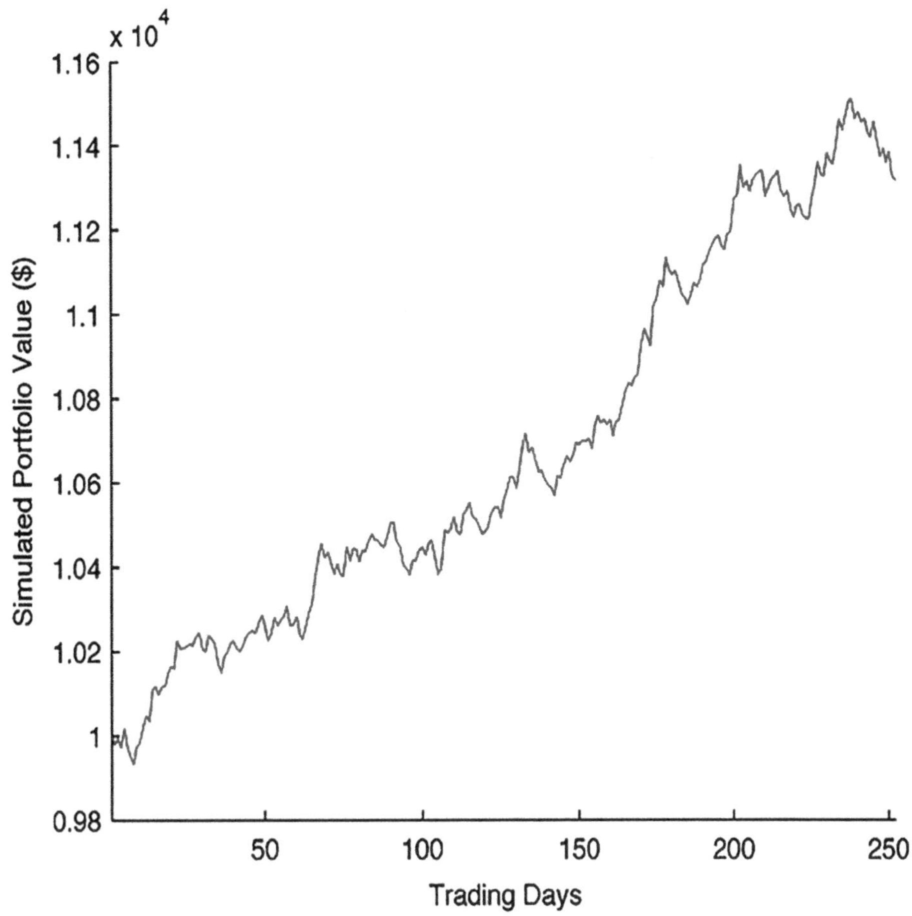

ity, which may or may not be directly observable from past return data.

FUTURE RESEARCH DIRECTIONS

The chapter recommends further study in financial risk management to investigate Martingale process for asset prices. The study also recommends further study in:

- Using time-varying parameters approach to investigate mean reversion and random walk for assets prices such as exchange rates and prices of precious metals such as gold.
- Using time-varying parameters approach to investigate mean reversion and random walk in futures price of crude oil.

CONCLUSION

In the paper, we put some arguments in favor of stochastic and behavioral finance. Namely, individuals make their predictions and decisions through a very complex system that is hard to be explained only through the set of differential equations. On the other hand, experiments have demonstrated that people usually also do not behave consistent in time, but use different ways of strategic thinking and reasoning, instead. This is especially true when dealing their wealth, which make the understanding of price movements much more complex. Although many attempts have been tried to define asset pricing through a kind of a stochastic process, i.e. Brownian motion or geometric Brownian motion, volatilities on the market indicate that new paradigm is needed.

When used to model the price of a security over time, the geometric Brownian motion process possesses neither the flaws of the Brownian motion process. Because it is the logarithm of the share prices that is assumed to be normal random variable, the model does not allow for negative share prices. Furthermore, because the values are in ratios, rather than differences of prices separated by a fixed amount of time that have the same distribution, the geometric Brownian motion makes what many feel is the more reasonable assumption.

The advantages of geometric Brownian motion are relatively easy involvement of calculation and do not need a lot of data to forecast the future closing price. It has been stated in the Martingale and Markov properties of geometric Brownian motion.

REFERENCES

Barone-Adesi, G., Bourgoin, F., & Giannopoulos, K. (1998). Don't look back. *Risk (Concord, NH), 11*, 100–104.

Barone-Adesi, G., Giannopoulos, K., & Vosper, L. (1999). VaR without correlations for non-linear portfolios. *Journal of Futures Markets, 19*, 583–602. doi:10.1002/(SICI)1096-9934(199908)19:5<583::AID-FUT5>3.0.CO;2-S

Blaug, M. (1962). *Economic theory in Retrospect*. Cambridge, Illinois: Cambridge University Press.

Brandão, L., Dyer, J., & Hahn, W. (2005). Using binomial trees to solve real-option valuation problems. *Decision Analysis, 2*(2), 69–88. doi:10.1287/deca.1050.0040

Brown, R. (1828). A brief account of microscopical observations made in the months of June, July and August 1827 on the particles contained in the pollen of plants. *Philosophical Magazine Series 2, 4*(21), 161–173. doi:10.1080/14786442808674769

Campbell, J. Y., Lo, A. W., & MacKinlay, A. C. (1997). *The Econometrics of Financial Markets*. Princeton: Princeton University Press.

Chaudhuri, K., & Wu, Y. (2003). Random-walk versus breaking trend in stock prices: Evidence from emerging markets. *Journal of Banking & Finance, 27*(4), 575–589. doi:10.1016/S0378-4266(01)00252-7

Eberlein, E., Frey, R., Kalkbrener, M., & Overbeck, L. (2007). Mathematics in Financial Risk Management. *Jahresbericht der Deutschen Mathematiker Vereinigung, 109*, 165–193.

Einstein, A. (1905). Uber die von der molekularkinetischen Theorie der Wärme geforderte Bewegung von in ruhenden Flüssigkeiten suspendierten Teilchen. *Annalen der Physik, 322*(8), 549–560. doi:10.1002/andp.19053220806

Fama, E. (1965). The Behavior of Stock-Market Prices. *The Journal of Business, 38*(1), 34–105.

Guermat, C., & Harris, R. (2002). Robust conditional variance estimation and value-at-risk. *Journal of Risk, 4*, 25–41.

Gujarati, D. (2004). *Basic Econometrics*. Tata: McGraw Hill.

Hull, J., & White, A. (1998). Incorporating volatility updating into the historical simulation method forvalue-at-risk. *The Journal of Risk, 1*, 5–19.

International Organization for Standardization (ISO). (2009a). *ISO Guide 73:2009 Risk Management Vocabulary*. Retrieved from http://www.iso.org/iso/iso_catalogue/catalogue_tc/catalogue_detail.htm?csnumber=44651

Kloman, H. (1999). Does risk matter? EARTH Matters, Special Edition on Risk Management, Lamont-Doherty Earth Observatory, Columbia University.

Lo, A. W., & MacKinlay, C. (1988). Stock Market Prices Do Not Follow Random Walks: Evidence from a Simple Specification Test. *Review of Financial Studies*, *1*(1), 41–66. doi:10.1093/rfs/1.1.41

Mandelbrot, B. B. (1963). The variation of certain speculative prices. *The Journal of Business*, *XXXVI*, 392–417.

McNeil, A., & Frey, R. (2000). Estimation of tail-related risk measures for heteroscedastic financial time series: An extreme value approach. *Journal of Empirical Finance*, *7*(3-4), 271–300. doi:10.1016/S0927-5398(00)00012-8

Mishra, A., Mishra, V., & Smyth, R. (2014). *The random-walk hypothesis on the Indian stock market* (Discussion Paper: 07/14). Monash University, Department of Economics.

Takayasu, M., Mizuno, T., Ohnishi, T., & Takayasu, H. (2005). *Practical Fruits of Econophysics*. Tokyo: Springer.

Venter, J., & Jongh, P. D. (2002). Risk estimation using the normal inverse Gaussian distribution. *Journal of Risk*, *4*, 1–23.

Wiener, N. (1923). Differential space. *Journal of Mathematics and Physics*, *58*, 131–174.

ADDITIONAL READING

Abraham, A., Seyyed, F. J., & Alsakran, S. A. (2002). Testing the random walk behavior and efficiency of the Gulf stock markets. *Financial Review*, *37*, 469–480.

Amanulla, S. (1997). *Asset price behaviour and stock market efficiency*. Ph.D. Dissertation, University of Hyderabad.

Berkowitz, J. (2001). Testing density forecasts, with applications to risk management. *Journal of Business & Economic Statistics*, *19*, 465–474.

Borges, M. R. (2011). Random walk tests for the Lisbon stock market. *Applied Economics*, *43*(5), 631–639.

Charles, A., & Darne, O. (2008). The random walk hypothesis for Chinese stock markets: Evidence from variance ratio tests. *Economic Systems*, *33*(2), 117–126.

Chesney, M., & Scott, L. (1989). Pricing European currency options: A comparison of the modified Black Scholes model and a random variance model. *Journal of Financial and Quantitative Analysis*, *24*, 267–284.

Dixit, A., & Pindyck, R. (1994). *Investment under Uncertainty*. Princeton, New Jersey: Princeton University Press.

Eberlein, E. (2001). *Application of generalized hyperbolic Lévy motions to finance. Lévy Processes: Theory and Applications*. Basel: Birkhäuser.

Hoque, H., Kim, J. H., & Pyun, C. S. (2007). A comparison of variance ratio tests of random walk: A case of Asian emerging stock markets. *International Review of Economics & Finance*, *16*(4), 488–502.

Karatzas, I., & Shreve, S. E. (1991). *Brownian Motion and Stochastic Calculus* (2nd ed.). Springer Verlag Press.

Morter, P., & Peres, Y. (2010). *Brownian Motion*. Cambridge Press.

Oksendal, B. K. (2002). *Stochastic Differential Equations: An Introduction with Applications*. Springer.

Revuz, D., & Yor, M. (1999). *Continuous Martingales and Brownian Motion* (3rd ed.). Springer Press.

Sigman, K. (2006). *Geometric Brownian motion*. Columbia University.

Stefano, M. I. (2008). *Simulation and Inference for Stochastic Differential Equations. Number XVIII in Springer Series in Statistics*. Springer Verlag.

KEY TERMS AND DEFINITIONS

Assets: An item of current or future economic benefit to an organization. Examples include: cash, short-term investments, accounts receivable, grants receivable, inventories, prepaid expenses, buildings, furniture, equipment, vehicles, and long-term investments.

Black Scholes Model: A model of price variation over time of financial instruments such as stocks that can, among other things, be used to determine the price of a European call option. The model assumes that the price of heavily traded assets follow a geometric Brownian motion with constant drift and volatility. When applied to a stock option, the model incorporates the constant price variation of the stock, the time value of money, the option's strike price and the time to the option's expiry. Also known as the Black-Scholes-Merton Model.

Markov Property: The term *Markov property* refers to the memoryless property of a stochastic process. It is named after the Russian mathematician Andrey Markov. A stochastic process has the Markov property if the conditional probability distribution of future states of the process (conditional on both past and present values) depends only upon the present state, not on the sequence of events that preceded it.

Option Pricing Theory: Any model- or theory-based approach for calculating the fair value of an option. The most commonly used models today are the Black-Scholes model and the binomial model. Both theories on options pricing have wide margins for error because their values are derived from other assets, usually the price of a company's common stock. Time also plays a large role in option pricing theory, because calculations involve time periods of several years and more. Marketable options require different valuation methods than non-marketable ones, such as those given to company employees.

Stochastic Differential Equation: It is a differential equation in which one or more of the terms is a stochastic process, resulting in a solution which is itself a stochastic process. They are used to model diverse phenomena such as fluctuating stock prices or physical systems subject to thermal fluctuations.

Stock Price: The cost of purchasing a security on an exchange. Stock prices can be affected by a number of things including volatility in the market, current economic conditions, and popularity of the company.

Volatility: It is a measure for variation of price of a financial instrument over time in finance.

Wiener Process: In mathematics, the Wiener process is a continuous-time stochastic process named in honor of Norbert Wiener. It is often called standard Brownian motion, after Robert Brown. It is one of the best known Lévy processes (càdlàg stochastic processes with stationary independent increments) and occurs frequently in pure and applied mathematics, economics, quantitative finance and physics.

Chapter 12
The Effects of Situational and Dispositional Factors on the Change in Financial Risk Tolerance

Jorge Ruiz-Menjivar
University of Georgia, USA

Wookjae Heo
University of Georgia, USA

John E. Grable
University of Georgia, USA

ABSTRACT

Utilizing the lens of Heider's (1958) attribution theory and Grable and Joo's (2004) conceptual framework, this chapter studies the effect of situational and dispositional attributions on changes in financial risk tolerance. Situational factors are assessed through changes in household situation and changes in macroeconomic factors. For dispositional factors, changes upon sensation seeking attitudes are explored. The data employed in this research come from the 1993, 1994, and 2006 National Longitudinal Survey of Youth (N = 5,449). Results from structural equation modeling indicate that changes in internal attributions have a significant and positive effect (coefficient = 0.12, p <0.01) on the change in risk tolerance, as is true for changes in external attributions where a significant effect is seen (coefficient = 0.30, p <0.01). Thus, the findings from this study support the conceptual framework premised on Heider's attribution theory and Grable and Joo's (2004) conceptual model.

INTRODUCTION

Financial risk tolerance (FRT) is a significant and influential factor affecting those decisions of an economic and financial nature. Importantly, the concept has been deemed as an associative and predictive factor of financial risk-taking behaviors. During the last few decades, the concept has earned consideration among financial professionals committed to advising consumers,

DOI: 10.4018/978-1-4666-7484-4.ch012

and for researchers dedicated to understanding and predicting individuals' financial behaviors. The evaluation, understanding, and measurement of the elusive FRT are ongoing endeavors in the fields of finance and economics.

FRT is the level of uncertainty an individual is willing to assume despite experiencing less advantageous outcomes in the pursuit of a most advantageous outcome (International Organization for Standardization, 2005). At the household level, FRT becomes a relevant influencer on decisions such as asset and retirement portfolio allocation, and strategies for achieving wealth, growth, and accumulation (Barsky, Juster, Kimball, & Shapiro, 1997). Typically, individuals with higher levels of FRT obtain higher returns in their investments over longer periods of time. This is consistent with the idea of risk-return trade-offs, which suggest that those riskier investments are associated with potentially higher returns. Nonetheless, not all consumers are high-risk takers. Indeed, rational consumers are intrinsically risk-averse and will tolerate only a certain level of risk for any given return.

Numerous factors have been reported as having an association with FRT. For example, the literature suggests an association between FRT and multidisciplinary factors (e.g., social, economic, demographic, psychological factors, etc.) such as life cycle variables, race and ethnicity, wealth, employment status, economic outlook, personality, and psychological traits, among others (Barsky et al., 1997; Grable, 2000; 2008; Grable & Lytton, 1999; 2001; Grable & Joo, 2004; Hanna & Lindamood, 2005; Sung & Hanna, 1996).

An aspect that has been of particular interest is the notion of FRT's stability or variability through time. This topic has created debate among academicians and professionals in the field (Grable, 2008; Sahm, 2007; Yao, Hanna, & Lindamood, 2004). While some maintain that FRT is a changeable attitude over time and attribute this elasticity to factors such as market conditions and sentiment, and expectation of the economy (Grable, 2000; 2008; Pan & Statman, 2010; Yao, Hanna, & Lindamood, 2004), others argue that FRT is relatively fixed over time (Gerrans, Faff, & Hartnett, 2012; Roszkowski & Cordell, 2009; Roszkowski, Delaney & Cordell, 2009; Sahm, 2007; Santacruz, 2009). In an effort to explore this topic further, the purpose of this study is to explore the research question of whether or not changes in circumstantial and internal variables can potentially affect the change in an individual's FRT.

BACKGROUND

Financial risk tolerance (FRT) is an important factor in the process of financial decision making under uncertainty. FRT refers to an individual's attitude towards financial risk, and the willingness to undertake more financial risk for the potential of obtaining higher returns. Barsky et al. (1997) express financial risk tolerance as the inverse of risk aversion—as viewed from an expected utility theory. Faff, Mulino, and Chai (2008) evaluate the link between FRT and risk aversion. Their findings suggest that both concepts are associated to a significant degree, especially when using questions regarding gambling to measure such concepts—as is the case in this study.

Regarding measurement of FRT, various instruments exist (see for example, Barsky et al., 1997; Grable & Lytton, 1999; Hanna, Gutter, & Fan, 2001). Despite these research instruments having been tested for validity and reliability, it is dubious as to the whether or not these instruments are measuring the same dimension of FRT (Ruiz-Menjivar, Blanco, Çopur, Gutter, & Gillen, 2014). A possible explanation for the discrepancy on measurements across instruments is the disagreement in terms of definition of FRT. For example, some researchers define it as an attitude while others conceptualize FRT as a trait. The use of different theoretical frameworks (e.g., economic theory, prospect theory) and/or the empirical approach used to create the instrument can also cause disagreements. Four approaches to measure FRT have been identified in the literature: (a) choice of type of investments and financial products, (b) hypothetical questions on risk/reward, (c) mixed measured, and (d) actual behavior (Hanna et al., 2001; Shelbecker & Roszkowski, 1993). In this study, we measure FRT using job gambling risk/reward hypothetical questions.

Multiple socioeconomic and demographic variables are associated with FRT. For instance, studies have found significant relationships between FRT and age (Sung & Hanna, 1996), gender (Grable & Lytton, 1999), race/ethnicity (Grable, 2008; Fan & Xiao, 2006; Sung & Hanna, 1996; Yao, Gutter, & Hanna, 2005), marital status (Roszkowski, Snelbecker, & Leimberg, 1993; Sung & Hanna, 1996), income and education (Grable, 2000; Grable & Joo, 2004), employment status (Hanna & Lindamood, 2005), and economic expectations (Grable, 2000), amongst others. Grable (2008) provides a summary of principal factors affecting FRT by reviewing 125 studies published between 1960 and 2006. His revision of the literature indicates that higher levels of FRT are strongly correlated with male gender, being single, and having a minimum educational attainment of a college degree. In further comparison, of individuals with lower versus higher levels of FRT, those with the higher levels are associated with greater net worth and income, higher levels of financial knowledge and financial satisfaction, larger household size, and greater economic expectations.

A long debated aspect of FRT is about the notion of whether or not FRT changes through time or remains static. Findings in the literature in terms of changes in FRT are mixed. For example, some studies have found that FRT is elastic through time (Grable, 2000; 2008; Pan & Statman, 2010; Yao et al., 2004). Yao and her associates evaluate changes in FRT trends from 1983 to 2001. Their findings conclude that FRT is overimpacted by economic events, and changes in FRT levels are reflected accordingly. They posit that the changes in FRT during the evaluated time period is consistent with the pattern of FRT increase when securities returns increase, and it decreases when returns decline. However, it is worth noting that Yao et al. use six waves of the cross-sectional Survey of Consumer Finances when analyzing these trends on FRT. Other cross-sectional studies suggest that factors such as emotion and economic circumstances affect the variation in risk tolerance (Grable, 2000, 2008; Pan & Statman, 2010). For example, using a sample of 2,734 investors, Pan and Statman (2010) posit that FRT changes due to market conditions and is significantly associated with emotions.

Per contra, other research studies suggest a relative stability in FRT (Gerrans, Faff, & Hartnett, 2012; Roszkowski & Cordell, 2009; Roszkowski, Delaney & Cordell, 2009; Sahm, 2007; Santacruz, 2009). For instance, utilizing a sample of college students, Roszkowski and Cordell (2009) find that relative FRT is significantly stable over a change of 269-814 days. Sahm (2007) uses panel data from the Health and Retirement Study to assess variation in risk tolerance through time (1992-2002). Sahm finds that, despite noted exceptions in some variables tested, overall relative risk aversion is stable over time. Moreover, she finds that risk tolerance decreases with age, and increases in the context of better economic conditions for macroeconomic conditions such as the stock market. Interestingly, Sahm's findings indicate that changes in wealth, and personal economic shock, such as job displacement, are not significantly associated to changes in FRT. A more recent study by Gerrans, Faff, and Hartnett (2012) uses a longitudinal panel of investors in order to assess changes in FRT during the global financial crisis. Their findings suggest that FRT is considerably stable over the analyzed period of time (2007-2009). They acknowledge that in a short period, FRT appears stable; nevertheless, they do not discard the possibility that FRT might be subject to change over longer period of time.

Conceptual Framework

The present research utilizes a conceptual framework based on the combination of both a) general elements borrowed from the main premises of Heider's (1958) attribution theory, and (b) the financial risk tolerance (FRT) model proposed in Grable and Joo (2004).

Heider's attribution theory is a well-known framework in the field of social psychology. The theory, in an effort to understand and explain behavior of the self and of others, proposes that individuals assign attributes to behavior and infer them as causal (Heider, 1958; Kelly, 1967; Kelley & Michela, 1980; Manusov & Spitzberg, 2008). Under the lens of Heider's frameworks, individuals consider two types of attribution: dispositional or situational. The former refers to factors such as personality traits, beliefs, and attitudes that are internal to the individual. Situational attributions, on the other hand, are those factors pertinent to the individual's environment or context (e.g., social, economic, cultural, familial situation and/or background) (Heider, 1958; DeLamater & Myers, 2011).

Further, Grable and Joo (2004) propose a multidisciplinary model, as it includes an amalgamation of financial, economic, psychological, and sociological variables. In their conceptual model, environmental factors are defined as those variables that involve quantifiable household financial situations, socio-economic status, and social changes such as marital status or household number change. In their model, income, net worth, financial knowledge, homeownership, education, and marital status constitute the environmental factors. They use biopsychosocial factors to refer to those internal variables that are pertinent to the individual's life such as personality and psychological traits (e.g., sensation seeking, self-esteem), attitudes, dogmas or beliefs, and/or factors in which an individual has little control (e.g., birth order, race/ethnicity, age, gender). In Grable and Joo's model, these biopsychosocial factors are represented by the following variables: age, gender, racial background, birth order, self-esteem, type A personality, sensation seeking, and financial satisfaction. It is worth noting that Grable and Joo's FRT model is premised on the risk attitude and risk taking behavior model presented by Irwin (1993). The latter is a causal model used to predict risk-taking behavior among adolescents (Irwin & Millstein, 1986).

In the conceptual model used in this study, we posit that the change in FRT is affected by shifts in an individual's dispositional and situational attributions. Contextually, in the model, dispositional attribution is represented by the personality trait of sensation seeking. In addition, situational attributions refer to the following variables: change in family size, residence type, net worth, inflation, and unemployment rates. Figure 1 illustrates the conceptual model proposed in the present study.

Situational Factors

Household Factors: Specific to the conceptual model in this study are net worth, family size, and homeownership—variables pertinent to the internal situation of the household. The literature supports a correlation between FRT and each of these household situation variables.

Using data from the 1998 Survey of Consumer Finances, Finke and Huston (2003) find a strong, positive relationship between net worth and FRT. Likewise, their results reveal that greater risk tolerance is associated to greater ownership of financial assets—a typically risky element of net worth. These results confirm previous findings on the relationship between FRT and net worth. For instance, Hanna, Gutter and Fan (2001) suggest a negative association between wealth and relative risk aversion.

Mixed results exist for FRT and household size. Grable (2008) reports that literature moderately supports the notion of a positive relationship between household size and FRT. Yet other studies suggest less willingness to take financial risks by larger households (Coleman, 2003; Gutter, Fox, & Montalto, 1999).

Figure 1. Proposed conceptual framework
Note: The proposed model hypothesizes that the change in Financial Risk Tolerance is influenced by shifts in an individual's dispositional and situational attributions—where dispositional attribution is represented by the personality trait of sensation seeking, and situational attributions refer to the following variables: change in family size, residence type, net worth, inflation, and unemployment rates.

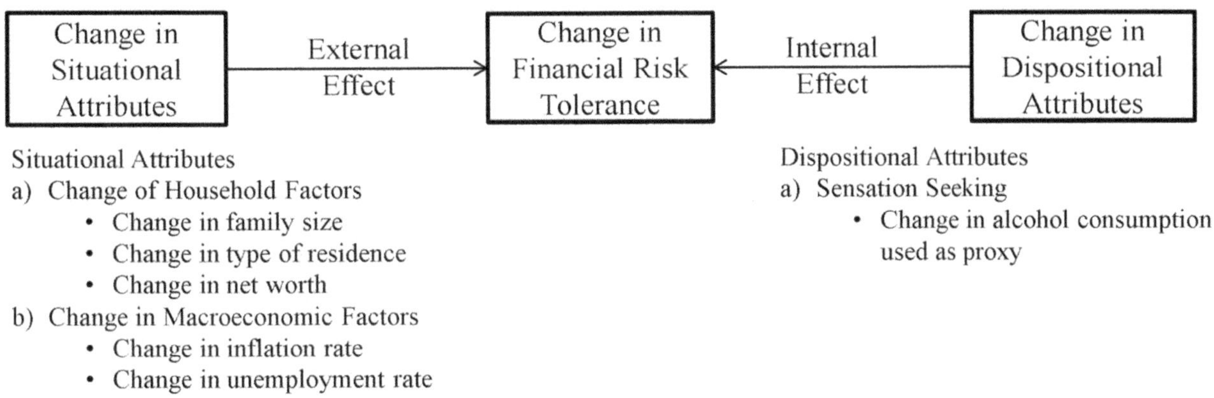

Finally, homeownership is another factor that has been found to be correlated with FRT; being a homeowner is associated to being more risk tolerant. However, the support in the literature about this relationship is low (Grable, 2008). Using data from several waves of the Italian Survey of Household Income and Wealth, Diaz-Serrano (2005), interestingly, shows that a household's risk aversion (when compared to market constraints) plays a stronger role in the relationship between income uncertainty and the likelihood of being a homeowner. It is worth noting that the literature strongly supports the positive relationship between predictable and stable income and high FRT.

Macroeconomic Factors: In the context of the proposed model, inflation rates and unemployment rates represent the macroeconomic variables external to the household. Brandt and Wang (2003) find that aggregate risk aversion is sensitive to the report of news on inflation where high aggregate risk aversion levels are associated to an unexpected increase in inflation. Expectation about the performance of the economy or economic outlook might capture, to some extent, expectation on inflation rates. Grable (2000) concludes that individuals with greater economic expectation tend to be more risk tolerant than their counterparts.

Regarding unemployment rates, Diaz-Serrano and O'Neill (2004) suggest a significant and positive association between risk aversion and the likelihood of being unemployed. Relatedly, Grable (2008) indicates that there is moderate evidence in the literature to suggest that being employed full-time is associated with increasing levels of FRT. In addition, in Grable (2000), results show that those individuals employed in professional occupations are typically more financially risk tolerant that those who have lower ranking occupations.

Dispositional Factors

Sensation Seeking and Risk Tolerance: For decades, sensation seeking has been a construct of considerable study in the field of personal psychology. The concept was first introduced and developed by the psychologist Marvin Zuckerman. This personality trait refers to the pursuit of sensations and experiences that involve novelty, complexity, and/or sensational intensity to the extent that an individual may be willing to assume physical, social, legal, or other types of risk (Horvath & Zuckerman, 1992; Zuckerman, 1969; 1979a; 1994; 2007; 2010; Zuckerman, Buchsbaum, & Murphy,

1980). Of note is that realization that risk itself is not the main factor that makes an individual engage in an activity. This main construct has been divided into four sub-factors: (a) thrills and adventure (activities or sports involving unusual sensations and risks beyond the conventional), (b) experience seeking (openness to experimenting with new types of sensations through music, art, or drugs), (c) disinhibition (seeking stimulating sensation and experiences in social situations such as parties or social drinking), and (d) boredom susceptibility (intolerance of monotonous and repetitive types of experiences).

In terms of financial risk, studies on gambling and sensation seeking have shown that individuals with high sensation seeking scores—especially those in the disinhibition factor—are more prone to gambling. Sensation seekers also underestimate the risks associated with gambling, and they tend to be more aware of the odds of winning or losing (Zuckerman, 1974; 1976; 1979a; 1979b). Moreover, sensation seekers tend to bet more while gambling and choose games with worse odds (Water & Kirk, 1968). Interestingly, when holding the perception of risk constant, those with higher levels of sensation seeking expect more pleasure and anticipate less anxiety when engaging in certain activities (Zuckerman, 1976; 1979a; 1979b; 2010; Roberti, 2004).

Further, Wong and Carducci (1991) evaluate the association between sensation seeking and financial risk tendencies in everyday financial decisions. Their study specifically uses 12 hypothetical financial decisions divided into the following categories: personal investment decisions (e.g., buying stocks, bonds, certificate of deposits and real estate), household affairs (e.g., buying car insurance, keeping appropriate liquidity in financial accounts), and gambling decisions (e.g., playing the lottery and card games). Consistent with the results of previous studies on the association between gambling and sensation seeking, Wong and Carducci find that, in general, those individuals with higher sensation seeking scores show greater financial risk tendencies when managing everyday financial situations. The study also finds that males are more prone to assuming greater risk in everyday financial decisions regardless of sensation seeking levels.

Purpose of the Study and Hypotheses

The purpose of this study is to evaluate the effects of changes in situational and dispositional attribution on changes in consumers' FRT. Based on Heider's (1958) attribution theory and the conceptual framework proposed in Grable and Joo (2004), we utilize a model in which situational factors are represented by changes in household situation (residence type, family size, net worth), by changes in macroeconomic factors (inflation rates and unemployment), and dispositional factors are measured by sensation seeking. The following hypotheses were tested:

H_1: Changes of situational factors significantly affect FRT

H_2: Changes of dispositional factors significantly affect FRT

METHODOLOGY

Dataset and Sample

Data used for this study come from the 1993, 1994, and 2006 National Longitudinal Survey of Youth 1979 cohort (NLSY79). Sponsored by the U.S. Department of Labor, this survey is a nationally representative sample of 12,686 young men and women (age 14-22 on December 31, 1978) living in the United States who were first interviewed in 1979. NLSY79 was conducted annually until 1994, and has been administered biannually thereafter. Although NLSY's main emphasis of investigation is labor force behavior, content of much broader nature is available in the survey. For instance, NLSY offers data pertinent to income and assets, health conditions, crime and substance abuse, fertility, and attitudes and expectations (e.g., risk aversion, time preference, time use, self-esteem, among others), along with a series of demographic questions.

Given the longitudinal nature of NLSY79, the employment of this survey is relevant for this study as the main purpose is to assess the relationship between changes in risk tolerance and changes in internal and external attribution variables. Nonetheless, as typical, we are not exempted of virtually ineluctable data constraints when using this dataset for the study. For example, the selection of NLSY79 waves for this study is primarily based on the availability of two of the main variables of interest—risk tolerance and alcohol consumption (used a proxy for sensation seeking). Questions on alcohol consumption are available only in the 1994, 2002, and 2006 waves. In the case of risk tolerance, a series of questions about income gambling for measurement of risk aversion are available in the 1993, 2002, 2004 and 2006 waves. Thus, in light of the constrained availability of key data, we use and match the answers of risk aversion questions from the 1993 wave to the data of the 1994 wave. This assumption may be perceived as a limitation in the study.

After accounting for factors such as survey attrition, missing data, and unavailability of variables in certain years, the total sample in this study totals 5,449 respondents. Table 1 offers the descriptive measures of the sample utilized in this study.

Measurement of Variables

Change in Risk Tolerance: Barsky et al. (1997) describe financial risk tolerance as the inverse concept of risk aversion. In this study, we adopt this perspective, and we discuss the paper in terms of risk tolerance. In order to measure risk tolerance, the following three questions are for measurement of risk tolerance:

1. "Suppose that you are the only income earner in the family, and you have a good job guaranteed to give you your current (family) income every year for life. You are given the opportunity to take a new and equally good job, with a 50-50 chance that it will double your (family) income and a 50-50 chance that it will cut your (family) income by a third. Would you take the new job?"
2. "Suppose the chances were 50-50 that it would double your (family) income and 50-50 that it would cut it in half. Would you still take the new job?"
3. "Suppose the chances were 50-50 that it would double your (family) income and 50-50 that it would cut it by 20 percent. Would you take the new job?"

The two-stage scoring process of respondents' risk tolerance is adopted from methodologies used in Barsky et al. (1997) and Heo, Grable, and Chatterjee (2013). Based on their responses to questions A and B, or A and C, participants are ordered in four different risk tolerance categories: very low-risk tolerance, low risk-tolerance, high-risk tolerance, and very high-risk tolerance (coded as 0, 1, 2, and 3 respectively).

The first stage in the scoring process lies on the answer indicated to question A. Those respondents who accept the job proposed in A are then asked question B. On the contrary, if respondents decline the job offered in A, then respondents are asked C. The second stage of the scoring process determines the risk tolerance categories of each respondent. Individuals answering "yes" to A and B are assigned to the "very high-risk tolerance" group. Participants who indicate "yes" to A, yet "no" to B are categorized as high-risk takers. In the case of those answering "no" to A and C, their risk tolerance is classified as low. Finally, those who respond "no" to A, but "yes" to C are considered very low-risk takers.

Table 1. Descriptive statistics: sample profile based on 2006 NLSY79 wave

Variables			
Race	**Description**	**Frequency (%)**	
Race Gender	Hispanic	1,003	(18.18)
	Black	1,541	(27.93)
	White & others	2,974	(53.90)
Gender Family Size	Male	2,742	(49.69)
	Female	2,776	(50.31)
Family Size Marital Status	1	1,092	(19.75)
	2	1,207	(21.87)
	3	1,181	(21.40)
	4	1,271	(23.03)
	5	504	(9.13)
	Over 6	263	(4.76)
Marital Status	Never Married	918	(16.64)
	Married	3,210	(58.17)
	Separated	268	(4.86)
	Divorced	1.047	(18.97)
	Widowed	74	(1.34)
Variables			
Net Worth	Description	Mean (SE)	
Net Worth	1993	51,277.47	(1798.56)
	1994	58,746.96	(1961.54)
	2002	168,836.30	(4458.79)

Note. *N*=5,449

Once respondents are assigned to their respective risk tolerance category for the years of the analysis, then we assess changes among a decade between 1994 and 2006. In terms of change in risk tolerance, seven different possibilities are considered. If risk tolerance has not increased or decreased during the period of the evaluation, then we assign those respondents to the "no change" group. In the case of those whose risk tolerance has increased, they were assigned into one of the following groups: small positive shift, moderate positive shift, and large positive shift. Similarly, for the respondents whose risk tolerance had decreased over the examined period of time, they are classified as the following: small, negative shift, moderate negative shift, and large negative shift. As a result, the risk tolerance is coded on a 7-point scale from -3 to 3.

Internal Attribution

Change in Sensation Seeking: This study uses alcohol consumption as a proxy for sensation seeking. Research shows that sensation seeking is associated to and predictive of alcohol consumption (Zuckerman, 1994; 2007). Particularly, alcohol drinking is an activity saliently related to the disinhibition sub-factor of sensation seeking

(Cohen & Fromme, 2002; Schwarz, Burkhart, & Green, 1978; Zuckerman, 1994; 1987; 2010; Zuckerman, Bone, Neary, Mangelsdorff, & Brustman, 1972). Earleywine and Finn (1991) indicate that the relationship between alcohol consumption and behavioral disinhibition is grounded in their respective relationships to sensation seeking. In addition to drinking, drug use and risky sexual behaviors might be deemed as core risk taking factors linked to impulsive sensation seeking, sociability, and aggression (Zuckerman & Kuhlman, 2000). Thus, given the limitation on sensation seeking measurement, we acknowledge that alcohol consumption comprises a small dimension of the general construct of sensation seeking. For the purpose of this study, then, sensation seeking should be thought of in terms of the disinhibition subscale portion of sensation seeking only, as that is the only area in which we are able to capture with the available data.

In order to measure the disinhibition sub-factor of sensation seeking, we use a question that asked participants to indicate whether or not they had consumed alcohol in the last 30 days. We code the attribution as ordered scale: 1 if there is an increase in alcohol consumption (increase in sensation seeking, for the purpose of this study), 0 if no change, and -1 if there is a decrease in alcohol consumption (decrease in sensation seeking).

External Attribution

Change of Residence Type: Respondents are initially assigned into either homeowner or non-homeowner groups (i.e., renters and others). After which, we evaluate changes of residency type over the respective time-period of analysis. Change of residence type is coded as ordered scale: 1 if a respondent has moved from non-homeowner to homeowner; 0 if no change; and -1 if the respondent has moved from homeowner to non-homeowner.

Change of Family Size: The reported number of household members is used in to order to determine the change of family size. Three ordered categories are created: an increase in the number members in the family, no-change, or a decrease in the number of members in the household (coded as 1, 0, and -1 respectively).

Change of Net Worth: NLSY79 provides respondents' net worth as a continuous measure with actual dollar amount in 1994 and in 2006. Changes of net worth between years of study coded as actual difference between 1994 and 2006. Specifically, changes of net worth uses subtraction from 2006 to 1994; therefore, the positive dollar amount denotes increasing net worth and the negative dollar amount tells decreasing net worth. In the model the actual dollar amounts are standardized.

Change of Inflation Rate: We use the Consumer Price Index (CPI)—an estimate of the change in the weighted average price of a basket of consumer goods and services— as a measure of "headline" inflation. In this study, the primary data from NLSY79 is combined with CPI data from the U.S. Bureau of Labor Statistics (BLS). NLSY79 offers data on the geographical regions wherein the respondents dwell. The regions are divided into the following: Northeast area, Midwest, South and West. BLS records annual CPI for each state. For the purpose of this study, we estimate the mean CPI for each region for the years 1994, and 2005, and assign these estimate values to respondents based on the area in which they resided during those years. After matching the data, we calculate the changes of CPI (changes of inflation rate, in the context of this study) for the period of 1994-2006. In the model, change of inflation rate is standardized.

Change of Unemployment Rate: The primary data from NLSY79 is combined with local area employment statistics from the U.S. Bureau of Labor Statistics (BLS). As previously mentioned, NLSY79 geographically localizes respondents in regions (i.e., Northeast, Midwest, South, and West). BLS, though, reports county-level annual unemployment rates for each state. Similar to the procedure adopted for the estimation of inflation rates, the mean value of all counties unemployment rates within each of the respective regions is calculated. The mean region-wise unemployment rate is then matched with respondents based on their respective residency during the years 1994, and 2006. Change of unemployment rate between 1994 and 2006 is calculated for each region. Same as CPI, change of unemployment rate is standardized in the model.

Analysis

This study employs structural equation modeling (SEM) to assess a model through which changes in financial risk tolerance (FRT) might be affected by dispositional and situational attributes. Table 2 displays the descriptive statistics of the change in the variables used in the SEM model. This hypothesized model is based on the conceptual framework that was fully detailed earlier in this paper. Figure 2 displays the hypothesized structural equation model. Based on Heider's (1958) attribution theory and Grable and Joo's (2004) model, we hypothesize that changes in dispositional and situation variables affect the change in FRT. As shown in figure 2, the latent variable of change in situational attributes is composed of two additional latent variables: changes of household situation and changes of macroeconomic factors. In addition, sensation seeking (proxied by alcohol consumption) represents the dispositional attributes of the model. Particularly, SEM is used to confirm the empirical model. In this study, maximum likelihood estimation is used as the basic estimation method of SEM. Since the present research uses various measures and scales in the model, maximum likelihood is an appropriate form of estimation. When using maximum likelihood estimation, however, SEM sometimes does not provide a smooth result (Ferron & Hess, 2007). To solve the estimation problem, Ferron and Hess suggest diverse strategies like changing the start value, screening the data for outliers, and optimizing the maximum number of iterations. This study employs the strategy of optimizing the maximum number of iterations based on maximum likelihood estimation. And, for this study, the optimized number of iterations is defined as that point where the model's fit is minimized. Precisely, a mid-way point was chosen as the optimization point for the best model fit.

RESULTS

In this section, we first discuss the assessment of the model's fit, and then provide the parameter values of the model and an interpretation of the direction for each significant coefficient in the model. Kenny (2014) refers to model fit as that model in which there is high capacity for consistency with the data such that it has reliability and reproducibility. No single, specific fit criterion exists that is universally accepted or used by academicians employing SEM. In practice, researchers generally assess various fit indices for the model in question. Bollen and Long (1993) provide a detailed description of several of the fit indices used in the literature, along with their respective suggested cutoff values. In this study, we use the following fit indices: Chi Square test, Comparative Fit Index (CFI), Root Mean Square Error of Approximation fit (RMSEA), and Standardized Root Mean Square Residual (SRMSR). As the Tucker Lewis Index (TLI) and CFI are both highly correlated (Kenny, 2014), only the CFI is reported and discussed in this section. Chi square test evaluates how well a proposed model fits the observed data. In the 1994-2006 model, the chi square value ($\chi 2 = 79.68$, $p < 0.01$) shows a poor fit for the model. Nevertheless, as Kenny (2014) explains, chi square test often finds statistical significance when using greater than 400 cases in structural equation modeling. As such, the chi-square test is often deemed unreliable as a test for a model's fit in structural equation modeling (Weston & Gore, 2006).

Table 2. Descriptive statistics: change in variables (from year 1994 to 2006)

Variables	Description	Frequency (%)	
Race	Hispanic	1,003	(18.18)
	Black	1,541	(27.93)
	White & others	2,974	(53.90)
Gender	Male	2,742	(49.69)
	Female	2,776	(50.31)
Family Size	1	1,092	(19.75)
	2	1,207	(21.87)
	3	1,181	(21.40)
	4	1,271	(23.03)
	5	504	(9.13)
	Over 6	263	(4.76)
Marital Status	Never Married	918	(16.64)
	Married	3,210	(58.17)
	Separated	268	(4.86)
	Divorced	1.047	(18.97)
	Widowed	74	(1.34)
Variables	**Description**	**Mean (SE)**	
Net Worth	1993	51,277.47	(1798.56)
	1994	58,746.96	(1961.54)
	2002	168,836.30	(4458.79)
	2006	237,051.00	(5992.86)

The CFI for the model is 0.929. Based on the criteria offered in Kenny (2014) and Kline (2011), the model's fit is marginal (between 0.90 and 0.95). The closer the RMSEA value is to 0.1, the poorer the fit of the model Kline. For the model, RMSEA is approximately 0.023. Based on the MacCallum, Browne, and Sugawara (1996) criteria for RMSEA, the fit is good for the model. Lastly, we assessed fit index, via SRMR, which resulted in a model fit of 0.022. This also supports that the model has a good fit as based on the criteria provided by Hu and Bentler (1999) and Kline where a good fitting model has an SRMR value of less than 0.08. Additionally, a low SRMR indicates that the observed and predicted correlations are tight. In summation, the model's fit is acceptable across all tested fit indices, save one, (chi square test). As such, we accept the feasibility of the proposed model and the conceptual framework for the use in the 1994 to 2006 NLSY79 dataset.

Figure 3 displays a diagram of the full model including standardized parameter estimates. As shown, the standardized direct effect of change of dispositional attributions has a positive and significant effect on the change of FRT (coefficient = 0.12, $p < 0.001$). An increase by one standard deviation in the change of dispositional attributes predicts a 0.12 standard deviation increase in the change of FRT. Moreover, the standardized direct effect of change of external attribution on the change of FRT is 0.30, significant at 99% confidence level. That is, an increase of one standard deviation in the change of situational attributes represents a 0.30 standard deviation increase in

Figure 2. Proposed Model of the Effect of Change of Dispositional and Situational Attributes in Financial Risk Tolerance

Note: Proposed path diagram is presented. Based on Heider's (1958) attribution theory and Grable and Joo's (2004) conceptual framework, the model used in this chapter posits that that changes in dispositional and situation variables affect the change in FRT. The latent variable of change in situational attributes is composed of two additional latent variables: changes of household situation and changes of macroeconomic factors. In addition, sensation seeking (proxied by alcohol consumption) represents the dispositional attributes of the model. Particularly, SEM is used to confirm the empirical model. In this study, maximum likelihood estimation is used as the basic estimation method of SEM.

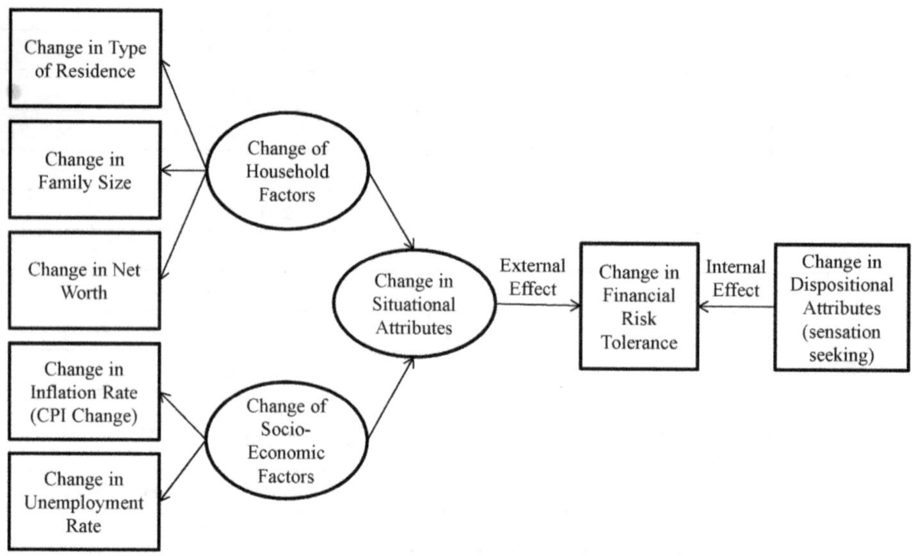

change for FRT. Therefore, the model indicates that both internal and external attributions that are affecting change in FRT between 1994 and 2006.

This explorative study evaluates a proposed model based on both attribution theory and Grable and Joo's (2004) model, wherein our main objective is to evaluate a model's fitness for predicting change in financial risk tolerance. Particular to this, is the greater concern about coefficient directionality rather than the interpretation of the parameters themselves.

As seen in figure 3, dispositional attributes (coefficient = 0.12, p <0.001) correlate positively to a change in FRT. As discussed earlier in this paper, sensation seeking, proxied by alcohol consumption, is used to represent dispositional factors. In this sense, the positive relationship of dispositional attributes to changes in risk tolerance indicates that higher alcohol consumption is correlated to a higher change in FRT. Situational attributes, similar to dispositional attributes, are positively and significantly correlated to a change in risk tolerance (coefficient = 0.30, p <0.001). The latent variable of situational attributes is composed of two other variables—change in household factors and change in macroeconomics factors. Changes in household factors (coefficient = 0.13, p <0.01) are positively correlated with the latent variable, situational attributes. However, the relationship between changes in macroeconomic factors and the latent situational attributes was not significant (-0.03, p >0.05). Despite this particular relationship not showing significance, the overall model's fit remains good in all tested indexes but one, chi square, where over-sensitivity given the use of SEM might be expected with chi square. As such, we accept the prospect of using the model with the NLSY79.

Further, change of net worth (coefficient = -0.24, p <0.001) and change of family size (co-

Figure 3. Result of Structural Equation Modeling for change of Financial Risk Tolerance

*Note: The full model including standardized parameter estimates is displayed. N=5,449; χ^2=79.68 (P<.001); RMSEA=0.023; CFI=0.929; TLI=0.929; SRMR=0.022. Ellipse=Latent variables, Rectangle= Observed variables. The standardized direct effect of change of dispositional attributions has a positive and significant effect on the change of FRT (coefficient = 0.12, p < .001). The standardized direct effect of change of external attribution on the change of FRT is 0.30, significant at 99% confidence level. Therefore, the model indicates that both internal and external attributions that are affecting change in FRT between 1994 and 2006. It is worth noting that for the latent variable of change in macroeconomic factors, both changes in inflation rate, and change in unemployment rate are significantly related to such latent construct. Nonetheless, the latter does not show a significant association to the latent variable of changes in situational factors. *p < .05. **p < .01. ***p < .001.*

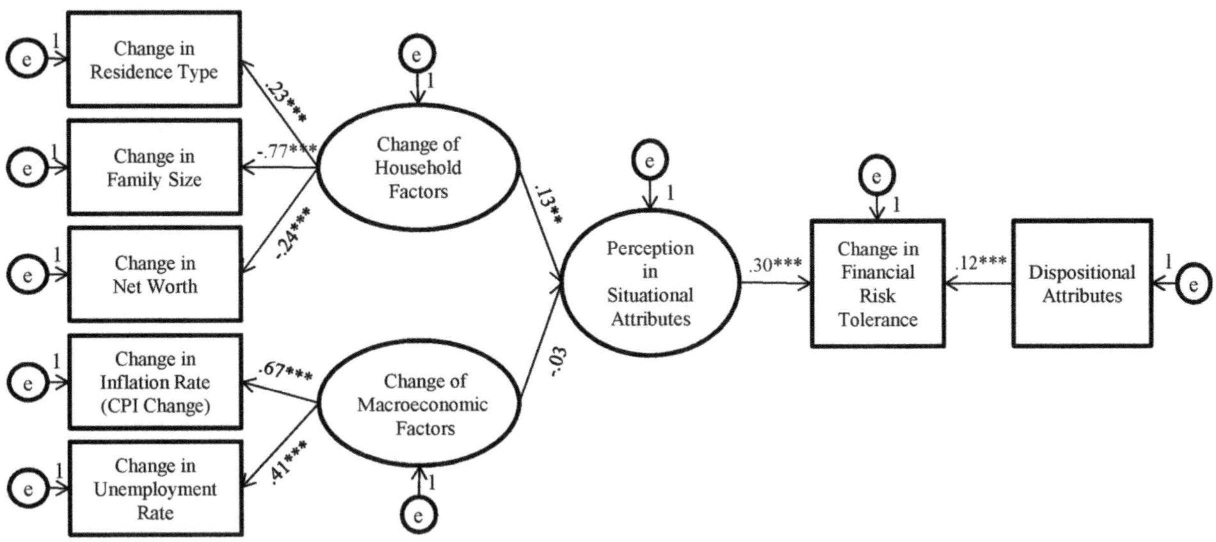

efficient = -0.77, *p* <0.001) are both negatively associated to the latent variable of changes of household factors. Then, a decrease in the change of net worth and family size are associated with higher change of FRT. On the other hand, a change in residence type (coefficient = 0.23, *p* <0.001) is positively related to the latent change in household factors. Thus, moving from non-homeowner to homeowner is associated with a higher change in FRT. For the latent variable of change in macroeconomic factors, both changes in inflation rate (coefficient = 0.67, *p* <0.001) and change in unemployment rate (coefficient = 0.41, *p* <0.001) are significantly related to the latent construct. Although these two factors are significant to the latent change in macroeconomic factors, the latter does not show a significant association to the latent variable of changes in situational factors. Therefore, making inferences in the directional relationship on the change in inflation and unemployment rate to the change in FRT is avoided as it could lead to erroneous conclusions.

DISCUSSION

In recent decades, financial risk tolerance (FRT) has received increasing attention by scholars and professionals in the fields of finance and economics. FRT's importance is seen in everyday money decisions and for making more complex financial choices in the marketplace (Grable, 2000; 2008). The exploration of FRT and its determinants are an ongoing effort in the finance and economic research community.

A problematic aspect of FRT, and one still under debate amongst academicians and professionals in the field, is the question as to whether FRT actually changes over time. The literature is equivocal on this. Those arguing for a fluid FRT over time cite factors such as changing market conditions and market sentiment (Grable, 2008; Yao, Hanna, & Lindamood, 2004), whereas others maintain that FRT is relatively stable, if not fixed, over time (Roszkowski & Cordell, 2009; Roszkowski, Delaney & Cordell, 2009; Sahm, 2007). We examine this further through evaluation of the effects of changes in situational (i.e., household situations and macroeconomic factors) and dispositional attributes (i.e., sensation seeking proxied by alcohol consumption) on the change in FRT utilizing a model premised on Heider's (1959) attribution theory and Grable and Joo's (2004) conceptual framework. Particularly, the viability of the proposed model is examined via structural equation modeling.

Using data primarily from NLSY79, we assess the effect of changes in situational and depositional attributes on the change in FRT from 1994 through 2006. The model's fit supports the use of the proposed conceptual framework and the data. The main findings indicate that positive and significant effects arise from both situational (coefficient = 0.30, $p < 0.001$) and dispositional attributes (coefficient = 0.12, $p < 0.1$) on the change in FRT. Otherwise stated, the greater the changes in dispositional and situational attributes, the greater the change in FRT. Moreover, we find that, in particular, the change of household factors significantly impact the change in FRT. But, changes of housing status, family size, and net worth are also associated to the change in FRT. For instance, shifting from a non-homeowner to a homeowner is associated to a greater variation in FRT. Conversely, changes in household size and net worth exhibit negative and significant correlation to changes in FRT.

A subtle but important phenomenon for discussion occurs here, in that, the macroeconomic factors, in turn, do not show any significant association to changes in situational factors. We speculate that this is do with the latent variable of macroeconomic factors being a composite of two merged variables, each comprised from a different source (Census Bureau data) to the main dataset (NLSY79). This non-statically significant result does not change the overall fit of the model however.

From the latent of dispositional attributes, a change in alcohol consumption (used as proxy for sensation seeking) exhibits a significant and positive association to a change in FRT where the greater the change in alcohol intake, the greater the change in FRT. And finally, of note, as this is an exploratory model of the prediction of change in FRT, the focus remains on interpretation of the directional relationship of the variables to the change in FRT rather than the interpretation of the coefficient. Accordingly, an accurate interpretation of the coefficient in SEM would require greater specificity and detail about the attributes in the dataset. We believe this to be a constraint in the present study. Further research should, undoubtedly, integrate additional attributes into the model; more in depth recommendations for future research will follow in the succeeding section.

In short, the findings of this exploratory study further contribute to the ongoing discussion about whether or not risk tolerance is stable or elastic over time. It provides an indication of the effects of changes in situational and dispositional factors on the change in FRT. The findings elicit important aspects pertinent to both research and academicians by providing potential, new directions for future research about the phenomena of FRT's elasticity, and for the applied fields by offering an insight into the temporal variation in risk tolerance—a significant factor for consideration when delivering recommendations about investment and portfolio allocation such that they are more closely aligned to consumers' needs and goals over time.

LIMITATIONS AND FUTURE RESEARCH

A main limitation in the study is a data limitation related to the unavailability of questions on financial risk tolerance in the four waves of the NLSY79 dataset—1993, 2002, 2004, and 2006, and the unavailability of questions on alcohol consumption in three waves—1994, 2002, and 2006. As such, we are compelled to limit the study to only those years for which both variables, FRT and alcohol consumption, were simultaneously available. Furthermore, to allow for evaluation in changes of FRT with the other variables through a consecutive period (1994 through 2006), we needed to match the 1993 data pertinent to the FRT questions to the 1994 wave data (as the FRT was not available in the 1994 wave). We acknowledge that this match may be presumptuous.

Another limitation in the present research relates to the measurement of dispositional attributes, specifically, that sensation seeking is proxied by alcohol consumption. Although alcohol consumption is often a variable used in the measurement of sensation seeking, and it is closely related to the disinhibition sub-factor of the construct, it is necessary to note that alcohol consumption represents a diminutive dimension of the conceptual spectrum of sensation seeking. We acknowledge that this is not an optimal substitution for sensation seeking. However, we are constrained in the sense that additional variables (e.g., drug use, risky sexual behaviors, practice of extreme sports/activities) are not available—at least not in the waves used in this study. Had additional variables been available, they might have been combined and afforded a fuller representation for sensation seeking.

Moreover, as discussed in previous sections, the relationship between the latent variable of situational attributions and the latent macroeconomic factors is not significant, though the model's fit is good. We surmise that a potential reason of this non-significant relationship is that both of the variables—change in inflation and unemployment rate—that compose the latent variables macroeconomic factors come from external data (U.S. Census Bureau), which is matched to the NLSY79 dataset for the purpose of the study. We are unable to make directional inferences about the relationship between the change of inflation and unemployment rate, and the change in FRT. The re-evaluation of these factors should be considered in future studies for change in FRT.

This study is an exploratory effort to evaluate the impact of internal and external variables in the change of FRT over time. Nonetheless, it is preliminary, and future research should consider the inclusion and analysis of more dispositional attributes in the model. Such attitudes might include psychological traits or personality traits found to be significantly related to risk tolerance (such as self-esteem and locus of control (Grable & Joo, 2004; McInish, 1982) which might provide further insight about FRT and its change over time. Moreover, when sensation seeking is part of the construct, it should be measured in a more comprehensive and diverse manner by taking into account sub-factors (e.g., thrill and adventure, experience seeking, disinhibition, and boredom susceptibility). Similar recommendations are extended for potential directions when considering situational attributes, whereupon education, marital status, socialization, and household income—all correlated to FRT—would provide an improved understanding about FRT. Finally, in this study, we evaluate goodness of fit of the proposed model and the direction of the change in situational and dispositional factors on the change in FRT. Nevertheless, given dataset limitations, we are unable to interpret the coefficients and thus examine how much change these variables are influencing FRT. This is a meaningful question that should be pursued in further research.

REFERENCES

Barsky, R. B., Juster, F. T., Kimball, M. S., & Shapiro, M. D. (1997). Preference parameters and behavioral heterogeneity: An experimental approach in the Health and Retirement Study. *The Quarterly Journal of Economics, 112*(2), 537–579. doi:10.1162/003355397555280

Bollen, K. A., & Long, J. S. (Eds.). (1993). *Testing structural equation models*. Newbury Park, CA: Sage.

Brandt, M. W., & Wang, K. Q. (2003). Time-varying risk aversion and unexpected inflation. *Journal of Monetary Economics, 50*(7), 1457–1498. doi:10.1016/j.jmoneco.2003.08.001

Bureau of Labor Statistics, United States Department of Labor. (2014). *Consumer Price Index*. Last modified October 13, 2013. http://www.bls.gov/cpi/

Bureau of Labor Statistics, United States Department of Labor. (2014). *Local Area Unemployment Statistics*. Last modified October 13, 2013. http://www.bls.gov/lau/#tables

Castanier, C., Le Scanff, C., & Woodman, T. (2010). Beyond sensation seeking: Affect regulation as a framework for predicting risk-taking behaviors in high-risk sport. *Journal of Sport & Exercise Psychology, 32*, 731–738. PMID:20980713

Cohen, E. S., & Fromme, K. (2002). Differential determinants of young adult substance use and high-risk sexual behavior. *Journal of Applied Social Psychology, 32*(6), 1124–1150. doi:10.1111/j.1559-1816.2002.tb01429.x

Coleman, S. (2003). Risk tolerance and the investment behavior of Black and Hispanic heads of household. *Financial Counseling and Planning, 14*(2), 43–52.

DeLamater, J. D., & Myers, D. J. (2011). Social Psychology (7th ed.). Belmont, CA: Wadsworth.

Diaz-Serrano, L. (2005). On the negative relationship between labor income uncertainty and homeownership: Risk aversion vs. credit constraints. *Journal of Housing Economics, 14*(2), 109–126. doi:10.1016/j.jhe.2005.06.002

Diaz-Serrano, L., & O'Neill, D. (2004). *The relationship between unemployment and risk-aversion* (IZA Discussion Paper No. 1214).

Earleywine, M., & Finn, P. R. (1991). Sensation seeking explains the relation between behavioral disinhibition and alcohol consumption. *Addictive Behaviors, 16*(3–4), 123–128. doi:10.1016/0306-4603(91)90004-2 PMID:2063699

Faff, R., Mulino, D., & Chai, D. (2008). On the linkage between financial risk tolerance and risk aversion. *Journal of Financial Research, 31*(1), 1–23. doi:10.1111/j.1475-6803.2008.00229.x

Fan, J. X., & Xiao, J. J. (2006). Cross-cultural differences in risk tolerance: A comparison between Americans and Chinese. *Journal of Personal Finance, 5*(3), 54–75.

Ferron, J. M., & Hess, M. R. (2007). Estimation in SEM: A concrete example. *Journal of Educational and Behavioral Statistics, 32*(1), 110–120. doi:10.3102/1076998606298025

Finke, M. S., & Huston, S. J. (2003). The brighter side of financial risk: Financial risk tolerance and wealth. *Journal of Family and Economic Issues, 24*(3), 233–256. doi:10.1023/A:1025443204681

Fuchs, G. (2013). Low versus high sensation-seeking tourists: A survey of backpackers' experience risk perception. *International Journal of Tourism Research, 15*(1), 81–92. doi:10.1002/jtr.878

Gerrans, P., Faff, R. W., & Hartnett, N. (2012, February). Individual financial risk tolerance and the global financial crisis. In *25th Australasian Finance and Banking Conference*. doi:10.2139/ssrn.1990811

Grable, J. E. (2000). Financial risk tolerance and additional factors which affect risk taking in everyday money matters. *Journal of Business and Psychology*, *14*(4), 625–630. doi:10.1023/A:1022994314982

Grable, J. E. (2008). Risk tolerance. In J. J. Xiao (Ed.), *Handbook of Consumer Finance Research*. New York, NY: Springer. doi:10.1007/978-0-387-75734-6_1

Grable, J. E., & Joo, S. (1999). Financial help-seeking behavior: Theory and implications. *Financial Counseling and Planning*, *10*(1), 25–38.

Grable, J. E., & Joo, S.-H. (2004). Environmental and biopsychosocial factors associated with financial risk tolerance. *Financial Counseling and Planning*, *15*(1), 73–88.

Grable, J. E., & Lytton, R. H. (1999). Financial risk tolerance revisited: The development of a risk assessment instrument. *Financial Services Review*, *8*(3), 163–181. doi:10.1016/S1057-0810(99)00041-4

Grable, J. E., & Lytton, R. H. (2001). Assessing the concurrent validity of the SCF risk tolerance question. *Financial Counseling and Planning*, *12*(2), 43–53.

Gutter, M. S., Fox, J., & Montalto, C. P. (1999). Racial differences in investor decision making. *Financial Services Review*, *8*(3), 149–162. doi:10.1016/S1057-0810(99)00040-2

Hanna, S. D., Gutter, M. S., & Fan, J. X. (2001). A measure of risk tolerance based on economic theory. *Financial Counseling and Planning*, *12*(2), 53–60.

Hanna, S. D., & Lindamood, S. (2005). Risk tolerance of married couples. In the *Proceedings of the Academy of Financial Services*, G2 (pp. 1-28).

Heider, F. (1958). *The psychology of interpersonal relations*. New York, NY: John Wiley & Sons. doi:10.1037/10628-000

Heo, W., Grable, J. E., & Chatterjee, S. (2013). Life insurance consumption as a function of wealth change. *Financial Services Review*, *22*(4), 389–404.

Horvath, P., & Zuckerman, M. (1993). Sensation seeking, risk appraisal and behavior. *Personality and Individual Differences*, *14*(1), 41–52. doi:10.1016/0191-8869(93)90173-Z

Hu, L. T., & Bentler, P. (1995). Evaluating model fit. In R. H. Hoyle (Ed.), *Structural Equation Modeling. Concepts, Issues, and Applications* (pp. 76–99). London: Sage.

International Organization for Standardization. (2005). *ISO 22222:2005 Personal financial planning: Requirements for personal financial planners.*

Irwin, C. E. (1993). Adolescence and risk taking: How are they related? In N. J. Bell & R. W. Bell (Eds.), *Adolescent risk taking*. Newbury Park, CA: Sage.

Irwin, C. E., & Millstein, S. G. (1986). Biopsychosocial correlates of risk-taking behaviors during adolescence: Can the physician intervene? *Journal of Adolescent Health Care*, *7*(Suppl), 82S–96S. PMID:3536822

Kelley, H. H. (1967). Attribution theory in social psychology. *Nebraska Symposium on Motivation*, *15*, 192–238.

Kelley, H. H., & Michela, J. L. (1980). Attribution theory and research. *Annual Review of Psychology*, *31*(1), 457–501. doi:10.1146/annurev.ps.31.020180.002325 PMID:20809783

Kenny, D. A. (2014). Measuring model fit [reference website]. Retrieved from http://davidakenny.net/cm/fit.htm

Kline, R. B. (2011). *Principles and Practice of Structural Equation Modeling* (3rd ed.). New York, NY: The Gulford Press.

MacCallum, R. C., Browne, M. W., & Sugawara, H. M. (1996). Power analysis and determination of sample size for covariance structure modeling. *Psychological Methods*, *1*(2), 130–149. doi:10.1037/1082-989X.1.2.130

Manusov, V., & Spitzberg, B. H. (2008). Attributes of attribution theory: Finding good cause in the search for theory. In D. O. Braithwaite & L. A. Baxter (Eds.), *Engaging Theories in Interpersonal Communication* (pp. 37–49). Thousand Oaks, CA: Sage. doi:10.4135/9781483329529.n3

McInish, T. (1982). Individual investors and risk-taking. *Journal of Economic Psychology*, *2*(2), 125–136. doi:10.1016/0167-4870(82)90030-7

Pan, C., & Statman, M. (2010). *Beyond risk tolerance: Regret, overconfidence, and other investor propensities* (Research Paper 10-05). SCU Leavey School of Business. Retrieved from http://papers.ssrn.com/sol3/papers.cfm?abstract_id=1549912

Popham, L. E., Kennison, S. M., & Bradley, K. I. (2011). Ageism, sensation-seeking, and risk-taking behavior in young adults. *Current Psychology (New Brunswick, N.J.)*, *10*(3), 184–193. doi:10.1007/s12144-011-9107-0

Roberti, J. W. (2004). A review of behavioral and biological correlates of sensation seeking. *Journal of Research in Personality*, *38*(3), 256–279. doi:10.1016/S0092-6566(03)00067-9

Roszkowski, M., & Cordell, D. (2009). A longitudinal perspective on financial risk tolerance: Rank-order and mean level stability. *International Journal of Behavioural Accounting and Finance*, *1*(2), 111–134. doi:10.1504/IJBAF.2009.027448

Roszkowski, M., Delaney, M., & Cordell, D. (2009). Intraperson consistency in financial risk tolerance assessment: Temporal stability, relationship to total score, and effect on criterionrelated validity. *Journal of Business and Psychology*, *24*(4), 455–467. doi:10.1007/s10869-009-9115-3

Roszkowski, M. J., Snelbecker, G. E., & Leimberg, S. R. (1993). Risk-tolerance and risk aversion. In S. Leimberg, M. Satinsky, R. LeClair, & R. Doyle (Eds.), *The Tools and Techniques of Financial Planning* (4th ed., pp. 213–225). Cincinnati, OH: National Underwriter.

Ruiz-Menjivar, J., Blanco, A., Çopur, Z., Gutter, M. S., & Gillen, M. (2014). A cross-cultural comparison of three risk tolerance measures: Turkey and The United States case. *International Journal of Research in Business and Social Science*, *3*(1), 1–14.

Sahm, C. (2007). How much does risk tolerance change? Finance and Economics Discussion Series 2007-66. Washington: Board of Governors of the Federal Reserve System; Available https://federalreserve.gov/Pubs/FEDS/2007/200766/200766abs.html

Santacruz, L. (2009). Effect of general economic mood on investor risk tolerance – implications for financial planning. *JASSA*, *1*, 35–42.

Schwartz, R. M., Burkhart, B. R., & Green, S. B. (1978). Turning on or turning off: Sensation seeking or tension reduction as motivational determinants of alcohol use. *Journal of Consulting and Clinical Psychology*, *46*(5), 1144–1145. doi:10.1037/0022-006X.46.5.1144 PMID:701550

Shelbecker, G., & Roszkowski, M. (1993). Risk tolerance and risk aversion. In S. R. Leimberg, M. J. Satinsky, R. T. LeClair, & R. J. Doyle (Eds.), *The tools and techniques of financial planning* (4th ed., pp. 213–225). Cincinnati, OH: National Underwriter.

Sung, J., & Hanna, S. (1996). Factors Related to Risk Tolerance. *Financial Counseling and Planning*, *7*, 11–20.

Waters, L. K., & Kirk, W. E. (1968). Stimulus-seeking motivation and risk taking behavior in a gambling situation. *Educational and Psychological Measurement*, *28*(2), 549–550. doi:10.1177/001316446802800242

Weston, R., & Gore, P. A. (2006). A brief guide to structural equation modeling. *The Counseling Psychologist*, *34*(5), 719–751. doi:10.1177/0011000006286345

Wong, A., & Carducci, B. J. (1991). Sensation seeking and financial risk taking in everyday money matters. *Journal of Business and Psychology*, *5*(4), 525–530. doi:10.1007/BF01014500

Yao, R., Gutter, M. S., & Hanna, S. D. (2005). The financial risk tolerance of Blacks, Hispanics, and Whites. *Journal of Financial Counseling and Planning*, *16*(1), 51–62.

Yao, R., Hanna, S. D., & Lindamood, S. (2004). Changes in financial risk tolerance, 1983-2001. *Financial Services Review*, *13*(4), 249–266.

Zuckerman, M. (1969). Theories of sensory deprivation. In I. J. P. Zubek (Ed.), *Sensory deprivation: Fifteen years of research* (pp. 407–432). New York, NY: Appleton-Century-Crofts.

Zuckerman, M. (1974). The sensation seeking motive. In B. Maher (Ed.), *Progress in experimental personality research*. New York, NY: Academic Press.

Zuckerman, M. (1976). Sensation seeking and anxiety, traits and states, as determinants of behavior in novel situations. In I. G. Sarason & C. D. Spielberger (Eds.), *Stress and anxiety*. Washington, DC: Hemisphere.

Zuckerman, M. (1979a). *Sensation Seeking: Beyond the Optimal Level of Arousal*. Hillsdale, NJ: Erlbaum.

Zuckerman, M. (1979b). Sensation seeking and risk taking. In C. E. Izard (Ed.), *Emotions in Personality and Psychopathology* (pp. 163–197). New York, NY: Plenum Press. doi:10.1007/978-1-4613-2892-6_7

Zuckerman, M. (1987). Is sensation seeking a predisposing trait for alcoholism? In E. Gottheil, K. A. Druley, S. Pashkey. & S. P. Weinstein (Eds.), Stress and Addiction (pp. 283-301). New York, NY: Bruner/Mazel.

Zuckerman, M. (1994). *Behavioural Expressions and Biosocial Bases of Sensation-Seeking*. Cambridge: Cambridge University Press.

Zuckerman, M. (2007). *Sensation Seeking and Risky Behavior*. Washington, DC: American Psychological Association. doi:10.1037/11555-000

Zuckerman, M. (2010). Sensation Seeking. Corsini Encyclopedia of Psychology. 1–4.

Zuckerman, M., Bone, R. N., Neary, R., Mangelsdorff, D., & Brustman, B. (1972). What is the sensation seeker? Personality trait and experience correlates of the Sensation Seeking Scales. *Journal of Consulting and Clinical Psychology*, *39*, 308–321.

Zuckerman, M., Buchsbaum, M. S., & Murphy, D. L. (1980). Sensation seeking and its biological correlates. *Psychological Bulletin*, *88*(1), 87–214. doi:10.1037/0033-2909.88.1.187

Zuckerman, M., & Kuhlman, D. M. (2000). Personality and risk-taking: Common biosocial factors. *Journal of Personality*, *68*(6), 999–1029. doi:10.1111/1467-6494.00124 PMID:11130742

KEY TERMS AND DEFINITIONS

Change in Financial Risk Tolerance: The idea that financial risk tolerance is a fluid attitude through time. Such elasticity is attributed to factors such as market conditions and sentiment, and expectation about the economy.

Dispositional Attributes: Factors such as personality traits, beliefs, and attitudes that are intrinsic to the individual.

Financial Risk Tolerance: The level of financial uncertainty an individual is willing to undertake for the potential of obtaining higher financial returns.

Situational Attributes: Factors pertinent to the individual's environment or context, which includes social, economic, cultural, and familial situation and background.

Chapter 13
Financial Well-Being among Young Employees in Malaysia

Mohamad Fazli Sabri
Universiti Putra, Malaysia

Nurul Farhana Zakaria
Universiti Putra, Malaysia

ABSTRACT

The purpose of this study is to identify the levels of financial literacy, money attitude, self-esteem, financial capability and financial well-being of young employees, to explore the differences in financial well-being based on demographic characteristics of young employees and to identify the determinants of financial well-being among young employees. The sample consists of 508 of young employees aged 40 and under in central zone of Malaysia, which selected through multi stage sampling technique. Data were collected through self-administered questionnaires. Financial literacy, domains in money attitude and financial capability had significant influence toward financial well-being whereby financial capability become a major contributing factor to the financial well-being. By understanding more about the determinants of financial well-being, it is hoped to help young employees to become financial prudence and in the long-run could decrease the number of young employees declared bankruptcy.

INTRODUCTION

Financial problems are not just the concerns of the poor. The declining employment opportunities, income instability and tough purchasing power of Malaysian households are among the important issues facing by families. As a result, these issues captured the attention of policy makers and educators. In recent times, economic changes have made an impact towards how the people spend, save, invest and manage risks in order to protect their standard of living especially in long-term plan.

Young or prime adult is generally a person in the age range of 20 to 40 whereby these individuals and households have relatively low incomes and few assets such as homes, savings and stocks. However, it is also a time when young adults make a decision and significant investments in their future and mostly require debt (Haveman& Wolff, 2005).

DOI: 10.4018/978-1-4666-7484-4.ch013

According to the report by Federation of Malaysian Consumers Associations (FOMCA) in 2011, many of those declared bankrupt due to credit card debt were under 40 years old and 72 percent of them have no retirement plans. Apart from that, it was reported that 47 percent of these young employees were in serious debt with monthly debt payment were 30 percent or more of their gross income and had enough savings on an average for only four months if they stop working. This is seen as unfavorable financial management activities especially for their long-term planning.

A survey of Financial Behaviors and Financial Habits of Young Workers was carried out by the Consumer Research and Resource Centre (CRRC) in 2012 among 1,000 respondents from urban area in Kuala Lumpur, Selangor and Putrajaya. It was reported that almost half of young workers aged between 18 and 35 years old were in serious debt whereby those earning between RM 2,000 and RM 3,000 per month had the most serious debt problem and it was likely due to acquiring assets like a house, car or getting married, thus increasing their loan repayment obligations. Apart from that, a study was done by Ramli, Sum, Manaf, Saad, Hussain and Lyndon (2011) toward married young employees in public sector. It was reported that their financial well-being was still in moderate level. It cannot be denied that high-cost of living in urban areas, increased cost of basic goods and amenities and financial dependents of households require them to survive and make a proper financial planning in order to ensure better financial well-being in the future.

Apart from that, the combination of financial problems such as high debt, low income, and low levels of financial literacy may adversely affect individuals' financial well-being. Income uncertainty, rising petrol prices and physical pain for instance, have a more drastic influence on well-being. The concept of well-being or people's perception on well-being may be varies and depend on change in the level of people life. In the past, well-being had a meaning of overall happiness or satisfaction with their financial status or assets. However, in present the concept of well-being has been expanded to material and non-material aspects of a person's perception from their financial status, improving their standards of living, ability to meet the needs, feeling safe, comfortable and satisfied with the income.

Today's young adults are clueless when it comes to their finances, retirement savings, smart investing, credit card and debt. There are still low in financial literacy among young adults especially when they were asked about interest rates, inflation and risk diversification. This is seen as an obstacle to the financial well-being as young adults are difficult in struggling to their own financial prosperity because they never learned how to budget and plan to achieve financial security. The increasing levels of compulsive buying among young adults have contributed to personal financial problems, personal bankruptcy filings and credit card debt (Roberts & Jones, 2011). Young people today face different financial challenges than their parents did. They also accumulate greater debt at younger ages, largely due to high college costs. More than ever, they need to gain skills to take a more active, responsible role in their personal finances. The inclination to view life events in a negative way also become a major impact on individual's well-being, thus override positive feelings and self-esteem when reporting felt distress. The effects of affectivity and self-esteem, employment commitment and financial strain become the predictor to financial well-being.

However, there has been scarce research on financial well-being in Malaysia particularly among young employees. Thus, this study explores the relationship between financial well-being to financial literacy, money attitude, self-esteem and financial capability among public and private employees in Malaysia. By understanding more about the contributions to the financial well-being, it is hoped to help young employees to become financial prudence and in the long run could decrease the number of young employees declared bankruptcy as the financial well-being concepts are intended to help people to satisfy with their financial status, improving their standards of living, able to meet the needs, feeling safe, comfortable and satisfied with the income.

OBJECTIVES

Due to the issue arise; this study is performed to obtain the specific objectives to determine the financial well-being of young employees as listed below:

1. To identify the levels of financial literacy, money attitude, self-esteem, financial capability and financial well-being of young employees.
2. To explore the differences in financial well-being based on demographic characteristics of young employees.
3. To identify the determinants of financial well-being among young employees.

LITERATURE REVIEW

Financial Well-Being

Impact on the financial well-being and quality of life among the employees have received the attention from researchers, financial educators, practitioners and policy makers. Before the mid-1990s, some researchers have made an effort to explain, predict or determine the relevant construct such as financial well-being, financial satisfaction and economic well-being whereby these terms have been used interchangeably one another. According to Joo (2008), financial well-being can be defined as a feeling of being financially healthy, happy and free from anxious and it is usually based on a subjective appraisal of individual's financial situation.

Past studies also have found that socio-economic factors such as age, number of household members, marital status, education level, income and home ownership affect the financial well-being.The perception of financial well-being in today's world have changed as the economic conditions, technology, values, culture and norms change among communities. The changing of location and time have made the people to be more aware of their satisfaction toward income and savings, safety and needs, comfortness of life and satisfaction with the distribution of income and bonuses. It is supported by Joo (1998) whereby the meaning of financial well-being in the past was about happiness or satisfaction with financial position or assets but at the present the individual's perception of material and spiritual aspects of one's financial situation has meant changing and to improve people's living standards.

Ramli et al. (2012) have conducted a research on quality of life and well-being among young adults in Malaysia. This study involved 250 public employees aged 40 years and below. Overall, the respondents were found to have a moderate level of financial well-being on their current financial situation. As young employees have a great potential in shaping the future development of the country, this study suggests that the factor that affect the quality of life and well-being of young employees should be investigated in more detail.

Financial Literacy

The terms of financial literacy, financial knowledge and financial education are often used interchangeably by the academic literature (Huston, 2010). According to American Institute of Certified Public Accountants (2003), financial literacy can be defined as the ability to effectively access and manage one's finance in order to achieve life goals and financial well-being.

Most of the previous studies were conducted by the practitioners in financial service industry and focus on money management and investment-related issues. The result of these studies shows that the participants generally answered fewer than 60% of the survey questions correctly. Meanwhile, according to the Survey of Adults Financial Literacy in Australia that conducted by ANZ Bank in 2011 showed that most Australian have basic financial literacy. Unfortunately, young people aged 18 to 34 years and those from low socio-economic background were facing difficulties in making decisions related to money management. The ignorance about basic financial concepts can somehow affect the retirement planning, the exclusion to participate in the stock market and lead to poor borrowing behavior (Lusardi, 2008).

In Malaysian context, the financial literacy among the young adults was still low and due to the lack knowledge on related issues such as credit card, loans and settlement, 70% of these young adults felt that their ability to manage their own finances were very poor and lead to a lower financial satisfaction. Apart from that, alarming by the issue of bankruptcy among the young adults, FOMCA has take the initiative to launch Financial Literacy Month whereby this effort is important in order to ensure their financial and personal well-being (FOMCA, 2011).

Hilgert, Hogarth and Beverly (2003) in their research stated that in order to improve the financial well-being, people need knowledge and skills in order to manage their personal and household finances. People who have greater knowledge and understanding about finances and possess financial management skills tend to make good financial decisions as it may lead to satisfaction in their life. Individuals will unable to choose the right savings or investments for themselves, and may be at risk of fraud, if they are not financially literate.

Money Attitude

In today's materialistic environment, the role of money is not limited as a medium of exchange but become means and an end for happiness and well-being. Money is a common language in consumer culture whereas attitude toward money expand its influence over every area of life such as savings, spending, ideology, work performance and attitude toward environment (Phau& Woo, 2008).

Nickerson, Schwarz and Diener (2007) attempted to relate the link between orientation toward money and life satisfaction. It shows that people with high materialism or obsessed with money were tend to be more satisfied with their finances due to their ability to afford their material desires. This result suggests that individual with high financial aspirations can affect their financial well-being. However, the financial aspirations must be realistic as it is important for both financial satisfaction overall life satisfaction.

However, virtually less attention has been given to the psychological and symbolic aspects of money in predicting financial well-being. The understanding of money attitude and the relationship of those attitudes toward financial well-being may help to see how the money variables that encompass the personality, cultural and economic are related to financial well-being.

Self-Esteem

High self-esteemprovides the basis for success in coping with daily life in a rapidly changing environment. Individualscan build their own self-esteem and parents can only lendsupports and influence in decisions and choices of leading a life.

Berk (2003) defines self-esteem as the evaluative aspect of the self-concept, and therefore theevaluation of a person's own competence, is related to accepting and approving of one's own characteristics. Meanwhile Williams (2001) defines self-esteem as greatly impacts individualsattitudes, emotional experiences, future behavior, and long-term psychological adjustments (van Zyl, Cronje, Payze, 2006).

Healthy self-esteem allows people the emotional self-confidence to go for their financial goals and dreams. Investing in financial self-esteem is about spending the time, energy and money to go forward, toward their financial goals with less doubt and indecision.Feeling prepared and competent can be a big boost to self-esteem. If they want to become more proactive with their financial life, it is time to invest in financial education.

Ever since the 1969 publication of The Psychology of Self-Esteem, wherein Branden (1971) posited that self-esteem was the single most important facet of personal well being, the self-esteem movement has been one of far-reaching influence.

Financial Capability

In general, there is no internationally accepted definition of financial capability. However, the core definition of this term is about having the knowledge, understanding, skills, motivation and confidence in making financial decisions which are appropriate subject to the one's personal circumstances (Atkinson & Messy, 2012). Basically, most of the studies on financial capability are focusing on four key components of financial capability which entails managing money, staying informed, planning ahead and choosing products (Financial Industry Regulatory Authority [FINRA], 2009 & OECD, 2005).

Johnson and Sherraden (2007) also shared the same views where they believed financial capability not only requires financial literacy but requires access to appropriate financial products. In other words, financial capability requires both the ability to act which is the knowledge, skills, confidence and motivation as well as the opportunity to act through the beneficial financial products offered by the financial institutions. Together with ability and opportunity, it will contribute to a person's financial well-being.

Surveys of young adults conducted by the Financial Services Authority (FSA) and other organizations in 2006 have found that a basic understanding of personal finance has been often poor, especially among those with few formal qualifications and those who are not in education, employment or training. Poor financial capability is a major cause of adults do not access and benefiting from financial services, leading to financial exclusion. It is estimated, for example, that two million adults in the UK do not have a bank account.

METHODOLOGY

Sample Design

The sample comprised of 508 employees in public and private sectors, in which 290 from public sectors and 218 from private sectors participated in the study. Samples were selected using multistage sampling technique in selecting the sample study in the center zone of Peninsular Malaysia namely Southern Perak, Selangor, Federal Territory of Kuala Lumpur, Federal Territory of Putrajaya and Northern Negeri Sembilan. A total of 600 young employees were selected as the respondents. Four states in the center zone was randomly selected in the first stage. Each state was targeted to obtain 150 respondents. The data were collected using self-administered questionnaire, which were distributed through human resource personnel of selected agencies. Consent to take part in the study was obtained prior to giving out the survey forms.Data was coded and analyzed using SPSS to identify direct and indirect determinants of financial well-being among young Malaysian employees.

INDEPENDENT VARIABLES

Financial Literacy

Financial literacy was measured by an instrument developed by Sabri, Masud and Paim(2006) based on the Malaysian context. The instrument consisted of 34 statements indicate the true, false or don't know answer relating to financial aspects covering general knowledge of personal finance, savings, investments, financial records, credit, retirement, banking system, wills and insurance. Each correct answer carried one point, incorrect (wrong) and "don't know" answers were given zero point. Item analyses with correctly identified items were summed and the score was transformed into a percentage. Higher percentage scores indicated higher level of financial literacy. In this section, financial literacy was divided into three categories, namely low mean score (0-10), medium mean score (11-21) and high mean score (22-34). The average score was 17.81, with a standard deviation of 5.53.

Money Attitude

Money attitude in this study was measured by adopting six dimensions from the Furnham's Money Beliefs and Behaviors Scale (MBBS) that comprises of obsession, retention, inadequacy, effort, power and security. Money attitude involved 24 items that describe the feelings and experiences of the respondents with a five point Likert scale from strongly disagree (1) to strongly agree (5). Factor analysis was applied to identify and analyze the dimensions of money attitude. The Kaiser-Mayer-Olkin test of the sample adequacy showed that the sample was sufficient at 0.818 (Hair, Anderson, Tatham& Black, 1992). Based on the latent root criterion whereby only factors with eigenvalue of greater than one were considered. Together they explained 56.49% of the total variance.

Self-Esteem

Self-esteem was based on acquired score from Self-Esteem Inventory, which consisted of 10 items. This questionnaire uses likert-scale with five responses from strongly disagree (1) to strongly agree (5). The higher the score means the higher the respondent's self-esteem, and the lower the scoremeans the lower the respondent's self-esteem. For the level of classifications of respondents' self-esteem, score between 10-23 is classified as affected by low self-esteem, 24-37 is classified as moderate self-esteem, and 38-50 is classified as high level of self-esteem.

Financial Capability

The employees' financial capability was measured by twenty statements comprising of four domains which are, managing money, staying informed, choosing products and planning ahead with a five-point-likert scale question. A financial capability score was computed by summing the averages score for all twenty items. Those who were not capable ended up towards the lower scores, while those who were more capable ended up towards the higher scores. The Cronbach's alpha reported was 0.89.

DEPENDENT VARIABLE

Financial Well-Being

The measurement of financial well-being in this study was based on Malaysian Financial Well-Being Scale (MFWBS) developed by Garman and Jariah (2006), which based on the adaptation of the Incharge Financial Distress / Financial Well-being (IFDFW) by Prawitz et al. (2006). This scale consists of 12 questions with 10 measurement scale with the scale "1" is the lowest score of well-being (very dissatisfied) and the scale "10" is the highest score of well-being (very satisfied). The average score and standard deviation were used to determine the levels of financial well-being. The Cronbach's alpha reported was 0.935.

Sample Characteristics

A total of 38.4% were male and 61.6% were female. The majority of the respondents were Malay ethnicity (90.4%). The mean age of the sample was 31.2 years (SD= 4.853, median age=31 years). The mean monthly household income of the respondents was RM4,937.66. Regarding marital status, more than half of the respondents (68.5%) reported that they were married.Their current income were enough to meet their basic needs while majority of them can do savings for at least 1 to 10% per month and their asset values more than outstanding debt.

RESULTS AND DISCUSSIONS

The Levels of Financial Literacy, Money Attitude, Self-Esteem, Financial Capability and Financial Well-Being of Young Employees

Based on the possible scores, the financial literacy scores were divided into three levels, namely low mean score (0-11), moderate mean score (12-22) and high mean score (23-34) in order to illustrate the level in which they fit. A total of 508 respondents answered all the 34 literacy questions. The higher percentage of them, 323 out of 508 (63.6%) were in the moderate level of financial literacy while 23.4% (n=119) had high financial literacy. Increased financial literacy has as positive impact on people's personal life whereby it helps to reduce social and psychological pressures (Fox, Bartholomae & Lee, 2005). In work life, higher financial literacy lead to higher efficiency and productivity and help employees to better understand benefits offered by the organization and improve their satisfaction (Brennan, 1998). This finding was similar with pilot survey conducted by the OECD in 2012 whereby they assessed the national level of financial literacy, which involved several countries such as Germany, Peru, Norway and Malaysia. Based on the pilot survey, Malaysia indicates moderate levels of financial literacy with 51% of knowledge scores.

Scores for each of each dimension in money attitude were based on the possible scores. Dimension with a high score representing a high level of the attitude. The respondents scored high on effort of money attitude (mean=16.9) and followed by retention of money (mean=10.7), obsession of money (mean=9.3) and lastly was inadequacy of money (mean=7.9). It can be concluded that the respondents believe the money they gain were based on their effort and ability. They deserved a good paid of salary as it in line with their level of education and the scope of task that assigned to them. The more effort that they put the high value of money that they perceived. The respondents were also be careful on their wealth and prefer not to spend their money on unnecessary things.

The scores of self-esteem were divided into three levels, namely low self-esteem (10-23), moderate self-esteem (24-37) and high self-esteem (38-50). The higher percentage of them, 271 out of 508 (53.3%) were in the moderate level of self-esteem while 45.7% (n=232) had high level of self-esteem.

Scores for each of the four domains in financial capability were computed by summing the average score for all of the items. A high score indicated the respondents were financially capable on that particular domain. It shows that scores for financial capability in managing money were the highest (mean=19) and followed by planning ahead (mean=17.82), choosing products (mean=17.02) and the least was staying informed (mean=16.04).In overall, 73.6% of the respondents were in moderate levels of financial capability. It can be conclude that the respondents able to keep up with their financial commitments without difficulty or with less struggle. The respondents were also capable in planning ahead even though they were still young. It indicates that the respondents realized that preparing for retirement should be started from the beginning of their working life. However, the findings showed that the respondents were less capable in choosing products and staying informed. People often do not understand the risk associated with products and services and some of them refused to seek for professional advice and they often buy products based on advice from non-professional such as friends or family. Since the financial service market has undergoing transformation to meet customers' changing needs, it is important to the individuals to seek advice from a professional as they can provide reassurance about their financial situation. It is supported by a finding from OECD (2012) whereby it shows that those who use financial advisors have more valuable pensions and more financially confident than those who do not.

The levels of financial well-being were classified into three levels, namely low (average score 12-47), moderate (average score 48-84) and high level (average score 85-120) . The results showed 27 respondents (5.3%) had an average score of 12-47. This shows that respondents have a low level of financial well-being. A total of 399 respondents (78.5%) had an average score of 48-84 and it showed that the respondents have a moderate level of financial well-being. The remaining 82 respondents (16.1%) had an average score between 85-120, which indicated they were in high level of financial well-being. This shows that the respondents were in moderate level of financial well-being. The composite score of the financial well-being among the respondents was 5.51. The data showed that on average the respondents were in the moderate level of financial well-being . However, compared with previous studies, this composite score in this study was lower than Zaimah findings (2011), Prawitz et al . (2006) and O'Neill et al . (2006) with each recorded 6.57, 5.7 and 5.53. This may happen due to the Malaysia's economic that undergo rapid changes in term of inflation rate and rising price of goods and necessities compared to the previous years.

The Differences In Financial Well-Being Based On Demographic Characteristics of Young Employees

An independent sample t-test was conducted to compare the financial well-being scores for male and female young employees. Table 1 showed that there was a significant difference in scores for male (M=70.10, SD=16.32) and female young employees (M=73.22, SD=13.79; $t(508) = 2.31$, $p=0.021$). The results revealed that there was a significant difference between male and female young employees, as female mean scores were greater in financial well-being than male.The result showed that female tend to be more financially well-being compared to male as they often deal with financial commitments and been in charge of the household budget that require them to maintain their financial stability and tend to take responsibility for their own well-being compared to male (Henry, Weber & Yarbrough, 2001).

Table 1. Gender comparisons for financial well-being

Gender	n	Mean	SD	t	Sig.
Male	195	70.1077	16.32	2.308	0.021
Female	313	73.2268	13.79		

*Significant p< 0.05

An independent sample t-test was conducted to compare the financial well-being scores for married and single young employees. Table 2 showed that there was a significant difference in scores for married (M=73.00, SD=14.11) and single status (M=70.14, SD=16.12; t (508) =1.97, p=0.04). The results revealed that there was a significant difference between married and single young employees. Married couples tend to be more financially well compared to the single young employees.Married couples typically manage their resources jointly thus allowing them to

Table 2. Marital status comparisons for financial well-being

Marital status	n	Mean	SD	t	Sig.
Married	335	73.003	14.11	1.974	0.04
Single	173	70.145	16.12		

*Significant p<0.05

adjust to the economic circumstances compared to the single one (Brines & Joyner, 1999).

A one-way between-groups analysis of variance was conducted to explore the financial well-being among the income groups. Income groups were divided into three based on monthly household income classification used for Malaysian in 10th Malaysia Plan which is low, middle and high (Group 1: less than RM1, 500; Group 2: RM1, 500 to RM3, 500; Group 3: Above RM3, 500). Table 3 revealed that there was a statistically significant difference at the $p< 0.05$ level in financial well-being for the three income groups [$F(2, 480)= 12.810$, $p=0.001$). Post-hoc comparisons using the Tukey HSD test indicated that the mean score for Group 3 (M=75.05, SD=13.99) was significantly different from Group 1 (M=65.92, SD=19.76) and Group 2 (M=69.51, SD=13.63). Meanwhile Group 1 (M=65.92, SD=19.76) did not differ significantly from Group 2 (M=69.51, SD=13.63). It shows that the respondents in high-income group were more financially well compared to the other groups.It shows that the respondents in high-income group were more financially well compared to the other groups. Incomes help people to meet their needs whereby people with greater incomes are more likely to be able to meet their needs such as a healthy food, safety, health and comfortable housing that lead to the subjective financial well-being compared to the lower incomes. It is supported by a study that conducted by Diener and Oishi (2000) in Japan, South Korea, China, and Singapore whereby increase in an individual's income results in higher well-being.

Table 3. Income group comparisons for financial well-being

Income group	n	Mean	SD	F	p
Low	57	65.92	19.764	12.810	0.000
Middle	179	69.52	13.633		
High	247	75.05	13.999		

*Significant $p<0.05$

Determinants of Financial Well-Being among Young Employees

Multiple regression analysis was used to explore the contributor factors toward financial well-being. Based on the multiple regression results in Table 4, the variables explained 38.7% of the variance of financial well-being. We found that all the demographic characteristics which were gender (male=1), marital status (married=1) and household income; financial status which were saving ratio, asset to debt ratio and income adequacy become the predictors to financial well-being. Apart from that, financial literacy, obsession of money attitude, retention of money attitude, effort of money attitude, managing money and planning ahead in financial capability also become the important predictors to financial well-being.By referring to the table of Coefficient, the Beta value shows which variable makes the strongest unique contribution to explain the dependent variable and the significant value will explain whether the variable make a significant unique contribution to the prediction of dependent variable. Overall, financial capability in managing money was the greatest predictor of financial well-being among young employees (Beta= 0.379).

Hira and Mugenda (2000) showed that satisfaction with the financial situation are significantly influenced by gender. This may happen due to different financial socialization between men and women. A number of studies regarding gender differences in financial well-being have shown that the economic well-being and financial behavior of men and women differ significantly (Newcomb &Rabow, 1999; Hira&Mugenda, 2000). Based on the result, it shows that male respondents were more financially well-being compared to the female respondents. It was supported by Gottschalck (2008) whereby it is believed that women hold lower levels of wealth and have significantly lower

Table 4. Multiple regression results of determinants of financial well-being

Variable	b	Beta	t	Sig.
Constant	-9.409		-1.275	0.203
Demographic characteristics				
Gender (Male)	-2.171	-0.071	-1.941	0.05*
Marital status (Married)	2.525	0.081	2.202	0.028*
Household income	2.659	0.126	3.261	0.001**
Financial status				
Saving ratio	6.855	0.115	3.102	0.002**
Asset to debt ratio	4.450	0.143	3.766	0.000**
Income adequacy	5.952	0.132	3.513	0.000**
Financial literacy	0.223	0.083	2.099	0.036*
Money attitude				
Obsession	-0.534	0.097	-2.383	0.018*
Retention	0.755	0.093	2.492	0.013**
Effort	0.942	0.182	4.444	0.000**
Inadequacy	-0.035	-0.005	-0.118	0.906
Financial capability				
Managing money	-1.697	0.379	-10.512	0.000**
Planning ahead	0.714	0.125	2.472	0.014**
Staying informed	-0.382	0.092	-1.838	0.067
Choosing products	0.163	0.029	0.551	0.582
Self-esteem	0.119	0.037	0.940	0.348

R= .638; R^2 = .408; Adjusted R^2= .387; F= 19.873; Sig. F=.000
$^{**}p<.01$, $^{*}p<.05$

earnings compared to men. Besides that, women may spend as many as five more years than men in retirement due to a longer life expectancies.

Apart from that, household income also make a unique contribution to financial well-being. The relationship betweeen income and well-being has been an area of interest among the researchers and modern economists. Undoubtedly, the objective indicator such as income can portray on people's living conditions (Wunder, 2008). Di Tella, Haisken-Denew and Macculoch (2005); Clark, Frijters, Shields (2006) had investigate the relationship between growth in income and subjective financial well-being. The empirical framework has includes income comparison in the multivariate regression analysis of subjective financial well-being. It shows that a positive correlation between income and financial well-being indicated that higher income could allow people to more comfortably meet their basic needs as well as to confer status advantages. Thus, incomes allow for greater self-actualization and more successful goal pursuits.

The results also indicated that financial literacy, obsession, retention and effort money attitude, financial capability in managing money and planning ahead were positively predicting financial well-being. Results indicated that those with higher level of financial literacy, positive money attitude and higher level of financial capability have greater financial well-being. Individuals who have knowledge on various aspects of finances, particularly in relation to their financial needs are more likely to make the right decisions and capable to use the skills to manage their personal finances. In addition, a positive attitude towards money such as retention and efforts money attitude can help the individual to manage their financial through budgeting and intensify their efforts to generate income and protect their future financial needs. However, self-esteem did not make any contribution on financial well-being of young employees.

IMPLICATIONS AND FUTURE DIRECTIONS

Financial management among young employees need to be emphasized in improving their ability to manage their finances and help to increase their financial well-being in the future. In view of the discussion above, there are some variables that begin to emerge from this analysis. These variables provide the basis for further analysis and guidance in developing recommendations for general financial education materials program for young employees.

Financial literacy of these young employees also remained at a moderate level, while some of the financial aspects were still in a low level The respondents also failed to give a correct answer regarding their purchasing power and misunderstood about the concept of investment whereby some of them believe that all investments are profitable to them. They also did not know that spending more than 40 percent of their income on installment is an unfavorable financial practice as they will unable to make their ends meet.

Due to this scenario, it is important to promote financial education to these young employees as this initiative will provide the necessary knowledge, skills and tools for them to make informed decisions with confidence. Apart from that, this initiative may highlight the importance of financial literacy as a living skills for the young employees to educate them on how to develop and maintain healthy financial behavior and habits for financial well-being.

The results of the financial capability clearly showed that young employees were generally good at managing money and planning ahead but improvement is desirable at the areas of staying informed and choosing products. Due to the complexity of financial products in the market, people are required to be careful in selecting and use a wide range of information to inform their choices. Therefore, this finding is necessary to the financial services industry. In our local context, Bank Negara Malaysia is one of the financial services that may help to provide consumers particularly the young adults to access to information on financial products and services. Perhaps with this effort it helps to equip the young adults with sufficient knowledge in order to understand the risks and obligations involve before they make an informed financial decision. Therefore, with the present of confidence and responsibility, the problem of financial exclusion among the young adults can be overcome.

The past studies on financial well-being. It may happen because of today's economic condition together with cost of living that increased tremendously. Therefore, it can be concluded that the results of this study can serve as a reference and guide to young employees to be more concern on the factors that can contribute or hinder the financial well-being. Workplace financial education programs could improve employees' financial problem and reduce their financial strain (Garman, Kim, Kratzer, Brunson, &Joo, 1999). Findings indicated that employees who attended financial education seminars and workshops reported less financial stress and greater financial well-being than those who did not (Garman, et al., 1999). In addition financial education programs at the workplace have been found to increase contributors' confidence in their financial practices and managements (Fletcher, Beebout, & Mendenhall,

1997; Bernheim, Garrett, & Maki, 2001). These findings suggest that any organizations in Malaysia may need to enhance their employee's financial literacy and capability in order to enhance the employees' financial well-being, as these factors will enhance financial behavior and decreases financial stress and problems.

This study involved only four states and focused on central zone of Peninsular Malaysia as the beginning. Financial constraint as well as time constraint also influenced this study. Therefore, this study was conducted only among young employees form both public and private agencies in the four states in the central zone of Peninsular Malaysia. It is recommended that in the future there will be a more detailed and extensive study which involve the whole states in Malaysia to be carried out. Cross-sectional design using a self-administered questionnaire with close-ended questions was used in this study. It is recommended that mixed method can be used in the future research. This approach is more comprehensive as in-depth analysis can help to tackle the problem arise from any relevant angle instead of looking at one point of view only. The integrating of qualitative and quantitative data collection and analysis may lead to greater validity and provides better understanding on the issue of financial well-being among the young employees.

REFERENCES

Atkinson, A., & Messy, F. (2012). Measuring Financial Literacy: Results of the OECD / International Network on Financial Education (INFE) Pilot Study. In OECD (Ed.), *OECD Working Papers on Finance, Insurance and Private Pensions* (Vol. 15). OECD Publishing.

Berk, L. E. (2003). *Child development*. Boston: Allyn and Bacon.

Bernheim, B. D., Garrett, D. M., & Maki, D. M. (2001). Education and saving: The long-term effects of high school financial curriculum mandates. *Journal of Public Economics*, *80*(3), 435–465. doi:10.1016/S0047-2727(00)00120-1

Branden, N. (1971). *The psychology of self-esteem: A new concept of man's psychological nature*. Bantam Books.

Brennan, K. A., Clark, C. L., & Shaver, P. R. (1998). Self-report measurement of adult attachment. *Attachment theory and close relationships*, 46-76.

Brines, J., & Joyner, K. (1999). The ties that bind: Principles of cohesion in cohabitation and marriage. *American Sociological Review*, *64*(3), 333–355. doi:10.2307/2657490

Clark, A. E., Frijters, P., & Shields, M. A. (2006). *Income and happiness: Evidence, explanations and economic implications*.

Consumer Research and Resource Centre. (2012). Report on the Survey of Financial Behaviours and Financial Habits of Young Workers. Accessed from http://www.crrc.org.my/crrc/A-report-on-the-survey-of-financial-behaviours-and-financial-habits-of-young-workers/pdf

Di Tella, R., & MacCulloch, R. (2006). Some uses of happiness data in economics. *The Journal of Economic Perspectives*, *20*(1), 25–46. doi:10.1257/089533006776526111

Diener, E., & Oishi, S. (2000). Money and happiness: Income and subjectivewell-being across nations. In E. Diener & E. M. Suh (Eds.), *Culture and Subjective Well-being* (pp. 185–218). Cambridge: MIT Press.

Federation of Malaysian Consumers Associations. (2011). Accessed from http://www.fomca.org.my/kewangan/images/stories/pub/FLM2011(ENG).pdf

FINRA Investor Education Foundation. (2009). *Financial Capability in the United States: National survey executive summary*. Washington, DC. Retrieved from www.finrafoundation.org/capability

Fletcher, C. N., Beebout, G., & Mendenhall, S. (1997). Developing and evaluating personal finance education at the worksite: A case study. *Personal Finances and Worker Productivity*, *1*(1), 54–59.

Fox, J., Bartholomae, S., & Lee, J. (2005). Building the case for financial education. *The Journal of Consumer Affairs*, *39*(1), 195–214. doi:10.1111/j.1745-6606.2005.00009.x

Garman, E. T., Kim, J., Kratzer, C. Y., Brunson, B. H., & Joo, S. H. (1999). Workplace financial education improves personal financial wellness. *Financial Counseling and Planning*, *10*(1), 79–88.

Gottschalk, P. (2008). The rising instability of US earnings. *The Journal of Economic Perspectives*, 3–24.

Hair, J. F., Black, W. C., Babin, B. J., & Anderson, R. E. (2010). *Multivariate data analysis: a global perspective*. Upper Saddle River, N.J.: Pearson.

Haveman, R., & Wolff, E. N. (2005). Who are the asset poor? Levels, trends, and composition, 1983-1998. *Inclusion in the American dream: Assets, poverty, and public policy* (pp. 61-86).

Henry, R. A., Weber, J. G., & Yarbrough, D. (2001). Money Management Practices Of College Students. *College Student Journal*, *35*(2).

Hilgert, M. A., Hogarth, J. M., & Beverly, S. G. (2003). Household financial management: The connection between knowledge and behavior. *Federal Research Bulletin*, *89*, 309.

Hira, T. K., & Mugenda, O. M. (2000). Gender Differences in Financial Perceptions, Behaviors and Satisfaction. *Journal of Financial Counseling and Planning*, *13*(2), 86–92.

Huston, S. J. (2010). Measuring financial literacy. *The Journal of Consumer Affairs*, *44*(2), 296–316. doi:10.1111/j.1745-6606.2010.01170.x

Johnson, E., & Sherraden, M. S. (2007). From financial literacy to financial capability among youth. *Journal of Sociology and Social Welfare*, *34*(3), 119–146.

Lusardi, A. (2008). *The importance of being financially literate*.

Masud, J. (2007, July). *Testing of Malaysia's Financial Well-Being Scale*. Paper presented in the Seventh Biennial Conference 2007 ACFEA, Purajaya, Malaysia.

Nickerson, C., Schwarz, N., & Diener, E. (2007). Financial aspirations, financial success, and overall life satisfaction: Who? and how? *Journal of Happiness Studies*, *8*(4), 467–515. doi:10.1007/s10902-006-9026-1

O'Neill, B., Sorhaindo, B., Prawitz, A. D., Kim, J., & Garman, E. T. (2006). Financial distress: Definition, effects, and measurement. *Consumer Interest Annual*, *52*, 1–8.

Organization for Economic Cooperation Development (OECD). (2005). Improving financial literacy: Analysis of issues and policies. Paris: OECD. *Psychology (Savannah, Ga.)*, *56*(3), 218.

Phau, I., & Woo, C. (2008). Understanding compulsive buying tendencies among young Australians: The roles of money attitude and credit card usage. *Marketing Intelligence & Planning*, *26*(5), 441–458. doi:10.1108/02634500810894307

Prawitz, A. D., Garman, E. T., Sorhaindo, B., O'Neill, B., Kim, J., & Drentea, P. (2006). InCharge financial distress/financial well-being scale: Development, administration, and score interpretation. *Financial Counseling and Planning*, *17*(1), 34–50.

Ramli, Z., Sum, S. M., Manaf, A. A., Saad, S., Hussain, M. Y., & Lyndon, N. (2012). Kualitihidupdankesejahteraanbelia: Kajiankeataspekerjasektorawam Malaysia. *Geografia: Malaysian Journal of Society and Space*, *8*(6), 150–156.

Roberts, J. A., & Jones, E. (2001). Money attitudes, credit card use, and compulsive buying among American college students. *The Journal of Consumer Affairs*, *35*(2), 213–240. doi:10.1111/j.1745-6606.2001.tb00111.x

Sabri, M. F., Masud, J., & Paim, L. (2006). *Financial Literacy, Attitude and Practice among Malaysian IPTs Students*. Serdang: UPM.

Van Zyl, J. D., Cronjé, E. M., & Payze, C. (2006). Low Self-Esteem of Psychotherapy Patients: A Qualitative Inquiry. *Qualitative Report*, 182–208.

Williams, N. (2001). *The Work We Were Born to Do*. London: Element Books.

Wunder, S., Engel, S., & Pagiola, S. (2008). Taking stock: A comparative analysis of payments for environmental services programs in developed and developing countries. *Ecological Economics*, *65*(4), 834–852. doi:10.1016/j.ecolecon.2008.03.010

ADDITIONAL READING

Bank Negara Malaysia. (2010).Annual Report. Accessed from http://www.bnm.gov.my/files/publication/ar/en/2010/ar2010_book.pdf

Basic Skills Agency and Financial Services Authority (2006).Adult Financial Capability Framework.

Cocco, J. F., & Gomes, F. J. (2012). Longevity risk, retirement savings, and financial innovation. *Journal of Financial Economics*, *103*(3), 507–529.

Cox, A., Hooker, H., Markwick, C., & Reilly, P. (2009). *Financial well-being in the workplace. Research report 464*. Sussex: Institute for Employment Studies.

Diener, E., & Biswas-Diener, R. (2002). Will money increase subjective wellbeing? *Social Indicators Research*, *57*, 119–169.

Furnham, A. (1999). The saving and spending habits of young people. *Journal of Economic Psychology*, *20*, 677–697.

Husniyah, A. R., & Fazilah Abdul Samad, M. (2009). The impact of financial management-practices on financial well-being of families in Malaysia. *JurnalPenggunaMalaysia*, *12*, 27–41.

Husniyah, A.R., & Syuhaily, O, Fazli, S. M., Amim, O. M., & Hariza, H. A. (2005). Gelagatperancangankewangankeluarga di Malaysia. *Malaysian Journal of Consumer and Family Economics*, *8*, 27–39.

Kempson, E., Collard, S., & Moore, N. (2005). *Measuring financial capability: An exploratory study*. Financial Services Authority. Consumer Research Report 37, June 2005.

Kim, J., Garman, E. T., & Sorhaindo, B. (2003). Relationships among Credit Counseling Clients' Financial Well- being, Financial Behaviors, Financial Stressor Events, and Health. *Financial Counseling and Planning*, *14*(2), 75–87.

Parrotta, J. L. & Johnson, P. (1998). *The impact of financial attitudes and knowledge on financial management and satisfaction of recently married individuals*.

Prince, M. (1993). Self-concept, money belief and values. *Journal of Economic Psychology*, *14*(1), 161173.

Sabri, M. F., & Falahati, L. F. (2013). Predictors of Financial Well-Being among Malaysian Employees: Examining the Mediate Effect of Financial Stress. *Journal of Emerging Economies and Islamic Research*, *1*(3).

Shim, S., Xiao, J. J., Barber, B. L., & Lyons, A. (2009). Path ways to life success: A conceptual model of financial well-being for young adults. *Journal of Applied Developmental Psychology*, *30*(6), 708–723.

Shuzen, N. (2009), *Credit Card Debt and You: Under-30s Under Siege*. Retrieved from http://www.mmail.com.my/content/credit-card-debt-and-you-under30s-under-siege

Srivastava, A., Locke, E. A., & Bartol, K. M. (2001). Money and subjective well-being: It's not the money, it's the motives. *Journal of Personality and Social Psychology*, *80*(6), 959.

Taylor, M., Jenkins, S., & Sacker, A. (2009). *Financial capability and wellbeing: Evidence from the BHPS* (Occasional Paper Series 34). London: The Financial Services Authority.

Teo, B. C. (2003). Money Attitude of Urban Malaysian Consumers. *Malaysian Journal of Consumer and Family Economics*, *6*, 62–77.

vonStumm, S., Fenton O'Creevy, M., & Furnham, A. (2012). Financial capability, money attitudes and socioeconomic status: Risks for experiencing adverse financial events. *Personality and Individual Differences*.

Yilmazer, T., & DeVaney, S. A. (2005). Household debt over the life cycle. *Financial Services Review-Greenwich*, *14*(4), 285.

KEY TERMS AND DEFINITIONS

Compulsive Buying: An unhealthy obsession with shopping that materially interferes with the daily life of the afflicted. This ailment goes beyond mere consumerism and is psychological in nature.

Financial Capability: Measure of knowledge, skills, attitude and behaviors to manage personal finance whereby knowledge is necessary to understand the financial products, terms and concepts, skills for the ability of budgeting and attitude as a willingness to spend time to keep track with finances (OECD, 2008).

Financial Literacy: Financial literacy can be defined as possessing of knowledge necessary in order to understand concepts related to finance (OECD, 2011).

Financial Well-Being: Financial well-being is defined as a state of being financially healthy, happy and free from worry and base on subjective appraisal of one's financial situation (Joo, 2008).

Money Attitude: Money attitude can be defined as a means of influence and protection and reflect to a personal dependence on money that lead to ongoing concern about money (Furnham, 1984).

Quality of Life: The Malaysian QoL is defined as encompassing personal advancements, a healthy lifestyle, access and freedom to pursue knowledge, and a standard of living which surpasses the fulfillment of basic needs of individuals and their psychological needs, to achieve a level of social well-being compatible with the nation's Aspirations (EPU, Malaysian QOL 2011).

Self-Esteem: A concept given by Branden (1969) that describes self-esteem as the experience of being competent to cope with the basic challenges of life and being worthy of happiness.

Chapter 14
Determinants of Financial Management Behaviors of Families

Gulay Gunay
Karabuk University, Turkey

Ayfer Aydiner Boylu
Hacettepe University, Turkey

Ahmet Oğuz
Karabuk University, Turkey

ABSTRACT

Today's family income management is a central resource for welfare of family members. This study was performed to test the reliability and validity of the Turkish version of the Financial Management Behavior Scale (FMBS) developed by Dew and Xiao (2011) to measure individual's saving, investment, and expenditure and debt behavior in family. It also examines the predictors of financial management behavior in family. The study was concluded over a total of 696 participants who are working at Government Office in Bursa-Turkey. The results of the factor analysis were composed of four subscales in accordance with original form of the scale. Reliability analysis showed that the FMBS had a high internal consistency (CronbachAlpha: .82; Split-half: .83) and split half reliability coefficient. The result of hierarchical regression analysis revealed that demographic characteristics, saving and investment decision, financial satisfaction and compared financial status were predicted of financial management behavior.

1. INTRODUCTION

Life satisfaction is one of the important measures of subjective well-being (Pavot & Diener, 1993). Given the positive effects of subjective well-being on several dimensions of life, researchers have become increasingly interested in studying specific factors that influence subjective well-being (Xiao et al., 2009). Environmental, social, cultural, and economic conditions are all under a permanent change due to globalization. Under these ever-changing conditions, in order for

DOI: 10.4018/978-1-4666-7484-4.ch014

families to maintain their current well-being or to improve it, it is necessary that obstacles standing in the way towards an increased well-being for individual family members be eliminated. In this regard, economic functions of families play an extremely important role in meeting their needs and wants that impact their overall quality of living (Terzioğlu, 1990, p.112; Özmete, 2004). However financial welfare of families is a more complex issues (Bailey, 1987), and families economic behaviors and financial satisfaction are most important determinants of welfare (Raijas, 2011; Bailey, 1987; Godwin, 1993). Families act in an environment of financing system which includes the pressure of the economic powers like the changing economic balances, increasing unemployment rate, changing purchasing power of money, inflationist pressures, increasing tax load, changing government policies, increasing interest rates, complicating consumer market, and the competence gradually increasing between the businesses (Goldsmith, 2000, p.108; Godwin, 1993; Terzioğlu, 1990, p.112; Bailey, 1987; Raijas, 2011). In such an environment, the behaviors of family related to usage of the income affect both of social and economic welfare of family and the national economy and welfare (Çopur & Şafak, 2000; Becker, 1988).

Much of the literature on family financial management is prescriptive in nature, including extensive discussion of what families should do in managing their financial resources. Despite the importance of effective financial management in families' lives, relatively little empirical research has focused on what families actually do. For instance, how meet family their needs? Is their income enough for meet their needs? How they use their income? Are they making saving with their finances resources? Why don't they make savings? Are they in debt? Are they satisfied with their financial situation? In other words, it's obvious that the financial decisions and behaviors of families will affect the macro micro economic decisions of families' life. Families have to manage their finance in one way or another. Some tend to save a lot, some like to collect information before each purchase, some like to follow their gut feelings (Fünfgeld & Wang, 2009). According to Gunnarsson and Wahlund (1997) households as being financial actors, more or less active and more or less conscious of their behaviors. Patterns of households' savings and debts may be viewed as expressing some sort of financial strategy, whether consciously or unconsciously practiced.

Therefore today's family, income organization is a central resource for welfare of family members (Raijas, 2011; Heimdal & Houseknecht, 2003). Hira and Mueller (1987) reported that improved money management practices are more important than increasing the resources. Improving money management could be help families cope with financial difficulties and meet family needs. Thus, it is necessary to plan the usage of income for today and future, and to create a successful balance between consumption and saving in order to develop the quality of life and provide the financial welfare (Çopur & Şafak, 2000).

The economic function of families is a determinant of the households and individuals level of living (Yadollahi et al. 2009; Goldsmith, 2000, p.108). For this reason, the economic activities of family like saving, expenditure, and debt propensities and capacities are vital elements of family life (Çopur & Şafak, 2000; Bailey, 1987).

Western sociological research over the last few years has found that patterns of financial management and expenditure decision-making vary between different cultures, across social classes and over time. The reason for this is the fact that financial management within families is a demanding task where various knowledge and skills are needed. Control of the household budget bestows both power and responsibility (Clarke, 2002). Also financial management is recognized as having both mental and physical components (Deacon and Firebaugh, 1988, p.7). In practice, financial management is influenced by various factors, such as marital status, family income, education and age of households, number of dependent children, and the family's phase of life, the needs of family members, and the amount of money available to allocate (Godwin, 1993; Hira, 1987; Sumarwan & Hira, 1993; Raijas, 2011).

The relationships between the financial sources, money management, financial conditions, problems, the economic stresses and pressures, and satisfaction levels of family have been analyzed for the last 50 years. Such researches have examined and identified demographic variables affect family economic status (Yadollahi et al. 2009), socioeconomic variables directly affect perceived income adequacy (Sumarwan & Hira, 1993), satisfaction from money management among dual-earner households (Hira, 1987), the relationship between adequacy of resources and socioeconomic and family composition characteristics (Çopur et al. 2009), how families manage their economic hardship (Beak & De Vaney, 2010), financial behavior and life satisfaction of college students (Xiao et al. 2009), financial management, financial problems and marital satisfaction among recently married university students (Kerkmann et al. 2000), the impact of financial attitudes and knowledge on financial management and satisfaction of recently married individuals (Parrotta & Johnson, 1998).

Financial situation of families have strongly and positively influenced by income (Yadollahi et al. 2009). Assessment of income adequacy can be a subjective measure of welfare (Ormsby & Fairchild, 1987). According to the studies income had a significant direct effect on financial satisfaction (Davis & Helmick, 1985; Sumarwan & Hira, 1993; Hira, 1987), financial decision making (Retting & Schultz, 1991) and preparation for financial emergencies (Sumarwan & Hira (1992).

Although financial satisfaction is positively related to income, it is not determined by income alone. Low income is not always associated with dissatisfaction nor does a high income guarantee economic satisfaction. Studies have shown that income only indirectly influences financial satisfaction (Hira & Mugenda, 1998). For example Marlowe and Godwin (1988) reported that income alone was not a good measure of families' financial welfare. Joo and Grable (2004) also reported that income had no direct effects on financial satisfaction. Families' income and finances can be changed depend on economic changing over the period changed in multiple and often overlapping domains, such as employment status, employment conditions, and savings, emergency funds and debt, all of which impacted the amount of income available to parents toward their goals and practices (Iversen et al. 2011). According to the literature financial satisfaction is associated with income and wealth and an individual's perceived financial needs. Dew and Xiao (2011) stated that consumer debt levels are positively related to anxiety. Further, assets and consumer debts are associated with relationship quality among married couples. Mugenda and her associates (1990) concluded that net worth, savings, monthly debt payments, and absence of financial difficulties were the main determinants of managers' satisfaction with financial status. Hanna et al. (1995) noted that persons having high outstanding debt have high interest rates and should, therefore, rationally consume less today to consume more in the future. Hira (1987) reported similar findings regarding the relationship between monthly debt payments, amount of money saved, and satisfaction with financial status. She found that money managers who made smaller monthly debt payments saved a larger amount of their income and were more satisfied with their financial status than were those who made higher monthly debt payments and saved a lower amount of their income. Sumarwan and Hira (1992) found in their study monthly debt payment had a significant but negative effect on satisfaction. Iversen and her associates (2011) had reported many families in her studies, during the downturn (2008-09) increased levels of debt, primarily from credit cards, which had become a largely unmanageable economic challenge for low- and middle-income households across the U.S.

2. HYPOTHESES

Financial management behaviors are extremely important in relation to the quality of life of families and thus of societies as a whole. In this study we determine the validity and reliability of Financial Management Behavior (FMBS) for Turkish population and to investigate the correlations between financial satisfaction and selected socio-economic and demographic characteristics in Turkey. Therefore, we test the following hypothesis:

H1: Financial management behavior would be positively associated withdemographic variables of families

H2: Financial management behavior would be positively associated with economic decisions taken from family

H3: Financial management behavior would be positively associated with financial satisfaction

H4: Financial management behavior would be positively associated with comparing family's financial situation.

3. RESEARCH METHOD

3.1. Sample

A questionnaire-based survey was employed as the method for collecting the data used in our study. Data were collected from a sample of individuals who are working as a staff at Bursa Government Tax Office in Turkey. Among the 1009 staff only 703 staff was married. A total of 696 completed and usable questionnaires were returned by the staffs producing a 98% response rate. Of the 696 staffs who responded to survey, 41.1% (n= 300) were female and 58.9% (n= 396) were male.

Participants were contacted in person and surveys were given individually. On arrival at their work sites, and following the researcher's self-introduction, the purpose of the study was explained. Participants were also informed that participation in the study was voluntary. After obtaining their consent, the survey packets, which subjects read and completed on their own, were distributed and then researchers collected all surveys once they were completed. 3 of the contacted individuals refused to participate and 4 individual was incompletely filled. Data were collected between Septembers to November 2011.

3.2. Instruments

Demographic Variables: This study included nine demographic variables: gender, age, education, income, length of marriage, employment status of the spouses in the family, number of children, family type, owning a house and other income sources.

Economic Decision-Making in Family: It was measured with four questions "Who does make the decisions on economic activities in your family in general?", "Who does make the decisions on expenditures in your family?", "Who does make the decisions on debts in your family?", "Who does make the decisions on saving and investments in your family?" (1=always women, 2=always man, 3=sometimes man, but mostlywomen, 4=sometimes women, but mostly man, 5=together with family members, 6=always man and women together).

Financial Satisfaction: Financial satisfaction was measured with 8 item forms layout by Hira and Mugenda (1998). In this study, responses were obtained from a series of statements seeking respondents' satisfaction with various aspects of their financial situation. These aspects included satisfaction with: 1. Meet needs and desires with current resources, 2. Increase the assets and improve the quality of life, 3. Regular monetary savings, 4. Current debt level, 5. Family's current financial situation, 6. Ability to meet long-term financial goals, 7. Ability to meet financial emergencies, and 8. Money management skills. The responses were recorded on a five-point Likert

Scale ranging from 1=very dissatisfied to 5=very satisfied. For the inferential statistics, the whole scale was used, and items summed, to obtain a financial satisfaction index (Hira and Mugenda, 1998). According to Hira and Mugenda (1998) the Cronbach's Alpha for the financial satisfaction was .89. In this study Cronbach's alpha coefficient was found .93.

Comparative Financial Situation: Comparative financial situation was measured with three questions. 1. Assess families' current financial situation compared with other families, 2. Assess families' current financial situation compared with their own situation before the time of study, 3. Assess their families' current financial situation compared with their expectations for the future from the time of the study. Responses were recorded on a five-point Likert Scale ranging from 1=Much Worse to 5=Much Better (Cronbach's Alpha coefficient was found .84).

Financial Management Behavior Scale (FMBS): FMBS was developed by Dew and Xiao (2011) to measure the overall behavior of the financial management. Financial Management Behavior Scale includes 15 items such as "Comparison shopped when purchasing a product or service" or "Contributed money to a retirement account". Responses were given on a 5-point Likert Scale range from "1=never" to "5=always". If the scores increased taken from the FMBS, participants' reported levels of savings increased and their reports of consumer debt decreased. The instruction for the three insurance items stated, "Please rate your behavior regarding insurance within the past year on a scale of 1 – 5." These items asked about the past year because sometimes insurance behaviors occur on an annual basis. The response set was the same as the other items. The insurance items queried participants about health insurance, property insurance, and life insurance. Each item consisted of concepts that were short, easy to understand, and limited to only one idea. Also, positive sentences and personal expressions were used.

Financial Management Behavior Scale was consisting of four factors. Factor 1 explained 30% of the variance. The authors referred to the factor "Savings and Investment Behaviors". Five saving and investment items loaded on this factor and the factor loading ranged from .69 to .78. Savings and Investment Behaviors explained 30% of the variance. Second factor named "Insurance Behavior" factor loading was between .74 and .85. This factor was explained 12% of the variance and consists of three items. Four items loaded on factor 3 (loadings between 64. and .73). It explained 9% of the total variance. This factor called "Cash Management". Last factor have been named as "Credit Management". Three positive credit management items loaded on factor 4 with loadings of .66 to .77. It explained 8% of the variance. Overall, the four factors explained 59% of the variance.

The full FMBS had a Cronbach's alpha of .81. Cronbach alpha scores were also calculated for the four subscales. The savings and investments subscale, the insurance subscale, cash management subscale and the credit management subscale Cronbach Alpha scores are .78, .73, .63 and .57 respectively.

3.3. Data Analysis

Data analysis began with calculating frequencies of the sample on all independent variables. One way variance analysis (ANOVA) were than used to compare variables of economic decisions making in the family and family management behavior scale. When the F test indicated significant (.05) mean differences on a given variable, Tukey's multiple comparison test was used to isolate the specific between-category means that were significantly different.

Correlation analyses were performed to determine the level and direction of the relationship between the dependent and independent variables, and Hierarchical Regression Analysis was used to determine the sequence of contribution for the variables. In this approach, independent variables were put into the regression analysis in a certain sequence to determine the model that best describes the dependent variable (Büyüköztürk, 2007, p.31). In this study, multiple-variable hierarchical regression analysis were performed to find out whether some variables related to FMBS such as; demographic variables (age, marital length, number of children, monthly income of the family, education, employment status of the spouses in the family, other income sources of the family), economic decision, expenditure decisions, debt decisions and savings and investment decisions, financial satisfaction and compared financial situation have any effect on the family management behavior or not.

4. RESULTS

The age of participants ranges from 21 to 62 years old, with 40.9 per cent between 41 and 50 years old (n=285). The mean age of the respondents was 41.3 years (SD=8.05). The proportion of people with a university degree (64.4%) was higher than other education degree. The finding reflected that 70.1 percent of the females and 61.4 percent of the males was graduated from bachelor's degree.

Among the participants incomes varied between 700TL – 9000TL (1$ is equivalent to about 1.90 TL- June, 2013) and the median income was 3742,5 (=1970 $). Both of male (81.3%) and female (84.3%) reported that their families are in middle-income level. Average marital length of the participants was 14.3(SD=8.62) and the average number of children was two ranging from 0 to 6 in the families'. About 28.9% of the participants had 1 child, 41.5% had 2, 14.3% had 3 or more, and 15.2% had no children. Approximately 80.3% of the individuals' families were in the expanding stage. In addition, the majority of the individuals lived in a nuclear family (92.2%). More than half of the participants (57.6%) reported that both of husband and wife works full-time, 30.5 per cent of the individuals reported that husband work full-time, wife does not (Table 1.).

Factor Analysis

The validity of the Turkish version of the Financial Management Behavior Scale was discussed in term of content validity and construct validity.

Content Validity: The FMBS had not previously been used in Turkey. It was developed in English for use in the United States by Dew and Xiao (2011). This measure was translated into Turkish and then back-translated into English by 3 academicians who were all proficient in both English and Turkish. Each of the 15 items that formed the scale was considered carefully to find its conceptual equivalent in Turkish to ensure that the concepts being measured were understood to be essentially the same by both English and Turkish speakers. Next step the Turkish version of the FMBS has been examined by financial management and financial counselors. The experts have agreed that the Turkish version of FMBS is suitable to use.

Construct Validity: Factor scores for the FMBS were calculated according to the domains of financial management behavior. Principal components factor analysis with a varimax rotation was used for this analysis. Before engaging in factor analysis, however, the Kaiser–Meyer–Olkin (KMO) value was computed to see if the data would be appropriate for factor analysis. Because the Bartlett's test (X^2=4830.2, df=105, p<.001) and KMO value for the inventory were found to be 0.84, it was concluded that factor analysis would be appropriate.

The results of principal components factor analysis of the FMBS, the scale was found to have a four-factor structure that had an eigenvalue of above 1 and that explained 67% of the total variance changing between 4.56 and 1.24. This rate of variance explained by four factors was at an acceptable level. The factor loading of the 15 items in the FMBS varied between 0.55 and 0.87.

Table 1. Demographic variables

Demographic Variables	N	%	M	SS	Range (Min – Max)
Age			40.1	8.1	21–62
≤ 30	100	14.4			
31 – 40	251	36.1			
41 – 50	285	40.9			
≥ 51	60	8.6			
Education					
Primary school (5 years)	10	1.4			
Secondary school (3 years)	15	2.2			
High school (3 years)	113	16.2			
Associate (2 years)	105	15.1			
Bachelor's (BA) (4 years)	424	60.9			
Master (MA) (2 years)	25	3.6			
Postgraduate (PhD) (4 years)	4	0.6			
Marital Length			14.3	8.6	1–40
≤5	138	19.8			
6 – 10	137	19.7			
11 – 15	103	14.8			
16 – 20	140	20.1			
≥ 21	178	25.6			
Monthly income of the family			3742.5	1351.3	700–9.000
Low	80	11.5			
Middle	575	82.6			
High	41	5.9			
Number of children			1.58	1.0	0–6
1	201	28.9			
2	289	41.5			
3+	100	14.3			
No children	106	15.2			
Employment status of the spouses					
Both spouses work full-time	401	57.6			
Husband work full-time, wife work part-time	62	8.9			
Husband works wife does not	212	30.5			
Wife work full-time	21	3.0			
Family Type					
Nuclear	54	7.8			
Extended	642	92.2			
Other income sources					

Continued on following page

Table 1. continued.

Demographic Variables	N	%	M	SS	Range (Min – Max)
Rent	108	15.5			
Interest	13	1.9			
Agricultural production	13	1.9			
Commercial revenue	16	2.3			
No other income sources	539	77.4			
More than one income source	7	1.0			

Factor 1, which is called "Saving and Investment", has an eigenvalue of 4.56, and explain of variance 30%. Items "8, 9, 10, 11, and 12" are grouped together under the head of this factor as they are in the original version of the form. The factor loading of the 5 items in the Savings and Investment vary between 0.55 and 0.87.

Factor 2 explained 20% of the total variance and had an eigenvalue of 3.07. The distribution of the items in the "Cash Management" subdimension differed from the original version of the form. The fifth item that was in the Factor 4 that is in the "Credit Management" subdimesion, of the original form (Paid off credit card balance in full each month) was instead a part of the subdimension Cash Management. The fact that this item appeared in a different sub-dimension can be explained by the circumstances of application themselves as well as by the fact that individuals are concerned about being able to maintain their daily lives given the socio-economic conditions of our times. Items that indicated cash management, such as keeping a financial record and paying bills on time, loaded on Factor 3 with loadings between 0.67 and 0.77.

Factor 3 had an eigenvalue of 1.30 and was found to account for 9% of the variance. Factor 3 was named "Insurance Behavior". This factor included "Maintained or purchased adequate property insurance like auto or homeowners insurance (loading: .83)", "Maintained or purchased adequate life insurance (loading: .85)" and "Maintained or purchased an adequate health insurance policy (loading: .83)" like the original scale.

The fourth and the last factor comprised the following two components: "Maxed out the limit on one or more credit cards" and "Made only minimum payments on a loan". It had an eigenvalue of 1.06. The loadings were 0.70 and 0.82. This factor was named "Credit Management," and it was found to explain 8% of the variance.

The reliability of Financial Management Behavior Scale was investigated by test re-test, Cronbach alpha, split-half. Cronbach's alpha was calculated for each subscale; Savings and investment behavior (.78), Cash management (.82), Insurance subscale (.85) and Credit management (.72). The Cronbach's alpha for the FMBS was .82 and split-half .83. These results suggest that the inner consistency of the scale is high. These analyses are interpreted to mean that the Financial Management Behavior Scale is reliable and valid for these subjects in Turkey.

The Relationship between Variables and FMBS

According to the findings it can be said that there was no significant relationship between participants' scores on the FMB Scale and gender ($t=1.039$, $df=694$, $p>0.05$). In the other words statistical analysis stated that the score of FMB Scale has no difference according to male (396) and female (300) participants.

Table 2. Factor analysis

Items of Financial Management (α=.83)	M(SS)	Factor 1	Factor 2	Factor 3	Factor 4	Corrected Item-Total Cor.
Cash management subscale (α=.78)						
1. Comparison shopped when purchasing a product or service	4.1 (1.1)		**.74**			.54
2. Paid all your bills on time	4.4 (1.0)		**.77**			.64
3. Kept a written or electronic record of your monthly expenses	3.4 (1.4)		**.68**			.46
4. Stayed within your budget or spending plan	3.9 (1.0)		**.77**			.63
5. Paid off credit card balance in full each month	4.2 (1.1)		**.67**			.54
Credit management subscale (α=.82)						
6. Maxed out the limit on one or more credit cards	2.5 (1.4)				**.70**	.56
7. Made only minimum payments on a loan [a]	2.2 (1.4)				**.82**	.56
Savings and investment subscale(α=.85)						
8. Began or maintained an emergency savings fund	3.0 (1.4)	**.63**				.59
9. Saved money from every paycheck	3.2 (1.3)	**.81**				.72
10. Saved for a long term goal such as a car, education, home, etc	3.2 (1.4)	**.87**				.72
11. Contributed money to a retirement account	2.4 (1.5)	**.55**				.58
12. Bought bonds, stocks, or mutual funds	2.7 (1.5)	**.67**				.46
Insurance subscale (α=.72)						
13. Maintained or purchased an adequate health insurance policy	1.8 (1.4)			**.85**		.59
14. Maintained or purchased adequate property insurance like auto or homeowners insurance	2.2 (1.5)			**.83**		.42
15. Maintained or purchased adequate life insurance	1.8 (1.4)			**.83**		.61
Eigen values		4.56	3.07	1.30	1.24	
% of Variance Explained by Factor		30.4	20.1	8.7	8.3	

[a]Reverse coded.

Results of the ANOVA displayed that general economic decision (F=1.519, df=695, p<0.05), expenditure decision (F=1.500, df=695, p<0.05), and saving and investment decisions (F=1.407, df=695, p<0.05), significantly (at .05) affected scores of FMB Scale. However there was no significantly relationship between debt decisions and participants' scores on FMB Scale. Given this results the first hypothesis (H_1) was partially accepted.

Table 3 examines the relationship between the economics decision-making in the family and FMBS scores. Those who make general economic decisions (M=51.8; SD=10.9), spending decisions (M=52.0; SD=11.0), saving and investment decisions (M=52.4; SD=11.7) with other family members were found to have a higher mean financial management behavior scale score. Also findings indicated that while making debt decisions with family members, FMBS score has

Table 3. Results of variance analysis between the variables economic decision making in the family and family management behavior scale

Variable	N	%	M	SD	F	Sig.
General Economic Decision					1.519	.035*
Always women	26	3.7	45.0	12.0		
Always man	75	10.8	45.5	11.2		
Sometimes man, but mostly woman	21	3.0	47.0	11.9		
Sometimes woman, but mostly man	57	8.2	45.1	11.5		
Together with family members	153	22.0	51.8	10.9		
Always man and woman together	364	52.3	50.7	11.6		
Expenditure decisions					1.500	.012*
Always women	25	3.6	42.7	9.9		
Always man	76	10.9	45.2	11.9		
Sometimes man, but mostly woman	16	2.3	50.4	9.7		
Sometimes woman, but mostly man	51	7.3	46.2	11.4		
Together with family members	148	21.3	52.0	11.0		
Always man and woman together	380	54.6	50.5	11.6		
Debt decisions					.959	.564
Always women	43	6.2	47.9	11.2		
Always man	59	8.5	50.9	12.7		
Sometimes man, but mostly woman	40	5.7	48.0	12.9		
Sometimes woman, but mostly man	45	6.5	51.2	11.6		
Together with family members	143	20.5	48.5	10.5		
Always man and woman together	366	52.6	50.1	11.8		
Savings and investment decisions					1.407	.029*
Always women	35	5.0	44.3	12.2		
Always man	160	23.0	45.0	11.9		
Sometimes man, but mostly woman	28	4.0	47.5	9.4		
Sometimes woman, but mostly man	43	6.2	47.2	9.9		
Together with family members	119	17.1	52.4	11.7		
Always man and woman together	311	44.7	52.1	11.9		

*p<0.05

decreased. Those who indicated that debt decisions are made "sometimes [by] woman, but mostly [by] man" (M=48.5; SD=10.5) has a higher mean FMBS score (Table 4). It can be said that second hypothesis (H_2) was not rejected.

Pearson Product Moment correlations were used to establish the relationship between the independent and dependent variables. Results presented in table 5. Findings showed that there was a significant and positive correlation between FMBS and monthly income (0.33, p<0.01), education (0.26, p<0.01), general economic decision (0.11, p<0.01), expenditure decisions (0.14, p<0.01), savings and investment decisions (0.18,

Table 4. Pearson product moment correlations between FMBS and independent variables

Variables	1	2	3	4	5	6	7	8	9	10	11	12	13	14
1. Age	1													
2. Marital length	.87**	1												
3. Number of children	.50**	.59**	1											
4. Monthly income of the family	-.06	-.07	-.07	1										
5. Education	-.09*	-.15**	-.13**	.34**	1									
6. Employment status of the spouses in the family	.17**	.20**	.20**	-.47**	-.20**	1								
7. Other income sources	-.08*	-.07	-.11**	-.11**	-.02	.02	1							
8. Economic decisions	.05	.04	.05	.06	.11**	-.04	.07	1						
9. Expenditure decisions	.06	.05	.01**	.06	.09*	-.05	.03	.81**	1					
10. Debt decisions	.03	.03	-.02	-.01	.08*	.05	.03	.03	.01	1				
11. Savings and investment decisions	.02	.01	.04	.09*	.11**	-.10**	-.02	.56**	.59**	.03	1			
12. Financial satisfaction	-.12**	-.13**	-.09*	.27**	.23**	-.21**	-.04	.07	.09*	-.08*	.14**	1		
13. Compared financial situation	-.03	-.05	-.01	.35**	.27**	-.24**	-.11**	.15**	.17**	-.02	.19**	.62**	1	
14. FMBS	-.13**	-.14**	-.09*	.33**	.26**	-.26**	-.06	.11**	.14**	-.05	.18**	.83**	.83**	1

*p<0.05; **p<0.01

p<0.01), financial satisfaction (0.83, p<0.01) and compared financial situation (0.83, p<0.01). However the correlation between FMBS and age (-0.13, p<0.01), marital length (-0.14, p<0.01), number of children (-0.09, p<0.05) and employment status of the spouses in the family (-0.26, p<0.01) was significant and negative relationship.

Hierarchical regression analysis was used to examine contributions of demographic and economic decision making variables to the variance in the FMBS. Means, standard deviations, and correlation coefficients for all variables are summarized in Table 6. For the first stage of the Hierarchical Regression Analysis, only the demographic factors, such as age, length of marriage, number of children, monthly income of the family, education, employment status of the spouses, and other income sources of the family were included to the analysis. In the second stage, general economic decisions, expenditure decisions, debt decisions and savings and investment decisions were added. At the third and last stage of the analysis, the independent variables financial satisfaction and compared financial situation of family were added to the regression along with the demographic factors and other independent variables. The determination coefficients (R^2) obtained in the end of three stages were compared and the variables evaluated for participant if these variables give information about their financial management behavior.

Demographic variables explains 16% of the effect of the total variance on the frequency of their financial management behavior for the participants (R=0.397, R^2=0.158, F= 18.376, p<.001). Table 6 gives the t-test results related to significance and the regression coefficient (β) standardized to test the effect of the independent variables, in the first stage of the analysis, on the financial management behavior.

The findings indicated that economic decisions variables explained variance rate was 18 percent (R=0.427, R^2=0.182, F= 13.862, p<.001) of the financial management behavior. Considering

Table 5. Hierarchical regression result for financial management behavior

	B	β	t	p	R	R²	F	Sig.
Model 1					**.397**	**.158**	**18.376**	**.000**
1. Age	-.077	-.053	-.739	.460				
2. Marital length	-.068	-.051	-.654	.513				
3. Number of children	.262	.023	.516	.606				
4. Monthly income of the family	.002	.215	5.121	**.000*** **				
5. Education	1.843	.157	4.149	**.000*** **				
6. Employment status of the spouses in the family	-1.395	-.117	-2.881	**.004** **				
7. Other income sources	-.256	-.033	-.925	.355				
Model 2					**.427**	**.182**	**13.862**	**.000**
8. Economic decisions	-.361	-.048	-.791	.429				
9. Expenditure decisions	.709	.092	1.496	.135				
10. Debt decisions	-.442	-.057	-1.625	.105				
11. Savings and investment decisions	.792	.112	2.563	**.011***				
Model 3					**.925**	**.855**	**308.720**	**.000**
12. Financial satisfaction	1.080	.507	26.799	**.000*** **				
13. Compared financial situation	1.927	.504	25.789	**.000*** **				

*p<0.05; **p<0.01; ***p<0.001

participant standardized regression coefficient (β) and the t-test results show that the relationships between the financial management behavior (β=.79, p<.05) and savings and investment decisions was statistically important.

The third stage was run by including financial satisfaction and compared financial situations regression equations. The results illustrated that the stage was significant (R=0.925, R^2=0.855, F=308.720, p<.001). The explained variance analysis was 86 percent. Additionally finding indicated that among the independent variables, the relationships between financial management behavior and financial satisfaction (β=.11, p>.001) and compared financial situation (β=1.93, p>.001) was statistically significant. According to the results of Hierarchical regression analysis the t-statistics of independent variables of financial satisfaction and compared financial situation is 26.799, 25.789 respectively. Since the p-value is smaller than 0.001 the hypothesis H_3 and H_4 can be accepted.

5. DISCUSSION

The level of income is directly related to determining the levels of meeting the needs of the family, as well as the health, education, social interaction, house, free time and general life style conditions. Therefore financial security is an important goal of families worldwide. However, in developing countries, it is often difficult to meet even basic needs, especially within the uncertainty of an inflationary condition in the economy (Ormsby & Fairchild, 1987). It is possible to discover numerous researches analyzing the economic activities of the families and the results of the economic activities in the developed and developing countries. Therefore the aim of the study was adopting the FMB scale (Dew & Xiao, 2011) for Turkish populations and determined demographic characteristics, family decision making structure, financial satisfaction and compared family financial situation can affect financial management behavior.

The factor analysis applied in order to determine the factor structure of the Turkishversion of the FMBS revealed that the scale had four factors like the original version. The rates of variance explained for by the four factors–savings and investment behavior, cash management, insurance behavior, credit management– were at an acceptable level. The four subscale has explained of total variance 67%.

The factor loading values for the four subscales of the FMBS varied between 0.55 and 0.87. When eliminating the items that did not measure the same structure in the factor analysis, special attention was paid to ensuring that items had a factor loading of over 0.45 in the factor that they were a part of, and that they had a high factor loading only in one factor. In social sciences the rates of variance that can be accounted for by between 40% and 60% are considered sufficient (Tavşancıl, 2006, p.84; Büyüköztürk, 2008, p.124). According to these results, the fact that items in all four subscales had a factor loading of over 0.45 shows that all items cohere with the structure that they are a part of.

Analyses of the data from 696 adults of diverse family compositions showed the FMB scale to be an acceptably reliable and valid measure in Turkish containing four financial management behaviors. These management behaviors are concluded to be saving and investment behavior, cash management, credit management and insurance behavior. Multiple factor loadings on certain questions suggest that financial management behaviors are likely to be interrelated. This is an expected result because management behaviors are conceptually related and at some point may even be interchangeable.

The relationship between FMBS scores and the economic decision-making suggests that those who make general economic decisions, spending decisions, saving and investment decisions together with all family members have higher FMBS scores. This result highlights the importance of sharing responsibilities concerning economic activities with other family members including children. The ANOVAs also showed significant (.05) differences in the financial management behavior according to general economic decisions, expenditure decisions, and savings and investment decision. The various studies that have been conducted also support this result (Erbil & Pasinoğlu, 2004; Şener & Terzioğlu, 2005; Ashby & Burgoyne 2008; Kabaklı Çimen, 2012; Kermann et al. 2000; Rettig et al., 1999). Thus, it is observed for both in this study and in other studies that the higher education level of the male and female, the higher their occupational statuses, the higher their level of income, the length of marriage; the higher women participation in the labor force increased women's participation economic decision making process in the family.

There is no single financial indicator of wellbeing that will always accurately measure the living standards of people. Income may be preferred as its level can be directly affected. But spending probably provides a better picture of long-run financial circumstances than income, since over the life course incomes tend first to rise sharply with age, and then decline in later life, but people use borrowing and saving to make sure that their spending is more even over time (Goodman & Oldfield, 2004).

When the relationship examined between independent variables and financial management behavior the correlations indicated that higher income, higher education level, give the general economic, expenditure and savings and investment decision with the family members, financial satisfaction and compared financial situation have positive affect financial management behavior than does married for many years, increase the number of children and non-employed female.

Based on adjusted regression coefficients, the order of significance among variables was as follows: monthly income of the family, education and employment status of spouses. When economic decision variables of general economic decisions, expenditure decisions, debt decisions and savings and investment decisions were added to the regression equation predicting FMB, this second model was significant as well (R=0.427, R^2=0.182, F= 13.862, p<.001). The new set of independent variables also accounted for 18% of the variance in the outcome variable. In the third stage including variables financial satisfaction and compared financial situation predicted FMB and this model was also significant (R=0.925, R^2=0.855, F=308.720, p<.001). The new variables have explained of the total variance 86 percent. Thus, the adjusted R-squared was significant; that is the addition of the financial satisfaction and compared financial situation variables increase the percentage of variance explained. Thus, income, education, employment status of the spouses, savings and investment decisions, financial satisfaction and compared financial situation were the variables making the most prediction of financial management behavior.

It is possible to discover results both supporting and not supporting the results in the literature. According Kim et al. (2003) pointed out that financial stressor events and financial behaviors are significant variables in explaining financial welfare. These results are consistent with findings reported by Xiao et al. (2006). Xiao et al. (2006) in fact found that positive financial behaviors do contribute to financial satisfaction among a sample of consumers who use credit counseling. Joo and Grable (2004) found that factors such as financial behaviors, financial stress, financial knowledge, financial solvency, risk tolerance, and demographic variables such as income and education, were all factors that significantly explained the level of financial satisfaction of individuals. Sumarwan and Hira (1993) reported that income and age were both positively and significantly related to satisfaction with financial status. Vera-Toscano et al. (2006), using data from a national survey in Spain, found that not only income but also income expectation affects financial satisfaction. According to Plagnol (2011) income has a positive relationship with the financial satisfaction because a higher level of financial satisfaction means increases in cumulated wealth. Alternatively, it may also be a case of decreases in liabilities experienced by individuals. Sighieri et al. (2006), using data from nine European countries, examined the relationship between income and financial satisfaction and found that income and satisfaction have a positive relationship up to a point and variables in the environment, such as differing household characteristics, explained 30% of the variances regarding financial satisfaction. In this study regression analysis revealed that financial behavior was affected not only by socio-economic characteristics but by financial satisfaction and compared financial situation and literature supported this results.

6. CONCLUSION AND IMPLICATIONS

These findings make an important point for financial advisors and educators: though both of individuals and families differ in some financial beliefs and behaviors. Finally, it is clear that current and future families need to receive education on financial issues. They should be taught how to manage their financial resources, they do make in an effective manner and how they can protect and elevate their financial welfare. Informative and awareness-raising educational programs need to be prepared and given to financial managers in the family about their very important issues. Such programs should include information such as money management, financial management, saving, investment, debt, consumption behavior, financial planning.

This research has several limits as every research has some. First of them is that the research covers only married female and male. The sample of the study included only individuals at Government Office, which limits the generalizability of the results. It is recommended to include other demographic variables (family life period, being married or divorced, or being re-married etc.) in the research. In addition, this research has been conducted in a country where the economic conditions are equal. In the new researches to be conducted, the financial behaviors and the financial satisfaction levels of the families living in countries having different socio-economic and socio-cultural characteristics, as well as different economic conditions can be compared.

This study aimed to determine validity and reliability of FMB scale for the Turkish form of the scale with a sample of adults having diverse demographic characteristics. In addition, this study is limited with the survey questions applied depending on the subject. The information, attitudes and behaviors can be measured or compared with different questions which can affect the financial behavior and the financial satisfaction levels (e.g. financial problems, stress sources, the economic conditions of the country and/or the scales related to the financial behaviors in the family) in the new studies to be planned. It is considered that this study constitutes a good infrastructure for the new studies to be conducted relating the subject.

REFERENCES

Ashby, K. J., & Burgoyne, C. B. (2008). Separate financial entities? Beyond categories of money management. *Journal of Socio-Economics*, *37*(2), 458–480. doi:10.1016/j.socec.2006.12.035

Baek, E., & DeVane, S. A. (2010). How do families manage their economic hardship? *Family Relations*, *59*(4), 358–368. doi:10.1111/j.1741-3729.2010.00608.x

Bailey, A. W. (1987). Social and economic factors affecting the financial welfare of families. *Journal of Home Economics*, *79*(2), 4–18.

Becker, G. S. (1988). Family economics and macro behavior. *The American Economic Review*, *78*(1), 1–13.

Büyüköztürk, Ş. (2008). Sosyal bilimleriçinveri analiz el kitabı [Handbook for the Social Sciences Data Analysis]. Ankara: Pegem Akademi Yayıncılık.

Clarke, S. (2002). Budgetary management in Russian households. *Sociology*, *36*(3), 539–557. doi:10.1177/0038038502036003003

Çopur, Z., & Şafak, Ş. (2000). Ailede gelirin kullanımına ilişkin karşılaşılan problemlerin incelenmesi [Examine the problems on using of the income in the families]. *Aile ve Toplum*, *2*(6), 7–14.

Çopur, Z., Şafak, Ş., Terzioğlu, G. R., & Dodder, R. A. (2009). Perception of adequacy of resources with a Turkish sample. *Journal of Family Issues*, *30*(12), 1624–1650. doi:10.1177/0192513X09334915

Davis, E. P., & Helmick, S. A. (1985). Family financial satisfaction: The impact of reference points. *Home Economics Research Journal*, *14*(1), 123–131. doi:10.1177/1077727X8501400112

Deacon, R. E., & Firebaugh, F. M. (1988). *Family research management* (2nd ed.). Boston: Allyn and Bacon Inc.

Dew, J., & Xiao, J. J. (2011). The financial management behavior scale: Development and validation. *Journal of Financial Counseling and Planning*, *22*(1), 43–59.

Erbil, N., & Pasinlioğlu, T. (2004). Kadının ailede karar vermeye etkisi [The efffect of the woman in decision making within the family]. *Journal of Anatolia Nursing and Health Sciences*, *7*(2), 1–11.

Fünfgeld, B., & Wang, M. (2008). Attitudes and behavior in everyday finance: Evidence from Switzerland. *International Journal of Bank Marketing*, *27*(9), 108–127.

Godwin, D. D. (1990). Family financial management. *Family Relations*, *39*(2), 221–228. doi:10.2307/585728

Goldsmith, E. B. (2000). *Resource management for individuals and families* (2nd ed.). Florida: Florida State University Wadsworth Thomson Learning.

Goodman, A., & Oldfield, Z. (2004). *Permanent differences? Income and expenditure inequality in the 1990s and 2000s* (Report Series No 66). Retrieved April 13, 2013, from www.ifs.org.uk/comms/r66.pdf

Gunnarsson, J., & Wahlund, R. (1997). Household financial strategies in Sweden: An exploratory study. *Journal of Economic Psychology*, *18*(2-3), 201–233. doi:10.1016/S0167-4870(97)00005-6

Hanna, Sh., Fan, J. X., & Chang, R. Y. (1995). Optimal life cycle savings. *Financial Counseling and Planning*, *6*, 1–15.

Heimdal, K. R., & Houseknecht, S. K. (2003). Cohabiting and married couples income organization: Approaches in Sweden and the United States. *Journal of Marriage and the Family*, *65*(3), 525–538. doi:10.1111/j.1741-3737.2003.00525.x

Hira, T. K. (1987). Satisfaction with money management practices among dual-earner households. *Journal of Home Economics*, *79*(2), 19–22.

Hira, T. K., & Mueller, M. J. (1987). The application of managerial systems to money management practices. *Iowa State Journal of Research*, *62*(2), 219–233.

Hira, T. K., & Mugenda, O. (1998). Predictors of financial satisfaction: Differences between retirees and non-retirees. *Financial Counseling and Planning*, *9*(2), 75–83.

Iversen, R. R., Napolitano, L., & Furstenberg, F. F. (2011). Middle-income families in the economic downturn: Challenges and management strategies over Time. *Longitudinal and Life Course Studies: International Journal*, *2*(3), 286–300.

Joo, S., & Grable, J. E. (2004). An exploratory framework of the determinants of financial satisfaction. *Journal of Family and Economic Issues*, *25*(1), 25–50. doi:10.1023/B:JEEI.0000016722.37994.9f

Kabaklı Çimen, L. (2012). Bir faktör olarak eğitimin kadının aile içi kararlara katılımı üzerine etkisi (The effect of education, as a factor, on the participation of women in domestic decisions). *International Journal of New Trends in Arts. Sports and Science Education*, *1*(2), 78–90.

Kerkmann, B. C., Lee, T. R., Lown, J. M., & Allgood, S. M. (2000). Financial management, financial problems and marital satisfaction among recently married university students. *Financial Counseling and Planning Education*, *11*(2), 55–64.

Kim, J., Garman, E. T., & Sorhaindo, B. (2003). Relationship among credit counseling clients' financial wellbeing, financial behaviors, financial stressor events, and health. *Financial Counseling and Planning*, *14*, 75–87.

Marlowe, J., & Godwin, D. (1988). The relationship of income and human capital to debt/asset ratio of farm families. *Home Economics Research Journal*, *17*(1), 93–109. doi:10.1177/1077727X8801700110

Mugenda, O. M., Hira, T. K., & Fanslow, A. M. (1990). Assessing the causal relationship among communication, money management practices, satisfaction with financial status, and satisfaction with quality of life. *Lifestyles: Family and Economic Issues*, *11*(4), 343–360. doi:10.1007/BF00987345

Ormsby, P., & Fairchild, T. G. (1987). Perceived income adequacy and selected financial management practices among families in Chile and Mexico. *Social Indicators Research*, *19*(3), 317–327. doi:10.1007/BF00300364

Özmete, E. (2004). Ailelerin öznel refah düzeylerine ilişkin bir değerlendirme (Evaluating the subjective well-being of families). *Aile ve Toplum Dergisi*, *2*(6), 23–31.

Parrotta, J. L., & Johnson, P. J. (1998). The impact of financial attitudes and knowledge on financial management and satisfaction of recently married individuals. *Financial Counseling and Planning*, *9*(2), 59–75.

Pavot, W., & Diener, E. (1993). Review of the satisfaction with life scale. *Psychological Assessment*, *5*(2), 164–172. doi:10.1037/1040-3590.5.2.164

Plagnol, A. C. (2011). Financial satisfaction over the life course: The influence of assets and liabilities. *Journal of Economic Psychology*, *32*(1), 45–64. doi:10.1016/j.joep.2010.10.006

Raijas, A. (2011). Money management in blended and nuclear families. *Journal of Economic Psychology*, *32*(4), 556–563. doi:10.1016/j.joep.2011.02.006

Rettig, K. D., Leichtentritt, R. D., & Danes, S. M. (1999). The effects of resources, decision making, and decision implementing on perceived family welfare in adjusting to an economic stressor. *Journal of Family and Economic Issues*, *20*(1), 5–34. doi:10.1023/A:1022163729635

Retting, K., & Schultz, C. (1991). Cognitive style preferences and financial management. *Financial Counseling and Planning*, *2*, 55–78.

Şener, A., & Terzioğlu, G. R. (2005). Determining the expenditure, investment and saving patterns in respect of family life cycles. *Aile ve Toplum Dergisi*, *2*(8), 53–59.

Sighieri, C., Desantis, G., & Tanturri, M. L. (2006). The richer, the happier? An empirical investigation in selected European Countries. *Social Indicators Research*, *79*(3), 455–476. doi:10.1007/s11205-005-5394-x

Sumarwan, U., & Hira, T. K. (1992). Credit, saving and insurance practices influencing satisfaction with preparation for financial emergencies among rural households. *Home Economics Research Journal*, *21*(2), 206–227. doi:10.1177/1077727X9202100205

Sumarwan, U., & Hira, T. K. (1993). The effects of perceived locus of control and perceived income adequacy on satisfaction with financial status of rural households. *Journal of Family and Economic Issues*, *14*(4), 343–364. doi:10.1007/BF01013984

Tavşancıl, E. (2006). *Tutumların ölçülmesi ve SPSS ileveri analizi (Measurement of attititudes and data analysis with SPSS)*. Ankara: Nobel Yayın Dağıtım.

Terzioğlu, G. R. (1990). Ailenin Ekonomik Faaliyetleri [Economic Activities of Families] (Pub. No: 10). Türkiye Aile Yıllığı. Ankara: Başbakanlık Aile Araştırma Kurumu Yayınları.

Vera-Toscano, E., Ateca-Amestoy, V., & Serrano-Del-Rosal, R. (2006). Building financial satisfaction. *Social Indicators Research*, *77*(2), 211–243. doi:10.1007/s11205-005-2614-3

Xiao, J. J., Sorhaindo, B., & Garman, E. T. (2006). Financial behavior of consumers in credit counseling. *International Journal of Consumer Studies*, *30*(2), 108–121. doi:10.1111/j.1470-6431.2005.00455.x

Xiao, J. J., Tang, C., & Shim, S. (2009). Acting for happiness: Financial behavior and life satisfaction of college students. *Social Indicators Research*, *92*(1), 53–68. doi:10.1007/s11205-008-9288-6

Yadollahi, M., Paim, L. H., Othman, M., & Suandi, T. (2009). Factors affecting economic status. *European Journal of Scientific Research*, *37*, 99–109.

ADDITIONAL READING

Bernstein, D. (2004). Household debt and IRAs: Evidence from the survey of consumer finances. *Financial Counseling and Planning*, *15*, 63–72.

Davis, E. P. (1992). Financial management practices among households with differing resource constraints. *Journal of Consumer Education*, *10*, 27–31.

Davis, E. P., & Weber, J. A. (1990). Patterns and obstacles to financial management. *Financial Counseling and Planning*, *1*, 41–51.

Dennis, M., & McCready, B. (2009). *Sample field report: Familial response to financial instability*. Menlo Park, CA: Knowledge Networks.

Dew, J. P. (2007). Two sides of the same coin? The differing roles of assets and consumer debt in marriage. *Journal of Family and Economic Issues*, *28*, 89–104.

Dew, J. P., & Xiao, J. J. (April, 2010). *The association between family financial declines, financial behaviors, and relationship satisfaction during the recession*. Paper presented at the annual conference of the American Council of Consumer Interests, Atlanta, GA.

Fitzsimmons, V. S., Hira, T. K., Bauer, J. W., & Hafstrom, J. L. (1993). Financial management: Development of scales. *Journal of Family and Economic Issues*, *14*, 257–274.

Frost, J. (1980). *Financial management practices and related factors in rural Guatemalan families*. Unpublished master's thesis, Brigham Young University, Provo, Utah.

Furnham, A. (1984). Many sides of the coin: The psychology of money usage. *Personality and Individual Differences*, *5*, 501–509.

Garasky, S., Nielsen, R. B., & Fletcher, C. N. (2008). Consumer finances of low-income families. In J. J. Xiao (Ed.), *Advances in consumer finance behavior research* (pp. 223–237). New York: Springer.

Garcia, J., & Draut, T. (2009). *The plastic safety net: how households are coping in a fragile economy*. New York: Demos.

Gauthier, A. H., Budd, J., Furstenberg, F. F., & Pacholok, S. (2010). Families, financial strain, and the economic crisis. Paper presented at the European Population Conference, September 2010.

Godwin, D. D., & Koonce, J. C. (1992). Cash flow management of low-income newlyweds. *Financial Counseling and Planning*, *3*, 17–43.

Grable, J. E., Park, J. Y., & Joo, S. H. (2009). Explaining financial management behavior for Koreans living in the United States. *The Journal of Consumer Affairs*, *43*, 80–107.

Hilgert, M. A., Hogarth, J. M., & Beverly, S. G. (2003). Household financial management: The connection between knowledge and behavior. *Federal Reserve Bulletin*, *89*, 309–322.

Joo, S. (2008). Personal financial wellness. In J. J. Xiao (Ed.), *Advances in consumer finance behavior research* (pp. 21–33). New York: Springer.

Kim, J., & Garman, T. E. (2003). Financial stress and absenteeism: An empirically derived model. *Financial Counseling and Planning*, *14*(1), 31–42.

Metzen, E. J. (1975). Relationship between assessed and perceived adequacy of family income. Paper presented at the annual meeting of the American Home Economics Association, San Antonio, Texas.

Musgrove, P. (1978). Determinants of urban household consumption in Latin America: A summary of evidence from ECIEL surveys'. *Economic Development and Cultural Change*, *26*, 441–465.

Perry, V. G., & Morris, M. D. (2005). Who is in control? The role of self-perception, knowledge, and income in explaining consumer financial behavior. *The Journal of Consumer Affairs*, *39*, 299–313.

Prochaska-Cue, K. (1993). An exploratory study for a model of personal financial management style. *Journal of Financial Counseling and Planning*, *4*, 111–134.

Rosen, D. L., & Granbois, D. H. (1983). Determinants of role structure in family financial management. *The Journal of Consumer Research*, *10*, 253–258.

Scannell, E. (1990). Dairy farm families' financial management. *Financial Counseling and Planning*, *1*, 133–146.

Servon, L. J., & Kaestner, R. (2008). Consumer financial literacy and the impact of online banking on the financial behavior of lower-income bank customers. *The Journal of Consumer Affairs*, *42*, 271–305.

Tang, T. L. P. (1995). The development of a short Money ethic scale. Attitudes toward money and pay satisfaction revisited. *Personality and Individual Differences*, *19*, 809–816.

Tufano, P., & Schneider, D. (2010). Supporting saving by low and moderate income families. *Focus (San Francisco, Calif.)*, *27*, 19–25.

Xiao, J. J. (2008). Applying behavior theories to financial behavior. In J. J. Xiao (Ed.), *Handbook of consumer finance research* (pp. 69–82). New York: Springer.

KEY TERMS AND DEFINITIONS

Budget: A quantitative financial plan for a defined period of time.

Consumption: The purchase and use of goods and services by individuals.

Desires: A sense of longing or hoping for a goods or services that is not necessary.

Life Satisfaction: A global assessment of a person's quality of life according to his chosen criteria.

Needs: Something that is necessary to live a healthy life such as food, shelter, and etc.

Quality of Life: An overall general well-being that is comprised of objective and subjective evaluations of physical, material, social, and emotional well-being together.

Saving: Income not spent, or deferred consumption.

Chapter 15
Is Technical Analysis Profitable even for an Amateur Investor?
Evidence from the Greek Stock Market (2002-12)

Vasileiou Evangelos
University of the Aegean, Greece

ABSTRACT

The purpose of this chapter is to examine if even the simplest trading rules could take advantage of the market's inefficiency and lead to profitable trading decisions. For this reason, this study examined the profitability of the simplest trading rules, using only the simple moving averages (SMA) rules that even an amateur investor could apply. In order to examine the specific issue a data sample from the Greek stock market during the period 2002-12 was used. The results suggest that even if one takes into account the most expensive transaction fees, the trading rules signal profitable investment decisions; therefore, even an amateur trader and/or investor who does not have a significant amount of money to invest (which may lead to reduced transaction costs) could take advantage of the market's inefficiency. Behavioral finance theories may provide some useful and alternative explanations regarding some of the reasons that contribute to the Greek stock market's inefficient environment.

1. INTRODUCTION

Technical analysis is a field of applied financial economics literature which gathers many conflicting opinions regarding the ability of the trading rules to present significant higher profits than the buy-and-hold strategy. If we assume that specific trading rules generate increased profits, this means that the study of the historical prices enables us to predict future prices, which is in contrast to Fama's (1970) efficiency market hypothesis (EMH). There are numerous studies which confirm that several simple or advanced trading rules (moving average, RSI index, MACD, stochastic rules etc.) enable the investors who apply them to increase their profits in several stock markets around the world (Brock, Lakonishock, & LeBaron(1992); Chong & Ng, 2008; Ulku & Prodan, 2013 etc.).

DOI: 10.4018/978-1-4666-7484-4.ch015

Scholars suggest that a crucial prerequisite in order to achieve profits using trading rules is the non-linearity in prices (Neftci, 1991). However, similar to most issues examined in finance, there are studies which disprove the aforementioned point. Usually, a friction point is that the transaction costs significantly reduce the trading rules profits[1]. Indicatively, Alexander (1961) presents that the trading rules outperform the buy-and-hold strategy, but Alexander (1964) re-examines his earlier findings including transaction costs and finds significant reductions in the trading rules profits. Fama & Blume (1966) suggest that technical rules fail to outperform the buy-and-hold strategy, but Sweeney (1988) questions their findings taking into account a later sample (1970-82).

The main objectives of this paper are to examine the following: (i) whether the simplest trading rules (simple moving average, SMA) or composite SMA rules enable us to predict the financial trend, which leads to increased profits in comparison to buy-and-hold trading strategy, (ii) how profitable could these rules be, and (iii) if even the financial crisis period could be profitable for someone who applies the examined strategies using derivatives. We examine the trading rules profitability taking a data sample from the Greek stock market during the period 2002-12 because there are recent studies which provide empirical evidence for the existence of calendar anomalies (Vasileiou & Samitas, 2014; Vasileiou, 2014 a,b), which is an indication for market inefficiency.

The rest of this paper goes as follows: Section 2 reports the trading rules and clearly defines the assumptions under which we examine their profitability. Section 3 briefly presents market information and describes the dataset. Section 4 presents the examined strategies, the theoretical and methodological background and their outcomes. Section 5 further discusses the empirical findings and links them to previous studies under a behavioral financial view. Finally, section 6 concludes the study.

2. TRADING RULES AND PRACTICAL ASSUMPTIONS DEFINITIONS

This paper examines the profitability of simple trading rules in the ATHEX. Therefore, we should declare the assumptions under which we examine the specific issue and clearly demonstrate how the individual investor can apply simple trading rules and present the final returns. Three main points should be noted in order to adequately present the results:

1. Which are the indexes in which we could apply the trading rules,
2. Which trading rules are simple and could be applied even by an amateur technical analyst-investor, and
3. Which are the possible trading strategies that could be applied.

Most of the studies that examine the Greek stock market use datasets from the Athens Exchange General Index (ATHEXGI) as a sample, which consists of the 60 largest companies stocks and is the most reliable indicator regarding the Greek stock market[2]. This means that a possible applied strategy may be that an investor holds a stocks' portfolio which simulates the ATHEXGI and when the trading signal suggest a sell period he sells the stock and deposits his money in Greek banks[3]. This could be named as the 1st strategy, but its main drawback is that an investor cannot gain profits from the sell period signals, by shorting the specific index because there is no future contract with the ATHEX as underlying value.

However, in the ATHEX derivatives exchange (ADEX) there are several financial products using as an underlying index the FTSE/ASE20, FTSE/ASE 40 or futures on stocks. Among them we finally chose to include the futures on FTSE/ASE20 index because this index presents increased correlation with the ATHEX GI 98.65% (e.g. the ATHEXGI and FTSE/ASE40 correlation is 87.41%).

The FTSE/ASE-20 index is based on the 20 largest ATHEX stocks; it was developed in 1997 by the partnership of ASE with FTSE International, it represents over 50% of ASE's total capitalization (ADEX official webpage www.adex.gr). It is worth mentioning that FTSE/ASE 20 on 3rd December, 2012 is renamed to FTSE/ASE Large Cap Index and consists of 25 of the largest and most liquid stocks that trade in the Athens Stock Exchange. The fact that this change happened during the last days of our sample enables us to assume that it does not influence the results.

The specific investment tool enables the investor to gain profits even when the financial trend is negative, either by selling his or her portfolio when the sell signal suggest it and he or she goes short on the FTSE/ASE20 index (2nd strategy presented by Table 4) or does all his or her investment movements using only FTSE/ASE 20 future contracts (3rd strategy presented by Table 5) by taking long and short positions.

Regarding the trading rules, we decide to examine the simplest among them and those that could easily be applied, even by amateur investors, who simply observe the market's performance. Therefore, we examine trading rules that are linked to the simple moving averages of 22, 56, 100, 150 and 200[4] days in order to include several investor groups (from short term to long term). Under these assumptions we may conclude if the trading rules generate significantly more profits even for the mean individual and without increased information investor.

Regarding the SMA trading rules we follow the Ulku & Prodan (2013) suggestion when today's closing price (P_t) crosses the n-simple moving average SMA(n) from below we buy, but when the P_t crosses the SMA(n) from above we sell[5]. The SMA(n) is defined from the following equation

$$\mathbf{SMA(n)} = \frac{P_{t-(n-1)} + P_{t-(n-2)} + \dots + P_{t-1} + P_t}{n} \quad (1)$$

We assume that the investor has always invested in the Greek stock market. This means that when the signal shows that he or she should sell, he or she takes a short position or sells the portfolio and deposits the funds in the Greek banking market. Regarding the trades' execution day we accept Ulku & Prodan's (2013) suggestion that the execution takes place at the closing price of the day on which the signal is generated, therefore the returns to a signal position start to accrue the next day.

3. MARKET INFORMATION, DATA, AND DESCRIPTIVE STATISTICS

Our samples consist of daily data information from the Greek stock market. The first time series we use consists of daily information of the ATHEXGI for the time span January 2002 to December 2012. We use the specific sample because during the aforementioned period in the Greek economy and the Greek stock market there are no significant regulatory or structural reforms that could significantly influence the investors behavior as Alexakis & Xanthakis (1995) suggest.

In this point we try to briefly present the recent reforms that have taken place in the ATHEX during the last decades. The Greek stock market was founded in 1876, as the Athens Stock Exchange (ASE). Despite the fact that the ASE is old, modernization took place during the 1990's. The most important reforms of the ASE's history are[6]:

1. The establishment, in 1991, of the first electronic trading system (ASIS) which replaces the open outcry method, while the newly founded Central Securities Depository (CSD) settles the transactions,
2. In 1999 the Athens Derivatives Exchange Clearing House (ADECH) and the Athens Derivatives Exchange (ADEX) start to operate and the first derivatives are traded in August 1999,

3. In the same year the electronic book entries in the Dematerialized Securities System (DSS) gradually replaces the paper depository receipts, while the OASIS replaces the ASIS as the electronic trading system,
4. In May 2001 the ASE upgrades to mature market,
5. In 2002 the "Athens Exchange"(ATHEX) is founded by the merging of the ASE and the ADEX,
6. In 2003 the Greek state withdraws its ownership stake from the ATHEX, while the ATHEX transfers its remaining regulatory responsibilities to the Hellenic Capital Market Commission (HCMC), and (vii) in 2008 starts the trading of the first Exchange Traded Fund (ETF).

The aforementioned market information enable us to assume that during the examined period (2002-12) there are not take place significant regulatory reforms, therefore the investors behavior are not influenced from them. In other words, there are not such financial reforms that could influence the trading activity (consequently the trading rules implementing or profitability).

Figure 1 depicts the ATHEXGI performance and the ATHEXGI returns charts, while Table 1 presents the descriptive statistics regarding the ATHEXGI returns for the sample's period.

The descriptive statistics show that the time series distribution presents increased kurtosis and the Jarque-Bera test confirms that the time series does not follow the normal distribution. Figure 1(b) shows that after 2008 the volatility is significantly increased, which is an indication that linear models may not be appropriate for the specific time series, which in turn may be an indication that trading rules may be profitable (Neftci, 1991)[7].

As we mention in section 2, some strategies make use of the FTSE/ASE20 index. For the examined period the FTSE/ASE20 index presents increased correlation with the ATHEX GI, which is 98%. Figure 2 presents the FTSE/ASE20 performance and the FTSE/ASE20 returns charts, while Table 2 presents the descriptive statistics regarding the FTSE/ASE20 returns for the sample's period.

The comments regarding the FTSE/ASE20 descriptive statistics are similar to the ones afore-

Table 1. Descriptive statistics of ATHEX GI returns during the period 2002-12

	Total Period (2002-12)
Mean	-0.000387
Standard Deviation	0.017577
Skewness	0.039841
Kurtosis	7.509174
Jarque-Bera	2325.42*
Q(1)	9.0279*
Q(2)	13.687*
Q(3)	14.815*
Q(4)	15.156*
Q(5)	15.508*
Observations	2,744

Note: * indicates 1% statistical significance level.

Table 2. Descriptive statistics of FTSE/ASE20 returns during the period 2002-12

	Total Period (2002-12)
Mean	-0.000560
Standard Deviation	0.020557
Skewness	0.196293
Kurtosis	7.731000
Jarque-Bera	2,576.671
Q(1)	6.2932**
Q(2)	13.894*
Q(3)	14.610*
Q(4)	14.790*
Q(5)	15.394*
Observations	2,744

Note: * indicates 1% statistical significance level.

Figure 1. ATHEXGI performance and the ATHEXGI returns charts

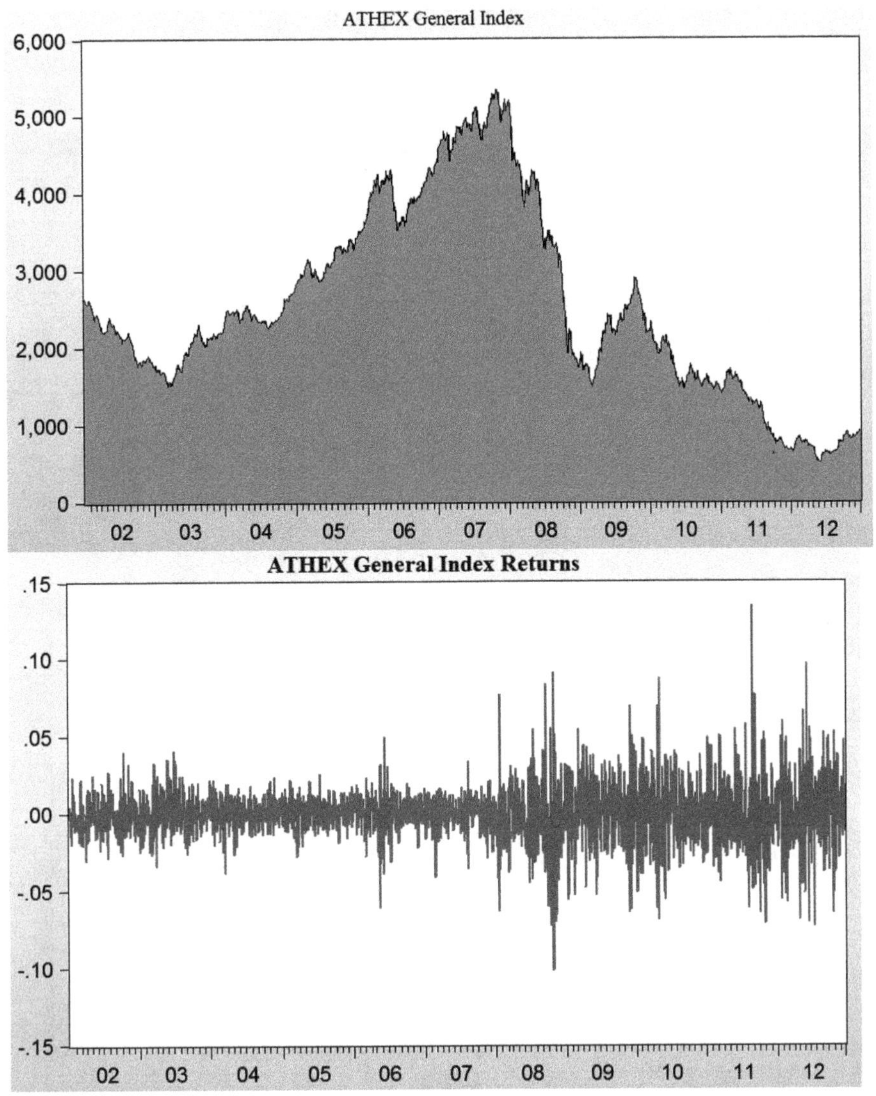

mentioned for the ATHEXGI, therefore we do not repeat them in order to save text space.

4. EXAMINED STRATEGIES, THE THEORETICAL BACKGROUND AND RESULTS PRESENTATION

Daily returns, as the descriptive statistics show, do not follow the normal distribution, which means that the standard t-test may be biased in assessing the statistical significance of trading rules' profits. Therefore, we employ the t-statistics obtained from a bootstrap simulation as suggested by Brock et al (1992) and are applied in many similar studies (Ulku & Prodan, 2013).

t-statistic for buys (sells) =

$$\frac{\mu_r - \mu}{(\sigma^2 / \mathrm{N} + \sigma^2 / \mathrm{N}_r)^{1/2}} \quad (2)$$

Figure 2. TSE/ASE20 performance and the FTSE/ASE20 returns charts

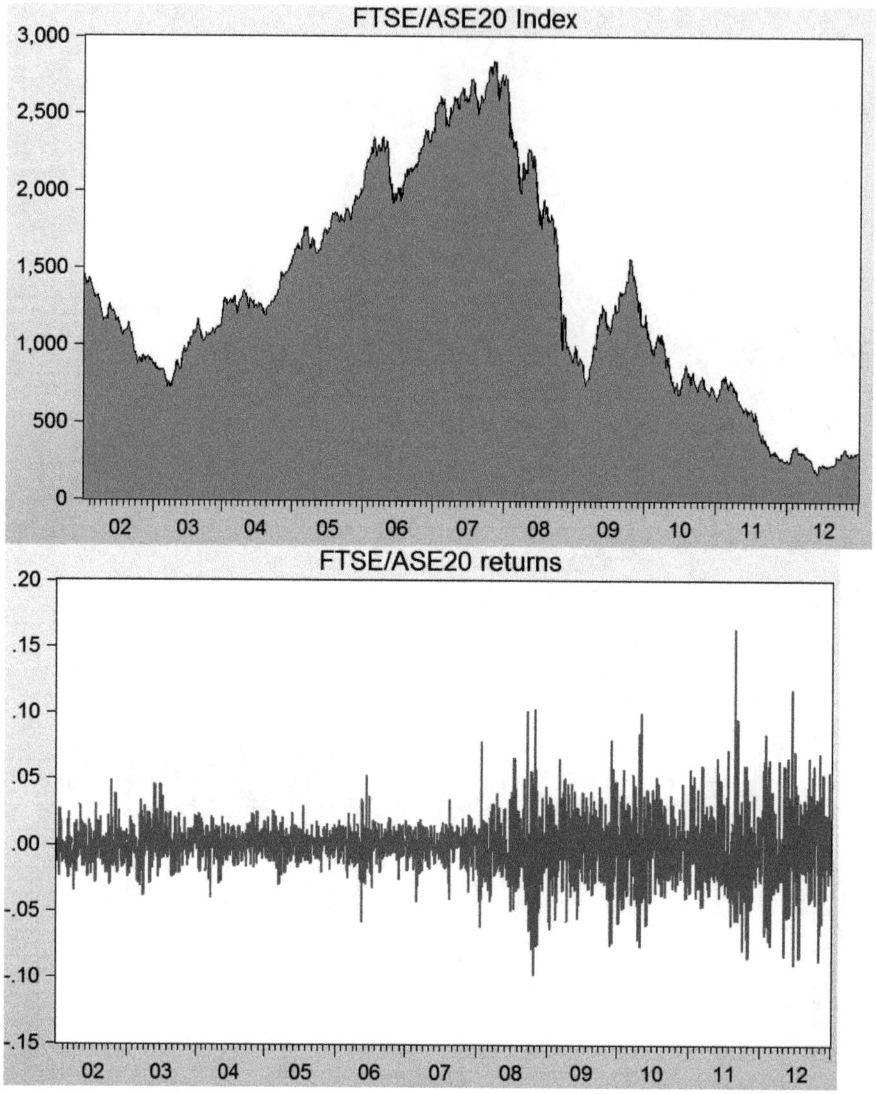

where μ_r and N_r are the mean return and number of signals for the buys or sells and μ and N are the unconditional mean and number of observations, while σ^2 is the estimated variance for the entire sample, and

t-statistic for buy - sells =

$$\frac{\mu_b - \mu_s}{(\sigma^2 / N + \sigma^2 / N_r)^{1/2}} \qquad (3)$$

where μ_b and N_b are the mean return and number of signals for the buys or sells and μ_s and N_s are the mean return and number of signals for the sells.

In order to present as much information as possible we present in each of the following tables:

1. The results regarding the SMA's length,
2. The daily buy, sell and the combined buy-sell returns (no commissions included) and the respective t-statistics[8],
3. The N(buy) and N(sell) periods' days,

Table 3. 1st Strategy's results

1st Strategy	Buy	Sell	Buy-Sell	N (Buy Period)	N (Sell Period)	S(Buy)	S(Sell)	Buy Period Positive Sessions Ratio	Sell Period Positive Sessions Ratio	Individual Investor's Returns
MA(22)	0.01041 (8.617)*	0.00023 (2.450)**	0.00546 (4.671)*	1,396	1,324	119	119	54.73%	53.93%	0.00089 (0.391)
MA(56)	0.00961 (5.574)*	0.00024 (1.570)	0.00509 (2.998)*	1,376	1,284	57	56	54.87%	53.50%	0.00274 (0.822)
MA(100)	0.00975 (3.967)*	0.00021 (0.884)	0.00546 (2.310)**	1,332	1,088	35	34	55.26%	53.03%	0.00384 (0.874)
MA(150)	0.00882 (7.161)*	0.00022 (2.070)**	0.00450 (3.893)*	1,290	1,304	22	22	55.58%	53.60%	0.00345 (1.473)
MA(200)	0.00690 (5.619)*	0.00020 (1.733)	0.00388 (3.023)*	1,317	1,080	23	22	55.20%	52.87%	0.00273 (1.137)

Notes: *, ** and *** marks indicate the 1%, 5% and 10% statistical significance for a two-tailed test. The figures inside the brackets are the t-statistics.

4. The buy/sell signals (S) that the indicators show,
5. The percentages of the successful positive returns sessions that according to the indicators suggestions, and
6. We present the returns taking into account the most expensive commissions[9].

Regarding the empirical findings we should focus on the results without commissions and the results with commissions. The specific comparison may be useful in order to examine that the lower the commissions are, another MA may produce more profits. In this way the presented results may be useful not only for the average individual investor, but also for other investors (institutional and/or individual) who pay significantly lower commission.

Table 3 presents the results if we follow the buy signal and we buy a stock portfolio which adequately stimulates the ATHEXGI, but when a sell signal arises the investor sells his or her portfolio and entrust these funds in a Greek bank savings account (1st strategy).

Among the MAs the results suggest that if somebody takes a long position, when the MA(22) indicate a buy signal, the buy period's returns are the highest in comparison to all the other examined MAs and give signals for 17.26% year returns. If we focus on the buy-sell returns the MA(22) and MA(100) indicators result in the same returns (13.64% per year). However, the commissions[10] reduce the final profits especially if the buy/sell signals are increased. The most profitable among all the examined MAs is the MA(100), because the reduced signals lead to reduced transactions and therefore reduced transaction costs, that ultimately increases profitability for the investor (9.60%).

Regarding the second strategy the MA(22) provides (commissions excluded), in time, information for the financial trend's change. The MA(22) signals give 26.03% returns on buy periods, 53.36% on sell periods and 39.33% for the combination of these signals. Similarly to the first strategy, the results suggest that the commissions[11] reduce the final profits (e.g. for the MA(22) the final profits when the commissions are included are 5.63%). Therefore, as the results suggest, when we include the commissions, the most profitable MAs signals are those that the MA(150) suggest (25.59%).

Table 4. 2nd Strategy's results

2nd Strategy	Buy	Sell	Buy-Sell	N (Buy Period)	N (Sell Period)	S(Buy)	S(Sell)	Buy Period Positive Sessions Ratio	Sell Period Positive Sessions Ratio	Individual Investor's Returns
MA(22)	0.01041 (8.617)*	0.02134 (15.236)*	0.01573 (13.938)*	1,396	1,324	119	119	54.73%	53.78%	0.00225 (0.985)
MA(56)	0.00961 (5.574)*	0.02007 (9.840)*	0.01466 (9.006)*	1,376	1,284	57	56	54.87%	52.96%	0.00785 (2.360)**
MA(100)	0.00975 (3.967)*	0.01969 (7.063)*	0.01422 (6.823)*	1,332	1,088	35	34	55.26%	53.22%	0.00962 (2.189)**
MA(150)	0.00882 (7.161)*	0.01747 (12.228)*	0.01064 (11.316)*	1,290	1,304	22	22	55.58%	53.37%	0.01024 (4.366)*
MA(200)	0.00690 (5.619)	0.01735 (11.616)*	0.01161 (10.321)*	1,317	1,080	23	22	55.20%	53.33%	0.00841 (3.507)*

Notes: *, ** and *** marks indicate the 1%, 5% and 10% statistical significance for a two-tailed test. The figures inside the brackets are the t-statistics.

The third strategy includes as underlying values only the FTSE/ASE20 and the MA(22) presents the most profitable signs if we combine the buy and sell signals (33.89%), but the transaction costs[12] of the 238 signals turn the final profits to negative returns. Similarly to the aforementioned strategies the most gainful profits, if we include the transaction costs in our results, are provided by longer last MA, which in our case is the MA(200) that presents 18.73% annual returns.

These results are consistent to previously examined studies for the ATHEX (Eriotis, Vasiliou, & Papathanasiou,2006; Vasiliou, Eriotis & Papathanasiou, 2008) which suggest that in the Greek stock market the MA trading rules are able to beat the buy-and-hold strategy, which is an indication for a violation of the EMH[13].

Table 5. 3rd Strategy's results

3rd Strategy	Buy	Sell	Buy-Sell	N (Buy Period)	N (Sell Period)	S(Buy)	S(Sell)	Buy Period Positive Sessions Ratio	Sell Period Positive Sessions Ratio	Individual Investor's Returns
MA(22)	0.00812 (7.069)*	0.01887 (12.634)*	0.01356 (10.095)*	1,344	1,376	119	119	53.94%	53.49%	-0.00431 (-1.890)***
MA(56)	0.00814 (5.127)*	0.01852 (9.039)*	0.01335 (7.312)*	1,324	1,334	65	64	54.08%	53.00%	0.00328 (1.056)
MA(100)	0.00824 (3.526)*	0.01925 (6.586)*	0.01318 (5.599)*	1,334	1,086	38	37	54.72%	53.22%	0.00662 (1.627)
MA(150)	0.00695 (2.738)*	0.01691 (5.095)*	0.01160 (4.171)*	1,290	1,129	28	27	55.04%	53.32%	0.00669 (1.407)
MA(200)	0.00600 (2.495)**	0.01691 (5.080)*	0.01094 (3.996)*	1,313	1,085	19	18	55.06%	53.55%	0.00749 (1.575)

Notes: *, ** and *** marks indicate the 1%, 5% and 10% statistical significance for a two-tailed test. The figures inside the brackets are the t-statistics.

Figure 3. Investors' participation per group in ASE (% Of total turnover)

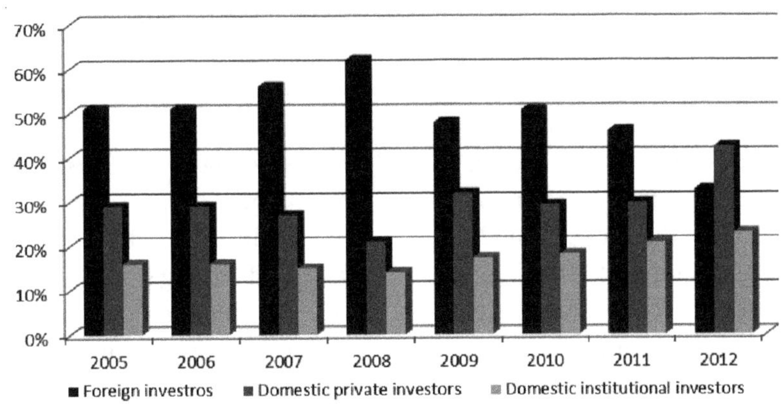

5. THE GREEK CASE UNDER A BEHAVIORAL FINANCE VIEW

At this point we present an explanation for the Greek stock market which is linked to the behavioral finance (BF) theory, but first we should define what BF is. As Shefrin (2000) briefly describes BF is the study of how psychology and other social sciences affect finance. In the case of the financial markets the psychological influence may be different depending on the trader types (institutional, individuals, foreign investors etc.)[14]. There are several aspects of the BF theory, but examining the Greek case we focus on the herding behavior, because it may be combined to previous studies that examine the Greek stock market. This section tries to present a wider explanation for these findings and to trigger some of the readers to examine new possible explanations for the financial issues which are mentioned below.

Regarding the Greek stock market, Vasileiou & Samitas, 2014; Vasileiou (2014 a,b) (hereafter VSV) examine the month and trading month effect, the day of the week effect and the turn of the month effect respectively for the Greek case during the same sample period 2002-12. They examined these calendar effects under the assumption that the Greek economy's trends influence them. Figure 1, depicts that the Greek stock market presents a period of long term growth (2002-07) and a period of long term recession (2008-12). VSV empirical findings confirm their assumption that the calendar anomalies patterns change depending on the financial trend. This means that the Greek stock market is inefficient, a conclusion that is consistent with the results we present above, because they mean that past values enable investors to predict the future values, which violates Fama's (1970) efficient market hypothesis.

One of the VSV findings that could be linked to BF theories is that the previous day returns positively influence the today returns especially during the growth period (this influence weakens during the recession sub-period). The positive coefficient of the previous day's return may not be explained only by the non-synchronous trading which is likely to characterize the less developed markets (Alexakis & Xanthakis, 1995), but also by the "positive feedback traders". Moreover, positive feedback trading may be the reason why the market decline (rise) may lead to further market decline (rise)[15].

This feedback strategy may be linked to the herding behavior, which could be the result of an increased number of investors who apply a feedback strategy[16]. Regarding the Greek case we note two studies that could confirm our assumptions: (i) Economou, Kostakis & Philippas (2011) provide evidence for herding effects in the Greek stock market during the period (1998-2008), and (ii) Merikas, Merikas, Vozikis & Prasad (2004), which study the behavior and the investment strategy of 150 experienced investors and found that almost one out of three Greek investors acts on the opinions of the firms majority stockholders (herding behavior), 30.7% of the Greek individual investors examine the past returns, 40% the recent trend, while 37.3% wants the "get rich quickly". These findings may be an indication that Greek individual investors examine the returns' pattern and want to follow the trend in order to prosper financially. Trading rules try to take advantage of the implied trend, therefore the trading rules profitability may be influenced from the herding effect, which may be an interesting issue for further research.

Moreover, the aforementioned findings are not only a possible (and alternative) explanation for the positive and statistically significant autocorrelation that VSV present, but also an explanation for the technical rules profitability. Similar to VSV question, if the change in the participants ratio (Figure 3) could be an explanation for the autocorrelation pattern, further study that will examines the trading rules profitability taking into account the participations ratio may be useful in order to draw useful conclusions for the trading rules-participants relationship.

6. CONCLUSION

This study tries to examine the simple trading rules profitability using as a sample the mature Greek stock market during the period 2002-12. The results suggest that the short-term MAs (commissions excluded) signal the most profitable transactions. The buy, sell and their combined returns are significantly different from the unconditional mean returns. If we include the most expensive transaction costs, mid and long term MAs are the most profitable for an amateur investor, because the transactions in this case are expensive and reduce the transactions' real returns.

Among the strategies for the average investor in the Greek stock market the combination of a stock portfolio during the buy period and a short position using derivatives is the most profitable. The second most profitable strategy is the trading using exclusively futures (2nd strategy), while the strategy of buying stocks and merely selling them when the trading signal suggests it, it does not present increased profitability, because it does not produce profits during the negative trend period.

In this study we try to present the results in such a way so that they may be useful to a wide range of investors and traders, because someone who may be charged with fees less than those we have used in our study may earn more profits than the presented or may follow a trading rule strategy that is more suitable to his or her needs[17]. Regarding the optimal method the buy, sell and buy-sell returns (without transaction cost) may be a guide.

The empirical findings are consistent with previously reported papers regarding the trading rules' profitability in the Greek stock market, but it is the first indication (to the best of our knowledge) for profits even for an amateur investor with a limited investment amount. The existence of significantly increased profits from the trading rules contradicts the Efficient Market Hypothesis, because investors gain profits if they study the historical prices.

The recent empirical findings suggest that the Greek stock market is inefficient and the trading rules enable even an amateur chartist to achieve significant returns, while there is evidence for herding behaviour (especially during the during the 2002-07 period) which contributes to the stock market's inefficiency environment.

ACKNOWLEDGMENT

I would like to thank Dr. Polychronopoulos Dimitrios for his support.

REFERENCES

Alexakis, P., & Xanthakis, M. (1995). Day of the week effect on the Greek stock market. *Applied Financial Economics*, *5*(1), 43–50. doi:10.1080/758527670

Alexander, S. S. (1961). Price movements in speculative markets: Trends or random walks. *Industrial Management Review*, *2*, 7–26.

Alexander, S. S. (1964). Price movements in speculative markets: Trends or random walks. No. 2. *Industrial Management Review*, *5*, 25–46.

Banerjee, A. (1992). A Simple Model of Herd Behaviour. *The Quarterly Journal of Economics*, *107*(3), 797–817. doi:10.2307/2118364

Brock, W., Lakonishock, J., & LeBaron, B. (1992). Simple technical trading rules and the stochastic properties of stock returns. *The Journal of Finance*, *47*(5), 1731–1764. doi:10.1111/j.1540-6261.1992.tb04681.x

Chong, T. T., & Ng, W. (2008). Technical analysis and the London stock exchange: Testing the MACD and RSI rules using the FT30. *Applied Economics Letters*, *15*(14), 1111–1114. doi:10.1080/13504850600993598

Economou, F., Kostakis, A., & Philippas, N. (2011). Cross-country effects in herding behaviour: Evidence from four south European markets. *Journal of International Financial Markets, Institutions and Money*, *21*(3), 443–460. doi:10.1016/j.intfin.2011.01.005

Eriotis, N., Vasiliou, D., & Papathanasiou, S. (2006). Testing Technical Anomalies in Athens Stock Exchange (ASE). *European Research Studies Journal*, *9*(3-4), 75–90.

Fama, E. (1970). Efficient Capital Markets: A Review of Theory and Empirical Work. *The Journal of Finance*, *25*(2), 383–417. doi:10.2307/2325486

Fama, E., & Blume, E. (1966). Filter rules and stock market trading. *The Journal of Business*, *39*(S1), 226–241. doi:10.1086/294849

Kwon, K., & Kish, R. (2002). Technical trading strategies and return predictability: NYSE. *Applied Financial Economics*, *12*(9), 639–653. doi:10.1080/09603100010016139

Merikas, A. A., Merikas, A. G., Vozikis, G. S., & Prasad, D. (2004). Economic factors and individual investor behaviour: The case of the Greek stock exchange. *Journal of Applied Business Research*, *20*(4), 93–98.

Neftci, S. (1991). Naive trading rules in financial markets and Wiener-Kolmogorov prediction theory: A study of "technical analysis.". *The Journal of Business*, *24*(4), 549–571. doi:10.1086/296551

Sentana, E., & Sushi1 W. (. (1991). Feedback traders and stock returns autocorrelations: Evidence from a century of daily data. *The Review of Economic Studies*, *58*, 547–563. doi:10.2307/2298011

Shefrin, H. (2000). *Beyond Greed and Fear: Understanding Behavioural Finance and the Psychology of Investing*. Cambridge, MA: Harvard Business School Press.

Sweeney, R. (1988). Some filter rule tests: Methods and results. *Journal of Financial and Quantitative Analysis*, *23*(3), 285–300. doi:10.2307/2331068

Ülkü, N., & Prodan, E. (2013). Drivers of technical trend-following rules' profitability in world stock markets. *International Review of Financial Analysis*, *30*, 214–229. doi:10.1016/j.irfa.2013.08.005

Vasileiou, E. (2014a). *Long Live Day of the Week Patterns and the Financial Trends' Role: Evidence from the Greek Stock Market during the Euro Era (2002-12)*. Retrieved from; doi:10.2139/ssrn.2338430

Vasileiou, E. (2014b). Turn Of the Month Effect and Financial Crisis: A new explanation from the Greek Stock Market (2002-2012). *Theoretical and Applied Economics*, *10*, 33–58.

Vasileiou, E., & Samitas, A. (2014). *Does the Financial Crisis Influence the Month and the Trading Month Effects?* Evidence from the Athens Stock Exchange. Retrieved from; doi:10.2139/ssrn.2345450

Vasiliou, D., Eriotis, N., & Papathanasiou, S. (2008). Technical Trading Profitability in Greek Stock Market. *The Empirical Economics Letters*, *7*(7), 749–756.

ADDITIONAL READING

Achelis, S. B. (2001). *Technical Analysis from A to Z*. New York: McGraw Hill.

Ackert, L., & Deaves, R. (2009). *Behavioural finance: Psychology, decision-making, and markets*. Boston, Massachusetts: Cengage Learning.

Barberis, N., & Thaler, R. (2003). A survey of behavioural finance. in Constantinides, M. Harris and R.M. Stulz (Ed.), Handbook of the Economics of Finance, volume 1, part B, p.p. 1053-1128, Amsterdam, Netherlands: Elsevier.

Blume, L., Easley, D., & O'hara, M. (1994). Market statistics and technical analysis: The role of volume. *The Journal of Finance*, *49*(1), 153–181.

Caparrelli, F., D'Arcangelis, A. M., & Cassuto, A. (2004). Herding in the Italian stock market: A case of behavioural finance. *Journal of Behavioral Finance*, *5*(4), 222–230.

De Bondt, W., Muradoglu, G., Shefrin, H., & Staikouras, S. K. (2008). Behavioural finance: Quo vadis? *Journal of Applied Finance (JAF)*, *18*(2), 7–21.

Dunbar, F. C., & Heller, D. (2006). Fraud on the market meets behavioural finance. *Delaware Journal of Corporate Law*, *31*(2), 455–532.

Edwards, R. D., Magee, J., & Bassetti, W. H. C. (2012). *Technical analysis of stock trends*. Boca Raton, FL: CRC Press.

Fama, E. F. (1998). Market efficiency, long-term returns, and behavioural finance. *Journal of Financial Economics*, *49*(3), 283–306.

Hudson, R., Dempsey, M., & Keasey, K. (1996). A note on the weak form efficiency of capital markets: The application of simple technical trading rules to UK stock prices-1935 to 1994. *Journal of Banking & Finance*, *20*(6), 1121–1132.

Kim, K. A., & Nofsinger, J. R. (2008). Behavioural finance in Asia. *Pacific-Basin Finance Journal*, *16*(1), 1–7.

Knorr Cetina, K., & Preda, A. (2004). *The sociology of financial markets*. Oxford, UK: Oxford University Press.

Konstantinidis, A., Katarachia, A., Borovas, G., & Voutsa, M. E. (2012). From efficient market hypothesis to behavioural finance: Can behavioural finance be the new dominant model for investing? *Scientific Bulletin–Economic Sciences*, *11*(2), 16–26.

McGoun, E. G., & Skubic, T. (2000). Beyond behavioural finance. *The Journal of Psychology and Financial Markets*, *1*(2), 135–144.

Mills, T. C. (1997). Technical analysis and the London Stock Exchange: Testing trading rules using the FT30. *International Journal of Finance & Economics*, *2*(4), 319–331.

Murphy, J. J. (1999). *Technical Analysis of the Futures Markets: A Comprehensive Guide to Trading Methods and Applications*. New York, NY: New York Institute of Finance.

Neely, C., Weller, P., & Dittmar, R. (1997). Is technical analysis in the foreign exchange market profitable? A genetic programming approach. *Journal of Financial and Quantitative Analysis*, *32*(04), 405–426.

Park, C. H., & Irwin, S. H. (2007). What do we know about the profitability of technical analysis? *Journal of Economic Surveys*, *21*(4), 786–826.

Pompian, M. M. (2006). *Behavioural finance and wealth management*. New Jersey: How to Build Optimal Portfolios That Account for Investor Biases.

Schindler, M. (2007). *Rumours in financial markets: Insights into behavioural finance*. Hoboken, New Jersey: John Wiley & Sons.

Shefrin, H. (2001). Behavioural corporate finance. *Journal of Applied Corporate Finance*, *14*(3), 113–126.

Shefrin, H., & Statman, M. (1994). Behavioural capital asset pricing theory. *Journal of Financial and Quantitative Analysis*, *29*(3), 323–349.

Shiller, R. J. (2003). From efficient markets theory to behavioural finance. *The Journal of Economic Perspectives*, *17*(1), 83–104.

Shleifer, A. (2000). *Inefficient markets: An introduction to behavioural finance*. Oxford, UK: Oxford University Press.

Statman, M. (1999). Behavioural finance: Past battles and future engagements. *Financial Analysts Journal*, *55*(6), 18–27.

Taylor, M. P., & Allen, H. (1992). The use of technical analysis in the foreign exchange market. *Journal of International Money and Finance*, *11*(3), 304–314.

Thaler, R. H. (Ed.). (2005). *Advances in behavioural finance* (Vol. 2). Princeton, NJ: Princeton University Press.

Wärneryd, K. E. (2001). *Stock-market psychology: How people value and trade stocks*. Cheltenham: Edward Elgar Publishing.

Wong, W. K., Manzur, M., & Chew, B. K. (2003). How rewarding is technical analysis? Evidence from Singapore stock market. *Applied Financial Economics*, *13*(7), 543–551.

KEY TERMS AND DEFINITIONS

Behavioral Finance: Is a field of the financial theory that tries to examine the humans' (occasionally we do not use the term investors) economic decisions taking into consideration factors that are not strictly linked to the quantitative finance. Behavioral finance uses knowledge from other scientific fields (e.g. psychology, neuroscience, sociology etc.) in order to give alternative explanations where the financial theory cannot.

Herd Behavior: Is the investors' tendency to follow the larger groups' decisions even if their own information and/or estimations do not suggest it.

Market Efficiency: Suggests that prices constantly reflect all the available information regarding a particular stock and/or the whole market; therefore it is extremely difficult for an investor to beat the market.

Technical Analysis: Assumes that stock market patterns tend to be constantly repeated and under this assumption tries to forecast the market trend using historical (price and volume) data.

Trading Rules: Are rules that technical analysts have defined through time and it is widely believed, if specific preconditions are met, they are able to adequately forecast future trends.

Weak Form Efficient: Market could be characterized as a stock market that enables the its participants to make systematically profitable decisions using only historical data. In this way investors are able to take advantage of the market inefficiency.

ENDNOTES

1 An interesting literature review studies regarding the specific controversial issues are presented in Kwon and Kish (2002).

2 Vasileiou (2014a) briefly present some of these studies.

3 We calculate the profits of the sell period using the mean saving daily returns from the Bank of Greece database. We use the savings returns because we want the funds to be available any time in order to use them when the signals suggest it.

4 We choose the 22-days SMA because it is considered by technicians to be the working days in a month. Alternatively the SMA (20) and the SMA (25) could be used. We examined both of them and the results are similar. A similar approach is followed by Ülkü & Prodan (2013).

5 This means that we close our position and we sell, therefore two transactions are needed in the case of the futures.

6 The primary source is gathered from the Hellenic Exchange Groups web site (http://www.helex.gr/web/guest/helex-history).

7 Vasileiou & Samitas (2014), Vasileiou (2014a,b) provide sufficient evidence that non-linear models are inappropriate for the examined data set (e.g. OLS estimations present ARCH LM effect, there is leverage effect etc.).

8 The presented results and the respective t-statistics are calculated regarding the 10-days returns similar to Brock et al (1992) which is commonly used in similar studies. In our comments we use the year returns which is calculated by the equation 250*(daily returns), because 250 is the number of the year's trading days.

9 The most expensive commissions are those that an individual investor pays. For stocks buy/sell transaction the maximum commission is about 0.5% for stocks trading (for somebody who invests an average amount of €2,500 which is less than the average transaction amount per investor share, data available upon request, source www.helex.gr) and 1% for the index trading (during the examined period we assume that the margin rate is 37.5%, source www.adex.ase.gr). Moreover, in contrast to other studies we include the custody fees 0.0040% per day. These commissions are the highest among several commissions, which are related to individual investors in the lowest scale of the investment funds. From discussions with several traders we conclude that the aforementioned fees are really the most expensive, in some cases we may be very strict and for this reason, in order to avoid any possible counterargument, we report and the returns if we exclude the commissions, so anyone who may be interested could examine which strategy and which MA better fits his or her investment profile.

10 The commissions regarding the first strategy are 0.50% on the returns if we buy or sell the portfolio.

11 The commissions regarding the second strategy reduce the returns for 1.45% because each sell/buy signal leads to a stock (0.50%) and future transactions (1%).

12 If we assume that the average transaction cost for a future contract is 1% (note 4) only the first transaction should be charged by 1% commission fee, but the other signals should be charged by 2 transactions of 1%, therefore 1.99% fees.

13 The results for both studies include significantly lower transaction costs, which may be more appropriate for the cases of the institutional investors and they do not include the custody fees. However, the returns they find in their studies are similar to those we find in ours.

14 In the Greek stock market the ratios depending on the group of participants significantly changed during the examined period (Figure 3).

15 Sentana & Wadhwani (1992) suggest "…if one set of traders follow a feedback trading strategy (i.e. they react to price changes), then returns will exhibit serial autocorrelation".

16 Banerjee (1992) characterizes herding behavior as: when people do what others are doing rather than using their information. This behavior is irrational and leads to inefficient equilibrium which, as we present above, the trading rules take advantage of.

17 For example: The manager of an equity mutual fund may gain more profits by following shorter term MA rules, because: (i) the commissions are significantly lower than those we have used in our study, and (ii) the longer term strategy has been built by the investment strategy and the stocks portfolio selection.

Section 4
Financial Industry

Chapter 16
The Philippine Health Care Delivery System and Health Expenditure

Abdulkadir Işık
Namık Kemal University, Turkey

Abdulhamid Mauyag Gunda
Namık Kemal University, Turkey

Birol Topçu
Namık Kemal University, Turkey

ABSTRACT

Health is recognized by the Philippine constitution as a basic human right. The Philippines, compared to most Asian countries, produces more and better human resources for health. However, the Philippines are challenged by attracting and retaining staff in the under-served areas of the country. Philippine allotted 4.2-4.4% of its GDP to health from 2009 to 2011. Furthermore, considerable inequities in health care access and outcomes between Socio-economic groups remain. The Phil Health's limited breadth and depth of coverage has resulted in high levels of out of pocket payments. The implementation of the reforms in financing, service delivery and regulation which are aimed to tackle the inefficiencies and inequalities in the health system has been challenged by the decentralized environment and the presence of private sector, often creating fragmentation and variation in the quality of health services across the country.

INTRODUCTION

The Philippines is the second largest archipelago on earth with 7,107 islands. It is positioned on the western edge of the Pacific Ocean on the South-eastern rim of Asia (PHSDP, 2012). It is a member of the Association of South-East Asian Nations or ASEAN. The country is made up of three major geographical regions namely: Luzon, Visayas and Mindanao. It has a total of 80 provinces, 138 cities and 1,496 municipalities. In 2010, the population of the Philippines was 92.3 million, with a growth rate of 1.9% per year. Half of the population lives in the urban areas and of that, 44% live in slums

DOI: 10.4018/978-1-4666-7484-4.ch016

(PHSDP, 2012). Christians make up the majority of the population and there is a Muslim minority concentrated in the southern part of the country. Additionally, the country is a home of 180 ethnic groups. Malays make up the majority and there are tribes of indigenous peoples in mountainous areas throughout the country (PHSDP, 2012).

Economically, the Philippines is considered as a developing country and is a lower middle-income economy in the South East Asia. Per capita Gross Domestic Product (GDP) is 2,918.13 US Dollars in the third quarter of 2013. The GDP growth rate is 7.025 in the same year. The annual per capital poverty threshold is P9,385 in 2012, slightly higher than that in 2009 which was P8,448. Average annual family income reached P206,000 in 2012, it is also higher than that of P173,000 in the year 2006. Unemployment rate in 2013 is 7.3% with a 0.3% increase from the 7.0% in 2012. Underemployment rate has decreased from 22.8% in 2012 to 19.2% in 2013 (NSCB, 2013).

The Philippines has had seven constitutions since 1897. In effect now, the one ratified by referendum in 1987, established a republican government patterned after that of the United States with a strong executive branch, a bicameral legislature, and an independent judiciary under a supreme court. It has had seven constitutions since 1897. In effect now, the one ratified by referendum in 1987, established a republican government patterned after that of the United States with a strong executive branch, a bicameral legislature, and an independent judiciary under a supreme court (PHSR, 2011).

Health service delivery is based on a Western biomedical model of health initially introduced during the Spanish colonial era and strengthened during American colonization. This Western system is superimposed on a pre-existing alternative model of health care based on a mix of folk and herbal medicines, religious beliefs, and traditional practices that has persisted throughout the country. Indicators of health status have steadily improved since the 1970s. The analysis of the country's demographic and health aspects show that it is going through a demographic and epidemiological transition, characterized by a decrease in fertility, increase in life expectancy and a substantial change in risk factors (PHSR, 2011). However, there is a high inequality in many health outcomes between socio-economic classes and disparities between geographical regions. The top five causes of death include heart and cerebrovascular diseases, malignant neoplasm, pneumonia, and tuberculosis. The top five causes of morbidity include acute respiratory infection, ALRTI and pneumonia, bronchitis, hypertension and acute watery diarrhoea (PHSDP, 2012).

THE PHILIPPINE HEALTH CARE DELIVERY SYSTEM

The Philippine health system has undergone changes and trends to meet the timely demand for it. In fact, there have been many legislative actions undertaken by the government to form the regulatory framework for the health system and public health in the country. Example of these are the Local Government code of 1991, National Health Insurance Act of 1995, Organ Donation Act (1991), Hospital Licensure Act, Pharmacy Act, Dangerous Drugs Act and many others.

Organization of the Health Care System

The Philippines provides recognition of health as a basic human right. Protection and promotion of the right to health of the people and instilling health consciousness among them have been guaranteed in the Article II, Section 15 of the Philippine Constitution. The Philippine health system consists of the public and private sector. The public sector consists of the Department of Health (DOH), Local Government Units (LGUs) and other national government agencies providing health services.

The Department of Health is the country's lead agency in health. The major mandate of DOH is provide national policy direction & develop national plans, technical standards & guidelines on health. It has a regional field office in every region and maintains specialty hospitals, regional hospitals and medical centers. It also maintains provincial health teams made up of DOH representatives to the local health boards and personnel involved in communicable disease control (NOH, 2005-2010).

With the devolution of health services under the 1991 Local Government Code, provision of direct health services, particularly at the primary and secondary levels of health care, is the mandate of LGUs. Under this set-up, provincial and district hospitals are under the provincial government while the municipal government manages the rural health units (RHUs) and barangay health stations (BHSs). In every province, city or municipality, there is a local advisory body to the local executive and the sanggunian or local legislative council on health-related matters (NOH, 2005-2010).

The passage of the 1995 National Health Insurance Act expanded the coverage of the national health insurance program to include not only the formal sector but also the informal and indigent sectors of the population. The program founded under the principle of social solidarity where the healthy subsidizes the sick and those who can afford to pay subsidize those who cannot. PhilHealth, a government-owned and controlled corporation attached to the DOH, is the agency mandated to administer the national health insurance program and ensure that Filipinos will have financial access to health services (NOH, 2005- 2010).

The private sector includes for-profit and non-profit health providers whose involvement in maintaining the people's health is enormous. Their involvement include providing health services in clinics and hospitals, health insurance, manufacture and distribution of medicines, vaccines, medical supplies, equipment, other health and nutrition products, research and development, human resource development other and other health-related services (NOH, 2005-2010).

Health Facilities and Services

The total number of hospital is 1,795. The 721 of this belongs to the government while 1,074 as private hospitals. The number of beds per 1000 population was 1.04 in 2008. The number of Barangay Health Stations (BHSs) was 17, 018 in 2008. And the Rural Health Units (RHUs) numbered 2,266 in 2005. In terms of government hospital beds, National Capital Region (NCR) has the most number of 27,779 beds followed by Region IV-A and Central Luzon at 9,459 and 8, 218 beds respectively. The regions with the least number of government hospital beds are Autonomous Region of Muslim Mindanao (ARMM) at 586 beds, CARAGA at 1,718 beds and Region IV-B at 2, 093 beds. The government hospital bed to population ratio is worst in ARMM with 0.17 per 1000 population while it is best in NCR with 2.47 per 1000 population. There is increasing trend in the number of BHSs from 15,343 in 2002 to 17,018 in 2008 and also an increased in the number of RHUs in the country from 1,879 in 2001 to 2,266 in 2005. NCR has the most number of RHUs while the Central Mindanao has the least number of RHUs. On the other hand, Region IV-A and Region IV-B have the most number of BHSs while NCR has the least (PSY 2004). On the average, each RHU serves around 41,000 people while each BHS serves around 5,100 people (PSY, 2004 & NOH, 2005-2010). Table 1 shows the number of beds and rate per 1000 population by region in 2008.

The DOH has existing policy to provide services under the National Mental Health Policy, the National Policy on Oral Health, including the Minimum Essential Oral Health Package of

Table 1. Numbers of beds and rate per 1000 population by region, Philippines, 2008

Region	Number of Beds	Rate per 1000 Population
I Ilocos	4,163	0.84
II Cagayan Valley	2,779	0.86
III Central Luzon	8,218	0.84
IV-A CALABRAZON	9,459	8.83
IV-B MIMAROPA	2,093	0.73
V Bicol	4,156	0.76
VI Western Visayas	5,114	0.78
VII Central Visayas	6,190	0.92
VIII Eastern Visayas	2,845	0.67
IX Zamboanga Peninsula	2,909	0.87
X Northern Mindanao	4,858	1.16
XI Southern M.	4,580	1.08
XII Central M.	3,180	0.94
NCR	27,779	2.47
CAR	2,472	1.52
ARMM	586	0.17
CARAGA	1,718	0.70
Philippines	**94,199**	**1.04**

Source: Department of Health

the DOH for children 2-6 years, and to overseas Filipino workers. However there is also a very limited dental and rehabilitative service in the public sector. The 7.76 million overseas Filipino workers face a wide range of occupational, mental, reproductive and sexual health-related problems, but currently receive almost no education or information and variable levels of insurance and support. Public facilities from both national and local governments provide free services including medicines and laboratory work up during outbreaks (e.g measles, dengue and flu) and other public health related events (PHSDP, 2012).

Health Information system including surveillance of diseases and other public health events are recorded and reported from the local surveillance units and through the Philippine Integrated Disease Surveillance and response to the DOH national surveillance unit. This serves as the data bank for the analysis of the health status of the local community as well as the national data for the health profile of the country especially those that will need immediate notification to WHO as a commitment for the implementation of International Health Regulation (2005).

In 2012 the DOH released a new classification system of hospitals and other health facilities with specific guidelines for scope of services and functional capacity for each classification, and overall operating standards. There is also an ongoing effort to upgrade government health facilities in line with the goal to achieve universal coverage (PHSD, 2012).

Health Human Resource

Human resources for health are central to managing and delivering health services. They are crucial in improving health systems and health services and in meeting the desired health outcome targets. Human resources for health are enormous but unevenly distributed in the country. Most health practitioners are in Metro Manila and other urban centers. Compared to most Asian countries, the Philippines is producing more and better human resources for health (NOH, 2005-2010).

The number of physicians per 100,000 populations slightly increased from 123.8 in 1998 to 124.5 in 2000, which translates into one physician for every 803 people in 2000. The number of dentist per 100,000 populations almost remained unchanged at 54.2 in 1998 and 54.4 in 2000 or one dentist per 1,840 people in 2000. The number of pharmacists per 100,000 populations improved slightly from 55.8 in 1998 to 58.1 in 2000. This means one pharmacist for every 1,722 people in 2000. The number of nurses per 100,000 popu-

Table 2. Classification and characteristics of health facilities and services in the Philippines, 2012

Facility	Number	Characteristics
		Hospitals
General Hospitals **Level 1 General Hospitals** **Level 2 General Hospitals** **Level 3 General Hospitals** **DOH Hospitals** **c. Specialty hospitals** **d. Other DOH Hospitals**	70 16 54	Most hospitals at all levels provide services for all kinds of illnesses, diseases, injuries or deformities. It has emergency and outpatient services primary care services, family medicine, pediatrics, internal medicine, obstetrics-gynecology, surgery including diagnostic and laboratory services, imaging facility and pharmacy. Hospitals Level 1 general hospitals also include: isolation facilities, maternity, dental clinics, 1 st level x-ray, secondary clinical laboratory with consulting pathologist, blood station, and pharmacy. Level 2 hospitals include level 1 services and departmentalized clinical services, respiratory units, ICU, NICU and HRPU, high risk pregnancy unit, tertiary clinical laboratory, and 2 nd level x-ray Level 3 hospitals include level 2 services and teaching/training, physical medicine and rehabilitation, ambulatory surgery, dialysis, tertiary laboratory, blood bank, 3 rd level x-ray A tertiary hospital which specializes in the treatment of patients suffering from a particular condition requiring a range of treatment (e.g. Phil. Orthopaedic Centre, National Centre for Mental Health); patients suffering from disease of a particular organ or groups of organ (e.g. Lung Centre of the Philippines, Phil. Heart Centre); or patients belonging to a particular group such as children, women, or elderly (National Children's Hospital, Dr. Jose Fabella Memorial Medical Centre). Tertiary care facilities located all over the country serving as referral hospitals in the different regions of the country and providing anticipated range of tertiary services.
		Other Health Facilities
Category A: Primary Care facility **Category B: Custodial care facility** **Category C: Diagnostic/ Therapeutic facility** **Category D: Specialized out-patient facility**		First contact facility offering basic services including emergency and normal delivery services. Includes: in-patient short-stay facilities, medical out-patients, overseas workers and seafarers facilities, and dental clinics. Provides long-term care for those with chronic or mental illness, substance/drug abuse treatment and rehabilitation, sanatorium/leprosarium, and nursing home facilities. Laboratory facilities, radiology including x-ray, and nuclear medicine facilities. Including for dialysis, ambulatory surgery, in-vitro fertilization, stem cell services, oncology and chemotherapy, radiation oncology, and physical medicine and rehabilitation. PNAC is a unit within the DOH responsible for promoting HIV/AIDs program and provides secretariat support to HIV/AIDs prevention and control, Diabetes Foundation, Heart Association and Philippine Coalition for the Prevention of NCDs are organizations with membership from the public and private sectors.

Source: Philippines Health Service Delivery Profile (PHSDP), 2012

lations almost remained constant from 442.7 in 1998 to 442.8 in 2000, a ratio of one nurse per 226 people for both 1998 and 2000 (SEAMIC, 2003 & NOH, 2005-2010).

In 2002, there are 3,021 doctors, 1,871 dentist, 4720 nurses and 16,534 midwives employed by LGUs. Other health personnel employed by LGUs consist of 3,271 engineers/sanitary inspectors, 303 nutritionist, 1,505 medical technologist, 977 dental aides and 2,808 non- technical staff. Assisting these health personnel at the grassroots are 195,928 volunteer barangay health workers and 54,557 birth attendants (FHSIS, 2002 & NOH, 2005-2010).

The Philippines has traditionally been a major source of health professionals to many countries because of their fluent English, skills and training, compassions, humaneness and patience in caring. The country is purportedly the leading exporter of nurses to the world (Aiken, 2004) and

Table 3. Summary of health services and providers in the Philippines, 2012

Health Services	Public Sector Provision	Private Sector Provision
	Health promotion	
Health education Family planning Maternity care Child care Nutrition and food safety Lifestyle-related or non-communicable diseases Communicable diseases Environmental Health and sanitation	Health centres Barangay health stations National programs and agencies provide technical support Activities are highly variable and depend on the local government unit Community health teams provide education and information at family levels in the community. They also work with poor families to determine health needs, services available and receive PhilHealth benefits Hospitals conduct multi media health promotion activities in their waiting areas, lobbies and OPDs Some LGU-operated birthing facilities Include: Pre-natal care for mothers, Iron Anti-rabies for animal bite centres UHC/KP focuses on the 5Million poorest	Family and community practitioners, paediatricians, obstetricians, physicians and some subspecialists Some organized NGOs initiate activities Large-scale programs are rarely provided by the private sector
	Disease Prevention	
Childhood immunization Tb, malaria, leprosy, filariasis, schistosomiasis, rabies, dengue fever, and SARS	Health centres Provincial hospital outpatient services and Animal Bite Treatment Centres National agencies provide technical support and supplies Support from the Global Fund for AIDS, Tuberculosis and Malaria Includes: Endemic areas are provided with anti- malaria drugs, schisto and filarial drugs, including soil-transmitted helminthiasis	Paediatricians clinics and private hospital outpatient services provide immunizations Private Animal Bite treatment Centres as stand alone clinics and those in private hospitals. Pulmonary specialists and some general practitioners participate in the DOTS program for
HIV and other Sexually Transmitted Infections (STI)	Display of IEC materials in some rural health units/ social hygiene clinics/city health offices; video showing in waiting areas	NGOs and Key Populations at higher risk for HIV Support Groups for Sex workers/Men having Sex with Men and People who inject drugs, and the young key populations conduct outreach work and peer education activities Some private hospitals display IEC materials; video showing in waiting areas
Environmental health and sanitation	Local governments, water districts, national agencies provide assistance in terms of water supply systems; sanitation systems; solid waste, hazardous waste, health care waste management systems; sewage and wastewater collection and treatment facilities; water and wastewater laboratories. DOH Environmental and Occupational Health Office provides technical support to LGUs.	Water utilities (e.g. Manila Water, Maynilad), NGOs for water and sanitation; water refilling stations, bottled water companies; solid waste and hazardous waste treatment and disposal services; septic tanks desludging services (e.g. Malabanan companies); sewage and wastewater treatment facilities; water and wastewater laboratories

Source: PHSDF, 2012

the second major exporter of physicians (Bach, 2003). Although the country is producing a surplus of health workers for overseas market since the 1960s, the large exodus of nurses in the last four years has been unparalleled in the migration history of the country. While Filipino physicians have been migrating to the United States since the 1960s and to the Middle East countries in the 1970s in steady outflows, the recent outflows are disturbing because they are no longer migrating as medical doctors but as nurses (NOH, 2005-2010).

Table 4. Summary of health services and providers in the Philippines, 2012

Health Services	Public Sector Provision	Private Sector Provision
Diabetes, hypertension, cancer and mental health	Health facilities at LGU levels National NCD program of the DOH provides technical support to local government units Hospitals at municipal/city, provincial and regional levels also provide disease-prevention related activities (e.g. smoking cessation advice, wellness clinic, etc.) The medicines program – Compack - for NCDs targets the 5 Million poorest as part of UHC/KP commodity support	Private general practitioners and Specialists in clinics and medical centres provide education and prevention programs. Some are linked to NGOs such as Diabetes Foundation, Philippine Heart Association, Philippine Coalition for the Prevention of NCDs, among others Private mental health facilities
Primary Services		
Outpatient, dental and laboratory services Disease programs like TB, Malaria, Dengue	Health centres Primary care hospitals other DOH-supported commodities – eg TB drugs, vaccines (DPT, OPB, measles, BCG, Hep B), also flu vaccines for indigent senior citizens	Clinics Hospitals
Secondary and Tertiary services		
Outpatient, Inpatient and hospital care Laboratory and special procedures Acute and emergency care Dental care Mental Health	Secondary and tertiary care hospitals, including very specialized care Hospitals Some health centres and hospitals Hospitals	Secondary and tertiary care hospitals, including very specialized care Hospitals Most dental care is by private practitioners in clinics and some hospitals Hospitals, Clinic/halfway homes
Rehabilitative Services		
Acute inpatient rehabilitation Long term care for the elderly and disabled Programs for the disabled Palliative care	Tertiary hospitals with specialist physicians and physical, occupational and speech therapists A few tertiary hospitals provide house visits and palliative care Some community-based care National Commission Concerning Disabled Persons coordinates implementation and enforcement of legislation A few tertiary hospitals Services are variable, highly dependent on the local government	Tertiary hospitals Some home-based care Several NGOs and foundations provide assistance This should be filled up. There are more of private partners doing work here. Hospitals

Source: PHSDF, 2012

HEALTH EXPENDITURE

The Philippine health financing involves different financial sources, regulatory bodies and health services providers. Generally, the four main sources are government (national and local), Social insurance (government and private), user fees or out-of-pocket (OPP) and the donors. The sources coming from donors is also called grants are those that come from philanthropists and charity organizations. The Department of Health (DOH) and the National Health Insurance Program or PhilHealth. Health services providers as we know includes the hospitals, the doctors and nurses.

The total health expenditure per capita is 8.1% in 2011. It has an annual growth rate of 7.2% in the period of 2009 and 2011. The Philippine had allotted 4.2-4.4% of its domestic growth product (GDP) to health in the same period of time. This share rose slightly compared to 3.9% in 2007 (figure number), but remains relatively low

Table 5. Number of government health workers, Philippines, 2008

Area	Doctors	Dentists	Nurses	Midwives
Philippines	2,838	1,891	4,576	17,437
NCR	590	498	723	1,135
CAR	89	40	131	637
I	159	105	259	1,014
II	97	65	196	839
III	278	176	441	1,662
IV-A	238	189	472	1,818
IV-B	83	68	142	555
V	157	85	273	1072
VI	234	123	401	1,775
VII	177	117	328	1,534
VIII	155	94	201	904
IX	100	44	203	697
X	138	74	241	1,052
XI	75	69	127	743
XII	113	56	194	876
ARMM	76	30	130	507
CARAGA	79	58	114	615

Source: Department of Health

compared with the WHO Western Pacific Region 2006 average of 6.1% this total health expenditure tallied an average annual growth rate of 9% in the period of 2009 and 2011.

The government total health expenditure on health amounted to 27% in 2011 from which 12.3% as a national government share and the remaining 14.7% by the local government share. From 2009 to 2011, the government expenditure on health has increased with an average annual growth rate of 14.6%. The government, as a whole, spent more on personal health care than the public health care each year from 2009 to 2011. More detailed expenditure accounts indicate that spending on hospitals dominated the government's personal health care expenditures.

In 1995, the National Health Insurance Program (NHIP) managed by Philippine Health Insurance Corporation (PHIC or PhilHealth) signaled the movement towards a single-payer Premium-based financing or insurance system. However, the current system continues to maintain a dual financing system existing parallel to each other (NOH, 2011-2016). This Social health insur-

Table 6. Health expenditures by source, 2009-2011

Sources of Funds	AMOUNT (in million pesos, at current prices) 2009 2010 2011	Growth Rate 2010-2011	Average Annual Growth Rate 2009-2011
GOVERNMENT	**88,722 101,378 116,443**	**14.9**	**14.6**
National Government	36,949 43,375 53,069	22.3	19.8
Local Government	51,773 58,003 63,364	9.2	10.6
SOCIAL INSURANCE	**27,897 33,925 39,126**	**15.3**	**18.4**
National Health Insurance Program	27,791 33,799 39,022	15.5	18.5
Employee's Compensation	107 126 104	17.1	1.1
PRIVATE SOURCES	**217,865 239,139 272,009**	**13.7**	**11.7**
Private Out-Of-Pocket	182,370 199,983 227,215	13.6	11.6
Private Insurance	6,083 6,401 7,222	12.8	9.0
HMO	18,199 21,170 24,570	16.1	16.2
Private Establishments	7,809 7,937 9,297	17.1	9.1
Private Schools	3,404 3,649 3,706	1.6	4.3
REST OF THE WORLD	**7,681 6,384 3,478**	**45.5**	**32.7**
Grants	7,681 6,384 3,478	45.5	32.7
ALL SOURCES	**342,164 380,826 431,047**	**13.2**	**12.2**

Source: National Statistical Coordination Board, 2013

Table 7. Total Health Expenditure, 2009-2011

Item	2009	2010	2011
THE (in million Pesos, at current prices)	342,164	380,826	431,585
THE Growth Rate (in percent, at current prices)		11.3	13.2
THE (in million pesos, at 2000 constant prices)	209, 147	226, 144	248, 585
Total Health Expenditure Growth		8.1	9.9
Per Capita Health Expenditure (in pesos, at current prices)	3,759	4,112	4,577
Per Capita Health Expenditure (in pesos, at 2000 constant prices)	2,298	2,442	2,639
Per Capita Health Expenditure Growth Rate (in percent, at current prices)		9.4	11.3
THE Per Capita		6.3	8.1
THE (in billion pesos, at current prices)	342.2	380.8	431.0
Gross Domestic Product (GDP, in billion pesos, at current prices)	8,0261.1	9,003.5	9,735.5
Gross National Income (GNI, in billion pesos, at current prices)	10,652.5	11,996.1	12,878.1
Health Expenditure (% of GDP)	4.3	4.2	4.4
Health Expenditure (% of GNI)	3.2	3.2	3.3

Source: National Statistical Coordination Board, 2013

ance program, known as PhilHealth, increased its share of total health spending at an average annual growth rate of 18.5% from 2009 to 2011. Public funding through PhilHealth has been expected to set the incentive environment in order to have a greater leverage and drive forward health system performance. However, the share of 9.1% remains low in relation to the 30% target set by DOH in the 1999 health reform agenda to reduce out-of-pocket share of total health expenditure.

Table 8. Source of financing during impatient visits, Philippines, 2008

Source of Payment	Confined in Private Hospitals (%)	Confined in Public Facilities
Salary/income	48	51
Loan	17	23
Savings	37	32
Donation	17	23
PhilHealth	51	24
SSS/GSIS	4	2
HMO	6	1
Others	0.82	0.32

Source: Raw data from National Demographic & Health Survey, NSO 2008

The private sector continues to be the dominant source of health care financing with financing with 63.1% share of the total health expenditure in 2011 and was slightly higher than the preceding year which was 62.8%. The private sector share on health spending has an annual growth rate of 11.7% from 2009 to 2011. Moreover, out-of-pocket or user fees continue to dominated the share of private sources and the total health expenditure as a whole with 57.2% and an annual growth rate of 11.6%. This trend of increased of OOP payments is quite alarming knowing that the Social insurance has been expanded in the recent years.

The high level of Out-Of-Pocket may lead to financial catastrophe and impoverishment. Table 5 validates the large contribution of OOP during confinement but it is significantly higher among patients confined in public facilities. Despite the safety nets, donations would still count as one of the major sources of financing.

Table 9. Distribution of out-of–pocket expenditure by components and by socio- economic status, in percent, Philippines. 2000-2009

Components	Poorest				Richest				Philippines			
	2000	2003	2006	2009	2000	2003	2006	2009	2000	2003	2006	2009
Medicines	74.2	75.0	73.5	74.7	59.5	59.7	59.1	57.2	67.6	66.6	66.6	65.7
Hospital charges	1.8	2.1	2.2	2.1	7.2	6.7	6.9	7.0	4.4	4.4	4.6	4.7
Medical & dental	6.0	5.3	5.6	6.2	19.8	18.6	18.0	16.7	12.5	12.6	11.6	11.5
Other medical goods	9.0	8.4	8.7	8.9	11.7	13.7	10.3	10.9	10.8	11.6	10.1	10.6
Other medical services	8.8	1.1	1.7	2.0	1.3	0.4	0.8	0.9	4.4	1.0	1.6	1.7
Contraceptive	0.3	8.0	7.4	5.0	0.5	0.8	1.4	2.0	0.5	3.9	3.6	3.1
Food supplement	-	-	0.9	1.1	-	-	3.0	5.4	-	-	1.9	2.7

Source: Raw data Family Income and Expenditure Surveys, 2000-2009

Looking at the components of Out-Of-Pocket by quantile, more than half of the medical expenditure was spent on medicine. However, share of medicine on the total medical expenditure was consistently higher among the poor compared to their richer counterparts. Expenditure on contraceptives was also higher among the poor on household (Lavado & Ulep, 2011).

CONCLUSION

The health service delivery in the Philippines is based on a Western biomedical model. Health functions are generally devolved to provinces and municipalities. As stated above, health service has evolved into dual delivery systems of public and private provision, covering the entire range of interventions with varying degrees of emphasis at different health care levels. Health status has improved over the last decades. Among the indicators of this improvement are the decreased in the infant mortality rate, decreased prevalence of communicable diseases and the increased in the life expectancy of the Filipinos. However, there are still many problems and challenges the country has to solve. For the inequities in access to health care services and outcomes between Socio-economic groups remain. This has been generally caused by the high cost of access and use of health care. Also, the high level of out of pocket payments brought about by the limited breadth and depth coverage of the PhilHealth, the country's social health insurance, is a heavy burden to the poor Filipinos. Despite being a major exporter of health workers, some rural and poor areas of the Philippines still face shortage of professional health workers. Thus, the government has to exert efforts in attracting and retaining staff in the under-served areas of the country. Another key challenge is the inefficiency in service delivery. This I believed is the result of an ineffective referral system and gatekeeping of the health system. Finally, reform efforts in financing, service delivery and regulation have been done to resolve these problems. However, implementation has been challenged by the decentralized environment and the presence of a large private sector, often creating fragmentation and variation in the quality of services across the country.

REFERENCES

Commission on Higher Education. (2009). *Statistics index*. Retrieved from http://www.ched.gov.ph/index.html

Department Of Health. (2009a). *Health indicators*. Retrieved from http://www.doh.gov.ph/research_statistics.html

Department Of Health. (2012). *National objectives for health 2011-2016*. Retrieved from http://www.doh.gov.ph/content/national-objectives-health-2011-2016.html

Department of Health. (2012). *Philippine health system at a glance*. Retrieved from http://www.doh.gov.ph/sites/default/files/3%20chapter1.pdf

National Statistical Coordination Board. (2010). *National statistical coordination board*. Retrieved from http://nscb.gov.ph/

National Statistical Coordination Board. (2013). *Philippine indicators for 2013*. Retrieved from http://www.nscb.gov.ph/stats/pnha/#sthash.CQmpSwVK_dpuf

Philippine Health Insurance Corporation. (2008). *PhilHealth annual report 2008*. Retrieved from http://www.philHealth.gov.ph/about_us/annual_report/ar2008.pdf

Philippine Health Insurance Corporation. (2009a). *Lifetime members*. Retrieved from http://www.PhilHealth.gov.ph/members/lifetime/index.htm

Philippine Overseas Employment Association. (2009). *Number of deployed nurses by top 10 destinations, New Hires, 2003-2009*. Retrieved from http://www.poea.gov.ph/stats/2009_OFW%20 Statistics.pdf

World Health Organization. (2007). *Philippine health information system: Review & Assessment*. Retrieved from http://www.who.int/healthmetrics/library/countries/HMN_PHL_Assess_Final_2007_07_en.pdf

World Health Organization. (2009b). *National health accounts: Country information*. Retrieved from http://www.who.int/nha/country/en/index.html

World Health Organization. (2012). *Health service delivery profile Philippines*. Retrieved from http://www.wpro.who.int/health_service_service_delivery_profile_philippines.pdf

ADDITIONAL READING

Abel-S, B. (1996). Assessing the experience of health financing in the United Kingdom. In D. W. Dunlop & J. M. Martins (eds.), An international assessment of health care financing, lessons for developing countries. The World Bank Washington.

Arbor, A. (1990). *Health administration*. Michigan University Press.

Behrman, J. R., & Deolalikar, A. B. (1988). The impact of economic adjustment programs on health and nutrition and seasonality. In D. E. Sahn and M. R. Reich (eds.), Health, nutrition and economic crisis: Approaches to policy in the third world. Dover Massachusetts: Auburn House.

Buxton, M. (1987). Developments in the teaching of health economics education, training and evangelism. G. T. Smith (ed.), Health Economics: Prospects for the future. Croom Helm Ltd.

Carrin, G. (1987). *Economic evaluation of health care in developing countries. Theory and Applications*. Croom Helm Ltd.

Cohen, D. R., & Henderson, J. B. (1988). *Health, prevention and economy*. Oxford University Press.

Cullis, J. G., & West, P. A. (1979). *The Economics of health: An introduction*. Martin and Robertson Company Ltd.

Culyer, A. J. V. D. Gaag & M. Perlman. (1981). Health, economics and health economics. North Holland Amsterdam.

Edgman, M. R., Moomaw, R. L., & Olson, K. W. (1996). Economics and contemporary issues. The Dryden Press.

Evans, R. G., & Law, M. M. (1996). The Canadian Health Care System: Where Are We and How Did We Get Here. In D. W. Dunlop and J. M. Martins (eds.), An International Assessment of Health Care Financing, Lessons for Developing Countries. The World Bank Washington.

Fausto, D. (1990). Italy, advances in health economics and health services research, comparative health systems: The future of national health care systems and economic analysis. In R. F. Scheffler and L.F. Rossitier (eds.), L.F. JAI Press Inc.

Ferranti, D. D. (1985). Paying for health services in developing countries: An overview, World Bank Staff Working Paper, No: 721, The World Bank.

Field, M. (1989). *Success and crisis in national health systems*. New York, London: Routledge.

Foland, S., Goodman, A. C., & Stano, M. (1997). *The Economics of Health and Health Care*. Upper Saddle River, NJ: Prentice Hall.

Fuchs, V. R. (1986). *The Health Economy*. Harvard University Press.

Fujino, S. (1987). Health economics in japan: prospects for the future. In G. T. Smith (Ed.), *Health economics: Prospects for the future*. London: Croom Helm.

Gertler, P., & Gaag, J. V. D. (1990). *The willingness to pay for medical care: Evidence from two developing countries*. Published for the World Bank The John Hopkins University Press.

Getzen, T. F. (1995). *Health Economics: fundamentals and flow of funds*. Temple University Press.

Griffiths, A., & Mills, M. (1980). Health sector financing and expenditure survey. K. Lee and A. Mills (eds.), Health economics of health in developing countries. Oxford University Press Oxford, 1980.

Hsiao, W. C. (1996). A Framework for assessing health financing strategies and the role of health insurance. In D. W. Dunlop and J. M. Martins (eds.), An International assessment of health care financing, lessons for developing countries. The World Bank Washington DC USA.

Isabel, S., & de Cassas, C. (1994). Health care in Latin America. In D. R. Phillips and Y. Verhasselt (eds.), Health and Development. Routledge. London and New York.

Kleczkowski, B. M. (1980). Technological imperatives and economic efficiency in health care, in economics and health policy. The council for International Organizations of Medical Sciences (CIOMS) and Sandoz Institute.

Kong-Kyun, R. (1971). *Health care economics: An Overview, economics in health care* (L. E. Weeks & H. J. Berman, Eds.).

Lee, K., & Mills, A. (1983). *Developing countries, health and health economics. The Economics of health in developing countries*. Oxford University Press.

Lewitt, R., Wall, A., & Appleby, J. (1996). *The reorganized national health service, (6. edition)*. Chapman and Hall UK.

Mach, E. P., & Smith, B. A. (1983). *Planning the finance of the health sector*. World Health Organization.

Martins, J. M., & Dunlop, D. W. (1996). Lessons learned. In D. W. Dunlop & J. M. Martins (Eds.), *An international assessment of health care financing, lessons for developing countries*. The World Bank.

Maynard, A. (1987). Health economics research in the UK. In G. T. Smith (eds.). Health Economics: Prospects for the future. New York.

Yang, B. (1996). Issues in health care delivery: The case of Korea. D. W. Dunlop and J. M. Martins (ed). An international assessment of health care financing, lessons for developing countries. The World Bank.

Zöllner, H. (1987). A European health policy 1980s and 1990s. G. T. Smith (ed). Health Economics: Prospects for the Future. Croom Helm Ltd.

KEY TERMS AND DEFINITIONS

Department of Health: The Department of Health is the Philippine's lead agency in health. The major mandate of DOH is provide national policy direction & develop national plans, technical standards & guidelines on health.

Health: According to the World Health Organization (WHO), "health is more than just the absence of illness or disability, but also is physical, spiritual and social well-being."

Health Economics: Health economics can be defined as the application of the rules of economics to the health services. It can also be defined as the efficient use of the resources allocated to the health sector.

Health Expenditures: According to U.S. National Library of Medicine, health expenditures occurs the amounts spent by individuals, groups, nations, or private or public organizations for total health care and/or its various components. These amounts may or may not be equivalent to the actual costs (Health Care Costs) and may or may not be shared among the patient, insurers, and/or employers.

Health Care System: The World Health Organization defines health care systems as follows: "A health system consists of all organizations, people and actions whose primary intent is to promote, restore or maintain health. This includes efforts to influence determinants of health as well as more direct health-improving activities. A health system is therefore more than the pyramid of publicly owned facilities that deliver personal health services. It includes, for example, a mother caring for a sick child at home; private providers; behavior change programmes; vector-control campaigns; health insurance organizations; occupational health and safety legislation. It includes inter-sectorial action by health staff, for example, encouraging the ministry of education to promote female education, a well-known determinant of better health."

Out-Of-Pocket: OOP is defined as payments made for health care services by patients or households. In general, OOP cost refers health expenses that are not covered by insurance.

Philippine Health Insurance Corporation: Philippine's national health insurance program aiming to provide affordable health care for the population with site location, service and contact information.

Chapter 17
The Analysis of Health Care Expenses of Turkey between 1990-2012

Hayriye Işik
Namık Kemal University, Turkey

Yaşar Akdağ
Hakkari University, Turkey

ABSTRACT

Health is described not only as the absence of disease and disability but also as physically, psychologically, and socially general well-being of people. Best practices of individuals and the society from the health services depend on taking the correct decisions on health policies. In addition, the thought that a country spending much on health services must have a perfect status of health should not be perceived as right. Effectiveness of the spending result in the efficient practices of these services. Although there have been many institutions carrying out the health services, it has been observed that the share separated for the health from the gross domestic product in Turkey increased until 2009 but decreased as of the mentioned year and it has been stated as low compared with the other countries. In this chapter the effectiveness of Turkey's health spending between 1999 and 2012 has been analysed from this view.

INTRODUCTION

Undoubtedly, health care services is the one of the most important requirement for individuals. Providing the health care to community is considering the of the essential government's function. To fulfill society's requirement, government make a high rate of expenditure to provide health care services. But the high level on health spending does not mean always better health condition for society.

Improving the health status and health care services is related the effectiveness of spending rather than quantity. Effectivity of health spending means more people can reach the more qualified health care service to the minimum cost. To achieve this goal the decision makers should define cost effective health policies, and both public and private sector health institutions should managed by this policies. On the other hand the individuals behavior patterns is the one of the other important factor.

DOI: 10.4018/978-1-4666-7484-4.ch017

In this study first determined the research resources of health spending in Turkey. The data of the study was taken the OECD, the World Bank and World Health Organization's statics. And Turkey's health expenses analysed by the spending indications, the ratio of GDP, public and private sectors spending, out of pocket spendings, per capita for different income groups and position among the other countries.

BACKGROUND

When examined the studies about the impact of increasing in health expenses on health status; it has been noticed that the direct increase or deduction of health expenses does not affect health status or average life expectancy in generally. It is observed that in the European Commission report's (2013) a deduction of health expenses due to disruption of public health reducing the preventive health service and it is increasing the health expenses in the long run. According to IMF Fiscal Monitor Report (April 2014) and Joumard, Andre, vand Nicq (2010) and Grigoli an Kapsoli's (2013) estimates shows that 50% increases in the health expenses could lead the one year increase in the average life expectancy. And in this context inefficiencies on health system reduce approximately 2 years of life expectancy based on health. It is suggested that the positive life expectancy outcomes of policies for decrease the inefficiencies on health system by 10% could be equivalent to increase health expenses potentially by 0.7% to GDP . On the other hand as the noted Gaynor (et all, 2012) it has been found an improvement of health outcomes without increasing cost in the England practice which incentive the competition in the hospital sector. But this effectivity only can be for private health expenses. In Turkey most of health expenses provided by public. It can be possible that creating a competitive environment lead to negative results because the low access to preventive and curative health services in developing countries such as Turkey. Therefore it can be mentioned that the interventions for health such as increasing and deduction of health expenses or creation a competitive health sector has negative effect on health status. It has been estimated that public health expenses increase by 3.5% to 4% in OECD countries according to OECD health systems report (2010). Beside the limit for increasing in the health expenses, the effectivity of health expenses become more important because of rapidly aging population and increases in medical technology device prices.

AN ANALYSIS OF TURKEY'S HEALTH SPENDING

In Turkey, the statistics of health spending and other statistics on health are published by the Turkish Statistical Institute, State Planning Organization, annuals of the Directorate of Refik Saydam Hıfzıssıhha Centre and Social Security Institution[1]. At an international level, the OECD, the World Bank, EUROSTAT and World Health Organization have extensive statistics on health.

As a result of publication of different statistics of health from different institutions in Turkey, a decision was taken to set a coordination for the purpose of standardization and also it was decided that the Turkish Statistics Institution would report the statistics of health spending and these reports would be sent to the international institutions. With the decision taken, other institutions would also support the Turkish Statistics Institution on this issue. In this study, because other units also have current data and for the purpose of reliability of the study, the data of the OECD, the World Bank and the World Health Organization were used in addition to the data of the Turkish Statistics Institution.

As is seen in Table 1, the total health spending was 4 billion 985 million TL in 1999 and increased up to 74 billion 189 million TL in 2012. Similarly, the health spending per capita was 79 TL in 1999 while it was 987 TL in 2012. The data above will be examined in detail below.

Table 1. Indications of the health spending in Turkey 1999 – 2012

	1999	2000	2001	2002	2003	2004	2005	2006	2007	2008	2009	2010	2011	2012
Total Health Spending														
Million TL	4 985	8 248	12396	18774	24279	30021	35359	44069	50904	57740	57911	61678	68607	76358
Million USD Dollar	11790	13140	10052	12389	16159	20975	26205	0599	38864	44364	37493	41067	40919	42376
Health Spending Per Capita														
Turkish Lira(TL)	79	128	190	284	363	443	516	635	725	812	804	845	928	1020
USD Dollar	186	204	154	188	242	310	382	441	553	624	521	563	553	566
The Total Health Spending to Gross Domestic Product Ratio %	4.8	4.9	5.2	5.4	5.3	5.4	5.4	5.8	6.0	6.1	6.1	5.6	5.3	5.4
The Public Health Spending to Total Health Spending Ratio %	61.1	62.9	68.1	70.7	71.9	71.2	67.8	68.3	67.8	73.0	81	78.6	79.6	76.8
The Household Health Spending to Total Health Spending Ratio %	29.1	27.6	22.8	19.8	18.5	19.2	22.8	22.0	21.8	17.4	14.1	16.3	15.4	15.4

Source: T.R. Prime Ministry, News Bulletin of Turkish Statistics Institution, Volume: 34, 18 February 2011, Volume: 15871, 10 October, 2013, Volume: 16161, 5 November, 2014.

As is seen in the Figure 1, when the data previously given as numerical is evaluated as proportionally, it has been observed that the total health spending to the gross domestic product ratio steadily increased until 2009 and then increased numerically but showed falling tendency proportionally to the gross domestic product. However in Turkey especially since 2008 health expenses is increasing but health expenses increasing ratio to GDP is tend to stop and after that tend to down. This situation does not seem significant when associated to the life expectancy of health.

Figure 1. The total health spending to gross domestic product ratio
Source: (T.R. Prime Ministry, Turkey Statistics İnstitution, News Bulletin, Volume: 29-34-15871-16161, 2010–2011-2013-2014.

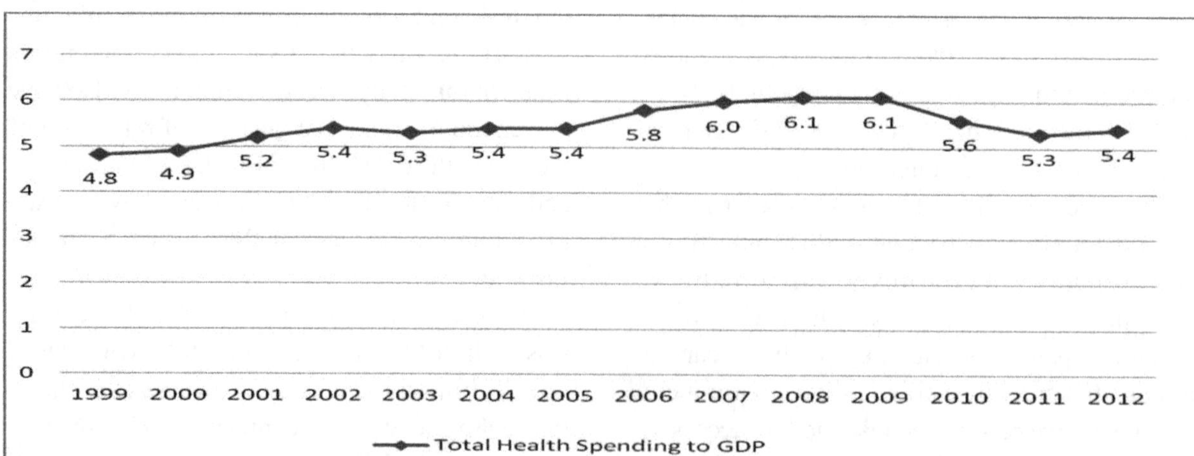

Figure 2. Average life expectancy in Turkey (1999-2012)
Source: Oecd Health Data: (http://stats.oecd.org/index.aspx?DataSetCode=HEALTH_STAT)

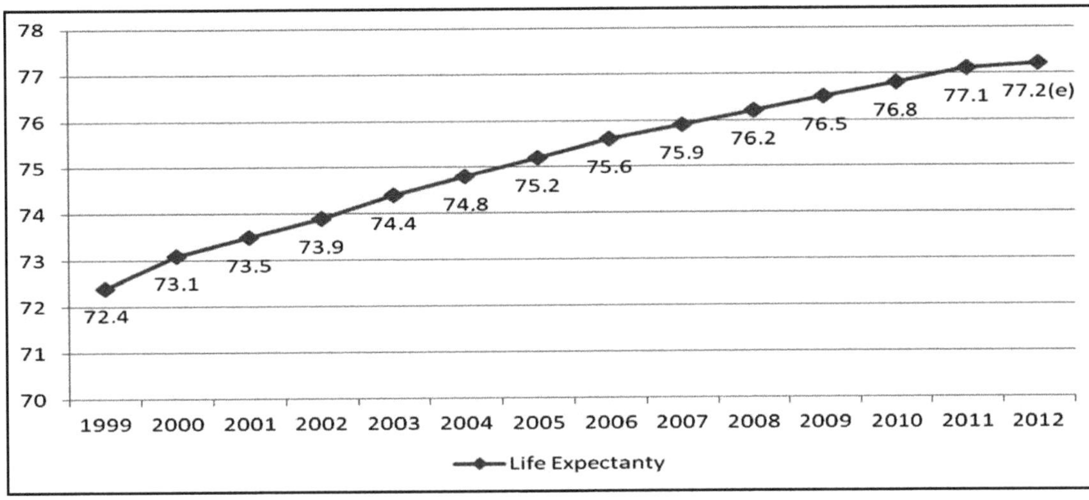

Life expectancy at birth is an important indicator that used to measure to socio-economic development levels, quality of life and mortality levels of countries. This indication can be obtained by life tables. Life expectancy data is collected and published by Turkey Statistical Institute in Turkey. In Figure 2 data was taken from OECD's statistics for integrity. Besides that, Turkey's 2013 life expectancy did not estimated in OECD data set but according to Turkey Statistical Institute data, life expectancy in Turkey for 2013 has been estimated 76,3. Additionally, Turkey Statistical Institute has the ratio of total health expenditure to GDP for 2013. Accordingly, the ratio of total health expenditure to GDP is 5,4 in 2013. Also data for the year 2012 is revised and these ratio (health expenditure / GDP ratio) that indicated earlier 5.4 was drawn to 5.2 by Turkey Statistical Institute.

As is seen in the Figure 2, in 2008 the health expenses ratio to GDP was 6.1% and in 2012 this ratio was decreased to 5.2% but according to OECD data life expectancy in Turkey was 76.2% in 2008 and 77.2 (estimated) in 2012. Between 2000 and 2012 life expectancy in Turkey is increased 3.5 years. The increasing in life expectancy can be explained by more effective health expenses of Turkey and ensuring the large scope of community's utilize the health services instead of increasing or decreasing of health expenses. In fact, recently entered into force "The Transformation Programme on Health" include the purpose of increasing to large scope of community's access on health services. Because in the long term, does not expect any rapid increasing in the health expenses.

The decreasing in the health expenses increase speed have been seen almost all around the world. It is seem that this situation make pressure all countries budgets for future (IMF, 2014: 29). But health reforms mostly are tended to increase the saving instead of effectivity of health expenses. Despite the deduction of health expenses leads to saving in the short run, the deduction of preventive health service and health development causes disruption of basic health services and community health, in the long run and it may cause increase in the public health expenses in the long run (European Commission, 2013). As is seen in Table 2, Korea had the lowest the total health spending to GDP (gross domestic product) ratio and Turkey also follows Korea in 1999. However, according to the data of 2011, Turkey had the lowest the

Table 2. The total health spending to gross domestic product ratio in the countries of OECD (1999-2012)

	1999	2000	2001	2002	2003	2004	2005	2006	2007	2008	2009	2010	2011	2012
Australia	7.8	8.0	8.1	8.4	8.3	8.5	8.5	8.5	8.6	8.8	9.0	8.9		
Austria	10.1	9.9	10.1	10.1	10.3	10.4	10.4	10.2	10.3	10.5	11.2	11.0	10.8	
Belgium	8.1	8.1	8.3	8.5	10.0	10.2	10.0	9.5	9.5	10.1	10.6	10.5 (d)	10.5 (d)	
Canada	8.9	8.8	9.3	9.6	9.8	9.8	9.8	10.0	10.0	10.3	11.4	11.4	11.2	11.2
Chili	6.6	6.6	6.8	6.7	7.5	7.1	6.6	6.3	6.5	7.1	7.9	7.4	7.5	7.6 (e)
Czech Republic	6.6	6.5	6.7	7.1	7.4	7.2	6.9	6.7	6.5	6.8	8.0	7.4	7.5	
Denmark	9.0	8.7	9.1	9.3	9.5	9.7	9.8	9.9	10.0	10.2	11.5	11.1	10.9	
Estonia	5.9	5.3	4.9	4.8	5.0	5.1	5.0	5.0	5.2	6.1	7.0	6.3	5.9	
Finland	7.4	7.2	7.4	7.8	8.2	8.2	8.4	8.3	8.0	8.3	9.2	9.0(e)	9.0(e)	9.1 (e)
France	10.1	10.1	10.2	10.5	10.9	11.0	11.0	11.0	10.9	11.0	11.7	11.7	11.6	
Germany	10.3	10.3	10.4	10.6	10.8	10.6	10.8	10.6	10.5	10.7	11.8	11.5	11.3	
Greece	8.6	7.9	8.8	9.1	8.9	8.7	9.7	9.7	9.8	10.1	10.2	9.5	9.1	
Hungary	7.2	7.0	7.1	7.5	8.3	8.0	8.4	8.3	7.7	7.5	7.7	8.0	7.9	7.8 (e)
Iceland	9.6	9.5	9.3	10.2	10.4	9.9	9.4	9.1	9.1	9.1	9.6	9.3	9.0	8.9 (e)
Ireland	6.1	6.1	6.7	7.1	7.4	7.6	7.6	7.5	7.9	9.1	10.0	9.3	8.9	
Israel	7.5	7.5	8.0	7.9	7.9	7.8	7.9	7.6	7.6	7.7	7.7	7.7	7.7	
Italy	7.8	8.1	8.2	8.3	8.3	8.7	8.7	8.8	8.5	8.9	9.4	9.4	9.2	9.2
Japan	7.5	7.7	7.9	8.0	8.1	8.1	8.2	8.2	8.2	8.6	9.5	9.6		
Korea	4.3	4.5	5.1	4.9	5.2	5.3	5.6	6.1	6.4	6.6	7.1	7.3	7.4	7.5 (e)
Luxemburg	5.8	7.5	7.4	8.3	7.7	8.2	7.9	7.7	7.1	7.2	8.0	7.2	6.6	
Mexico	5.1	5.1	5.5	5.6	5.8	6.0	5.9	5.7	5.8	5.8	6.4	6.2		
Netherland	8.1	8.0	8.3	8.9	9.8	10.0	10.9	10.7	10.8	11.0	11.9	12.1	11.9	
New Zealand	7.5	7.6	7.7	8.0	7.9	8.3	8.4	8.8	8.5	9.3	10.0	10.2	10.3	
Norway	9.3	8.4	8.8	9.8	10.0	9.7	9.0	8.6	8.7	8.6	9.7	9.4	9.3	9.4
Poland	5.7	5.5	5.9	6.3	6.2	6.2	6.2	6.2	6.3	6.9	7.2	7.0	6.9	
Portugal	8.0	9.3	9.3	9.3	9.8	10.1	10.4	10.0	10.0	10.2	10.8	10.8	10.2	
Slovak Republic	5.8	5.5	5.5	5.6	5.8	7.2	7.0	7.3	7.8	8.0	9.2	9.0	7.9	
Slovenia	7.9	8.3	8.6	8.6	8.6	8.4	8.4	8.3	7.9	8.3	9.2	8.9	8.9	8.8 (e)
Spain	7.3	7.2	7.2	7.3	8.2	8.2	8.3	8.4	8.5	8.9	9.6	9.3		
Sweden	8.2	8.2	8.9	9.2	9.3	9.1	9.1	8.9	8.9	9.2	9.9	9.5	9.5	
Switzerland	10.2	10.2	10.6	10.9	11.3	11.3	10.9	10.4	10.2	10.3	11.0	10.9	11.0	11.3 (e)
Turkey	4.8	4.9	5.2	5.4	5.3	5.4	5.4	5.8	6.0	6.1	6.1	5.6	5.3	5.4
United Kingdom	6.9	7.0	7.2	7.6	7.8	8.0	8.3	8.4	8.5	9.0	9.9	9.6	9.4	
United States of America	13.6	13.7	14.3	15.2	15.7	15.7	15.8	15.9	16.2	16.6	17.7	17.7	17.7	

Source: OECD Health Data, November 2011, www.oecd.org, www.worldbank.org.
The Data of 2005 and afterwards have been updated by www.oecd.org

Figure 3. The public health spending and private sector health spending to the total health spending ratio
Source: Turkey statistics institution, news bulletin, Volume: 29, 34, 15871 and 16161, 2010 – 2011- 2013-2014

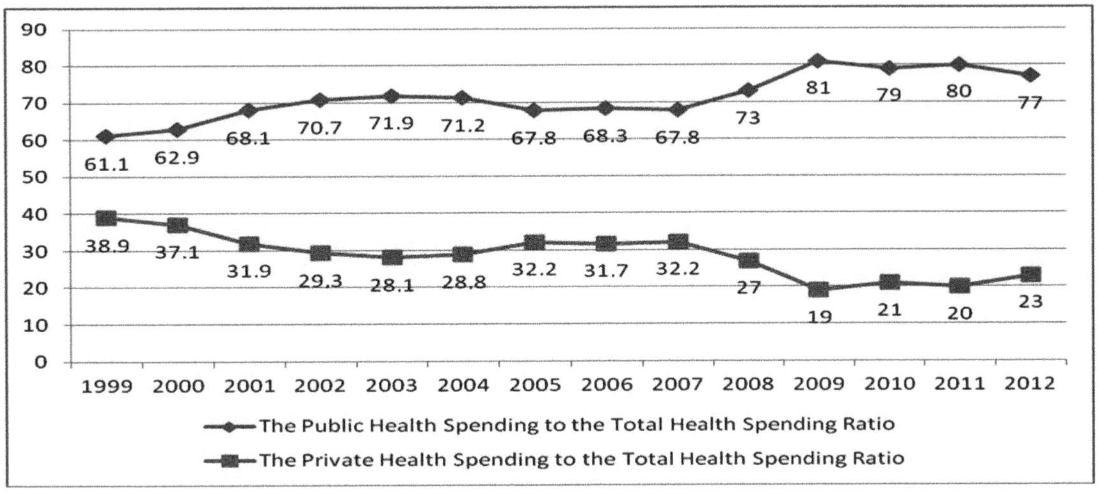

total health spending to GDP ratio. It has been estimated that the rapid development of Turkey and the structural changes conducted in the field of health services will increase this ratio relatively. Although a numerical increase occurred, this rapid development and the structural changes reduced GDP ratio. In many of the OECD countries where regulations were carried out in the field of health services, especially after 2009 the total health spending to GDP ratio reduced. However, in 2009 the total health spending to GDP ratio was 9.6% on average in the OECD countries and also reduced to 9.3% in 2011. Similarly, this ratio was 6.1% in 2009 in Turkey and reduced to 5.3% in 2011 (5.2% in 2012). In Table 2, the mentioned comparison was conducted for the year of 2011 because the data of 2012 of all the countries could not be obtained.

It is of much importance to know the shares of public and private sectors within the total health spending. In Figure 3, the shares of public and private sectors within the total health spending are given separately.

As is seen in Figure 3, of the total health spending 61.1% was met by the public and 38.9% was met by the private sectors in 1999. However these rates were 81% and 19%, respectively. It has been estimated that the highest public share occurred in 2009 as a result of the arrangements carried out in the field of health services. The public share increased in the short period of time; however, it has been stated that the private sector health spending had a tendency in steadily increasing and it has been also estimated that the share of the private sector will increase in the long term when it is considered that many of the arrangements conducted in the field of health services have been oriented to privatization. The share of the private sector within the total health spending in 2012 was 15 billion 404 million TL and at the rate of 21%.

It is of much importance to know the rates of the out-of-pocket expenses as much as the importance of knowing the share of the public and private sector within the total health spending in a country. Being aware of these rates is significant in the social state understanding for indicating that the government fulfills its responsibilities to which degree and also it is important for estimating the burden of the health sector on the public sector (Çelik, 2011: 301). According to IMF report (2010:16) between 2011 and 2030 public health expenses will increase by 1% to GDP in the developing countries and this ratio estimated

Figure 4. Out-of-pocket health spending to the total health spending ratio
Source: Turkey Statistics Institution, News Bulletin, Volume: 29 – 34- 15871-16161, 2010 –2011-2013-2014

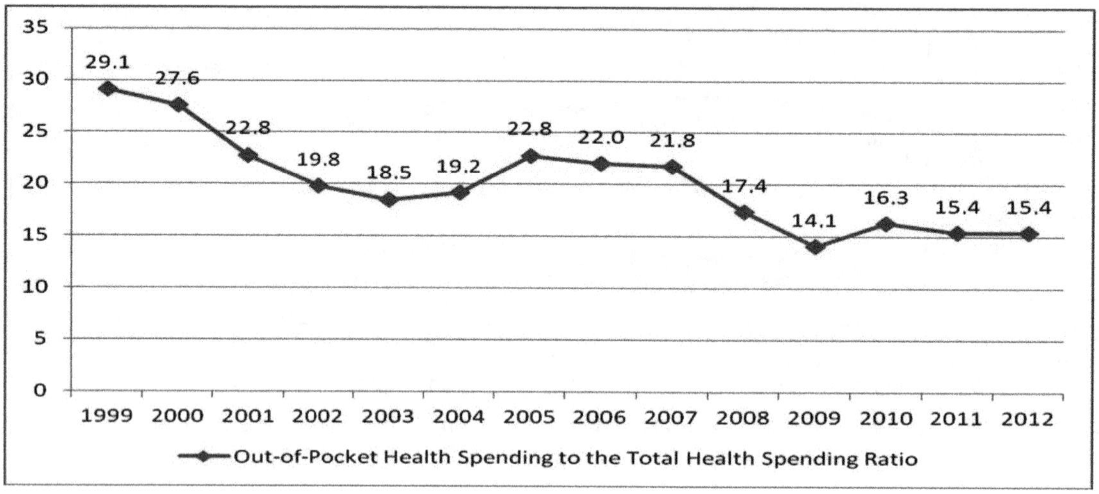

1.3% for Turkey. In the same way OECD is determined this ratio between 3.5% and 4% for 2050. Turkey's macro-economic indicators raises the possibility of this forecast. In fact earlier studies showed that growth have a significant effect on health expenses.

In Turkey, the data of the out-of-pocket expenses was obtained via the household budget questionnaire completed by the Turkish Statistics Institution. As is seen in Figure 4, the out-of-pocket health expenses to the total health spending ratio reduced at 13.7 point from 1999 until 2012 and was calculated as 15.8 in 2012. The OECD average for the out-of-pocket health expenses were determined as 19.6 (OECD Health Statistics, 2013). Steadily reducing of the household out-of-pocket health expenses in Turkey and this rate's being below OECD average and also less leaning of the government to the household compared with most of the OECD countries indicate that the govern-

Figure 5. 2011 Health spending levels of the countries per capita according to the income groups
Source: World Bank (http://www.worldbank.org)

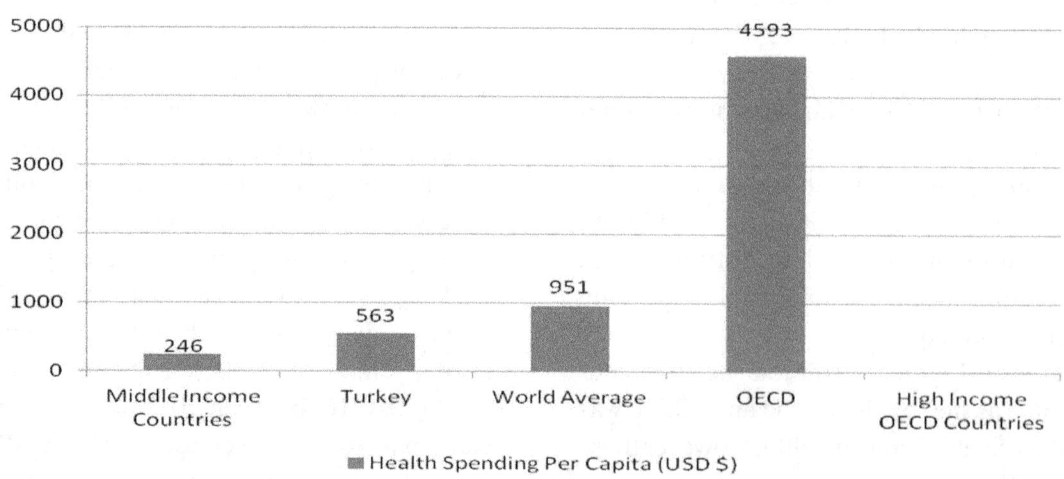

Figure 6. 2012 The distribution of current health expenses to the finance subsidiaries
Source: Turkey Statistics Institution, News Bulletin, Volume: 15871, 2013

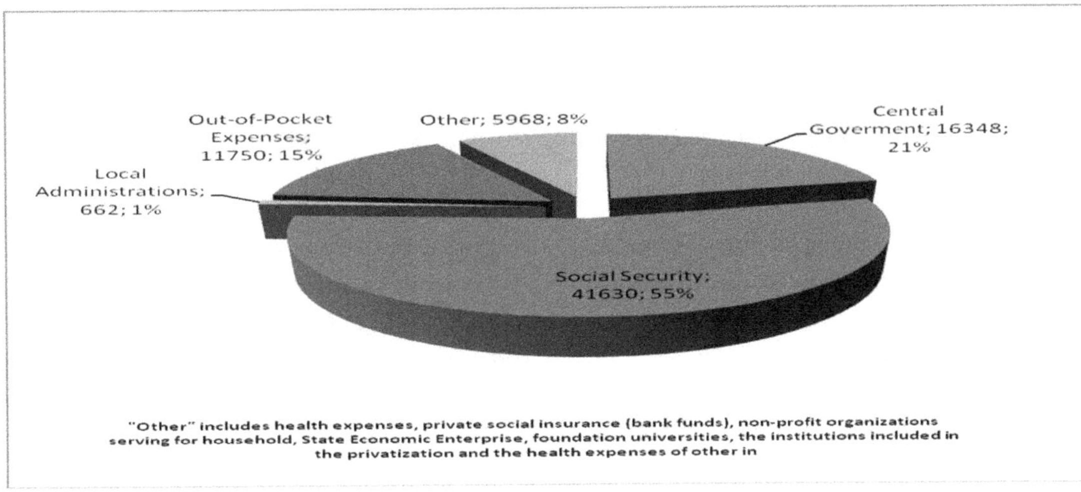

ment act within the framework of social state understanding. However, along with the entering into force and implementation of the provisions of the General Health Insurance in 2012, it has been estimated that especially premium payments of health insurance and patient shares will increase out-of-pocket health expenses.

Comparing the health spending levels of a country in terms of the similar income groups and other income groups is quite important. As is seen in Figure 5 that we prepared by using the data of the World Bank of 2011, there is a correlation between the income level and health expenses of a country. In addition, the total health spending to GDP ratio was 5.3 in Turkey in 2011. The health spending per capita in Turkey is in a better situation compared with middle income countries. However, when compared with the OECD countries, both the health expense per capita and its ratio to GDP is much lower in Turkey.

To determine which institution is effective in health spending, it is required to examine the distribution of total health expenses in terms of the finance subsidiaries. The distribution of total health expenses in Turkey in terms of the finance subsidiaries is given in Figure 6 below.

As is stated previously, the total health expense in 2012 was 76 billion 358 million TL. Of this expense, 72 billion 820 million TL was for the current health expenses and 3 billion 538 million TL was for the investment expense on health. Within the current health expenses, hospitals, nursing care at home, retail sale and other presenters of medical equipment, the presentation and management of public health programs, general health management, insurance and 7 separate items with one category that could not be classified. In 2012, health expense of central government was 16 billion 348 million TL, of local administrations was 662 million TL, of social security institution was 41 billion 630 million TL and of private sector was 17 billion 718 million TL. Here, the key point is the increase of the burden on the Social Security Institution compared with the previous years.

CONCLUSION

In Turkey, health expenses to GDP ratio steadily increase until 2008; however, it was cut down after 2009. According to the analysis conducted with the data of the World Bank, World Health Organization, OECD and Turkey Statistics Institution, the total health sending of Turkey to GDP ratio was 6.1 in 2009 and 5.6 in 2010 and 5.3 in 2011 and 5.2 in 2012. As a result of the current regulations conducted in the field of health services, the health expenses increased numerically; however, the total health expenses to GDP ratio reduced. According to the existent data, the health expense to GDP ratio in Turkey is quite below the average of the OECD. It was thought that the amendments made within the framework of Transformation of Health would increase the health expenses. However, the increase in the health expenses may not be an indication of a better health status. The increase in the health expenses does not always reflected as an improvement in real terms. Particularly, the increase in the expenses in the health systems that are convenient for corruptions does not mean that the accesses to these services also have advanced. There exist countries that have less health expense and have much better health status compared with the countries that have much health expense. This shows us that only health expenses are not a measure for health status. Efficient use of the expenses is significant. Also, the regulations conducted in the field of health services in Turkey reduced the health expenses (GDP%) rather than increasing. The decreases in these numbers indicate an improvement in the mentioned services. Indeed in the most of earlier studies it was estimated that the inefficiency of health expenses have negative effect on average life expectancy and reducing this inefficiency has equal to increasing health expenses to a level. Saving in the health expenses also reducing the expenses but this may cause disruption of preventive health service and effect common health in negative way.

Reducing expenses could pressure in curative health services so without a good analysis process, decrease in the expenses can be conduct increase in the expenses in the long run. So it is inconvenient to saving by health spending on an important issue such as health. In recent years it was observed that even though decreasing in the health expenses level to GDP, life expectancy is increasing in Turkey. This observation could be show the importance of effectivity which described above. According to the estimates (OECD, 2010) for future years (to 2050), and in the light of available data, there is no other way except provide the effectivity in the health expenses because of the limited increase ability of the public health expenses, rapidly aging population and the technology used in the health services become expensive. However it should be considered that dangerous consequences of competition and excessive marketing for health services while provide the effectivity for health expenses. In fact the "Transformation Programme on Health" in Turkey have been criticized for encouraging to commercialization and marketing of health care services. At this point, it is important to establishment of public balance in terms of service priority for access to health service while providing the effectivity in health care services.

Health expenditure topics such as relations between economic growth rate and health spending, the discrimination of public and private health expenditures, the effect of health expenses on life expectancy are promising research topic for developing counties. Macroeconomic balance of the economy, social- economic development, social security approach is extremely significant for public health and associated with health policy. Actually, not only Turkey but also for all developing country the health expenditures has importance. It is recommended for researchers who will work on this issue to use multiple sources and compares the world and local data.

REFERENCES

Çelik, Y. (2011). *Sağlık Ekonomisi*. Ankara: Siyasal Bookstore.

European Commission. (2013). Report on Public Finances in European Monetary Union European Economy (No.4/2013). Brussels: Directorate General for Economic and Financial Affairs.

Grigoli, F., & Kapsoli, J. (2013), *Waste Not, Want Not: The Efficiency of Health Expenditure in Emerging and Developing Countries* (IMF Working Paper 13/87). Washington.

IMF (2010). *Macro-Fiscal Implications of Health Care Reform in Advanced and Emerging Economies.*

IMF (2014). *Fiscal Monitor.* April 2014.

Joumard, I., Andre, C., & Nicq, C. (2010), *Health Care Systems: Efficiency and Institutions* (Working Paper No. 769). Paris: Economics Department, Organisation for Economic Co-operation and Development.

OECD. (2010). *Health Care Systems: Efficiency and Policy Settings.* OECD Publishing.

OECD. (2013). *Health at a Glance, OECD Indicators.* Retrieved from http://www.oecd-ilibrary.org/social-issues-migration-health/health-at-a-glance-2013_health_glance-2013-en

OECD. (2011, November), *OECD Health Data.* Retrieved from www.oecd.org

Turkey Statistics Institution (2012, April), *Türkiye İstatistik Yıllığı 2011.* Ankara: Turkey Statistics Institution Printing.

Turkey Statistics Institution News Bulletin. (2010, February). *Sağlık Harcama İstatistikleri 2007.* Ankara: World Bank Statics. Retrieved from, www.worldbank.org

Turkey Statistics Institution News Bulletin (2011, February). *Sağlık Harcama İstatistikleri 2008.* Ankara.

Turkey Statistics Institution News Bulletin (2013, October). *Sağlık Harcama İstatistikleri 2009 2010 2011, 2012.* Ankara.

Turkey Statistics Institution News Bulletin. (2014, November). *Sağlık Harcama İstatistikleri 2013.* Retrieved from http://www.tuik.gov.tr/PreHaberBultenleri.do?id=16161

World Health Organization. (n.d.). Retrieved from, www.who.org

ADDITIONAL READING

Akdağ, Y. (2012). The Measurement of Effect of Health Expenditures on Quality of Life: The Case of Denizli, Unpublished master's thesis, University of Pamukkale, Denizli.

Altay, A. (2007). Sağlık Hizmetlerinin Sunumunda Yeni Açılımlar ve Türkiye Açısından Değerlendirilmesi. *Journal of Court of Accounts, 64*, 33–58.

Arrow, K. J. (1963). Uncertainty and the Welfare Economics of Medical Care. *The American Economic Review, 53*(5), 941–973.

Başar, D., Brown, S., & Hole, A. R. (2012). *Out-of-Pocket Health Care Expenditure in Turkey: Analysis of the Household Budget.* Sheffield Economic Research Paper Series. Retrieved June 12, 2014, from http://eprints.whiterose.ac.uk/74495/1/serps_2012020.pdf

Belek, İ. (2009). *Sağlığın Politik Ekonomisi (Sosyal Devletin Çöküşü).* İstanbul: Yazılama Bookstore.

Berger, M., & Messer, J. (2002). Public Financing of Health Expenditure, Insurance, and Health Outcomes. *Applied Economics, 34*(17), 2105–2113. doi:10.1080/00036840210135665

Blomqvist, A., & Carter, R. (1997). Is Health Care Really a Luxury? *Journal of Health Economics, 16*(2), 207–229. doi:10.1016/S0167-6296(96)00534-6 PMID:10169095

Burman, L. E., & Phaup, M. (2012, June). Tax Expenditures, the Size Efficiency of Government, and Implications for Budget Reform. *Tax Policy and the Economy, 26*(1), 93–124. doi:10.1086/665504

Ceritoğlu, E. (2012). *Health Expenditures Risk, Purchase of Private Health Insurance, and Precautionary Saving in Turkey*. Central Bank of the Republic of Turkey, Retrieved April 12, 2014, from, http://www.tcmb.gov.tr/research/discus/2012/WP1222.pdf

Clements, B. J., Coady, D., & Gupta, S. (Eds.). (2012). *The Economics of Public health Care Spending in Advanced and Emerging Economies*. Washington: International Monetary Fund.

Commission on Macroeconomics and Health. (2001). *Macroeconomics and Health: Investing in Health for Economic Development*. Retrieved April 4, 2014 from http://whqlibdoc.who.int/publications/2001/924154550x.pdf

Cremieux, P. Y., Oulette, P., & Pilon, C. (2000). Health Care Spending As Determinants of Health Outcomes. *Health Economics*, *8*(7), 627–639. doi:10.1002/(SICI)1099-1050(199911)8:7<627::AID-HEC474>3.0.CO;2-8 PMID:10544328

Cutler, D. M., & Sahni, N. R. (2013). If Slow Rate of Health Care Spending Growth Persists, Projections May Be Off by $770 Billion. *Health Affairs*, *32*(5), 841–850. doi:10.1377/hlthaff.2012.0289 PMID:23650316

Deloitte. (2012, June). *Turkey Life Science and Healthcare Report*. Retrieved from, http://www.yased.org.tr/webportal/English/haberler/basin_bultenleri/Documents/Turkey_Life_Science_and_Healthcare_Report_2013_02_28.pdf

Evans, D. B., & Associates. (2000). *The Comperative Efficiency of National Health Systems in Producing Health: An Analysis of 191 Countries* . (GPE Discussion Paper Series, No. 29). Geneva: WHO.

Feldstein, P. J. (2007). *Health Policy Issues, an Economic Perspective*. Washington, D.C.: Aupha Press.

Gaynor, M., Propper, C., & Seiler, S. (2012), *Free to Choose? Reform and Demand Response in the English National Health Service* (NBER Working Paper, No.18574). Cambridge, Massachusetts: National Bureau of Economic Research.

Gupta, S. (2010). Effects of Development Assistance on Domestic Health Expenditure. *Lancet*, *376*(9741), 593–594. doi:10.1016/S0140-6736(10)61297-4 PMID:20728755

Hatwig, J. (2008). What Drive Health Care Expenditure? - Boumol's Model of 'Unbalanced Growth' Revisited. *Journal of Health Economics*, *27*(3), 603–623. doi:10.1016/j.jhealeco.2007.05.006 PMID:18164773

Hunter, R. (2013). Turkey's Health Care Reform: The 2023 Challenge. *Turkish Policy Quarterly*, *12*(2). Retrieved from, http://www.turkishpolicy.com/dosyalar/files/vol_12-no_2-hunter.pdf

Hurst, J. (2002). Performance measurement and improvement in OECD health systems: Overview of issues and challenges. In *Measuring Up: Improving Health System Performance in OECD Countries*. Paris: OECD.

Hussey, P. S., de Vries, H., Romely, J., Wang, M. C., Chen, S. S., Shekelle, P. G., & McGlynn, E. A. (2009). A Systematic Review of Health Care Efficiency Measures. *Health Services Research*, *44*(3), 784–805. doi:10.1111/j.1475-6773.2008.00942.x PMID:19187184

Joumard, I., André, C., Nicq, C., & Chatal, O. (2008). *Health Status Determinants: Lifestyle, Environment, Health Care Resources and Efficiency* (Economics Department Working Papers, No. 627). Paris: OECD.

Mathauer, I., & Wittenbecher, F. (2013). Hospital Payment Systems Based on Diagnosis-Related Groups: Experiences in Low- and Middle- income Countries. *Bulletin of the World Health Organization*, *91*(10), 746–756. doi:10.2471/BLT.12.115931 PMID:24115798

Mladovsky, P., Srivastava, D., Cylus, J., Karanikolos, M., Evetovits, T., Thomson, S., & Mckee, M. (2012). Health Policy Responses to the Financial Crisis in Europe. In European Observatory on Health Systems and Policies and Health Evidence Network (No. 5). Copenhagen: World Health Organisation Regional Office for Europe.

Morgan, D., & Astolfi, R. (2013), *Health Spending Growth at Zero* (Health Working Paper, No. 60) Paris: OECD.

Mutlu, A. (2006). Küresel Kamusal Mallar Bağlamında Sağlık Hizmetleri ve Çevre Kirlenmesi: Üretim, Finansman veYönetim Sorunları. *Journal of Public Finance*, *150*, 53–78.

Mutlu, A., & Işık, A. (2012). *Sağlık Ekonomisine Giriş*. Bursa: Ekin Bookstore.

OECD. (2010 October). *Improving Value in Health Care: Measuring Quality*. Forum on Quality of Care, Paris. Retrieved June 24, 2014 from http://www.oecd.org/health/ministerial/46098506.pdf

OECD. (2014). *How Does Turkey Compare? OECD Health Statistics 2014*. Retrieved June 24, 2014 from, http://www.oecd.org/els/health-systems/Briefing-Note-TURKEY-2014.pdf

OECD, World Bank. (2008). *OECD Sağlık Sistemleri İncelemeleri, Türkiye*. Retrieved from, http://siteresources.worldbank.org/TURKEYINTURKISHEXTN/Resources/455687-1235059017165/OECDReviewsOfHealthSystemsTurkey-tr.pdf

Penner, S. (2003). *Introduction to Health Care Economics and Financial Management: Fundamental Concepts with Practical Application*. Philadelphia: Lippincolt Williams and Wilkins.

Pritchett, L., & Summers, L. H. (1996). Wealthier is Healthier. *The Journal of Human Resources*, *31*(4), 841–868. doi:10.2307/146149

Ryu, A. J., Gibson, T. B., McKellar, M. R., & Chernew, M. (2013). The Slowdown in Health Care Spending in 2009-11 Reflected Factors Other than the Weak Economy and Thus May Persist. *Health Affairs*, *32*(5), 835–840. doi:10.1377/hlthaff.2012.1297 PMID:23650315

Samuelson, P. A. (1958). The Pure Theory of Public Expenditure. *The Review of Economics and Statistics*, *36*(4), 387–389. doi:10.2307/1925895

Savedoff, W. (2003). How Much Should Countries Spend on Health? (WHO Discussion Paper, 2.) Geneva. Retrieved July 2, 2014 from, http://www.who.int/health_financing/en/how_much_should_dp_03_2.pdf

Snow, W. F. (1921, July). Federal Expenditures for Public Health. *Proceedings of the Academy of Political Science in the City of New York*, *9*(3), 194–198. doi:10.2307/1172189

Stiglitz, J. E. (2000). *Economics of the Public Sector*. New York: W.W. Norton & Company Inc.

Sulku, S. N., & Bernard, D. M. (2012). Financial Burden of Health Care Expenditures: Turkey. *Iranian Journal of Public Health*, *41*(3), 48–64. PMID:23113149

Tokgöz, E. (1987). İktisat Biliminin Yeni Uygulama Alanı: Sağlık Ekonomisi. *Journal of Istanbul University Faculty of Economics*, *45*(1-4), 12–20.

Wendt, C. (2009). Mapping European Health Care Systems: A Comperative Analysis of Financing, Service Provision and Access to Healthcare. *Journal of European Social Policy*, *19*(5), 432–445. doi:10.1177/0958928709344247

WHO. (2013, August). Research for Universal Coverage: World Health Report, Retrieved June 2, 2013,Retrieved from, http://apps.who.int/iris/bitstream/10665/85761/2/9789240690837_eng.pdf?ua=1

WHO. (2014). World Health Statistics, Retrieved July 4, 2014, Retrieved from, http://www.who.int/gho/publications/world_health_statistics/2014/en/

Wolf, C. (1993). *Markets or Governments, Choosing between Imperfect Alternatives*. Cambridge: MIT Press.

KEY TERMS AND DEFINITIONS

Effectiveness: Effectiveness is defined to achieve the intended results.

Efficiency: Efficiency can be defined as optimization of resources. In this chapter efficiency refers the least waste of health sources.

GDP: The monetary value of all the finished goods and services produced within a country's borders in a specific time period.

Health Economics: Health economics is a branch of economics which aims to produce using the highest level of health care with most economical (efficient, effective, rational) resources allocated to health sector and crates best way to divide them for community and the members of social groups.

Health Spending Per Capita: Portion of total health expenditure for each individual person.

Health Spending: All of spending which aim to protect the health promotion or prevention, improvement, maintenance, nutrition and emergency programs are regarded as health spending.

Life Expectancy: Life expectancy is a statistical indicator that showed life time for an infant. The Turkey Statistical Institute defines as the average life years for an infant which exposed to age specific mortality rate in a specific periods during the life time.

Out-Of-Pocket Health Spending: OOP is defined as payments made by the patient directly or households.

Private Sector Health Spending: The spending which held by economy that is not state controlled, and is run by individuals and companies for profit.

Public Health Spending: The part of health spending hat is run completely by the government.

ENDNOTES

1 Directorate of Refik Saydam Hıfzıssıhha Centre, was repealed in the recent organization structure of the Ministry of Health.

Chapter 18
Financial Development and Energy Consumption in Turkey:
Empirical Evidence from Cointegration and Causality Tests

Murat Çetin
Namık Kemal University, Turkey

Eyyup Ecevit
Erciyes University, Turkey

Fahri Seker
Bozok University, Turkey

Davuthan Günaydin
Namık Kemal University, Turkey

ABSTRACT

This chapter investigates the cointegration and causal relationship between financial development and energy consumption in the case of Turkey over the period 1960-2011. In doing so, the ARDL bounds testing and Johansen-Juselius approaches to cointegration and Granger causality test based on vectorerror correction model are employed. The empirical results show that the series are cointegrated. The empirical results also show a positive and statistically significant relationship between financial development and energy consumption in the long run. In addition, a unidirectional causality running from financial development to energy consumption is found in the short and long run. Thus, this chapter provides an empirical evidence that financial development is a determinant of energy consumption in Turkey. This chapter also presents some implications for Turkey's energy policy.

INTRODUCTION

Investigating the determinants of demand for energy has been a major focus of research topic in developing countries for several reasons. Firstly, since energy is a key factor of the production, its resources may affect economic growth and development of a country (Squalli, 2007; Stern, 2010). Secondly, some developing countries such as Turkey, China and India have been growing

DOI: 10.4018/978-1-4666-7484-4.ch018

rapidly. This increases the demand for energy in those countries. As indicated in Turkey report presented by US Energy Information Administration (2013) Turkey has witnessed the fastest growth in energy demand over the last two years in the OECD. In addition, Turkey which imports majority of its oil, natural gas and hard coal supplies is expected to double energy demand over the next decade. Thus, it is very important issue to deal with the dynamics of energy consumption for Turkish economy.

Turkey has also implemented a macroeconomic strategy regarding cautious structural and fiscal reforms since 2002. Through this strategy, Turkey has been one of the major recipients of foreign direct investment (FDI) and integrated with the globalized world economy accelerated by Turkey's EU accession process. One of the main aims of these structural and fiscal reforms is to increase the efficiency and resiliency of the financial sector. These reforms have reinforced the macroeconomic structure of the country. Therefore Turkey has experienced rapid economic growth between 2002 and 2012 with an average annual real GDP growth of 5 percent. These significant improvements in the Turkish economy have also enhanced foreign trade. Turkey's exports reached USD 151.7 billion by the end of 2013, up from USD 36 billion in 2002 (OECD, 2013; Macroeconomic Outlook Report, 2012). Thus, as well as demand for energy, financial development, economic growth and foreign trade appear as important policy dynamics of Turkish economy.

In recent years, the role of financial development as a determinant of energy consumption has been investigated in energy literature (Sadorsky, 2010a; Shahbaz & Lean, 2012; Islam, Shahbaz, Ahmed & Alam, 2013; Mudakkar, Zaman, Shakir, Arif & Naseen, 2013; Coban & Topcu, 2013). However, as seen from Table 1, none of the previous studies examine this relationship in the case of Turkey in spite of the considerable increases both in its financial development and demand for energy in the last decade. Therefore, this study basically investigates the long-run and causal relationship between financial development and energy consumption by adding real income and trade openness as potential determinants to function for energy consumption in Turkey over the period 1960-2011.

In this study, firstly, using the ARDL bounds testing and Johansen-Juselius approaches to cointegration, we have tested the long-run relationship between the variables. Secondly, we have tested the causal relationships by Granger causality test based on vector error-correction model (VECM). The study is a single country analysis. Since there is limited empirical evidence on the link between financial development and energy consumption for Turkish economy, this study is expected to make a contribution to the existing literature and reveal some policy implications. Especially, if financial development is found to affect energy consumption then this relationship can affect energy policies of Turkish economy.

LITERATURE REVIEW

The literature examining the dynamics of energy consumption first focuses on the link between economic growth and energy consumption (Wandji, 2013; Shahbaz, Zeshan & Afza, 2012). Theoretically, growth hypothesis implies that decreasing energy consumption may reduce economic growth, whereas the conservation hypothesis suggests a causality running from economic growth to energy consumption (Squalli, 2007; Stern, 2010). Payne (2010) and Wandji (2013) suggest uni-directional causality running from energy consumption to economic growth, whereas Belloumi (2009); Shahbaz et al. (2012) and Bozoklu & Yilanci (2013) reveal bi-directional causality between the variables. On the other hand, several studies (e.g. Ghani, 2013; Sadorsky, 2012; Shahbaz, Nasreen & Ling, 2013) examine the relationship between foreign trade (trade openness) and energy consumption. Ghani (2013) investigating the impact of liberalization on energy consumption shows an empirical evidence that trade liberalization does not affect energy consumption in developing countries. In the long run, Sadorsky (2012) using panel data techniques for 7 South American countries finds bidirectional causality between foreign trade and energy consumption. Employing panel data methodologies for 91 high, middle and low income countries, Shahbaz et al. (2013a) suggest bi-directional causality between trade openness and energy consumption in the long run.

In energy literature, the relationship between financial development and energy consumption has been recently investigated by several studies (e.g. Shahbaz, Islam & Islam, 2010; Sadorsky, 2011; Al-Mulali & Lee, 2013). Financial development implies a country's decision to allow and promote financial activities. These include increases in foreign direct investment, banking and stock market activity (Sadorsky, 2011). It is accepted as one of the key elements of economic development. According to several researches (e.g. Goldsmith, 1969; McKinnon, 1973; Shaw, 1973; Levin, 1997) financial development may increase the efficiency of capital accumulation, the country's saving and investment. Therefore, it has a positive effect on economic growth. In addition, financial development may promote financial innovation and the adoption of advanced technology (Baier, Dwyer & Tamura, 2004; Shahbaz, 2012).

Financial development may also enhance the economic efficiency of a financial system. This creates a number of advantages including a reduction in borrowing costs and financial risk, access to greater financial capital and the newest energy-efficient products. Thus, it may affect economic activity and energy demand of a country (Sadorsky, 2010a; 2011). Islam et al. (2013) suggest that financial development encourage industrial growth and generates demand for new infrastructure. Therefore, it positively affects energy consumption. Sadorsky (2011) explains how financial development might influence the demand for energy in great detail. Firstly, a developed financial system facilitates consumers' borrowing for their wants and needs. This is called as direct effect. Secondly, when there is improved financial development, businesses can access to financial capital easily and cheaply. This is known as business effect. Thirdly, financial development increases stock market activity and therefore develops stock market. A developed stock market generally affects the confidence of consumers and businesses. This may create a wealth effect. So, economic activity and the demand for energy may increase through these three effects (Sadorsky, 2011).

In twenty-two emerging economies Sadorsky (2010a) finds that the impact of financial development on energy consumption is positive and statistically significant in the long-run. Employing the data from 9 Central and Eastern European frontier economies and system GMM approach, Sadorsky (2011) shows the same result. Similarly, in Pakistan Shahbaz et al. (2010), in Tunisia Shahbaz & Lean (2012), in Malaysia Tang & Tan (2014), and in Malaysia Islam et al. (2013) reveal a significant and positive effect of financial development on energy consumption. They also find a bi-directional casual relation between the variables. In Pakistan Mudakkar et al. (2013), in 19 selected countries Al-Mulali & Sab (2012a) and in China Shahbaz, Khan & Tahir (2013) show the same causality findings. In Malaysia Islam, Shahbaz & Alam (2011), in China Zang, Fan & Chang (2011), in Sri Lanka and India Mudakkar et al. (2013) show a unidirectional causality running from financial development to energy consumption.

Al-Mulali & Sab (2012b) indicate that energy consumption increases financial development in the long-run for 30 Sub-Saharan African countries. Coban & Topcu (2013) find no significant relationship between the variables in the EU27. However, the empirical results present an evidence of the impact of the financial development on energy consumption in the old members. Using the panel data from selected SAARC countries,

Table 1. Summary of the studies on financial development-energy consumption relation

Authors	Country	Period	Financial Development Indicators	Methodology	Results
Shahbaz & Lean (2012)	Tunisia	1971-2008	Domestic credit to private sector	ARDL, Johansen, VECM	FD ↔ EC FD has positive effect on EC
Islam et al. (2013)	Malaysia	1971-2009	Domestic credit to private sector	ARDL, VECM	FD ↔ EC FD has positive effect on EC
Tang & Tan (2014)	Malaysia	1972-2009	Money and quasi money, liquid liabilities, domestic credit to private sector, domestic credit provided by the banking sector	ARDL, Johansen, VECM	FD ↔ EC FD has positive effect on EC
Zang et al. (2011)	China	1992-2009	Stock market scale	Granger causality	FD → EC
Shahbaz et al. (2013b)	China	1971-2011	Domestic credit to private sector	ARDL, Johansen, VECM	EC → FD
Mudakkar et al. (2013)	SAARC countries	1975-2011	Money and quasi money, liquid liabilities, domestic credit claims on private sector, domestic credit provided by the banking sector	Johansen, Toda-Yamamoto and Dolado-Lutkephol	FD ↔ EC in Pakistan FD → EC in India and Sri Lanka
Sadorsky (2011)	Central and Eastern European countries	1996-2006	Financial system deposits, deposit money bank assets, liquid liabilities, deposit money bank assets, private credit by deposit money banks	Panel system GMM	FD has positive effect on EC
Sadorsky (2010a)	22 Emerging countries	1990-2006	FDI, deposit money bank assets, stock market capitalization, stock market total value traded, stock market turnover ratio	Panel system GMM	FD has positive effect on EC
Coban &Topcu (2013)	EU countries	1990-2011	Deposit money bank assets, financial system deposits, liquid liabilities, private credit, concentration ratio, stock market capitalization	Panel system GMM	FD has positive effect on EC
Al-Mulali & Sab (2012a)	19 selected countries	1980-2008	Broad money, domestic credit provided by banking sector, domestic credit to private sector	Pedroni cointegration, Panel Granger	FD↔EC
Al-Mulali & Sab (2012b)	Sub-Saharan countries	1980-2008	Broad money, domestic credit to the private sector	Pedroni cointegration, Panel Granger	FD ↔ EC EC has positive effect on FD
Al-Mulali & Lee (2013)	GCC countries	1980-2009	Domestic credit to private sector	Pedroni cointegration, Panel VECM, Panel DOLS	FD ↔ EC FD has positive effect on EC
Khan et al. (2013)	SAARC countries	1975-2011	Broad money, liquid liabilities, domestic credit provided by banking sector and domestic credit to private sector	Pedroni cointegration, Pooled regressions	FD has positive effect on EC

Note: The results show the long run findings. → indicates a one way causal relationship, and ↔ indicates a bi-directional causal relationship. FDis financial development and ECis energy consumption.

Khan, Khan, Zaman, Khan & Zahoor (2013) find that financial development has a larger impact on increasing energy consumption, followed by GDP per capita and FDI. They also indicate a unidirectional causality from energy consumption to financial development in Nepal. Finally, in GCC countries Al-Mulali & Lee (2013) show that financial development increases energy consumption in the short and long-run.

The rest of this study is organized as follows. Section 2 reviews the literature. Section 3 describes data and empirical specification. Section 4 presents econometric methodology used in the study. Empirical findings are reported in Section 5. Section 6 concludes the study.

DATA AND EMPIRICAL SPECIFICATION

In this study, the relationship between financial development, real income, trade openness and energy consumption is investigated. We employ annual data covering the period 1960-2011 taken from the World Development Indicators (WDI) online database (2013). The sample is selected on the basis of data availability for Turkey. All data are transformed to natural logarithmic because log-linear specification provides a better result compared with the linear functional form. Modified from Islam et al. (2013); Mudakkar et al. (2013) and Shahbaz & Lean (2012), the consumption function for energy can be expressed as follows:

$$lnEC_t = \alpha_0 + \alpha_1 lnGDP_t + \alpha_2 lnFD_t + \alpha_3 lnTR_t + \varepsilon_t \quad (1)$$

where *EC* is per capita energy consumption (kg of oil equivalent) and *FD* is financial development. Domestic credit provided by banking sector as share of GDP (*FD1*), domestic credit to private sector as share of GDP (*FD2*) and money and quasi money as share of GDP (*FD3*) are the proxies for financial development (Khan et al., 2013; Mudakkar et al., 2013). Therefore, we will investigate the relationship between financial development and energy consumption for three cases. *GDP* is per capita real income (constant 2005 international dollars) and measures the economic growth (Shahbaz & Lean, 2012). *TR* is trade openness (foreign trade, % of GDP) (Sadorsky, 2012; Shahbaz et al., 2013b). α_1, α_2 and α_3 are the slope coefficients and ε_t is the error term assumed to be normally distributed with zero mean and constant variance. Table 2 presents the descriptive statistics and correlation matrix of the variables used in the analysis. The results of correlation matrix indicate the existence of a positive link between financial development and energy consumption. Energy consumption also is positively correlated with economic growth and trade openness. The results also show a positive association between all the independent variables.

METHODOLOGY

We apply the ARDL bounds testing procedure developed by Pesaran, Shin & Smith (2001) to establish the existence of cointegration relationship between the variables owing to its many advantages over the alternatives. Firstly, according to standard cointegration methods such as Engle-

Table 2. Descriptive statistics and correlation matrix(1960-2011,Observ.:52)

Statistics/Variables	ln*EC*	ln*GDP*	ln*FD1*	ln*FD2*	ln*FD3*	ln*TR*
Mean	6.698	8.393	3.486	2.942	3.294	3.187
Std. dev.	0.394	0.355	0.306	0.275	0.353	0.661
Min.	5.951	7.747	2.968	2.540	2.680	1.744
Max.	7.354	9.037	4.243	3.911	4.027	4.032
ln*EC*	1.000					
ln*GDP*	0.992	1.000				
ln*FD1*	0.669	0.696	1.000			
ln*FD2*	0.581	0.619	0.694	1.000		
ln*FD3*	0.926	0.939	0.778	0.697	1.000	
ln*TR*	0.923	0.907	0.560	0.449	0.869	1.000

Granger (1987) and Johansen-Juselius (1990) the variables should be integrated at unique level of integration. Whereas, the ARDL can be applied irrespective of whether the regressors are $I(0)$ or $I(1)$. Secondly, it is possible to estimate the short and long-run parameters of the model simultaneously through an unrestricted error correction model (UECM) derived from the ARDL model. So, the UECM integrates the short-run dynamics with the long-run equilibrium. Thirdly, the ARDL provides more robust and better results for finite and small sample sizes. Finally, all the variables are assumed to be endogenous in this procedure (Pesaran & Shin, 1999; Panopoulou & Pittis, 2004). The equation of UECM for the ARDL bounds approach is modelled as:

$$\Delta lnEC_t = \beta_0 + \sum_{i=1}^{m}\beta_{1i}\Delta lnEC_{t-i} + \sum_{i=0}^{m}\beta_{2i}\Delta lnGDP_{t-i} + \sum_{i=0}^{m}\beta_{3i}\Delta lnFD_{t-i} + \sum_{i=0}^{m}\beta_{4i}\Delta lnTR_{t-i} + \gamma_1 lnEC_{t-1} + \gamma_2 lnGDP_{t-1} + \gamma_3 lnFD_{t-1} + \gamma_4 lnTR_{t-1} + \mu_t \quad (2)$$

where β_0 is the drift component and μ_t is error term assumed to be independently and identically distributed. The coefficients of γ_1, γ_2, γ_3 and γ_4 denote the long run relationship while the coefficients of β_1, β_2, β_3 and β_4 represent the error correction dynamics in Eq. (2).

In the first stage of the ARDL bounds testing procedure, we estimate the Eq. (2) by ordinary least square (OLS) method. Here, the F-statistic is calculated for joint significance of the coefficients of the lagged level of the variables to test the null hypothesis of no cointegration $H_0: \gamma_1 = \gamma_2 = \gamma_3 = \gamma_4 = 0$ against the alternative of $H_1: \gamma_1 \neq \gamma_2 \neq \gamma_3 \neq \gamma_4 \neq 0$. We compare the computed F-statistic with the critical bounds developed by Pesaran et al. (2001) to determine the existence of a long-run relationship among the variables. These are known as the upper critical bound (UCB) and lower critical bound (LCB). If the computed F-statistic is higher than the UCB, then there exists a long-run relationship between the variables. There is no a long-run relationship between the variables if the computed F-statistic is less than the LCB. If the computed F-statistic falls between the LCB and UCB, it is said that the result is inconclusive. Some diagnostic tests can be applied to investigate the robustness of the ARDL model. These tests check normality of error term, serial correlation, functional form and heteroscedisticity. In addition, we conduct the cumulative sum of recursive residuals (CUSUM) and squares of sum of recursive residuals (CUSUMsq) tests developed by Brown, Durbin & Evans (1975) to test the stability of the ARDL parameters.

The long-run relationship between the variables can be estimated after the selection of the ARDL model by SBC or AIC. An alternative way to determine the existence of a long-run relationship between the variables is to test the significance of error correction term (*ECT*)'s coefficient. Thus, error correction model (ECM) based on ARDL model are estimated and short-run dynamics are obtained. A general ECM of Eq. (2) is expressed as follows:

$$\Delta lnEC_t = \alpha_0 + \sum_{i=1}^{m}\delta_{1i}\Delta lnEC ?_{t-i} + \sum_{i=0}^{n}\delta_{2i}\Delta lnGDP_{t-i} + \sum_{i=0}^{p}\delta_{3i}\Delta lnFD_{t-i} + \sum_{i=0}^{r}\delta_{4i} lnTR_{t-i} + \phi ECT ?_{t-1} + \varepsilon_t \quad (3)$$

where ε_t is white noise residual term and Δ is the first difference operator. The ECT_{t-1} indicates the speed of the adjustment and shows how quickly the variables return to the long-run equilibrium. The coefficient of ECT_{t-1} is expected to be statistically significant and negative. To investigate the goodness of the ECM model some diagnostic and stability tests are applied as in ARDL model.

As well as the ARDL bounds testing approach, this study also employ the Johansen-Juselius cointegration test to provide a sensitivity check for the cointegration results. This methodology is based on the vector autoregression (VAR) of order p given by

$$\Delta y_t = \mu + \Pi y_{t-1} + \sum_{i=1}^{p-1} \Gamma_i \Delta y_{t-i} + Bz_t + ?\varepsilon_t \quad (4)$$

where y_t is a vector of variables that are integrated of order one, ε_t is a vector of innovations and Bz_t is a vector of deterministic variables.

$$\Pi = \sum_{i=1}^{p} A_i - I$$

and

$$\Gamma_i = -\sum_{j=i+1}^{p} A_j$$

If the coefficient matrix Π has reduced rank $r<n$, then there exist nxr matrix α and β each with rank r such that $\Pi = \alpha\beta'$ and $\beta' y_t$ is stationary. $r$is the number of cointegrating relationships, the elements of α are known as the adjustment parameters in the vector error correction model and each column of β is a cointegrating vector. It can be shown that for a given r, the maximum likelihood estimator of β defines the combination of y_{t-1} that yields the r largest canonical correlations of Δy_t with y_{t-1} after correcting for lagged differences and deterministic variables when present. Johansen's procedure estimates the significance of these canonical correlations and thereby the reduced rank of the Πmatrix. Johansen-Juselius propose two different likelihood ratio tests: the trace test and maximum eigenvalue test, shown in equations (5) and (6) respectively.

$$J_{iz} = -T\sum_{i=r+1}^{n} \ln(1-\hat{\lambda}_i) \quad (5)$$

$$J_{max} = -Tln\left(1-\hat{\lambda}_{r+1}\right) \quad (6)$$

where T is the sample size and $\hat{\lambda}_i$ is the ith largest canonical correlation. The null hypothesis for trace test is r cointegrating vectors which is tested against its alternative of n cointegrating vectors. The null hypothesis for maximum eigenvalue test is r cointegrating vectors which is tested against its alternative of $(r+1)$ cointegrating vectors.

The ARDL bounds testing and Johansen-Juselius approaches for cointegration can be used to investigate the presence of a long run relationship between the variables. However, these methods do not inform about the direction of causality. Engle & Granger (1987) indicate that if the variables are cointegrated, they should have an error correction representation. In this causality test ECT_{t-1} is included to the VAR system as an additional variable. Thus, VECM causality approach is known as augmented Granger causality test. We employ Granger causality test based on VECM to determine the existence of the causal relationship between the variables. This model is as follows:

$$\begin{bmatrix} \Delta lnEC_t \\ \Delta lnGDP_t \\ \Delta lnFD_t \\ \Delta lnTR_t \end{bmatrix} = \begin{bmatrix} \varnothing_1 \\ \varnothing_2 \\ \varnothing_3 \\ \varnothing_4 \end{bmatrix} +$$

$$\sum_{i=1}^{p} \begin{bmatrix} \alpha_{11}(L)\alpha_{12}(L)\alpha_{13}(L)\alpha_{14}(L) \\ \alpha_{21}(L)\alpha_{22}(L)\alpha_{23}(L)\alpha_{24}(L) \\ \alpha_{31}(L)\alpha_{32}(L)\alpha_{33}(L)\alpha_{34}(L) \\ \alpha_{41}(L)\alpha_{42}(L)\alpha_{43}(L)\alpha_{44}(L) \end{bmatrix} \begin{bmatrix} \Delta lnE_{t-1} \\ \Delta lnGDP_{t-1} \\ \Delta lnFD_{t-1} \\ lnTR_{t-1} \end{bmatrix}$$

$$+ \begin{bmatrix} \gamma_1 ECT_{t-1} \\ \gamma_2 ECT_{t-1} \\ \gamma_3 ECT_{t-1} \\ \gamma_4 ECT_{t-1} \end{bmatrix} + \begin{bmatrix} C_1 \\ C_2 \\ C_3 \\ C_4 \end{bmatrix} + \begin{bmatrix} \mu_1 \\ \mu_2 \\ \mu_3 \\ \mu_4 \end{bmatrix} \quad (7)$$

where ECT_{t-1} is the lagged residual generated from the long-run association. Δ is the a difference operator; C_1, C_2, C_3 and C_4 are constants; and μ_1, μ_2, μ_3 and μ_4 are error terms assumed to be N $(0,\sigma)$. The VECM approach includes both the short and the long-run causal relationships. A significant *t*-statistic on the coefficient of ECT_{t-1} indicates that there is a long-run causality between the variables. A significant *F*-statistic on the first differences of the variables shows the existence of a short-run causality between the variables.

EMPIRICAL FINDINGS AND DISCUSSION

We begin the analysis by using the Augmented Dickey-Fuller (1979) ADF, Phillips-Perron (1988) PP and Kwiatkowski, Phillips, Schmidt & Shin (1992) KPSS unit root tests to examine the stationarity of the variables. Unlike ADF and PP tests the null hypothesis is stationarity in KPSS test. The outcome of these unit root tests is reported in Table 3. The results reveal that all the variables

Table 3. Unit root tests results

Regressors	ADF Test Statistic	PP Test Statistic	KPSS Test Statistic
ln*EC*	-0.889	-0.903	0.961
ln*GDP*	-0.324	-0.251	0.969
ln*FD1*	-0.385	-0.478	0.574
ln*FD2*	0.154	0.034	0.476
ln*FD3*	-0.842	-0.309	0.930
ln*TR*	-1.845	-1.851	0.923
Δln*EC*	-6.861***	-6.857***	0.087***
Δln*GDP*	-7.130***	-7.136***	0.058***
Δln*FD1*	-6.688***	-6.683***	0.171***
Δln*FD2*	-6.236***	-6.234***	0.291***
Δln*FD3*	-9.209***	-12.217***	0.179***
Δln*TR*	-7.023***	-7.104***	0.114***

Note: The unit root tests have an intercept. The optimum lag order is selected automatically by usingthe SBC for ADF test and the bandwidth is selected by using the Newey-West method for PP and KPSS tests. *** denotes significant at 1% level.

are stationary in their first differences indicating that they are integrated at $I(1)$. The results also lead us to apply the ARDL and Johansen-Juselius approaches for cointegration.

In the ARDL bounds testing, we select the optimum lag order by using AIC. After selecting lag order for the ARDL model, our computed *F*-statistics are compared with LCB and UCB generated by Pesaran et al. (2001). The calculated *F*-statistics of Eq. (2) are presented in Table 4 as all cases. The results indicate an evidence of the long-run relationship between financial development, real income, trade openness and energy consumption because the computed *F*-statistic is greater than UCB. In all cases, the significantly negative coefficients obtained for (ECT_{t-1}) also support the existence of cointegration relationship at 1% level of significance. The diagnostic tests presented in the lower part of Table 4 indicate that all the models pass the diagnostic tests for normality of error term, serial correlation, heteroskedasticity and model specification.

Table 4. ARDL cointegration test results

	Max. Lag	Opt. Lag	F-Statistics	ECT_{t-1}(t-ratio)	Result
Case 1	5	(4,5,3,5)	7.165***	-0.842(-6.950)***	Cointegration
Case 2	5	(4,4,5,5)	5.249**	-0.516(-6.088)***	Cointegration
Case 3	3	(3,0,3,2)	6.667***	-0.305(-7.094)***	Cointegration

Critical Values for F-statistics	Lower $I(0)$	Upper $I(1)$
1%	5.17	6.36
5%	4.01	5.07
10%	3.47	4.45

Diag. Test Statistics	R^2	F-Statistic	*J-B Normality Test*	*ARCH LM Test*	*Ramsey RESETtest*	*B-G LM Test*
Case 1	0.914	9.798[0.00]	1.074[0.584]	1.377[0.240]	0.984[0.332]	0.035[0.850]
Case 2	0.902	8.465[0.00]	1.545[0.461]	0.096[0.756]	0.139[0.712]	0.032[0.856]
Case 3	0.857	12.062[0.00]	0.088[0.956]	0.986[0.320]	3.144[0.086]	1.154[0.282]

Note: Values in brackets are p-values. *** and ** denote significant at 1% and 5% levels. The critical values are obtained from Pesaran et al. (2001, p.301), critical values for the bounds test: case V: unrestricted intercept and unrestricted trend

The Johansen-Juselius cointegration approach is also employed to complement the findings of ARDL bounds testing for cointegration. The Johansen-Juselius procedure requires that the variables should be integrated at $I(1)$. The unit root tests validate the use of this cointegration test. The optimum lag order is selected by using multivariate VAR model based on SBC. The results of the trace and maximum eigenvalue statistics reported in Table 5 indicate the presence of cointegration relationship between the variables in all cases. In other words, the results show an evidence of at least one cointegration vector for case 1 and 2. The results also show that there are at least three cointegration vectors for case 3.

Having found the long-run relationship in all cases, we can estimate long and short-run coefficients in the equations. Table 6 provides the long-run estimation results based on ARDL approach along with diagnostic test statistics such as serial correlation, functional form, normality and heteroscedasticity. The results show that all the variables are statistically significant and have the expected signs in all cases. Our central interest is the long-run relationship between financial development and energy consumption. The coefficients of ln*FD1*, ln*FD2* and ln*FD3* with respect to ln*EC* are positive and significant indicating that financial development contributes to energy consumption in the long-run. The results imply

Table 5. Johansen-juselius cointegration test results

Hypotheses	Trace Statistic	5% CV	Max. Eigen Value	5% CV
Case 1: lnEC, lnGDP, lnFD1 and lnTR. Lag 2				
R=0	72.041***	63.876	47.163***	32.118
$R\leq1$	24.877	42.915	14.689	25.823
$R\leq2$	10.188	25.872	7.580	19.387
$R\leq3$	2.607	12.517	2.607	12.517
Case 2: lnEC, lnGDP, lnFD2 and lnTR. Lag 3				
R=0	60.461*	63.876	34.824***	32.118
$R\leq1$	25.637	42.915	13.858	25.823
$R\leq2$	11.778	25.872	8.765	19.387
$R\leq3$	3.013	12.517	3.013	12.517
Case 3: lnEC, lnGDP, lnFD2 and lnTR. Lag 4				
R=0	96.625***	63.876	42.188***	32.118
$R\leq1$	54.437***	42.915	29.072**	25.823
$R\leq2$	25.364*	25.872	20.525**	19.387
$R\leq3$	4.839	12.517	4.839	12.517

Note: Test statistics show the results of the model with constant and trend. ***, ** and * denote significant at 1%, 5% and 10% levels, respectively.

Table 6. Long-run estimates based on selected ARDL models

Regressors	Case 1	Case 2	Case 3
ln*GDP*	2.184(15.234)***	1.886(6.735)***	2.419(5.544)***
ln*FD1*	0.065(2.810)***		
ln*FD2*		0.179(1.664)[a]	
ln*FD3*			0.306(2.256)**
ln*TR*	0.330(9.172)***	0.260(4.498)***	0.392(4.557)***
C	-11.758(-10.019***	-9.634(-4.529)***	-14.346(-3.934)***
Diagnostic Test Statistics			
R^2	0.998	0.998	0.998
Adj-R^2	0.997	0.997	0.997
F-statistic	898.752[0.000]	735.941[0.000]	1615.319[0.000]
J-B normality test	1.464[0.480]	1.535[0.464]	0.203[0.903]
ARCH LM test	1.499[0.220]	0.266[0.605]	0.655[0.418]
Ramsey RESET test	0.235[0.632]	0.245[0.624]	2.640[0.113]
B-G LM test	0.105[0.745]	0.000[0.985]	0.068[0.793]

Note: Values in brackets are *p*-values. Values in parenthesis are *t*-statistics. ***and ** denote significant at 1% and 5% levels. [a] indicates significant at 11% level.

that financial development is a determinant of energy consumption in the case of Turkey. The coefficient value of 0.065, 0.179 and 0.306 for ln*FD1*, ln*FD2* and ln*FD3*, respectively, suggests that a 1% increase in domestic credit provided by banking sector, the domestic credit to private sector and money-quasi money leads to around 0.065%, 0.179% and 0.306% increase in energy consumption, respectively. Furthermore, in all cases the significant positive coefficients of ln*GDP* and ln*TR* with respect to ln*EC* suggest that energy consumption increases with the increase of real income and trade openness. The results confirm the validity of hypotheses of economic growth and trade-led energy consumption in Turkish economy.

The results of serial correlation, functional form, normality and heteroscedasticity reported in the lower part of Table 6 reveal that the underlying models pass all the diagnostic tests. We also apply the CUSUM and CUSUMsq tests to

Figure 1. CUSUM and CUSUMsq for Case 1

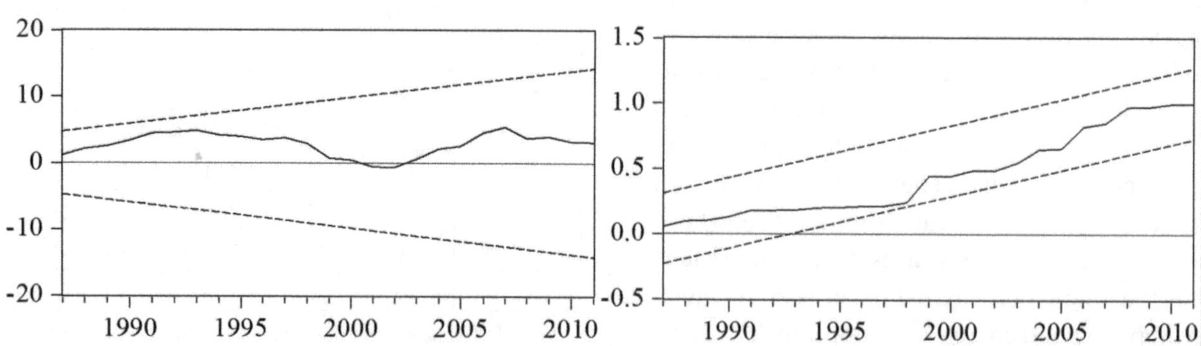

Figure 2. CUSUM and CUSUMsq for Case 2

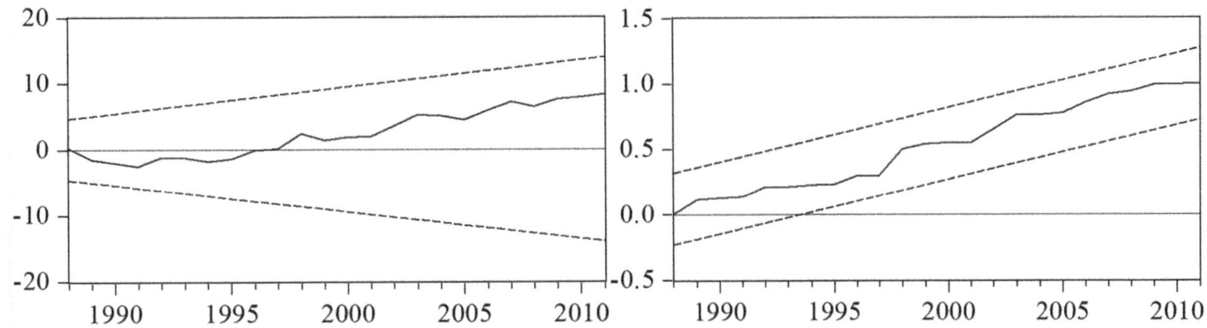

investigate the stability of long-run coefficients. The plots of CUSUM and CUSUMsq statistics for all cases are reported in Figure 1, 2 and 3. The results imply that the estimated parameters are stable over the period because the plots of both CUSUM and CUSUMsq fall inside the critical bounds of 5% significance. Thus, we can use the estimation results of the ARDL model for policy implication in the case of Turkey.

Table 7 reports the short-run estimation results in ECM along with some diagnostic tests. The results show an insignificant relationship between financial development and energy consumption in the short-run. Similar to the long-run results, in all cases, the short-run results indicate that there is a positive and significant relation between real income and energy consumption. In addition, it is found that trade openness is positive linked with energy consumption. Based on these empirical findings, higher economic growth and trade openness will result more energy consumption in Turkey. On the other hand, the coefficients of ECM_{t-1} are found to be statistically significant with negative sign in all cases implying that energy consumption is corrected from the short towards long-run equilibrium by 84%, 52% and 31%, respectively each year.

The existence of a long-run relationship between financial development, real income, trade openness and energy consumption implies that there is at least one way directional causal relationship between the variables. The results of short and long-run Granger causality based on VECM are summarized in Table 8. In the long run we find unidirectional Granger causality running from financial development, real income and trade openness to energy consumption for case 2 and 3. This indicates that financial development, economic growth and trade openness cause energy consumption. In all cases, we also find unidirec-

Figure 3. CUSUM and CUSUMsq for Case 3

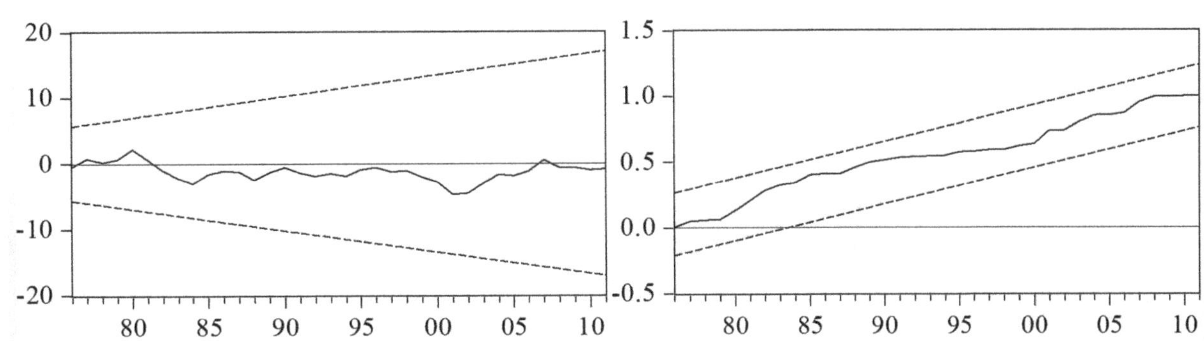

Table 7. Short-run estimates based on selected ARDL models

Regressors	Case 1	Case 2	Case 3
ΔlnGDP	0.795(11.257)***	0.784(9.670)***	0.708(8.717)***
ΔlnFD1	-0.004(-0.213)		
ΔlnFD2		0.031(1.301)	
ΔlnFD3			0.007(0.292)
ΔlnTR	0.121(5.840)***	0.093(4.507)***	0.090(4.552)***
ΔC	-0.033(-5.023)***	-0.015(-6.088)***	-0.016(-3.004)***
Diagnostic Test Statistics			
R^2	0.911	0.900	0.852
Adj-R^2	0.858	0.836	0.818
F-statistic	17.471***	14.073***	25.041***
RSS	0.007	0.007	0.011
SE of regression	0.015	0.017	0.017

Note: Values in parenthesis are *t*-statistics. *** denotes significant at 1% level.

tional Granger causality running from financial development to energy consumption in the short run. Thus, the study presents an evidence that financial development cause energy consumption in both the short and long run.

CONCLUSION AND POLICY IMPLICATIONS

The basic motivation for this study is the lack of studies that investigate the relationship between financial development and energy consumption in the case of Turkey. The study examines this relationship by adding real income and trade openness to the empirical analysis for 1960-2011 period. Before testing for cointegration and causality relationships, ADF, PP and KPSS unit root tests are applied. The results suggest that all series are stationary in their first differences, hence validate the use of ARDL bounds testing and Johansen-Juselius approaches for cointegration. The cointegration tests reveal the presence of a long-run relationship between the variables. We find that the impact of financial development, real income, and trade openness on energy consumption is positive and statistically significant. This implies that financial development, economic growth, and trade openness increase energy consumption in Turkey in the long-run.

The Granger causality test based on VECM reveals long-run unidirectional causality from financial development, real income and trade openness to energy consumption indicating that financial development, economic growth and trade openness cause energy consumption. We also find unidirectional causality running from financial development to energy consumption in the short run. Thus, the study provides an evidence that financial development cause energy consumption in the case of Turkey over the period. The coefficients of estimated *ECTs* are also negative and statistically significant at 1% level of significance indicating that any deviation from the long-run equilibrium between variables is corrected for each period to return the long-run equilibrium level. In addition, we find that long-run parameters are stable over the period implying that the estimation results of the ARDL model can be used for policy implication in case of Turkey.

Turkey's energy demand has been permanently increasing in last two decades. Moreover, finan-

Table 8. VECM granger causality results

Dependent Variable	Short-Run Granger Causality					Long-Run Granger Causality	
	Δln*EC*	Δln*GDP*	Δln*FD1*	Δln*FD2*	Δln*FD3*	Δln*TR*	ECT_{t-1}(t-ratio)
Case 1: Energy consumption, real income, domestic credit provided by banking sector and trade openness							
Δln*EC*	-	2.495*	2.184*	-	-	1.907	-0.991
		[0.059]	[0.089]			[0.130]	(0.331)
Δln*GDP*	2.210*	-	2.367*	-	-	1.495	0.955
	[0.086]		[0.070]			[0.228]	(0.348)
Δln*FD1*	0.491	1.026	-	-	-	0.425	0.395
	[0.779]	[0.424]				[0.826]	(0.696)
Δln*TR*	0.511	1.034	0.196	-	-	-	0.026
	[0.764]	[0.420]	[0.960]				(0.978)
Case 2: Energy consumption, real income, domestic credit to private sector and trade openness							
Δln*EC*	-	0.876	-	2.488*	-	1.636	-1.948*
		[0.511]		[0.059]		[0.188]	(0.063)
Δln*GDP*	0.901	-	-	2.036	-	1.349	0.227
	[0.496]			[0.109]		[0.278]	(0.821)
Δln*FD2*	0.331	0.420	-	-	-	1.024	1.482
	[0.888]	[0.829]				[0.425]	(0.151)
Δln*TR*	1.149	2.051	-	0.862	-	-	-1.301
	[0.362]	[0.107]		[0.520]			(0.205)
Case 3:Energy consumption, real income, money-quasi money and trade openness							
Δln*EC*	-	0.301	-	-	6.189***	1.538	-1.979*
		[0.823]			[0.001]	[0.222]	(0.055)
Δln*GDP*	1.555	-	-	-	3.778**	0.644	0.572
	[0.218]				[0.019]	[0.591]	(0.570)
Δln*FD3*	1.233	0.281	-	-	-	0.301	-0.703
	[0.312]	[0.838]				[0.824]	(0.486)
Δln*TR*	0.297	0.751	-	-	0.753	-	0.997
	[0.827]	[0.529]			[0.528]		(0.325)

Note: Values in brackets are p-values for Wald tests with F distribution. The optimum lag is based on AIC. Δ represents the first difference operator. ***, ** and * denote significant at 1%, 5% and 10% levels, respectively.

cial development, economic growth and trade openness positively affect energy consumption in Turkish economy. The empirical results indicate that financial development is a determinant of energy consumption. Therefore, the projections regarding energy demand in Turkey should include financial development indicators used in the study. Otherwise, actual energy demand may be underestimated. Turkey should perform an appropriate energy policy without compromising outward-oriented trade, growth and financial development policies. Firstly, the government should direct the financial institutions to invest in energy infrastructure to meet the rising demand for energy. Secondly, the government should explore the new alternative energy resources such as hydroelectric, thermal and wind power plants and increase the share of renewable sources in the energy efficiency/saving projects. Finally, some measurements that enhance the energy efficiency and reduce the wastage of energy should be taken.

REFERENCES

Al-Mulali, U., & Lee, J. Y. M. (2013). Estimating the Impact of the Financial Development on Energy Consumption: Evidence from the GCC (Gulf Cooperation Council) Countries. *Energy*, *60*, 215–221. doi:10.1016/j.energy.2013.07.067

Al-Mulali, U., & Sab, C. N. B. C. (2012a). The Impact of Energy Consumption and CO_2 Emissions on the Economic and Financial Development in 19 Selected Countries. *Renewable & Sustainable Energy Reviews*, *16*(7), 4365–4369. doi:10.1016/j.rser.2012.05.017

Al-Mulali, U., & Sab, C. N. B. C. (2012b). The Impact of Energy Consumption and CO_2 Emissions on the Economic Growth and Financial Development in the Sub Saharan African Countries. *Energy*, *39*(1), 180–186. doi:10.1016/j.energy.2012.01.032

Baier, S. L., Dwyer, J. G. P. Jr, & Tamura, R. (2004). Does Opening a Stock Exchange Increase Economic Growth? *Journal of International Money and Finance*, *23*(3), 311–331. doi:10.1016/j.jimonfin.2004.01.001

Belloumi, M. (2009). Energy Consumption and GDP in Tunisia: Cointegration and Causality Analysis. *Energy Policy*, *37*(7), 2745–2753. doi:10.1016/j.enpol.2009.03.027

Bozoklu, S., & Yilanci, V. (2013). Energy Consumption and Economic Growth for Selected OECD Countries: Further Evidence from the Granger Causality Test in the Frequency Domain. *Energy Policy*, *63*(C), 877–881. doi:10.1016/j.enpol.2013.09.037

Brown, R. L., Durbin, J., & Evans, J. M. (1975). Techniques for Testing the Constancy of Regression Relations over Time. *Journal of the Royal Statistical Society. Series B. Methodological*, *37*, 149–163.

Chow, G. (1960). Test of Equality between Sets of Coefficients in two Linear Regressions. *Econometrica*, *28*(3), 591–605. doi:10.2307/1910133

Coban, S., & Topcu, M. (2013). The Nexus between Financial Development and Energy Consumption in the EU: A Dynamic Panel Data Analysis. *Energy Economics*, *39*, 81–88. doi:10.1016/j.eneco.2013.04.001

Dickey, D. A., & Fuller, W. A. (1979). Distribution of the Estimators of Autoregressive Time Series with a Unit Root. *Journal of the American Statistical Association*, *74*, 427–431.

Engle, R. F., & Granger, C. W. J. (1987). Cointegration and Error Correction Representation: Estimation and Testing. *Econometrica*, *55*(2), 251–276. doi:10.2307/1913236

Ghani, G. M. (2013). Does Trade Liberalization Effect Energy Consumption? *Energy Policy*, *43*, 285–290. doi:10.1016/j.enpol.2012.01.005

Goldsmith, R. (1969). *Financial structure and development*. New York: Yale University Press.

Hansen, B. E. (1992). Tests for Parameter Instability in Regressions with I(1) Processes. *Journal of Business & Economic Statistics*, *10*, 321–335.

Islam, F., Shahbaz, M., Ahmed, A. U., & Alam, M. M. (2013). Financial Development and Energy Consumption Nexus in Malaysia: A Multivariate Time Series Analysis. *Economic Modelling*, *30*, 435–441. doi:10.1016/j.econmod.2012.09.033

Islam, F., Shahbaz, M., & Alam, M. (2011). *Financial Development and Energy Consumption Nexus in Malaysia: A Multivariate Time-Series Analysis. MPRA Paper 28403*. Germany: University Library of Munich.

Johansen, S., & Juselies, K. (1990). Maximum Likelihood Estimation and Inferences on Cointegration. *Oxford Bulletin of Economics and Statistics*, *52*, 169–210. doi:10.1111/j.1468-0084.1990.mp52002003.x

Khan, M. A., Khan, M. Z., Zaman, K., Khan, M. M., & Zahoor, H. (2013). (in press). Growth Factors Determining Financial Development Impact on SAARC's Energy Demand: Energy-starved or Energy-efficient Region? *Energy Policy*. doi:10.1016/j.enpol.2013.07.135

Kwiatkowski, D., Phillips, P. C. B., Schmidt, P., & Shin, Y. (1992). Testing the Null Hypothesis of Stationarity against the Alternative of a Unit Root. *Journal of Econometrics*, *54*(1-3), 159–178. doi:10.1016/0304-4076(92)90104-Y

Levine, R. (1997). Financial Development and Economic Growth: Views and Agenda. *Journal of Economic Literature*, *35*(2), 688–726.

Macroeconomic Outlook Report. (2012). Republic of Turkey Ministry of Finance Strategy Development Unit, May-June, Vol. 19, 1-15. Retrieved from http://www.maliye.gov.tr/Lists/TabMenuIcerik/ Attachments/107/Macroeconomic%20Outlook%20Report%20may-june%202012.pdf

McKinnon, R. (1973). *Money and capital in economic development*. Washington, DC: Brookings Institution.

Mudakkar, S. R., Zaman, K., Shakir, H., Arif, M., Naseen, I., & Naz, L. (2013). Determinants of energy consumption function in SAARC countries: Balancing the odds. *Renewable & Sustainable Energy Reviews*, *28*, 566–574. doi:10.1016/j.rser.2013.08.006

OECD. (2013). OECD. *Economic Outlook*, *2013*(1).

Panopoulou, E., & Pittis, N. (2004). A Comparison of Autoregressive Distributed Lag and Dynamic OLS Cointegration Estimators in the Case of a Serially Correlated Cointegration Error. *The Econometrics Journal*, *7*(2), 585–617. doi:10.1111/j.1368-423X.2004.00145.x

Payne, J. E. (2010). On Biomass Energy Consumption and Real Output in the US. Energy Sources. *Economics. Planning and Policy*, *6*, 47–52.

Pesaran, M. H., & Shin, Y. (1999). An autoregressive distributed lag modeling approach to cointegration analysis. Econometrics and Economic Theory in 20th century: The Ragnar Frisch Centennial Symposium, eds. S. Strom, Cambridge University Press, Cambridge. doi:10.1017/CCOL521633230.011

Pesaran, M. H., Shin, Y., & Smith, R. (2001). Bounds Testing Approaches to the Analysis of Level Relationships. *Journal of Applied Econometrics*, *16*(3), 289–326. doi:10.1002/jae.616

Phillips, P. C. B., & Perron, P. (1988). Testing for Unit Roots in Time Series Regression. *Biometrika*, *75*(2), 335–346. doi:10.1093/biomet/75.2.335

Sadorsky, P. (2010a). The Impact of Financial Development on Energy Consumption in Emerging Economies. *Energy Policy*, *38*(5), 2528–2535. doi:10.1016/j.enpol.2009.12.048

Sadorsky, P. (2010b). Trade and Energy Consumption in the Middle East. *Energy Economics*, *33*(5), 739–749. doi:10.1016/j.eneco.2010.12.012

Sadorsky, P. (2011). Financial Development and Energy Consumption in Central and Eastern European Frontier Economies. *Energy Policy*, *39*(2), 999–1006. doi:10.1016/j.enpol.2010.11.034

Sadorsky, P. (2012). Energy Consumption, Output and Trade in South America. *Energy Economics*, *34*(2), 476–488. doi:10.1016/j.eneco.2011.12.008

Shahbaz, M. (2012). Does Trade Openness Affects Long Run Growth? Cointegration, Causality and Forecast Error Variance Decomposition Tests for Pakistan. *Economic Modelling*, *29*(6), 2325–2339. doi:10.1016/j.econmod.2012.07.015

Shahbaz, M., Islam, F., & Islam, M. M. (2010). The Impact of Financial Development on Energy Consumption in Pakistan: Evidence from ARDL Bounds Testing Approach to Cointegration. In: *Proceedings of the Second International Conference on the Role of Social Sciences and Humanities in Engineering (ICoHSE)*, 12-14 November 2010, Penang, Malaysia.

Shahbaz, M., Khan, S., & Tahir, M. I. (2013b). The Dynamic Link between Energy Consumption, Economic Growth, Financial Development and Trade in China: Fresh Evidence from Multivariate Framework Analysis. *Energy Economics*, *40*, 8–21. doi:10.1016/j.eneco.2013.06.006

Shahbaz, M., & Lean, H. H. (2012). Does Financial Development Increase Energy Consumption? The Role of Industrialization and Urbanization in Tunisia. *Energy Policy*, *40*, 473–479. doi:10.1016/j.enpol.2011.10.050

Shahbaz, M., Nasreen, S., Ling, C.H., & Sbia, R. (2013a). *Causality between Trade Openness and Energy Consumption: What Causes What in High, Middle and Low Income Countries*. (MPRA No. 50382, pp. 1-47).

Shahbaz, M., Zeshan, M., & Afza, T. (2012). Is Energy Consumption Effective to Spur Economic Growth in Pakistan? New Evidence from Bounds Test to Level Relationships and Granger Causality Tests. *Economic Modelling*, *29*(6), 2310–2319. doi:10.1016/j.econmod.2012.06.027

Shaw, E. (1973). *Financial deepening in economic development*. New York: Oxford University Press.

Squalli, J. (2007). Electricity Consumption and Economic Growth: Bounds and Causality Analyses of OPEC Countries. *Energy Economics*, *29*(6), 1192–1205. doi:10.1016/j.eneco.2006.10.001

Stern, D. I. (2010). *The Role of Energy in Economic Growth* (USAEE-IAEE Working Paper, No. 10-055, pp. 1-55).

Tang, C. F., & Tan, B. W. (2014). The Linkages among Energy Consumption, Economic Growth, Relative Price, Foreign Direct Investment, and Financial Development in Malaysia. *Quality & Quantity*, *48*(2), 781–797. doi:10.1007/s11135-012-9802-4

US Energy Information Administration. (2013). Turkey Report 2013. Retrieved from http://www.eia.gov/countries /analysisbriefs/Turkey/turkey.pdf

Wandji, Y. D. F. (2013). Energy Consumption and Economic Growth: Evidence from Cameroon. *Energy Policy*, *61*, 1295–1304. doi:10.1016/j.enpol.2013.05.115

World Bank World Development Indicators Database. (2013). Retrieved from http://data.worldbank.org/data-catalog/world-development-indicators

Zhang, Y., Fan, J., & Chang, H. (2011). Impact of China's Stock Market Development on Energy Consumption: An Empirical Analysis. *Energy Procedia*, *5*, 1927–1931. doi:10.1016/j.egypro.2011.03.331

ADDITIONAL READING

Belaisch, A., & Zanello, A. (2006). Deepening Financial Ties. *Finance & Development*, *43*(2), 16–19.

Chtioui, S. (2012). Does Economic Growth and Financial Development Spur EnergyConsumption in Tunisia? *J. Econ. Int. Financ.*, *4*(7), 150–158. doi:10.5897/JEIF12.014

Claessens, S., & Feijen, E. (2007). *Financial Sector Development and the Millennium Development Goals* (World Bank Working Paper No. 89).

Dan, Y., & Lijun, Z. (2009). *Financial Development and Energy Consumption: An Empirical Research based on Guangdong Province*. Paper presented at International Conference on Information Management, Innovation Management and Industrial Engineering, ICIII, 3, 102-105.

Ekholm, T., Ghoddusi, H., Krey, V., & Riahi, K. (2013). The Effect of Financial Constraintson Energy-climate Scenarios. *Energy Policy*, *59*, 562–572. doi:10.1016/j.enpol.2013.04.001

Fatai, K., Oxley, L., & Scrimgeour, F. G. (2003). Modeling and Forecasting the Demand for Electricity in New Zealand: A Comparison of Alternative Approaches. *Energy*, *24*, 75–102.

Gurley, J. G., & Shaw, E. S. (1955). Financial Aspects of Economic Development. *The American Economic Review*, *45*, 515–538.

Huang, H., & Zhang, H. H. (2010). Energy Industry Development and Financial Support: A Panel Data Analysis. *Journal of Guangdong University of Finance*, *25*(4), 89–99.

Inglesi-Lotz, R. (2013). *On the Causality and Determinant of Energy and Electricity Demand in South Africa: A Review. Workingpaper: 14*. South Africa: University of Pretoria.

Jalil, A., & Feridun, M. (2011). The Impact of Growth, Energy and Financial Development onthe Environment in China: A Cointegration Analysis. *Energy Economics*, *33*(2), 284–291. doi:10.1016/j.eneco.2010.10.003

Kaifeng, L., Hongyuan, Z., & Guiyu, C. Z. (2012). Analysis of Relationship between China's Energy Investment and Financing and the Development of Energy Industry. *Energy Procedia*, *14*, 655–661. doi:10.1016/j.egypro.2011.12.991

Kakar, Z. K., Khilji, B. A., & Khan, M. J. (2011). Financial Development and Energy Consumption: Empirical Evidence from Pakistan. International Journal of Trade. *Economics and Finance*, *2*(6), 469–471.

Ozturk, I., & Acaravci, A. (2013). The Long-run and Causal Analysis of Energy, Growth, Openness and FinancialDevelopment on Carbon Emissions in Turkey. *Energy Economics*, *36*, 262–267. doi:10.1016/j.eneco.2012.08.025

Ryan, R., & Campbell, N. (2012). Spreadingthenet: The multiple benefits of energy efficiency improvements. International Energy Agency, OECD/IEA, France.

Xu, S. (2012). The impact of financial development on energy consumption in China based on SYS-GMM estimation. *Adv. Mater. Res.* 524-527.

Zaman, K., Khan, M. M., & Saleem, Z. (2011). Bivariate Cointegration between Energy Consumption and Development Factors: A Case Study of Pakistan. *International Journal of Green Energy*, *8*(8), 820–833. doi:10.1080/15435075.2011.602157

KEY TERMS & DEFINITIONS

ARDL Bounds Testing: ARDL bounds testing approach is a cointegration method developed by Pesaran et al. (2001) to test presence of the long run relationship between the variables. This procedure, relatively new method, has many advantages over the classical cointegration tests. Firstly, the approach is used irrespective of whether the series are I(0) or I(1). Secondly, unrestricted error correction model (UECM) can be derived from the ARDL bounds testing through a simple linear transformation. This model has both short and long run dynamics. Thirdly, the empirical results show that the approach is superior and provides consistent results for small sample.

Energy Consumption: Energy consumption is the consumption of energy or power. Per capita or total energy use can be employed in empirical analyses.

Financial Development: Financial development means some improvements in producing information about possible investments and allocating capital, monitoring firms and exerting corporate governance, trading, diversification, and management of risk, mobilization and pooling of savings, easing the exchange of goods and services. These financial functions affect savings andinvestment decisions, and technological innovationsand hence economic growth.

Turkey: Turkey is one of the developing countries which are rapidly growing such as China and India. Turkey has been one of the major recipients of FDI and integrated with the globalized world economy accelerated by Turkey's EU accession process. It has experienced rapid economic growth between 2002 and 2012 with an average annual real GDP growth of 5 percent. In addition, Turkey's foreign trade has developed from the year of 2002. Nowadays, energy, financial development, economic growth and foreign trade are seen as crucial policy areas in Turkey.

Vector Error Correction Model: Generally, after examining the long-run relationship between the variables, standard Granger causality based on VAR system or Granger causality based on vector error correction model are used to determine the direction of causality between the variables. If there is a cointegration between the variables, vector error correction model can be used. This method is known as augmented Granger causality test. In this approach, error correction term (ECT) is added to the VAR system. The significance t-statistic on the parameter of ECT indicates that there is an evidence of the existence of the long run relationship and long run causality between the variables.

Chapter 19
Investor Sentiment and Stock Returns:
Out of Sample Evidence

Serkan Yılmaz Kandır
Çukurova University, Turkey

Veli Akel
Erciyes University, Turkey

Murat Çetin
Namık Kemal University, Turkey

ABSTRACT

In this chapter, the authors investigate the relationship between investor sentiment and stock returns in an out of sample market, namely Borsa Istanbul. The authors use the Consumer Confidence Index as an investor sentiment proxy, while utilizing BIST Second National Index as a measure of small capitalized stock returns. The sample period spans from January 2004 to May 2014. By using monthly data, the authors employ cointegration test and error–correction based Granger causality models. The authors' findings suggest that there is a long-term relationship between investor sentiment and stock returns in Borsa Istanbul. Moreover, a unidirectional causal relationship from investor sentiment to stock returns is also found.

INTRODUCTION

Efficiency of the capital markets is a widely debated topic in finance literature. The first view suggests that capital markets are efficient and security prices reflect all available information. Nevertheless the second approach comes up with a different explanation. This approach denies the efficiency of the capital markets. A number of market anomalies are used as evidence against the efficiency of the capital markets. Moreover, reasons as well as existence of market anomalies are widely investigated. Attempts to explain market anomalies on a rational ground failed in some occasions. On the contrary, sentiment is found to exacerbate anomalies (Stambaugh, Yu, & Yuan,

DOI: 10.4018/978-1-4666-7484-4.ch019

2012). Thus, physiological explanations appeared as a remedy to clarify the roots of deviations from market efficiency. Kahneman and Tversky (1979) is a pioneering study that introduces investor psychology as a significant factor in capital markets and the area is referred to as behavioral finance.

Aim of this study is to investigate the relationship between investor sentiment and stock returns in Borsa İstanbul. The sample period extends from January 2004 to May 2014. We use Consumer Confidence Index as an investor sentiment proxy, while BIST Second National Index is used to measure small capitalized stock returns. We employ cointegration test and error–correction based Granger causality models by using monthly data. The majority of relevant empirical studies use sorted portfolio returns for measuring returns of small capitalized firms. Instead we use an index that exclusively reflects performance of small capitalized firms, namely BIST Second National Index. Furthermore, a great body of literature employs market-driven sentiment measures to proxy investor sentiment. Up to our best knowledge, this study is the first to establish a connnection between consumer confidence index and a market index designed for small firms.

The rest of the paper is organized as follows. The next section examines investor sentiment issue. The third section summarizes the literature. The fourth section presents the methodology and data. And the fifth section reports the empirical results. The last section concludes the paper.

INVESTOR SENTIMENT

Behavioral finance approach includes a number of sub-theories. The term "noise" has a unique position among these theories. The term noise is originated by Black (1986) and it refers to "incorrect signals" shared among the participants of the capital markets. The investors who try to exploit noise are called noise traders. Moreover, noise trading cannot be attributed to specific group investors. On the contrary, noise trading may have a pervasive character across the capital markets. Thus, diversifying the noise originated security price deviations would not be possible. In this manner, noise would earn a systematic character as a source of risk and it should be involved in the return generation processes. Limited arbitrage makes it easier for noise trading to impact asset prices (Shleifer & Summers, 1990).

Although noise introduces additional risks, investors in fact benefits from its existence. As noise originates from incorrect signals, information reflects the correct signals in the market. However, the potential problem arises from the correctness of the signals reaching the marketplace. If every market participant trades on the correct signals, nobody would find counterparty. Since all participants share the very same information, all expectations regarding the future would be the same. This harmony in expectations would prevent security trades. Nevertheless, if some of the participants make noisy decisions, they would constitute ideal counterparties for rational investors. As a result, we may expect a positive association between the volume of noise trading and the liquidity of the general market. However, since the correct signals do not guarantee a good return, rational investors would not be able to fully exploit the incorrect expectations of the noise traders. Security prices would always reflect noise as well as information (Black, 1986, p.530-532).

De Long, Shleifer, Summers and Waldmann (1990) associate noise trading with investor sentiment. Beginning with the separation between rational investors and noise traders suggested by Black (1986), they attempt to better explain the motives behind the noise traders. De Long et al. (1990) suggest that rational expectations determine the decisions of rational investors. On the contrary, noise traders' investment decisions are influenced by their sentiment. Sentiment determines the level of expectations of noise traders and these expectations may be lower or higher than the rational level. Since rational investors and noise traders make transactions with their own motives, market prices reflect correct and incorrect signals. Nevertheless, if sentiment of the noise traders has a pervasive impact on majority of the stocks, the risk arising from the sentiment of the noise trades would not be diversified. Barber, Odean and Zhu (2009) find a correlated investment behavior among individual investors and report psychological factors as the main source of these correlated trades. As a result, investor sentiment appears as an additional source of risk that should be priced in the market. Furthermore, investor sentiment does not seem to be restricted with local markets. Baker, Wurgler and Yuan (2012) find that investor sentiment has a forecasting ability of global stock returns. Another important issue is related with the size of the impact of noise traders on the general market equivalence. Mendel and Shleifer (2012) conjecture that noise traders have disproportionately (relative to their size in the market) high impact on market equilibrium.

Although arbitrage activities of rational investors is thought to be a potential tool for stabilizing market demand, limits to arbitrage prevent rational investors' willingness to take position against noise traders (Baker & Wurgler, 2007, p.130). The most important limit to arbitrage is that riskless arbitrage would not be possible with irrational demand of noise traders. Although mean reversion is generally valid for rational investors, it may not exist for noise traders. If negative sentiment of noise traders drive security prices down, this pessimism would not revert to mean. Moreover, prices would decline further due to long-lasting pessimism of noise traders. Thus, a mean-reversion based strategy to take position against noise traders may not work properly (De Long et al., 1990, p.705). Another finding supporting this thought is that investor sentiment impairs the conventional risk-return relationship (Yu & Yuan, 2011). Thus, rational expectations would not be sufficient to make abnormal returns in a market, where investor sentiment prevails.

After documenting the existence of noise trading, another question remaining is related with the stock preferences of noise traders. A widely documented interest is that individual investors (noise traders) invest heavily in small capitalization stocks (Lee, Shleifer, & Thaler, 1991). Another finding associated with noise traders' portfolios is that riskier stocks are preferred by noise traders (Trueman, 1988).

A growing body of literature investigates the relationship between investor sentiment and stock returns. However, majority of these studies examine the existence of investor sentiment effect in developed countries they find that investor sentiment is an indicator for stock returns (Lee et al., 1991; Leonard & Shull, 1996; Baker & Wurgler, 2006; Bathia & Bredin, 2013). Nevertheless, some of the empirical studies do not find such a predictive ability of investor sentiment (Elton, Gruber, & Busse, 1998; Doukas & Milonas, 2004; Kling & Gao, 2008; Canbas & Kandir, 2009).

Recently, empirical studies tend to establish a relationship between investor sentiment and consumer confidence (Charoenrook, 2005; Qiu & Welch, 2006; Lemmon & Portniaguina, 2006; Schmeling, 2009; Bathia & Bredin, 2013). This relationship may be logical since both terms refer to similar economic agents. Investor sentiment theory classifies noise traders as individuals or retail investors whereas the surveys designed for calculating consumer confidence indices aim households or individuals. Thus perceptions of individuals about current and expected economic conditions measured by consumer confidence index may be aligned with the interests of retail investors. Moreover, Fisher and Statman (2003) find that consumer confidence indices in the USA are associated with American Association of Individual Investors Sentiment Index designed for directly measuring investor sentiment. On the other hand, theoretical explanations are possible about the role of consumer confidence in stock pricing. There are two channels through which we can establish the connection between stock prices and consumer confidence. The first reason is that higher stock prices mean higher wealth. In turn, we may expect a positive sentiment among investors. The second motive is that investors may interpret higher stock prices as a sign of improving economic conditions in the future (Jansen & Nahuis, 2003, p.90). Beside theoretical advantages, the favorable position of consumer confidence comes from its availability. As of 2007, consumer confidence surveys are regularly conducted in at least forty-five countries around the world (Curtin, 2007). Furthermore, predictive ability of consumer confidence is not limited with stock market. Household spending may be estimated by consumer sentiment (Carroll, Fuhrer, & Wilcox, 1994). Likewise, consumer confidence may help estimating other economic indicators, such as interest rates (Bram & Ludvigson, 1998).

LITERATURE REVIEW

Investor sentiment literature employs some typical investor sentiment proxies. Closed-end fund discount has a prominent role in a majority of the empirical studies. Lee et al. (1991) investigate the association between stock returns and closed-end fund discount in USA. Their findings demonstrate that closed-end fund discount shares a significant relationship with small stock returns. In the same manner, Leonard and Shull (1996) use closed-end fund discount as a proxy of investor sentiment and find that investor sentiment is an important factor for NYSE stocks.

Beside the studies revealing the importance of investor sentiment in the pricing process of securities, some others report a limited impact. Elton et al. (1998) detect that other pricing factors play a more significant role than investor sentiment in stock pricing. Likewise, Doukas and Milonas (2004) find sector indices to be more important than closed-end fund discount in explaining Greek stock returns. Although they employ a number of various sentiment proxies Brown and Cliff (2004) fail to report predictive power of investor sentiment for future stock returns. Kling and Gao (2008) do not report an ability of investor sentiment to predict future Chinese stock returns. Moreover, Canbas and Kandir (2009) also report a bidirectional relationship between investor sentiment and stock returns in Turkey. Stock returns are found to impact investor sentiment.

Another strand of literature employs mutual fund flows as a sentiment proxy. Brown, Goetzmann, Hiraki, Shiraishi and Watanabe (2003) find daily mutual fund flow as a significant investor sentiment proxy in USA and Japan. Likewise, by using mutual fund flows as a proxy of investor sentiment, Chi, Zhuang and Song (2012) document a significant impact of investor sentiment on Chinese stock returns. Similarly, Ben-Rephael, Kandel and Wohl (2012) employ mutual fund flows as sentiment indicator and detect a significant sentiment influence on small and growth US stocks. These findings do not seem surprising or interesting, since Indro (2004) defines mutual fund flows as a reasonable proxy of investor sentiment.

Share turnover is another investor sentiment proxy. Baker and Stein (2004) employ share turnover as an investor sentiment Proxy and find a predictivie power of sentiment for future US market returns. Chen, Chen and Lee (2013) examine the distinctions among industries in terms of sensitivity to investor sentiment proxied by turnover. By considering several industries from 11 Asian countries, they contend that investor sentiment influences industry returns at different levels.

Investor sentiment indices and a group of proxies are employed in some studies. Neal and Wheatley (1998) use three investor sentiment proxies, namely closed-end fund discount, mutual fund redemptions and odd-lot sales to purchases ratio. They find that all proxies except odd-lot sales to purchases ratio affect stock returnsBaker and Wurgler (2006) generate an investor sentiment index based on six investor sentiment proxies, namely closed-end fund discount, share turnover, IPO data, share of equity issues in total security issues and dividend premium. Although some control variables are used in the model, investor sentiment effect is found to exist. Corredor, Ferrer and Santamaria (2013) find that investor sentiment has a pervasive impact on stock returns in four markets, namely France, Germany, Spain and UK. They employ various sentiment measures, the sentiment index constructed by Baker and Wurgler (2006), and consumer confidence index. However, findings show variability in terms of significance among countries. Baker, Wurgler and Yuan (2012) extend the literature by investigating the existence of investor sentiment in a global context. By constructing one global and separate sentiment indices for six developed markets, they find that investor sentiment has forecasting ability of stock returns both in local and global markets.

IPO activities also appear as a sentiment proxy in a number of studies. Dorn (2009) find investor sentiment as the basic motive behind the demand of retail investors for IPOs in Germany. Alimov and Mikkelson (2012) document a relationship between investor sentiment and IPO volume in the USA. Moreover, post IPO performance is also found to be impacted by investor sentiment. Likewise, Jiang and Li (2013) establish a connection between investor sentiment and IPO pricing in Hong Kong stock market. Neupane, Paudyal and Thapa (2014) examine the sources of demand for participating IPO activities in India and find that although rational explanations are available for institutional investors; investor sentiment is the main determinant of retail investment activities.

Recently, a growing body of literature attempts to construct a relationship between and investor sentiment and consumer confidence. Ottoo (1999) detects a contemparenous relationship between changes in consumer confidence and changes in stock market index. Lettau and Ludvigson (2001) examine the impact of consumption on US stock returns and detect predictibility power of consumption for not only stock returns but also interest rates. Likewise, Fisher and Statman (2003) find that consumer confidence predicts future stock returns in the USA. Jansen and Nahuis (2003) investigate the relationship between consumer confidence and stock returns in 11 European countries. In most of the countries, Stock returns are found to Granger-cause consumer confidence at short horizons. Charoenrook (2005) examines association between change in consumer confidence and stock returns. Analysis results show that consumer confidence estimates future stock returns. Qiu and Welch (2006) answer three main questions. First, closed-end fund discount is not found to be good proxy of investor sentiment, while consumer confidence index is correlated with sentiment index. Moreover, consumer confidence is capable of estimating small firm returns. Lemmon and Portniaguina (2006) demonstrate that investor sentiment forecasts returns of small stocks and the stocks ignored by institutional investors in USA. Schmeling (2009) reports investor sentiment measured by consumer confidence index as a significant predictor future returns in 18 developed countries. Chen (2011a) examines the relationship between stock returns and consumer confidence in the USA. Findings demonstrate that there is a bidirectional relationship between consumer confidence and stock returns. Chen (2011b) documents an adverse impact of negative consumer sentiment on S&P 500 returns for 1978-2009 periods. Bathia and Bredin (2013) investigate the impact of investor sentiment on stock prices in G7 countries. By using several sentiment proxies including consumer confidence, they find investor sentiment, particularly consumer confidence influence stock returns.

DATA AND METHODOLOGY

The sample period spans from January 2004 to May 2014. Monthly data of two variables, namely BIST Second National Index (XIU) and Consumer Confidence Index (CCI) are used. Thus total number of observations is 125. The choice of time period is determined by the availability of CCI data. In Turkey, CCI has been calculated since the beginning of 2004.

The first variable, namely Consumer Confidence Index (CCI) is used as an investor sentiment proxy. CCI is an economic indicator that reflects the expectations of consumers for the future (Fisher & Statman, 2003). CCI is calculated by using Monthly Consumer Tendency Survey data. Monthly Consumer Tendency Survey aims to measure present situation assessments and future period expectations of consumers' on personal financial standing and general economic course and to determine consumers' expenditure and saving tendencies for near future. The survey is applied to persons at the age of 16 and above as a representative of the household in urban and rural areas of Turkey. The person is randomly selected by the data entry programme (Turkish Statistical Institute).

Consumer Confidence Index is calculated by the following sub-items (Turkish Statistical Institute):

- Financial situation expectation of household over the next 12 months
- General economic situation expectation over the next 12 months
- Number of people unemployed expectation over the next 12 months
- The probability of saving over the next 12 months

Consumer Confidence Index takes values between 0 and 200. If it is above 100, it means consumer confidence is optimistic, if it is below 100, consumer confidence is pessimistic (Turkish Statistical Institute).

Since the survey is applied to households, CCI is related with individual or retail investors rather than institutional investors. This characteristic of CCI makes it a proxy candidate of investor sentiment. Recently, a number of studies employ CCI to proxy investor sentiment (Charoenrook, 2005; Qiu & Welch, 2006; Lemmon & Portniaguina, 2006; Schmeling, 2009; Bathia & Bredin, 2013). Consumer confidence Index data are derived from Turkish Statistical Institute.

Since small stocks are intensively traded by retail investors, they constitute an ideal research area for investor sentiment. In order to isolate small stocks from big ones, a particular index is employed, namely BIST Second National Index. The index consists of the stocks of companies traded on the Second National Market. Second National Market includes small and medium sized companies, companies temporarily or permanently de-listed from the Second National Market, and companies that fail the National Market's listing criteria are traded on the Second National Market. Thus, the stocks that are included in BIST Second National Index are rather small stocks. As of May 2014, while the market value of the companies listed in National market approaches 530 billion TLs, the market value of the companies listed in Second National market cannot reach 19 billion TLs. The difference is also reflected in avarage firm size. While average firm size is in national market is about 2.3 billion TLs, average capitalization for a Second National Market firm is approximately 220 milyon TLs. This difference in size makes BIST Second National Index an ideal indicator for following price movements of small capitalization stocks. BIST Second National Index (XIU) data come from Borsa Istanbul internet site (http://borsaistanbul.com/en/indices/index-data).

We employ cointegration and error correction methods to investigate the relationship between investor sentiment and stock returns. Since both of the methods depend on stationarity of series. Thus, at the first step, stationarity of the series is examined by Augmented Dickey–Fuller (ADF) test (Dickey & Fuller, 1979) and Phillips–Perron (PP) test (Phillips & Perron, 1988).

A possible solution for nonstationarity problem may be taking differences of the economic series and using them in the regression analysis.

Table 1. Summary statistics

Variables	Mean	Maximum	Minimum	Std. Dev.	Observations
XIU	25396,83	58108,72	8528,64	8196,82	125
CCI	77,84	98,68	55,66	8,98	125

XIU is the BIST second national market index and CCI is the consumer confidence index.

However, this naïve strategy is alleged to cause loss of valuable information. In order to avoid losing information, cointegration analysis is widely employed. According to cointegration analysis, a linear combination of series may be stationary, even though the single series are nonstationary (Engle & Granger, 1987, p.275).

In the cointegration analysis, the existence and the number of cointegrating vectors are tested. Johansen (1988, 1991) and Johansen and Juselius (1990) introduce two statistics to test for cointegrating vectors. These statistics are maximum eigenvalue (λ_{max}) and trace (λ_{trace}). If these tests indicate the existence of statistically significant cointegrating vectors, a long-run relationship is hypothesized among the variables.

Granger causality test is widely used in investigating causality relationship among variables (Granger, 1969). Nevertheless, Granger causality test requires stationarity of series. If series are not stationary and are not cointegrated, differencing is maintained for Granger causality test. On the other hand, if series are nonstationary but cointegrated, Granger causality test would not be an ideal solution. In this case, error correction model (ECM) introduced by Engle and Granger (1987) is used for testing causality. ECM would be specified as follows (Granger, 1988):

$$\Delta Y_t = \alpha + \sum_{i=1}^{m} \beta_i \Delta X_{t-i} + \sum_{i=1}^{n} \delta_i \Delta Y_{t-i} + \lambda_1 EC_{t-1} + \varepsilon_t \quad (1)$$

$$\Delta X_t = \alpha + \sum_{i=1}^{l} \beta_i \Delta X_{t-i} + \sum_{i=1}^{p} \delta_i \Delta Y_{t-i} + \lambda_2 EC_{t-1} + \nu_t \quad (2)$$

where, ECt-1 is the error correction term obtained from the cointegration vector, β, δ and λ are parameters to be estimated.

EMPIRICAL RESULTS

At the first step, descriptive statistics of the data are summarized and stationarity of series is examined. Then cointegration and error correction results are reported. Table 1 presents summary statistics.

Mean CCI level is about 78, whereas maximum and minimum CCI levels are about 99 and 56, respectively. Since CCI never reaches 100, Turkish consumers seem to be pessimistic. Although there are variations in CCI, pessimism generally dominates. The average level of XIU exceeds 25.000 with maximum and minimum values of aproximately 58.000 and 8.500, respectively. Moreover, XIU seems to be much more volatile when it is compared with CCI. Table 2 presents unit root test results.

Panel A of Table 2 summarizes ADF and PP unit root test results at levels. When test results are examined both two series seem to be nonstationary at 95% significance level. Whereas unit root test results for in Panel B imply completely different results. ADF and PP test findings reveal that both series are stationary for first difference

Table 2. Unit root test results

Panel 1. Results at Levels				
	ADF		PP	
Variables	Constant	Constant and Trend	Constant	Constant and Trend
XIU	-2,651	-2,635	-2,323	-2,311
CCI	-2,615	-2,503	-2,309	-2,081
Panel 2. Results at First Difference				
	ADF		PP	
Variables	Constant	Constant and Trend	Constant	Constant and Trend
XIU	-8,448*	-8,417*	-8,344*	-8,310*
CCI	-8,698*	-8,728*	-8,437*	-8,462*

XIU is the BIST second national market index and CCI is the consumer confidence index.
* denotes significance at 5%.

of the series. Thus, both XIU and CCI series are integrated of order 1 ($I(1)$). Since both series are $I(1)$, existence of a long-run relationship between XIU and CCI may be investigated by cointegration analysis. The lag order used in the Johansen test is determined by the Schwarz information criterion (Schwarz, 1978). Cointegration test results are reported in Table 3.

Findings in Table 3 demonstrate that both trace and maximum eigenvalue test statistics reject the null of zero cointegrating vectors. On the other hand, the hypothesis that there is one cointegrating vector cannot be rejected. These results reveal that there is a cointegration relationship between XIU and CCI. In other words there is a long-term relationship between the variables. Since we observe a cointegration relationship, we test the direction of the relationship by using vector error correction model and present findings in Table 4.

As can be seen from Table 4, error correction parameter for ΔXIU is negative and significant at 5%. This finding implies that there is a causal relationship between XIU and CCI. In other words, investor sentiment tends to impact small stock returns. However, error correction parameter for ΔCCI does not seem to be significant at the 5%. This means the causal relationship is not a bidirectional one. Stock returns do not appear to influence investor sentiment. This finding is in line with a number of empirical studies (Charoenrook, 2005; Qiu & Welch, 2006; Lemmon & Portniaguina, 2006; Schmeling, 2009; Bathia &

Table 3. Johansen cointegration test results

Variables	Hypotheses	Eigen Values	Trace Statistic	Critical Value (%5)	P Value	Lag Length
XIU-CCI	H_0: r=0 H_a: r≤1	0,138 0,051	24,763* 3,841	15,494 6,493	0,002 0,108	1
Variables	**Hypotheses**	**Eigen Values**	**Max-Eigen Statistic**	**Critical Value (%5)**	**P Value**	**Lag Length**
XIU-CCI	H_0: r=0 H_a: r≤1	0,072 0,049	18,271* 3,841	14,265 6,493	0,011 0,108	1

XIU is the BIST second national market index and CCI is the consumer confidence index.
* denotes significance at 5%.

Table 4. Estimation of error correction model

	EC_{t-1}	α	ΔXIU_{t-1}	ΔCCI_{t-1}	F Statistic
ΔXIU	-0,141* (-3,185)	-9,198 (-0,315)	0,335* (3,751)	-0,042 (-0,641)	6,353*
ΔCCI	0,007 (0,320)	-0,157 (-0,734)	-2,576 (-0,212)	0,203* (2,285)	3,438*

XIU is the BIST second national market index and CCI is the consumer confidence index.
The numbers inside parentheses below the estimated coefficients are the *t*-statistics.
* denotes significance at 5%.

Bredin, 2013). This result supports the view that investor sentiment can impact prices of assets that are primarily owned by noise traders. Consistent with this suggestion, sentiment component of confidence also forecasts returns on stocks predominantly held by individuals.

CONCLUSION

In this paper, we examine the relationship between investor sentiment and stock returns in Turkey. Our sample spans from January 2004 to May 2014. Consumer Confidence Index is used as the proxy of investor sentiment and BIST Second National Index reflects small capitalized stock returns. We employ cointegration method as well as error correction method.

Our findings suggest that there is a long-term relationship between investor sentiment and stock returns. Furthermore, the causal relationship is from investor sentiment to stock returns, but not vice versa.

This study contributes to the current literature in three dimensions. First, we employ a survey based investor sentiment measure instead of proxies based on market data. Second, the finding that investor sentiment predicts stock prices introduces significant implications for portfolio management. CCI may serve as a leading indicator to determine appropriate timing for both individual and institutional investors. Finally, investor sentiment seems to be an additional systematic risk factor in the market. Thus diversification would not serve eliminating noise trader risk. In turn, noise trader risk should be priced appropriately.

We analyze a single segment of Turkish market. Results may differ for other markets and different market segments. We may examine whether effects of investor sentiment are systematically correlated accross the aggregate stock market. Furthermore, a possible association between consumer confidence and other asset types may also be investigated.

REFERENCES

Alimov, A., & Mikkelson, W. (2012). Does favorable investor sentiment lead to costly decisions to go public? *Journal of Corporate Finance*, *18*(3), 519–540. doi:10.1016/j.jcorpfin.2012.02.004

Baker, M., & Stein, J. (2004). Market liquidity as a sentiment indicator. *Journal of Financial Markets*, *7*(3), 271–299. doi:10.1016/j.finmar.2003.11.005

Baker, M., & Wurgler, J. (2006). Investor sentiment and the cross section of stock returns. *The Journal of Finance*, *61*(4), 1645–1680. doi:10.1111/j.1540-6261.2006.00885.x

Baker, M., & Wurgler, J. (2007). Investor sentiment in the stock market. *The Journal of Economic Perspectives*, *21*(2), 129–151. doi:10.1257/jep.21.2.129

Baker, M., Wurgler, J., & Yuan, Y. (2012). Global, local, and contagious investor sentiment. *Journal of Financial Economics*, *104*(2), 272–287. doi:10.1016/j.jfineco.2011.11.002

Barber, B., Odean, T., & Zhu, N. (2009). Systematic noise. *Journal of Financial Markets*, *12*(4), 547–569. doi:10.1016/j.finmar.2009.03.003

Bathia, D., & Bredin, D. (2013). An examination of investor sentiment effect on G7 stock market returns. *European Journal of Finance*, *19*(9), 909–937. doi:10.1080/1351847X.2011.636834

Ben-Rephael, A., Kandel, S., & Wohl, A. (2012). Measuring investor sentiment with mutual fund flows. *Journal of Financial Economics*, *104*(2), 363–382. doi:10.1016/j.jfineco.2010.08.018

Black, F. (1986). Noise. *The Journal of Finance*, *41*(3), 529–543. doi:10.1111/j.1540-6261.1986.tb04513.x

Bram, J., & Ludvigson, S. (1998). Does consumer confidence forecast household expenditure? A sentiment index horse race. *FRBNY Economic Policy Review*, *4*, 59–78.

Brown, G. W., & Cliff, M. T. (2004). Investor sentiment and the near-term stock market. *Journal of Empirical Finance*, *11*(1), 1–27. doi:10.1016/j.jempfin.2002.12.001

Brown, S. J., Goetzmann, W. N., Hiraki, T., Shiraishi, N., & Watanabe, M. (2003). *Investor sentiment in Japanese and U.S. daily mutual fund flows* (NBER Working Paper, No. 9470).

Canbas, S., & Kandir, S. Y. (2009). Investor sentiment and stock returns: Evidence from Turkey. *Emerging Markets Finance & Trade*, *45*(4), 36–52. doi:10.2753/REE1540-496X450403

Carroll, C. D., Fuhrer, J. C., & Wilcox, D. W. (1994). Does consumer sentiment forecast household spending? If so, why? *The American Economic Review*, *84*(5), 1397–1408.

Charoenrook, A. (2005). *Does sentiment matter?* (Working Paper, No: 3301937). Vanderbilt University. Retrived from http://apps.olin.wustl.edu/workingpapers/pdf/2008-12-003.pdf

Chen, M., Chen, P., & Lee, C. (2013). Asymmetric effects of investor sentiment on industry stock returns: Panel data evidence. *Emerging Markets Review*, *14*, 35–54. doi:10.1016/j.ememar.2012.11.001

Chen, S. (2011a). Consumer confidence and stock returns over market fluctuations. *Quantitative Finance*, *12*(10), 1–13.

Chen, S. (2011b). Lack of consumer confidence and stock returns. *Journal of Empirical Finance*, *18*(2), 225–236. doi:10.1016/j.jempfin.2010.12.004

Chi, L., Zhuang, X., & Song, D. (2012). Investor sentiment in the Chinese stock market: An empirical analysis. *Applied Economics Letters*, *19*(4), 345–348. doi:10.1080/13504851.2011.577003

Corredor, P., Ferrer, E., & Santamaria, R. (2013). Investor sentiment effect in stock markets: Stock characteristics or country-specific factors? *International Review of Economics & Finance*, *27*, 572–591. doi:10.1016/j.iref.2013.02.001

Curtin, R. (2007). Consumer sentiment surveys: World review and assessment. *Journal of Business Cycle Measurement and Analysis*, *1*(1), 7–42. doi:10.1787/jbcma-v2007-art2-en

De Long, J. B., Shleifer, A., Summers, L. H., & Waldmann, R. J. (1990). Noise trader risk in financial markets. *Journal of Political Economy*, *98*(4), 703–738. doi:10.1086/261703

Dickey, D. A., & Fuller, W. A. (1979). Distribution of the estimators for autoregressive time series with a unit root. *Journal of the American Statistical Association*, *74*(366), 427–431. doi:10.2307/2286348

Dorn, D. (2009). Does sentiment drive the retail demand for IPOs? *Journal of Financial and Quantitative Analysis*, *44*(1), 85–108. doi:10.1017/S0022109009090024

Doukas, J. A., & Milonas, N. T. (2004). Investor sentiment and the closed-end fund puzzle: Out-of-sample evidence. *European Financial Management*, *10*(2), 235–266. doi:10.1111/j.1354-7798.2004.00249.x

Elton, E. J., Gruber, M. J., & Busse, J. A. (1998). Do investors care about sentiment? *The Journal of Business*, *71*(4), 477–500. doi:10.1086/209754

Engle, R. F., & Granger, C. J. W. (1987). Co-integration and error correction: Representation, estimation and testing. *Econometrica*, *55*(2), 251–276. doi:10.2307/1913236

Fisher, K. L., & Statman, M. (2003). Consumer confidence and stock returns. *Journal of Portfolio Management*, *30*(1), 115–127. doi:10.3905/jpm.2003.319925

Granger, C. W. J. (1969). Investigating causal relations by econometric models and cross-spectral methods. *Econometrica*, *37*(3), 424–438. doi:10.2307/1912791

Granger, C. W. J. (1988). Some recent development in a concept of causality. *Journal of Econometrics*, *39*(1-2), 199–211. doi:10.1016/0304-4076(88)90045-0

Indro, D. C. (2004). Does mutual fund flow reflect investor sentiment? *Journal of Behavioral Finance*, *5*(2), 105–115. doi:10.1207/s15427579jpfm0502_4

Jansen, W. J., & Nahuis, N. J. (2003). The stock market and consumer confidence: European evidence. *Economics Letters*, *79*(1), 89–98. doi:10.1016/S0165-1765(02)00292-6

Jiang, L., & Gao, L. (2013). Investor sentiment and IPO pricing during pre-market and aftermarket periods: Evidence from Hong Kong. *Pacific-Basin Finance Journal*, *23*, 65–82. doi:10.1016/j.pacfin.2013.01.006

Johansen, S. (1988). Statistical analysis of cointegration vector. *Journal of Economic Dynamics & Control*, *12*(2/3), 231–254. doi:10.1016/0165-1889(88)90041-3

Johansen, S. (1991). Estimation and hypothesis testing of cointegration vectors in gaussian vector autoregressive models. *Econometrica*, *59*(6), 1551–1580. doi:10.2307/2938278

Johansen, S., & Juselius, K. (1990). The full information maximum likelihood procedure for inference on cointegration with applications to the demand for money. *Oxford Bulletin of Economics and Statistics*, *52*(2), 169–210. doi:10.1111/j.1468-0084.1990.mp52002003.x

Kahneman, D., & Tversky, A. (1979). Prospect theory: An analysis of decision under risk. *Econometrica*, *47*(2), 263–292. doi:10.2307/1914185

Kling, G., & Gao, L. (2008). Chinese institutional investors' sentiment. *International Financial Markets. Institutions and Money*, *18*(4), 374–387. doi:10.1016/j.intfin.2007.04.002

Lee, C., Shleifer, A., & Thaler, R. H. (1991). Investor sentiment and the closed-end fund puzzle. *The Journal of Finance*, *46*(1), 75–109. doi:10.1111/j.1540-6261.1991.tb03746.x

Lemmon, M., & Portniaguina, E. (2006). Consumer confidence and asset prices: Some empirical evidence. *Review of Financial Studies*, *19*(4), 1499–1529. doi:10.1093/rfs/hhj038

Leonard, D. C., & Shull, D. M. (1996). Investor sentiment and the closed-end fund evidence: Impact of the January effect. *The Quarterly Review of Economics and Finance*, *36*(1), 117–126. doi:10.1016/S1062-9769(96)90032-0

Lettau, M., & Ludvigson, S. (2001). Consumption, aggregate wealth, and expected stock returns. *The Journal of Finance*, *56*(3), 815–849. doi:10.1111/0022-1082.00347

Mendel, B., & Shleifer, A. (2012). Chasing noise. *Journal of Financial Economics*, *104*(2), 303–320. doi:10.1016/j.jfineco.2011.02.018

Neal, R., & Wheatley, S. M. (1998). Do measures of investor sentiment predict returns? *Journal of Financial and Quantitative Analysis*, *33*(4), 523–547. doi:10.2307/2331130

Neupane, S., Paudyal, K., & Thapa, C. (2014). Firm quality or market sentiment: What matters more for IPO investors? *Journal of Banking & Finance*, *44*, 207–218. doi:10.1016/j.jbankfin.2014.04.010

Ottoo, M. W. (1999). *Consumer sentiment and the stock market* (Finance and Economics Discussion Paper, No. 60). Federal Reserve Board. Retrieved from http://www.federal-reserve.gov/pubs/feds/1999/199960/199960abs.html

Phillips, P., & Perron, P. (1988). Testing for a unit root in time series regression. *Biometrika*, *75*(2), 335–346. doi:10.1093/biomet/75.2.335

Qiu, L. X., & Welch, I. (2006). *Investor sentiment measures*. (SSRN Working Paper, No: 589641).

Schmeling, M. (2009). Investor sentiment and stock returns: Some international evidence. *Journal of Empirical Finance*, *16*(3), 394–408. doi:10.1016/j.jempfin.2009.01.002

Schwarz, G. (1978). Estimating the dimension of a model. *Annals of Statistics*, *6*(2), 41–464. doi:10.1214/aos/1176344136

Shleifer, A., & Summers, L. H. (1990). The Noise trader approach to finance. *The Journal of Economic Perspectives*, *4*(2), 19–33. doi:10.1257/jep.4.2.19

Stambaugh, R. F., Yu, J., & Yuan, Y. (2012). The Short of it: Investor sentiment and anomalies. *Journal of Financial Economics*, *104*(2), 288–302. doi:10.1016/j.jfineco.2011.12.001

Trueman, B. (1988). A theory of noise trading in securities markets. *The Journal of Finance*, *43*(1), 83–95. doi:10.1111/j.1540-6261.1988.tb02590.x

Yu, J., & Yuan, Y. (2011). Investor sentiment and the mean–variance relation. *Journal of Financial Economics*, *100*(2), 367–381. doi:10.1016/j.jfineco.2010.10.011

Yu, J., & Yuan, Y. (n.d.). *BIST Second National Index data from Borsa Istanbul*. Retrieved from http://borsaistanbul.com/en/data

Yu, J., & Yuan, Y. *Consumer Confidence Index data from Turkish Statistical Institute*. Retrieved from http://www.turkstat.gov.tr/Start.do

ADDITIONAL READING SECTION

Abarbanell, J. S., & Bernard, V. L. (1992). Tests of analysts' overreaction / underreaction to earnings information as an explanation for anomalous stock price behavior. *The Journal of Finance*, *47*(3), 1181–1207.

Barberis, N., Shleifer, A., & Vishny, R. (1998). A model of investor sentiment. *Journal of Financial Economics*, *49*, 307–343.

Bikhchandani, S., Hirshleifer, D., & Welch, I. (1992). A theory of fads, fashion, custom and cultural change as informational cascades. *Journal of Political Economy*, *100*(5), 992–1026.

Bikhchandani, S., Hirshleifer, D., & Welch, I. (1998). Learning from the behavior of others: Conformity, fads, and informational cascades. *The Journal of Economic Perspectives*, *12*(3), 151–170.

Bikhchandani, S., & Sharma, S. (2001). Herd behavior in financial markets. *IMF Staff Papers*, *47*(3), 279–310.

Bodurtha, J. N., Kim, D., & Lee, C. M. C. (1995). Closed-end country funds and U. S. market sentiment. *Review of Financial Studies*, *8*(3), 879–918.

Burch, T. R., Emery, D., & Fuerst, M. E. (2003). What can "nine-eleven" tell us about closed-end fund discounts and investor sentiment. *Financial Review*, *38*, 515–529.

Chan, L. K. C., Jegadeesh, N., & Lakonishok, J. (1996). Momentum strategies. *The Journal of Finance*, *51*(5), 1681–1713.

Chen, N., Kan, R., & Miller, M. H. (1993a). Are the discounts on closed-end funds a sentiment index? *The Journal of Finance*, *48*(2), 795–800.

Chen, N., Kan, R., & Miller, M. H. (1993b). Yes, the discounts on closed-end funds are a sentiment index: A rejoinder. *The Journal of Finance*, *48*(2), 809–810.

Chopra, N., Lee, C. M. C., Shleifer, A., & Thaler, R. H. (1993a). Yes, the discounts on closed-end funds are a sentiment index. *The Journal of Finance*, *48*(2), 801–808.

Chopra, N., Lee, C. M. C., Shleifer, A., & Thaler, R. H. (1993b). Summing up. *The Journal of Finance*, *48*(2), 811–812.

Conrad, J., & Kaul, G. (1998). An anatomy of trading strategies. *Review of Financial Studies*, *11*(3), 489–519.

Daniel, K., Hirshleifer, D., & Subrahmanyam, A. (1998). Investor psychology and security market under and overreactions. *The Journal of Finance*, *53*(6), 1839–1885.

De Bondt, W. F. M., & Thaler, R. (1985). Does the stock market overreact? *The Journal of Finance*, *40*(3), 793–805.

De Bondt, W. F. M., & Thaler, R. (1987). Further evidence on investor overreaction and stock market seasonality. *The Journal of Finance*, *42*(3), 557–581.

De Bondt, W. F. M., & Thaler, R. (1990). Do security analysts overreact? *The American Economic Review*, *80*(2), 52–57.

Fisher, K. L., & Statman, M. (2000). Investor sentiment and stock returns. *Financial Analysts Journal*, *56*(2), 16–23.

Goldberg, J., & Nitzsch, R. (2002). *Behavioral Finance* (2nd ed.). England: John Wiley & Sons, Ltd.

Jegadeesh, N. (1990). Evidence of predictable behavior of security returns. *The Journal of Finance*, *45*(3), 881–898.

Jegadeesh, N., & Titman, S. (1993). Returns to buying winners and selling losers: Implications for stock market efficiency. *The Journal of Finance*, *48*(1), 65–91.

Jegadeesh, N., & Titman, S. (1995). Overreaction, delayed reaction, and contrarian profits. *Review of Financial Studies*, *8*(4), 973–993.

Jegadeesh, N., & Titman, S. (2001). Profitability of momentum strategies: An evaluation of alternative explanations. *The Journal of Finance*, *56*(2), 699–720.

Kelly, M. (1997). Do noise traders influence stock prices? *Journal of Money, Credit and Banking*, *29*, 351–363.

Lehmann, B. N. (1990). Fads, martingales, and market efficiency. *The Quarterly Journal of Economics*, *105*(1), 1–28.

Malkiel, B. G. (1977). The valuation of closed-end investment company shares. *The Journal of Finance*, *32*(3), 847–859.

Scharfstein, D. S., & Stein, J. C. (1990). Herd behavior and investment. *The American Economic Review*, *80*(3), 465–479.

Shefrin, H. (2000). *Beyond Greed and Fear: Understanding Behavioral Finance and the Psychology of Investing* (1st ed.). USA: Harvard Business School Press.

Shefrin, H., & Statman, M. (1985). The disposition to ride winners too long sell losers too soon: Theory and evidence. *The Journal of Finance*, *41*(3), 774–790.

Thaler, R. (1985). Mental accounting and consumer choice. *Marketing Science*, *4*(3), 199–214.

KEY TERMS AND DEFINITIONS

Behavioral Finance: A study of the way in which psychology inflences the behavior of market practitioners, both at the individual and group level, and the subsequent effect on markets.

Borsa Istanbul: Borsa İstanbul brings together all the exchanges operating in the Turkish capital markets under a single roof.

Consumer Confidence Index: An economic indicator that reflects the expectations of consumers for the future.

Investor Sentiment: A belief about future cash flows and investment risks that is not justified by the facts at hand.

Stock Returns: The gain or loss of a stock in a particular period.

Chapter 20
The Analysis of 2008 Global Crisis in Terms of the Sustainability of Public Debt Stock and Budget Deficits of PIIGS Countries Panel Data Analysis

Binhan Elif Yilmaz
Istanbul University, Turkey

Ferda Yerdelen Tatoglu
Istanbul University, Turkey

Sinan Ataer
Istanbul University, Turkey

ABSTRACT

In this chapter, we have focused the impacts of 2008 global crisis on the debt policies and the sustainability of debts in the PIIGS Countries. For that, the circumstances of the global crisis are examined, and the economic condition before the crisis is handled. As a main objective, the public debt indicators of PIIGS Countries are pointed out. The ratios and budget units are evaluated in terms of sustainability of debts. While making these evaluations and examinations our method was panel data analysis which can be found at the end of this chapter. In this method, public debt ratios and the sustainability conditions of the public debts in the PIIGS Countries are used as the determinants of public debts sustainability.

BACKGROUND

The house prices got moved downwardly after the explosion of the bubbles at the house prices in U.S.A. According to S&P/Case-Shiller House Prices Index, the rapid increase at the house prices since 2002 reversed with the rapid decrease after the year of 2006. The index indicates the house prices at the February of 2008, %13 decreased in contrast with the same time of past year, after

DOI: 10.4018/978-1-4666-7484-4.ch020

six month the ratio was %18. These declines decreasingly continued through the 2009. Finally, while the house prices decreasing, failure to pay off debts of the low income citizens, let the financial institutions in a hard position. After the failure debts, the houses are conscripted, during the conversion into cash of the houses the excess supply occurred and this affected the prices more decreasingly.

The global financial crisis erupted in September 2008 with the collapse of Lehman Brothers, largely as a result of accumulating defaults on mortgages and derivative products. The ensuing financial sector crisis quickly led to a significant decline in credit to the private sector as well as to a sharp rise in interest rates. The resulting collapse in U.S. financial institutions led to a collapse of equity markets and of international trade and industrial production and spread to other advanced economies as well as to emerging markets and developing countries. Real growth around the world declined sharply below projections and advanced economies, including the U.S., entered into a recession. Only China and developing Asia maintained strong growth (Matheson, 2013, p.3).

IMF forecast that the world economy would achieve the lowest growth since 2009 with 3,3 per cent. The Fund, which lowered the growth forecast from 3,5 per cent to 3,3 per cent, stated that the risk of global deceleration is high (IMF, 2012, p. 190). According to IMF World Economic Outlook Update January 2013, the growth rate of developed countries was 1, 6 per cent, whereas it was 6, 3 percent for developing countries and emerging markets in 2011. In 2012 the rate of developed countries was 1, 3 per cent while it was 5, 1 per cent for developing countries and emerging markets. IMF forecast the 2013 growth rate of developed countries as 1, 4 per cent and for developing countries and emerging economies this rate would be 5,5 per cent. IMF's forecast of EU for 2013 has been revised downward since October 2012 and the forecast is 0, 2 per cent (Yılmaz; 2013, p. 231).

Liberalising capital movements created pressure both on American and European banking systems and European banks dominating the international markets were affected negatively and the crisis globalised (Akçay, 2012, p. 266). Rapid falls in the prices of assets affected all national and international investors. Hence, when problems emerging in loan market spread capital markets, an atmosphere of uncertainty and loss of credibility affected loan markets, interbank markets and capital markets, obstructed corporations which operate in international markets from finding new funds. This situation put extra pressure on banks' capital competence ratios, caused financial decay, bankrupts and bank mergers. The financial destabilisations that occurred in the financial markets of U.S.A. firstly spread to the developed economies of the Western Europe. Almost all the fiscal systems of countries impacted by the domino effects of the crisis. The European banking system that was in a dominant position at the international markets, seriously affected by the crisis by the October 2008.

The countries that their competition power weakened and their public finance indicator deformed against the developed economies in the European Union, today they are in a concern in terms of sustainability of their public debts.

The use of shared currency and the monopoly execution of monetary policy by the European Central Bank for the Eurozone countries cause the tight connections between those countries and make a Eurozone country easily affected from the other Eurozone country's negative situation. The negative situations rapidly spreads in Eurozen by that way.

Besides that, the high integration level of financial sectors and real sectors increases the level and quickness of affection between the members of European Union. On the other hand, the countries that adopted the public debts as a usual public income after passing Euro currency and decreased costs of debts today became the lead actors of European debt crisis.

The subject actors, were under the umbrella of Euro with the two strongest member of Euro as Germany and France, gained confident of international investors and reached the debt income in a positive atmosphere and with low costs. The opportunity of finding debts with low costs for these countries caused higher public expenditure and was as incentive factor on financing budget deficits with this cheap way.

The absence of competition and often devaluations for taking the growth advantages back of these countries, directed them to the domestic demand and public expenditures by the reason of maintain their economic growth after the obligation to apply a unique monetary policy. These countries choose the way that higher public debts once financial environment was suitable for that.

Thus, the debt crisis that occurred in Greece at the second half of 2010, covered the Eurozone countries and in fact threatened the future of economic and monetary union in Europe.

Since public debts, which are already very high in PIIGS countries, generally have negations in terms of the structure of debts (term structure, currency structure, local-foreign creditors and interest structure of contracts) in majority of these countries, the financial fragility has rapidly increased in the aforementioned countries from 2008 until today. The difficulty of PIIGS countries to convert their debts left the financial institutions that keep the bonds of these countries in a difficult situation, as well. Thus, the European banking system has taken a great risk.

The expander policies that applied for restabilisation and eliminate the depressive effects of the global crisis on the economy, caused to giving fiscal discipline up. Not only in U.S.A., several simulative preventions to domestic demand in every country that effected by the crisis, ruined public budgets. Public debts are chosen for financing budget deficits. Higher public debt stocks increased the concerns about maintenance of debts and reduced the confident in Europe countries in debt.

Public finance dynamics were negatively affected by global crisis, too. Budget deficits escalated to 12% since 2009 while they are 2% of national income in the USA. Public debt stock exceeded 100% in 2011 while it was 55% of national income in 2007 in the USA. Eurozone countries which have a significant position in the expansion area of the crisis became the main actor of the global crisis as the most recessed countries among the developed economies and whose budget deficits and public debt stock hit record high. Since Euro is the shared currency in the Eurozone and mentioned countries' economies are strictly depended to each other, adverse events happened one of the Eurozone countries expanded rapidly among other Eurozone countries. As a matter of fact the debt crisis broke out in Greece in the second quarter of 2010 affected the other Eurozone countries in a short span of time, led to adverse events in PIIGS countries (Portugal, Ireland, Italy, Greece, Spain) and Maastricht criteria was violated continuously.

In Portugal, while budget-national income ratio was 4.6% (surplus) in 2006, deficit was 10,2% of national income. In 2014, budget deficit is expected as 4,2% of national income. While budget in Ireland is 2,9% surplus in proportion to national income in 2006, budget deficit hit record high in 2010: %30 of national income. In Ireland, budget deficit is expected as 4% of national income in 2014. In Italy, budget started to have a deficit before the crisis. In 2006, as budget had a deficit 3,4% ratio of national income, budget deficit rose to 5,4% of national income in 2009. The budget deficit of Italy estimated as %2,3 of its national income. Greece is one of the countries that has budget deficit before crisis. The global crisis rapidly increased the budget deficits. The budget deficit of Greece that realized as %6 in 2006, increased to %15,6 in 2009. It is estimated to decrease under %2,6 in 2014.

Spain had made a budget surplus as %2,4 in 2006. But Spain got far away from fiscal discipline and in 2011, Spain's budget deficit realized as

%11.2 of its national income. This ratio estimated as %7 in 2014. (European Commission, Economic and Financial Affairs, AMECO database).

PIIGS countries could not reach and provide the Maastricht criteria's in terms of public debt stocks. The public debt stock / national income ratio realized as %69,4 in 2006 for Portugal. This ratio increased till %108,3 in 2011. The subject ratio estimated about %124,3 in 2014 for Portugal.

Before the crisis, Ireland could reach the Maastricht Criteria with a ratio %24,6 for public debt stock / national income ratio. In 2011, this ratio became going further %100. Ireland's ratio expected as %120 for the year of 2014.

In Italy, public debt stock / national income ratio was realized as %106 in 2006 and %120 in 2011. The subject ratio is expected as %132 in the year of 2014.

Greece is the lead actor of the debt crisis in Europe with its record level of debt. Greece's public debt stock / national income ratio was realized as %107 in 206 and this ratio had increased to %170 in 2011. There is a strong expectation about this ratio as %175 for the year of 2014.

Spain was one of the countries that reached criteria for this ratio before the crisis but in 2011 the subject ratio increased to %70 and estimated as %97 for the year of 2014 (European Commission, Economic and Financial Affairs, AMECO database).

OBJECTIVE OF THE STUDY

In this study the effects of the global economic crisis on the PIIGS (Portugal, Ireland, Italy, Greece, Spain) countries' budget deficit and debt stock will be examined by using Panel Data Analysis over the period 1983-2012.

DATA AND METHODOLOGY

Literature Review

First studies related with sustainability of debts depend on stationarity tests. Hamilton and Flavin researched the stationarity of debt stock of USA for 1962-1984 periods and concluded that the budget deficit was sustainable. Kremers (1989) stated by using the ratio of outstanding external debt of USA to the GDP for 1920-1981 periods that the budget deficits were not sustainable. The later studies continued with researching the existence of a long term relationship between the income and expense. In this context, the cointegration relation between deficit, debt stock and interest payments or public expenditures including interest was researched. The aforementioned method was used by Trehan Walsh (1991), Hakkio and Rush (1991), Ahmed and Rogers (1995). In another method used by Bohn (1998) the feedback effect from debts to budget deficits was tested. In the analysis the existence of a negative relationship between debt stock and budget deficits which means the increase in debt stock was researched.

When the literature was examined related with the sustainability of debts time series studies were coincided for countries one by one and it was observed that European Union countries were mostly incorporated to the studies performed with panel data. No studies related with PIGS countries were coincided.

Application and Conclusions

In this part of the study, in order to test the sustainability indicators stated by Kremers, Hamilton and Flavin and Trehan and Walsh, some tests will be made for PIGS countries.

In literature in order to test whether the debts are sustainable or not various tests are suggested which basically depends on unit root and cointegration analyses. Initial tests researched the stationarity conditions of debt stock and the ratio of debt stock to gdp. If the series of ratio of debt stock to gdp is stationary it fulfils the debt sustainability condition of Kremers, if the first difference of debt stock series is stationary it fulfils the debt sustainability condition of Hamilton and Flavin. In later studies, (Trehan and Walsh) the long term relationship between debt stock and surplus series and in this context cointegration tests took part.

Econometrically first of all panel unit root tests are being used in order to test the stationarity of debt stock, ratio of debt stock to gdp and surplus variables. d_{it} shows the series of debt stock (country i=1,…,5 and time t=1980,...,2013), the existence of unit root in the series can be tested by the basic Augmented Dickey Fuller (ADF) specification for panel data.

$$\Delta d_{it} = \alpha_i + \rho_i d_{it-1} + \lambda_t + \sum_{j=1}^{mlag_i} \beta_{ij} \Delta d_{it-j} + \varepsilon_{it} \quad (1)$$

This specification allows the lag length according to cross section units. There are various unit root tests using different null and alternative hypotheses:

Hypotheses (A): H_0: $\alpha_{i1}=0$ for all i versus H_1: $\alpha_{i1}<0$ for all i
Hypotheses (B): H_0: $\alpha_{i1}=0$ for all i versus H_1: $\alpha_{i1}<0$ for some i
Hypotheses (C): H_0: $\alpha_{i1}<0$ for all i versus H_1: $\alpha_{i1}=0$ for all i

While hypotheses (A) is used for Levin et al. (2002) panel unit root test; hypotheses (B) is assumed in Im et al. (2003) and Fisher type tests (ADF–Fisher and PP-Fisher) proposed by Maddala and Wu (1999) and Choi (2001). Hypotheses (C) is used in Hadri (2000) panel unit root test.

LLC and Hadri unit root tests among aforementioned tests are known as first generation tests which do not allow correlation between units and do not also allow autoregressive term (ρ) to take value according to units as well. IPS and Fisher type tests on the other hand allow autoregressive term to take value according to units. As the CADF test of Pesaran is designed so as to take the correlation between units into consideration, it is assumed as second generation test and its null hypothesis indicates the existence of unit root.

Pedroni (1999), with the aim of investigating the existence of the cointegration relation among variables in the panel data, suggested seven both parametric and non-parametric Philips-Perron type panel cointegration tests that suggests "no cointegration" in its null hypothesis and permits heterogeneity in the alternative hypothesis (four of them are panel and three of them are group test statistics). Pedroni (1999) presented critical values for the conditions of with and without intercepts and deterministic trends in his paper. Kao (1999), on the other hand, suggested a ADF based panel cointegration test with a null hypothesis that similarly suggests "no cointegration". Similarly Westerlund (2007), suggested 4 panel cointegration tests depending on error correction model in order to test the existence of cointegration in panel data. While autoregressive parameter is not allowed to be changed according to units in panel variance ratio statistics, autoregressive parameter changes from unit to unit in group average variance ratio statistics.

RESULTS

We use annual unbalanced panel data from 1983 to 2012 for PIGS Countries (Ireland, Italy, Spain, Greece, Portugal). The variable that we consider are the debt stock (d_{it}), debt/GDP (dg_{it}) and the primary surplus (s_{it}).

Table 1. Pooled unit root tests

Test	dg_{it}	d_{it}	Δd_{it}	s_{it}	Δs_{it}
Levin, Lin & Chu t-stat	0.9275	0.8073	0.0000	0.0400	0.0000
Lm, Pesaran & Shin W-stat	0.9708	0.6913	0.0026	0.0252	0.0000
ADF-Fisher Chi-square	0.8756	0.2534	0.0000	0.0556	0.0000
PP-Fisher Chi-square	0.9905	0.8343	0.0000	0.1109	0.0000
Pesaran CADF	0.605	0.8870	0.0010	0.1860	0.0000
Hadri Z-stat	0.000	0.000	0.1179	0.000	0.7931

The null hypothesis in Hadri-Z test that series are stationary and in other tests the null hypothesis that series are non-stationary.

First, we apply several panel unit root tests for the series, the pooled and individual panel unit root tests results are represented in Table 1 and Table 2 respectively. The lag orders are chosen by schwarz information criterion and the values in the tables are probability values. Pooled unit root test results show that the series of ratio of debt stock to gdp is not stationary so that the sustainability condition of Kremers cannot be fulfilled for PIGS countries. On the other hand debt stock series is not stationary on the level but it becomes stationary when its first difference is taken. Therefore the sustainability condition of Hamilton and Flavin is fulfilled.

According to ADF and PP (Philips Perron) individual panel unit root tests results, debt/GDP series for all countries are not I(0) in 5% significance level. We can say by virtue of these results that sustainability hypothesis for Kremers is not accepted in all PIGS countries. When the sustainability condition of Hamilton and Flavin is evaluated separately for each country, it can be said that debts are sustainable only in Ireland according to ADF Fisher unit root test results while debts are sustainable in Ireland and Italy according to Philips Perron panel unit root result. In remaining countries (Greece, Spain and Portugal) debts are not sustainable according to conditions of both Kremers and Hamilton & Flavin.

The sustainability condition of Kremers and Hamilton&Flavin takes unit root tests as a basis however more advanced techniques are used in following studies. According to Trehan and Walsh, if the debt stock and noninterest budget expenditure are conintegrated, the debts are sustainable. In Table 1, unit root tests which are precondition

Table 2. Individual unit root tests

	ADF Fisher Unit Root Test			PP Unit Root Test		
Country	dg_{it}	d_{it}	Δd_{it}	dg_{it}	d_{it}	Δd_{it}
Ireland	0.2777	0.3076	0.0001	0.6605	0.6211	0.0001
Greece	0.9727	0.9848	0.2461	0.9721	0.9976	0.2443
Spain	0.5656	0.0648	0.1116	0.6931	0.4961	0.1090
Italy	0.4084	0.3140	0.2079	0.6017	0.4889	0.0381
Portugal	0.9841	0.9959	0.7662	1.0000	0.9997	0.1062

The null hypothesis in tests the null hypothesis that series are non-stationary

Table 3. Panel cointegration results (d_{it}, s_{it})

Pedroni Panel Cointegration Test	Panel v	Panel rho	Panel PP	Panel ADF	Group rho	Group PP	Group ADF
	1.0779 (0.1405)	**-0.79618 (0.2130)**	**-0.8837 (0.1884)**	**-1.0160 (0.1548)**	**0.5798 (0.7190)**	**-0.4264 (0.3349)**	**-0.9764 (0.1644)**
Westerlund Panel Cointegration Test	**Panel t**	**Panel a**			**Group t**	**Group a**	
	0.776 (1.000)	0.808 (0.994)			0.049 (1.000)	0.635 (0.999)	
Kao Panel Cointegration Test				**ADF**			
				-1.3521 (0.0882)			

for cointegration take place. As mentioned earlier, debt stock series is not stationary on the level while its first difference is a stationary series. When surplus series is examined it is also observed that this series is also not stationary on the level (except LLC and IPS tests) but it becomes stationary when its first difference is taken. After it is understood that both series are I(1) panel cointegration tests were used in order to test whether there is a long term relationship between them or not.

In Table 3, 7 panel cointegration test statistics of Pedroni, 4 panel cointegration test statistics of Westerlund and 1 panel cointegration test statistic of Kao and also probability values in brackets take place. According to all results the null hypothesis indicating the existence of long term relationship between surplus and debt stock is not refused; a long term relationship between the aforementioned series is not present. Therefore the sustainability condition of Trehan and Wals is not fulfilled.

Econometric Conclusion

In this study, the sustainability condition of Kremers, Hamilton and Flavin and Trehan and Wals in PIGS countries between years 1980 and 2013 was examined. According to both two analyses except the sustainability condition of Hamilton and Flavin, results support each other and it is observed that the debts are not sustainable in aforementioned countries in the mentioned date interval. When the results of Hamilton and Flavin are examined in detail, it is concluded that debts in Ireland and Italy are sustainable as the first difference of the debt stock series is stationary.

REFERENCES

Akçay, B. (2012). *21. Yüzyılın İlk Finansal Krizi* (p. 266). Ankara: Seçkin Yayıncılık.

European Commission. *Economic and Financial Affairs, AMECO database*. Retrieved from: http://eu.spindices.com/indices/real-estate/sp-case-shiller-20-city-composite-home-price-index

Insider Mortgage Finance (2010). In *The Mortgage Market Statistical Annual* (Vol. 1). Bethesda, MD: Insider Mortgage Finance Publishing.

International Monetary Fund. (2012, October). World Economic Outlook, Coping with High Debt and Sluggish Growth (p. 190).

Lin, J. Y., & Treichel, V. (2012, January). *The Unexpected Global Financial Crisis, Researching Its Root Cause* (Policy Research WP: 5937). The World Bank.

Matheson, T. (2013). *The Global Financial Crisis: An Anatomy of Global Growth.* IMF WP: 13/76, March.

Yılmaz, B. E. (2013). Reflections of the Global Economic Crisis on the Countries of PIIGS and Turkey's Macroeconomic Variables. *Marmara Üniversitesi İktisadi ve İdari Bilimler Dergisi, 34*(1), 231.

ADDITIONAL READINGS

Allen, L. (2013). *The Global Economic Crisis: A Chronology*. London: Reaction Books Ltd.

Allen, W. A. (2013). *International Liquidity and the Financial Crisis*. Cambridge University Press.

Authers, J. (2013). *Europe's Financial Crisis: A Short Guide to*. New Jersey, USA: FT Press.

Berend, I. (2013). *Europe in Crisis: Bolt from the Blue*? Routledge, Taylor and Francis Group.

Blaese, J. D. (2012). *International institutions and the power of the EU*. Anchor Academic Publishing.

Blinder, A. S. (2013). *After the Music Stopped: The Financial Crisis, The Response and the Work Ahead*. USA: Penguin Press.

Desai, P. (2011). *From Financial Crisis to Global Recovery*. New York: The Columbia University Press.

Eichengreen, B., & Park, B. (2012). *The World Economy after the Global Crisis*. Singapore: World Scientific Publishing Co.

Farlow, A. (2013). *Crash and Beyond: Causes and Consequences of the Global Financial Crisis*. Oxford University Press.

Hieronymi, O., & Stephanou, C. (2012). *International Debt: Economic, Financial, Monetary, Political and Regulatory Aspects*. Palgrave Macmillan.

Nayak, S. (2013). *The Global Financial Crisis: Genesis, Policy Response and Road Ahead*. Springer.

KEY TERMS AND DEFINITIONS

Global Crisis: This term directly references to the global economic crisis which occurred in 2008 at USA and covered all of the world next years.

PIIGS: This abbreviation is occurred by the first letters of Portugal, Ireland, Italy, Greece and Spain which are the leading actors of the European debt crisis.

Public Debt Stock: This term indicates the total amount of the debts of governments. This is an important indicator to evaluate the debt sustainability of a country and gives significant expressions about the weakness or strong sides of an economy.

Sustainability: Sustainability is a term that shows how long an economy can bring the negative indicators without stepping into a crisis.

Section 5
Behavioral Corporate Finance

Chapter 21
State Financed Social Housing Model in South Africa Requires Capacity Building Injection

Vuyisani Moss
National Department of Human Settlements, South Africa

Hasan Dinçer
Istanbul Medipol University, Turkey

Ümit Hacıoğlu
Istanbul Medipol University, Turkey

ABSTRACT

This chapter is based on the premise of Social Housing Institutions (SHIs) sustainability mechanisms. It is informed largely by National Housing Finance Corporation's (NHFC's) research findings on social housing developments commissioned on its behalf. The broad aim of the study was to conduct an audit survey through a critical appraisal and analysis of one of South Africa's social housing projects. The methodological approach was primarily through a thorough literature and documentation review this study had examined in addition to quantitative findings; the definition of social housing as a concept and how it has been operationalized in different markets. According to the findings the low levels of employment, low levels of income and the lack of industries in the area suggest that the affordability levels of the project tenants are low.

INTRODUCTION

Any form of housing, property investment in particular is a function of a country's macro-economic activity, levels of its employed population, GDP growth plus budget and expenditure framework. The Gross Domestic Product (GDP) in South Africa expanded to an annualized 3.8% in the fourth quarter of 2013 (National Treasury, 2014). The GDP growth rate in South Africa is reported by the Statistics South Africa to have averaged 3.2% from 1993 until 2013.

By March 1996 the country's GDP growth rate recorded an all-time high of 7.6% while a

DOI: 10.4018/978-1-4666-7484-4.ch021

Table 1. GDP growth rate of selected country comparison in Africa: 2004-2013

	2004	2005	2006	2007	2008	2009	2010	2011	2012	2013 est
Angola	10.2	20.9	19	23.2	13.8	2.4	3.4	3.9	7.9	8.2
Nigeria	10.5	6.5	6	6.4	6	7	8	7.4	6.6	6.7
Botswana	2.6	4.8	8.3	8.9	3.7	-7.9	8.1	8	5.8	5.6
Burundi	4.8	0.9	5.4	3.5	4.9	3.8	4.8	4.2	4.3	4.6
Chad	34.3	7.9	2.7	8.4	3.4	4.1	14	1.6	7.2	7.4
Comoros	1.9	2.8	2.6	0.8	0.6	1.1	2	2.6	2.7	3.2
Egypt	4.1	4.5	6.8	7.1	7.3	4.9	4.8	1.8	2.2	2
Equatorial Guinea	38	9.7	1.3	21.4	10.7	4.6	-0.5	7.7	5.5	4.9
South Africa	4.6	5.3	5.6	5.5	3.6	-1.5	3.1	3.5	2.5	2.8
Zimbabwe	-6.9	-2.2	-3.5	-3.7	-17.7	6.3	9.6	10.6	4.4	5
Ghana	5.6	5.9	6.4	6.5	8.4	4	8	14.4	7.1	8
Kenya	5.1	5.9	6.3	7	1.5	2.7	5.8	4.4	4.2	4.5
Tanzania	7.8	7.4	6.7	7.1	7.4	6	7	6.4	6.4	6.9
Uganda	5.8	10	7.1	8.1	10.4	4.1	6.2	5.9	4.4	4.9
Rwanda	7.4	9.4	9.2	7.6	11.2	6.2	7.2	8.3	7.7	7.1

Source: GDPAfDB Statistics, SARB

negative growth of 2.70% was posted in March 2009. South Africa's export-based economy is the largest and most developed in Africa. The graph below demonstrates that even though South Africa has the biggest economy in the continent, its GDP growth is lagging behind other African countries. The countries comprising the top five ranking led by South Africa are Nigeria, Egypt, Algeria and Angola had shown exceptional economic growth in recent years. Equatorial Guinea recorded the continents' highest GDP rate of 38% in 2004 and being the worst performing economy as reflected in the graph.

South Africa's GDP growth rate by peer comparison had been tepid and lackluster. It is in Southern African states that SA's GDP growth rate had been gloomy comparatively speaking and Angola's economy has grown consistently over the measured period. Even the bottom ranked country, Comoros (in terms of economic size, investor confidence and country risk profile) is expected to contend well relative to South Africa and it has not been exposed to any negative growth rate over the last few years.

BACKGROUND

As stated by Statistics South Africa economic overview report, (2014) the Gross Domestic Product (GDP) in South Africa expanded 2.0% in the fourth quarter of 2013. The GDP annual growth rate in South Africa averaged 3.19% from 1994 until 2013, reaching a historical high of 7.10% in the fourth quarter of 2006 and a recorded a negative growth of 2.70% in the second quarter of 2009. South Africa is still regarded as the biggest economy in Africa even though the Nigerian economy is reportedly to have surpassed that of SA this year (2014). The largest sector of the economy is services which accounts for around 73.0% of GDP.

Within services, the most important are finance, real estate and business services (21.2% of GDP); government services (13.6% of GDP); wholesale, retail and motor trade, catering and accommodation (12.5% of GDP). Financial reforms and prioritizing housing in the national account has resulted in improved material conditions of those beneficiaries accessing housing subsidies in South

Africa. For instance, of the R1.25 trillion budgeted for the 2014/15 financial year, the government would be spendingapproximately R143-billion towards housing and community amenities. A 2011 study commissioned by Kayamandi Development Services on the economic impact and expenditure of housing delivery programmes had found that from April 1994 to April 2010 revealed that a total of R115.6 billion had been spent on housing, which equaled 2 371 777 units delivered at an average annual rate of 148 236 housing units (Kayamandi Report, 2011).

International Context of Social Housing

Most of the governments in Western Europe after the Second World War embarked on ambitious social housing programmes as much of the investment went into the reconstruction of infrastructure and industries. Government intervention came in the form of rent control as scarcity continued to increase prices beyond the affordability of the general population. Subsidies for investment in housing were also granted and social housing attained prominence in the bid to accelerate housing provision. Priemus&Dieleman (1997) note that in seeking to achieve quantity, quality was largely comprised in dwellings designed to provide accommodation to low income households. Priemus (1997) further notes that the countries with the largest absolute numbers of social housing stock are Germany, United Kingdom, France and the Netherlands. However, the countries with the largest proportion of social housing as a percentage of the total housing stock in Western Europe are the Netherlands, Sweden, UK, Denmark, Austria, France and Germany. In fact, Smith and Oxley (1997) note that the Netherlands' social housing sector is the largest in Europe. In 1993, about 41 percent of Netherlands' total housing stock was in the social rented sector.

In Britain housing has been part of the welfare state particularly after 1945. Yet what is notable is that housing operated within a loose laissez-faire framework of central influence rather than stricter control applying to the social insurance and social assistance (Hugo, 2004). Welfarism in housing was reflected in rent control policies and the policies on rent for council housing which emerged after the Second World War. In calculating the level of rent benefits required in the post-war period, Britain used the level of rents in the period just before the war. When rent control was introduced in 1945, about 62% of dwellings were rented from private landlords. The introduction of legislation to reduce rent control (1954) resulted in the decline of tenure in the private rental sector.

The British approach of addressing housing needs through the public sector in the form of local government meant that housing provision was linked to the public sector financing regime and what Murie (1997) refers to as the Public Sector Borrowing Requirement (PBSR). This link to the public sector financing meant that the provision of public housing was subject to the restrictions imposed by the PSBR. On the development of the social rented sector in the Netherlands, Krythoff (2008) remarks that the sector experienced an exponential growth after the Second World War from 12% in 1947 to 1990 when its overall market share represented 41% of the housing stock. However the shifts in housing policies and strategies after 1990 have reduced the market share of social housing to about 37% which is still large when compared to other European countries. Priemus (2003) argues that the Netherlands rental market can be considered a unitary rather than a dual rental market. While the Dutch social rental sector might be considered to be anti-market but it still conforms to market principles.

There are a range of factors that explain the rapid growth of the social rented sector in the Netherlands. Firstly, between 1945 -1990 the Netherlands had an acute shortage of housing and policy instruments and strategies focused on addressing the housing shortage through mass housing. Straub (2002) argue that the provision of social housing, regulation of rents and allocation of subsidies are interventions within the housing market to ensure access and affordability. Analysts such as Murie (1997) and Velzen (1997) postulate that social housing in the UK and Sweden respectively will increasingly become the option for the poor. Initially social housing accommodated highest income households. In France in 1973, there was a radical shift when social housing increasingly became the accommodation option for the lowest income quartiles. A similar trend is observed for Britain where social housing is said to have broken the distinction between the low and high income households. Macro-economic policies that encouraged home-ownership and the sale of council housing in the UK resulted in a decline in the overall market share of social housing. In discussing social housing Priemus (1997) delineates the characteristics that distinguish the social rented sector in the Netherlands:

- The housing was built with state financing;
- It was subsidized by the national government;
- The principal and administrator was either the local authority or non-profit housing association;
- Rents were set below the prevailing market rates (housing need > housing demand);
- The dwellings were meant for low-income households.

The approach of the Netherlands to public financing of social housing was to set up a guarantee scheme to allow housing associations access private funds for new developments. Thus the cost of private loans is no longer a criterion for the definition of social housing.

In establishing the concept of social housing, Priemus (1997) argues that social housing exists only to the extent that housing providers build and manage good quality dwellings for the low-income populations and that such groups have preference in accessing the accommodation. Priemus (1997) further notes that social housing is made possible by the subsidy mechanism in the Netherlands. The author aptly observes that, 'an unsubsidized social rented sector is not a feasible option. In other words, social housing is often subsidized housing, but subsidization is not a necessary condition for a dwelling to be classified as social rented housing' (Priemus 1997,p.555). Such an assertion resonates considerably in the South African context of housing subsidy. The South African subsidized model provides fully for those households and individuals with no income and very low income plus the social housing concept is operationalized within the partial subsidy regime for low and middle income earners.

Social Housing in South Africa

Social Housing, according to the original Toolkit developed by the Social Housing Foundation (SHF) is "a particular approach to affordable housing whose core intention is to provide low to moderate income households with an affordable housing option". Embraced by this approach are a range of other services which include provision of community development services and empowerment benefits, and promote a lifestyle which is conducive to community living. Social housing is distinct from other low to moderate-income housing as it involves the residents in the on-going management of their housing.

There are two main features of Social Housing:

- It is located in a formally recognized and accredited institution; Residents are somehow involved, to a greater or lesser degree, in the overallmanagement of their arrangements; and
- The social housing component is the state's heavily subsidized instrument.

The local government has put a high emphasis on the regeneration of the inner city. An important part of this program is the development of the social housing.

The local Government Green Paper on Social Housing in the Inner City of May 1998 states, 'Social housing represents an important opportunity to achieve both the objectives of housing delivery and urban regeneration'. The term social housing is used locally to describe a very broad range of housing delivery and management mechanisms, aimed at housing the lower income part of the market, but which are all characterized by the fact that it is subsidized with the institutional subsidy provided under national subsidy scheme.

The Green Paper on Social Housing further states that social housing is a recent phenomenon in South Africa and there is little knowledge of policy or experience to guide its development. The Green Paper suggests a supportive approach and a number of importantrecommendations on the facilitation and promotion the social housing sector are made.

The original classification of social housing sector was before the Legislative regulatory changes were characterized by institutions that differ in terms of the following:

- Legal form (Private companies, section 21 companies and co-operatives);
- Tenure options (Rental, Co-operatives, Rent - to - Buy and Installment sale); and,
- Type of development (Greenfields, Refurbishments, Conversion and Upgrade).

The institutions also differ according to their stage of development with the followingdiscernible categories:

- Potential Social Housing institutions representing institutions that have expressed an intention to pursue social housing delivery but have not yet registered a legal entity for social housing;
- Emerging Social Housing Institutions being those institutions that have formally registered a legal entity for social housing but have not yet developed anyhousing stock; and,
- Established Social Housing Institutions being those institutions that are formally registered legal entities, owning and/or managing housing units.

In strictest definition, social housing- a heavily subsidized real estate component is defined as 'a rental or co-operative housing option for low income persons at a level of scale and built form which requires institutionalized management and which is provided by accredited social housing institutions or in accredited social housing projects in designated restructuring zones' (Department of Human Settlements, 2005). The social housing definition conforms to the idea of putting in place an institutional framework to ensure that rental housing is held as a public good for the benefit of the poor. For an institution to qualify for accreditation to provide social housing it must be 'a legal entity established with the primary objective of developing and/ or managing housing stock that has been funded through the grant programmes.

The Targeted Market

The low and middle income groups in the social housing policy are described as those with household income is below R7500 per month. Income mix prescriptions for individual projects specify segments of participants for different income categories within this broad band and ensure a good spread across the range of R1,500 to R7,500. Under the capital housing subsidy scheme, one of the requirements for eligibility is that one has to have dependents in addition to being over 21 years. This criterion does not apply to the beneficiaries of social housing.

The target market segment of social housing is individuals rather than households; access is not pegged on having dependents among other issues. Social housing targets individuals as well as households, thus it is more inclusive and the requirements more accommodating than other types of subsidy. The social housing policy estimated an increase of 7% in the demand for the social rented sector between 2001 and 2011. While the policy specifies the target for social housing, the same policy also stipulates that the purpose of social housing is restructuring and not mass delivery (DOH, 2005). Restructuring in social housing is conceptualized in terms of the income, and racial mix of the tenants in each development.

The policy clearly notes that there is need to avoid the concentration of low income individuals in the housing developments as this is likely to increase the proportion of subsidies required and also create spaces of social exclusion. Although the targeted beneficiaries of social housing in South Africa are persons earning between R1500 to R7500, the policy notes that most of the beneficiaries of social housing have been persons earning approximately R3500. The tendency for persons earning close to the threshold for the subsidy has meant that social housing institutions are unable to attract a large proportion of the housing subsidy. Social housing providers have also tended to draw tenants earning above the subsidy thus putting social housing institutions on a collision course with the government.

The specific guiding principles of social housing in South Africa include:

- Ensuring transparency, accountability, and efficiency in the administration and management of social housing;
- Promotion of the use of public funds in a way that stimulates and/ or facilitates private sector investment and participation in social housing sector;
- Operate within the provisions of the constitution (1996) the Public Finance Management Act (PFMA) and other statutory procurement prescripts.

The Social Housing Act (2008) (RSA, 2008) stipulates that institutions must be accredited with the Social Housing Regulatory Authority (SHRA) and ensure compliance with the provisions of the Social Housing Act (2008) which among others include meeting the core mandate of acquiring, developing and managing social housing projects for low income communities with the support of local authorities. The initial focus of social housing was that the targeted beneficiaries and individual dwellings but, the shift to projects has meant that great attention had to be paid to the public environment where the projects are located.

Funding of Social Housing Projects

Social housing has since 1994 been financed by the National Department of Housing (DOH), now Department of Human Settlements (DHS) under the Housing Subsidy Scheme (HSS). Given that the goal of social housing is restructuring, the policy (2005) makes a shift from a single-pronged financing approach to a multi-pronged approach that does not only include subsidy financing but also debt funding and public-private partnerships. Social housing continues to be financed from the fiscus through the HSS which is allocated to the provinces and is managed by the individual provinces. However a second way in which social housing is financed is through the Human Settlement Redevelopment Programme (HSRP) which includes a fixed component, that is, the restructuring component (DOH, 2005, p.2; RSA, 2008). The HSRP is managed the DHS and under this programme the local authorities are required to apply with a business plan for access to the standard/fixed restructuring grant. The standard component restructuring grant is managed by the DHS. The role of the provinces is to administer the disbursement of the fixed grant to various municipalities. This is also complimented profoundly by National Housing Finance Corporation (NHFC) debt funding model.

The second component of the social housing capital grant- the variable component is administered by the provinces or local authorities and derived from the equitable share of housing budget allocated to the provinces on each funding cycle (DOH, 2005; RSA, 2008). Provinces or accredited local municipalities are required to allocate part of their budget to the social rented sector. The funds allocated to the social rented sector are distributed in terms of institutional subsidies which are also used outside the restructuring zones. The second component of the social housing grant is used within the restructuring zones as top-up to increase the affordability of the social rented dwellings thus helping reach the neediest targets. There is a cap on the top-up component of the social housing grant. Other ways of toping up include the free allocation of land for social housing by local authorities or monetary contributions. While not obliged to make contributions, local authorities, national DHS and provincial departments can make contributions to the capital costs of social housing.

The Form of Tenure

In terms of the social housing policy, rental tenure does not include the option for immediate individual ownership if the social housing is developed using the state housing grant. Where social housing units have to be transferred to individual ownership, this is "only possible with the express permission of the regulator, and on the assumption that a portion of the subsidy will be repaid to bring the actual subsidy received in alignment with the other subsidy instruments of government (such an institutional subsidy" (DHS, 2009, p.18). According to the Social Housing Regulations (2012), the gross rentals charged should be able to cover the operating costs and also not exceed 33% of the total monthly household income of the tenant. In terms of the tenant mix, the Regulations (2012) require that at least 30% of units in social housing be allocated to households earning less than R3500 per month and only a maximum of 70% of the units can be allocated to households earning between R3500 and R7500. Social housing is not eligible to households earning more than R7500.

The notable characteristics of the social housing model can be summarized as follows:

- The housing built with state financing;
- It subsidized by the national government;
- The principal and administrator is either the local authority or non-profit housing association;
- Rents are set below the prevailing market rates (housing need > housing demand);
- The dwellings are meant for low-income households

Estimated Project Development Cost

Social housing institutions in the form of housing associations are required to develop affordable rental housing units for low-income tenants. Given that the institutional subsidy is often insufficient to build quality rental accommodation, the housing associations often have to source top-up finance from capital markets. In the case of the studied project the top-up finance was loaned by an investor which provided a loan of R22 million. The housing project was developed as follows.

Table 2. Development cost

Unit Type/ Dwelling	Number of units	Average development cost	Total development cost in million Rands
30 m^2 Low spec	118	37 483.07	4, 423.002
30 m^2 Semi Detached	86	46 743.50	4, 019.855
30 m^2 Detached	225	46, 378.65	10, 435.196
40 m^2 Semi Detached	46	53, 159.44	2, 44.334
40 m^2 Detached	102	52, 519.99	5, 357.039
54 m^2 Semi Detached	8	61, 131.64	489.045
54 m^2 Detached	91	60, 464.53	5, 502.181

Findings of the Study

When the total sample size of 618 is disaggregated the results show that the vast majority were Colored (99 per cent or 612), while 3 out of the 618 were Africans and only 1 was an Indian / Asian respondent. More females (63.4 per cent/392) than males (36.6% / 226) participated in the survey. More than half (54.9 per cent/339) of the respondents were married compared to 44.2 per cent or 273 that were single. About six (1 per cent) of the respondents interviewed refused to disclose their marital status.

Household Size

The survey requested information on the inhabitants of each household unit including their names, ages, gender, race, marital status, citizenship and social welfare status.

The distribution of household size shows that the largest size of an individual household in all of the 618 units was ten (10) and the smallest was nought (0). Further analysis suggests that there are mostly four (4) residents over 15 in a household, with a mean average of 3.55.

Table 3. Demographics

Race	n	%
African	3	0.5
Coloured	612	99.0
Indian/Asian	1	0.2
White	0	0
Other	2	0.3
Gender		
Male	226	36.6
Female	392	63.4
Marital Status		
Married	339	54.5
Single	273	44.2
No response	6	1.0

Table 4. Demographics

Residents	Males	% of males	Females	% of females
2618	1238	47.3	1380	52.7

Employment Status

The employment numbers show that the proportion of unemployed (46.0 per cent or 284 respondents) is more than the employed (41.3 per cent or 255 respondents). Further analysis of the employment status of respondents reveals that of the 41.3 per cent that is employed, 7.8 per cent (48) is self-employed on a part-time basis. About 33.2 per cent (205) of the respondents indicated that they were unemployed and looking for employment. In addition, 5.4 per cent (33) of the respondents are permanently disabled, while larger proportions of housewives are also looking for work (3.2 per cent or 20). There are also 7.3 per cent (45) respondents either on pension, studying or in some form of activity which is not defined as employed.

Income Levels

While 21.03% of the residents had a monthly household income of less than R1 000, the majority of residents (58.57%) had a monthly household income of between R1 000 and R5 000. A small proportion (6.47%) had a monthly household income of between R5 000 and R10 000, while an even smaller proportion (0.48%) had a monthly household income of between R10 000 and R20 000.

The monthly personal income is somewhat differently distributed. The majority (46.76%) of respondents had a personal income of less than R1 000, the next largest group (39.16%) had a personal income of between R1 000 and R5 000, followed by a small group (4.37%) that had a personal income of between R5 000 and R10 000, whilst the

Table 5. Household income

Household Income	Frequency	Per Cent
R2 001 – R3 000	100	16.18
R1 001-R1 500	95	15.37
R1 501 – R2 000	84	13.59
R3 001 – R5 000	83	13.43
Refuse to answer	77	12.46
R751 – R1 000	44	7.12
R501 –R750	39	6.31
R5 001 – R7 500	30	4.85
No income	28	4.53
R1 – R500	19	3.07
R7 501 – R10 000	10	1.62
Uncertain/Don't know	6	0.97
R10 001 – R15 000	2	0.32
R15 001 – R20 000	1	0.16

highest income level was between R10 000 and R15 000 which composed 0.16% of respondents. Census 2011 showed that the majority (61.0%) of the residents in the designated municipality have monthly incomes less than R1 600 per month.

Total Monthly Household Income

Comparison of Affordability Levels of Residents Who Own The Unit With Those Who Rent

The majority of residents 526 (85.11%) own the unit, with the rest of the residents renting (11.81%), sub-letting (0.65%) or having other forms of occupation (2.43%). It is worth noting here that the project provided social housing for rent so that once tenants had proved their credit worthiness after paying rent for four years, they could then apply for a loan to purchase the unit. The proportion of those who indicated ownership represents households that accessed the housing subsidy and have been living in the units as the original tenants of the project. The majority of residents (77.51%) also agree or even strongly agree that ownership is a good form of home occupation. The majority of households, a total of 323 (85.90%), are not up to date with their rent/bond repayments. Most of these, a total of 232 of all households (52.59%), have fallen behind in the previous year.

The main reasons residents provide in 20 for the difficulty in making rent or mortgage payments are due to reasons other (37.22%) than unemployment (14.24%), other debts or responsibilities (7.12%), unexpected utility bills (5.99%),working fewer hours/less overtime (2.27%), illness (2.27%), increases in rent/bond repayments and domestic problems (0.97%), in that order. There are 436 units (71.13%) that have been repaired by residents themselves. Most households (50.97%) found it very difficult to pay for those repairs.

Affordability Levels of Tenants In Terms of Their Ability to Service Mortgages

From the audit survey a mere 34% of the tenants earn more than R3000. This implies that the tenants can afford to pay rent in the project quite comfortably. In terms of the social housing policy, the target market for social housing are individuals earning between R1500 to R7500. The findings of this study point to high levels of unemployment and low levels of income. Majority earn less than R5000. This finding is supported by the key informant interviews which suggest that although at the start of the project most tenants had employment, the situation changed with the closure of factories in the area. This had resulted in some tenants moving out and renting out their units at rates higher than what the project was charging for rent.

Tenants who moved out of the area to seek employment had resorted to asking other people to house-sit for them so that they would retain their dwellings. While this was done with good intention, the strategy had backfired on some of the original tenants as those house-sitting demanded to be recognized as tenants. A small number had sold the units. The tenants without income had resorted to encouraging others not to pay their rent. At the current income levels the high unemployment rates, the tenants cannot afford the dwellings in which they live. The lack of affordability is compounded by the unwillingness to pay rent in some instances.

Strategic Recommendations

In summing up, by means of recommendations as emerged from the findings, fundamental are interventions geared towards maintaining the sustainability of social housing projects. There are quite a number of interventions that should be adopted by various stakeholders to ensuring the existence of healthy relationships among all participants. Amongst such important initiatives are the one highlighted below.

Proper comprehension of social housing instrument;

- Strong acquaintance of social housing policy and its regulatory frameworks including the value of subsidy ;
- Robust and well accustomed residential committees liaising directly with all stakeholders;
- Existence of trustworthiness and honesty across all key participants;
- Training and empowerment of occupant both owners and tenants;
- Clear understanding of tenure options and implications thereof;
- Good management skills for each social housing project;
- Ongoing consultative engagements of key stakeholders on critical matters;
- Constant appraisal of tenants profile and earnings;
- Resultant impact of non-payment behavior;
- Clarification on roles and responsibilities;
- Coach and empower prospective homeowners about the cost of ownership and obligations;
- Mentor and empower tenants about rent issues and potential escalations
- Strive to build, maintain and reinforce relationships between projects management and residents through clear communication and other ways.

CONCLUSION

This study set out to assess the current status of the tenants. The study through the survey findings has shown that most tenants currently living in the project earn low incomes; the rate of unemployment is high and the levels of education moderate. The closure of factory industries in the area had exacerbated the challenge of unemployment as some tenants have had to move out of the area to seek employment elsewhere. Given the high rate of unemployment and the low levels of income, the affordability levels of the tenants are low.

There are those who genuinely cannot afford the units in which they live. In such instances, such households should be allocated alternative accommodation. There are households which are struggling and can with difficulty afford to meet their rental obligations. Such tenants should be afforded an opportunity to pay their rent and continue to live in the development. There are also those who can afford to pay rent comfortably and such individuals must be allowed to pay their rental arrears and the new rent be set up by the investor.

In analyzing the current status of the project and the affordability levels, it is evident that whether tenants are able to resume rent payment or not, there is generally an unwillingness to resume payment and this has been partly explained in terms of non-payment behavior coupled with requisite management skills and lack capacity building to empower tenants and borrowers about responsibilities and corresponding obligation of tenancy and ownership. In the absence of such a will, the sustainability of these projects remains a challenge and that create financial vulnerability and cash flow problems of managing agents. Most importantly and fundamental in this sector is that prospective investors are deterred and discouraged by such patterns.

REFERENCES

Department of Human Settlements. (2004). "Breaking New Ground": A Comprehensive Plan for the Development of Sustainable Human Settlements. Pretoria.

Department of Human Settlements. (2005). Social Housing Policy for South Africa: Towards an Enabling Environment for Social Housing Development. Pretoria.

Department of Human Settlements. (2011). Annual Report 2011/13. Pretoria.

Hugo, P. (2004). Dutch Housing Allowances: Social Housing at Risk. *International Journal of Urban and Regional Research*, *28*(3), 706–712. doi:10.1111/j.0309-1317.2004.00545.x

Kayamandi Development Services. (2011). *Economic Impact and Expenditure of Housing Delivery Programmes from 1994 to 2010. National Department of Human Settlements*. Pretoria: NDHS.

Kruythoff, H. (2008). *Tenant Participation in the Netherlands: The role of Laws, Covenants and (power) Positions*. Housing Studies.

National Housing Finance Corporation, (2013). *Report of Tenant Audit Survey for Housing Association*.

National Treasury. (2014). *Finance Minister's Budget Policy Statement, 2014/15*. Cape Town: Parliament.

Priemus, H. (2003). Dutch Housing Associations: Current Developments and Debates. *Housing Studies*, *18*(3), 327–351. doi:10.1080/02673030304237

Priemus, H., & Dieleman, F. (1997). Social Rented Housing: Recent Changes in Wester Europe-introduction. *Housing Studies*, *12*(4), 421–425. doi:10.1080/02673039708720907

Social Housing Foundation (Social Housing Regulatory Authority). (2003). *Social Housing Toolkit for Housing Associations*. Retrieved from wwww.shra.org.za

South African Reserve Bank (SARB). (2013). *Quarterly Report, December*. Pretoria: Government Publishers.

Statistics South Africa. (2014). *Economic Overview: Practice Forex Trading*. Pretoria: Statistics South Africa Publishers.

Straub, A. (2002). Strategic Technical Management of Housing Stock: Lessons from Dutch Housing Associations. *Building Research and Information*.

KEYTERMS AND DEFINITIONS

Mortgage: A mortgage is a legal agreement or a kind of loan, which is used by purchasers to raise money to buy the property or to raise funds for any purpose. Mortgage assuresfinancing the purchase of real estate with specified payment periods and interest rates. Mortgage conveys the conditional right of ownership on a property by its owner to a lender.

Project Development: Project development is the process and the facility of planning, organizing, coordinating, and controlling the resources to accomplish specific goals. The process takes a transportation improvement from concept through construction. It has six phases; initiation, definition, design, development, implementation and follow-up phases.

Real Estate: Real estate is the property which consists of land, the buildings or housing in general and immovable property on it. Real estate can include business or residential properties. Examples of real estate include undeveloped land, houses, office buildings and factories.

Social Housing: Social housing is low rents permission on a secure basis to the people who are struggling with housing costs. It is a form of housing tenure which may be owned and managed by the state to let affordable housing.

South Africa: Republic of South Africa (RSA) is a country with close to 53 million people and has a multiethnic society, cultures, languages, and religions.

Chapter 22
Post-Offering Operating Performance of Reverse LBOs:
An Update

Sevilay Gümüş
Hacettepe University, Turkey

ABSTRACT

This chapter reports on the post-offering performance of 114 US firms that went public between 2000 and 2008 following leverage buyouts. The objective of this paper is to examine accounting performance of following reverse leverage buyouts compared to the industry competitors before, at the time of, and the following four years after initial public offering. In addition to accounting performance measures, capital expenditures, working capital and employment levels are also compared to rival firms. The evidence indicates that the RLBO corporations have superior accounting performances compared to their industries exact year of IPO and following years after public offering. Also, the RLBO corporations have less operating income compared to the reverse leverage buyout firms in previous studies, but have more operating income and operating cash flows than their industry counterparts. The RLBO firms typically make less capital expenditure except the IPO year and four years after the initial public offering.

1. INTRODUCTION

In last two decades, intense public examinations have surrounded around the reverse leverage buyout phenomenon that had been previously bought out by another corporation or special private equity entrepreneurs and investors. The goal of reverse leverage process differs from one company to another, while it is also related to firms' sizes. The initial purpose of Leverage Buyout process is to reduce inefficiencies and to improve performance.

Happern, Kieschnick & Rotenberg (1999) find that the leverage buyout companies have better growth prospects and lower Tobin q values than the rest of the publicly traded firms in associated industries. Similarly, Jensen (1989) documents leverage buyout companies haveless motivation problems especially in the sectors with less growth opportunities. Moreover, Degeorge & Zeckhauser (1993) cite that the accounting performances of

DOI: 10.4018/978-1-4666-7484-4.ch022

reverse leverage buyout corporations exceed their counterparts in the year before and at the time of the initial public offering, but deteriorate thereafter.

Kaplan (1997), in explaining the trends in 1980s, gives important clues about the RLBOs behavior in general:

In the first half of the 1980s, the LBO insights led to great success. Buyout companies experienced improved operating profits and few defaults. Adjusting for the overall stock market or industry these early buyouts generated abnormally positive returns. Because the overall stock market increased over this period, buy out sponsors earned substantial nominal returns

In this paper, 144 reverse leverage buyout corporations that returned to initial public trading between 2000 and 2008 are examined. We examine the performanceof these reverse LBOs as well as the changes in their organizational structures(in terms of leverage and employment level). In addition tothe expenditure decisions of the reverse leverage buyout firms, the working capital management is also investigated in order to have a better understanding on the position of the reverse leverage buyout companiescompared to their industry counterparts. We also analyze the degree of changes in performance and change in the working capital management associated to the changes in organizational structure. To perceivethe relationships between change in performance and change in debt, capital expenditures, working capital and employment management, sectional and cross sectional analysis are conducted.

The results show a decrease in the mean leverage ratio, although the leverage level of reverse LBO firms remains high compared to their industry peers. However, the reverse LBO sample used in this paper has lower debt level compared to the ones in the past studies. The change in debt/capital of post-IPO period was found as -23% by Holthausen & Larcker (1996), but we find -35% or -36.45% for/with the firms (including the those have zero debt mentioned in their 10-Ks) which can be seen from the Table 2 Panel A. Moreover, the accounting performance of reverse leverage buyout firms has better position than the industry counterparts (the evidences suggest a weakness in performance in the second year) and continue to outperform throughout the years. Also, the evidence shows that the reverse leverage buyout corporations spent less on capital expenditures than their peers in associated industries, except the year of the public offering and four years after the initial public offering differently than Hotlhausen & Larcker (1996) as mentioned earlier. With respect to working capital management, the evidence suggests that reverse leverage buyout companies carry less working capital than their industry equivalents. It needs to be mentioned that although the RLBO corporations increase their working capital, the working capital remains at a lower level than peer firms. In terms of employment intensity, there is not much difference found between reverse LBO firms' staffing level and their associated industries. Yet, the evidence refers a continuous increase in employment level starting from the two years after initial public offering and shows continuity to four years after the offering.

The plan of this paper is as follows: the next section covers conceptual issues and the literature review. The third section discusses the role of the leverage level in reverse leverage buyout firms. Section three states the formal hypotheses. Section four discusses data and methodologies which are used in this study. The results are given in section five, with subsections discussaccounting performance, median levels of working capital, capital expenditures and employment level are analyzed. Section six concludes the paper.

2. CONCEPTUAL ISSUES AND LITERATURE REVIEW

An original initial public offering, IPO, represents a first sale of common stock or sharesto public by growing firm. The purpose of it may differ in terms of the firms' sizes, so the issuer may often be young or relatively small firm, which may desire to expand firm's capital, as well as large but privately-held firm, which may wish to be converted into a public firm. The public corporation often believes the importance of using media exposure and visibility as an effective marketing tool of the firm. Since the corporation has an ability to increase its investors' share liquidity and enable the diversification of entrepreneurs' wealth as well as founders', the public firm generally obtains a lower cost of capital. However, some disadvantages of initial offering also exist. Disadvantages of an IPO include transaction cost, ongoing fees and expenses in providing information to equity markets and regulators, and reduction in the control of the firm to outsiders (Hogan, Olson & Kish, 2001). In addition, the publicly quoted company with dispersed ownership may suffer from a higher degree of managerial discretion resulting from a lack of monitoring which may lead to "empire building" to the detriment of shareholders' value (Renneboog & Simons, 2005).

A leveraged buyout, be shorten as LBO, steps into a role when opportunity to add value arises. LBO, once described as "bootstrapping", represents an equity control of afinancial sponsor when a major portion of purchase is financed by borrowing. In fact, the term of LBO does not only refer public to private transformation, which we address in this paper, but also refers an increase in leverage due to acquisitions. The central purpose of going from public to private can be explained with several different reasons such as capital relocation, wealth transfer from bondholders to shareholders, tax savings and reduction of agency cost. Nevertheless, "wealth gain" is generally accepted as the basis of those transactions.

Even though, the early versions of LBO seen in 1960s, American corporate sector faced almost 2000 leverage buyout activities in 1980s.Jensen (1989) observedthat LBO-like organizations reduced their incentive problems faced by more traditional corporate organizations. Normally typical leverage buyout companies have finer growth prospects and lower Tobin q values than the rest of the publicly traded firms of the equal size in the same industry (Halpern, Kieschnick&Rotenberg, 1999). Thus, "going public" or "public offering" plays a significant role for the entrepreneurs and financial sponsors on this stage. Jensen (1989, p.61) describes this circulation as "eclipse of the public corporation". Kaplan (1991) researched 183 leverage buyout companies that went public between 1979 and 1986, and observed that a significant amount of leverage buyout companies went public again. Similarly, Ainina & Mohan (1991)explains the main motivation of private corporations' going public desire with revolving door policy, which states a process which implies superior information held by insiders who decide when to exit and to enter the public market. Kosedag, Mehran & Qian (2009) similarly use Ainina and Mohan's statement in order to complete Bruton, Keels & Scrifres (1999)'s idea of complete cycle and refer to reverse leverage buyouts as the last component of this cycle.

The procedure of obtaining cash to decrease firm's debt by turning privately held companyinto a public company, which was publicly traded before, is expressed as reverse leverage buyout. RLBO firms are the companies which were taken private in a LBO and then reenter public markets in order to acquire the same or even better benefits than original IPO. Even though some scientists claim this private to public transformation should better be fast, Cao (2007) claims this quick flip may increase doubts on whether buyout sponsors have time to make enough improvements on operation or not.

As one of the results of this"revolving door" process, insiders may use the advantage of "going public" decision earlier than the rest of the market and take advantage of the situation by purchasing the corporation's stock while they are low and selling them when the prices are high. However, reverse leverage buyouts differ from original initial public offerings in the amount of information available to investors in the period before to the IPO (Hogan,Olson & Kish, 2001). Muscarella and Vetsuypens (1989) figuredthat reverse-LBO firms have considerably less informational asymmetry than the ones gone public for the first time. This can be interpreted as the intensity of under-pricing more observable in original IPOs rather than reverse-LBOs. On a similar pattern, Kaplan and Stein (1991) stated that the afterward leverage buyout companies aregetting greater values and can be able to finance with publicly issued debt with a much greater extent than were earlier deals. Moreover, Mian & Rosenfeld (1993) investigated 85 firms which were operated roughly between the years of 1982 to 1990, and stated that the offerings notably and significantly outperform compared to their stock market peers. While Long and Ravenscraft (1993) documented contradictory evidence about the improvement in cash flow subsequently to initial public offering, Holthausen & Larcker (1996) found supporting evidence that reverse leverage buyout corporations show better operating performance (operating cash flow and operating earnings) in the post-IPO period against their industry counterparts. Also, Holthausen & Larcker (1996) found that the reverse leverage buyout firms spend less on capital expenditures than the median firms in their industry before making initial public offering, but the expenditures return to median level of the industry equivalents after the initial public offering.

3. FORMAL HYPOTHESES STATEMENT

An investigation of reverse leverage buyout firms can give us someadditional information about the extent to which leverage level provide advantageous inducements within business or organization. Holthausen & Larcker (1996) find that mean leverage ratio has decreasing path from the year before IPO to after. Thus, we detail our analysis based on this believe to mean leverage ratios of debt/capital changes compared to the year prior to initial public offering.

$H_{1,o}$ = *There is no decrease in mean leverage ratio of the reverse leverage buyout companies in time compared to the year before initial public offering.*

$H_{1,a}$ = *There is a decrease in mean leverage ratio of the reverse leverage buyout companies in time compared to the year before initial public offering.*

Since the accounting performances (operating earnings before depreciation, interest and taxes and operating cash flow before interest and taxes) allow us to compare the performance level of RLBO companies to their associated industries, we believe that the accounting performance measures can provide better and more accurate results on whether reverse LBO firms are outperforming compared to their industries or not. Degeorge & Zechauser (1993) claim reverse LBO firms' accounting performances outperform only before they went public, while both Hotlhausen&Larcker (1996) and Mian&Rosenfeld (1993) claim that the reverse leverage buyout companies exceed their industry peers on performances.

$H_{2,o}$ = *Accounting performances of RLBO corporations does not show any difference from the accounting performance oftheir industry peers*

$H_{2,a}$ = *Accounting performances of RLBO corporations does show differences from the accounting performances of their industry peers*

Kaplan (1989), Smith (1990) and Muscrealla & Vetsupens (1990) state that firms have some ability to lower some of their expenditures (such as capital expenditure) on discretionary items after an LBO. For that reason, we examine the capital expenditure/asset changes and compare them with the related industry in order to have better understanding on whether they are different from their industries peers and whether the patterns observed change over time.

$H_{3,o}$ = *Reverse LBO firms have no dissimilarities from their industry counterparts'median level in terms of spending on capital expenditures*

$H_{3,a}$ = *Reverse LBO firms have dissimilarities from their industry counterparts' median level in terms of spending on capital expenditures.*

The working capital is examined in this analysis to see whether the reverse leverage buyout firms have similar working capital in their structure to their industry counterparts and when it is increasing or decreasing before, at the time, or after initial public occurred since Holthausen & Larcker(1996) documents that the reverse leverage buyout firms have significantly smaller amounts of working capital than their industry counterparts both before and after initial public offering. Also, they find in the same research that amount of reverse LBO firms' working capital increase after the public offering.

$H_{4,o}$ = *RLBO corporations carry similar working capital to their industry equivalents*

$H_{4,a}$ = *RBLO corporations does not carry similar working capital to their industry equivalents*

According to Holthausen & Larcker (1996), staffing level of reverse leverage buyout companies is not different from their counterparts either before or after the public offering. For that reason, we examine how employment level changes in and over time, and whether reverse leverage buyout firms differ from their peers in terms of employment level after the offering.

$H_{5,o}$ = *Reverse leverage buyout companies employment level is not different than their industries.*

$H_{5,a}$ = *Reverse leverage buyout companies employment level is different than their industries.*

In this study this kind of analysis is made because the firms' performance levels possibly be different (significantly better or worse) than their industries throughout the years from the prior to IPO, at the time of IPO, +1, +2, +3, +4 years after initial public offering while the year -1 (prior to IPO year) used as a benchmark. We examine the changes in accounting performance between year -1 and +1 or between years -1 and the average of years +1 and +4 in order to see which independent variable is related to which accounting performance by how much and are there any unusual path compared to the results of the statements mentioned above. We also consider regression patterns where we can control industry performance to come up with better evidences.

$H_{6,o}$ = *Change in accounting performances (measured from one year before to one up to four years after the reverse LBO) is unrelated to change in leverage*

$H_{6,a}$ = *Change in accounting performances (measured from one year before to one up to four years after the reverse LBO) is related to change in leverage*

$H_{7,o}$ = *Change in accounting performances (measured from one year before to one up to four years after the reverse LBO) is unrelated to change in capital expenditures*

$H_{7,a}$ = *Change in accounting performances (measured from one year before to one up to four years after the reverse LBO) is related to change in capital expenditures*

$H_{8,o}$ = *Change in accounting performances (measured from one year before to one up to four years after the reverse LBO) is unrelated to change in working capital*

$H_{8,a}$ = *Change in accounting performances (measured from one year before to one up to four years after the reverse LBO) is related to change in working capital*

$H_{9,o}$ = *Change in accounting performances (measured from one year before to one up to four years after the reverse LBO) is unrelated to change in employment level*

$H_{9,a}$ = *Change in accounting performances (measured from one year before to up to four years after the reverse LBO) is related to change in employment level*

4. DATA AND METHODOLOGY

The sample is built from 114 reverse leveraged buyouts from 2000 to 2009.We include only US corporations,eliminating those that have foreign investment before, after or at the time of reverse leverage buyout process. Additionally, since the time range of the analysis covers recent period and the databases only give the data till at the end of 2008, some of the corporations are excluded from the study or analyzed in the time period without considering the years after 2008.

The acquired data represents all initial public offerings (IPOs) of leverage buyouts (LBOs) which are listed by Hoover's IPO central, Thomson Reuters and Security Exchange Commission's IPO fillings.Originally, 270 IPO firms areobtained from those lists for the time period of January 1, 2000 and December 31, 2009. Since SDC stopped identifying reverse LBOs in its database as of 1999 and Thomson Reuters' database is not capable of identifying reverse leverage buyout corporations,we have to check the IPO samples and identify firms to obtain trustable sample. The sample is checkedagainst 10-Ks of the each firm for each year individually from SDC Corporate database, Dow Jones News Service and Factiva for the firms' stories in order to control whether the corporations, which we found as RLBO firms, are really reverse leverage buyout firms or not.

Table 1. The table presents a distribution calendar for leveraged buyout (LBO) and the following initial public offering for the sample of 114 corporations.

Calendar Year	LBO	IPO	Calendar Year	LBO	IPO
1983	1	0	1996	5	0
1984	0	0	1997	8	0
1985	1	0	1998	7	0
1986	0	0	1999	14	0
1987	0	0	2000	12	7
1988	2	0	2001	10	10
1989	1	0	2002	16	8
1990	2	0	2003	12	7
1991	0	0	2004	9	23
1992	1	0	2005	11	25
1993	0	0	2006	0	25
1994	0	0	2007	1	5
1995	0	0	2008	1	4

*The IPOs of the RLBOs showed in the Table 1 occurred between January 1, 2000 and December 31, 2008. 114 LBO firms versus 114 IPO firms

The reason behind of checking the sample against 10-Ks is that a firm is identified as a reverse LBO if 10-K's indicates that it existed previously or a public company.

Leverage changes (as a part of the organizational structure) before, at the time and after IPO with explanatory statistics are also examined in this study. The leverage is defined by Holthausen & Larcker as "the sum of long term debt, short term debt, capitalized leases, and redeemable preferred stock divided by the sum of long term debt, short term debt, capitalized leases, redeemable preferred stock and the book value of common equity" (1996). Therefore, we use their definition to conduct the leverage changes analysis in this study.

In order to reach RLBOs' relative operating performances, operating income and operating cash flows are used as accounting measures. As

Holthausen & Larcker (1996) mentioned the common stock returns did not use for this evaluation since "any expected decline in the performance of the company due to its reversion to a public corporation should be impounded in the offering price, so that changes in the organizational structure observed at the IPO should be uncorrelated with subsequent return".

While the operating income before depreciation, interest and taxes divided by total assets (directly taken from COMPUSTAT as OPINC/assets) is taken as the first accounting ratio, operating cash flow before depreciation, interest and taxes divided by total assets (directly taken from COMPUSTAT as OCF/asset) is the second accounting ratio used in this analysis to measure accounting performances. COMPUSTAT describes operating cash flow before, interest and taxes divided by total assets as income before depreciation plus decrease in accounts receivable plus decrease in inventory plus increase in accounts payable plus increase in other current liabilities plus decrease in other current assets.

Also, it should not be forgotten that while year -1 represents the year of initial public offering, year 0 presents the fiscal term which IPO occurred. As Holthausen & Larcker (1996) explained, there is no control either on or over the Year 0 in terms of operating results since some firms might be private or public at the time of IPO. The years after initial public offering represents not numbers of years after the process and going public, but the performance over the number of fiscal years with in that company went public.

Moreover, in this analysis, unadjusted measure is used in order to perceive the reverse-LBO corporations' performances. Industry-adjusted is used simply to understand whether the firms are better or worse comparing to their industries' performances. To obtain industry adjusted, first the RLBO companies' associated four digit SIC codes is found and then the sectors, which the reverse LBO firms are in based on their 4 digits codes, are classified from the whole COMPUSTAT universe between 1999 to 2008. If the number of the firms in the sector related to their SIC codes are less than five, less digit SIC codes are used to obtain the industry medians. For instances, if in the classification of 3 digits codes do not have enough companies to estimate the industry median, 2 digits SIC codes associated with the companies are used. When Table 4 shows RLBO firms and industry adjusted based on these firms related sectors based on the classification mentioned above, Table 5 presents RLBO firms and industry-adjusted medians based on just with the two digit SIC codes associated with the reverse leverage buyout companies' sectors.

The reason of using different SIC codes is to get better understanding on the results about the industry as a whole. Besides, it should also be mentioned that for having Table 4 figures or results SAS computer program is used. However, in order to control the results obtained from SAS and re-find the medians for the whole industry based on the corporations' 2 digit SIC codes, the data from COMPUSTAT universe between 1970 and 2009 is acquired and eliminated up/down to the period of 1999 to 2008 for the whole COMPUSTAT universe based on the mentioned 2 digits SIC codes. The obtained results and the difference found can also be seen on Table 5. Such difference found cause it should not be forgotten that the most of the companies which we have worked on are acquired or bought-out immediately after/ or went bankruptcy immediately or for a while later. Since the accounting data of those firms are not generally obtainable because of mentioned reasons earlier, the observations used in this study are also available across the years.

Table 2. The table presents leverage changes (as a part of the organizational structure) before, at the time and after IPO with explanatory statistics.

Panel A			
Debt to capital for all RBLO firms in the analysis	**mean**	**median**	**stdev**
Pre -IPO debt / capital	0.7977	0.7375	0.5587
IPO Year debt / capital	0.7060	0.5580	1.4423
1 Year after IPO debt / capital	0.5386	0.5010	0.3740
2 Years after IPO debt / capital	0.5135	0.5000	0.3419
3 Years after IPO debt / capital	0.5050	0.4900	3.3074
4 Years after IPO debt / capital	0.6187	0.5270	0.4113
Post -IPO debt /capital	0.4633	0.5092	0.9752
Change in debt/ capital	-0.3343	-0.2283	0.4165
# of observations for whole RLBO firms*	**114**	**114**	**114**
Panel B			
Debt to capital of all RLBO firms with non-zero debt level	**mean**	**median**	**stdev**
Pre -IPO debt / capital	0.8267	0.7455	0.5472
IPO Year debt / capital	0.7526	0.5735	1.4777
1 Year after IPO debt / capital	0.5597	0.5105	0.3654
2 Years after IPO debt / capital	0.5302	0.5000	0.3343
3 Years after IPO debt / capital	0.5477	0.5010	3.3841
4 Years after IPO debt / capital	0.6330	0.5290	0.4048
Post -IPO debt /capital	0.5586	0.5348	0.3469
Change in debt/ capital	-0.2055	-0.1908	-0.0267
# of observations for the firms explained above*	**108**	**108**	**108**
Panel C			
Debt to capital of the companies which have completed Post-IPO	**mean**	**median**	**stdev**
Pre -IPO debt / capital	0.7642	0.7255	0.3737
IPO Year debt / capital	0.5839	0.5585	0.3418
1 Year after IPO debt / capital	0.5449	0.5045	0.3427
2 Years after IPO debt / capital	0.5273	0.5120	0.3507
3 Years after IPO debt / capital	0.5437	0.5160	0.3653
4 Years after IPO debt / capital	0.6187	0.5270	0.4113
Post -IPO debt /capital	0.5586	0.5348	0.3469
Change in debt/ capital	-0.2055	-0.1908	-0.0267
# of observations which have +4 years*	**44**	**44**	**44**
Panel D			
Debt to capital of the companies which have only 3 years after IPO	**mean**	**median**	**stdev**
Pre -IPO debt / capital	0.7647	0.6570	0.8169
IPO Year debt / capital	0.4501	0.4770	0.3038
1 Year after IPO debt / capital	0.3923	0.4050	0.2698
2 Years after IPO debt / capital	0.3934	0.4880	0.2632
3 Years after IPO debt / capital	0.4071	0.4270	5.4583
Post -IPO debt /capital	0.0420	0.4817	1.8453

continued on following page

Table 2. Continued

Change in debt/ capital	-0.7227	-0.1753	1.0284
# of observations which have +3 years*	**25**	**25**	**25**
Panel E			
Debt to capital of the companies which have only 2 years after IPO	**mean**	**median**	**stdev**
Pre -IPO debt / capital	0.9958	0.8950	0.6070
IPO Year debt / capital	1.1963	0.6175	2.8824
1 Year after IPO debt / capital	0.5924	0.4740	0.3602
2 Years after IPO debt / capital	0.6056	0.4880	0.3713
Post -IPO debt /capital	0.5990	0.4905	0.3607
Change in debt/ capital	-0.3968	-0.4045	-0.2463
# of observations which have +2years*	**26**	**26**	**26**

*The number of observations represents how many reverse -LBO firms was/is actually performing during this period. Since our time range is 2000- 2009, and some of the companies went public/became reverse-LBO closer to the end of our research date, the number of the firms which have 2 years after IPO are greater than the ones have only 3 years after offering. (For example if a firm went public in 2006, it will have only 2 years after IPO since 2009 10-Ks are not published till the time when the research was conducted)

Pre-IPO debt/capital is the sum of long term debt, short term debt, capitalized leases and redeemable preferred stock divided by the sum of long term debt, short term debt, capitalized leases and redeemable preferred stock plus the book value of common equity immediately prior to IPO

Post-IPO debt/capital is the sum of long term debt, short term debt, capitalized leases and redeemable preferred stock divided by the sum of long term debt, short term debt, capitalized leases and redeemable preferred stock plus the book value of common equity immediately after to IPO

5. RESULTS

5.1. Mean Leverage Ratio of Reverse Leverage Buyout Firms

Table 2 presents leverage changes (as a part of the organizational structure) before, at the time and after IPO with explanatory statistics. So, the mean leverage ratio (these ratios are based on book values (Holthausen & Larcker,1996) decreases from 79.77% before IPO to 46.33% in post-IPOwhile the post-IPO covers the years immediately after public offering. Therefore, we re-calculate the ratios while excluding those firms have zerodebt. The resulting firms exhibit that the mean leverage ratio falls from 82.67% prior to the IPO to 55.86% in post- IPO period with this method. The median of all RLBO corporations declines from 73.75% before IPO to 50.10% immediately after initial public offering.

Shown in Table 2 Panel A, each year after initial public offering has lower mean and median leverage compared to the mean and median levels in the year prior to the IPO. The other interesting result is that while three years after public offering has notably lower mean and median leverage ratios, four years after the offering firms exhibit slightly higher leverage than immediately preceding year. And these four years after IPO results are closer to the onesobtained for the year of initial public offering. We investigate the reason of having such a lower mean average ratio for three years after initial offering, and we figure out that one of the Reverse LBO firms created the problem and distorts the mean leverage ratio. For fixing the dilemma, this firm is excluded from the analysis and the mean leverage ratio is re-find. While the mean leverage ratio increases to 50.50%, the median does not significantly change. The median increases from 49% to only 49.20% after the adjustments are made. However, these results are not shown in the table for not to create any confusions. Our study's results show similarities with Holthausen & Larcker's study (1996) in terms of the mean average ratios. However, the post

IPO debt/capital ratio is slightly higher in Holthausen & Larcker's analysis the mean leverage ratio for 1983-1988 period compared to our study. The change in debt/capital is found as -23% by Holthausen & Larcker (1996) while we find -35% or -36.45% for/with the firms (including the those have zero debt mentioned in their 10-Ks) which can be seen from the Table 2 Panel A. Thus, the evidences might be interpreted as while the reverse LBO firms have more debt in their capital between 1983 and 1988, they become more risk averse and use less debt in their capital between 1999 to 2008 period since the reverse LBOs in our sample has slightly lower percentages on the debt leverage. Moreover, the evidences may also be interpreted or they may be suggest eitherthe reverse leverage buyout firms have become more and more risk averse in years after they went public or the market tolerate less debt in time.

We also take the analysis one step further and find the mean leverage ratios for the companies which have four full years after the initial public offering(only 44 firms), the companies which have only three years after initial public offering (25 firms) and the ones have only two years after initial public offering (26 firms). The logic behind make such an additional analysis is to have better understanding and to check whether the companies which have full data for after public offering process are given similar results or not, since some of the reverse leverage buyout corporations went bankruptcy or acquired by another firm immediately after or after they went public. Table 2 Panel C presents the leverages based on this classification. The mean leverage ratio of the corporations which have four full years after the initial public offerings decreases from 76.42%prior to the IPO to 58.39% after the IPO. Similarly, the mean leverage ratio declines from 76.47% prior to IPO to 4.20% after IPO for the firms which have three years after initial public offering. The reason of having such a low mean average ratio for the corporations which have three years after IPO is only because a great amount of negative debt leverage of the one single company as it was explained earlier. After the execution of this specific firm (for the health of the study), the mean average ratio increases up to 40.71% for three years after IPO. Following to the adjustment made, it found that the pattern of the mean average ratio behavior before and after the initial public offering stays the same. As it can be seen from Table 2 Panel E, similar patterns are observed for the companies which have two years after the initial public offering process. Thus, this evidence might suggest the reverse leverage buyout corporations become more risk averse in time, and start using less debt in their capital between 1999 to 2008 periods.

5.2. The Accounting Performance of Reverse Leverage Buyout Firms

In order to reach RLBOs' relative operating performances, operating income and operating cash flows are used as accounting measures of this study. Even though OCF and OPINC ratios seem closely related, the main dissimilarity between them is OCF ratio purges more accounting accruals, and it shows more variability by smoothing earnings relative to cash flow compared to OPINC as it was very well stated by Holthausen & Larcker (1996). Table 3presents median and mean of two accounting performance measures from the year before the IPO, which is stated as Year -1, to four years after the initial public offering. The mean for operating cash flow before depreciation, interest and taxes shows little difference across year, but increases from the year -1 to 4 years after public offering. However, as it can be seen from Table3 Panel A, the third year of OCF/asset shows negativity. The reason is the firm which lowers also debt/capital mean average ratios 3 years after initial offering as it explained in the result section mean leverage ratio subsection. If this firm is excluded from the

Table 3. The table presents median and mean of two accounting performance measures from the year before the IPO, which is stated as Year -1, to four years after the initial public offering.

Panel A			
Operating Cash Flow before interest and taxes/asset for all RBLO firms in the analysis	**mean**	**median**	**stdev**
Pre -IPO OCF / Assets	0.0701	0.0909	0.2499
IPO Year OCF /Assets	0.0864	0.0914	0.1500
1 Year after OCF /Assets	0.0923	0.1093	0.1769
2 Year after OCF /Assets	0.0863	0.0891	0.1623
3Year after OCF /Assets	0.1102	0.1061	1.0446
4 Year after OCF /Assets	0.0939	0.0913	0.1091
Post -IPO OCF/Assets	0.0654	0.1064	0.3657
Change in OCF/Assets	-0.0047	0.0155	0.1158
# of observations for whole RLBO firms	**114**	**114**	**114**
Panel B			
Operating Income before depreciation, interest and taxes/asset for all RBLO firms in the analysis	**mean**	**median**	**stdev**
Pre -IPO OPINC/Assets	0.1009	0.1297	0.2675
IPO Year OPINC/Assets	0.1474	0.1493	0.1310
1 Year after OPINC /Assets	0.1438	0.1519	0.1917
2 Year after OPINC /Assets	0.1263	0.1408	0.2103
3Year after OPINC /Assets	0.1450	0.1347	0.9685
4 Year after OPINC /Assets	0.1501	0.1338	0.0980
Post -IPO OPINC/Assets	0.1076	0.1429	0.3693
Change in OPINC/Assets	0.0068	0.0131	0.1019
# of observations for whole RLBO firms	**114**	**114**	**114**

OPINC/asset: Operating earnings before depreciation, interest and taxes deflated by total assets

OCF/asset: Operating cash flow before interest and taxes deflated by total asset

*Exact definition of OCF from Compustat is that operating income before depreciation (data item #13)plus decrease in account receivable (Data item # 2) plus decrease in inventory (data 3) plus increase in accounts payable (Data item #70) plus increase in other current liabilities (data 72) plus decrease in other current assets (Data item # 68) taxes to asset (OPINC/assets) for the third year after public offering. Such a big difference emanates because of the one singlecompany's announced data which can be easily obtained from COMPUSTAT. This gap also proves that one firm's abnormal movements can affect the entire RLBO universe used and the calculations based on that.

computations, the mean of OCF/asset slightly and notably increases up to 11.10%, while the change in OCF/assets goes up from -0.0047 to 0.0088. The mean, goes up from 2.96 to 14.50% for operating income before depreciation, interest and

Additionally, it should not be forgotten that while year -1 represents the year of initial public offering, year 0 presents the fiscal term which IPO occurred, and there is no control either on or over the Year 0 as it was previously explained.

Moreover in this analysis, unadjusted measure is used in order to perceive the reverse-LBO corporations' performances. To obtain industry adjusted, associated SIC codes are found and then the sectors are classified from the whole COMPUSTAT universe between 1999 and 2008. The obtained results are shown on Table 5, and as it can be seen Table 4 industry adjusted numbers are different than the ones in the Table 5. The rationale under it is, two digits SIC codes cover more firms and

Table 4. The table shows RLBO firms and industry adjusted based on these firms related sectors.

Panel A							
Results on levels of accounting performance based on various SIC codes associated with the firms							
	Year -1	**Year 0**	**Year 1**	**Year 2**	**Year 3**	**Year 4**	**Avg. years +1 to +4**
Median level of OCF/asset Firm	0.090909[b]	0.091427[b]	0.109304[b]	0.089063[b]	0.106074[a]	0.091289[b]	0.1064[a]
Industry adjusted*	0.0510[b]	0.0438[b]	0.0612[b]	0.0610[b]	0.0700[b]	0.0532[b]	0.0614[b]
# of observations**	114	113	106	95	69	44	106
Median level of OPINC/asset Firm	0.129746[b]	0.149344[b]	0.1519[b]	0.1408[a]	0.1347[a]	0.1338[b]	0.142895[a]
Industry adjusted	0.036118[b]	0.031522[b]	0.055825[b]	0.042905[b]	0.043393[b]	0.036697[b]	0.046[b]
# of observations**	114	112	107	96	70	44	105

Panel B						
Results on the change in accounting performance based on various SIC codes associated with the firms						
	Year -1 to year 0	**Year -1 to year 1**	**Year -1 to year 2**	**Year -1 to year 3**	**Year -1 to year 4**	**Year -1 to avg. years +1 to +4**
Median change in OCF/asset Firm	0.0041[b]	0.0124[b]	0.0075[b]	0.0074[b]	0.0175[a]	0.0085[b]
Industry adjusted	0.024[b]	0.032[b]	0.036[b]	0.0403[b]	0.0361[b]	0.037[b]
Median change in OPINC/asset Firm	0.0155[b]	0.0247[b]	0.0132[b]	0.0085[b]	0.0375[a]	-0.0135[b]
Industry adjusted	0.0056[b]	0.0153[b]	0.0086[b]	0.0005[c]	-0.0009	0.0132[b]

**The number of observations are for the firms' performances and the industry adjusted performance

* The industry adjusted performance is calculated by using the medians of both OCF/asset and OPINC/asset for the firms in various SIC codes

as it is explained in the study. In order to find the industry adjusted OCF/asset or OPINC/asset performance in given time period, the industry

performance is subtracted from the OCF/asset or OPINC/asset of individually each of the reverse leverage buyout firm.

[a]Significantly different from zero at 0.01 level (two-tailed t-test)

[b]Significantly different from zero at 0.05 level (two-tailed t-test)

[c]Significantly different from zero at 0.1 level (two-tailed t-test)

give undetailed, and more general results since the only 2 digit of the 4 digit SIC code is taken. In addition, since we also want to know whether the current RLBO firms are behaving similarly as the firms in the past or parallel to the past researches indicates, we used similar testing methods like other researchers used to use.

Based on the two-digit SIC codes (Table 5), the median industry-adjusted OCF/asset for year-1 is calculated as 0.019 while the median OCF/asset for RLBO firms at year -1 is 0.0909. The median industry-adjusted OPINC/asset for year -1 is 0.019 while the median OPINC/asset for RLBO firms at year -1 is 0.1297. The evidences depend on computations suggest that we have 2% better OCF/asset and 1% better OPINC/assets industry medians compared to Holthausen & Larcker (1996). Based on 4 digit SIC codes (when the

Table 5. The table presents RLBO firms and industry-adjusted medians based on just with the two digit SIC codes associated with the reverse leverage buyout companies' sectors.

Panel A							
Results on levels of accounting performance based on 2-digit SIC codes associated with the firms							
	Year -1	**Year 0**	**Year 1**	**Year 2**	**Year 3**	**Year 4**	**Avg. years +1 to +4**
Median level of OCF/asset Firm	0.090909[b]	0.091427[b]	0.109304[b]	0.089063[b]	0.106074[b]	0.091289[b]	0.1064[a]
Industry adjusted*	0.0189[b]	0.0160[b]	0.0306[b]	0.0172[b]	0.0319[c]	0.0370[b]	0.0236[b]
# of observations**	114	113	106	95	69	44	106
Median level of OPINC/asset Firm	0.129746[b]	0.149344[b]	0.1519[a]	0.1408[b]	0.1347[b]	0.1338[b]	0.142895[a]
Industry adjusted	0.018951[b]	0.036465[b]	0.068477[b]	0.047632[c]	0.049717[b]	0.053057[b]	0.043[b]
# of observations**	114	112	107	96	70	44	105

Panel B						
Results on the change in accounting performance based on 2-digit SIC codes associated with the firms						
	Year -1 to year 0	**Year -1 to year 1**	**Year -1 to year 2**	**Year -1 to year 3**	**Year -1 to year 4**	**Year -1 to avg. years +1 to +4**
Median change in OCF/asset Firm	0.0041[b]	0.0124[b]	0.0075[b]	0.0074[b]	0.0175[b]	0.0085[b]
Industry adjusted	0.002	0.018[b]	0.003[b]	-0.0002	0.0023[b]	-0.002
Median change in OPINC/asset Firm	0.0155[b]	0.0247[b]	0.0132[b]	0.0085[b]	0.0375[a]	-0.0135[b]
Industry adjusted	0.0130[b]	0.0198[b]	0.0211[b]	0.0074[c]	0.0179[b]	0.0156[b]

**The number of observations are for the firms' performances and the industry adjusted performance

* The industry adjusted performance is calculated by using the medians of both OCF/asset and OPINC/asset for the firms in 2-digit SIC codes

as it is explained in the study. In order to find the industry adjusted OCF/asset or OPINC/asset performance in given time period, the industry performance is subtracted from the OCF/asset or OPINC/asset of individually each of the reverse leverage buyout firm.

[a]Significantly different from zero at 0.01 level (two-tailed t-test)

[b]Significantly different from zero at 0.05 level (two-tailed t-test)

[c]Significantly different from zero at 0.1 level (two-tailed t-test)

digit of codes vary related with the number of firms in industry as it was explained above and can be seen from Table 4 Panel A),

the median industry-adjusted OCF/asset for year-1 is 0.0510 when the median OCF/asset for RLBO firms at year -1 is 0.0909. The median industry-adjusted OPINC/asset for year -1 is 0.03618 while the median OPINC/asset for RLBO firms at year -1 is 0.1297. Thus, the OCF/asset and OPINC/asset of the reverse leverage buyout firm is slightly higher than the median levels associated with them, so the evidences might be interpreted as of outperforming compared to their industries. However, since the year- 1 represents the year before initial public offering, the levels may be influenced by the following public offering process. For that reason, the public offering year which is year 0 should also be investigated. Based on two digit SIC codes (table 5 Panel A), the median industry-adjusted OCF/asset for year 0 is obtained as 0.016 while the median OCF/asset for RLBO firms at year -1 is found as 0.0914.

The median industry-adjusted OPINC/asset for year -1 (Table 5 Panel B) is 0.036 while the median OPINC/asset for RLBO firms at year -1 is 0.1493. Yet, from various SIC codes (Table 4 Panel A), depending on the number of firms in associated industry, the median industry-adjusted OCF/asset for year 0 is 0.0438 when the median OCF/asset for RLBO firms at year -1 is 0.0914. The median industry-adjusted OPINC/asset for year -1 is 0.0315 while the median OPINC/asset for RLBO firms at year -1 is 0. 1493.As it can be seen, the initial public offering year shows similar positive and superiorpattern with the year before initial public offering. Parallel path was observed by both Holthausen & Larcker (1996)'s studies except their Reverse LBO firms' median level of OCF/asset and median level of OPINC/assets were notably higher than our reverse LBO firms' median levels for the both accounting measurement. The difference of their accounting measurements' median levels and our accounting measurements' median level is fluctuating between as lower as 5% to as higher as 10%. Therefore, the interpretation ofthese significant differences can be stated as the reverse leverage buyout corporations which have been operated between 1999 and 2008 have less operating income compared to the reverse leverage buyout firms which had been operated between 1983 and 1988, but have more operating income and operating cash flows than their industry counterparts.

We also conducted two-tailed t-test assuming unequal variances to test the performance between the companies and the associated industries. According to the results be seen from both Table 4 and 5, the reverse-LBO corporations persist on outperforming in their industries for four years after the initial public offering occurred while their median industry adjusted performances for OCF/asset and OPINC/asset notably differ from zero for each year before, at the time and after initial public offering. Unlikely to the past researches, for instance in Holthausen & Larcker(1996) found some performance weakness observed in the third year after public offering, we observe a performance weakness two years after IPO especially for OPINC/asset ratio the reverse leverage buyout firms.

Panel Bs on the both Table 4 and 5 shows the changes in the accounting performance for both the reverse leverage buyout firms and the industry adjusted from the year prior to IPO and throughout the years. When Panel A only shows observations in any given year, panel B represents changes between the years, so available data from year -1 to another year (such as year 0, year +1, year +2 and so on). The reason of conducting such an analysis is that the intensity of RLBO firm performance can possibly be superior or inferior to its industry throughout years before IPO, at the time of IPO, and +1, +2, +3, +4 years after IPO. In this analysis, year -1 is used as a benchmark.

Change in both four years after initial public offering and three years after IPO process performance weakness are observed compared to the associated industries. Unlikely from Holthausen & Larcker's studies(1996) on this subject, the median changes for both OCF/Asset and OPINC/Asset show stronger changes in performance throughout the years for the reverse LBO firms. While Holthausen & Larcker's have -0.047 for the year -1 to year 0 for OCF/asset, we have 0.0155 for the year -1 to year 0. Also, according to their result while the median change for OCF/asset for year -1 to year 1 was -0.062, we have 0.0247 as the median change for OCF/asset for year-1 to year +1. Also, while the median changes for firms in both OCF/asset and OPINC/asset show negativity except the median change of OPINC/asset for year -1 to year 0. But, more surprisingly Holthausen & Larcker's the firm median change in OPINC/assets has lower performance in each year after initial public offering compared to the prior public offering year. However, for our sample, each individualyear after initial public offering have better performances (except the second year for both OCF/asset and OPINC/asset) in terms of the median changes for the reverse LBO firms between 1999 and 2008.

Moreover, while the industry adjusted for 1983-88 period shows negativity for almost each year from year -1 for both the median changes of OCF/asset and OPINC/asset except the year -1 to 0 for OPINC/asset median change, the industry adjusted in our study shows positivity in median changes for all years of OCF/asset, but only shows negativity in from year -1 to year 4 for OPINC/asset as it can be seen from the Table 4, Panel B. However, based on the 2-digit SIC codes which can be seen from Table 5 Panel B, the only negativity for the industry adjusted is the one in the median changes of OCF/asset for year -1 to year 3.For sure we should mentioned that the industry adjusted is expected to be lower because of the way of its calculations, since in order to obtain industry adjusted performances; the industry median OCF/asset or OPINC/asset performances, which are calculated by using the firms' related SIC codes, are subtracted from OPINC/asset or OCF/asset of each reverse leverage buyout firm.

5. 3. Median Levels of Capital Expenditures, Working Capital and Employment

In this study, in addition to accounting performance, working capital management, employment level and the expenditures on capital equipment are also investigated. We examine whether the capital expenditures, working capital and staffing management patterns of the reverse leverage buyout firms are different from their industry counterparts and whether these patterns change throughout the years. Table 6 presents the changes of means, medians and their related standard deviations of capital expenditures, working capital and employment for each year individually from the year before initial public offering to 4 years after offering. For both working capitals, capital expenditures and employment the year before public offering have lower means and medians than the year of public offering and the each year after the offering. As it can be seen from Table 6 Panel A, the capital expenditures mean in the year before IPO is 0.0545 when the capital expenditures mean of four years after public offering is 0.0762. Also, the working capital mean in the year before IPO is -0.0112 while the working capital mean of four years after initial offering is 0.1148. On the similar way, the mean of employment level in the year before IPO is 0.0046 for our obtained reverse LBO firms when the mean of employment increases to 0.0085 four years after offering. However, for the exact year of initial public offering occurred, greater mean than the years after the initial public offering is observed. The mean of capital expenditures increases to 0.0809, but after that it starts to decline. A similar observation is also found for the working capital. At the year of public offering, the mean of working capital goes up to 16.10%, but after that it shows remarkable decreases in following years.

Nevertheless, when we look at the post-IPO terms in general, we detected that the capital expenditures mean before the public offering year is higher than the post-IPO period mean. But,the capital expenditure median in year prior to IPO is almost 5% lower than the post-IPO period. Similarly, both the mean and the median of RLBOs' working capital and the employment level in the year before the initial public offering have lower percentages than the mean and the medians of post-IPO period.

Table 7 Panel A illustrates the median level of capital expenditures, working capital and employment level for both the reverse LBO corporations and the associated industries for the year before, at the time and each year after initial public offering. As it also can be seen from the related table, even though there is not much difference with the capital expenditure and the industry counterparts similar to Holthausen & Larcker'sfindings (1996); the reverse LBO firms still spent less on capital equipment than their industry. Yet, for the exact year of IPO and following years after public of-

Table 6. The table presents the changes of means, medians and their related standard deviations of capital expenditures, working capital and employment for each year individually from the year before initial public offering to 4 years after offering.

Panel A			
Capital expenditures/asset for all RBLO firms in the analysis	**mean**	**median**	**stdev**
Pre -IPO Capital expenditures / Assets	0.0545	0.0304	0.0575
IPO Year Capital expenditures/Assets	0.0809	0.0334	0.1237
1 Year after IPO Capital expenditures/Assets	0.0760	0.0391	0.0971
2 Years after IPO Capital expenditures/Assets	0.0739	0.0405	0.0911
3 Years after IPO Capital expenditures/Assets	0.0723	0.0480	0.0751
4 Years after IPO Capital expenditures/Assets	0.0762	0.0570	0.0860
Post -IPO Capital expenditures/Assets*	0.0480	0.0760	0.0913
Change in Capital expenditures/Assets**	0.0304	0.0760	0.0913
Panel B			
Working Capital/asset for all RBLO firms in the analysis	**mean**	**median**	**stdev**
Pre -IPO Working Capital / Assets	-0.0112	0.0552	1.4918
IPO Year Working Capital/Assets	0.1610	0.1098	0.2324
1 Year after IPO Working Capital /Assets	0.1445	0.1002	0.1837
2 Years after IPO Working Capital /Assets	0.1230	0.0900	0.2107
3 Years after IPO Working Capital /Assets	0.1321	0.1129	0.1807
4 Years after IPO Working Capital /Assets	0.1148	0.1186	0.2839
Post -IPO Working Capital /Assets*	0.1301	0.1050	0.1799
Change in Working Capital /Assets**	0.1413	0.0498	-1.3119
Panel C			
Employees/asset for al RLBO firms in the analysis for all RBLO firms in the analysis	**mean**	**median**	**stdev**
Pre -IPO Employees / Assets	0.0046	0.0014	0.0078
IPO Year Employees /Assets	0.0070	0.0032	0.0113
1 Year after IPO Employees /Assets	0.0069	0.0032	0.0111
2 Years after IPO Employees /Assets	0.0075	0.0033	0.0115
3 Years after IPO Employees /Assets	0.0074	0.0033	0.0117
4 Years after IPO Employees /Assets	0.0085	0.0030	0.0145
Post -IPO Employees /Assets*	0.0069	0.0034	0.0109
Change in Employees /Assets**	0.0023	0.0020	-0.0078

* post-IPO represent the average of one year after initial offering to four years after offering
** change values represent post-IPO values minus pre-IPO values
Pre-IPO values represent the values of the year before the initial public occurred

fering, the authors did not find much difference between the firms and their industries. But, in our study, we find that except the year of public offering and the four years after offering, the reverse leverage buyout firms spend little more on capital equipments than their industry counterparts in +1,

Table 7. The table illustrates the median level of capital expenditures, working capital and employment level for both the reverse LBO corporations and the associated industries for the year before, at the time and each year after initial public offering.

Panel A							
Results on the level of capital expenditures, working capital and employment							
	Year -1	**Year 0**	**Year 1**	**Year 2**	**Year 3**	**Year 4**	
Median level of capital expenditures/asset Firm	0.0304[a]	0.0341[a]	0.0405[a]	0.04145[b]	0.0494[b]	0.0586[a]	0.076243[a]
Industry adjusted*	-0.0021	-0.0005	0.0089[b]	0.0026[b]	0.0007	-0.0026	0.004
# of observations**	114	114	108	97	70	44	
Median level of working capital/asset Firm	0.0552[a]	0.1098[a]	0.1012[a]	0.0900[a]	0.1129[a]	0.1186[a]	0.105[a]
Industry adjusted	-0.03476	(0.09875)[a]	(0.08459)[a]	(0.09261[a]	(0.09684)[a]	(0.09661)[a]	(0.047)[b]
# of observations**	114	114	108	97	70	44	
Median level of employees/asset Firm	0.001442[b]	0.003188[b]	0.0032[b]	0.0033[b]	0.0033[b]	0.0030[b]	0.003408[b]
Industry adjusted	0.0001	0	0	0.0001	0.00015	0.00018	0.0001
# of observations**	114	114	108	97	70	44	

Panel B						
Results on the change in capital expenditures, working capital and employment						
	Year -1 to year 0	**Year -1 to year 1**	**Year -1 to year 2**	**Year -1 to year 3**	**Year -1 to year 4**	**Year -1 to avg. years +1 to +4**
Median change in capital expenditures/ asset Firm	0.0024[b]	0.0028	0.003	0.0063	0.0108[b]	0.0049
Industry adjusted	(0.0005)[b]	(0.0005)[a]	-0.0004	-0.0069	-0.0002	-0.003
Median change in working capital /asset Firm	0.0016	0.0123	0.0242	0.0366	0.0150[b]	-0.0005
Industry adjusted	0.0038[b]	0.0379[b]	0.0434[b]	0.0638[b]	0.0492[b]	0.0265[b]
Median change in employees /asset Firm	-0.000011	0.000101	0.000052	0.000136	0.000692	0.000046
Industry adjusted	-0.0001	0.000012	0.000175	0.000144	0.00027	0.000082[c]

*Parentheses stand for negative number in this table

[a]Significantly different from zero at 0.01 level (two-tailed t-test);[b] Significantly different from zero at 0.05 level (two-tailed t-test)

[c]Significantly different from zero at 0.1 level (two-tailed t-test)

+2+3 years. In this point, we should remind the facts that the lower the capital expenditure, the higher the free cash flow and the income since free cash flowis the amount that a company generates after laying out the money required to maintain or increase its assets, and the higher the free cash flow, the stronger the company's Balance Sheet.

In terms of working capital, the reverse leverage buyout firms in our time range have less working capital in their structurecompared to their industry since the industry adjusted percentages are all negative. Thus, the evidence might suggest that reverse leverage buyout companies are more sufficient than their industry peers. Even more surprising result is that

almost all of the industry medians for working capital are almost two times greater than the firms' medians.

Since there is not muchdifference observed between the reverse leverage buyout firms and their associated industries on the employment level, we can say that there is not much evidenceof layoffs found. Yet, starting from two years after initial public offering to four years after offering the employment level is increased.

5.4.Sectional and Cross-Sectional Analyses

In this study, we try to find the firm characteristics that affect accounting performance (OCF/asset and OPINC/asset) and debt/capital, working capital/asset, capital expenditures/asset and employees/asset. Table 8 presents how much debt/capital, capital/asset, capital expenditures/asset and employees/asset in the each year before, at the time and after IPO is correlated to OCF/asset and OPINC/asset in each year before, at the time and after the public offering.

Table 8 Panel A shows,the OCF/asset and debt/capital, the t-stat of the year at the time of IPO and the t-stat of three years after offering are way greater than 1.96 in absolute term. The specified years' p values are also smaller than the alpha equal to 0.001, so we can consider them as meaningful and significant in 0.001 level which is accepted as highly significant level. However, when the test can only have 22.84% explanatory power for the initial public offering year, it has year 97.63% prediction power in the third year after the IPO. Yet, for OPINC/asset and debt/capital, not only the year of public offering and three years after offering, but also the year before initial offering is significant, while the year 0 and +3 are 99.999% and the year before IPO is 95% significant.

For the relation between OCF/assets and capital expenditures/assets, we can say that the relation is not significant either at 5% or at 10% significance level, but it is significant only two years after initial offering at 80% level. Similar pattern is observed for the relationship between OPINC/asset and capital expenditures. Working capital and OCF/asset show 99.999% significant relation in the year prior to IPO, at the year of IPO and two years after. Three years after the initial public offering working capital/asset and OCF/asset have correlation at 98%.Nevertheless, OPINC/asset and working capital/asset in prior to IPO has 99.999% significance, the year of IPO and +2 and +3 years are significant at 95% (Table 8 Panel C). Additionally, as it seen from Table 8 Panel D, while the OCF/asset and employment level shows 95% significant relationship at the year of public offering +1 and +2have 95% significant correlation while the year prior to IPO and four years after the offering shows 90%. OPINC/asset and employment level shows 98% significance while the year prior to IPO and two years after initial public offering shows 90% significant correlation.

We also examined in the changes in performance of the reverse LBO firms which can be explained by changes in leverage and working capital management, expenditures on capitalequipment and employment level. Table 9 illustrates these sectional variations in changes. While the change in debt/capital from -1 to +1 shows 95% significant relation with both OCF/asset from -1 to +1 and

Table 8. The table presents how much debt/capital, capital/asset, capital expenditures/asset and employees/asset in the each year before, at the time and after IPO is correlated to OCF/asset and OPINC/asset in each year before, at the time and after the public offering.

Panel A						
Dependent Variable	**Intercept**	**Adjusted R^2**	**P Value**	**T Stat**	**Debt/Capital Regression Coefficient**	**Independent Variable**
OCF/asset prior to IPO	0.02087	0.010309	0.143	1.5	0.06175756	Debt/capital prior to IPO
OCF/asset in year of IPO	0.12197	0.228372	5.E-08	-5.8	-0.05044016	Debt/capital in year of IPO
OCF/asset 1 year after IPO	0.09014	-0.00954	0.932	0.1	0.00395581	Debt/capital 1 year after IPO
OCF/asset 2 years after IPO	0.09972	-0.0077	0.597	-0.5	-0.02608694	Debt/capital 2 years after IPO
OCF/asset 3 years after IPO	-0.0495	0.976398	4.E-58	54	0.31201388	Debt/capital 3 years after IPO
OCF/asset 4 years after IPO	0.12281	0.007969	0.253	-1.2	-0.04671336	Debt/capital 4 years after IPO
Intercept stands for the coefficient value of the intercept.						
OPINC/asset prior to IPO	0.02291	0.033123	0.029	2.2	0.09772993	Debt/capital prior to IPO
OPINC/asset in year of IPO	0.17975	0.267704	3.E-09	-6.5	-0.04762718	Debt/capital in year of IPO
OPINC/asset 1 year after IPO	0.12507	-0.00476	0.482	0.7	0.03504885	Debt/capital 1 year after IPO
OPINC/asset 2 years after IPO	0.10068	-0.00374	0.424	0.8	0.05048689	Debt/capital 2 years after IPO
OPINC/asset 3 years after IPO	-0.0049	0.979091	1.E-60	58	0.29180143	Debt/capital 3 years after IPO
OPINC/asset 4 years after IPO	0.13178	-0.01213	0.495	0.7	0.02485719	Debt/capital 4 years after IPO
Intercept stands for the coefficient value of the intercept.						

Panel B						
Dependent Variable	**Intercept**	**Adjusted R^2**	**P Value**	**T Stat**	**Capx */ Asset Regression Coefficient**	**Independent Variable**
OCF/asset prior to IPO	0.04963	-0.00137	0.36	0.9	0.37603713	Capx/asset prior to IPO
OCF/asset in year of IPO	0.07414	0.006302	0.194	1.3	0.1496158	Capx/asset in year of IPO
OCF/asset 1 year after IPO	0.08041	-0.00323	0.419	0.8	0.14384372	Capx/asset 1 year after IPO
OCF/asset 2 years after IPO	0.06502	0.013531	0.132	1.5	0.27609693	Capx/asset 2 years after IPO
OCF/asset 3 years after IPO	0.06163	-0.00886	0.537	-0.6	-1.02910156	Capx/asset 3 years after IPO
OCF/asset 4 years after IPO	0.08289	-0.01785	0.648	0.5	0.08764918	Capx/asset 4 years after IPO
*Capx = capital expenditures						
OPINC/asset prior to IPO	0.08093	-0.00268	0.405	0.8	0.36573552	Capx/asset prior to IPO
OPINC/asset in year of IPO	0.14319	-0.00786	0.722	0.4	0.03589374	Capx/asset in year of IPO
OPINC/asset 1 year after IPO	0.14588	-0.0089	0.814	-0.2	-0.04539843	Capx/asset 1 year after IPO
OPINC/asset 2 years after IPO	0.09925	0.01284	0.137	1.5	0.35252025	Capx/asset 2 years after IPO
OPINC/asset 3 years after IPO	0.10059	-0.00805	0.513	-0.7	-1.00444411	Capx/asset 3 years after IPO
OPINC/asset 4 years after IPO	0.15549	0.004503	0.278	-1.1	-0.19289778	Capx/asset 4 years after IPO

continued on following page

Table 8. Continued

*Capx = capital expenditures						
Intercept stands for the coefficient value of the intercept.						
Panel C						
Dependent Variable	**Intercept**	**Adjusted R^2**	**P Value**	**T Stat**	**Wacp / Asset Regression Coefficient**	**Independent Variable**
OCF/asset prior to IPO	0.07236	0.758371	1.E-36	19	0.14626293	Wacp**/asset prior to IPO
OCF/asset in year of IPO	0.1358	0.178741	2.E-06	-5	-0.33424348	Wacp/asset in year of IPO
OCF/asset 1 year after IPO	0.11199	0.010823	0.146	-1.5	-0.1454953	Wacp/asset 1 year after IPO
OCF/asset 2 years after IPO	0.12084	0.075296	0.004	-2.9	-0.23991072	Wacp/asset 2 years after IPO
OCF/asset 3 years after IPO	-0.2249	0.062948	0.021	2.4	1.6009161	Wacp/asset 3 years after IPO
OCF/asset 4 years after IPO	0.09319	-0.02354	0.917	0.1	0.00623341	Wacp/asset 4 years after IPO
Intercept stands for the coefficient value of the intercept.						
OPINC/asset prior to IPO	0.10323	0.745051	3.E-35	18	0.15518694	Wacp /asset prior to IPO
OPINC/asset in year of IPO	0.16687	0.034229	0.028	-2.2	-0.14027824	Wacp /asset in year of IPO
OPINC/asset 1 year after IPO	0.15593	-0.00281	0.404	-0.8	-0.09053541	Wacp /asset 1 year after IPO
OPINC/asset 2 years after IPO	0.16013	0.039318	0.029	-2.2	-0.23744069	Wacp /asset 2 years after IPO
OPINC/asset 3 years after IPO	-0.1713	0.068762	0.016	2.5	1.54215574	Wacp /asset 3 years after IPO
OPINC/asset 4 years after IPO	0.14711	-0.0232	0.961	0	-0.00264878	Wacp /asset 4 years after IPO
** Wcap = Working capital						
Intercept stands for the coefficient value of the intercept.						
Panel D						
Dependent Variable	**Intercept**	**Adjusted R^2**	**P Value**	**T Stat**	**Emp/ Asset Regression Coefficient**	**Independent Variable**
OCF/asset prior to IPO	0.04911	0.012118	0.125	1.5	4.60311471	Emp***/asset prior to IPO
OCF/asset in year of IPO	0.06869	0.026746	0.046	2	2.50004558	Emp/asset in year of IPO
OCF/asset 1 year after IPO	0.06995	0.026558	0.05	2	3.00441807	Emp /asset 1 year after IPO
OCF/asset 2 years after IPO	0.06275	0.033414	0.04	2.1	2.95849269	Emp/asset 2 years after IPO
OCF/asset 3 years after IPO	-0.0142	-0.0147	0.99	1	0.13994739	Emp/asset 3 years after IPO
OCF/asset 4 years after IPO	0.08128	0.025415	0.153	1.5	0.99276236	Emp/asset 4 years after IPO
Intercept stands for the coefficient value of the intercept.						
OPINC/asset prior to IPO	0.0749	0.01911	0.076	1.8	5.68678777	Emp/asset prior to IPO
OPINC/asset in year of IPO	0.1233	0.069023	0.003	3.1	3.22998959	Emp/asset in year of IPO
OPINC/asset 1 year after IPO	0.11785	0.033784	0.032	2.2	3.58526974	Emp/asset 1 year after IPO
OPINC/asset 2 years after IPO	0.09818	0.028883	0.923	1.9	3.64544157	Emp/asset 2 years after IPO
OPINC/asset 3 years after IPO	0.03678	-0.01457	0.923	-0.1	3.75933267	Emp/asset 3 years after IPO
OPINC/asset 4 years after IPO	0.14648	-0.02321	0.965	0	0.03056323	Emp/asset 4 years after IPO

*** Emp= Employees
Intercept stands for the coefficient value of the intercept.
All the P values are for the independent variables.
All the t-values are for the independent variables.

OPINC/asset from -1 to +1, the change in debt/capital from -1 to average of one years after initial offering to four years after offering shows 99.99% significant relationship with both OCF/asset and OPINC/asset from -1 to average of years +1 to +4. However, neither capital expenditure from year -1 to +1 nor capital expenditure from year -1 to average of one to four years after public offering show any significant relation with neither OCF/asset from year -1 to year +1 nor OCF/asset from year -1 to average of one to four years

after public offering. The correlation between capital expenditure and OPINC/asset reflects similar path in terms of no significance. On the other hand, both working capital from year -1 to +1 and the working capital from -1 and average of one to four years after public offering show highly significant (99.99%) relationship with both OCF/asset from -1 to +1, OCF/asset from -1 and average of one to four years after offering, OPINC/asset from -1 to +1 and OPINC/asset from -1 and average of one to fouryears after offering. Meanwhile, employment level change in years shows no significant relation with OCF/asset change in years, but as it can be seen from Table 8 Panel D, while employment level has no significant correlation in prior year to IPO, there is a significant relationship between employment level and both OCF/asset and OPINC/asset in the year and one year after public offering. Yet, employment level from prior IPO to one year after offering has 95% significant correlation with OPINC/asset from prior IPO.

We also checked whether there is any relationship between debt/capital and both working capital and capital expenditures (Table 8 Panel E) or not. Between the years of prior to initial offering to one year after offering there is no significant correlation observed between debt/capital and neither with capital expenditure/asset nor with working capital/asset. The evidences shows almost similar pattern for the years between prior to IPO to average of the years after offering.

Cross sectional analysis is also conducted to investigate cross-sectional variation in the change in performance of the reverse leverage buyout firms which can be explained by changes in leverage, expenditures in capital, working capital and employment level. In order to conduct this analysis, accounting performance measures are assumed as a good reflector of firms' performances. Evidence of the significance of the accounting performance measures is documented in random samples by investigating the relation between change in independent variables and change in accounting performances. As it was also mentioned by Holthausen & Larcker (1996), if there is any reduction in the leverage is necessary to have better performance, we should detect positive coefficient on the leverage when OCF/assets and OPINC/assets are dependent variable. Yet, if there is a great amount of leverage be seen, reducing the leverage from the structure should increase the performance and the leverage coefficient should be negative. We assume that the optimal organizational structure (in terms of debt) does not change at the time of reverse LBO in order to make this assumption. Further, parallel to Holthausen &Larcker's study conducted in 1996, if an increase in capital expenditure, there could be sing of poorer performance while increase or a positive coefficient in working capital can be good sign for the companies' performances since if current assets do not exceed current liabilities, then firm may run into trouble paying back creditors in the short term.In the cross sectional analysis, the accounting performances (OCF/assets and OPINC/asset) between the year before IPO and one year after the offering, and between the year prior to IPO and average of one year and four years after the initial public offering are taken as dependent variables while debt/capital (leverage), working capital/asset, capital expenditures and employment level between the year prior to IPO and one year after IPO are taken as independent variables.

As it can be seen from Table 10, while the coefficients of leverage for both OPINC/assets

Table 9. The table illustrates the sectional variations in changes.

Panel A					
Independent Variable					
Dependent Variable	**Intercept**	**Change in Debt/Capital from -1 to +1**	**Adj. R^2**	**F-Stat**	**t-stat of Debt/Capital**
Change in firm OCF/assets from year -1 to +1	0.03652	0.070270026	0.033541	3.887024	1.971553734
Change in firm OPINC/assets from year -1 to +1	0.060157	0.087851827	0.035872	5.204346	2.2813035
Dependent Variable	**Intercept**	**Change in Debt/Capital from -1 to Avg. +1 to +4**	**Adj. R^2**	**F-Stat**	**t-stat of Debt/Capital**
Change in firm OCF/assets from year -1 to the average of years +1 to +4	0.03845	0.108798591	0.398283	70.5005	8.396457841
Change in firm OPINC/assets from year -1 to the average of years +1 to +4	0.047316	0.100485483	0.307583	47.64279	6.902375436
Panel B					
Independent variable					
Dependent Variable	**Intercept**	**Change in Capital Expenditure/Asset from -1 to +1**	**Adj. R^2**	**F-Stat**	**t-stat of Capx/Capital**
Change in firm OCF/assets from year -1 to +1	0.017406	-0.101122259	-0.0073	0.181032	-0.42547868
Change in firm OPINC/assets from year -1 to +1	0.038735	-0.269820794	0.00089	1.100619	-1.04910402
Dependent Variable	**Intercept**	**Change in Capital Expenditure/Asset from -1 to Avg. +1 to +4**	**Adj. R^2**	**F-Stat**	**t-stat of Capx/Capital**
Change in firm OCF/assets from year -1 to the average of years +1 to +4	-0.00358	0.174944782	-0.00346	0.6383	0.798936818
Change in firm OPINC/assets from year -1 to the average of years +1 to +4	0.015778	-0.166176843	-0.00455	0.524458	-0.72419489
Panel C					
Independent variable					
Dependent Variable	**Intercept**	**Change in Working Capital/ Asset from -1 to +1**	**Adj. R^2**	**F-Stat**	**t-stat of Working Capital/Asset**
Change in firm OCF/assets from year -1 to +1	0.001896	0.097434009	0.523321	125.057	11.18288902
Change in firm OPINC/assets from year -1 to +1	0.019589	0.102565292	0.490616	109.8364	10.48028806
Dependent Variable	**Intercept**	**Change in Working Capital/ Asset from -1 to Avg. +1 to +4**	**Adj. R^2**	**F-Stat**	**t-stat of Working Capital/Asset**
Change in firm OCF/assets from year -1 to the average of years +1 to +4	0.021068	-0.142307654	0.475004	96.00167	-9.79804408
Change in firm OPINC/assets from year -1 to the average of years +1 to +4	0.029084	-0.116498239	0.286461	43.15374	-6.56915051

continued on following page

Table 9. Continued

Panel D					
Independent ariable					
Dependent Variable	**Intercept**	**Change in Employees/Asset from -1 to +1**	**Adj. R^2**	**F-stat**	**t-stat of Employees/Asset**
Change in firm OCF/assets from year -1 to +1	0.009738	3.066698524	0.007196	1.819029	1.348713697
Change in firm OPINC/assets from year -1 to +1	0.023894	5.273181853	0.034855	5.080855	2.254075238
Dependent Variable	**Intercept**	**Change in Employees/Asset from -1 to Avg. +1 to +4**	**Adj. R^2**	**F-stat**	**t-stat of Employees/Asset**
Change in firm OCF/assets from year -1 to the average of years +1 to +4	-0.00804	2.445236384	-0.00144	0.837069	0.914915002
Change in firm OPINC/assets from year -1 to the average of years +1 to +4		3.069633339	0.00236	1.26732	1.125753062
Panel E					
Independent Variable					
Dependent Variable	**Intercept**	**Change in debt/capital from -1 to +1**	**Adj. R^2**	**F-stat**	**t-stat of debt/capital**
Change in firm working capital/ assets from year -1 to +1	0.221401	0.269923936	0.004735	1.537589	1.239995626
Change in firm capital expenditure/assets from year -1 to +1	0.017545	0.000980207	-0.00889	0.00378	0.061479994
Dependent Variable	**Intercept**	**Change in Debt/Capital from -1 to Avg. +1 to +4**	**Adj. R^2**	**F-Stat**	**t-stat of Debt/Capital**
Change in firm working capital/ assets from year -1 to the average of years +1 to +4	0.21627	0.196184448	0.003913	1.443953	1.201645891
Change in firm capital expenditure/ assets from year -1 to the average of years +1 to +4	0.017517	0.013696468	0.02216	3.560884	1.887030438

Average +1 to +4 is the simple average of OPINC/asset (OCF/asset, working capital/asset, capital expenditure/asset, employment level/ asset) over the time period consisting of the first fiscal year after the IPO to the fourth fiscal year after IPO.

between the year before IPO and one year after the offering and OCF/assets between the year before IPO and one year after the offering are positive as well as the coefficient of OPINC/ assets between the year prior to IPO and average of one year and four years after the initial public offering, the coefficient of debt/capitalfor OCF/ assets between the year prior to IPO and average of one year and four years after IPO is negative. However, the evidences suggest that the changes in the leverage levels seem unimportant since their t-stat is notably small.

Even though, the coefficients of capital expenditure for both accounting performance between the specified years show positivity, the OCF/assets accounting performance between the year prior to IPO and average of one year and four years after the initial public offering is significant at 99.998% level when OPINC/assets between the year prior to IPO and average of one year and four years after the initial public offering is 99% significant. While OCF/assets between the year prior to IPO and one year after IPO is 90% significant, OPINC/assets between the year before IPO and one year after the

Table 10. The table presents OPINC/assets and OCF/ asset from -1 to 1 and +1 to +4

	Intercept	Change in Debt/ Capital	Change in Capex/Asset	Change in Emp/asset	Change in Wacp /Asset	Adj. R2	F-Stat.
OPINC/asset from -1 to+1	0.0112	0.02569	0.20486	4.58722	0.15176	0.51	27.78
*	-0.42583	-0.71881	-0.97201	-2.474	-10.05049		0
OCF/asset from -1 to +1	-0.01002	0.00421	0.36575	0.48824	0.15745	0.55	33.61
*	(-0.4194)	-0.1295	-1.9098	-0.2898	-11.4751		0
OPINC/asset from -1 to avg.+1 to +4	-0.01863	0.02482	0.70382	2.87733	0.1537	0.49	25.93
*	(-0.6720)	-0.65893	-3.16858	-1.47239	-9.65756		0
OCF/asset from -1 to avg.+1 to +4	-0.04081	-0.01121	0.76111	0.97235	0.15282	0.48	25.1
*	(-1.4794)	(-0.29917)	-3.44292	-0.49995	-9.64848		0

(*) states t-test results for each independent variable in the cross sectional analysis

offering is insignificant with capital expenditures/ assets. On the other hand, the working capital is highly significant (99.999%) and meaningful for both accounting performances for the both specified periods. However, the employment level only shows significant result for OPINC/assets between the year before IPOand one year after the offering, even though the coefficient of it is positive for both accounting performances for the both specified periods. Since the evidences suggest that the accounting performances (forspecifically this sample) used in the cross sectional analysis are not reliable as the ones we used for the firms in general.

6. CONCLUSION

In this paper, it was examined operating performance and capital structure for as well as capital expenditures, working capital and employment management for a reverse leverage buyout sample between 2000 and 2008. The major findings in the paper are that the firms continuously outperform their industry peers for the following four years of initial public offering, while the average debt/capital level decreases in years. Even though Degeorge & Zechauser (1993) claims reverse LBO firms' accounting performances outperform only before they went public, we find similar to Hotlhausen & Larcker (1996) and Mian & Rosenfeld (1993) that the reverse leverage buyout companies exceed their industry peers on performance. Moreover, the evidences suggest a performance weakness in the second year of an IPO while they are still exceeding their counterparts on performance.

Thus, we reject the null hypothesis ($H_{1,o}$) of there is no decrease in mean leverage ratio of the reverse leverage buyout companies since the mean average ratios for debt/capital at the time of initial public offering and the years after that are lower than the mean average ratio of debt/capital in the year before IPO.

$H_{1,o}$ = *There is no decrease in mean leverage ratio of the reverse leverage buyout companies in time compared to the year before initial public offering.*

$H_{1,a}$ = *There is a decrease in mean leverage ratio of the reverse leverage buyout companies in time compare to the year before initial public offering.*

Moreover, we reject the null hypothesis of accounting performances of RLBO corporations does not show any difference from the accounting performance of their industry peers since the evidences mentioned above suggest a difference.

$H_{2,o}$ = *Accounting performances of RLBO corporations does not show any difference from the accounting performance of their industry peers*

$H_{2,a}$ = *Accounting performances of RLBO corporations does show differences from the accounting performances of their industry peers*

With regard to capital expenditure, we find that the reverse leverage buyout firms typically spent less on capital equipment than their counterparts except the ones in our results which differ from the year of initial public offering and four years after the IPO. Holthausen & Larcker (1996) who claimed that the reverse leverage buyout firms spent less on capital expenditures prior to IPO compare to the industry equivalents, while there is no difference for the later years. Since, we find that the mean level of capital expenditures is continuously decreasing after the year of the IPO while the capital expenditure median levels in +1, +2, +3 years after IPO almost stay the same. With these outcomes, we achieve similar findings to the past studies of Kaplan (1989), Smith (1990) and Musceralla & Vetsuypens (1990) that young public corporations overinvest in capital expenditures even though they also specified that the reverse leverage buyout companies have some abilities to lower some of their expenditures after leverage buyout process. Furthermore, with respect to working capital management, the evidence suggests that reverse leverage buyout companies carry less working capital than their industry equivalents. Our results are similar to Holthausen & Larcker (1996) on working capital since they also found additionally, based on their sample between 1983 and 1988, that the reverse LBO firms was carrying approximately half of the working capital carried by their industry counterparts. In terms of employment management of the reverse leverage buyout firms, there is not much difference observed for reverse LBO firms' staffing level and their industry peers' level. Yet, the evidence refer a continuous increase in employment level starting from the two years after initial public offering and continue to four years after the offering.

For those reasons, we reject the third null hypothesis which is reverse LBO firms have no dissimilarities from their industry counterparts' median level in terms of spending on capital expenditures. The evidence suggests that the year before and the year of IPO reverse leverage buyout firms have less capital expenditures and until the fourth year after the public offering they spent little more compared to their industry peers. In addition, we also reject the fourth null hypothesis since the evidence reflects that reverse LBO firms carries less working capital compared to their industry peers. However, in terms of employment level, we accept the fifth null hypothesis since we could not find any significant evidence against the statement.

$H_{3,o}$ = *Reverse LBO firms have no dissimilarities from their industry counterparts' median level in terms of spending on capital expenditures*

$H_{3,a}$ = *Reverse LBO firms have dissimilarities from their industry counterparts' median level in terms of spending on capital expenditures.*

$H_{4,o}$ = *RLBO corporations carry similar working capital to their industry equivalents*

$H_{4,a}$ = *RBLO corporations does not carry similar working capital to their industry equivalents*

$H_{5,o}$ = *Reverse leverage buyout companies employment level is not different than their industries.*

$H_{5,a}$ = *Reverse leverage buyout companies employment level is different than their industries.*

We also conducted sectional and cross-sectional regression analyses, and based on these analyses, the evidences suggest that debt/capital and working capital/assets are highly correlated with accounting performances while neither capital expenditure/assets not employees/asset are related. So, our results give contradictory suggestions about Holthausen & Larcker (1996) comment on a little correlation between capital expenditures/ asset and debt/capital between the years of prior to initial offering to one year after offering.

So, the null hypothesis ($H_{6,o}$) of change in accounting performances (measured from one year before to one up to four years after becoming reverse IPO) is unrelated to change in leverage is also rejected since the evidence reflects a significant association between debt/capital and the accounting performances. But, we accept the null hypothesis ($H_{7,o}$) of change in accounting performances (measured from one year before to up to four years after becoming reverse LBO) is unrelated to change in capital expenditures since the evidences stated earlier show that there is no relation between the capital expenditure/assets and accounting performances either in any of year related with IPO or in any of year period specified earlier. On the other hand, we reject the null hypothesis ($H_{8,o}$) change in accounting performances (measured from one year before to one up to four years after the reverse LBO) is unrelated to change in working capital since there is significant association found between accounting performances from one year prior to IPO to one up to four years after the IPO. However, while we are accepting the $H_{9,o}$ (stated below), we should also mention the fact that there is an evidence of a significant association between the accounting performances and the employment level between the prior year of IPO and the year after IPO.

$H_{9,o}$ = *Change in accounting performances (measured from one year before to one up to four years after the reverse LBO) is unrelated to change in employment level*

$H_{9,a}$ = *Change in accounting performances (measured from one year before to up to four years after the reverse LBO) is related to change in employment level*

Overall, the results in this paper add some strong evidences of positive association between debt leverage and performance level as well as working capital and performance level of the reverse leverage buyout firms.

ACKNOWLEDGMENT

This chapter is an unpublished Master thesis submitted in order to fulfillment of the requirements of the Drexel University LeBow College of Business for the degree of Master in Finance.

REFERENCES

Ainina, M. F., & Mohan, N. K. (1991). When LBOs go IPO. *Journal of Business Finance & Accounting*, *18*(3), 393–403. doi:10.1111/j.1468-5957.1991.tb00602.x

Bruton, G. D., Keels, J. K., & Scrifes, E. L. (1999). The ethics of the complete management buyout cycle: A multi perspective analysis. *Journal of Business Ethics*, *19*(4), 403–413. doi:10.1023/A:1005987208869

Cao, J. X. (2007). *Do Buyout Sponsors Time RLBO to Exit?* (Working paper, pp. 1-20). Singapore Management University.

Degeorge, F., & Zeckhauser, R. (1993). The reverse LBO decision and firm performance: Theory and evidence. *The Journal of Finance*, *48*(4), 1323–1348. doi:10.1111/j.1540-6261.1993.tb04756.x

Halpern, P. (1999). On the heterogeneity of leveraged going private transactions. *Review of Financial Studies*, *12*(2), 281–309. doi:10.1093/rfs/12.2.281

Hogan, K. M., Olson, G. T., & Kish, R. J. (2001). A comparison of reverse leveraged buyouts and original initial public offers: Factors impacting their issuance in IPO market. *Financial Review*, *38*(3), 1–18. doi:10.1111/j.1540-6288.2001.tb00017.x

Holthausen, R. W., & Larcker, D. F. (1996). The financial performance of reverse leveraged buyouts. *Journal of Financial Economics*, *42*(3), 293–332. doi:10.1016/0304-405X(96)00884-7

Jensen, M. (1989). Takeovers: Their causes and Consequences. *The Journal of Economic Perspectives*, *2*(1), 21–48. doi:10.1257/jep.2.1.21

Jensen, M. C. (1989). Eclipse of public corporations. *Harvard Business Review*, *67*, 61–75.

Kaplan, S. N. (1989). The effects of management buyouts on operating performance and value. *Journal of Financial Economics*, *24*(2), 217–254. doi:10.1016/0304-405X(89)90047-0

Kaplan, S. N. (1991). The staying power of leverage buyouts. *Journal of Financial Economics*, *29*(2), 287–314. doi:10.1016/0304-405X(91)90004-4

Kaplan, S. N. (1997). The evaluation of US corporate governance: We are all Henry Kravis now. *Journal of Private Equity*, *1*, 7–14. doi:10.3905/jpe.1997.409664

Kaplan, S. N., & Stein, J. D. (1991). *The evolution of buyout pricing and financial structure in the 1980s* (Discussion Paper). University of Chicago

Kosedag, A., Mehran, J., & Qian, J. (2009). Reverse-LBOs, re-LBOs and informational asymmetry hypothesis of LBO transactions. *Managerial Finance*, *35*, 716–728.

Long, W. F., & Ravenscraft, D. J. (1993). LBOs, Debt and R&D Intensity. *Strategic Management Journal, 14 (summer)*, 119-135.

Mian, S., & Rosenfeld, J. (1993). Takeover activity and the long run performance of reverse leverage buyouts. *Financial Management*, *22*(Winter), 46–57. doi:10.2307/3665576

Muscarella, C. J., & Vetsuypens, M. R. (1989). The under pricing of 'second' initial public offerings. *Journal of Financial Research*, *12*(3), 183–192. doi:10.1111/j.1475-6803.1989.tb00512.x

Muscarella, C. J., & Vetsuypens, M. R. (1990). Efficiency and organizational structure: A study of reverse LBOs. *The Journal of Finance*, *45*(5), 1389–1413. doi:10.1111/j.1540-6261.1990.tb03720.x

Renneboog, L., & Simons, T. (2005). *Public-to-Private Transactions: LBOs, MBOs, MBIs and IBOs* (Discussion paper 2005-23). Tilburg University, Tilburg Law and Economic Center

Smith, A. J. (1990). Corporate ownership structure and performance: The case of management buyouts. *Journal of Financial Economics*, *27*(1), 143–164. doi:10.1016/0304-405X(90)90024-T

ADDITIONAL READING

Bowman, R. G., & Graves, L. (2005). *Reverse Leverage Buyouts: Timing and Underpricing* (Working Paper). University of Auckland.

Cao, J., & Lerner, J. (2009). The Performance of Reverse Leveraged Buyouts. *Journal of Financial Economics*, *91*(2), 139–157.

Cao, J. X. (2010). IPO Timing, Buyout Sponsors' Exit Strategies and Firm Performance of RLBOs. *Journal of Financial and Quantitative Analysis*, *46*, 1001–1024.

Cook, J. P., & Officer, D. T. (1996). Is Underpricing a Signal of Quality in "Second Initial Public Offerings"? *Quarterly Journal of Business and Economics*, *35*(1), 67–78.

Gombola, M., Chou, D. W., & Liu, F. Y. (2005). Earnings Management and Stock Performance of Reverse Leveraged Buyouts. *Journal of Financial and Quantitative Analysis*, *41*(2), 407–438.

Klasa, S. (1998). *LBO's, reverse LBO's and the reduction of agency problems*. Masters Thesis, Concordia University.

Noronha, G., & Yung, K. (1997). Reverse LBO Underpricing: Information Asymmetry or Price Support? *Journal of Applied Business Research*, *13*(3), 67–78.

Ritter, J., & Loughran, T. (2004). Why Has IPO Underpricing Changed Over Time? *Financial Management*, *33*(3), 5–37.

Spiros, K. (1998). *Operating Performance of Reverse Leveraged Buyouts and Underwriter Prestige*. Masters thesis, Concordia University.

Wright, M., Robbie, K., Thompson, S., & Starkey, K. (2006). Longevity and the life-cycle of management buy-outs. *Strategic Management Journal*, *15*(3), 215–227.

KEY TERMS AND DEFINITIONS

Initial Public Offering: A first sale of common stock or shares to public by private firm. Also referred to as a public offering.

Leverage Buyout: An equity control of a financial sponsor when a major portion of purchase is financed by borrowing. In fact, the term of LBO does not only refer public to private transformation, but also refers an increase in leverage due to acquisitions. Also referred to as "bootstrapping."

Reverse leverage Buyout: The process of turning privately held company which was publicly traded beforeinto a public company.

Chapter 23
Emotional Intelligence Skills, Leadership, and Conflict in Effective Decision Making Process

Burcu Hacioğlu
Society for the Study of Business and Finance, Turkey

Ümit Hacıoğlu
Istanbul Medipol University, Turkey

Hasan Dinçer
Istanbul Medipol University, Turkey

Pelin Şahin Yarbağ
Beykent University, Turkey

Türker Tuğsal
Beykent University, Turkey

ABSTRACT

There are plenty of researches about EI which have focused on EI and strategic decision making, management capabilities, transformational leadership, managerial traits, personality dimensions. This chapter is putting forth the relationship between EI and managing conflict by theoretical research. In the chapter the authors firstly reiterated the theoretical studies, state the necessity of having high level of EI for accomplishing the decision making process and discuss the relationship between EI, managers and managing conflict. To conclude, the authors state that managers having high EI can understand and evaluate the conflicts among employees and encourage their followers in struggling; with comparison to the ones having low EI.

DOI: 10.4018/978-1-4666-7484-4.ch023

INTRODUCTION

As a result of globalization, it is required for all managers, administrative officers and even employees to have high level of EI for accomplishing the decision making process to contribute to the success of long term strategy planning and implementation process. There are plenty of academic studies supporting that managers who have high level of EI can make good decisions. As it is emphasized in Doğan and Demiral's study, it is not enough to have employees who have high level of IQ or technical and mental talents to be able to increase success, provide efficient and productive performance, and create customer satisfaction. Besides, organizations need to employ emotional and social individuals who can know or manage their own emotions, and also understand what others feel (Dinçer et. al., 2011).

The necessity of innovative management strategies and also employees who are open to innovations has been started to be more of an issue for the companies in the competitive environment emerged by the impact of globalization factor, because dynamic changes and developments in the field of technology owing to this fierce competition affect almost all sectors seriously. In short, organizations should renew employees' work processes and methods taking either internal or external needs or expectations to become a dominant player in the market. To this respect employees need to be motivated in terms of all work conditions to search out new work methods or generate new ideas including innovative approaches. Thus, it will be easier for them to present their innovative work behaviors accordingly.

The original exploration of this chapter is putting forth the relationship between Emotional Intelligence (EI) and managing conflict by theoretical research. This paper is organized into four sections and proceeds as follows. We first carefully reiterated the theoretical studies. Section 2 shows background and literature; section 3 discusses the relationship between Emotional Intelligence (EI), managers and managing conflict; and finally section 4 concludes the study.

1. EI Theoretical Framework

Success of business, in today's corporate life, depends on a good manager. When two organizations whose sources and abilities are similar have been compared, the one which has a good manager reaches success whereas the other in the hand of a bad manager paints a hopeless picture (Çelikten & Çelikten, 2007). Erdem (1997) states that managers' job is creating effective teams with their knowledge, skills, attitudes and approaches towards problems. An effective organization is provided by high motivation. Managers are responsible for motivating their workers and make them do their work voluntarily. Therefore; in the organization motivated workers will perform the aims of establishment

Managers should make strategic plans independent from the circumstances they are in (Aslan et al., 2007). They should find ways to make negative conditions turn to opportunities and can find ways or solutions not intuitionally but by using scientific methods. Ay and Karadal (2003) states that managers should have knowledge in order to evaluate the behaviors of followers. A manager who doesn't know himself could not have knowledge of others' behaviors and could not make evaluations as well. Tosun (1992) states definitions of managers in many ways. Management is an activity of bringing production factors together effectively. Management is a period of coordination of cooperation efforts done to reach an aim. Another definition is that management is an activity of convincing people to cooperation in the cause of reaching a common aim. A further one is management is an art of providing maximum results by minimum effort thereby providing the most happiness, wealth to employers and employees and the best service possible to public. Yet another one is management is a period to make someone do a work voluntarily.

In organizations the success or failure of cooperation for providing organizational aims can be subjected to the authority. The reason lying behind this idea is that the authority is related with the determination of responsibilities in the organization, minimizing or destroying disagreement due to different ideas and being the aims of organization at the forefront. That's why authority is not constant, unchangeable situation that is possession of some certain people (Papatya, 1997). In this situation, when a manager or a person using this authority remains incapable, besides efforts of manager within the establishment is also ineffective. This ineffectiveness causes insufficiency of motivation, lack of success in supervision and lack of using sources economically and rationally in reaching target aims.

In the past a lot of managers provided a kind of trust to make people believe that they were infallible. In those kind of situations the manager becomes a symbol of sense of embracement for the group. The authority depending on trust and adopted authority are strengthened in both two sense (Eren, 2010).A group which adopts its leader, increasingly trust its leader more and the critics about the adopted leader show decrease in this dimension

In order to reach some certain aims, making right decisions about using people, material sources, equipment, stocks, auxiliary materials and time in an effective manner is called management (Eren, 2010).For taking out management period, there should be a person in command of the person who is in leader position and decides about product factors. A person who influences his employees by using their activities in order to perform some certain aims even there is not any other source or material equipment.

Philosophers, who are in thought of perceiving management as a period, define management as total effort of right manipulation of a group of people to provide certain aims and cooperation between them (Şimşek, 2010). As a period, management is used for the situations in which reaching determined aims with the cooperation of others are provided. According to Uğurluoğlu and Çelik (2009) organizations can continue their strategic management periods successfully by following efficient ways. Senior managers must show a way to the organization by using their strategic leadership status in the establishment in order to form vision and mission. All the people in the organization who work for certain aim want to obtain their working strategies and act according to certain vision by considering strategic leaders as a guide.

The most important factor for the existence of management is efficiency. The management should provide its efficiency to show its existence under no circumstances. For this efficiency the precautions that are taken in technology are necessary. Besides technology and rationalization, workforce must show efficiency (Kaynak, 1975). The high quality of accordance among individuals and their satisfaction are the basic factors of workforce efficiency. The other requirement of management that is necessary to continue its existence is the continuity of two basic factor that we mentioned previously. In short, as the management fulfills these requirements, it should continue the period by providing motivation with the same requirements.

Many definitions on management concept can be done. In general it can be said that manager tries to reach targets by showing effort to reach certain aims with the help of cooperation of a group of people or via other people (Bakan, 2008). In short a manager is responsible for providing a balance. He should provide accordance between the technology, aim, structure of organization and people having different qualifications. A professional manager obtains this duty as his job. This success depends on his talent of influencing and providing others towards an organizational aim. A professional manager does not show a success of influencing or directing not just by using his authority. Apart from being a classical manager, having certain talents is the necessity of management mentality.

The communication inside organization must continue from one manager to another after that from one worker to another. As organization continues to grow, the communication within organization becomes difficult. Thus, the quality of organizational communication becomes more necessary (Eroğluer, 2011). The most effective factor on the motivation of worker is the communication and sharing between worker and the manager. For this reason the most important factor in increase of motivation is fulfilling the expectations of workers. The expectations of workers are the fair distribution of gained rights among workers (Baz, Kaya & Savaş, 2011). In this decision mechanism the basis between employees and employer must be maintained strongly. Organizational justice which is one of the most effective factors on the behaviors and attitudes of workers is an important subject that should be considered with importance by managers. An act of representing an organization in an establishment, coordinating the Works of employees and directing them toward aims is known as management. The manager is the person who has the leading role in organizations, provides people act within certain aims and is responsible for creating effective organization. Performing of organizational aims shows parallelism with the efficiency level of managers (Çırpan & Koyuncu, 1998). That's why one of the most important job of a manager is performing the aims of establishment together with the aims of employees. Since managers are in a status of taking decisions about the whole of organization, its parts, other employees and environmental relationships apart from their own subjects, they are expected having a high sense of self. The most important means of manager to evaluate himself according to other people is the self. Since the self develops differently for each manager, it shows different reflections for different decisions which must be taken in or out of organization. A developed self when it shapes as a perception for others, has an important place in directing relations and taking decisions (Çakmak & Kara, 2011).

There have been plenty of researches in the field of emotional intelligence (see Table 1). These researches have focused on EI and strategic decision making (Dinçer et al., 2011); EI and management capabilities (Behbahani, 2011); EI and transformational leadership (Cavazotte, Moreno, Hickmann, 2012); EI profiles and managerial traits (Siegling, Sfeir, Smyth, 2014; Siegling, Nielsen, Petrides, 2014); EI and personality dimensions (Sarawati et. al., 2013); EI and professional success (Obradovic et. al., 2013).

Emotional intelligence is important factor on the success of individual's social life and business life. Plenty of studies on this issue has increased in recent years. When analyzing studies about emotional intelligence's influences, results are generally similar. Considering the variety of definitions in the literature, they are all based on three models generated by Mayer and Salovey, Goleman, Bar-on.

For the first time, the term "emotional intelligence" is used by Mayer and Salovey They define it as "a kind of talent to observe one's own and others' emotions, to recognize them and to use this information to guide one's thinking or actions" (Mayer & Salovey, 1993; Dinçer et. al., 2011). According to Mayer and Salovey there are four main abilities. These abilities are "perception of emotions; use of emotions for inspiration; understanding of emotions; and regulation of emotions for the enrichment of personal development and social relations" (Mayer & Salovey, 1993). Therefore, the one who has these abilities manage to overcome such problems more effectively with comparison to others who has not.

Goleman states that emotional intelligence is "something which helps one understand his own emotions, show empathy and control them in such a way that they facilitate his life and contribute him in any case (Dinçer et. al., 2011). Goleman's model consists of five abilities which of them are "self-awareness, self-regulation, motivation, empathy, and social talents" (Rahim & Psenicka, 2002).

Bar-on defines emotional intelligence as "relating and understanding others, while adapting and coping with potential problems around his environment in order to become more successful in

Table 1. Literature review and selected studies on emotional intelligence

Author(s)	Aim of the Research	Methodology	Findings and Results
Hasan Dinçer, Gülşah Gencer, Nazife Orhan, Kevser Şahinbas (2011)	Significance of emotional intelligence on strategic decision making.	Descriptive statistics, Mann-Whitney Test	When the degree of EI increases, the level of innovative work behaviors also increases and vice versa.
Ali Akbar Behbahani (2011)	The relationship between emotional intelligence and management capabilities.	Emotional IntelligenceQuestionnaire	Significant relationship between emotional intelligence with its components.
Flavia Cavazotte, Valter Moreno, Mateus Hickmann (2012)	The effects of intelligence, personality traits and emotional intelligence on transformational leadership.	SEM	The leadership effectiveness, is a direct function of a leader's transformational behaviors, and is an indirect function of individual differences.
A.B. Siegling, Mireille Sfeir, Hedley John Smyth (2014)	The trait EI profiles of a general managerial sample.	ANCOVA	Managers' global trait EI scores were significantly higher than those of the normative sample.
Siti Sarawati Hj. Johar, Ishak Mad Shah, Zainudin Abu Bakar (2013)	The personality dimensions' impact through the perspective of emotional intelligence of leaders in organization.	Theoretical	The stability dimensional from the perspective of neuroticism personality among the leaders is to be the main catalysts.
Vladimir Obradovic, Petar Jovanovic, Dejan Petrovic, Marko Mihic, Zorica Mitrovic (2013)	Correlation between project managers' emotional intelligence and their professional success.	Theoretical	The empirical research reveals that there is a very high positive correlation between emotional intelligence and professional success
A.B. Siegling, Charlotte Nielsen, K.V. Petrides (2014)	Trait emotional intelligence can differentiate between leaders and non-leaders.	Logistic-regression model	The leadership and management positions require high trait EI.

dealing with environmental demands" (Şahinkaya, 2006). Bar-on's model has five abilities. These are namely "social talents, interpersonal talents, adaptability dimension, overcoming stress and finally general mood" (Bar-on&Parker, 2000).

2. Emotional Intelligence and Conflict Management Relations

Some technological developments have negative effect on relations of people and individualize them. As a result of this, a confliction arouses among working people in establishments. To increase the performance of workers, the establishment should conflict among people under control.

Conflict can be defined in general as an interactive period that comes out as a result of incompatibility and disagreement. It is a dynamic among people that shapes inner and outer conditions of people and affects the performance of people either positive or negative way. A conflict which comes out in every relations and interactions is an inevitable fact. Despite of its negative effects, the constructiveness or destructiveness of conflict is related to the conflict management skills of people. Interestingly, the relationship between Emotional Intelligence (EI) and managing conflict may find justification from the management capabilities, managerial traits and professional success discussed in Behbahani (2011); Siegling, Sfeir, Smyth (2014); Siegling, Nielsen, Petrides (2014); Obradovic et al. (2013).

Persuasion, conflict management and ability of gathering people around common aim are the basic instruments of a manager. In order to bring emotions to the same frequency and establish a successful communication, a leader should realize his feelings (Ülker, 2008). The managers who have an ability of bringing people in common by understanding the difference of point of views, can direct the latest thoughts and feelings towards the common aim of the group after he solve conflict by making people talk (Tuna, 2008). Whatever the area is, one of the most important subjects that a manager has to study on is the increase the success of workers. To provide this, as a manager is expected to take precautions to solve conflicts, the employees are expected to show the necessary effort, perform their duties and be ready for the increase or decrease of demand (Aktaş & Gök 2010).

Listening to people totally and sending convincing messages is known as communication. The people, who have strong mutual communication, easily solve problems, provide open communication by recording emotional clues and being ready any kind of good or bad news has this talent (Goleman, 2012). Providing a solution to disagreement during communication is known as conflict management. One of the characteristics of people who have talents in solving is to soothe the parties by obtaining problem during development.

To evaluate the emotions of opponent in the right way is an important factor for success. The people, who do this best, can analyze the most important points and compromise about those important points whereas they force the opponent for devotion about the less important subjects (Goleman, 2012).Kaya and Kozak (2006) states that managers having high emotional intelligence can understand and evaluate the conflicts among workers, any kind of conditions that has to be overcome, relations and interactions which have profit potential better and easier than the ones having low emotional intelligence.

In whichever department or among whoever the conflict takes place, the effective management of conflict is possible with exact evaluation (Akkirman, 1998). An effective management is necessary to be provided from the beneficial sides of workers whereas their harmless sides are reduced.

Managers can reduce conflicts within organization or provide trust among workers by showing behaviors preventing gossips and warning workers about this subject (Bektaş & Erkal 2007).To decrease the conflicts due to the lack of communication within organization, managers should increase their efficiency in accordance (Tuna, 2009). As the accordance and optimism levels of managers increase, the cooperative working of people in different status and ranks increase in the same level.According to Akkirman (1998) there is a requested conflict on a certain level for organizational efficiency is expressed in studies. The good management of conflict provides the motivation of trends such as newness, change and creativity, coming up new ideas and o positive effect on organization by increasing organizational cooperation. All of them are the most important sign that show the contribution of effective managed conflicts to organization development and advancement.

3. EI and Leadership Relationship

Although the concept of leadership firstly was used at the beginning of 19th century in political articles about English parliament, it actually came out in 1300s and it is the most popular subjects that have been worked on for a long time (Akbaba & Erenler, 2008).

If it is necessary to make a few definitions of leadership; leadership is coming forefront of a single person among employees during right control period of social movements (İbicioğlu et al., 2009). In another definition leadership means to direct and convince people on previously determined route (Çelik & Sünbül, 2008). According to Eren (2010) leadership means: "The total of information and talents to gather people around a certain aims and move them to perform those aims". According to another definition, move audiences toward a certain aim, convey the sincerity to opponents, a talent of assigning different meanings to the behaviors come out in different situations (Bakan, 2008).

When the definitions in different sources are considered, there lies an attracting of emotions of other people in the basis of leadership. How and why leaders attract others, which functions play role in this attraction and which source powers they use in attracting others become the subjects of latest studies about leadership. Leadership can occur in any ranks of organization and in order to have leaders' qualities, it is not necessary to be a senior officer. The importance is directing people to determine aims by making them follow you (Demir, Yılmaz & Çevirgen, 2010).

The basic aim in leadership behavior is to affect the activities of workers. The strategy, behavior, tactics of leader is to provide the values, beliefs and behaviors of workers as well as their success in doing work and accordance with others. It is important that the behaviors and strategies of leader must be perceived in the right way by workers in the sense of ethics in order to fulfill what is expected from them (Arslantaş & Dursun, 2008). Although there are some studies about individual and situational determiners of ethics in leadership, it has not been exactly found if ethic leadership behavior affects individual behavior.

A leader can observe and evaluate affective emotional flows in general of the group well and can also study how his behaviors are affective on these. The most important method of gaining trust of a leader is to sense these feelings and behave in a way that shows them to be understood (Goleman, 2012).A leader is the main source of emotional situation in the organization and reflects his experience as a mirror. Being guidance in group requires this emotional transfer and plays an important role in obtaining the route with workers. The behavior of leader is related to the manners in relations with person following him and the group he is working with. The good fulfilling of duties of workers to provide the aims of organization is related to the behaviors of leader. This causes the researchers to search this subject and make classifications. The leader behavior is examined into two groups as human based and work based (Taş & Önder, 2010).Good leaders go around mostly than mean leaders and ask questions about their families and personal problems. Also they form an open system by rousing they want to know about the developments in their lives. This continuity of two way communication provides continuous information of all people in senior staff (Goleman, 2012).Since something which is not done alone, it is very important to provide sharing and cooperation and this important duty is the basic function of leadership (Ülker, 2008).

Team working, directing target, forming vision, establishing available teams for work and transforming of authority and responsibility is important in leadership. Also this leadership brings different point of views. In changing based leadership it is a basic characteristic to provide opportunities in order to improve their capacities and form different point of views (Taş & Önder, 2010). Leaders encourage their workers in struggling, taking risks and using authority. They provide their workers to show a higher performance than it is expected. A leadership behavior which is used in this way provides to manage his own duties and responsibilities rather than following workers.

The leaders, who are sensitive to the emotions of others, know themselves well and are able to control their feelings, establish a close relationship with their workers and strengthen it in time (Sosik & Megerian, 1999).Leaders are the people who can put creativity into the organization. They make a necessary route way by taking the existing creativity out. Leaders encourage their workers who are coming with beneficial ideas by affecting their creativity directly or indirectly (Cengiz, Acuner & Baki, 2006).

Change Agent

Change agent means to start or manage change. The individuals who have got this effectiveness are the ones who provide and defend change by eliminating conditions preventing change. Effective change leaders have characteristics such as high self-confidence, directing political relations within the organization according to his intuitions, high level of impressiveness, dependency and high level of motivation (Goleman, 2012). Leaders can realize new ideas and working styles however they aren't generally the ones that start change and it is not necessary for them to be reformists. Traditional management is not enough in changing organizations. There needs a charismatic leaders in organizations entering changing period.

Cooperation

The most important dimensions that affect success are behaviors such as assistance, sharing and cooperation. It is possible for establishment managers to evaluate these behaviors more important than the productivity of establishment.

For the continuous development of productivity, the continuity of accordance, solidarity and cooperation of workers matters the most. These kind of behaviors keep the collective conscious keeps labor force all together. The previous studies show that the military activities in military organizations are closely related to supplementary emotional intelligence talents such as cooperation, friendship, solidarity, motivation rather than having a technical talent (Acar, 2001).

Concern is an expression that provides us to undertake the responsibility of the things we have to do. The yarest people to spend time and effort to help their colleagues are the concerned ones. They know the importance of cooperation to contribute the bigger aims of establishment rather than focusing on their own works (Goleman, 2012).

Team Skills

Today establishments need the talents and skills of all workers rather than individual efforts of managers. Çetin (2009) states that the continuous development basic job period provides rivalry advantage so establishments need to get right benefit from every level of workers in every rank. The future establishments will grow directly proportional with the workers' right usage of talents or will diminish. To name amounts of people as team there must have some basic characteristics of these team members. When disciplined behaviors are discussed, amounts of people can get the characteristics of team. Teams are separated from group in terms of obtaining a common aim, reaching a consensus and making supplementary works. Also, when there needs a strong leadership characteristics, in teams leadership is done alternatively.

In terms of the rightness of decisions, it is very important to examine the subject from every point of view before taking it. At the end of this kind of study, the team members will be aware of subjects, ready to the conditions that can happen later and are in communication with each other. In all kinds of work done with cooperation, the key provision is continuous informing system. Each team member should be informed on the same level continuously (John, 1995).

The importance of emotional intelligence is also important for the emotional intelligence of teams. Each of the emotional intelligence talent develops on each other and form a kind of continuity.

The self-conscious behavior of team members provide them to evaluate each other better and get close to each other with empathy. The empathic behaviors of team members provide a continuous positive atmosphere. Besides, they can manage the relations with the outer world and among themselves effectively. Having a social consciousness provides team having an effective communication with other parts of organization.

The biggest profit of team work is to maintain the common aim and this power to achieve it. In this kind of team individuals get more profit. In order to provide this synergy there need to have an exchange of ideas, correcting mutual mistakes and solving problems at the right time (Çetin, 2009). In order to benefit from this synergy, the people should be chosen from the people that can complete each other. By this created synergy positive results can be taken for the sake of establishment as well as positive motivation of workers.

4. Effective Decision Making Process with Multiple Skills

Emotions are known as the feelings that make people ready for people, objects or facts. They are as important as cognitive and behavioral factors and they direct the behaviors of individuals in perception and manner development period. In accordance of relations and surrounding, the factors which direct the individual is emotions. The feelings give the sense of satisfaction or sadness. A part of human life is under the effect of some feelings and emotions (Doğan & Özdevecioğlu, 2009). Emotions will be the part of organizational state in business life which takes the biggest part of people's lives. Because of these reasons emotions cannot be thought independent and apart from organizations. Although the behaviors in organizations are proper to logic, mind and system, emotions like sadness or jealousy happens as frequent as they happen in daily life

People are not machines. It is not possible to enter establishment by leaving them out. People can sometimes be sad or angry and those feelings can be related to establishment or daily problems. Whatever the reason is the mood that the person is in will affect his efficiency and the relations with his colleagues (Akın, 2004).

So it is very important for establishments that the managers are having an emotional practicum and workers having emotional maturity.

What is expected from managers for working condition is emotional maturity (Baltaş, 2001). According to the survey done on ten young managers who were expected to be successful but unfortunately weren't, there found four characteristics that cause their failure. These characteristics are: being unsuccessful in relations with people, being dominant, having conflicts with the superiors and over ambitious. Managers who know his and others' feelings, and sensitive to demands and needs of other people can establish relations depending on trust. In this direction despite of hard conditions, they can provide motivation, express his feelings openly, direct his workers and customers to the required results and solve conflicts with satisfactory solutions. People who have developed emotional intelligence have great contribution to the success of organization (Çetinkaya & Alparslan, 2011).

Ability of controlling feelings is the most important and basic characteristic of emotional intelligence. The feeling of a person is the basic factor in every decision and behavior and the success of leaders is the result of management of their emotional world. According to Baltaş (2013) the feelings must be used according to the aim. If they are used according to the aim, they show a way and increase efficiency. The managers having high emotional levels, benefit from his emotions in taking decisions, avoid negative emotions, understand the opponents' feelings and manage them well. Workers take their leaders as a model. The leader has an importance for the people around them and they are an example for others. In order to influence people and create the highest performance in organizations leadership characteristics are needed. If the intelligence level of a leader is high, he can manage the people around them accordingly (Özer, 2010).

Management effectiveness is known as regulating management activities according to make people work. Since managers are directly responsible for management activity, they need to have some talents and capabilities. It is expressed today that the behaviors of managers are affective on workers determine the success of the individual and organization (Erçetin, 2000). The manager must be aware of what is expected from him, choose his behaviors carefully and these behaviors have to be effective. Leaders firstly take the feelings and thoughts of workers then their behaviors into consideration with their sense of empathy. With their strong senses and strong emotional worlds they can influence and direct crowds. The leaders are expected to show social understanding and strong emotional management. The expectations related to being strategic, controlling, follower of a project as well as influencing, advancing positive behaviors, participating of opponents and creating estimation increases day by day. So the emotional intelligence talents of leaders come to forefront (Edizler, 2010). The increase attention to manage social and individual complex relations related to emotional intelligence level off a leader, makes the role of emotions in organizations important.

Managers should be well equipped about the job satisfaction, sense of belonging to working place, accordance to changing conditions and organization structure and directing of emotions. When it is looked at this period, the importance of emotion management, the positive emotional capitals such as toleration, optimism, belonging form a social capital for individual and organizations (Töremen, 2008).

The most important characteristics that managers has to acquire is the communication in the working place as well as offering working suggestions that prevents negative factors such as tension and conflict and behaving according to this by learning emotions. The most important factors that can be gained by improving of emotional intelligence are known as coping with change, accordance, behaving with control when necessary and behaving consistent during decision period (Arıcıoğlu, 2002). In development of emotional intelligence concept, some assumptions about the consistency of emotional intelligence and various measurements are used. What is important is to evaluate it with objective and significant criteria. Today, managers' being ineffective in relations and emotional management and giving importance about gaining experience mostly on technical and work qualities can cause some negativity. These problems are managers cannot provide workers' expectations, the increase in pressure on workers, ineffective prizing, managers cannot feel themselves together with their workers and the trust problem between the manager and the worker (Töremen, 2008).

The leader who is aware of his self-realization knows what he can or cannot do and continues his studies in order to improve his insufficient sides. Since these leaders are good listeners they can understand the unspoken feelings of workers and their point of views. They can also read the most important relationships among people as well as realize the capacity of workers (Beceren, 2013). They can use talent and ability capacity of the organization well. Being dominant on these subjects make them to trust his colleagues, establishment and himself as well as become ready for the duties over him. A leader who achieves these can form the balance of the group well, use the group efficiently and his social intelligence must be more developed than others. His success among people have also gain importance besides craft knowledge and skills of a person. In today's management success concept the superiority and success of teams gain importance rather than work and personal characteristics. The way of success of team work which is one of the most important factor in providing organizational aims, needs team workers having high emotional intelligence level. Nowadays human relations become more important than mental characteristics (Çetinkaya & Alparslan, 2011).

The previous studies show that the workers who have the highest working performance, have got emotional intelligence. Today organizations activate with teams rather than work as an individual and they become successful by this synergy (Çetinkaya & Alparslan, 2011). In order to get this success, relations must be provided effective and right by bringing characteristics such as accordance in team working and colleagues to the forefront.

CONCLUSION

To sum up, the main aim of this paper is putting forth the relationship between Emotional Intelligence (EI) and conflict management with theoretical research. In today's corporate life, success of business depends on a proficient manager. Managers should have knowledge in order to evaluate the behaviors of followers. A manager who doesn't know himself, is not able to know others' behaviors and even not able to make evaluations. When a manager remains incapable, this ineffectiveness causes insufficiency of motivation, lack of success, lack of using sources economically and rationally in reaching target aims.

In today's global business world, it is required for all managers, administrative officers and even employees to have high level of EI for accomplishing the decision making process. It is no longer enough to have employees who have high level of IQ or technical and mental talents. Besides, organizations need to employ emotionally and socially competent individuals who can manage their own emotions, and also others'.

Conflict shapes inner and outer conditions of people and affects the performance of people either positive or negative way. Despite the fact that it has negative effects, these constructive or destructive effects of conflict depends on manager's conflict management skills. The managers, who have an ability of bringing people in common by understanding the difference of point of views, can solve conflicts. Managers having high emotional intelligence can understand and evaluate the conflicts among employees, with comparison to the ones having low emotional intelligence.

Last but not least, with a view to transformational leadership, leaders encourage their followers in struggling, taking risks and using authority. The leaders, who are sensitive to the emotions of others, know themselves well and are able to control their feelings, establish a close relationship with employees. The most important characteristics that managers have to acquire is the communication in the work place as well as having suggestions that prevent negative factors such as tension and conflict. The most important factors that can be gained by improving of emotional intelligence are known as coping with change, accordance, behaving with control when necessary and behaving consistent during decision period. To conclude, we should emphasize the importance of Emotional Intelligence (EI) over conflict management as a leadership trait.

REFERENCES

Acar, F. T. (2001). *Duygusal zekâ yeteneklerinin göreve yönelik ve insana yönelik davranışları ile ilişkisi: banka şube müdürleri üzerine bir alan araştırması*. Unpublished PhD Thesis, İstanbul Üniversity.

Acar, F.T. (2002). Duygusal zekâ ve liderlik. *Social Sciences Institute, 12.*

Akbaba, A, & Erenler, E. (2008). Otel işletmelerinde yöneticilerin liderlik yönelimleri ve işletme performansı ilişkisi. *Turizm Araştırmaları Dergisi, 19*(1).

Akın, M. (2004), İşletmelerde duygusal zekânın üst kademe yöneticiler ile astları arasındaki çatışmalar üzerindeki etkileri, (Kayseri'deki büyük ölçekli işletmelerde bir uygulama). Unpublished PhD Thesis, Anadolu Üniversity, Social Sciences Institute.

Akkirman, A.D. (1998). Etkin çatışma yönetimi ve müdahale stratejileri. *Dokuz Eylul University Economics and Administrative Sciences Faculty Journal, 13*(2).

AktaşA.GökB.(Eds.).(2010). Örgütsel bağlılığın işgören başarımı üzerindeki etkisi: Antalya'daki A grubu seyahat acentesi çalışanları üzerine bir araştırma.*11. National Tourism Congress*, 2-5 Dec. 2010, Kuşadası (1).

Arıcıoğlu, A. M. (2002). Yönetsel başarının değerlendirilmesinde duygusal zekânın kullanımı: Öğrenci yurdu yöneticileri bağlamında bir araştırma. *Akdeniz University Economics and Administrative Sciences Faculty Journal*, (4).

Arslantaş, C. C., & Dursun, M. (2008). Etik liderlik davranışının yöneticiye duyulan güven ve psikolojik güçlendirme üzerindeki etkisinde etkileşim adaletinin dolaylı rolü. *Anadolu Üniversity Social Sciences Journal, 8*, 1.

Ay, Ü.,& Karadal, H. (2003). Yönetici yaşam biçimleri ile yöneticinin etkinliği ve iş tatmini arasındaki ilişki: Tekstil, çimento, sigorta ve gıda sektöründe bir araştırma. *Erciyes Üniversity Economics and Administrative Sciences Faculty Journal, 20*.

Bakan, İ. (2008). Örgüt kültürü ve liderlik türlerine ilişkin algılamalar ile yöneticilerin demografik özellikleri arasındaki ilişki: Bir alan araştırması. *KMU Economics and Administrative Sciences Faculty Journal, 10*(14).

Baltaş, A. (2001). *Değişimin içinden geleceğe doğru*. İstanbul: Remzi Publishing.

Baltaş, A. (2013). *Ekip liderinin el notları*. Retrieved from http://www.baltas-baltas.com/web/makaleler/l_1.htm

Bar-On, R., & Parker, J. D. A. (2000). *The handbook of emotional intelligence*. New York: Jossey-Bass Company.

Baz, M., Kaya, S., & Savaş, K. (2011). *İşveren ve işgören ilişkileri* (Vol. 1). Academic Social Sciences Journal.

Beceren, E. (2013). *Lider dediğin*. Retrieved from http://www.egedesonsoz.com/yazar/Lider-dedigin-/6243

Behbahani, A. A. (2011). A comparative study of the relation between emotional intelligence and employee's performance. *Procedia: Social and Behavioral Sciences, 30*, 386–389. doi:10.1016/j.sbspro.2011.10.076

Bektaş, M., & Erkal, P. (2007). Kamu ve özel sektörde çalışan büro elemanlarının etik olaylara bakış açısı üzerine bir araştırma: Balıkesir ve Burdur illeri çalışması.*VI. National Bureau Management and Secretarial Congress,* Ankara.

Çakmak, Z., & Kara, H. (2011). Yöneticilerde benlik algılamalarının belirlenmesi: Sanayi örgütlerinde bir araştırma. *Dumlupınar Üniversity Social Sciences Journal, 30*, 301–310.

Cavazotte, F., Moreno, V., & Hickmann, M. (2012). Effects of leader intelligence, personality and emotional intelligence on transformational leadership and managerial performance. *The Leadership Quarterly, 23*(3), 443–455. doi:10.1016/j.leaqua.2011.10.003

Çelik, C., & Sünbül, Ö. (2008). Liderlik algılamalarında eğitim ve cinsiyet faktörü: Mersin ilinde bir alan araştırması. *Süleyman Demirel Üniversity Economics and Administrative Sciences Faculty Journal, 13*(3), 49–66.

Çelikten, M., & Çelikten, Y. (2007). Televizyon programlarında çizilen öğrenci, öğretmen ve yönetici profilleri. *Social Sciences Institute Journal, 23*(2), 369–378.

Cengiz, E., Acuner, T., & Baki, B. (2006). Liderlerin sahip oldukları duygusal zekânın örgütsel yaratıcılık üzerine etkileri: Bir model önerisi. *Atatürk Üniversity Social Sciences Institute Journal, 7*(1), 421–433.

Çetin, C. (2009). *Liderlik stilleri, değişim yönetimi ve ekip çalışması*. İstanbul: İTO Publishing.

Çetinkaya, Ö., & Alparslan, A. M. (2011). Duygusal zekânın iletişim becerileri üzerine etkisi: Üniversite öğrencileri üzerinde bir araştırma. *Süleyman Demirel Üniversity Economics and Administrative Sciences Faculty Journal, 16*(1), 363–377.

Çırpan, H., & Koyuncu, M. (1998). İşletme kültürünün alt kademe yöneticileri üzerindeki etkisi: Bir örnek olay çalışması. *Kırıkkale Üniversity Economics and Administrative Sciences Faculty Journal, 2*(9), 223–230.

Demir, C., Yılmaz, M.K., & Çevirgen, A. (2010). Liderlik yaklaşımları ve liderlik tarzlarına ilişkin bir araştırma. *Alanya Management Faculty Journal, 2*(1).

Dinçer, H., Gencer, G., Orhan, N., & Şahinbaş, K. (2011). The significance of emotional intelligence on the innovative work behavior of managers as strategic decision-makers. *Procedia: Social and Behavioral Sciences, 24*, 909–919. doi:10.1016/j.sbspro.2011.09.052

Doğan, S., & Demiral, Ö. (2007). Kurumların başarısında duygusal zekânın rolü ve önemi. *Management and Economics Journal, 14*(1), 209–230.

Doğan, Y., & Özdevecioğlu, M. (2009). Pozitif ve negatif duygusallığın çalışanların performansları üzerindeki etkisi. *Selçuk Üniversity Economics and Administrative Sciences Faculty Social and Economical Researches Journal, 12*(18), 165–190.

Edizler, G. (2010). Karizmatik liderlikte duygusal zekâ boyutuyla cinsiyet faktörüne ilişkin literatürsel bir çalışma. *Selçuk Communication Journal, 6*(2).

Erçetin, Ş. (2000). *Lider sarmalında vizyon*. Ankara: Nobel Yayın Dağıtım.

Erdem, A. R. (1997). İçerik kuramları ve eğitim yönetimine katkıları. *Pamukkale University Education Faculty Journal, 3*(1), 68–77.

Eren, E. (2010). *Örgütsel davranış ve yönetim psikolojisi*. İstanbul: Beta Publishing.

Eroğluer, K. (2011). Örgütsel iletişim ile iş tatmini unsurları arasındaki ilişkiler: Kuramsal bir inceleme. *Ege Academic View Journal, 11*(1), 121–136.

Goleman, D. (2012). *Duygusal zeka neden IQ' dan daha önemlidir?* (B. S. Yüksel, Trans.). İstanbul: Varlık Publishing.

İbicioğlu, H., Özmen, H. İ., & Taş, S. (2009). Liderlik davranışı ve toplumsal norm ilişkisi: Ampirik bir çalışma. *Süleyman Demirel Üniversity Economics and Administrative Sciences Faculty Journal, 14*(2).

Johar, S. S., Shah, I. M., & Bakar, Z. A. (2012). The impact of emotional intelligence towards relationship of personality and self-esteem at work place. *Procedia: Social and Behavioral Sciences, 65*(3), 150–155. doi:10.1016/j.sbspro.2012.11.104

Kaya, İ., & Kozak, M. A. (2006). *Kariyer uygulamaları ve duygusal zekâ: Beş yıldızlı otel işletmesinde bir araştırma. III*. Postgraduate Tourism Students Research Congress National Free Proceedings.

Kaynak, T. (1975). Beşeri ilişkiler açısından yönetim ve verimlilik. *İstanbul University Management Faculty Management Economics Institute Journal, 1*(2).

Mayer, J. D., & Salovey, P. (1993). The intelligence of emotional intelligence. *Intelligence, 17*(4), 433–442. doi:10.1016/0160-2896(93)90010-3

Obradovic, V., Jovanovic, P., Petrovic, D., Mihic, M., & Mitrovic, Z. (2013). Project managers' emotional intelligence-A ticket to success. *Procedia: Social and Behavioral Sciences, 74*, 274–284. doi:10.1016/j.sbspro.2013.03.034

Özer, İ. Ç. (2010). *Duygusal zeka ile liderlik tarzları arasındaki ilişki*. MA thesis. Marmara University.

Papatya, G. (1997). İşletmelerin örgütsel verimliliğine ulaşmada yetki devri sorunu ve yönetici engeli –motivasyon kuramları bağlamında. *Süleyman Demirel Üniversity Economics and Administrative Sciences Faculty Journal, 2*, 127–146.

Rahim, M. A., & Psenicka, C. (2002). A model of emotional intelligence and conflict management strategies: A study in seven countries. *The International Journal of Organizational Analysis, 10*(4), 302–326. doi:10.1108/eb028955

Şahinkaya, B. (2006). *Yöneticilik ve liderlikte duygusal zekâ*. MSc Thesis, Balıkesir Universitesi Natural Sciences Institute.

Siegling, A. B., Nielsen, C., & Petrides, K. V. (2014). Trait emotional intelligence and leadership in a European multinational company. *Personality and Individual Differences, 65*, 65–68. doi:10.1016/j.paid.2014.01.049

Siegling, A. B., Sfeir, M., & Smyth, H. J. (2014). Measured and self-estimated trait emotional intelligence in a UK sample of managers. *Personality and Individual Differences, 65*, 59–64. doi:10.1016/j.paid.2014.01.027

Şimşek, Ş. (2010). Yönetim ve organizasyon (12th Edition). Konya: Eğitim Akademi Publishing.

Sosik, J. J., & Megerian, L. E. (1999). Understanding leader emotional intelligence and performance. *Group & Organization Management, 24*(3), 367–390. doi:10.1177/1059601199243006

Taş, A., & Önder, E. (2010). Yöneticilerin liderlik davranışlarının personel iş doyumuna etkisi. *Electronic Social Sciences Journal, 9*, 17–30.

Töremen, F. (2008). Yönetimde etkili bir yaklaşım: Duygu yönetimi. *Kuramsal Eğitimbilim, 1*(1).

Tosun, K. (1992). İşletme yönetimi (6th Edition). Ankara: Savaş Publishing.

Tuna, Y. (2008). *Örgütsel iletişim sürecinde yöneticilerin duygusal zekâ yeterlilikleri*. PhD. Thesis, Eskişehir Anadolu University.

Tuna, Y. (2009). Örgütsel iletişim sürecinde yöneticilerin duygularını yönetebilme yeterlilikleri. *Selçuk Communication Journal, 5*(4).

Uğurluoğlu, Ö.,& Çelik,Y. (2009). Örgütlerde stratejik liderlik ve özellikleri. *Hacettepe Health Management Journal, 12*(2).

Ülker, H. İ. (2008). Kurumsal liderlikte duygusal yeterlilik. *Economic and Social Researches Journal, 4*(2), 74–84.

KEY TERMS AND DEFINITIONS

Change Agent: Change agent defines starting, managing change. Effective individuals have characteristics such as high self-confidence and impressiveness, dependency and motivation.

Conflict: Conflict is an interactive period that comes out as a result of incompatibility and disagreement and affects the performance of people either positive or negative way.

Emotional Intelligence: Emotional Intelligence is a skill of perceiving, understanding, using and regulating own and others' emotions so as to develop personal and social relations; moreover, overcoming problems.

Manager: Manager is the person who provides maximum results by minimum effort thereby providing the most happiness, wealth to employers and employees; besides he performs these by convincing people to cooperation in the cause of reaching a common aim.

Chapter 24
Proactive Organizational Structure in Financial System

Korhan Arun
Namık Kemal University, Turkey

Tekin Yenigün
Namık Kemal University, Turkey

ABSTRACT

Technology alters the structure of the systems in the finance and service sectors. Nevertheless, technology has been chancing operating systems and as a source to the emergence of new business models. The boundaries of departments in enterprises are weakened and disappeared, these changes give rise to the emergence of showing less commitment in the behavior of employees. In modern business the survival of the organizations does not seem possible, which see success in reactive behavior of the strategy-structure-interaction classical triple. Critical success factor is based foresight and proactivity in all areas of operations including organizing. In this chapter, enterprise organizations' financial departments and resulting changes of structures of the financial sector entities, the effects of this structural changes in the operation system with the new business models is discussed, the tips on how financial system's agencies and departments can fulfill the requirements of proactive nature revealed is studied.

1. INTRODUCTION

In the war for future existence all institutions, including financial institutions, feel the need of converting the structures such as growth, downsizing, merger, change of administration, organizational inefficiencies as internal factors besides technological, social, legal and other environmental changes such as external reasons,.

Change, is seen as an important opportunity and threat, need to cope in today's organizations. Nowadays everything in the world is shifting. The environment is undergoing change with everything in. Change in the environment of the organization, it is necessary to also change strategy to be followed. Strategies vary, but the main goal of the organization is not changed: To make a viable and successful strategy. For Practicable and successful strategy, strategy consistent with an organizational structure is required. Succinctly environmental changes affect strategies, thus the structure of the organization

DOI: 10.4018/978-1-4666-7484-4.ch024

The traditional organizational structure was based on, command-and-control paradigm and the understanding that perceives the organization as a mechanical process. The traditional organizational structure has lost its effectiveness today. Nowadays, all organizations are in the trend and need of developing effective organizational structures that make it possible to achieve the goals. The most important element of business life, the financial sector, cannot be abstracted from these conditions. Changes in the organizational structure of the financial sector affect the entire business life and spearhead the entire industry.

The financial sector is generally considered the most globalized of all economic sectors. Money is easily digitalized and is therefore highly mobile via information and communication technology. For this reason, it is generally believed that the spread of telecommunications together with the ongoing deregulation in Europe will have an enormous impact on the financial sector and financial centers (Alessandrini et al., 2009, p.278).

The financial services sector can be the most effective economic sector in advanced economies. . In the advanced economies-like the United States- the financial sector employs more people than manufacturing of apparel, automobiles, computers, pharmaceuticals and steel combined; 5,4 million people are employed by financial services firms in the U.S. financial services account for almost 5% of Gross Domestic Product in the U.S., about 5.5% in Germany, 3.5% in Italy, and similar statistics are found in other European Union economies with highly developed intermediaries. (Harker & Zenios, 1998)

In the United States in 1934, there were over 14,000 commercial banks, while the figure has decreased by each year. The mid-1980s, the number of U.S. commercial banks has dropped by about 50 percent. When it comes to 2004 the number of commercial banks in the U.S. is around 7,000. (Source: Federal Deposit Insurance Corporation) But, the number of bank branches has risen considerably even as the number of banks has declined. The average number of branches per bank was only about one at 1934, but about 11 at 2007 (Source: Federal Deposit Insurance Corporation).

Table 1. Changes in the U.S. banking industry 1979-1994

Item	1979	1994
Total number of banking organizations	12.463	7.926
Number of small banks	10.014	5.636
Industry gross total assets (trillions of 1994 USD)	3.26	4.02
Industry assets in small banks	13.9%	7.0%
Total number of employees	1.396.970	1.489.171
A number of automated teller machines	13.800	109.080
Cost (1994 USD) of processing a paper check	0.0199	0.0253
Cost (1994 USD) of an electronic deposit	0.0910	0.0138

(Berger et al., 1995, pp. 55-218).

The change, above-mentioned, to be implemented, after the 1980s the most important tools in the hands of the organizations and managers have been a strategy. Strategies are both plans for the future and patterns from the past (Mintzberg, 1987, p.67). So it can be useful to analyze strategy in a historical process.

Following the lines of the historical development of the idea of strategic management development can be considered as three main periods:

1. Strategic planning conception period (1960-1980),
2. Competitive strategy, conception period (1980-1990),
3. Basic competency based on strategy period (From 1990s till Now) (Barca, 2009, pp.35-51).

When Fifty years progress in the field of strategic management kept in view, it is seen that changing environmental conditions rather than the theoretical quest, led to the development and change of the main dynamics. This can be seen as a condition that is expected because of the nature of strategy is required to be very sensitive to changes in the environment. This cause intellectual progress has led to the emergence from adaptation to the environment as a result of the struggle rather than mental activity. Parallel to changing environmental conditions, concept of strategies has changed significantly. The change in this understanding has been reflected in how strategies be formulated. A general conclusion that can be drawn here, due to changing environmental conditions in the coming time understanding, new strategies and formulations can be expected to come up. From the perspective of the managers what important is to anticipate the direction of change or will be informed quickly. Because now and in the future, the secret to being successful and sustaining it is shifting to keep to the route of the race of learning. Learn faster than their competitors and practitioners who will go ahead. And so, in the next period necessary to be found out of tracing what might happen of strategic insight that will give direction to the management, and the success of future-oriented thinking and acting strategically (Barca, 2009, pp.51-52).

Business leaders have worked to create efficiencies and tried to cut costs with technology investment and standardization. For a time, this strategy created advantage, but it also sapped flexibility. In order to survive and thrive amid constant change, companies must reclaim the right balance of standardization and flexibility and build strategic and operational agility into their business foundations. To achieve these goals, agility must be built into an organization's very foundation from strategy to design, people, process and supporting technology. (Keçecioğlu & Çiçek, 2012, p.295). The importance of strategy and strategic management in obtaining the Sustainable competitive advantage is undeniable. A sustainability conscious company should be proactive at all levels and various sectors (Habisch et al., 2005, p.130).

2. STRATEGY AND PROACTIVE ORGANIZATIONS

At the corporate level in strategy-structure relationship that leads to performance, structure follows strategy (Chandler, 1962). If the strategy - structure fits it will tend to improve performance (De Laurentis, 2005, p.10).

Strategic management analyzes the process that shows future goals of an organization's that wants to reach and how to reach this goal (Barry, 1986, p.10). Naturally, this analysis includes the organizational structure that yields to strategic goals to be achieved. Although there are a lot of factors that affect the strategic objectives of the organization, among these, environmental factors (technology, market, regulatory, etc.) And changes in these environments are important so the strategic behavior varies from responding to customer preference to anticipating these requests for gaining adaptive behavior (McIntyre, 2009, p.11; Morel-Guimaraes, 2005, p.292).

In addition, the relationship between organizational structure and innovation that has been demonstrated in many studies, conducted. For example, Gardener (1994) views that organizational structures may be changed to help induce innovation and respond to external innovation demands. In another study, also made important issues in the global economy has been demonstrated on a sectorial basis. In a study conducted in 2013 under the Global Challenges Top 729 CEOs were asked about priorities in the global economy. The responses received are shown in Table 2. (2014, May, retrieved from https://www.conference-board.org/retrievefile.cfm?filename=CEO-Challenge-Charts-and-Tables_FINAL1.pdf&type=subsite).

Table 2. Priorities in the global economy

Human Capital and Operational Excellence Are The Top Global Challenges for 2013	Sectors				
Global Rank N=729	**Challenges 2013**	**General Score**	**Manufacturing n=256**	**Financial Services n=92**	**Non-Financial Services n=361**
1	Human Capital	2.44	1	4	1
2	Operational excellence	2.10	2	3	4
3	Innovation	1.99	3	6	3
4	Customer relationships	1.72	6	2	2
5	Global political/economic risk	1.68	4	5	6
6	Government Regulation	1.55	7	1	5
7	Global Expansion	1.31	5	10	7
8	Corporate brand and reputation	0.92	9	9	8
9	Sustainability	0.82	8	8	9
10	Trust in business	0.46	10	7	10

According to the survey responses of CEOs working in the financial sector differentiate is observed than CEOs in other sectors. CEOs in the financial sector see the factors of importance in order: government regulation, respectively, customer relationships, operational excellence, human capital, global political/economic risk issues. It can be seen that of matters deemed important, except Government regulations, can be achieved with an effective organizational structure. Also in the financial sector "operational excellence" activities including organizational structure, emerges as the 3rd most important activity.

While the boundaries of competitiveness have changed in today's business life, other tools in the hands of the firms and managers to achieve their goals alongside with strategy is organizational structure. Within the framework of the organizational literature theorists have found different approaches to organization in the structure-strategy-effectiveness frame.

The term structure refers to the more or less stable relationships among parts of any system or entity. Organizational structure has two layers: social, the division of labor, including the differentiation of work tasks and the specialization of laborers, and physical as arrangement in space and time. (Hatch & Cunliffe, 2013).

Commonly used dimensions of organizational social structure are Administrative component, Differentiation, Integration, Centralization, Standardization, and Formalization, Specialization (Hatch & Cunliffe, 2013, p.95).

Debate on financial organizations has intensified through the years. While competing opportunities emerged, degree of concentration is not enough for the competitive environment banks operate in so not able to change market, organizations have made structural decisions (Alessandrini et al., 2009, p.136). Also new technologies, globalization, social rights and responsibilities push finance organizations evaluate their structures. Change is a proactive behavior (Gibson et al., 2009, p.488) so systems and people are more proactive and adaptable to changing circumstances (Laegaard & Bindslev, 2006, p.10).

Organizational structure has two layers: social, and physical (Hatch & Cunliffe, 2013) to have a proactive organization these two layers also must be proactive. For example, organizations with every creative way for product performance can step forward in a proactive way (Manring, 2003, p.213). Proactivity is taking the initiative to solve problems and anticipate future events before they happen, instead of reacting to an already existing problem or waiting for a difficult situation to occur (Mynatt, 2009).

Proactive Organizations shape their environment to facilitate improving performance. On the other hand, less proactive organizations, like people show little initiative, tending to passively adapt to their conditions rather than convert those (Crant & Bateman, 2000, p.65).

Granted the current economic state of affairs, the financial managers are determined to be more concentrated on the process and cost reduction. However, the stillness of the same managers about regulating the structure of the financial units is surprising. The results obtained in the studies indicate that, despite the financial crisis of 2008, financial companies have not made changes in their organizational structure to improve the performance (McKinsey Global Survey Results, 2009). This can be said to arise from reducing the costs of companies in times of crisis rather than engaging in large-scale organizational development activities. But the fact that this incorporates a dichotomy. Basic condition to survive, even before earlier than the crisis time, is the following of the organization's proactive strategy. Companies following Proactive strategies are affected less by crises, companies are suffering more from the crisis that are not proactive. More damaged in the crisis are unlikely to become proactive, before the impact of the crisis passes. In this dichotomy of the company to come out of this impasse will be possible by managing both strategy and organizational structure.

This is not an easy job to be done. Because; two of them are becoming particularly visible among the various consequences of the complex reorganization in the banking industry. First, banks are growing and more hierarchically complex. Second, banks are expanding geographically and consequently able to lend at larger distances. (Alessandrini et al., 2009, p.58).

Duty to manage large and complex structures in this procedure is becoming more difficult, that the people who live all over the world are customers / potential customers and the burden on societies to put forth new financial products.

The Capacities of a Proactive Company

(Araujo & Gava, 2012, p.44) identified eight different capacities for market proactiveness:

1. Capacity for dealing with risk.
2. Capacity for dealing with mistakes.
3. Capacity for visualizing future realities.
4. Capacity for managing short-term pressure.
5. Capacity for proactively innovating.
6. Capacity for managing in a flexible way.
7. Capacity for proactively leading.
8. Capacity for identifying and developing proactive people.

The effective exercise of these eight capacities reveals a new way of thinking, a proactive mindset different from what's found in companies aimed exclusively at responding to the market's demands. This new mindset is essential to the execution of proactive strategies, and above all, to achieve positive results. Observe the differences between proactive and reactive mentalities in regard to the eight

Proactive and reactive mindsets also correspond to very different strategic visions listed capacities (in Table 3) (Araujo & Gava, 2012, p.45)

Brockbank's view to proactivity on the basis of HRM is as shown below. Accordingly, the organization behavior is shaped in four stages. Operational reactivity, operational proactive-

Table 3. Differences between proactive and reactive mindsets

Capacities	Reactive Mindset	Proactive Mindset
How does the company deal with risk?	The urge for immediate financial results inhibits risk taking.	The company encourages risk taking on the search for change.
How are mistakes handled?	In theory faults are accepted, but mistakes are actually punished.	Mistakes are regarded as learning and growth opportunities.
When formulating its strategies, does the company consider future realities?	The strategic perspective is centered on current threats and opportunities.	The company is continually trying to imagine new market realities.
Does pressure for short term results hinder anticipation of the future?	Further gains are less important than current results.	Current results are often sacrificed for future gains.
Is innovation a market driven process?	Usually innovation is an answer to market demands.	Innovation is a process aimed at breaking current market patterns.
Do excessive bureaucracy and rules inhibit the free flow of ideas?	The operational *status quo* obstructs presentation of new approaches and ideas.	People are free to express their ideas and opinions.
What is the leadership style?	Traditional leadership focused on control and hierarchy.	Transformative leadership based on autonomy and freedom.
How does the company regard proactiveness at the level of individuals?	Proactiveness is an innate trait.	Proactiveness must be stimulated and developed.

ness, strategic proactivity and strategic reactivity. According to this, Brockbank, represents that strategically proactive will get the competitive advantage. The difference between reactive and proactive management is, reactive managers' focus on now and daily processes, but proactive managers look for the future and doing things in a creative way (Cook et al., 2004, p.1).

In this case, being proactive is an important element for the success of businesses. Being proactive should not be understood simply in the sense of being strategically proactive. Proactivity incorporates a range of management skills (Finney, 2008, p.154). Greater proactive involvement of HR required to match the variety and complexity of the challenging business environment (Finney,

Figure 1. HR competitive advantage index
(Brockbank, 1999, p. 340).

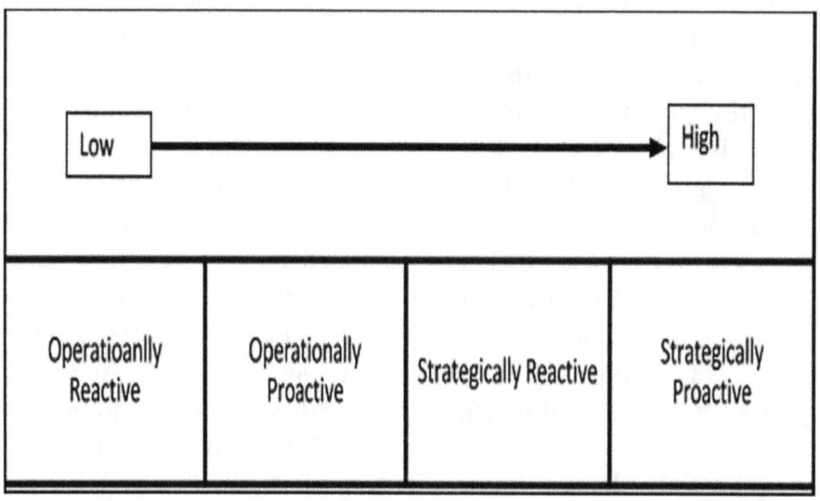

Figure 2. The four dimensions of proactive management
(Araujo & Gava, 2012, p.48).

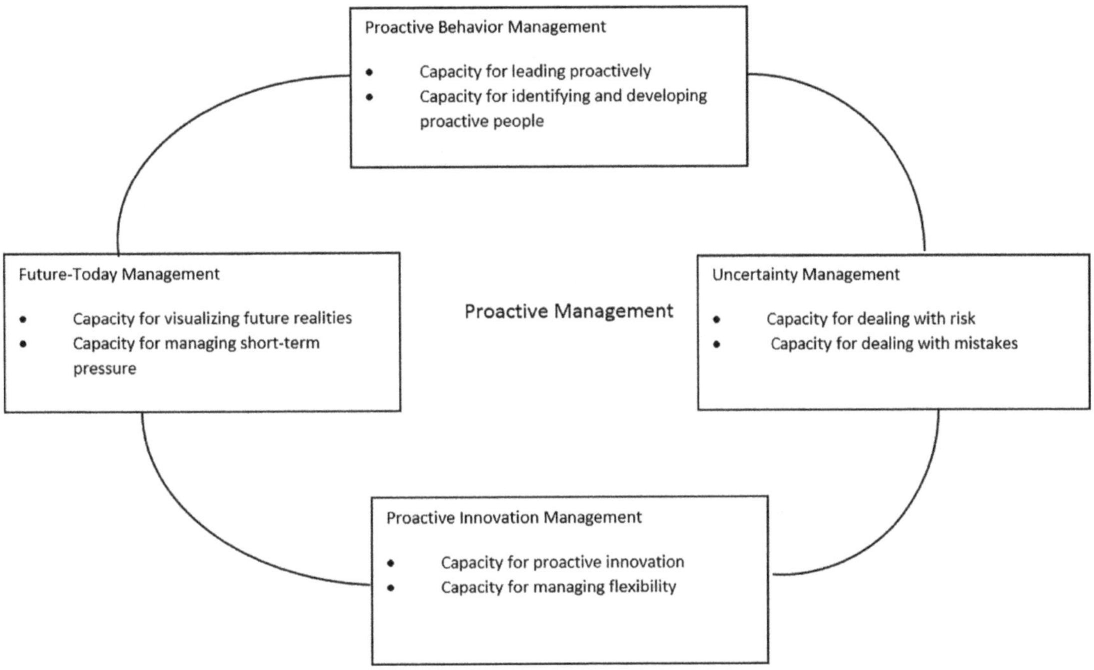

2008, p.43; Barney, 2010, p.78; Weijermars, 2011, p.76). Araujo and Gava (2012) examined Proactive Management in the form of four dimensions. Actually, these four dimensions refer to a paradigm.

The number of banks in Turkey with the relationship between the various variables are as shown in Table 4.

The number of bank branches and the number of staff are important in determining the organizational structure of banks as financial institutions have been evaluated. As success criteria of Banks'; total deposits, total assets, net income, total equity and shared capital are being determined the analysis of banks by considering all Banks in Turkey, the relationship between the number of branches and total number of employees and total deposits, total assets, net income, total equity and share capital were examined and the results presented were obtained in Table 4. Accordingly, the number of branches and personnel of banks' was significantly correlated of the variables that are designated as the criteria for success. In today's business life, customer expectations should be taken into consideration, banks which have the potential to reach a maximum of customers, appear to be more effective. Financial institutions that want to be successful in the future, should take into consideration when creating the organizational structure can be stated as important.

As seen from the Table 4 number of staff significantly correlated with the earnings of the banks. Because the creative energy of human capital allows organizations to stay continuously competitive (Rud, 2009, p.17).

3. FUTURE RESEARCH DIRECTIONS

Customer expectations, and the business process will continue to change so in the future organizational structures of banks` branches will change regionally. Companies` competitive strength is not

Table 4. The relationship among number of employees and branches and with various variables

Independent Var.	Dependent Var.	Correlation	R^2	ADJ. R^2	F	Sig.
# of Branches	Total Deposits	0.979	0.959	0.958	998.554	0,000
# of Personnel	Total Deposits	0.975	0.951	0.950	838.186	0,000
# of Personnel	Total Assets	0.972	0.945	0.943	733.815	0,000
# of Branches	Total Assets	0.967	0.935	0.934	621.335	0,000
# of Personnel	Net Profit	0.953	0.908	0.906	424.297	0,000
# of Branches	Net Profit	0.944	0.890	0.888	348.807	0,000
# of Personnel	Total Shareholders' Equity	0.938	0.880	0.877	315.941	0,000
# of Branches	Total Shareholders' Equity	0.920	0.847	0.843	237.701	0,000
# of Personnel	Share Capital	0.647	0.419	0.405	30.989	0,000
# of Branches	Share Capital	0.605	0.366	0.351	24.771	0,000

just coming from what they have but their ability to act proactively across multiple functional areas. Getting this ability; strategy, organizational structure and HR, all need covalent bonds.

Besides the power and the ability of leadership should be researched on how to promote proactive behavior.

In this context, it is necessary to research the contribution of HR to organizational structure change-strategy interrelation.

4. CONCLUSION

Nowadays success of financial businesses versatile pass from becoming more customer focused, developing new financial products and being able to create strategies. Selection, employment and keeping of human resources capable of carrying out the strategy, creation of reward system to make it successful the appropriate strategy will facilitate the achievement of the target. If the human resources are selected from individual that are appropriate to constantly change, there will be no resistance to change and proactive organizational structure will likely be able to adapt to change as required.

Decision support, system architecture as to achieve the creation of strategies to reach the goals and objectives emerges as a supportive element of success. When viewed in the context of structure-strategy, interaction, organizational structures, planned to support customer-focused strategy and practices, can be shown as one of the most important critical success components. Whenever way structure-strategy, interaction is adopted, proactive strategy, will require proactive an organizational structure along with that. Customer-oriented and innovative financial institutions need to proactive planning (Wezel, 2006, p.264) in this framework will implement organizational structures that support proactive strategy. In this case the direction of the interaction will be;

Customer Expectations → Strategy → Selection of Human Resource → Organizational Structure

However, the innovation is affecting the structure of all these factors. This is the first step of the Lisbon strategy for the competitiveness of the European Union and achieving the target of full employment. In a globalized and fast changing economy, European companies must increase R&D spending in order to ride competition successfully, and they have to speed up the diffusion

Figure 3. The scope of the current-strategic balance

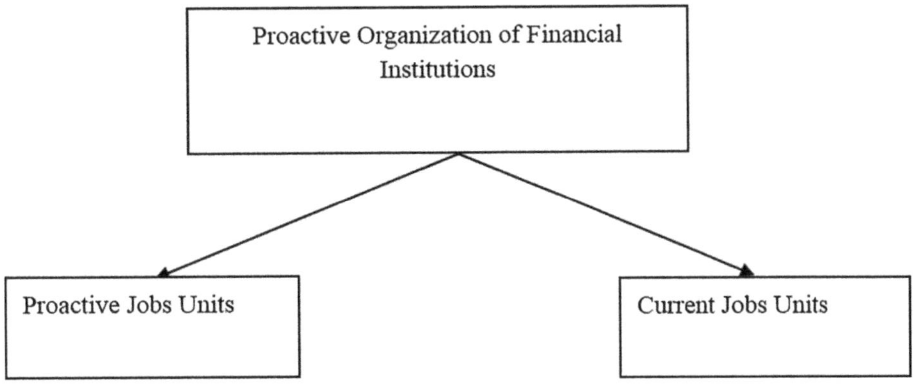

of new technologies and the introduction of new products. To this end, the removal of all bottlenecks in front of the creation and adoption of creativity has been a key policy (Alessandrini, 2009, p.75)

The primary elements that lead banks to restructure themselves into well-defined segments can be summed up as: competition, more and more segment based investor analysis, sustainability of operation and development alternatives, demand for dedicated services at a full cost, increased importance of service quality in customers' choice, critical mass in all market segments, accountability and higher visibility of each business line, potential to streamline holding structures (De Laurentis, 2005, p.10).

The organizational structure to meet the two requirements that are needed because the execution of the current work is also concerned for financial institutions. Within the scope of the Current-strategic balance, organizational structure of financial institutions should be evaluated as stated in Figure 3.

All financial constitutes, should take into account of these considerations in this framework for proactive restructuring and are required to highlight these issues on their strategies. Because "to try to manage the future" is a risky situation, but it is a risky situation than ever not to try (Drucker, 2000, p.17).

REFERENCES

Alessandrini, P., Fratianni, M., & Zazzaro, A. (2009). *The Changing Geography of Banking and Finance*. Springer.

Alessandrini, P., Fratianni, M., & Zazzaro, A. (Eds.). (2009). *The Changing Geography of Banking and Finance*. Springer.

Araújo, L., & Gava, R. (2012). *Proactive Companies How to Anticipate Market Changes*. U.K.: Palgrave Macmillan. doi:10.1057/9780230363014

Barca M., (2009). Stratejik yönetim düşüncesinin gelişimi [History of strategic management development]. *Ankara Sanayi Odası Dergisi*, Nisan, Mayıs, Haziran, 35-51.

Barney, M. (2010). *Leadershıp @ lnfosys*. Penguin Group.

Barry, B. W. (1986). *Strategic Planning Workbook for Public and Nonprofit Organizations* (p. 10). St. Paul: Amherst Wilder Foundation.

Berger, A. N., Kashyap, A. K., Scalise, J. M., Gertler, M., & Friedman, B. M. (1995). The Transformation of the U.S. banking industry: What a long, strange trip it's been. *Brookings Papers on Economic Activity*, *2*(2), 55–218. doi:10.2307/2534612

Brockbank, W. (1999). If HR were really strategically proactive: Present and future directions in HR's contribution to competitive advantage. *Human Resource Management, 38*(4), 337–352. doi:10.1002/(SICI)1099-050X(199924)38:4<337::AID-HRM8>3.0.CO;2-5

Chandler, A. D. (1962). *Strategy and Structure*. Cambridge, MA: MIT Press.

Cook, S., Macaulay, S., & Coldicott, H. (2004). *Change Management Excellence Using the Four intelligences for Successful Organizational Change*. Kogan Page Limited.

Crant, J. M., & Bateman, T. S. (2000). Charismatic leadership viewed from above: The impact of proactive personality. *Journal of Organizational Behavior, 21*(1), 63–75. doi:10.1002/(SICI)1099-1379(200002)21:1<63::AID-JOB8>3.0.CO;2-J

De Laurentis, G. (Ed.). (2005). *Strategy and Organization of Corporate Banking, Springer Theoretical Drivers of Divisionalization*. Springer. doi:10.1007/b138020

Drucker, P. (2000). *Yüzyıl Için Yönetim Tartışmaları* [Management Discussions for the 21st Century, 2nd edition]. Baskı, İstanbul, Çev. İrfan Bahçıvangil, Gülenay Gorbon, Epsilon Yayınları.

Finney, M. I. (2008). *Building High-Performance People and Organizations* (Volume 1 the New Employer-Employee Relationship). Praeger Perspectives.

Gibson, J. L., Ivancevich, J. M., Donnelly, J. H., & Konopaske, R. (2009). *Organizations: Behavior, Structure, Processes* (14th ed.). McGraw-Hill.

Habisch, A., Jonker, J., Wegner, M., & Schmidpeter, R. (2005). *Corporate Social Responsibilities across Europe*. Springer Germany. doi:10.1007/b138371

Harker, P. T., & Zenios, S. A. (1998). *What Drives the Performance of Financial Institutions*, Working Paper, the Wharton School, University of Pennsylvania.

Hatch, M. J., & Cunliffe, A. L. (2013). *Organization Theory Modern, Symbolic, and Postmodern Perspectives* (3rd ed.). UK: Oxford University Press.

Kaliski, B. S. (2007). *Encyclopedia of Business and Finance* (2nd ed., Vol. 2). J–Z, Thomson Gale.

Keçecioğlu, T., & Çiçek, A. (2012). Örgüt DNA'sına Yerleşen Yeni Bir Kavram ve Marka: Örgütsel ve Stratejik Çeviklik (Örgütsel Bağışıklık Sistemini Güçlendirmek). *Marmara Üniversitesi İ.İ.B. Fakültesi Dergisi, 33*(2), 295–308.

Lawrence, P. R., & Lorsch, J. W. (1967). *Organization and Environment: Managing Differentiation and Integration*. Boston: Harvard Business School Press.

Manring, S. L. (2003). How Do You Create Lasting Organizational Change? You must first slay Grendel's Mother. *Research in Organizational Change and Development, 14*, 195–224. doi:10.1016/S0897-3016(03)14083-9

McIntyre, J. R., Ivanaj, S., & Ivanaj, V. (2009). *Multinational Enterprises and the Challenge of Sustainable Development*. Cheltenham, UK: Edward Elgar.

McKinsey Global Survey Results. (2009). April retrieved from http://www.mckinsey.com/

Mintzberg, H. (1987). Crafting Strategy. *Harvard Business Review, 87*(4), 67.

Morel-Guimaraes, L., Khalil, T. M., & Hosni, Y. A. (2005). Management of Technology Key Success Factors for Innovation and Sustainable Development. Selected Papers from the *Twelfth International Conference on Management of Technology*. Elsevier.

Mynatt, J. (2009). *Encyclopedia of Management* (6th ed.). Gale, Cengage Learning.

Rud, O. P. (2009). *Business Intelligence Success Factors Tools for Aligning Your Business in the Global Economy*. Wiley.

Rumelt, R. P. (1974). *Strategy, Structure and Economic Performance*. Boston, MA: Division of Research, Harvard Business School.

van Wezel, W., Jorna, R., & Meystel, A. (2006). Planning. In *Intelligent Systems Aspects, Motivations, and Methods*. Hoboken, NJ: John Wiley & Sons, Inc.

Weijermars, R. (2011). *Building Corporate IQ: Moving the Energy Business from Smart to Genius Executive Guide to Preventing Costly Crises*. Springer.

ADDITIONAL READING

Baba, V. V., Tourigny, L., Wang, X., & Liu, W. (2009). Proactive Personality and Work Performance in China: The Moderating Effects of Emotional Exhaustion and Perceived Safety Climate. *Canadian Journal of Administrative Sciences*, *26*, 23–37.

Bateman, T., & Crant, J. M. (1999). Proactive Behavior: Meaning, Impact, Recommendations. *Business Horizons*, *42*(3), 63–68.

Bindl, U. K., & Parker, S. K. (2011). In S. Zedeck (Ed.), *Proactive work behavior: Forward-thinking and change-oriented action in organizations* (Vol. 2, pp. 567–598). APA handbook of industrial and organizational psychology Washington, DC: American Psychological Association.

David, F. R. (2011). *Strategic Management: Concept and Cases*. Boston: Prentice Hall.

Drazin, R., & Howard, P. (1984). Strategy Implementation: A Technique for OrganizationalDesign. *The Columbia Journal of World Business*, *19*, 40–46.

Grant, R. M. (2004). *Contemporary Strategy Analysis* (3rd ed.). Oxford: Blackwell Business.

Meadows, D. H. (2008). *Thinking in Systems a Primer*. Chelsea, Vermont: Green Publishing.

Miles, R., & Charles, S. (2003). *Organizational Strategy, Structure, and Process*. New York: McGraw-Hill.

Porter, M. E. (1998). *On Competition*. USA: Harvard Business Review.

Repetto, R., & Austin, D. (1999). Estimating the financial effects of companies´ environmental performance and exposure. *Greener Management International*, *27*, 97–110.

Simmering, M. J. (2014). Reactive vs. Proactive Change Encyclopedia of Business (2nd ed.). Retrieved from http://www.referenceforbusiness.com/management/Pr-Sa/Reactive-vs-Proactive-Change.html

Strickland, L. (2006). *Changing from a Reactive to a Proactive stance in business F.O.C.U.S.* Resource, Inc. Retrieved from http://carolinanewswire.com/news/

UNEP. (n.d.). *UNEP Finance Initiative: Innovative financing for sustainability*. Retrieved from www.unepfi.org/

Wheelen, T. H., & Hunger, J. D. (2006). *Strategic Management and Business Policy-Concepts and Cases*. New Jersey: Pearson.

Zhiang, L., & Carley, K. (1993). Proactive or reactive: An analysis of the effect of agent style on organizational decision-making performance. *Intelligent Systems in Accounting, Finance & Management*, *2*, 271–287.

KEY TERMS AND DEFINITIONS

Organization: An entity, structured and managed for pursuing the collective goals to meet economic needs that can be affected by environment.

Organizational Structure: A hierarchical arrangement of relationships between the different activities and the members, and subdividing and assigning roles, responsibilities, and authority to carry out different tasks.

Proactive Organizational Structure: Arranging structure at all stages and sectors to execute proactive strategies in a way that encompass anticipatory and influential actions on the surroundings to facilitate improving performance.

Proactiveness: An action that expects change and as involving the careful creation of modifications. Company's early response to signals of coming change is anticipation as creation of change itself is called influence.

Strategy: Making trade-offs in competing operational effectiveness for the conception of a unique and valuable position, requiring a different circle of actions.

Chapter 25
Financial Implications of Relationship Marketing in Airline Business

Hasan Dinçer
Istanbul Medipol University, Turkey

Ümit Hacıoğlu
Istanbul Medipol University, Turkey

Aydın Özdemir
Beykent University, Turkey

ABSTRACT

Relationship marketing promises a change from vendor, product and price centered marketing concept to a new people, long-term relationships and value centered marketing concept for airline companies in search of a messiah who will rescue them from bleeding to death because of monopolized supply market, duplicated services, financial crises, heavy pressure of competition and low profit margins. In this chapter, definitions and short background of relationship marketing are revised by focusing on components of the concept and relations with customer loyalty, customer value and basic notions. A glance at the airline industry takes place with a focus on relationship marketing and airline business on the basis of implication aspects such as frequent flyer programs, global distribution systems and internet. Specifically, domains of relationship marketing concept on the airline business are analyzed in detail specific to cost and profitability balance.

INTRODUCTION

Technological change brought by globalization, the pressure of population growth, inflation, and hard competition have forced companies to stand strong and sustain their activities in the middle of a high flow rate. In order to stand strong in the middle of this flow rate, companies have to strengthen their roots which are their customers.

While in the beginning of the century production was the center of industrialization in 1900's the center of companies turned into sales. In 1950s

DOI: 10.4018/978-1-4666-7484-4.ch025

companies started to diversify their marketing applications and marketing centered companies started to appear. 1990s was the beginning of new experience in other words the beginning of customer era. (Palmatier, 2008, p.12). Nevertheless, increase in diversity of service and goods, distribution, dazzling increase in price and communication opportunities and hard competition conditions increased the amount of accessibility for service and goods for all income levels. Competition caused by goods and service inflation has increased the quality of goods and service relation in this area. It is very common to reach and experience desired goods easily both by virtual or real communication channels. In this marketing atmosphere formed by conditions that we stated above customers desire to buy the feeling of "satisfaction". Customers replaced the meaning of goods and service. Therefore marketing has to take customer relations into consideration instead of goods and service (Kotler& Keller, 2009, p.14).

It is very difficult for companies to find new customers in global arena, besides losing their customers is a matter of life and death for them. Looking from another aspect, it means that if companies want to have more advantages than the others it depends on their long life relationship with their customers. Today's business world is based on relationship with customers not the operations. All these marketing conditions have changed and evolved marketing literature, so relationship marketing has taken over. (Payne, Christopher, Clark, & Peck, 1999)

Marketing success of companies is related to their customer relations and their ability to be different from their competitors. Considered from this aspect the strategy of having long life relationship with customers and relationship marketing has become the center of marketing strategies. Relationship marketing which puts customers in the center of marketing takes customer loyalty as the most important factor for profitability. It is accepted that value given to customers and their loyalty will give competitive priority to companies in long term period. Gummesson describes this new process as "interaction and joint value creation" (Gummesson, 2002).

Relationship marketing is not a program to be implied in current marketing programs; on the other hand it means change in whole business strategies. Basically, trust and relations web which have been main principles of trade in eastern societies are applied to western trade principals which are based on distrust and solid engagement. (Gummesson, 2002) Product and seller based trade and marketing have lost power in nowadays world. Companies started to explore and institutionalize customer centered marketing which was taken from eastern societies.

The purpose of this article is to put the clock back the formula which has a potential of creating customer retention, customer loyalty and customer value and as result of this chain is to create profitability for airlines. As a result, according to Berry's expression "the spirit and heart of relations marketing is based on customers when they become customers" (Gruen, 1995, p.449).

1. BASIC PRINCIPALS OF RELATIONS MARKETING

1.1 Definitions of Relations Marketing

Relations marketing showed up in 1980s and still it doesn't have a generally accepted definition. There are several reasons of not having a proper definition of relations marketing. The reasons are not theoretical or practical inadequate but it is because of diversity and multifunctional structure of relations based marketing (Grönroos, 1994).

Direct marketing which was applied for centuries was replaced after industrial revolution with such a solid and mechanical marketing perception. After this change, human factor was redefined and imprisoned in specific roles. After industrial revolution, technology, individualization and internet revolution started to shape relations marketing by putting human factor into the center of focus (O'Malley &Tynan, 2000).

During this formalization period Bagozzi in 1975 open a discussion about relations marketing by putting "change (mutual communication)" into center of its definition (Man, 1998). Berry outlines service marketing and how to have long life customer relations and how to improve and develop them (Man, 1998, p.10).

- Finding a basic product or service to build customer relation,
- Adjusting the relation according to individual customers,
- Enriching the basic product or service,
- Pricing strategies to increase customer loyalty,
- Marketing for employees, employee satisfaction.

According to Grönroos who is taken as a reference nowadays business relation is mutual relation on both customer and company side and it is profitable for both sides. This mutual relation should be built and sustained with the intention of profit making for both sides. Grönroos, additionally to customers he puts B2B, distribution channels, employees, and competitors into relations perspective. In relations marketing, he also points that all departments of a company have to work in harmony. (Grönroos, 1994).

While Gummesson, who works on the subject, defines relations marketing as a long term relationship between seller and customer, he associates it with profitability. Another definition by Gummesson for relationship marketing is based on interactivity by relations and web network. He is the first person to state and offer that marketing relations should be put on an order according to their priorities (Gummesson, 2002).

According to Morgen and Hunt (1981) all activities in order to establish, maintain and develop successful business relations are relationship marketing. They put at the center trust which leads to cooperative and productive relations (Morris, Brunyee, & Page, 1998).

Among all mentioned definitions first time Manroe (1991) stated the "value of exchange" and formulated customer value by distributing value into cost per customer. Manroe interested in what customer gives to company and cost of it, simply (Dodds, Monroe, & Grewal, 1991).

Ravald and Grönroos mostly studied on time concept in relationship marketing and focused on effect of time on creating value. They argue repeated relations in time create customer value. With a wider scope, Evans and Laskin focuses on relationship marketing as creating service partnerships, supporting employees, total quality management and by using all these assets to create customer satisfaction, loyalty and profit increase (Ravald & Grönroos, 1996).

Despite all efforts and definitions are made in time are far from to create a common and de facto definition, yet. As in the given statistics in Figure 1, intangibility of the term is certified by the rareness of the words agreed on. However, most common explanation is focusing on retention of customers. ŞükranKaraca's extensive definition shines out because of facing implication of the concept. She builds its definition creating value by promise, trust, loyalty, and retaining this value for long run (Karaca, 2010).

Consequently, relationship marketing is a concept aims to reduce costs and creating value, creating, maintaining long run relationships on a continuous win-win balance. In other words relationship marketing is a kind of consciousness that points how to gather all pieces currently on the stage but not used productively.

1.2 Relationship Marketing in Pieces

It is essential to understand components of relationship marketing content of the definition. Even in the definition of the term there is no consensus yet, however 6 elements which concept consists

Figure 1. Content analysis of definitions of relations
Source: Morris, Brunyee, & Page, 1998, p.361.

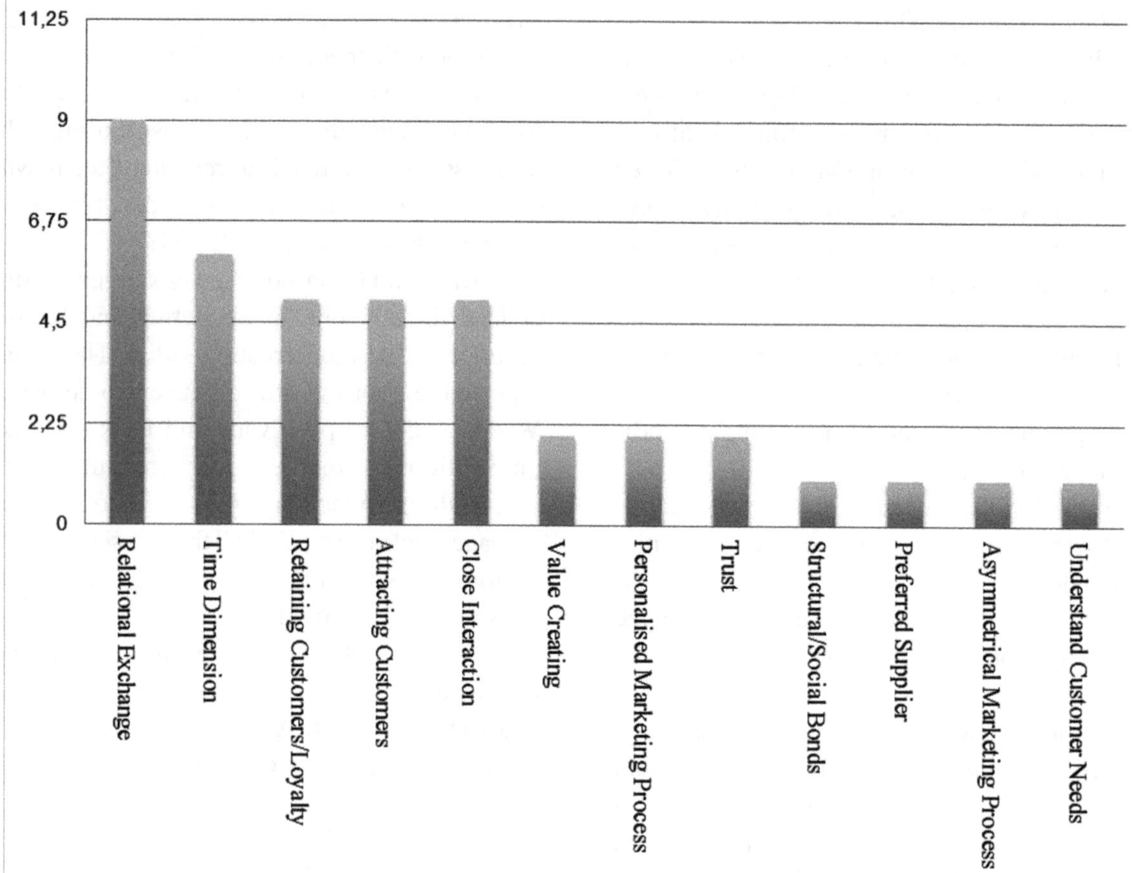

of had a general acceptance. Morgan and Hunt firstly stated these 6 elements but the last version which has a general acceptance was created by Sin and Tse. A company who accepts relationship marketing concept should invest on these areas shown in Figure 2 (Morgan & Hunt, 1994; Sin, Tse, Yau, Chow, Lee, &Lorett, 2005).

Between company and customer the first condition is trust. Not only in relationship marketing but also in all relational subjects of marketing trust has a big reputation. Although it has an abstract connotation, with very simple scales and surveys it can be measured and be converted into solid numbers (Sin, Tse, Yau, Chow, Lee, & Lorett, 2005).

Bonding or commitment rise upon trust and common aims and benefits between organization and customers. Communication both formal and informal with all possible channels is a company's weapon of attack and also defense, besides it's a pool where a company must pour its investments. Companies should invest this area in all possible ways. Shared values, are agreements between company and the customer on what is important to not, or what is true or not. Empathy is another concept that must be institutionalized and must accepted as the judge of relations or any problems that may rise among company and customer. Reciprocity is a value, must place instead of company

Figure 2. Components of relationship marketing
Source: Sin, Tse, Yau, Chow, Lee, & Lorett, 2005, p.187.

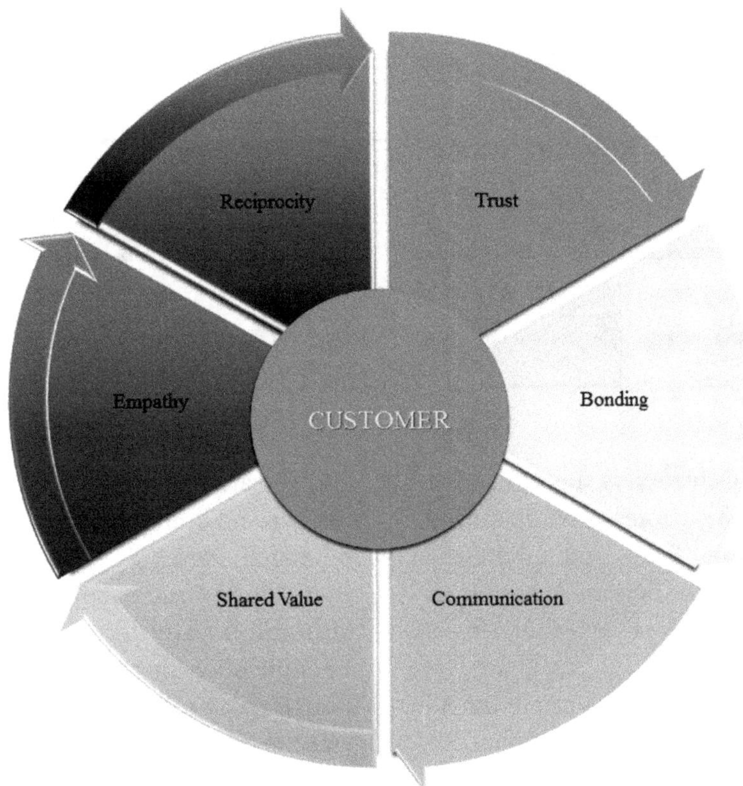

centered marketing concept. Reciprocity must find its meaning in last few years and became a buzzword as "win-win" (Sin, Tse, Yau, Chow, Lee, & Lorett, 2005).

All six components, discussed above are also can be used as scales of relationship marketing application. Moreover it is a compass for companies how to distribute its marketing resources or they are elements a marketing campaign must include in order to be named as a relationship marketing campaign.

1.3 Relationship Marketing and Customer Loyalty

Creating and maintaining long and beneficial relations mostly thought with customer loyalty and customer satisfaction is also accepted as the first step of it. Because there is a general opinion that customer satisfaction triggers purchasing behavior and this opinion mostly true but a dozen of researched shows that customers can defect without a distinction weather satisfied or not. Variety of alternatives, price and some other must take into consideration (Payne, Christopher, Clark, & Peck, 1999).

It is very clear that customer loyalty increases customers' relation time with the company and lowers price sensibility and also feedback of these customers have positive effect on development of product or processes. This overlap with relationship marketing makes it more valuable. For instance, Sheraton hotels spend 50 million dollars for its loyalty program per year (Karaca, 2010).

A survey on customer loyalty made by Jones and Sasser shows that if defection cost for cus-

Figure 3. Building value of customer
Source: Adapted from Kotler, Marketing Management, Millennium Edition, 2000, p.35.

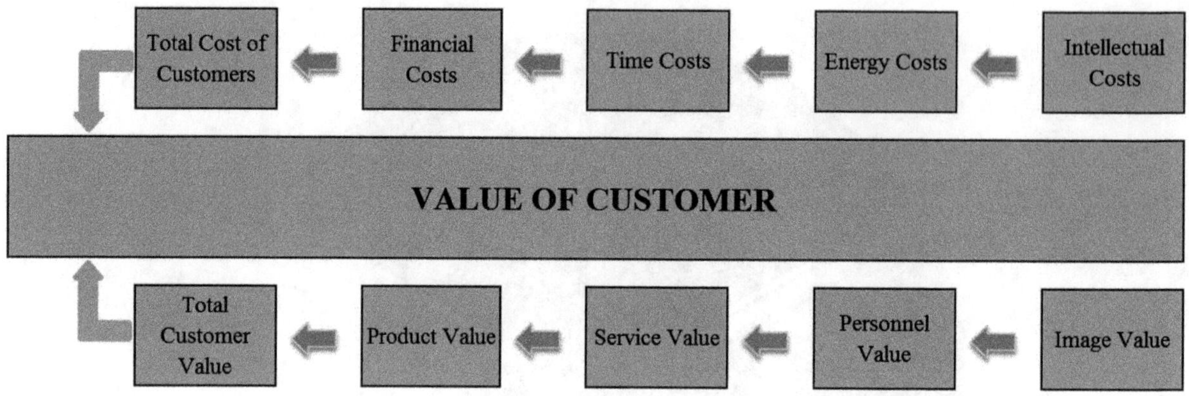

tomer is low only loyal customers stays loyal. As a result of this research customers are classified according to their loyalty levels and purchasing behaviors. Metaphors that authors use really reflect the function of groups well (Jones & Sasser, 1995).

1. **Apostles:** Loyal customers, volunteered brand ambassadors, triggers of word-of-mouth.
2. **Mercenaries:** Price sensibility is high, loyal as long as satisfied, always in expectation from the company.
3. **Hostages:** Customers who have to stay loyal because defection cost is high. Satisfaction is low.
4. **Terrorists:** Aware of market and alternatives well. Seize every opportunity and in seek of new opportunities. Technology addicted and very high in using internet in daily life.

Relationship marketing also uses criteria of price sensibility and price incentives for customer loyalty. For instance, FFPs rewards customers with free flight tickets, extra luggage rights, lounge etc. but as long as customers buy from the company. Social relations are one another way to build customer loyalty (Leick, 2007). For example, banks or cell phone operators assign a dedicated staff for same customers. They address customer by name and celebrated special days and anniversaries. This method is effective mostly in market and some products were competition is not much dense.

Customer satisfaction, customer value, and customer loyalty terms have the biggest share in application of relationship marketing. These functions also have very simple measurements and can be tracked by surveys any time moreover these results will be a compass for relationship marketing. Rewarding mechanism inside organizations must be placed on results of these scales. For example Kentucky fried Chicken restaurants rewards branch managers who had high scores of customer satisfaction by 35% net salary increase each month (Karaca, 2010).

Airlines should lead all other sectors by designing measurements for each step of service. From reservation to airport check-in and to the end of flight every step must have own assessment channels. Today some airlines has such applications, while you buy a ticket at the end of reservation a small survey exists on the internet page or if the channel is call-center at the end of conversation they forward you for another survey (Belobaba, Odoni, & Barnhart, 2009). During the flight with a form on board or inside the airlines' magazine, or on entertainment system screen or within mobile applications customers forced to step up scale. Without omitting a step in all levels development and enhancements are done. Companies not only have to provide customer satisfaction and loyalty but also must reward customers for their complaints, and feedbacks (Taneja, 2010).

1.4 Stages of Development

For years, exchange is accepted as the core of marketing but it is clear that the relationship between seller and the consumer do not end with it. When global oil crisis rose in 1970s, energy cost of companies reflected to prices and companies could manage to survive with deep wounds. Customer retention notion was very popular in those years (Egan, 2011).

Term is used by Berry first in 1983 and focused on making customer relations attractive, developing and maintaining (Berry, 1983, 2000, 2002).

Grönroos and Gummeson defined the term "defining relations with customers, establishing, maintaining and increasing" (Grönroos, 1994).

Years after WWII market boom was only on manufacturing, selling and face to face or one toone marketing.1960s industrial markets, relations increased intellectual and practical experience of marketing. By 1970s' highly political atmosphere, focused came on non-governmental organizations but with 1980s markets meet the word globalism and global markets, management of diversities. Besides service sector became "in" but when in 1990s' marketing concept's mechanical and product centered structure disturbed "human" factor (Gummesson, 2002; Alabay, 2010; Selvi, 2007; Palmatier, 2008).

From 1950s to current day the center of marketing has changed from product to organization itself and finally back to people again. Just like the concept of market also customer concept is changed too much. Today's customers are well educated, demanding, suspicious, and have no mercy for waiting or time loss (Arslan, 2008).

Third and most determinant chance is on technology and namely internet. Internet is just like a new marketing karma which bring all classical and relational marketing elements together. Today people, product, promotion, price and more all in the internet and the internet himself.

Consequently, relationship marketing had six stages until today starting with Berry, Grönroos and Gummeson's approach mostly from service sector point of view and second stage where focused was on mostly inter organization relations mostly in 1980s. With the third stage effective and productive relations started to be discussed lately network of relations term added to the concept and with the fifth stage relations role started to be discussed in value chain (Berry, 1995; Grönroos, 1994).Sixth stage is going to be the merge of internet and all past experiences.

1.5 Purposes of Relationship Marketing

Relationship marketing aims to create values which make customers loyal and guarantee profit in long run. Relationship marketing concept accepts fixed production overhead as opportunities to build and maintain relationships. At the very beginning, relationship marketing should aim to define and group customers who produce net profit and who does not, which will point "right" customers for the airline. In other words, Relationship marketing orientation must have a well prepared scale to group customers according to why they should stay and go, who they are and what they produce and at the bottom line what is the lifetime value for the company (Gilbert, 1996; Selvi, 2007).

In today's market conditions, average customer defection rate is defined as 10%. Relationship marketing can help organization to find out which customers are inclined to leave and why. So, organization can decide how to keep and lock the customers in (Man, 1998).

Relationship marketing gives importance to customer share instead of market share and so gives companies a new type of measurement of success (Şendur, 2009). From this point of view objectives of relationship marketing are defined as (Selvi, 2007, pp.33-46).

- Customer retention, finding new markets and customers,
- Establishing cooperation's,
- Increase service quality,
- Ensure customer satisfaction,
- Increase net profit,
- Establish trust,
- Long term customer relations.

Copulsky and Wolf explains objectives of relationship marketing is a combination of direct marketing, CRM, sales promotions, advertisement in order reach high profit rates by gaining customer retention, satisfaction, loyalty (Copulsky & Wolf, 1990; Voss & Voss, 1997).

1.6 Types of Relationship Marketing

Types of Relationship Marketing vary according to point of view just as the definition of it. If it is considered as a strategy, the ideal approach will be to apply different marketing applications according to product and market segmentation. Rowe and Barnes popularize relationship marketing strategies into four main categories (Rowe & Barnes, 1998, p.288).

1. **Locking Customers In:** Organization must use all marketing resources and benefits in order to build strong relationships with customers but control of relationships are still in the hands of organization. Organization builds high walls to lock customer in by creating high costs for customer defection.
2. **Customer Retention:** Same focus with the previous item but this strategy indicates to place resources in order to keep profitable customers in.
3. **Database Marketing:** Indicates placing resources in order to a list which is formed by a database research. The main focus of this database work should be on characteristics and choices of customers.
4. **Strong, Close, and Positive Relations:** Apart from one-way and single channel communications this strategy indicates to build multi-channel and interactive relations.

Except from the last one, all strategies given above are organization centered or flow of the relations is one-way such as from organization to customer. Besides, in these first three strategies organization is the center and benefit of the company is underlined. Only the last strategy depends on win-win situation. The thing must be discussed is not the superiority of any one but advantages and special usage areas of each one has. It has to be considered which one is used at which level (Rowe & Barnes, 1998). For instance, customer retention is ideal for cost reduction.

Gummeson has a simpler and definition centered classification that he divides strategy into three (Gummesson, 1998, p.243):

1. **Market Relations:** Relations work in market, mostly likely relations with customer-seller, competitors etc. environments.
2. **Mega Market Relations:** Social relations' level which are built with authorities, media etc.
3. **Nano Marketing Relations:** Organization level relations which are conducted with employees.

Gummeson's classification approaches relationship marketing as the management of sales, society, market and organizational relations. Zineldin has created a more quality based strategy mostly depends on customer satisfaction, long term profitability and other environments such as banks, vendors to create "5Q" approach. (Zineldin, 2000, p. 24).

Q1 Product Quality: Quality of product or service with a technical point of view which is "what" a customer buys from the organization actually.

Q2 Process Quality: Functional quality of "how" a customer buys a product or service from the organization.

Q3 Infrastructure Quality: Exchange of information, experience, know-how, technology and motivation.

Q4 Interaction Quality: Interactional relations consists of information, financial assets etc.

Q5 Environment Quality: Environment which parties operate and in cooperation. The quality of this environment has a direct impact on quality of organization and customer relationships.

Concisely, Zineldin builds relationship marketing types on a set of inner organization relations, customer satisfaction, process improvements and employee satisfaction. Likewise, Zineldin gives responsibility in organization to every unit and individual for all these five strategies (Zineldin, 2000).

Gruen has drawn attention to a different spot and the distinction between B2B and B2C market environments. Gruen defines relationship marketing in B2B markets as "partnership" and in B2C markets as "membership" (Gruen, 1995).Considering airline business these definitions finds well its equivalent as FFP's.

1.7 From Kotlerism to Relationship Marketing

Traditional or classic marketing concept is designed mostly to achieve goals set by the seller side. This concept underestimates customer behaviors, away from interaction and puts customer in a position that needs to be managed or shepherd. On the other hand, relationship marketing estimates a transformation from so-called Kotlerist approach which is short-term, seller centered, to a new form of marketing which is long term relations (Zineldin & Philipson, 2007).

Kotlerist marketing concept can be described as hunter-gatherer era of marketing where movement and continuous search for new markets and customers is a matter of survival. So popular cliché of "swim or sink" fits here well (Kotler, 2000; Kotler & Keller, 2009; Kumar, Scheer, & Kotler, 2000).Simple measurement of this concept is sales increase rates besides except from sales, all other facilities and services of the organization are accepted as auxiliary and cost producers. Going through the same metaphor, relationship marketing can be described as settled land or early agricultural era of mankind. Relationship marketing is settled and trying to produce maximum benefit from a pre-defined land. In order to survive hunters are still active but some farmers also trying to domesticate captured preys. Performance measurement of this concept is rate of customer retention and return of investments. Main purpose of this era is to create customers who are always profitable, stable and loyal to the organization (Grönroos, 1994).

Classic concepts puts customer in a passive position where he has to accept offered 4P of marketing or deny. The entire role he has in this process is limited by choosing. Considering the post war era environment where this concept was born it can be accepted as reasonable but in today's internet shaped limitless market atmosphere it is now insufficient. In order to resolve this insufficiency, new elements were added by theoreticians such as "people", "physical environment" and "Process". Today it is almost accepted as classic concept with "8P" of marketing. Yet, new addings were not to cover today's needs "4C" (consumer, cost, communication, convenience) concept was born in the hands of Robert F. Lauterborn (Schultz, Tannenbaum, & Robert, 1993).

Focusing on each element of 4P concept it can be pictured the transformation (Figure 4). Product element can be match-up with customer

Figure 4. Change of marketing concepts

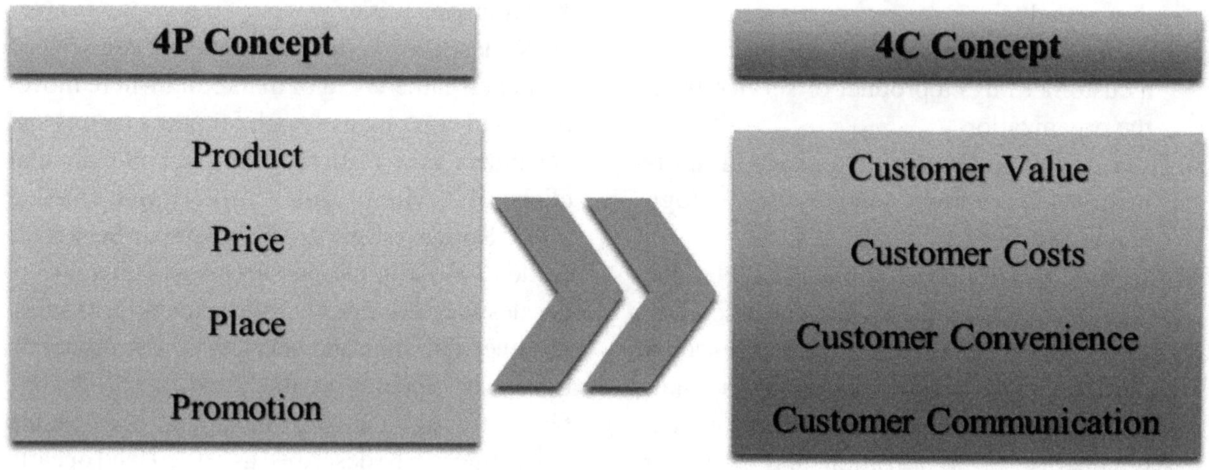

value in relationship marketing where product or service has to create also a value for the customer. Customer Cost in classical 4P concept is accepted as the reciprocity of price which is providing the best priced service or product customer demands (Alabay, 2010).

Convenience for the customer stands for distribution element in 4C concept and can be formulated as getting the right product or service in right time to the right customers. Customer communication can be replaced with Promotion element in 4C concept. Customer communication means informing customers instead of convincing them, briefly (Schultz, Tannenbaum, & Robert, 1993).

One another concept is customer relations which relationship marketing put forward. It is commonly accepted that in today's market place it is not possible to create competitive advantages or differentiate by product or service itself (Hennig-Thurau, Gwinner, & Gremler, 2002). In todays' market conditions only way to differentiate is customer centered approaches. To be explained in detail, it can be possible by segmenting customers into micro sectors, than to create value by products or services according to their demands and creating interactive relations with customers that will build long and beneficial relationships for both sides. This formula can be offered as the new form of profit maximization. It should be kept in the mind always that relationship marketing based upon relations which will cover all life cycle of customer. Relationship marketing requires "special" relations instead of "good "relations like the one in 4P concept (Gruen, 1995).

While traditional marketing is focused on finding new customers and market share, relationship marketing is focused on customer retention and putting all organization resources to provide this. On the other hand, 4P concept is sharpened by competition while relationship marketing puts spot on cooperation and win-win situations. Traditional marketing gives particular importance on seller's needs and demands, but relationship marketing prioritise customers' needs and demands. It is the product or service in 4P concept which shapes marketing activities as in relationship marketing it is customer and customer value (Selvi, 2007).

As a result of comparing old and new concepts of marketing, it can be sum up relationship marketing seeks for creating new values for customers, who are not the people who buys but also who defines the value. Relationship marketing points all life time trade of customers not the short time

Figure 5. Difference approaches to marketing concept
Source: Gummesson, Making Relationship Operational, 1994, p.9.

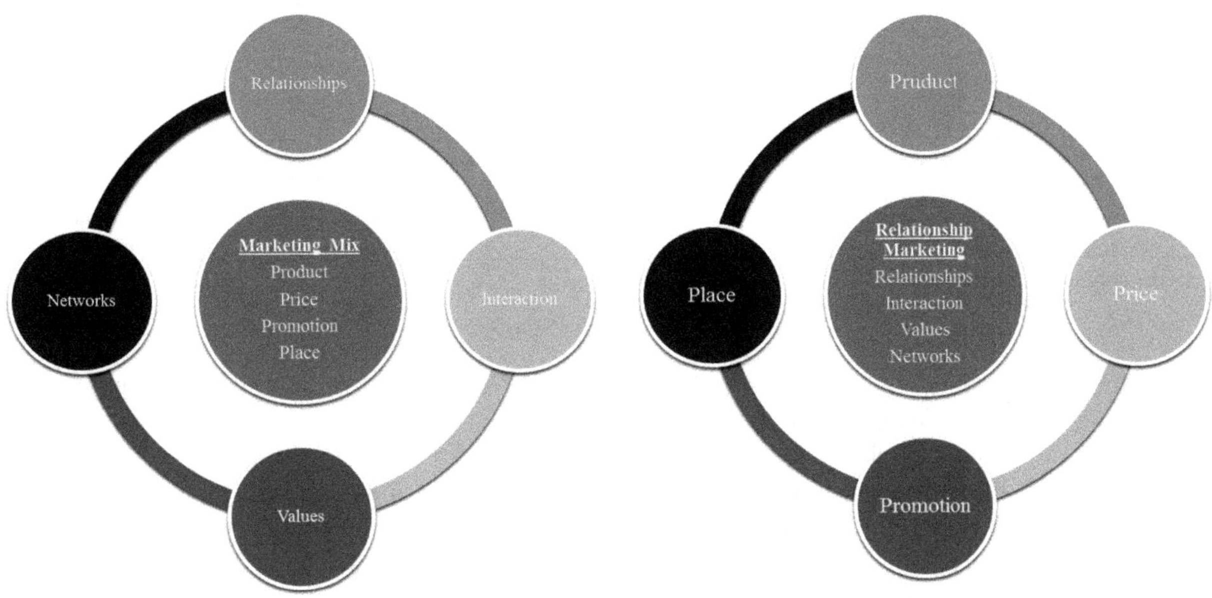

purchases. Relationship marketing changed the center of gravity of marketing from seller to the customer, in other words from product to relations, from competition to cooperation (Table 1).

1.8 Relationship Marketing as a Competitive Advantage?

In new economic environment, customer who had freedom and power is now more demanding and asking relations from organizations. This also means that Kotlerist concept of marketing is not valid anymore (Sindell, 2000).

Competitive advantage mostly comes in sight when an organization finds out a creative strategy and application which opponents do not apply. In other words competitive advantage strategies Works until opponents imitate them. What make a strategy valuable are its effects on profitability, utilizing opportunities within or out of organization environment and cost cutting effects. Remembering "locking in strategy" previously stated where customers stays in and avoid of defection not to pay for finding new sources and new relationships (Rowe & Barnes, 1998).

If marketing here underlines "defection obstacles" and increases cost of defection. FFP which airlines are using for years can be the best example. In order to gain points and free flight tickets customers stays in the system but this application lost its top place on the list as a competitive advantage for year ago. It is not only imitated but also became a "standard" for all airlines even for a small carrier who has few aircrafts also has its own FFP program. So, imitation has a very destructive power. IBM applied locking customers

Table 1. From 4P to relationship marketing

Marketing Mix (4P)	Relationship Marketing
One-way	Interactive
On-and-off Communication	Continuous Communication
Product Centered	Customer Centered
Quality is for Quality Department	Quality is for All
Competition	Cooperation
Price	Value

Source: Adapted from Selvi, 2007, p.23.

in strategy for years. Customers could not break out even if they are not happy with product or services and stayed loyal involuntarily. However, this relationship has destroyed by entrance of new competitors into the market with similar product and services, as result of this IBM in 1993 had a dive from peak to the bottom and company market value fall from 106 million dollar to 30 Million dollar (Rowe & Barnes, 1998).

Customer retention strategy underlines the cost of retention of current customers instead of cost of finding new customers. Organizations especially who has direct access to retail market keep records of their customers in detail such as communication information, some personnel information etc. in order to create tools in marketing activities (Rowe & Barnes, 1998).

Even if it seems as a very strong competitive advantage for organizations to use these databases and create customized products and services for their customers due to its R&D and application costs it can be used by very few companies. Producing a product or service in small amounts means high cost rate per unit. According to airlines who serve millions of customers each year this is also another challenge to apply strategy (Kanagal, 2005).

All strategies stated has both advantages and disadvantages but is there a strategy which will be close, stable and creating benefit for both sides, moreover could this strategy can be a competitive advantage?

Consequently, creating a customized strategy which will be a response to this question shall have high and costly barriers of customer defection, second has a wide and detailed database of customers where keeps all necessary to support marketing efforts. Third, top management of organization must build strong and close relations with the units and individuals who have direct contact with customers. Considering airline business, check-in staff, cabin attendants, and call centers can best examples. As the last, organization must develop benefits and positive surprises for customers randomly. It is for sure that such a marketing strategy is going to lock in and retain customers also creates financial performance with reduce costs and keeps away from price competition.

1.9 Relationship Marketing Karma

Relationship marketing considered in Ceterus Paribus condition, where cultural and industrial variables are reset, rise upon six pedestals. Hansen (2000) as a reference to classical marketing karma named it as "6I" Marketing Concept. Intention, Interaction, Integration, Information, Investment, Individuality are proposed as new marketing paradigm (Karaca, 2010, p.445).

- **Information:** This element is known as also "database marketing". Today's technological potential and software availabilities with a limited afford, millions of can be processed within minutes. This opportunity gives airlines to create and customize, segmented all information it has and create micro markets as target.
- **Investment:** So called revolution in marketing actually happened in perception of customer but as the market is customer itself, it should be divided into pieces must be segmented and classified so placing an organization's resources and efforts must be conducted according to this classification. From this point of view, placing resources equally among customers will be wasting and so will cause customer defection in the end.
- **Individuality:** Relationship marketing requires having an aspect of seeing each customer as a niche market. Aside from product customizations, only applications which succeeds to make customers feel special or the product is customized for the customer.
- It is a very interesting point that airlines that serves millions of customers each year has a wide and detailed database collected from reservation systems and FFPs however very few of them have staff employed and systems to study this data and harvest useful marketing clues to feed marketing units. Airlines yet did not degrade marketing efforts from mass marketing size to individualism but in an effort to survive has to come this point soon.
- **Interaction:** Interaction also claimed as a most distinctive element between classic marketing concept and relationship marketing. Internet, mobile applications and social media tools creates a platform where multichannel, interactive, social and multi-layer communication and sharing is possible with a cheap and simple way. So this platform is no more a billboard or an option but an obligation.
- Interaction has also a meaning of communication between all layers of organization and society. This creates an opportunity gap for relationship marketing. For instance, a random Office staff's or front desk secretary's attitude can be affective more than a company worth of millions. Remembering the core of relationship marketing strategy, which was human, without limitations and prejudices enables this marketing concept work. According to latest researches of purchasing decision makers in airline business, it is surprisingly stated that even front desk personnel has an effect on to share travel budget among airlines. Because of this in previous years airlines started to offer incentives not only the travel agents but also their staff (Doganis, 2006).
- **Integration:** Communication platforms where all parties are met also provide a place to meet on a common point which is "product". Especially in B2B markets integration take place as a result of long relationship where information, experience and resources shared.
- **Intention:** Common ground of relationship marketing is named as "trust". In sales and distribution channels the message of the company and one-way dictation of messages irritate customers anymore and has a negative effect on purchasing attitude. Also, today organizations are not only the constitutions that sell products but also have social responsibilities and environmental awareness. So, organizations have to state their intentions clear and briefly if they want to have a long time relationship.

1.10 Problems of Implication

The first and most obvious problem occurs in the process of relationship marketing concept is the wide gap between theory and practice. This gap occurred because lack of well-prepared application process and strategies and also dedicated and trained staff. Second common problem is trying to apply relationship marketing strategies for all customer groups. Every method could not be the best one for all customer segments. Companies should keep always in their minds that investing on low-profit customers is simply wasting. Besides, sometimes companies give importance and locate company resources excessively on the customer side and destroy financial balance (Selvi, 2007).

Third, return of investment in relationship marketing occurs in long-run so financial assets and resources must be placed on the ruler of time and campaigns according to these criteria (Hennig-Thurau, Gwinner, & Gremler, 2002).

Relationship marketing has a direct correlation with level of development. In Palmer's study on application of relationship marketing practices intercultural base, it is stated that, when level of development increases, customers' interest on companies' or products' functional or emotional importance also increase. Markets' culture, economic, political and technological infrastructures have a determining role on marketing practices (Palmer, 1995).

Finally, organizations should consider relationship marketing concept as a change of perception and strategy so it needs radical organizational changes. Airlines' organizations and formation are qualified by international organizations and rule makers (Alliances, IATA, EASA, and FAA etc.) This left very small room for airlines to create their own unique organizational structure.

2. CAN RELATIONSHIP MARKETING PUSH BACKAIRLINES FOR TAKE OFF? RELATIONSHIP MARKETING IN AIRLINE BUSINESS

2.1 Overall Picture of the Industry

Looking for the close traces of this ambiguous product, it can be seen a struggle against economic crises, epidemics, accidents but still attractive and still brilliant. Airline product concept is accepted among service sectors but considering specifications of the product, it is not very easy to classify it. This product first of all is not solid and customer does not have chance to see or experience it before consuming. Neither it can be packed nor shipped to the consumer. This is a special product where producing and consuming occurs in the same time lap (Shaw, 2007).

In the near history of the industry, sector faced its biggest financial crisis. Just a year before the 9/11 sector has a volume of 1, 82 billion passengers but just after the event it dropped to 1.79 billion passengers. Net profit of the sector dropped from 3, 7 billion dollars to -11, 3 billion dollars. Before 9/11 sector was growing with a rate of 8, 6% but after it fell down to a rate of -2,7%. But real shock wave came later with bankruptcies, decrease in traffic rates and a tragic decrease on barely surviving net profit rate with 1,1% fell to -4,2%(IATA, 2010).

Just after the 9/11, industry started to a session of recovery. Actually industry's playground has narrowed by new rules, increased security and safety precautions, new navigation applications. Airline industry with a dead cat bounce found a new way to survive and rose with mergers, partnerships and "low cost carriers". Solely, another beat was on the way. In 2008/9 global financial crisis, airlines were hit by another shock wave. This wave was lethal for some airlines and ended up with bankruptcy or turned them state-run companies. Following year European Volcano/ ash cloud crisis did not even let industry trying to stand up. To sum up, previous 10 years in industry were shaped by all possible type crises (even with volcano eruptions) and made permanent changes in the structural and financial forms of airlines. New forms of airlines were born and some old big guys (Pan Am, Iberia, Swiss etc.) left the stage. Center of gravity of travel routes also moved from Atlantic to Europe and then now moving to Far East through Middle East (Shaw, 2007; Doganis, 2006; IATA, 2011).

Nowadays, apart from the low cost carriers airlines can be classified by their styles, products and way of doing business. American Carriers, which have large but relatively old fleet, multi hub, static and Atlantic based and generally do not have ambition to compete European Carriers. American Airlines, Delta and United are foremost representatives of this group. This group sells the image of "American" as American Airlines says (Doganis, 2005).

European Carriers have large fleets but flexible and renewing. Multi hubs and flying too many destinations enjoying having share from the traffic from west to east. They are still rule makers in Europe and mandating regions, they have a weakness of having very shallow local market and threat of Gulf Carriers. Still making money from far-old dominions. Lufthansa, British Airways, Air France are foremost carriers. This group sells the image of "European Quality" (Doganis, 2005).

Gulf Carriers, which are led by Emirates, Qatar and Etihad are relatively new in the market but had a good share. Well managed corporate structures by European CEO's, which powered by oil fields with large wide-body dominated fleets, shake the statue of European carriers. Currently picking fruits of geographical advantage and rising trend of Gulf countries but having no local market is their Achilles' heel. This group of carriers sells pure luxury (O'Connell, 2011).

Another group which can be named as new players rising from middle east, far east and mostly from Latin Americas. Most outstanding ones among them are Turkish Airlines, TAM, and Asiana. Speaking on Turkish Airlines, which has a new dynamic and flexible fleet where can make operations with narrow body aircrafts to all Europe, Russia and many countries of middle east, CIS and Africa (Doganis, Flying off Course, The Economics of International Airlines, 2005). This airline has the true geopolitical advantage comparing to all other carriers also has a very strong local market. Mostly managed by young managers Turkish Airlines, is the real threat for both European and Gulf carriers. This airline has a very unique service and business concept fed by a strong culture so other carriers are not accustomed to deal with. Turkish Airlines serves western quality with oriental luxury (Uslu, Durmuş, & Kolivar, 2013).

Another major change in the industry is on customer purchasing habits which are shaped by internet and mostly technology. Travel agents and airline offices are leaving their places to mobile applications, virtual agents, and internet sites (Doganis, 2005).

David Wessels from Pennsylvania University conducted a very remarking study on 1.406 random participants. Regarding to results of the study it is stated that 30% of today's customers certainly visit web sites like Expedia, Orbitz, Kayak, etc. where all possible airline choices are offered and ranked by price. On purchasing stage, 41% of subjects use these web sites. However, crucial point in this part is 80% of subjects always put the airline which they have FFP membership. From this point of view relationship marketing implications' center is to be FFPs (Wessels, 2006).

Another significant point in Pennsylvania University's study that major criteria in purchasing process of airline customers are schedule, price and

FFPs. As a matter of fact results from a narrowed down study group of leisure travelers shown that FFPs are more important than safety. Also another result derived from the study is corporate travelers' have more loyalty and less price sensitivity which explains airlines' special interest in this group of customer (Wessels, 2006, p.9).

Airlines growth rate has a parallel progress with GDPs. Thus, airline industry have had four recessions, two global financial crisis, two gulf wars, one oil crisis and a few epidemics (SARS, Bird Flu etc.) and such an impact of 9/11 miraculously could manage to grow with a rate of 5%. However this rate is raised by developing Middle East and Far East markets. In financial portrait of industry starting from last ten years it can be seen a loss of 50 Billion Dollars. Loss in the 2008/9 crisis only is 11 Billion Dollars that Passenger capacity fell 7% and Cargo capacity 10% (IATA, 2010).

Considering the general portrait of the industry which is full of crises and problems, airlines are heading for stabile and steady sources of income. Just for this reason airlines re-focusing on productivity of customer incomes. It can be said that even if relationship market has a background of 30 years, airlines are discovering this concept nowadays.

2.2 Airline Economy 101

Airline product has high price sensitivity and under direct effect of travel time, schedule, and of course demographic variables. (Holloway, 2008).

Focusing on other financial area, costs and specifically capital costs which are 15% of total costs just after the leading cost factor which is fuel have a percentage of 30%. Labor costs, marketing and distribution, navigation, airline taxes are following these major costs. Under such a pressure of cost, airlines make yield management and flexible pricing strategies. Revenue management departments' main philosophy is to sell as much as possible in high fare classes and later on filling the rest by selling low fares (Belobaba, Odoni, & Barnhart, 2009).With this approach, in high fare class capacity is high and low fare class's capacity is designed low and also has time restrictions(IATA, 2012).

Other elements are sales channels and currency problems. As a result of operating in many countries and selling in many different currencies creates a loss in total. Airlines have to deal with this problem. Competition deeply affected by economic crisis or natural disasters, epidemics and has a very distributed organization structure make airline business very fragile. Even under these circumstances airline industry created a volume of 367 Billion Dollars in 2012 (IATA, 2013).

Main financial pans of airline business are divided into operational and financial revenues or costs. Financial revenues and costs are same as any corporate at any industry. Operational revenues can be summed up as, Scheduled flight revenues, charter revenues, cargo revenues, mail, excess luggage and additional revenues. Operational costs are fuel, maintenance, airport and slot costs, handling and catering, cabin and cockpit staff costs, fleet costs, staff costs and insurance costs (Shaw, 2007).

Financial performance of the network can be evaluated and routes can be classified according to the yield and Revenue per Available Seat Kilometer (RASK) achieved on routes (Figure 6).

2.3 Relationship Marketing and Airlines

Airlines managed to reach today by assistance of genuine marketing inventions such as FFPs, capacity control, flexible fare systems, product (Cabin) segmentation, and reservation and distribution systems. All these inventions inspired other industries and applied in many different forms in daily life.

Today, airlines standing on cross-roads again because the sector is shared and dominated between two main aircraft manufacturers (Boeing, Airbus) airlines serves almost with same design

Figure 6. Network structure and performance
Source: Serpen, 2013, p.15.

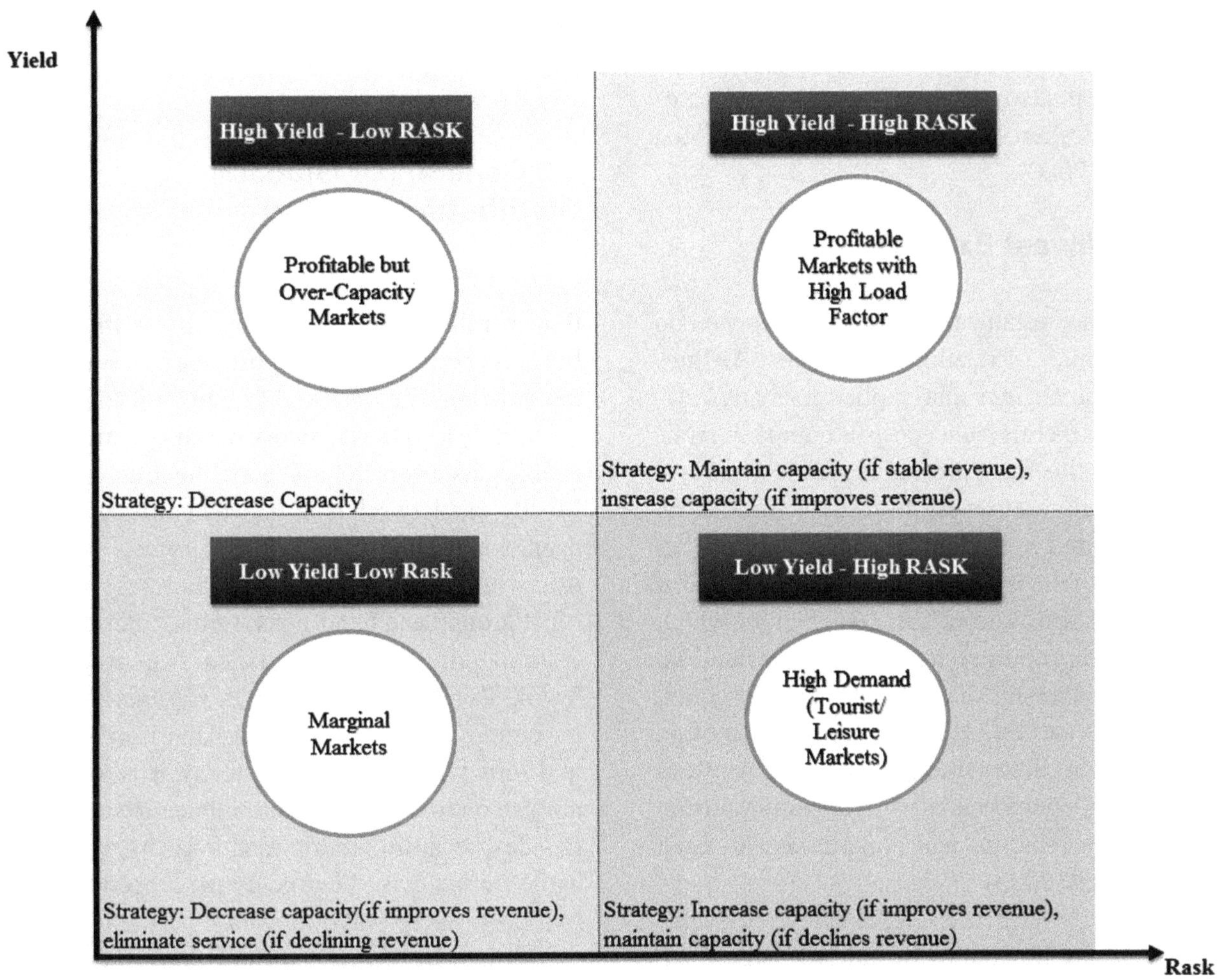

aircrafts, same services, same seats, same foods, even the hairstyle of cabin attendants are the same. Under a massive competition pressure, they have to survive with a very slight margin of profit but increasing costs day by day. So, airlines will decide whether they will try to survive in this market with the same concept or they will re-design and allocate old marketing weapons with the touch of relationship marketing (Pilarski, 2007).

According to Hennig and Hansen, availability of capacity, punctuality, safety, security, on board service are today minimum requirements or musts which airlines have to provide for sure. Not fulfilling any of them will cause drastic loss of customers for airlines but fulfilling all of them will not create a competitive advantage. Because of this reason, airlines re-considering relationship marketing merged with new technological opportunities. In 1990s American Airlines and British Airways started to shape marketing strategies with relationship marketing concept and segmented their customers. İn 1996 Lufthansa established "Target Customer Unit" and institutionalized micro segmentation, one to one marketing and customer value processes (Hennig-Thurau, Gwinner, & Gremler, 2002).

Lufthansa use a scale for long, to group its customers in FFP according to value and purchasing attitudes (Figures 7 and 8). Such an organization and dense effort requires dedicated time and staff but it is also valuable because it allocates marketing resources to right customer (Thorsten & Hansen, 2000).

2.4 Southwest Example

Success of an organization is always depends on inner dynamics of relations. Southwest Airlines is one of the airlines that applied formally relationship marketing concept as a company strategy. Today this most profitable airline's name is mentioned almost in every publication in industry. Jody H. Gittell in his book explains Southwest's success with its mastering on creating and maintaining relations and claims four factors which are leadership, culture, strategy and coordination.

Under leadership title it should not be forgotten Southwest's ex CEO H.Kelleher's creation of an atmosphere of information, common respect and sharing. Kelleher formulated organization culture focusing on relations and commitment to each other (Gittell, 2003).

Strategy is defined as long run tactics to maintain relations in Southwest culture (Figure 9). Coordination in Southwest defined relations not only inside company but especially other circle of the company such as unions, airport employees, and other airlines. Southwest takes on the principle of relations in every direction and level but not a hierarchical one (Gittell, 2003).

What Southwest earns with such a concept is efficiency, dedication, short ground times, more cycles in a day. It is well known by airport personnel that different from other airline staff, Southwest's' staff meets, jokes and "listens" them. Such courtesies worth millions in airport atmosphere where minutes means millions of dollars.

To sum up, what Southwest did is to put human and relations at the center and created such an organization culture, not works and procedures. However, as a result of this relationship approach relations make works and procedures easier and faster (Gittell, 2003). Southwest knows well "know-how" but also they developed a "know-who" perception.

2.5 General (Or Global?) Distributing Systems

General Distributing Systems are worth to mention in relationship marketing efforts in airline business because of its importance as a source of information, statistics and as market itself.

Simply a GDS is network based system which enables its users to make online transactions. Mostly the network is in between airlines, travel agents, and all sort of airport services. A GDS offers an online and real time link to vendors. Most ground and handling systems, catering, operational, financial and statistical systems are fed by GDS's (Belobaba, Odoni, & Barnhart, 2009).

First GDS was developed by American Airlines in 1960s with "Sabre" and today it is airlines' number one distribution, communication channel. Besides, because of the domination of a few GDS's in the market, it is a huge cost pan competing with fuel cost. Sabre was followed by Apollo which established by United Airlines, later on, Delta, Northwest and TWA created their own system named as "Worldspan". In Europe in 1987 nine airlines led by British Airlines and KLM created "Galileo" and four other airlines led by Lufthansa answered by "Amadeus" (Buhalis, 2003).

That is to say, in the research made by McKensey for IATA, it is stated as the most valuable item in value chain of airline industry. Airlines or carriers are coming far behind in this value chain after GDS's, travel agents, Cargo companies, finance, aircraft manufacturers, and airports.

In early stages GDS's were small software systems under airlines but because of the conflict on "to be seen on the first place" judicial process started and lasted for years but at the end it was claimed against competition law in USA. As a

Figure 7. Airline value pyramid
Source: Adapted from Hennig-Thurau, Gwinner, &Gremler, 2002, p.323.

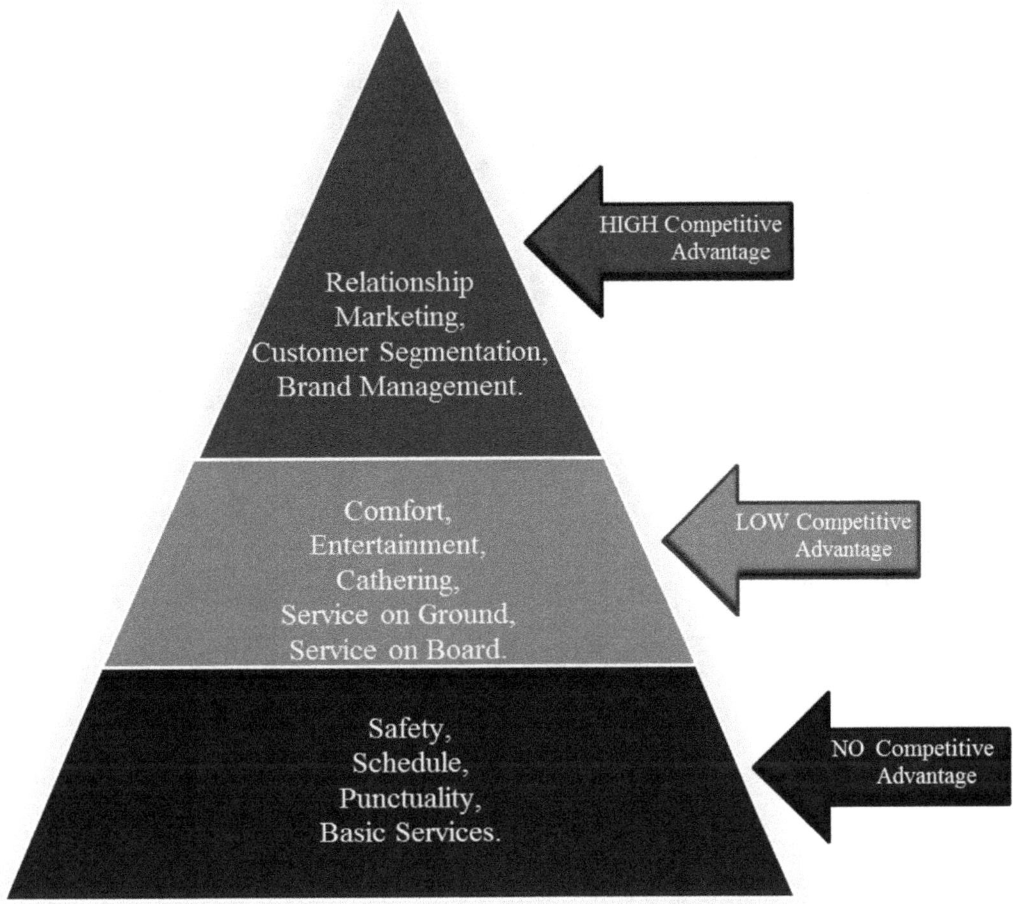

result of this they split up from airlines. (McKensey and Company, 2011).

In order to picture size of GDS's this "old" example can give idea about today's GDS's. In 1995 Sabre that was created and developed by American Airlines had reached the size which it serves in 54 countries on 130.000 terminals which contains 20.000 travel agents with all details, 57 rent a car companies, 50 touring organizations, 22.000 hotels all around the World, 641 airlines with all schedules, flight, pricing etc. Sabre in those years was a system which makes 2.700 transactions per second and files 750.000 passengers all reservation and personal data. Today GDS's are such huge systems (Gummesson, 1994, p.36).

For airlines using a global GDS also means buying a cost per reservation (weather it is ticketed or not), sharing its own customers data and could not find priority or ranking problems nevertheless if airlines use their own "in-house" reservation system they can keep all these advantages on their own side but this means also cannot reach such a big pool of travel agents, sales channels etc. or never be able to reach such terminal numbers.

Today, especially some low cost carriers leading by Easy Jet refuse to be in GDS's and insisting on their own sales channels. It is for sure that they are followed by legacy carriers enviously.

Figure 8. Customer segmentation and loyalty in airline business
Source: Hennig-Thurau, Gwinner, &Gremler, 2002, p.327.

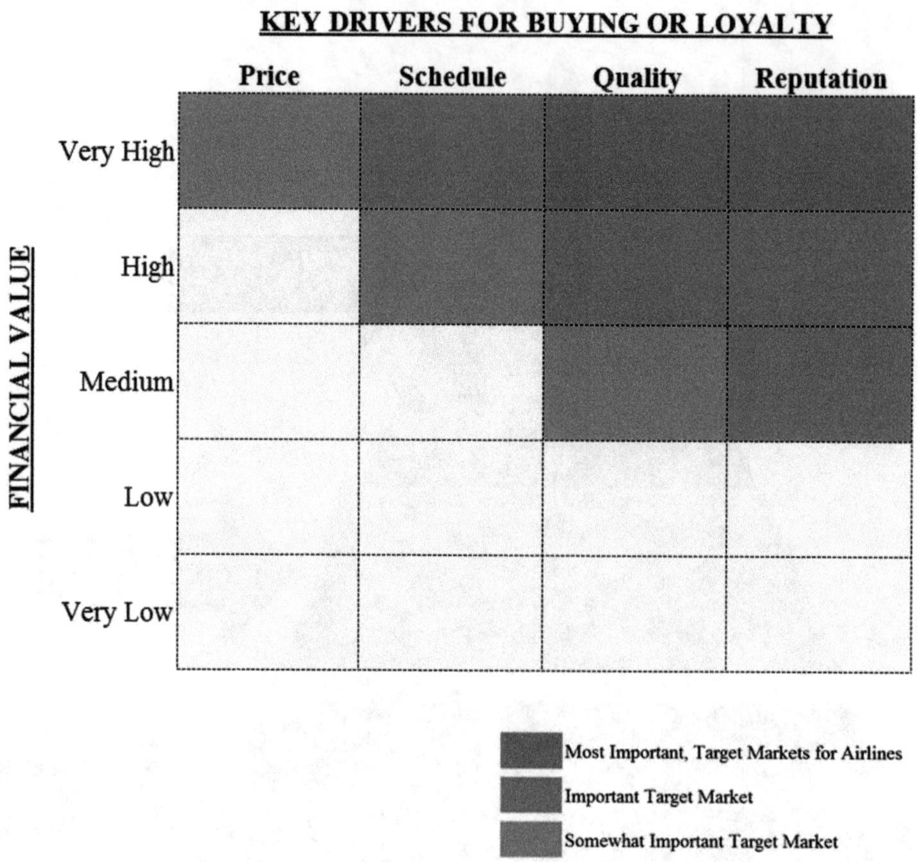

Figure 9. Relationship marketing strategy
Source: Adapted from Gittell, 2003, p.55.

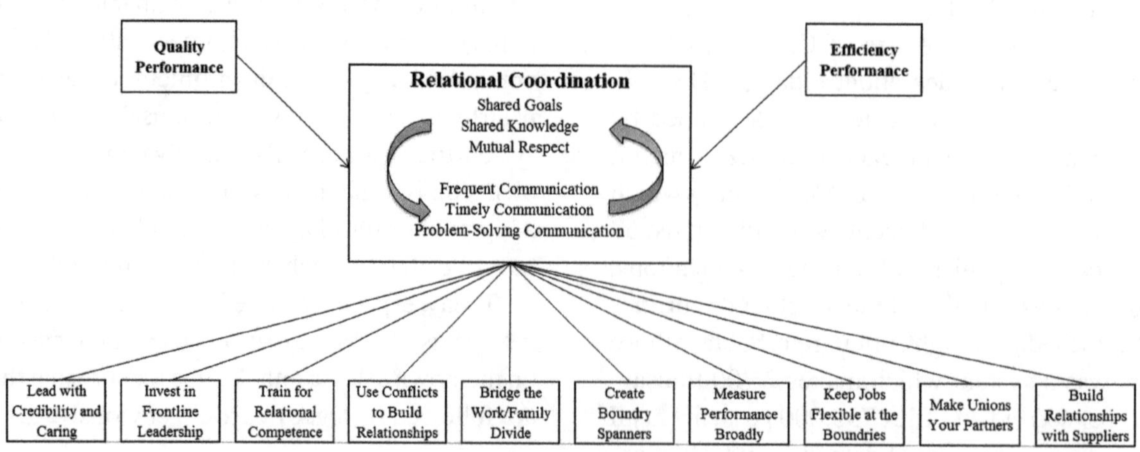

2.6 Frequent Flyer Programs (FFP)

2.6.1 Evolution of FFPs

First FFPs start in 1970s with Southwest's "Sweetheart stamps". Logically this application led to today's FFPs. The system used to work as collecting a defined number of stamps by each flight was converted to a free ticket.

Of course just like all successful invention it was imitated. American Airlines started in the same year "discount coupons" and followed by Western Airlines who gifts a 50 Dollar discount check after a passenger flied 5 times. Within all these primitive applications the idea was same and clear as much as today. The idea of FFPs is "rewarding repeated purchase behavior". On the other hand, due to technological insufficiency and lack of regulations it was hard to keep a campaign in tune with FFPs. FFPs were open defenseless to fraud and forgery of documents which used to cost airlines millions in those years. However, the real threat was usage of these programs without financial assessment namely, there was simply enough miles/credits cumulated in PanAm's FFP, "World Pass" to make all fleet operate a full month for free (Gilbert, 1996).

Maturity era started with American Airline's "AA Advantage Club" in 1981. Just five years later 24 national carriers of 27 in USA had FFPs just like this program and reached 22 million members. Growing each year it became such a complex structures. They made marriages with banks and payment cards and every card producing miles by every cent spent by the user. Besides, these credits or miles can be spent as a currency out of airlines for shopping, accommodation, rent a cars (Gilbert, 1996).

Inside airline alliances these FFPs became a covetable value or alliances integrated all members FFPs which each other. Shaw states this best as "FFPs are the glue of airline alliances." (Shaw, 2007, p.128).

Taking into account all of these today FFPs are the new currencies and have very complicated relations within financial systems and they became independent structures in airline industry but still needs the re-consideration with the touch of relationship marketing.

2.6.2 FFPs: Burden or Weapon?

FFPs are seen as the way of locking customers in or loyalty programs for airlines there are many ambiguous points in it. First of all unredeemed miles of airlines are growing with a snowball effect every day and became a heavy financial burden. Gillberts (1996) determination on the subject with an example is very interesting that if it is asked from airlines to redeem or melt all cumulated miles in a day they would need 600.000 Boeing 747s which will fly all day around the World. In other words today airlines can manage to melt only 25% of cumulated miles (Gilbert, 1996).

Another problem is corporates that finances business travels complaints about not having control on spending of miles. Companies paying for travels but benefit of these travels are spent by individuals because of FFP systems. This need forced many airlines to create special FFPs or memberships for companies (Holloway, 2008).

Governments are another party who puts a in a claim for benefits of FFPs. Governments see FFP miles as financial assets and want to excise them. Countries like UK which establishes its tax system on term of "benefit" and excises even mobile phone lines given by companies, vehicles for managers, bonus payments. So it is expected in such countries in short term that to excise benefits rise from use of FFP membership (Liston-Heyes, 2002).

On the side of airlines, miles causing another financial pressure. Unredeemed miles are converted as a currency and stays as "debt" on airlines balance-sheets which has a negative pressure on financial statement. After 2008/9 global financial crisis these huge amounts drew attention on board rooms and had the priority (Doganis, 2006).

International organizations and governments make new regulations in order to justify competition conditions for airlines. Nowadays, FFPs especially running by airlines under the roof of IATA, it is loudly discussed on charges of being against competition law and equality. Actually all FFPs are strong in their homeland or hub and do not provide living space for other airlines (Gilbert, 1996; Liston-Heyes, 2002).

In economic cycle of airlines, obviously, all FFPs work almost in same style, offer similar rewards and this raise competition threshold and increase customer retention cost.

As a result, FFPs shall be seen separate products of airlines which have financial roots and application availability in relationship marketing. FFPs will be successful if they can provide customer loyally, retention and reorder. In other words, FFPs have promising opportunities for airlines if they can be used as marketing tool.

2.6.3 Discussing FFPs in Relationship Marketing

Definition of FFPs and relationship marketing is overlapping on customer loyalty, customer retention and long run relationships. In order to renovate FFPs today there must be some certain steps to take from relationship point of view.

First of all, airlines while rewarding by FFPs must be generous to its customers. Putting strict and narrow time limitations for spending miles is not a good way of rewarding. Besides, the biggest problem from customer's side seems like finding available seat to spend miles as free tickets in certain seasons and destinations. Yield management departments are involuntary to give seats for FFP mile redemption in a top destination or high season but it must be remembered by these units that these customers must be seen as passengers already paid their seats in time (Shaw, 2007).

The most common reward in FFPs is free tickets but relationship marketing concept requires individualism and differentiation. So, airlines have to have a range of rewards from customized gifts or rewards to free tickets and actually must reward them by offering freedom of choice. As Shaw examples it will not be attractive for a passenger who flies 30 times in a year rewarding with a 31st flight (Shaw, 2007)

Additionally, today lots of airlines let their customers to change, share or sell their accumulated miles with other members. Airlines also can create some customized solutions for these demands. For example, airlines can promote members to spend their miles in low seasons when they have more empty seats. Airlines can make a setting if the member wants to fly in high season or fully booked top destinations have to spend more miles. In order to support weak or new destinations for airline members can be promoted to fly these destinations with spending very few miles. There can be created campaigns for specific destinations on mile spending (Holloway, 2008).

Mostly accumulated miles expire in three years which is an application that members do not like. This can be solved as miles can be kept unless member makes one flight per year. This would be just for both sides.

On balance-sheet of airlines balance of unredeemed miles can be converted also to relationship marketing tools. In order to melt this iceberg airlines have to inform their customers regularly and in different communication channels. There should open spending channels out of free flights and these channels must be less costly comparing to free flight tickets. There are some examples which bring relationship marketing, advertising, social responsibility and of course melting heavy burden of miles. When a customer starts reservation on the internet site of the airline, on routing step, an automatic system calculates total carbon emission of this possible flight per passenger and offers planting tree or trees on behalf of passenger in exchange for an amount of miles of course. This example application creates a feeling of doing something good for him and the environment and increase credibility of airlines ad also creates a win-win situation for all (Shaw, 2007).

Airlines can offer customers to join campaigns of charity or let them make donations to some charity or NGOs by spending from accumulated miles with a rate of exchange that company will decide. At the airport step of travel passengers should have availability to spend miles by limousine services, car parks or to get access to lounges. Besides a source of complaint, excess baggage fees can be made by miles and this can create another win-win situation.

On the stage of purchasing tickets there shall apply different rates, such if the customers choose to buy from airlines own channels such as internet site, sales Office, call center more miles would be earned and if other channels preferred less miles would be earned. This application will create a visible impact on cost area.

Another suggestion is enabling customers to be able make their shopping's with miles in certain internet sites. There is a common interest for airline promotional materials in public and this can be converted to an advantage by selling them and make it can be paid by miles. Airlines usually organize trips for corporates or staff of travel agents, airports etc. to their home based city and airline facilities such as operation, hangars, flight training centers, catering units and giving them chance to touch airline "product". These organizations are named as "fam trips" and mostly applied for B2B level. In order to make it a more profitable tool of marketing it must be adapted to B2C level. Melting miles by using this can be an option too. Today some airlines selling simulator flight hours in their flight training centers. Considering the crowded community of virtual airlines and pilots this would have an advertisement impact also.

All cases given above are examples for airlines to melt their mile icebergs without stepping out their main activities. Each example if considered with the impact of social media and advertisement support are nominees of being great campaigns or social media phenomenon's.

Consequently, FFPs are not only databases for airlines but has a potential of being source of information, analyses, segmentation and application instruments for relationship marketing. FFP members shall also be used as a pool for application of campaigns, surveys, new product launches.

2.7 Internet and Social Media

Internet is vital for relationship marketing just like it is a de facto of success for all industries today, not because it is a sales channel but also it is a multichannel, interactive and totally free place of share. From company perspective, customers today can access within minutes to cheapest product, can compare with related ones, can read and join user comments about the product even can order from all over the World and this makes traditional marketing karma dysfunctional. Especially the generation born in between 1997 to 1994 that also named as "Generation Y" use internet with all aspects in daily life to talk, meet, work, pleasure, shopping etc. purchasing power of this Generation Y is predicted 200 Billion dollars (İlban & Kaşlı, 2013).

So called word of mouth marketing has a more intense meaning with internet because in a latest survey related to the subject today's consumers consulting with a rate of 92% to their friends, colleagues or families moreover 73% admits that reading user comments in internet affects their choices and purchase behavior. Internet as a sales channel has reached 15% in total personal spending (İlban & Kaşlı, 2013).

A new updated survey on the subject made by Bright Local in USA, 83% of consumers read user comments about local companies and regarding to same survey 73% of total admits reading positive comments about the company increases trust to the company. Nielsen focuses on advertisement with its survey of "Trust on Advertisement" that studied with 28.000 internet users in 56 different countries. After family and friends who has an influence power with 92%, internet comes with 70% (Gazete Vatan, 2014).

Coming back to airlines, they will not reach their targets or will not turn into profit until they change their perception of internet and social media and abandon to try internet as a one-way channel to carry their messages from company to customers. Airlines should consider internet as a multi-channel real time communication channel, of course an advertisement area, a discussion forum, a CRM center, a sales channel, a distribution channel, a newspaper, TV channel, radio dedicated to airline, a place where you can meet and spend time with people(Chaffey, Ellis-Chadwick, Johnston, & Mayer, 2006).

For instance, Etihad Airlines makes announcement about itself and customers from twitter, for instance flight delays, cancellations. Airline replies all tweets and comments on Facebook one by through the channel "Etihad Help. Last year Turkish Airlines put its name on the top by a customer complaint made airborne during a flight from Istanbul on a social media channel. Just a few minutes after related department get in contact with the aircraft and inform cabin crew about the situation of passengers. Passenger's complaint had solved and informed also from same media channel within minutes during a flight. When passenger shared his complaint about something on Twitter it was a CRM issue but the way Turkish Airlines solved it is a good example of relationship marketing concept (kokpit.aero, 2013).

In 2008, Dave Carroll took a flight from Chicago to Halifax with United Airlines and gave its guitar to baggage because it was not allowed to the cabin because of its size, naturally. After the flight airline delivered the guitar broken. Related department in the airport offered to Carroll 250 dollars but actual price of it was more than 3.000 dollars. Passenger could not convince the airport about the real value of his instrument and backs to home with anger and disappointment. He wrote a song named "United breaks guitars" and after recording it uploaded to YouTube. In the first few days 150.000 people watched the video, later on news, and shows followed. United tried to cover but it was late. Just four days after the flight airlines value drop 10% of its value and lost 180 million dollars. This is a very solid example of how a CRM without awareness of relationship marketing (kokpit.aero, 2013).

Today American Airlines everyday replies 30.000 tweets one by one; KLM employs 60 experts in social media department. In addition to previous sections where from traditional marketing mix to relationship marketing is given, in this section with contemporary examples how CRM applications and relationship marketing should integrate is given (SocialBakers, 2014).

Consequently, today in such internet pages like Expedia, Orbitz all airlines are given according to best connection, schedule and price options from city A to city B. Airline logos are put side by side on a two dimension plane with prices and schedules under them. This is the simplest version of airline product. Because of the current market conditions and some sectorial peculiarities there is not much difference between airlines. In this case the most reasonable advice for airlines is to accept and immediately take necessary steps through relationship marketing concept.

3. FINANCIAL EFFECTS OF RELATIONSHIP MARKETING: IMPLEMENTATION MODEL FOR AVIATION INDUSTRY

3.1 Domains of Relationship Marketing

Adapting a cliché to the industry, A. M. Pilarski says in his book "Why Can't We Make Money in Aviation?" (Pilarski, 2007, p.9).

If you want to make millions in aviation, you must risk investing billions.

This is, in fact, a to-the-point statement underlining how bad the situation is considering the cost category of the industry, but still just points to the tip of the iceberg.

On the basis of three assertions, that even the small revisions to be made by the firm at the relations level could create great effects (Reinchheld, Markey, &Hopton, 2000, p.135).

1. It is less costly to serve long-term customers,
2. Loyal customers are less sensitive to price changes,
3. Loyal customers are voluntary marketing advocates.

In a 5-year study on loyal customers, Reinartz and Kumar have examined the customers with minimum 2-year commercial relation, accepting them as loyal customer, and observed that they have had positive effects on all cost items of the firm in different ratios (Sorce, 2002).

The domains of the relationship marketing, or in other words, expectations with regard to which domains will undergo changes in consequence of application of the relationship marketing are greatly important for effectiveness.

Among the studies conducted on this issue, especially Erdal Arlı's study conducted in Turkey is remarkable. The companies where the relationship marketing study would be conducted were given the simplest values, and the results of application were categorized by domains. As the relationship marketing practices, simple tactics such as customer retention, asking their wishes and needs, easy terms of payment, regarding the customers as members or stakeholders, remembering their special days, esteeming, offering special services, complaint handling, and one-to-one contact have been applied by the participant firms (Arlı, 2012). The results have had significant effects firstly on the repurchase criterion: an increase by 52.2%. The percentage in the categories such as satisfaction with management, intention to recommend, etc. has reached 80%. Briefly, it has been understood that even the basic practices that are in fact the simplest requirements of enterprise marketing but also cross-pathing with the relationship marketing have rather significant effects on the customers (Arlı, 2012).

The studies conducted indicate that the longer the relation lasts, the bigger is the gain. The possible reasons behind that are the decreases in the marketing costs, the decrease in the rate of leaving customers, and the increase in the SOW rate (Gummesson, 2002).

3.1.1 Effects of Relationship Marketing on Cost

Considering the abovementioned profile, for the present-day enterprises like the aviation industry trying to cope with heavy and multi-volume cost items, the most important cost item, among the visible ones, is in fact the customer defection.

For instance, an airline company's average annual customer defection rate is estimated to be 5%. Considering a medium-sized airline company carrying 32,000,000 passengers a year on average, this 5% defection corresponds to 1,600,000 passengers. Likewise, if we take the gross value as 1,000 dollars, the loss of the enterprise seems to be 1.6 billion dollars. Supposing, rather optimistically, that the profit margin of the company is 10%, the net loss of the company seems to be 160 million dollars. Although the ratios in this example are a little higher than the average, it will not be difficult to say that a company that might come to such ratios rather easily will go bankruptcy or at least be in a financially bad situation (Gupta, et al., 2006).

For another example, 15,30Billion TL out of Turkish Airlines' 18,77 Billion TL revenue for the year 2013 is the cost of the sales. And 1,94 Billion TL out of TL 3.47 billion gross profit seems to be the marketing expenditures (Turkish Airlines,

Figure 10. The chain of productivity
Source: Hanssens & Dekimpe, Models for the Financial-Performance Effects, 2008, p.502.

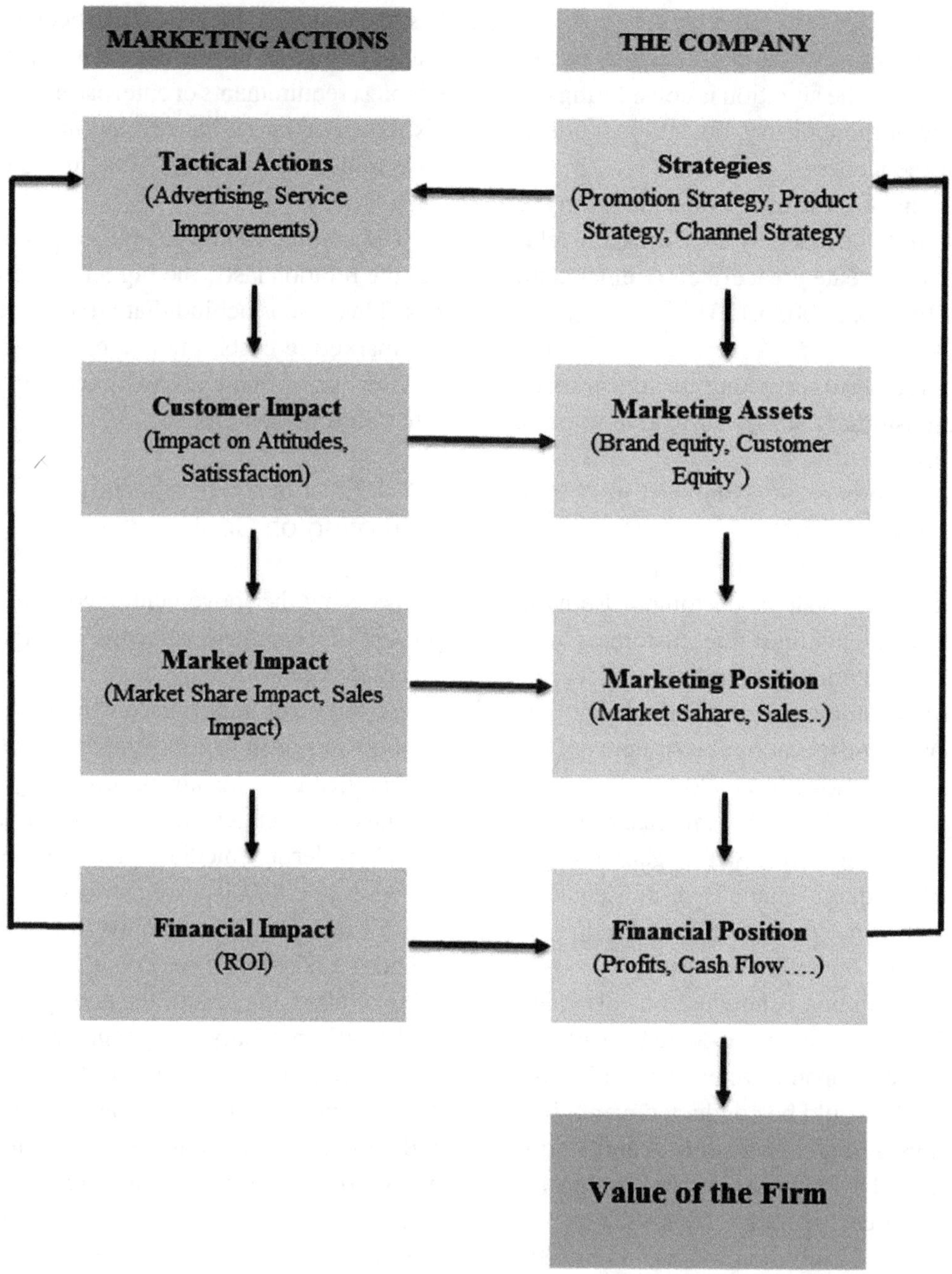

2014, March.).A relation with an enterprise, continued on the basis of long-term and mutual gains, will mean, first of all, a decline in the time cost. The customer will save the operating costs of finding new seller, such as time, labor, technology, transportation, etc.

Additionally, it must be remembered that the risk to be created by new customers also has its own cost. Although it has worn down today due to trust factor, the "open account" system applied in business life in Middle East societies deserves a review from the point of view of cost.

As per the principle that says the relationship marketing is to do marketing after the customer has become customer', the cost of the marketing efforts made to retain the customers in hand will be one-seventh of the cost of acquiring new customers (Grönroos, 1994).

Since the way of value creation passes through benefit creation, it is natural to regard it as a cost as well. However, the point to be reached is to create a value that can be the long-term value boosting the company's performance and providing the customer with benefit. Grönroos defines relationship costs as follows (Ravald & Grönroos, 1996, p.29).

- **Direct Relationship Costs:** The costs such as office, personnel, and system investments emerging with the supply of an idea, product or service.
- **Indirect Relationship Costs:** The costs such as incorrect billing, delayed deliveries, etc. caused by wrong execution of the supply function.
- **Psychological Costs:** The costs of safety precautions caused by the worries about whether the supplier can fulfill its promise, or whether it can solve the problems.

Decreasing the abovementioned cost types means creating a customer value without offering any additional benefit. This can be made possible through several changes to be made in the internal and external service quality and processes in the simplest and leanest manner. Activation of the strategies such as effectiveness, flexibility and zero customer loss in the areas of production, distribution and after-sales services will have reflections on the company's overall profitability. Grönroos mentions safety, security and credibility as the common costs that enable to establish long-term relationships and must be shared by the seller and the customer (Ravald & Grönroos, 1996; Grönroos, 2004).

3.1.2 Effects of Relationship Marketing on Profitability

The fundamental mission of marketing is to create or stimulate demand; thus, measuring the resulting sales and revenues under the marketing heading will not give the correct results. The effects of the marketing efforts must be searched in the sales and earnings of the company. In the US, the total value of the yearlong advertising and promotional activities is 10 trillion dollars, which corresponds to 10% of the Gross National Product. These figures and activities are regarded as the investments that must increase the profitability (Hanssens & Dekimpe, 2008).

The conventional profitability flow diagram starts with innovation, and this is the stage where the customers' demands and needs are also identified (Figure 11). Better products and services are offered to the customer at better rates and quality, and this creates a good experience for the customers. The satisfied customers are more loyal, and this returns to the company as the high repetition order rates and positive word-of-mouth marketing. Thus, the company that has up-sell and cross-sell items increases its profitability. And the increased profit finances the innovation to develop better products and services for the customer (Kumar, Pozza, Peterson, & Shah, 2009).

The Sprint Nextel example is included herein particularly for the questions it has caused. This company serves 53 million customers, and decided to cut off 1000 of them. Typical Nextel customer pays the company 55 dollars a month, 24 dollars of which seems to be profit. The company found out that this 1000-person group has called the customer services department several times a month, talked for 8 to 12 minutes on average, and complained about various services continuously. Since each minute in the customer services costs 2 dollars to the company, considering the fact that the said customer group does not yield any profit to the company, Sprint Nextel fired them following a radical decision strongly criticized in the indus-

Figure 11. Conventional path to profitability
Source: Kumar, Pozza, Peterson, & Shah, 2009, p.148.

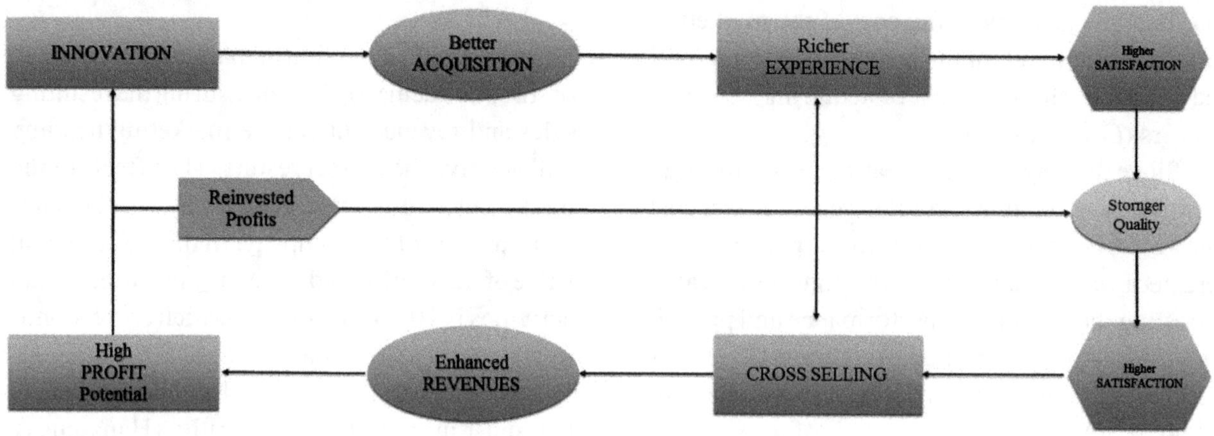

try. This example is important as it questions the relations in the classical, conventional profitability diagram. In his study of 1996, Reicheld observed a 60% defection among the satisfied customers as well. The author who gave examples from the automobile industry observed that only 40% of the customers who are 85% to 95% satisfied with the car they bought the same brand vehicle again (Kumar, Pozza, Peterson, & Shah, 2009).

A high amount of resources is used to create loyalty, or investments are made to increase the customer satisfaction in the aviation industry as well, but the profitability keeps being low. The factors such as time, connection type and quality, aircraft type, hub, etc. that affect the customer preferences despite the factors such as loyalty and satisfaction should also be regarded as standby diverters (Shaw, 2007).

In fact, such diversions occur as the customer satisfaction and loyalty are not connected to profitability in the first place. Therefore, discrimination between less and more profitable customers in the airline companies must be perceived as a compulsion. According to the classical FFP understanding, each customer gains as many miles as he flies, and this is generally the same for everyone (Gilbert, 1996). However, the purchasing processes are ignored at this stage. In such a situation, the relationship marketing prescribes analyzing the passenger firstly, drawing a conclusion by analyzing his flight segment, price class and amount of his ticket, and his previous buying behaviors. Likewise, numerous airlines have started to apply this. In previous years, the Continental Airlines has stated that it would reward the mile system on the basis of three statuses it has determined; likewise, Turkish Airlines changed its mile system by shifting to the price class, i.e. a rewarding system based on the amount paid by the customer, at the beginning of the year 2014(www.new-milesandsmiles.com, 2014). Thus, the mile accumulation will be diminished at the mile winning stage, and the frequent flyer loyal passenger will have a bigger share of the mile pie. And since the segment enjoying the bigger share of the mile pie is also the frequent flyer loyal segment, such miles will also be spent at a higher rate. What the airlines should do at this final point is to channel such accumulated miles to non-flying alternatives or idle routes.

According to the Pareto Principle, 20% of the customers generate 80% of the revenue. This 20% slice can be considered as the first, business or Premium class passengers or the passenger groups with high price class value such as the corporate, seamen, etc. Kumar's study measures the customer value in CLV, i.e. Customer Lifetime Value, from the relationship marketing perspective. In consequence of his study, Kumar has found out that, in parallel to the Pareto Principle, the 20% customer segment, i.e. the first two decile groups generate 95% of the company's revenue (Kumar, 2009).

In that case, companies who want to increase such type of customers of theirs must focus on and analyze their existing customers first, and then chase the customers that match the profile of such type of customers. The customers in this category will pioneer the companies about for which types of products and services they must apply innovations. For instance, as the first airline company offering the first lie-flat seats, British Airways owes this innovation to its first and business class passengers. Innovations made and the goods and services supplied considering the profitable customers will make contributions to both the total CLV and the company's overall profitability (Kumar, Pozza, Peterson, & Shah, 2009). The customer segmentation and tactics prepared from this viewpoint are shown in Figure 12.

Obviously, the success of the abovementioned scheme and segmentation depends on the organizational changes and qualified labor force to apply such patterns. Having applied the relationship marketing principles in compliance with the abovementioned tactics, IBM achieved a 20-million-dollar revenue growth in the year 2008 (Kumar, Pozza, Peterson, & Shah, 2009).

It is Monroe who has mentioned the exchange value in these exchanging processes for the first time and formulated the customers' customer value acquired in the simplest form. Having tried to attribute a numerical value by dividing the acquired values by the paid cost, Monroe has summarized the value as an evaluation of the customer's perception of what he has given and what he has received. (Man, 1998) On the other hand, a strong relationship set will facilitate the lives of the retail or corporate customers as it decreases the time to make a decision, because it creates a positive expectation for an award or feedback like the airline FFPs in consequence of an action or purchasing.

Considering from the perspective of the seller or the service provider, on the other hand, it is important as it reminds that the real motivation is "profit", though it seems rather difficult and costly to go beyond the motto of "Market share is everything" continuing for years (Bareika, 2010).

In consequence of this study conducted on over 100 companies from 20 different industries, it has been discovered that if the companies can decrease their customer defection rates by 5%, they can achieve a revenue growth by 25 to 85%. This study, which is capable alone to emphasize the importance of the relationship marketing, has revealed that not only the loyal customers yield more revenue in time, but also the cost of customer retention is much lower than the cost of gaining new ones. During another study conducted on a bank, it has been observed that if the customer defection rate is decreased from 20% to 10%, the average relationship period of a customer is extended from 5 years to 10 years, and that the average total profit per customer rises from 135 dollars to 300 dollars. If the defection rate can be decreased by 5% more, the profit rises from 300 dollars to 525 dollars by 75% increase (Reichheld & Sasser, 1990).

On the basis of the abovementioned two studies, it is possible to conclude that:

- The long-term customers are less sensitive to price changes,
- The long-term customers can perform free word-of-mouth marketing,
- The long-term customers tend to place more frequent, more steady, and less costly orders.

The long-term customers tend to buy additional products or services more rapidly and easily, and, as a general conclusion, their Life Time Values are higher.

Figure 12. The new path to profitability
Source: Kumar, Pozza, Peterson, & Shah, 2009, p.151.

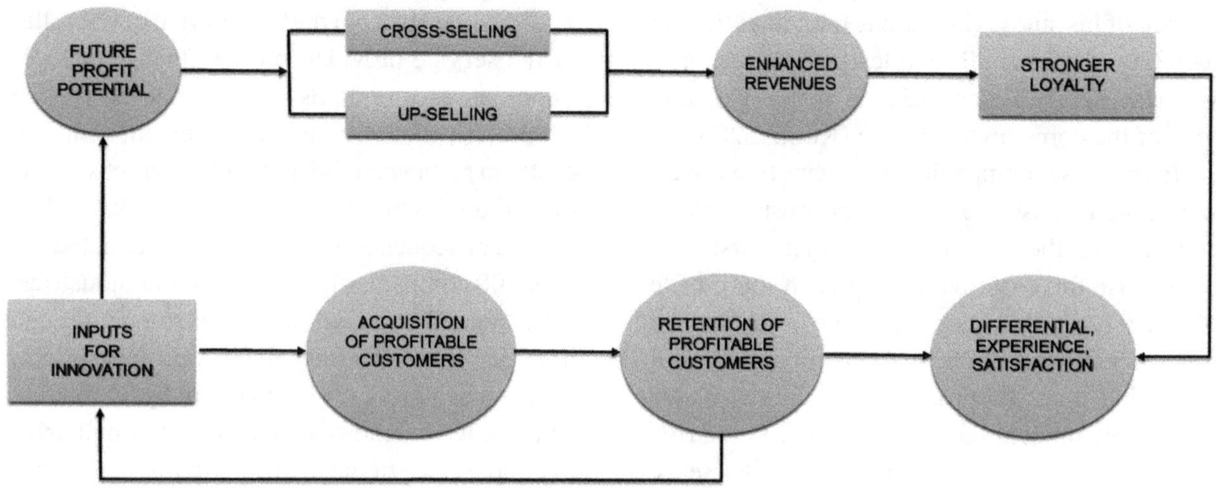

As confirmed by Grönroos, after the first few successful communications, if the customer is satisfied, he starts to trust the supplier, becomes more tolerant towards the supplier, and refrains from complaining, or in other words, he may give the supplier a chance to solve the potential problems. The customer also keeps buying from the same supplier and provides the supplier with other job opportunities through the word-of-mouth marketing (Karaca, 2010).

3.2 Financial Scales of Relationship Marketing

"You cannot manage something you cannot measure", says an old management adage. Even an in-house scale to be developed by the company itself, without the requirement of universal consent, will assist the company in positioning its resources more effectively. Besides, this scale will also be a motivation and rewarding tool for the company.

Since the marketing measures are generally abstract and their effects or returns are mostly protracted, a tendency of measuring them as based on financial data has emerged. The most commonly used measurement units are market share, cost reduction, sales growth rates, and return on investment (ROI). Life Time Value (LTV), which is mentioned frequently with the relationship marketing today, can also be included in this group (Sin, Tse, Yau, Chow, Lee, & Lorett, 2005; Hallowell, 1996; Lindgreen & Crawford, 1999).

As particular to airlines, the following scales can be concretized through the information sources like booking systems and FFPs:

1. **Customer Loyalty:** Whether the customer maintains his existence and the relationship within the unit of time.
2. **Customer Share:** The customer share is calculated by proportioning the gain brought to the company by a customer within the unit of time to the total.

The performance measurement is based on each customer's value and share according to the relationship marketing understanding, though it is based on the market share in the conventional marketing understanding.

3.2.1 Return on Relationship (ROR)

One of the leading theoreticians of the relationship marketing, Gummesson has adapted the Return on Investment (ROI) concept to the relationship marketing as shown in Figure 13.

The long-term net financial return on the network of relationships established and maintained by an enterprise is called the Return on Relationship Investment (ROR). Gummesson's description corresponds to satisfaction, loyalty and profitability in practice. ROI is a cost-based evaluation grounded in the return on the marketing campaign. What is important here is to calculate the cost items correctly and in detail whenever possible (Gummesson, 2002).

Four basic criterions must always be considered:

1. **Costs of Customer Acquisition and Break-Even:** The point of maximum cost to bear to acquire a customer.
2. **Depreciation Curves:** The indicator analyzing the customers' tendencies to depreciate in time, because the customers may lose their profitability in time. In the case of airlines, it is necessary to keep an eye on the passive members considering FFPs in particular, because the marketing strategy is based on the reason of this passivity: either the member has other memberships or he is really passive (Belobaba, Odoni, & Barnhart, 2009).
3. **Life Time Value:** Life time values of customers must be calculated to be able to calculate the costs and gains of the acquisition and retention activities. Customer lifetime value (CLV) is generally defined as the present value of all future profits obtained from a customer over his life of relationship with the firm (Gupta, et al., 2006).It is possible to make a comparison among the airlines in particular today, thanks to the joint mile programs applied in codeshare flights and carrier alliances. The mile values that have become a currency so can be calculated in CPM (Cents per mile) and RPM (Revenue per mile). In the simplest way, the average LTV is calculated by multiplying the number of the customer's purchases within a certain period of time by the profit per unit. For example, the LTV value of a customer who has made 15 purchases in 2 years:
4. LTV=15 x 1.45 (Profit Per Unit) =21.75 dollars. It is normal that some customer groups give negative values in consequence of this calculation. This indicator indicates the need to increase the number of customers as a unit. In detail, the formula is (Gupta, et al., 2006; 141):

$$CLV = \sum_{t=0}^{T} \frac{\left(p_{t-c_t}\right) r_t}{\left(1+i\right)} - AC$$

- c_t = direct cost of servicing the customer at time t,
- i = discount rate or cost of capital for the firm,
- r_t = probability of customer repeat buying or being "alive" at time t,
- AC =customer acquisition cost,
- T =time horizon for estimating CLV.

3.2.2 Relationship Marketing Scale

The effects of the relationship marketing practices on the company performance and the environmental factors in the process, the study conducted by Akyol and Ataman (2007) (Küçükkancabaş, Akyol, & Ataman, 2007) in Turkish beverage industry is a guiding one. The questionnaire used in 130 interviews made in various geographical regions basically deals with trust, loyalty, communication, shared values, empathy and reciprocity that are the basic factors of the relationship mar-

Figure 13. Return on relationship model
Source: Kanagal, 2005, p.9.

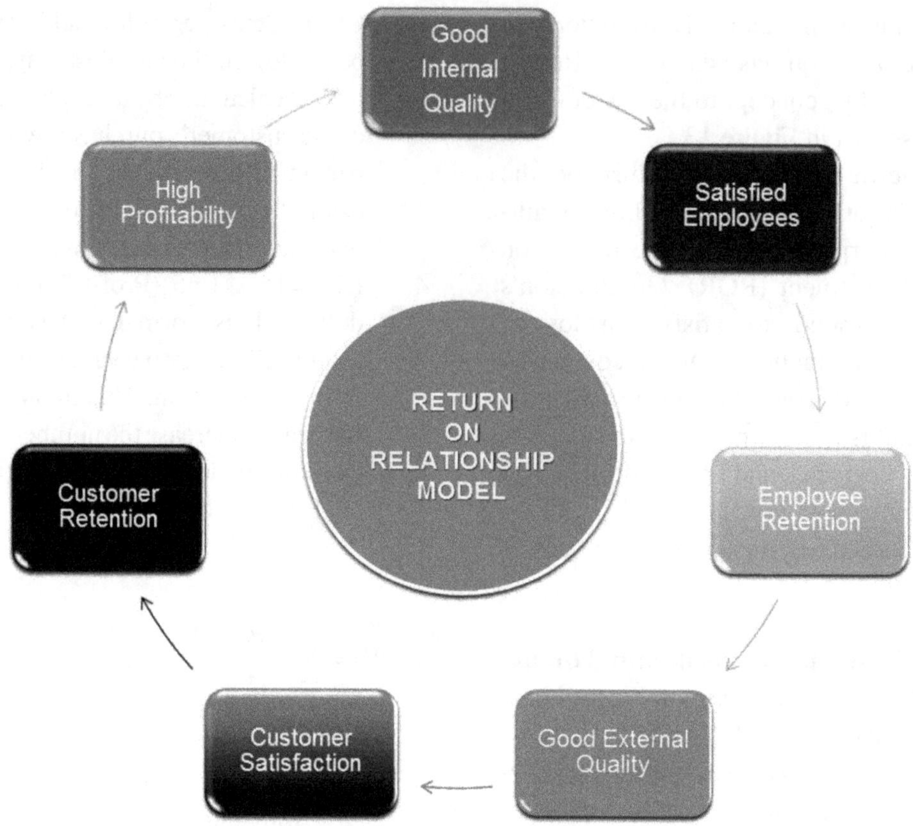

keting. The financial indicators used in the survey completed using the 5-point Likert scale were the sales growth rates and the market share. This study is about the relationship marketing where the subjective inputs generate objective values, and the results of such marketing. The strong results acquired have failed to decrease the effects of the market fluctuations and the other environmental effects. However, the common values, empathy and loyalty have appeared to be the strongest factors while reciprocity, communication and trust have fallen rather behind.

3.2.3 Loyalty Scale

Although loyalty, as evoked by its name, is an abstract notion, it is a measurable and concrete notion in the relationship marketing as it has concrete indicators such as the Share of Wallet (SOW), payments to Premium services, and repetition orders. This scale, generally accepted for its behavioral aspects and repurchasing indicator, can be measured through simple survey methods and repetition orders accessible through databanks and accounting records (Gupta, et al., 2006). For the aviation industry, the survey must include such headings as the service quality, preference, Premium classes and products, trust, difference and convenience (Network, timetables, vacant seats, hub or airports flied, etc.).

3.3 Relationship Strategies for Airlines

Today, the airlines pursue different strategies to come out of the turbulence in the industry. The relationship marketing as a focusing strategy has recently found a place in the market in corporate sense, while the cost leadership or differentiation is the most preferred strategies.

The primary method used by the airlines to differentiate in terms of cost is to ensure lowering fleet costs. This method applied successfully by the low cost airlines particularly provides a considerable cost advantage by singularizing all cost items such as spare parts, maintenance, training, etc. through a single type of aircraft. Since there is no producer in the industry at the same scale with Airbus and Boeing, this method is restricted (Doganis, 2006).

Considering the differentiation strategy, the innovation expenditures and risk await the carriers. This differentiation may sometimes gain favor in the type of aircraft. The favorite airplane of the recent years Airbus A380 has brought a breath of fresh air to the market. The comfort and luxury brought into the forefront by the Gulf carriers today constitute a conscious differentiation strategy.

A shift from the classical marketing concept and the operational structure organized as per this understanding to the relationship marketing strategy means a rearrangement of the entire organization. The first thing coming to mind when it is the reorganization within the frame of relationship marketing is the fallacy of a customer relations department becoming the center of gravity of the company. It is necessary to make clear that the relationship marketing refers to the relations of all units with all business circles. The results of the relationship marketing provide the aviation industry with returns in very short times (Grönroos, 1999).

According to Rapp, an airline company that will apply the relationship marketing concept has to understand the headings presented herein, and ensure that the same are accepted throughout the corporate (Rapp, 2000, pp.328-330):

1. It is necessary to establish customer relations rather than customer databanks, The customer information collected through the airline company's booking systems, call centers, FFPs are nothing but burden for the company, unless it is used as marketing tool.
2. The information must be used to improve the service quality, the airline companies must gather information on their customers, especially the valuable customers from whom they earn considerable revenue, but such information must be used to improve its relations and service quality, otherwise the regularly sent template mails are worthless. When the companies have an opportunity to receive data on the market or themselves from the customers via complaints, mails, etc., they must make sure to use it. The present-day mobile applications and social media channels are appropriate channels for this purpose.
3. It is necessary to find out and focus on the roots of the customer's certain attitudes,
4. The relationship-based measurement units must be used, In case of the airlines, the relationship marketing must measure the segment-based, long-term values, and LTV must also be added to indicators such as occupancy, supplied seats, mileage, etc.
5. The long-term relationship marketing programs instead of the one-time ones must be developed and it must be remembered that the relations can be developed in time, step by step, strategically and within the scope of a program, as is the case with the personal relations.

It is necessary to ensure differentiation in relationships and services by utilizing the FFP systems detailed above. It is mandatory to base diversification of the products and services on the current and prospective customers' demands. Likewise, it is necessary to find out and utilize the life time value of each customer in the system. It is known that several airline companies sort the customers in their registered customer pools by different criteria through the computer systems running on the FFP system, and generate a life time value to be used by the analysts by giving point to every piece of information they have. This system, the customer's frequency of travelling, the price class used for ticketing during his travels, his destinations and flying periods are scored separately, and other than the same, his personal information is also utilized, and his residential location and the real estate values at this location, the agency card, if any, otherwise the credit card, he has used while buying a ticket are also scored. Obviously, what lies beneath all this scoring is the customer's earning value in the eyes of the company. The biggest obstacle to make the most of the FFPs by the airlines is the worry about taking the FFPs out of their principal activity area, i.e. the airport.

Consequently, the application areas of the Relationship Marketing can be reduced to the following three categories according to Palmatier and Houston (2006, p.479).

3.3.1 Financial Relationship Marketing Programs

Such a program rewards the customer loyalty with financial benefits. It has a Taylorian approach, which regards money as the most important motivator. The airline companies have been applying this through discounts, award tickets, incentives, etc. Aside from being easy to copycat by the rivals, it can be seen as a point of loss as it stimulates the price sensitivity, because the customer may shift easily to another carrier offering more affordable prices or better financial benefits.

3.3.2 Social Relationship Marketing Programs

They can be considered as activities ensuring that the customers can have social connections with the airline company or disregard the competitors' offers. In the aviation industry, there are applications that cannot be copycatted with the same effect, such as agency dinners, familiarization trips, sponsorships, golf tournaments, etc. Especially the activities in this group will create the difference when they are coordinated with a relationship marketing awareness.

3.3.3 Structural Relationship Marketing Programs

The activities during which the customer is supported with the systems, devices, or products assisting him in improving his own efficiency or effectiveness. The advertising materials, office products or designs, booking system installations provided by the airline companies to their agencies free of charge can be evaluated within this category. (Palmatier, Gopalakrishna, & Houston, 2006).

The study conducted by Palmatier, Gopalakrishna and Houston (2006) has revealed that the social relationship marketing practices are more effective on the profitability especially within the B2B environment. At the same time, it has been observed that its effects appear in the short run, though it promotes the long-lasting customer loyalty (Palmatier, Gopalakrishna, & Houston, 2006).

3.4 A Relationship Implication Model for Airlines

The company must aspire to accessing a segment that is low in quantity but high in value, and brings revenue to the company, in addition to its on-going efforts for new customer acquisition and market expansion. The marketing resources must be positioned relative to this new segmentation. Within the frame of the Pareto Principle, the easiest way to do this is to use the large databases of the airline companies.

- Airlines' Website Records,
- GDS, Booking System Records,

- CRM Records,
- Call Centre Records,
- Social Media Records.

The list in hand will transform from the alphabetical form to a list of values as per the scoring system created by the company in consequence of the assessments and analyses to be made on the databases. The company must establish the scoring system in line with its own purposes and interests, but it must basically include the following breakdown for sure:

3.4.1 Database Search

- **Passenger Information:** Number of Passengers, Residence City, Residence Neighbourhood, Occupation, Age, Marital Status, Extra Services (Golf Clubs, Wheelchair, etc.)
- **Flight Information:** Long Haul/Short Haul/Domestic/Beyond, Destination City, Destination KM, Cabin Class, (First, Business, Comfort, Economy), Fare Class
- **Sales Information:** POS (Point of Sale), Which flight within the current year, which flight in total, Sales Channel (Airline company Website, Agency, Virtual Agency, Call Centre, etc.)
- **Payment Information:** Payment Source (Individual, Corporate), Payment Method (Cash, Credit Card, Debit Card, FFP Miles, Paypal, etc.)
- **FFP Information:** FFP Type (Carrier's or Alliance's Card), FFP Status (Gold, Silver, Classic, Corporate Club), Total Active Miles.

Surely, when each piece of information obtained from the data repositories in hand is given a point, the travelling frequency, cabin and price classes, and active miles of the customer will receive the highest point values. Therefore, they will be the determinant values. The scoring of the other information can be changed in line with the importance of such information for different domains. In consequence of this scoring, the material value of each passenger for the company in question will have appeared to a great extent. This can be achieved rather rapidly and effectively through new software and applications to be articulated to or fed by the current systems thanks to the present-day software opportunities. When millions of passengers carried for one year are sorted in descending order according to the abovementioned criteria, the target customers who yield the real gain to the company will have been identified (McKensey and Company, 2011).

3.4.2 Re-Segmentation

In consequence of the customer value research, the value sorting can be realized and divided into percentiles. However, the right thing to do is a re-segmentation over this sorting so that it can constitute a target for the marketing units. The first segmentation value of an airline organization dispersed through various countries will be the geographical location. Then, sub-sections can be created on the basis of the criteria such as the travel purpose, business or personal travels, etc. Since the developing airline companies that have sufficient area to grow are always focused on growth, they do not give due importance to this application. The companies that have left this work to FFPs and CRM units believe that the FFPs cage the customers naturally and thus ensure the continuity. However, their current structures wait in the wings to generate more income with the touch of relationship marketing than what they can earn through growth (Teichert, Shehu, & von Wartburg, 2008).

The re-segmentation is quite valuable as it will have identified the target customers for each unit of the organization in the form of concrete name lists.

3.4.3 Analysis of the Valuable Customer Behaviors

Following the scoring, sorting and valuing processes, the customers have been divided into certain micro-segments. There are two probabilities relating to the customers ranking low within the percentiles, i.e. the sorting. The first one is that the customer has already reached the peak of his current potential, that is, maximum revenue is derived from the unit, but its potential is low. The second probability is the fact that the airline company itself is not much preferred by the customer, that is, its Share of Wallet is low (Gruen, 1995). The real target for the company is the customers in this group. At this point the airline company must find out why the groups prefer or do not prefer the airline company, what they are satisfied with, what they are complaining about through different surveys it will carry out through different communication channels (internet, social media, personal interviews, etc.), and it must set its strategy separately for each micro-segment on the basis of the results of such surveys (Leick, 2007).

The motives to prefer that are still effective though not determinant any more in case of the airline companies are tariffs, price, flexibility, FFP, the rate of timely departures, the cabin services and catering, and finally the ground handling services. Differentiation in these services provided by each airline company in standard is now possible only in the manner of offering such services and the communication with the customer while offering them.

A sort of SWOT analysis to be acquired this way will have a say in setting of the short and long-term targets of the company as well as repositioning of its resources.

3.4.4 Re-Organization and Implementation

The customer valuation, micro-segmentation, survey and repositioning works performed will bring along organizational changes as well. Accordingly, the red-tape in the FFP units must be decreased, and such units must be converted into units analyzing the customers and generating marketing materials, thus yielding gain to the company, instead of performing works that are used very limitedly by the card-issuing banks, rent-a-car companies, and the customers. At the moment, the FFPs have turned into compulsory but non-yielding units for the companies because of their current cumbersome structures and the financial burden caused by the accumulated miles. Even the mile depleting efforts can turn into high-yield values for the company just with the touch of Relationship Marketing (Gilbert, 1996). From this point of view such applications can be conducted:

When the customer's destination is determined at the ticketing phase, the system calculates the amount of carbon to be released at that travel automatically through the data such as flight distance, aircraft type, and average load factor. Then, the airline company suggests you to make a donation to an environmentalist organization or plant one or more than one sapling on your behalf against some of your miles. As per the mutual gain principle of the relationship marketing, both the passenger and the airline company generate joint gain over the environmentalist message on the one hand, and a great contribution is made to the customer loyalty on the other hand.

As is the case in this example, the customer can be guided to use the option of donating to the international aid organizations such as UNICEF, Red Cross, or the institutions like the local zoo, schools, etc. at the cost of some of his miles. Alternatively, certain airline promotional products that are in great demand may be sold, or a Fam trip covering the hangar, training, technical, kitchen, etc. departments of the airline company may be suggested. A full flight simulator (FFS) flight to be offered against a high amount of miles at the training facilities will receive great attention. As can be seen in all the above mentioned examples, the value the airline has or can access easily at present have been approached again with the relationship marketing perspective, and turned into values to generate mutual benefits and customer loyalty.

Likewise, the CRM units must have a structure enabling them to acquire customers and guide the other units and marketing units generating values for the acquired customers to make improvements, instead of being units trying the solve the customer complaints through formal and predetermined communication channels. At present, the CRM units respond every customer and every incident in the same way due to their mandatory procedures, and use the same compensation rates for all customers. With the customer value motivation and increased initiatives and authorities, they will cease to be a back office only and turn into an active marketing unit for the company.

In addition to the abovementioned existing units, a "Social Media Management" must be established (if not established already), thus ensuring 24-hour, uninterrupted and centralized management of the social media channels. American Airlines spends 20 minutes on average to answer the customer questions on Twitter, and is closely followed by KLM with 66 minutes (Social Bakers, 2013).Both airlines have established in-house departments in charge of this operation, and made a great progress on this issue.

Within the scope of re-organization, in case of a customer previously recorded and valued in the general distribution systems, the relevant units must be granted the initiative to offer this customer various extras such as awards, discounts, etc. If it is possible to annotate the passenger's PNR, which is not a difficult and costly change in systematic terms, he can be hosted in line with his customer position from ticketing to check-in, or even when he is aboard. For example, the call center, check-in officers or the pursers must definitely be authorized to do aboard last minute upgrade. In relation to this application, the airline companies must develop sub-programs or applications requiring membership. Such actions that can be described as efforts to raise the previously mentioned defection barrier will increase the passenger loyalty (Shaw, 2007).

Secondly, high-rate and frequent channels of communication with the customers must be sought. As a great channel that can meet this need fully, the social media are available to airline companies. For example, it is necessary to organize "Fam Trips", which are made in-house rather frequently, for the passengers as well, and to develop methods to give the passengers a chance to see the inside of the company or touch the product.

Services offered in standard by the airlines such as catering, onboard entertainment, etc. must be turned into an experience, thus achieving the differentiation. At present, the airline companies look alike from foods to aircraft types, from seats to advertisements, from uniforms to even smiles. In such an environment, differentiation can be achieved through understanding the precious value of "localness" and the high quantity-quality of the relations established with the customers. This is the factor behind the success and unique cabin experience of Turkish Airlines that have made a big break in recent years. From the catering concept to crew uniforms, airplane appearance to interior cabin designs, the company gives its passenger the message of difference under the motto of "Oriental Luxury with Western Quality".

In consequence, all of the abovementioned application models describe for the airline companies how to access the new source of income, which they have but cannot utilize. A long-term relationship built on mutual gain, which is the essence of the relationship marketing, can be transformed into revenue and profit that are the purpose of foundation of the company only through these stages. Otherwise, it will be nothing more than an abstract understanding and theory.

REFERENCES

Alabay, M. N. (2010). The process of transition from traditional marketing to a new one. *Suleyman Demirel University Journal of Faculty of Economics and Administrative Sciences*, *15*(2), 213–235.

Arlı, E. (2012). Effect of relationship marketing applications on re-purchasing intention, advising intention and satisfaction in marina management. *Anadolu University Journal of Social Sciences*, *13*(1), 61–76.

Arslan, A. (2008, July 25). Boosting relationship marketing. *Electronic Journal of Social Sciences*, *7*(25), 139–156.

Bareika, G. (2010). Customer Equity in Airline Industry. Master's Thesis, Universiteit van Amsterdam.

Belobaba, P., Odoni, A., & Barnhart, C. (2009). *The Global Airline Industry*. West Sussex: John Wiley & Sons. doi:10.1002/9780470744734

Berry, L. L. (1995). Relationship marketing of services: Growing interest, emerging perspectives. *Journal of the Academy of Marketing Science*, *23*(4), 236–245. doi:10.1177/009207039502300402

Berry, L. L. (2002). Relationship marketing of services: Perspectives from 1983 and 2000. *Journal of Relationship Marketing*, *1*(1), 59–77. doi:10.1300/J366v01n01_05

Berry, L. L., Parasuraman, A., & Zeithaml, V. A. (1983). Service firms need marketing skills. *Business Horizons*, 28–31.

Buhalis, D. (2003, November 13). *eAirlines: Strategic and tactical use of ICTs in the airline industry*. Guildford, England, UK.

Chaffey, D., Ellis-Chadwick, F., Johnston, K., & Mayer, R. (2006). *Internet Marketing: Strategy, Implementation and Practice* (3rd ed.). Essex: Prentice Hall.

Copulsky, J. R., & Wolf, M. J. (1990). Relationship marketing: Positioning for the future. *The Journal of Business Strategy*, *11*(4), 16–20. doi:10.1108/eb060069 PMID:10106864

Dodds, W. B., Monroe, K. B., & Grewal, D. (1991, August). Effects of price, brand, and store information on buyers' product evaluations. *JMR, Journal of Marketing Research*, *28*(3), 307–319. doi:10.2307/3172866

Doganis, R. (2005). *Flying off Course, The Economics of International Airlines*. New York: Routledge.

Doganis, R. (2006). *The Airline Business*. New York: Routledge.

Egan, J. (2011). *Relationship Markering: Exploring relational strategies in marketing*. Essex: Pearson.

Freiberg, K., & Freiberg, J. (1996). *Nuts! Southwest Airlines' Crazy Recipe for Business and Personal Success*. Austin, Texas: Bard Press.

Gazete Vatan. (2014, Ocak 13). *Türkiye'nin alışveriş istatistiği*. Retrieved Mayıs 17, 2014, from http://haber.gazetevatan.com/turkiyenin-alisveris-istatistigi/600264/184/haber

Gilbert, D. C. (1996). Relationship marketing and airline loyalty schemes. *Tourism Management*, *17*(8), 575–582. doi:10.1016/S0261-5177(96)00078-7

Gittell, J. H. (2003). *The Southwest Airlines Way*. New York: McGraw-Hill.

Grönroos, C. (1994). From marketing mix to relationship marketing: Towards a paradigm shift in marketing. *Management Decision*, *32*(2), 4–20. doi:10.1108/00251749410054774

Grönroos, C. (1999). Relationship marketing: Challenges for the organization. *Journal of Business Research*, *46*(3), 327–335. doi:10.1016/S0148-2963(98)00030-7

Grönroos, C. (2004). The relationship marketing process: Communication, interaction, dialogue, value. *Journal of Business and Industrial Marketing*, *19*(2), 99–113. doi:10.1108/08858620410523981

Gruen, T. W. (1995). The outcome set of relationship marketing in consumer markets. *International Business Review*, *4*(4), 447–469. doi:10.1016/0969-5931(95)00026-7

Gummesson, E. (1994). Making relationship operational. *International Journal of Service Industry Management*, *5*(5), 5–20. doi:10.1108/09564239410074349

Gummesson, E. (1997). Relationship marketing as a paradigm shift: Some conclusions from the 30R approach. *Management Decision*, *35*(4), 267–272. doi:10.1108/00251749710169648

Gummesson, E. (1998). Implementation requires a relationship marketing paradigm. *Journal of the Academy of Marketing Science*, *26*(3), 242–249. doi:10.1177/0092070398263006

Gummesson, E. (2002). Relationship marketing in the new economy. *Journal of Relationship Marketing*, *1*(1), 37–57. doi:10.1300/J366v01n01_04

Gummesson, E. (2002). *Total Relationship Marketing*. Oxford: Butterworth-Heinemann.

Gupta, S., Hanssens, D., Hardie, B., Kahn, W., Kumar, V., Lin, N., & Sriram, S. (2006, November). Modeling customer lifetime value. *Journal of Service Research*, *9*(2), 139–155. doi:10.1177/1094670506293810

Hallowell, R. (1996). The relationships of customer satisfaction, customer loyalty, and profitability:an empirical study. *International Journal of Service Industry Management*, *7*(4), 27–42. doi:10.1108/09564239610129931

Hanssens, D. M., & Dekimpe, M. G. (2008). Models for the Financial-Performance Effects. In B. Wieranga (Ed.), *Handbook of Marketing Decision Models* (pp. 501–523). Los Angeles: Springer ScienceþBusiness Media. doi:10.1007/978-0-387-78213-3_15

Hennig-Thurau, T., Gwinner, K. P., & Gremler, D. D. (2002). Understanding relationship marketing outcomes. *Journal of Service Research*, *4*(3), 230–247. doi:10.1177/1094670502004003006

Hollensen, S. (2010). *Marketing Management, A Relationship Approach* (2nd ed.). Essex: Prentice Hall.

Holloway, S. (2008). *Straight and Level: Practical Airline Economics* (3rd ed.). Aldershot, Hampshire: Ashgate.

Hooley, G., Piercy, N. F., & Nicoulaud, B. (2008). *Marketing Strategy and Competetive Positioning* (4th ed.). Essex: Prentice Hall.

Hougaard, S., & Bjerre, M. (2002). *Strategic Relationship Marketing*. Heidelberg: Springer. doi:10.1007/978-3-540-24813-2

IATA. (2010). *Annual Report 2010*. Berlin: June.

IATA. (2011). *The Impact of September 11 2001 on Aviation*. IATA.

İlban, M. O., & Kaşlı, M. (2013). A model of commitment for Generation Y: A survey on airline companies. *Istanbul University Journal of the School of Business*, *42*(1), 133–152.

Jones, T. O., & Sasser, W. E. (1995, November-December). Why Satisfied Customers Defect. *Harvard Business Review*, 88-99.

Kanagal, N. (2005). Role of Relationship Marketing in Competitive Marketing Strategy. *Journal of Management and Marketing Research*, 1-17.

Karaca, Ş. (2010). Hizmet Sektöründe İlişki Pazarlaması. *Selçuk ÜNiversitesi İİBF Sosyal ve Ekonomik Araştırmalar Dergisi*, *13*(9), 440–455.

kokpit.aero. (2013, Ağustos 21). *Kokpit.aero*. Retrieved Haziran 21, 2014, from http://kokpit.aero/index.php?route=content/flight_fear&flight_fear_id=55

Kotler, P. (2000). *Marketing Management, Milennium Edition*. Upper Saddle River, New Jersey: Prentice-Hall, Inc.

Kotler, P., & Keller, K. L. (2009). *Marketing Management*. New Jersey: Prentice Hall.

Küçükkancabaş, S., Akyol, A., & Ataman, B. M. (2007, August 15). *Examination of the effects of the relationship marketing orientation on the company performance*. Springer Science+Business Media.

Kumar, N., Scheer, L., & Kotler, P. (2000). From Market Driven to Market Driving. *European Management Journal*, *18*(22), 129–142.

Kumar, V., Pozza, I. D., Peterson, J. A., & Shah, D. (2009). Reversing the Logic: The Path to Profitability through Relationship Marketing. *Journal of Interactive Marketing*, 147–156.

Lee, D. (2007). *The Economics of Airline Institutions, Operations and Marketing*. Cambridge, USA: Elsevier.

Leick, R. (2007, October). *Building Airline Passenger Loyalty through an Understanding of Customer Value: A Relationship Segmentation of Airline Passengers*. PhD Thesis, Cranfield University.

Lindgreen, A., & Crawford, I. (1999). Implementing, Monitoring and Measuring Programme of Relationship Marketing. *Marketing Intelligence & Planning*, 231–239.

Liston-Heyes, C. (2002). Pie in the sky? Real versus perceived values of air miles. *Journal of Consumer Policy*, *25*(1), 1–26. doi:10.1023/A:1014594718701

Man, L. W. (1998). *Relationship marketing: the case of Cathay Pacific*. Hong Kong: The University of Hong Kong.

Maxim, A. (2009). Relationship Marketing: A New Paradigm in Marketing Theory and Practice. University of Iasi, 287-300.

McKensey and Company. (2011, October). Sales 2.0 For Airlines. *Cost Analyse*. McKensey and Company.

Michael, H., & Morris, J. B. (1998). Relationship marketing in practice. *Industrial Marketing Management*, *27*, 360–361.

Morgan, R. M., & Hunt, S. D. (1994). The commitment-trust theory of relationship marketing. *Journal of Marketing*, *58*(3), 20–38.

Morris, M. H., Brunyee, J., & Page, M. (1998). Relationship marketing in practice: Myths and realities. *Industrial Marketing Management*, *27*, 359–371.

O'Connell, J. F. (2011). The rise of the Arabian Gulf carriers: An insight into the business model of Emirates Airline. *Journal of Air Transport Management*, 339–346.

O'Malley, L., & Tynan, C. (2000). Relationship marketing in consumer markets: Rhetoric or reality? *European Journal of Marketing*, *34*(7), 797–815.

Palmatier, R. W. (2008). *Relationship Marketing*. Cambridge, MA: Marketing Science Institute.

Palmatier, R. W., Gopalakrishna, S., & Houston, M. B. (2006). Returns on business-to-business relationship marketing investments strategies for leveraging profits. *Marketing Science*, *25*(5), 477–493.

Palmatier, R. W., Scheer, L. K., Houston, M. B., Kenneth, R. E., & Gopalakrishna, S. (2007). Use of relationship marketing programs in building customer-salesperson and customer-firm relationships: Differential influences on financial outcomes. *International Journal of Research in Marketing*, 210–223.

Palmer, A. J. (1995). Relationship Marketing:Local Implementation of a Universal Concept. *International Business Review*, *4*(4), 471–481.

Payne, A., Christopher, M., Clark, M., & Peck, H. (1999). *Relationship marketing for competetive advantage*. Oxford: Butterworth-Heinemann.

Peter, M. S. (2007). *Airline Finance*. Hampshire: Ashgate.

Pilarski, A. M. (2007). *Why Can't We Make Money in Aviation?* New York: Ashgate.

Rapp, R. (2000). Customer Relationship Marketing in the Airline Industry. In U. Hansen & T. Hennig-Thurau (Eds.), *Relationship Marketing* (pp. 317–330). Berlin, Heidelberg: Springer-Verlag.

Ravald, A., & Grönroos, C. (1996). The value concept and relationship marketing. *European Journal of Marketing*, *30*(2), 19–30.

Reichheld, F. F., & Sasser, W. E. (1990). Zero Defections: Quality Comes to Services. *Harvard Business Review*, 3-8.

Reinchheld, F. F., Markey, R. G., & Hopton, C. (2000). The Loyalty Effect: The Relationship Between Loyalty and Profits. *European Business Journal*, 134-139.

Rowe, W. G., & Barnes, J. J. (1998). Relationship Marketing and Sustained Competitive Advantage. *Journal of Market Focused Management*, *2*, 281–297.

Schultz, D. E., Tannenbaum, S. I., & Robert, F. L. (1993). *Integrated Marketing Communications*. Lincolnwood: NTC Business Books.

Selvi, M. S. (2007). *İlişkisel Pazarlama*. Ankara: Detay Yayıncılık.

Şendur, F. (2009). The Importance of Creating customer Value in Relational context of Marketing: A Research on Bank Sector. *Master Thesis*, 25-29. Balıkesir, turkey: Balıkesir University.

Serpen, E. (2013, November 21). Airline Business and Financial Planning. *Aviation Economics and Financial Analysis*. Istanbul: Istanbul Technical University.

Sharma, A., Tzokas, N., Saren, M., & Kyziridis, P. (1999). Antecedents and Consequences of Relationship Marketing. *Industrial Marketing Management*, 601–611.

Shaw, S. (2007). *Airline Marketing and Management*. Hampshire, England: Ashgate Publishing Company.

Sin, L. Y., Tse, A. C., Yau, O. H., Chow, R. P., Lee, J. S., & Lorett, L. B. (2005). Relationship marketing orientation: Scale development. *Journal of Business Research*, (58): 185–194.

Sindell, K. (2000). *Loyalty Marketing for the Internet Age: How to Identify, Attract, Serve, and Retain Customers in an E-Commerce Environment: Search Results*. Chicago: Dearborn Trade Pub.

Social Bakers. (2013, April 01). *Havadaki Rekabet Sosyal Medya'da Nasıl?* Retrieved June 18, 2014, from http://www.pazarlamasyon.com/2013/02/havadaki-rekabet-sosyal-medyada-nasil/

SocialBakers. (2014). *Statistics*. Retrieved April 27, 2014, from Social Bakers: http://www.socialbakers.com/twitter/group/brands/tag/airlines/

Sorce, P. (2002). *Marketing Strategies that Build Customer Commitment and Loyalty*. Rochester, New York: Printing Industry Center.

Taneja, N. K. (2010). *Looking Beyond the Runway*. Farnham: Ashgate.

Teichert, T., Shehu, E., & von Wartburg, I. (2008). Customer segmentation revisited: The case of the airline industry. *Transportation Research*, 227–242.

Thorsten, H.-T., & Hansen, U. (2000). *Relationship Marketing*. Berlin, Heidelberg: Springer.

Turkish Airlines. (2014, March.). *Turkish Airlines 2013 Annual Financial Statement*. Istanbul: Turkish Airlines.

Uslu, A., Durmuş, B., & Kolivar, B. K. (2013). Analyzing the Brand Equity of Turkish Airlines Services: Comparing the Japanese and Turkish Perspectives. *9th International Strategic Management Conference* (pp. 446-454). Istanbul: Procedia - Social and Behavioral Sciences.

Verhoef, P. C. (2003). Understanding the effect of customer relationship management efforts on customer retention and customer share development. *Journal of Marketing*, *67*, 30–45.

Voss, G. B., & Voss, Z. G. (1997). Implementing a relationship marketing program: A case study and managerial implications. *Journal of Services Marketing*, *11*(4), 278–298.

www.new-milesandsmiles.com. (2014, april 28). *Miles and Smiles*. Retrieved May 21, 2014, from Turkish Airlines: http://www.turkishairlines.com/tr-tr/kurumsal/haberler/miles-smiles/pek-yakinda-miles-smilesta-yeni-bir-donem-yeniliklerle-basliyor

Wessels, D. (2006). *Consumer Loyalty in the Airline Industry*. Philadelphia: University of Pennsylvania.

Zineldin, M. (2000). Total relationship management (TRM) and total quality management (TQM). *Managerial Auditing Journal*, *2*, 20–28.

Zineldin, M., & Philipson, S. (2007). Kotler and Borden are not dead: Myth of relationship marketing and truth of the 4Ps. *Journal of Consumer Marketing*, 229–241.

KEY TERMS AND DEFINITIONS

Deregulation: Airline deregulation is the process of removing government-imposed rules and restrictions mostly on financial structure of airlines and slot rights, pricing and operational regulations of airlines. The term was born with "1978 Airline Deregulation Act" when control over air travel industry passed from the political to the real market and today it is identified with liberalization acts in sector. Deregulation process in USA also triggered the deregulation acts all over the World and helped to shape of free market conditions.

European Volcano/Ash Cloud Crisis: In 5th of April 2010, the volcano Eyjafjallajökull in Island started eruption and massive and dense volcanic ash clouds caused to stop air traffic in busiest air space of the world. All flights from or to major European airports have stopped and millions of passengers to be stranded in airports. This was the largest air traffic shut-down since World War II in Europe. IATA estimated that during this closure (5th to 21st of April, 2010) 100,000 flights were cancelled in total, and 10 million people stranded or unable to board their flights. According to IATA data Airlines lost 1.7 Billion Dollars, and Airports lost 250 million Euros. Specifically, low cost carriers which have inter Europe flights had the worse hit comparing to legacy carriers. Low cost carriers cancelled %61 of their flights. Besides, 75% of European and 30% of total worldwide airline capacity was cut during this period.

Kotlerist Marketing Concept: The concept named as also the marketing mix or 4P Concept. According to Philip Kotler, Marketing is defined as a social and managerial process by which individuals and groups obtain what they need and want through creating, offering and exchanging products of value with others is known as Marketing. The base of marketing is defined as exchange in this concept. Price, product, promotion, and place are major components. The four Ps can be expanded to the seven P's or eight P's according to different nature of services. Kotler also explains marketing as a social process.

Life Time Value: LTV is a way of measurement that can be defined as the net profit attributed to the entire future relationship with a customer. In other words, LTV is the financial value of a customer relationship, based on the present value of the future cash. This measurement focuses on long-term value of their customer relationships and defines the upper limit of spending to acquire new customers.

Low Cost Carriers: Low-cost carriers or low-cost airlines are airlines offer comparatively low prices but offer fewer comforts such low leg rooms, no on board meals. LCCs charge for all extra services such as meal, baggage. LCCs mostly has dense schedules for specific destinations with high turn around rates or prefer not to fly major airports. Especially after 9/11, LCCs had their golden age. In order to keep fleet costs low they use single type of aircraft. Southwest, Ryanair, and Easyjet are leading LCCs.

Pareto Principle: At the beginning of the century, first, it is mentioned by an Italian economist Vilfredo Pareto in order to formulate unequal distribution of wealth and resources in Italy. He finds out that twenty percent of the people owned eighty percent of the wealth. So, this was the base of so called 80/20 principle. Lately in 1940s, Joseph Juran, working on the theory of "vital few and trivial many" studied Pareto's work and named it as Pareto Principle. He applied Pareto's observations about economics to a broader body of work.Juran's observation of the "vital few and trivial many" states the principle that %20 of something always are responsible for %80 of the results.

Relational Coordination: Relational coordination is a research model which is developed and proposed by Gittell in 2002. The model is used to assess organizational coordination in four airlines in the United States. The idea of relational coordination is based on the interactive nature between both relationships and communication in business environment. A higher level of relational coordination will then affect organizational outputs as in efficiency and quality in operations. Relational coordination can be used for measuring and analyzing the communication and relationships networks through which work is coordinated across functional and organizational boundaries.

Share of Wallet: SOW is a term which refers to customers' total spending that a business captures in the products or services that it offers. As a performance scale it shows the amount of business in percentage that a company gets from a specific customer. This scale can be used to increase repurchase, customer loyalty, and find marketing opportunities. Moreover, SOW indicates unmet needs that the product is not satisfying.

Word of Mouth: WOM is an expected marketing outcome which becomes a marketing technique also by oral or written recommendations made by a satisfied customer to the prospective customers of a product or service. It is accepted as the most effective form of promotion. As a marketing tool WOM is an interactive process such that customers are collaborating with the business, product or service for which they have derived enough satisfaction that they are willing to speak out about it and even recommend it to others.

Chapter 26
Overconfident CEO Appointments:
Determinants and Consequences on Competitors

Neslihan Yilmaz
Bogazici University, Turkey

ABSTRACT

This chapter analyzes the determinants of overconfident CEO appointments and the effect these appointments on competitor stock performance during managerial turnover within the firm. It also analyzes the turnovers that take place in S&P 500 firms and find that an overconfident successor appointed to the firm pertains to a significant positive impact on competitor's stock price. The author also finds that when the outgoing CEO is overconfident it is more likely for the firm to have an overconfident successor.

1. INTRODUCTION

Recent behavioral studies show that overconfident managers engage in overinvestment and make value destroying acquisitions, consequently, the appointment of an overconfident CEO pertains to a significant negative impact on firm's stock price whereas others argue that it might be desirable for a firm to hire an overconfident manager as he can result in greater innovative success of the firm.[1] Yet, we do not know much about the determinants of having an overconfident CEO in the firm and how the competitors of the firm are affected by the appointment of an overconfident CEO. Since a CEO plays a crucial role in setting and implementing the strategy and actions of a firm, and most firms do not operate in monopolistic markets, understanding the determinants of CEO overconfidence and its effect on competitor stock prices would also appear to be an important issue for investigation.

We study the turnover sample of CEOs employed by S&P 500 firms from 1996 to 2006 as in Mazzeo and Yilmaz (2014). Mazzeo and Yilmaz (2014) find that when an overconfident CEO is appointed to the firm there is a significant negative impact on firm's stock price. The proxy for overconfidence is from Malmendier and Tate (2005) who use CEO option holdings data to measure CEO overconfidence and consider overconfidence

DOI: 10.4018/978-1-4666-7484-4.ch026

as the persistent failure of the manager to reduce his exposure to company-specific risk. Using an event study methodology to calculate turnover abnormal returns of the competitor, we identify interesting findings. First, we find that successor overconfidence has a significant impact; when an overconfident CEO is appointed to the firm the abnormal return on the immediate competitor stock increases at the time of the succession announcement. Next, we examine the determinants of having an overconfident CEO appointed to the firm and find that the outgoing CEO being overconfident increases the likelihood, whereas, the outgoing CEO having an MBA degree pertains to a lower probability of having an overconfident successor.

The findings of this paper contribute to the growing behavioral corporate finance literature. Beginning with Roll (1986), studies examine the role of managerial irrationality in corporate finance. In general findings suggest that overconfident managers may be detrimental to firm value (e.g., Ben-David et al., 2007; Malmendier and Tate, 2008) and the market reacts negatively to the appointment of an overconfident CEO (Mazzeo and Yilmaz, 2014).However, some studies argue that it might be desirable for a firm to hire an overconfident manager as he can increase firm value (e.g., Englmaier, 2004; Gervais et al., 2011;Hirshleifer et al., 2012). This study complements the literature by measuring the biased managerial beliefs and examining the determinants of overconfident CEOs appointed to the firm.

The results of this paper also contribute to the research on product market competition. While several studies focus on the effect of competition on managerial turnover, this paper focuses on the consequences of CEO turnover on competitors by examining the repercussions of CEO overconfidence on competitor's abnormal stock return when a turnover takes place within the firm.[2]

2. RELATED LITERATURE AND HYPOTHESES DEVELOPMENT

2.1 Competitor Abnormal Returns

The existing CEO turnover literature provides us a context in which to think about the consequences of overconfidence on the firm itself during CEO turnover. However, further analysis is yet to be done on the effect on firm's rivals although there is a continuous interaction between firm and its rivals unless the firm is in a monopolistic market. The post-turnover actions of the successor CEO may affect the firm's rivals as well as the firm. In his study, Katz (1991) demonstrates that when contracts are unobservable, agents may act as pre-commitment devices. The rationale is that the contract distorts the agent's behavior - he acts as if the marginal costs were higher - and the contract has indirect strategic effects as other players in the market take the change in the agent's actions into account. Miller and Pazgal (2002) contend that managers' types, attitudes toward relative performance as aggressive or cooperative, can also be used as a strategic commitment device that can change firm profits.

Findings of the behavioral corporate finance literature are inconclusive about the possible direction of the reaction to overconfident successor CEO announcements. Several empirical studies show that overconfident CEOs are detrimental to firm value as they may engage in activities that deviate from maximizing shareholder value such as overinvestment and value destroying mergers and acquisitions. Consequently, the competitor of the firm may benefit from this negative effect if the firm with overconfident CEO makes value destroying acquisitions and perform poorly in the long run (Lang and Stulz, 1992; Laux et al., 1998). The competitors in the industry would benefit from the underperforming firm, for example, through gains in market shares. Alternatively, the competitor itself may become a target for the firm in the future and enjoy possible overestimation of its value by firm's overconfident CEO. We refer to this possibility as the *positive competitor abnormal returns hypothesis*. Under this hypothesis, we expect a positive reaction for competitor's stock when an overconfident successor is appointed to the CEO post within the firm. On the other hand, if the overconfident CEO may hurt firm value the competitor of the firm may also be hurt from this negative effect (Akhigbe et al., 1997; Tawatnuntachai and D'Mello, 2002). One possible explanation is that the overconfident CEO appointed to the firm may convey information to the market about the overconfidence of the CEOs of rival firms in the industry. If the firm has an overconfident CEO, the rivals may as well have such executives as their CEOs which in turn may hurt competitor performance. We refer to this possibility as the *negative competitor abnormal returns hypothesis*. Under this hypothesis, we expect a negative reaction for competitor's stock when an overconfident successor is appointed to the CEO post within the firm.

An alternative possibility on the effect of managerial overconfidence on firm performance is suggested by Goel and Thakor (2008). In their theory work, the authors develop a model in which overconfident manager has a higher probability of being promoted to the CEO post under value-maximizing corporate governance. They argue that overconfident manager sometimes makes value-destroying investments but a risk averse CEO's overconfidence has a nonmonotonic positive effect on firm value since it offsets some of the manager's risk aversion. Gervais et al. (2011) also argue theoretically that overconfident manager overestimates his ability to reduce risk, thus, may make capital budgeting decisions that are in better interest of shareholders. A rational, unbiased and risk averse manager may forego some risky but valuable projects if his compensation is not properly adjusted by shareholders. On the other hand, overconfident manager thinks his information allows him to know the likely outcome of risky projects with better precision, therefore, he is less reluctant to take risky projects. Also, in their empirical work, Hirshleifer et al. (2012) use option and press-based overconfidence proxies and show that overconfident CEOs results in greater innovative success for given research and development expenditures in innovative industries since overconfidence increases investment in risky projects. The authors measure innovative success in terms of the number of patents applied and the total citation count of the patents, and classify an industry as innovative if the average citation count per patent for the industry is greater than the median average citations across all industries. Consequently, we may expect the firm benefiting from the appointment of an overconfident CEO. In line with the previous arguments for both hypotheses, the competitor may be hurt by or benefit from the positive effect of the overconfident CEO on firm performance.[3] The competitor may be hurt by an overconfident CEO in the firm if overconfident CEO improves firm value, thus, hurt the competitor through, for example, gains in market shares. Alternatively, an overconfident CEO appointed to the firm may imply that the CEOs of rival firms are also overconfident, and if overconfident CEOs are good for firm performance they may also be good for competitors' performance.

2.2 The Appointment of Overconfident CEOs

Baker et al. (2006) argue that in order for the overconfident manager to have an impact, corporate governance is assumed to be limited in its ability to constrain him into making rational decisions. This could occur if the standard incentive contracts have little effect or boards are behaviorally biased or are not independent of management. One implication of these findings is that as the independence of the board of directors decreases, the probability of having an overconfident CEO appointed to the office increases. We label this possibility as the *appointment of overconfident CEOs*. One possible explanation is that if the board of directors is not independent and an overconfident incumbent wants another overconfident CEO to succeed him, he may influence the board into appointing an overconfident CEO.

3. DATA

3.1 Sample Selection

We identify all the CEO changes that take place in S&P 500 firms during the time period between 1996 and 2006.[4] We collect the announcement dates of each succession through news searches in Dow Jones Factiva during the time period. In order to analyze the effect of CEO overconfidence on turnover abnormal returns, we need to determine the overconfidence of both the incoming and the outgoing CEO. The option information required to calculate the overconfidence proxies of both the incoming and outgoing CEOs is obtained from Thomson Reuters' Insider Derivative Transactions. In addition, we supplement the data with personal information of the CEOs using Marquis Who's Who, Forbes annual compensation surveys, and firms' official websites. The information on the board of directors and institutional shareholders are from Risk metrics and CDA/Spectrum, respectively. The accounting data is from Compustat and the stock price data is from and CRSP.

The competitor information is from Hoover's. We use the Hoover's website instead of the SIC codes, which give a more general list of all the available competitors, in order to identify the immediate competitor of the firm.[5] The Hoover's website provides information on more than 20 million public and private firms in the United States and abroad. For each firm, detailed information including its strategies and background, sales and employment figures, top management as well as its competitors are listed. The competitors list consists of two parts; top competitors and all the competitors. The top competitors are the three closest rivals in the industry while the full list includes all the available rivals. For example, for General Motors Corporation the top three competitors are Ford motor Company, Chrysler LLC, and Toyota Motor Corporation. The full list of competitors includes all the car manufacturers available in the industry such as BMW AG, Honda Motor Company, Volkswagen AG, and Kia Motors Corporation.

In order to identify the immediate competitor for each firm, first we search through the top competitors list and identify the single competitor that is publicly traded and also does not have any announcements on the succession day. If more than one competitor is available, we randomly choose one of them. If none is available from top competitors, we go to the full list and find the next closest competitor in terms of business description and size.

We eliminate observations without valid information on both the incoming and the outgoing CEOs' option grants prior to the day of turnover announcement in order to assess CEO overconfidence. We include only the observations with both the outgoing CEO's departure and the successor's appointment announcements are concurrent. This allows us to control for both the incoming and the outgoing CEO characteristics while examining the abnormal returns. When the announcements are not made at the same time, in almost all of the cases, the departure of the outgoing CEO is announced first and no information is available on the incoming CEO. Therefore, one cannot control for the successor overconfidence.

3.2 Overconfidence Measure

We measure managerial overconfidence of both the incoming and the outgoing CEO in terms of the moneyness of options granted to the executive prior to the turnover announcement. When the incoming CEO is an outsider, we consider the option data available in the previous firm. Our proxy for overconfidence is from Malmendier and Tate (2005). Malmendier and Tate (2005) explain that a risk-averse CEO should exercise his options early if the stock price is sufficiently high as he is under-diversified because he cannot trade his option grants or hedge the risk by short-selling firm stock. In addition, the value of his human capital is closely linked to the firm's performance.

In order to construct the Holder 67 proxy for overconfidence, Malmendier and Tate (2005) examine the first year all options are at least partially exercisable, year 5. Then, they identify the benchmark of 67% for the minimum percentage in-the-money at which the CEO should exercise his vested options. This benchmark used is from Hall and Murphy (2002) who estimate the value of non-tradable options to an undiversified and risk averse executive. The 67% benchmark corresponds to a CEO with a relative risk aversion coefficient of 3 and a percentage of wealth in company equity equal to 66%. Following Malmendier and Tate (2005), we classify a CEO as overconfident, or the dummy variable Holder 67 equals one, if the CEO persistently (i.e., more than twice) exercises options later than suggested by the threshold moneyness level of 67%. The rationale is that the CEO is overconfident in his ability to keep the firm's stock price rising and profit from expected price increases.

3.3 Control Variables

In order to test our hypotheses, we include the relevant control variables from the related literature. Studies show that nature of the turnover, the successor being an outsider to the firm and corporate governance mechanisms may affect firm abnormal returns during CEO turnover.[6] In our analyses, we control for nature of the succession, whether it is forced or voluntary when examining turnover abnormal returns. We classify a succession as forced if it is reported that the CEO is forced or fired from the position, or the news implies that he was forced, or he is retiring but did not announce the departure at least six months in advance. We also include whether incoming CEO is an outsider to the firm, i.e., with the firm for one year or less at the time of the appointment, whether he has dual role or holds an MBA degree.[7] Furthermore, our baseline abnormal returns model includes monitoring mechanisms of the competitor; the percentage of outsiders on the board of directors and the institutional ownership percentage of total shares, in particular, in order to control for the effect of governance mechanisms on the market reaction to the turnover news. Lastly, we include CEO age and CEO tenure in the firm, if he is an insider of the firm, in our analysis.

We also control for the different announcements made by the firm experiencing the turnover, concurrent with the turnover announcement such as dividend payments, stock repurchases and earnings. We classify news as positive, negative or ambiguous depending on the content. For example, news about a higher earnings level than the target is considered as positive news and the Positive News dummy equals one whereas missing the target is bad news, Negative News dummy equals one. Any combination of the positive and negative news so that we cannot classify as either is considered as ambiguous and the Ambiguous dummy equals one. Finally, we control for competitor size, performance as wells as the competition in the industry. We use the natural logarithm of the book value of assets as the basic measure of competitor size. Competitor performance is measured by the industry-adjusted return for the fiscal year prior to the year during which the CEO change takes place minus the value-weighted 2-digit SIC code industry return for the same period. HHI (Herfindahl-Hirschman Index) proxies for the level of competition in the industry and is equal to the summation of the squared percentage market shares of all the firms in an industry, which is defined by the 2-digit SIC code. The market share of each firm is the sales of the firm divided by the total sales in the industry. As the HHI value gets lower, showing that the industry concentration is lower, the competition gets higher.

3.4 Summary Statistics

Table 1 contains the summary statistics (before industry-year adjustments) for the sample of CEO successions occurring from 1996 through 2006. The average successor overconfidence equals 0.38 whereas it is 0.46 for the outgoing CEO, both indicating that we do not have too many overconfident managers in the sample. 7% of new CEOs are outsiders, and on average, the insiders have been with the firm slightly over 14 years. The outgoing CEOs, on the other hand, have an

Table 1. Summary statistics

	Mean	Std. Dev.	Min.	Max.	Obs.
Successor CEO					
Incoming Holder 67	0.38	0.49	0	1	108
Outsider	0.07	0.26	0	1	108
Dual Role	0.27	0.44	0	1	108
MBA	0.35	0.48	0	1	108
Tenure	14.59	10.68	1	38	108
Age	51.48	5.85	37	68	108
Outgoing CEO					
Outgoing Holder 67	0.46	0.50	0	1	108
Dual Role	0.87	0.34	0	1	108
MBA	0.34	0.48	0	1	108
Tenure	22.78	12.29	2	49	108
Age	59.92	6.08	39	71	108
Succession					
Forced	0.07	0.26	0	1	108
Firm Announcements					
Positive News	0.16	0.13	0	1	108
Negative News	0.02	0.13	0	1	108
Ambiguous	0.03	0.16	0	1	108
Competitor					
Pct Outsider	49.87%	35.30%	0.00%	89.01%	108
Institutional Ownership	55.96%	27.59%	0.00%	100.00%	108
Assets ($M)	101,375	292,669	53	1,494,037	108
Industry-Adjusted Return	0.03	0.19	-0.67	0.81	108
HHI	0.06	0.06	0.01	0.45	108

Incoming and Outgoing Holder 67 are the overconfidence measures of the successor and outgoing CEO, respectively. Outsider is a binary variable and is equal to 1 if the successor is from another firm or with the firm for one year or less. Dual Role is equal to 1 if the CEO holds both the chairman and CEO post. MBA is equal to 1 if the CEO holds an MBA degree. Tenure is the total number of years the CEO is with the firm. Forced takes the value 1 it is reported that the CEO is forced or fired from the position, or the news imply that he was forced, or he is retiring but did not announce the departure at least six months in advance. Positive News, Negative News and Ambiguous are dummy variables that are equal to 1 if there are other announcements concurrent with the turnover announcements which are positive, negative or ambiguous in content, respectively. Pct Outsider is the percentage of outside directors on the board of directors and Institutional Ownership is the percentage of total amount of shares owned by institutions. Size is the total amount of assets in million dollars. Industry-Adjusted Return is the stock return for the fiscal year prior to the year during which the CEO change takes place minus the value-weighted 2-digit SIC code industry return for the same period. HHI and is equal to the summation of the squared percentage market shares of all the firms in an industry, which is defined by the 2-digit SIC code.

average tenure of almost 23 years. A substantial number of outgoing CEOs, 87% % in contrast to 27% of the successors, holds dual roles. Furthermore, the average incoming CEO is 51 while the outgoing CEO is 60 years old.

Most often the CEO seems to leave voluntarily; just 7% of the successions are classified as forced. On average, the competitors have 50% of outsiders on their boards of directors and56% of institutional share ownership. Furthermore, the sample firms' competitors are typically quite large with the mean total assets of $101 billion. Besides, the low mean HHI of 0.06 implies a competitive environment in the industries the firms are operating.

Table 2 presents the pairwise correlation coefficients among CEO overconfidence measures and control variables. In Panel A, the results for overconfidence measures and personal characteristics are listed while in Panel B, the correlations among over confidence measures and succession, competitor and competition characteristics are listed. Panel A presents that the correlation coefficient between the Incoming and Outgoing Holder 67 is quite large and statistically significant at 1% level. Incoming Holder 67 is negatively correlated with successor holding dual role, tenure and being an outsider, whereas, the Outgoing Holder 67 is negatively correlated with successor tenure.

4. METHODOLOGY AND RESULTS

To examine the effect of CEO overconfidence on turnover abnormal stock return of the competitor, we use the following regression specification:

$$CAR_i = \beta_1 + \boldsymbol{Holder67}'_i\boldsymbol{B}_2 + \boldsymbol{X}'_i\boldsymbol{B}_3 + \varepsilon_i \quad (4)$$

The cumulative abnormal return CAR for each competitor *i* is calculated using the market model where the market is the CRSP value-weighted market index. The event day is the day the firm announces the turnover news. We calculate the cumulative abnormal returns over a two-day period, including the day of and the day prior to the turnover announcement (-1, 0).[8] ***Holder67*** is the set of overconfidence measures; the overconfidence of both the incoming and the outgoing CEO, and ***X*** is the set of additional controls used in the regression; CEO, succession, competitor and competition characteristics. In the estimations performed, we correct the regression error structure for arbitrary heteroskedasticity.

4.1 Competitor Abnormal Returns

Table 3 reports the results of the analysis of the relationship between CEO overconfidence and abnormal returns of the immediate competitor for different specifications. The estimates of the regression of the abnormal returns on CEO characteristics are reported in column 1. We extend the regression model to include variables related to succession, competitor and competition characteristics in columns 2 and 3, respectively. In all cases, the coefficients on the Incoming Holder 67 are positive and statistically significant, suggesting that the market reacts positively when an overconfident CEO is appointed to the firm. Since overconfidence is public information (Malmendier and Tate, 2005), following the findings of Mazzeo and Yilmaz (2014), the positive coefficient on the Incoming Holder 67indicates that when an overconfident manager is announced to be the next CEO of the firm, the investors anticipate his possible future actions deviating from shareholder value maximization and expect a positive effect on the competitor of the firm.

The positive sign for the competitor in contrast to the negative one for the firm in Mazzeo and Yilmaz (2014) implies that in terms of the intra-industry information transfers, there exists a competitive effect for the immediate competitor. In other words, the link between the returns of firms releasing information and those of their rivals

Table 2. Correlations

Panel A: CEO Overconfidence and Personal Characteristics

N=108	Incoming Holder 67	Outgoing Holder 67	Incoming Dual Role	Incoming MBA	Incoming Tenure	Incoming Age	Outgoing Dual Role	Outgoing MBA	Outgoing Tenure	Outgoing Age
Incoming Holder 67	1.00									
Outgoing Holder 67	0.67***	1.00								
Incoming Dual Role	-0.22**	-0.09	1.00							
Incoming MBA	0.10	0.07	0.08	1.00						
Incoming Tenure	-0.26***	-0.27***	0.16 0.24	0.13	1.00					
Incoming Age	-0.19	-0.14	0.24**	0.04	0.15	1.00				
Outgoing Dual Role	0.02	0.08	0.05	0.05	0.01	0.08	1.00			
Outgoing MBA	-0.16	-0.03	0.05	0.16	0.02	-0.03	0.05	1.00		
Outgoing Tenure	-0.03	-0.03	0.22	0.05	0.15	0.06	0.10	-0.11	1.00	
Outgoing Age	-0.04	-0.05	-0.05	-0.10	0.16	0.11	0.12	-0.13	0.27***	1.00

Panel B: CEO Overconfidence and Turnover, Competitor and Competition Characteristics

N=108	Incoming Holder 67	Outgoing Holder 67	Incoming Outsider	Outgoing Forced	Outsider(%)	Institutional Ownership (%)	Assets	Industry-Adjusted Return	HHI
Incoming Outsider	-0.22**	-0.12	1.00						
Outgoing Forced	-0.00	0.03	0.32***	1.00					
Pct Outsider	-0.03	-0.11	0.03	-0.07	1.00				
Institutional Ownership (%)	0.09	-0.06	-0.01	-0.02	0.62***	1.00			
Assets	-0.20	-0.22	-0.06	0.09	0.13	-0.11	1.00		
Industry-Adjusted Return	0.00	0.12	-0.14	-0.13	-0.06	-0.06	-0.03	1.00	
HHI	0.21**	0.11	-0.13	-0.12	0.18	0.14	0.14	-0.08	1.00

Incoming and Outgoing Holder 67 are the overconfidence measures of the successor and outgoing CEO, respectively. Dual Role is equal to 1 if the CEO holds both the chairman and CEO post. MBA is equal to 1 if the CEO holds an MBA degree. Tenure is the total number of years the CEO is with the firm. Outsider is a binary variable and is equal to 1 if the successor is from another firm or with the firm for one year or less. Forced takes the value 1 it is reported that the CEO is forced or fired from the position, or the news imply that he was forced, or he is retiring but did not announce the departure at least six months in advance. Pct Outsider is the percentage of outside directors on the board of directors and Institutional Ownership is the percentage of total amount of shares owned by institutions. Size is the total amount of assets in million dollars. Industry-Adjusted Return is the stock return for the fiscal year prior to the year during which the CEO change takes place minus the value-weighted 2-digit SIC code industry return for the same period. HHI and is equal to the summation of the squared percentage market shares of all the firms in an industry, which is defined by the 2-digit SIC code.*, **, *** denote statistical significance at the 10%, 5%, and 1% levels, respectively.

suggest that while the arrival of an overconfident CEO is bad news for the firm, it is good news for the competitor. One possible explanation for the competitive effect is that the rival would benefit from the underperforming firm, for example, it may gain market share in the industry. Alternatively, the competitor itself may become a target for acquisition by the firm in the future and benefit from the possible overestimation of its value by the firm's overconfident CEO.

The coefficient of Incoming Holder 67 equals 0.019, which indicates that when the overconfidence of the successor increases by 1 standard deviation, the abnormal return increases by about

Table 3. Effect of CEO overconfidence on competitor abnormal returns

	(1)	(2)	(3)
Incoming Holder 67	0.0135 (1.54)	0.0166 (1.85)*	0.0190 (1.87)*
Outgoing Holder 67	-0.0038 (-0.50)	-0.0071 (-0.98)	-0.0085 (-1.14)
Incoming Age	0.0004 (0.74)	0.0007 (1.27)	0.0007 (1.12)
Outgoing Age	-0.0005 (-1.02)	-0.0006 (-1.32)	-0.0006 (-1.34)
Incoming Tenure	0.0001 (0.29)	0.0001 (0.21)	0.0008 (0.19)
Outgoing Tenure	-0.0001 (-0.16)	-0.0002 (-0.37)	-0.0002 (-0.44)
Incoming Dual Role	0.0040 (0.43)	0.0075 (0.72)	0.0061 (0.66)
Outgoing Dual Role	0.0023 (0.24)	0.0005 (0.06)	0.0008 (0.09)
Incoming MBA	0.0022 (0.31)	0.0009 (0.11)	0.0005 (0.07)
Outgoing MBA	0.0058 (0.85)	0.0060 (0.85)	0.0062 (0.88)
Incoming Outsider		0.0040 (0.37)	0.0041 (0.38)
Outgoing Forced		-0.0143 (-1.42)	-0.0155 (-1.38)
Industry-Adjusted Competitor Return		0.0341 (2.02)**	0.0326 (1.90)*
Positive News			0.0063 (0.63)
Negative News			-0.0026 (-0.18)
Pct Outsider			0.0010 (0.08)
Institutional Ownership			-0.0151 (-0.90)
Size			0.0004 (0.20)
HHI			-0.0199 (-0.40)
Number of Obs.	108	108	108
R-squared	0.0367	0.0832	0.0961

The analysis is for CAR (-1, 0), the cumulative abnormal return for the competitor over the two day period between the day before the announcement of the CEO turnover and the announcement day. Incoming and Outgoing Holder 67 are the overconfidence measure of the successor and outgoing CEO, respectively. Tenure is the total number of years the CEO is with the firm. Dual Role is equal to 1 if the CEO holds both the chairman and CEO post. MBA is equal to 1 if the CEO holds an MBA degree. Outsider is a binary variable and is equal to 1 if the successor is from another firm or with the firm for one year or less. Forced takes the value 1 it is reported that the CEO is forced or fired from the position, or the news imply that he was forced, or he is retiring but did not announce the departure at least six months in advance. Industry-Adjusted Competitor Return is the competitor stock return for the fiscal year prior to the year during which the CEO change takes place minus the value-weighted 2-digit SIC code industry return for the same period. Positive News and Negative News are dummy variables that are equal to 1 if there are other announcements concurrent with the turnover announcements which are positive and negative in content, respectively. Pct Outsider is the percentage of outside directors on the board of directors and Institutional Ownership is the percentage of total amount of shares owned by institutions. Size is the total amount of assets in million dollars. t-statistics are reported in parenthesis. HHI and is equal to the summation of the squared percentage market shares of all the firms in an industry, which is defined by the 2-digit SIC code. *, **, *** denote statistical significance at the 10%, 5%, and 1% levels, respectively

1%. This is an important effect as the average daily return on the S&P 500 index and individual firms in the index between 1996 and 2006 are around -2 and 10 basis points, respectively.[9] Overall, these findings provide evidence for the *positive competitor abnormal returns hypothesis*.

Similar to the findings of Mazzeo and Yilamz (2014), the coefficients show that the Outgoing Holder 67 has no significant effect and it is theIncoming Holder 67 that matters.[10] Turning to the controls other than those for overconfidence, we find that the industry-adjusted 1-year stock return of the competitor helps predict abnormal returns; the better the competitor's performance, the higher the abnormal returns. This implies that the competitor with a higher performance during the year prior to the CEO change in the firm benefits from the succession event. For example, it is possible that during the uncertainties that may follow the turnover process, the competitor will gain market share.

Overall, our findings show that the overconfidence of the successor CEO is important not only for the firm itself but also for its immediate competitor. The market is aware of the actions of overconfident CEOs and this is reflected in the stock prices during CEO successions.

4.2 Determinants of Successor Overconfidence

In this section, we examine the driving forces that may lead to the appointment of an overconfident successor. We estimate a logit model for the binary dependent variable Incoming Holder 67 that takes a value of 1 if the incoming CEO is overconfident and 0 otherwise. The control variables are the outgoing CEO, competitor and competition characteristics.

Table 4 reports the logit estimates. The results of the analysis in column 1 indicate that Outgoing Holder 67 has a significant positive effect on the probability of having aoverconfident incoming CEO. This is consistent with the statistics in Table 2 which illustrate that Incoming and Outgoing Holder 67 are highly correlated. The possibility of having an overconfident incoming CEO is more pronounced when the firm already has an overconfident incumbent. This might be a result of the actions of a powerful incumbent who may favor an overconfident successor. This provides evidence for the *appointment of overconfident CEOs hypothesis*.

We extend the model to include variables related to turnover, competitor and competition characteristics in columns 2 and 3, respectively. After we add the remaining controls, Outgoing Holder 67 still significantly predicts a higher probability of having an overconfident successor. In addition, the coefficient of Outgoing MBA is significant; if the outgoing CEO holds an MBA degree the likelihood of having an overconfident successor decreases. One possible explanation for the significant Outgoing MBA coefficient is that an MBA degree may correspond to a better knowledge and understanding of the value maximizing actions a CEO should take. In particular, if overconfident CEOs may deviate from shareholder value maximization, the outgoing CEO with an MBA degree may even try to avoid an overconfident successor.

5. CONCLUSION

Empirical behavioral corporate finance studies on the interaction between overconfident CEOs and firm policies often conclude that overconfident CEOs either hurt or improve firm value. However, we do not know much about the determinants of having an overconfident successor appointed to the firm or how an overconfident is perceived to effect the immediate competitor of the firm in the market. In this paper, we examine empirically whether overconfidence has any impact on competitor abnormal returns when a CEO turnover takes place within the firm and the important factors that contribute to the appointment of over-

Table 4. Logit estimation of having overconfident successors

	(1)	(2)	(3)
Outgoing Holder 67	3.6126 (5.54)***	3.8097 (5.43)***	4.0282 (5.09)***
Outgoing Age	-0.0002 (-0.01)	0.0002 (0.01)	-0.0060 (-0.13)
Outgoing Tenure	-0.0197 (-0.85)	-0.0224 (-1.00)	-0.0282 (-1.22)
Outgoing Dual Role	-0.1972 (-0.22)	-0.2039 (-0.21)	-0.3463 (-0.29)
Outgoing MBA	-1.2459 (-1.90)*	-1.2782 (-1.88)*	-1.4468 (-1.93)*
Outgoing Forced		-0.7240 (-0.87)	-0.9005 (-1.10)
Industry-Adjusted Competitor Return		-1.7491 (-1.45)	-1.7001 (-1.39)
Positive News			-0.2231 (-0.21)
Pct Outsider			-1.5882 (-1.40)
Institutional Ownership			2.7259 (1.91)
Size			0.0082 (0.05)
HHI			8.4439 (1.43)
Number of Obs.	108	108	108
Pseudo R-squared	0.3999	0.4118	0.4618

Outgoing Holder 67 is the overconfidence measure of the outgoing CEO. Tenure is the total number of years the CEO is with the firm. Dual Role is equal to 1 if the CEO holds both the chairman and CEO post. MBA is equal to 1 if the CEO holds an MBA degree. Forced takes the value 1 it is reported that the CEO is forced or fired from the position, or the news imply that he was forced, or he is retiring but did not announce the departure at least six months in advance. Industry-Adjusted Competitor Return is the competitor stock return for the fiscal year prior to the year during which the CEO change takes place minus the value-weighted 2-digit SIC code industry return for the same period. Positive News is a dummy variable that equals 1 if there are other announcements concurrent with the turnover announcements which are positive in content, respectively. Pct Outsider is the percentage of outside directors on the board of directors and Institutional Ownership is the percentage of total amount of shares owned by institutions. Size is the total amount of assets in million dollars. t-statistics are reported in parenthesis. HHI and is equal to the summation of the squared percentage market shares of all the firms in an industry, which is defined by the 2-digit SIC code. *, **, *** denote statistical significance at the 10%, 5%, and 1% levels, respectively

confident successors. First, we find evidence that successor overconfidence has a significant positive effect on competitor abnormal returns; when an overconfident CEO is appointed to the firm, the competitor stock price increases. Next, we examine the factors that may lead to the appointment of an overconfident successor and find that the possibility of having an overconfident incoming CEO is more pronounced when the firm already has an overconfident incumbent, whereas, the likelihood decreases if the outgoing CEO holds an MBA degree.

Taken as a whole, our findings suggest that overconfidence matters not only for the firm but also for its competitor. The close competitor of the firm seems to benefit from an overconfident CEO appointed to the firm as the competitor may better perform in the presence of an overconfident successor taking actions that could be detrimental to firm value, for example, the competitor may capture a higher share in the market. Moreover, when a firm has an overconfident CEO, it is more likely to have another one succeeding him. Also, CEO MBA education may prove to be useful in order to decrease the likelihood of having overconfident successors.

Our results indicate that overconfidence should be accounted for in the CEO appointment and contracting practices. Furthermore, better examining the underlying factors that lead to the positive effect on the competitor overconfidence would be very interesting to look at and may help us better understand overconfidence and its consequences.

REFERENCES

Agrawal, A., & Knoeber, C. R. (1996). Firm performance and mechanisms to control agency problems between managers and shareholders. *Journal of Financial and Quantitative Analysis*, *31*(3), 377–397. doi:10.2307/2331397

Akhigbe, A., Madura, J., & Whyte, A. (1997). Intra-industry effects of bond ratingadjustments. *Journal of Financial Research*, *20*(4), 545–561. doi:10.1111/j.1475-6803.1997.tb00265.x

Baker, M., Ruback, R. S., & Wurgler, J. (2006). Behavioral corporate finance: A survey. In E. Eckbo (Eds.), The Handbook of Corporate Finance: Empirical Corporate Finance (pp. 146-178). New York: Elsevier/North Holland.

Ben-David, I., Graham, J. R., & Harvey, C. R. (2007). *Managerial overconfidence and corporate policies* (NBER Working Paper No. 13711).

Bertrand, M., & Schoar, A. (2003). Managing with style: The effect of managers on firm policies. *Quantitative Journal of Economics*, *118*(4), 1169–1208. doi:10.1162/003355303322552775

Borokhovich, K. A., Parrino, R., & Trapani, T. (1996). Outside directors and CEO selection. *Journal of Financial and Quantitative Analysis*, *31*(3), 337–355. doi:10.2307/2331395

DeFond, M. L., & Park, C. W. (1999). The Effect of competition on CEO turnover. *Journal of Accounting and Economics*, *27*(1), 35–56. doi:10.1016/S0165-4101(98)00044-5

Denis, D. J., & Denis, D. K. (1995). Performance changes following top management dismissals. *The Journal of Finance*, *50*(4), 1029–1057. doi:10.1111/j.1540-6261.1995.tb04049.x

Doukas, J. A., & Petmezas, D. (2007). Acquisitions, overconfident managers and self-attribution bias. *European Financial Management*, *13*(3), 531–577. doi:10.1111/j.1468-036X.2007.00371.x

Englmaier, F. (2004). *A strategic rationale for having overconfident managers* (Unpublished results). Harvard University, Cambridge, MA.

Fee, C. E., & Hadlock, C. J. (2000). Management turnover and product market competition: Empirical evidence from the U.S. newspaper industry. *The Journal of Business*, *73*(2), 205–243. doi:10.1086/209640

Gervais, S., Heaton, J. B., & Odean, T. (2011). Overconfidence, compensation contracts, and capital budgeting. *The Journal of Finance*, *66*(5), 1735–1777. doi:10.1111/j.1540-6261.2011.01686.x

Goel, A. M., & Thakor, A. V. (2008). Overconfidence, CEO selection, and corporate governance. *The Journal of Finance*, *63*(6), 2737–2784. doi:10.1111/j.1540-6261.2008.01412.x

Gottesman, A., & Morey, M. (2010). CEO educational background and firm financial performance. *Journal of Applied Finance (JAF)*, *20*(2), 70–82.

Graham, J. R., & Harvey, C. R. (2001). The theory and practice of corporate finance: Evidence from the field. *Journal of Financial Economics*, *60*(2-3), 187–243. doi:10.1016/S0304-405X(01)00044-7

Hall, B. J., & Murphy, K. J. (2002). Stock options for undiversified executives. *Journal of Accounting and Economics*, *33*(1), 3–42. doi:10.1016/S0165-4101(01)00050-7

Hirshleifer, D., Low, A., & Toeh, S. H. (2012). Are overconfident CEOs better innovators? *The Journal of Finance*, *67*(4), 1457–1498. doi:10.1111/j.1540-6261.2012.01753.x

Huson, M. R., Malatesta, P. H., & Parrino, R. (2004). Managerial succession and firm performance. *Journal of Financial Economics*, *74*(2), 237–275. doi:10.1016/j.jfineco.2003.08.002

Katz, M. L. (1991). Game-playing agents: Unobservable contracts as precommitments. *The Rand Journal of Economics*, *22*(3), 307–328. doi:10.2307/2601049

Lang, L. H. P., & Stulz, R. M. (1992). Contagion and competitive intra-industry effects ofbankruptcy announcements: An empirical analysis. *Journal of Financial Economics*, *32*, 45–60. doi:10.1016/0304-405X(92)90024-R

Laux, P., Starks, L. T., & Yoon, P. S. (1998). The relative importance of competition and contagion in intra-industry information transfers: An investigation of dividend announcements. *Financial Management*, *27*(3), 5–16. doi:10.2307/3666270

Malmendier, U., & Tate, G. (2005). CEO overconfidence and corporate investment. *The Journal of Finance*, *60*(6), 2661–2700. doi:10.1111/j.1540-6261.2005.00813.x

Malmendier, U., & Tate, G. (2008). Who makes acquisitions? CEO overconfidence and the market's reaction. *Journal of Financial Economics*, *89*(1), 20–43. doi:10.1016/j.jfineco.2007.07.002

Mazzeo, M. A., & Yilmaz, N. (2014). The effect of CEO overconfidence on turnover abnormal returns. *Journal of Behavioral and Experimental Finance*, *3*, 11–21. doi:10.1016/j.jbef.2014.07.001

Miller, N., & Pazgal, A. (2002). Relative performance as a strategic commitment mechanism. *Managerial and Decision Economics*, *23*(2), 51–68. doi:10.1002/mde.1045

Parrino, R. (1997). CEO turnover and outside succession a cross-sectional analysis. *Journal of Financial Economics*, *46*(2), 165–197. doi:10.1016/S0304-405X(97)00028-7

Pfeffer, J., & Salancik, G. R. (1977). Organization context and the characteristics and tenure of hospital administrators. *Academy of Management Journal*, *20*(1), 74–88. doi:10.2307/255463 PMID:10305921

Tawatnuntachai, O., & D'Mello, R. (2002). Intra-industry reactions to stock split announcements. *Journal of Financial Research*, *25*(1), 39–57. doi:10.1111/1475-6803.00003

ADDITIONAL READING

Adams, R. B., Almeida, H., & Ferreira, D. (2007). Understanding the Relationship Between Founder CEOs and Firm Performance (Working Paper). University of Queensland, New York University and London School of Economics.

Alpert, M., & Raiffa, H. (1982). A Pogress Report on the Training of Probability Assessors. In D. Kahneman, P. Slovic, and A. Tversky (Eds.), Judgement Under Uncertainty: Heuristics and Biases (pp. 294-305).Cambridge: Cambridge University Press.

Anderson, R. C., & Reeb, D. M. (2003). Founding family ownership and firm performance: Evidence from the S&P 500. *The Journal of Finance*, *58*, 1301–1329.

Beatty, R., & Zajac, E. J. (1987). CEO change and firm performance in large corporations: Succession effects and manager shifts. *Strategic Management Journal*, *8*, 305–317.

Bonnier, K., & Bruner, R. F. (1989). An Analysis of Stock Price Reaction to Management Change in Distressed Firms. *Journal of Accounting and Economics*, *11*, 95–106.

Brickley, J. A., Coles, J. L., & Jarrell, G. (1997). Leadership Structure: Separating the CEO and Chairman of the Board. *Journal of Corporate Finance*, *3*, 189–220.

Davidson, W. N., Worrell, D. L., & Cheng, L. (1990). Key Executive Succession and Stockholder Wealth: The Influence of Successor's Origin, Position and Age. *Journal of Management*, *16*, 647–664.

Fischhoff, B., Slovic, P., & Lichtenstein, S. (1977). Knowing with Certainty: The Appropriateness of Extreme Confidence. *Journal of Experimental Psychology. Human Perception and Performance*, *3*, 552–564.

Friedman, S. D., & Singh, H. (1989). CEO Succession and Stockholder Reaction: The Influence of Organizational Context and Event Content. *Academy of Management Journal*, *32*, 718–744.

Goyal, V. K., & Park, C. W. (2002). Board Leadership Structure and Chief Executive Turnover. *Journal of Corporate Finance*, *8*, 49–66.

Heaton, J. B. (2002). Managerial Optimism and Corporate Finance. *Financial Management*, *31*, 33–45.

Hilary, G., & Menzly, L. (2006). Does Past Success Lead Analysts to Become Overconfident? *Management Science*, *52*, 489–500.

Jayaraman, N., Khorana, A., Nelling, E., & Covin, J. (2000). CEO Founder Status and Firm Financial Performance. *Strategic Management Journal*, *21*, 1215–1224.

Johnson, W. B., Magee, R. P., Nagarajan, N. J., & Newman, H. A. (1985). An Analysis of the Stock Price Reaction to Sudden Executive Deaths: Implications for the Managerial Labor Market. *Journal of Accounting and Economics*, *7*, 151–174.

Kim, Y. (1996). Long-Term Firm Performance and Chief Executive Turnover: An Empirical Study of the Dynamics. *Journal of Law Economics and Organization*, *12*, 480–496.

Lin, Y., Hu, S., & Chen, M. (2005). Managerial Optimism and Corporate Investment: Some Empirical Evidence From Taiwan. *Pacific-Basin Finance Journal*, *13*, 523–546.

Morck, R., Shleifer, A., & Vishny, R. W. (1988). Management Ownership and Market Valuation: An Empirical Analysis. *Journal of Financial Economics*, *20*, 293–315.

Murphy, K. J., & Zimmerman, J. L. (1993). Financial Performance Surrounding CEO Turnover. *Journal of Accounting and Economics*, *16*, 273–316.

Palia, D., Ravid, S. A., & Wang, C. (2008). Founders versus Non-Founders in Large Companies: Financial Incentives and the Call for Regulation. *Journal of Regulatory Economics*, *33*, 55–86.

Perez-Gonzalez, F. (2006). Inherited Control and Firm Performance. *The American Economic Review*, *96*, 1559–1589.

Reinganum, M. R. (1985). The Effect of Executive Succession on Stockholder Wealth. *Administrative Science Quarterly*, *30*, 46–60.

Russo, J. E., & Shchoemaker, P. J. H. (1992). Managing Overconfidence. *Sloan Management Review*, *33*, 7–17.

Svenson, O. (1981). Are We All Less Risky and More Skillful than Our Fellow Drivers? *Acta Psychologica*, *47*, 143–148.

Taylor, S. E., & Brown, J. D. (1988). Illusion and Well-Being: A Social Psychological Perspective on Mental Health. *Psychological Bulletin*, *103*, 193–210.

Villalonga, B., & Amit, R. (2004). How Do Family Ownership, Management, and Control Affect Firm Value? *Working Paper,* Harvard Business School.

Warner, J. B., Watts, R. L., & Wruck, K. H. (1988). Stock Prices and Top Management Changes. *Journal of Financial Economics*, *20*, 461–492.

Weinstein, N. D. (1980). Unrealistic Optimism About Future Life Events. *Journal of Personality and Social Psychology*, *39*, 806–820.

Weisbach, M. S. (1988). Outside Directors and CEO Turnover. *Journal of Financial Economics*, *29*, 431–460.

KEY TERMS AND DEFINITIONS

CEO Overconfidence: Irrational managerial behavior.

Executive Compensation: CEO payment and benefits.

Management Turnover: CEO succession.

Product Market Competition: Firm and its competitors in the industry.

ENDNOTES

1. Papers in the literature include, among others, Ben-David et al. (2007), Malmendier and Tate (2008), Englmaier (2004), Gervais et al. (2011), Hirshleifer et al. (2012) and Mazzeo and Yilmaz (2014).
2. One of the main findings is that turnover is more likely in more competitive industries (e.g., Pfeffer and Salancik (1977); Parrino (1997); DeFond and Park (1999); Fee and Hadlock (2000))
3. In our study, the size of the data limits us to further divide our observations into industry subgroups.
4. The start of the sample period is dictated by the availability of the option data from Thomson Reuter's Insider Derivative Transactions. We consider the CEO turnovers that take place only in S&P 500 firms for practical reasons since we hand collect the data on announcement dates as well as the CEO and succession characteristics.
5. Our findings do not change if we include the two-digit SIC industry codes.
6. Denis and Denis (1995), Jenter and Kanaan (2010), Borokhovich et al. (1996), Huson et al. (2004), Adams and Mansi (2009), Agrawal and Knoeber (1996), Jenter and Lewellen (2010) and Kaplan and Minton (2012)), respectively.
7. Graham et al. (2001) argue that CEOs with MBA degrees are more likely to use sophisticated techniques when calculating the cost of equity capital. Bertrand and Schoar (2003) find a positive relationship between MBA graduation and corporate performance; the return on assets is higher for MBA graduates, however, Gottesman and Morey (2010) find that firms managed by CEOs with MBA degrees do not perform better.
8. When the turnover is announced after the market is closed, weconsider the next business day as day zero.
9. From CRSP between 1996 and 2006.
10. As explained in Mazzeo and Yilmaz (2014), one possible explanation for having only the successor but not the outgoing CEO's overconfidence significantly reducing the returns, is the age of the outgoing CEOs. On average, an Outgoing CEO is 60 years old, and in most firms CEOs tend to retire after this age. Thus, even prior to the succession announcement, the market may anticipate that the outgoing CEO is going to leave the office soon. Consequently, when the succession news is released, Outgoing Holder 67 may not have as significant impact on the abnormal returns as the Incoming Holder 67.

Compilation of References

2013. İnsani gelişme raporu Güney'in yükselişi Farklılıklar dünyasında insani gelişme. (2013). İnsani gelişme raporu'ndaki muhtelif göstergelerle ilgili açıklama notu. [2013 human development report. The rise of the south: Human progress in a diverse world.explanatory note on 2013 HDR composite indices]. Retrieved January 27, 2014, from http://www.tr.undp.org/content/dam/turkey/docs/Publications/hdr/T%C3%BCrkiye%20De%C4%9Ferlendirmesi.pdf

Abreu, M., & Mendes, V. (2012). Information, overconfidence and trading: Do the sources of information matter? *Journal of Economic Psychology*, *33*(4), 868–881. doi:10.1016/j.joep.2012.04.003

Acar, F. T. (2001). *Duygusal zekâ yeteneklerinin göreve yönelik ve insana yönelik davranışları ile ilişkisi: banka şube müdürleri üzerine bir alan araştırması*. Unpublished PhD Thesis, İstanbul Üniversity.

Acar, F.T. (2002). Duygusal zekâ ve liderlik. *Social Sciences Institute, 12.*

Ackert, L. F., & Church, B. K. (2006). Firm image and individual investment decisions. *Journal of Behavioral Finance*, *7*(3), 155–167. doi:10.1207/s15427579jpfm0703_4

Agrawal, A., & Knoeber, C. R. (1996). Firm performance and mechanisms to control agency problems between managers and shareholders. *Journal of Financial and Quantitative Analysis*, *31*(3), 377–397. doi:10.2307/2331397

Ainina, M. F., & Mohan, N. K. (1991). When LBOs go IPO. *Journal of Business Finance & Accounting*, *18*(3), 393–403. doi:10.1111/j.1468-5957.1991.tb00602.x

AK Parti 2023 Siyasi Vizyonu. (2012). Siyaset, toplum dünya.

Akbaba, A, & Erenler, E. (2008). Otel işletmelerinde yöneticilerin liderlik yönelimleri ve işletme performansı ilişkisi. *Turizm Araştırmaları Dergisi*, *19*(1).

Akçay, R. C. (1994). *Çanakkale ilinde görev yapan öğretmenlerin emekliliğe hazırlık eğitimine ihtiyaçları* [The needs of teachers working in Çanakkale for preparation training for retirement]. Unpublished doctoral dissertation, University of Ankara, Turkey.

Akçay, B. (2012). *21. Yüzyılın İlk Finansal Krizi* (p. 266). Ankara: Seçkin Yayıncılık.

Akhigbe, A., Madura, J., & Whyte, A. (1997). Intra-industry effects of bond ratingadjustments. *Journal of Financial Research*, *20*(4), 545–561. doi:10.1111/j.1475-6803.1997.tb00265.x

Akın, A. (2012). Toplumsal cinsiyet ve yaşlılık [Gender and old age]. In D. Aslan, & M. Ertem (Eds.), *Yaşlı Sağlığı: Sorunlar ve Çözümleri* [The Elderly Health: Problems and Their Solutions]. Halk Sağlığı Uzmanları Derneği [Public Health Professionals Associations]. Retrieved May 13, 2014, from http://halksagligiokulu.org/anasayfa/components/com_booklibrary/ebooks/yasl%C4%B1saglgiyeni16.7.2012.pdf

Akın, M. (2004), İşletmelerde duygusal zekânın üst kademe yöneticiler ile astları arasındaki çatışmalar üzerindeki etkileri, (Kayseri'deki büyük ölçekli işletmelerde bir uygulama). Unpublished PhD Thesis, Anadolu Üniversity, Social Sciences Institute.

Akkirman, A.D. (1998). Etkin çatışma yönetimi ve müdahale stratejileri. *Dokuz Eylul University Economics and Administrative Sciences Faculty Journal*, *13*(2).

Aktan, C. C., & Şen, H. (2009). Ekonomik Kriz: Nedenler ve Çözüm Önerileri, Yeni Türkiye Dergisi 2002/1. In Bilge, O. (Eds.), Ekonomik krizlerin yoksulluk üzerine etkileri. Sosyal yardım uzmanlık tezi Başbakanlık Sosyal Yardımlaşma ve Dayanışma Genel Müdürlüğü, Ankara.

AktaşA.GökB. (Eds.). (2010). Örgütsel bağlılığın işgören başarımı üzerindeki etkisi: Antalya'daki A grubu seyahat acentesi çalışanları üzerine bir araştırma. *11.National Tourism Congress*, 2-5 Dec. 2010, Kuşadası (1).

Alabay, M. N. (2010). The process of transition from traditional marketing to a new one. *Suleyman Demirel University Journal of Faculty of Economics and Administrative Sciences*, *15*(2), 213–235.

Alagh, Y. K. (1992). Growth performance of the Indian economy, 1950-89: Problems of employment and poverty. *The Developing Economies*, *30*(2), 97–116. doi:10.1111/j.1746-1049.1992.tb00007.x

Albayrak, C. (2012). Küreselleşme ve ekonomik krizin iş hukukuna etkisi. *Türkiye Barolar Birliği Dergisi*, *98*, 166–202.

Albert, L. C. (2006). *A three part study on the relationship between retirement planning and health.* Unpublished doctoral dissertation, University of South Florida, United States of America.

Alessandrini, P., Fratianni, M., & Zazzaro, A. (2009). *The Changing Geography of Banking and Finance*. Springer.

Alexakis, P., & Xanthakis, M. (1995). Day of the week effect on the Greek stock market. *Applied Financial Economics*, *5*(1), 43–50. doi:10.1080/758527670

Alexander, S. S. (1961). Price movements in speculative markets: Trends or random walks. *Industrial Management Review*, *2*, 7–26.

Alexander, S. S. (1964). Price movements in speculative markets: Trends or random walks. No. 2. *Industrial Management Review*, *5*, 25–46.

Alimen, N., & Bayraktaroğlu, G. (2011). Consumption adjustments of Turkish consumers during the global financial crisis. *Ege Academic Review*, *11*(2), 193–203.

Alimov, A., & Mikkelson, W. (2012). Does favorable investor sentiment lead to costly decisions to go public? *Journal of Corporate Finance*, *18*(3), 519–540. doi:10.1016/j.jcorpfin.2012.02.004

Al-Mulali, U., & Lee, J. Y. M. (2013). Estimating the Impact of the Financial Development on Energy Consumption: Evidence from the GCC (Gulf Cooperation Council) Countries. *Energy*, *60*, 215–221. doi:10.1016/j.energy.2013.07.067

Al-Mulali, U., & Sab, C. N. B. C. (2012a). The Impact of Energy Consumption and CO_2 Emissions on the Economic and Financial Development in 19 Selected Countries. *Renewable & Sustainable Energy Reviews*, *16*(7), 4365–4369. doi:10.1016/j.rser.2012.05.017

Al-Mulali, U., & Sab, C. N. B. C. (2012b). The Impact of Energy Consumption and CO_2 Emissions on the Economic Growth and Financial Development in the Sub Saharan African Countries. *Energy*, *39*(1), 180–186. doi:10.1016/j.energy.2012.01.032

Alpert, M., & Raiffa, H. (1982). A progress report on the training of probability assessors. In D. Kahneman, P. Slovic, & A. Tversky (Eds.), *Judgment under uncertainty: Heuristics and biases* (pp. 294–305). Cambridge, UK: Cambridge University Press. doi:10.1017/CBO9780511809477.022

Altınok, S. (1999). Stagflasyon ve Stagflasyona Karşı Uygulanan Politikalar. *Selçuk Üniversitesi Sosyal Bilimler Enstitüsü Dergisi*, *4*, 59–72.

Altman, M. (2012). Implications of behavioural economics for financial literacy and public policy. *Journal of Socio-Economics*, *41*(5), 677–690. doi:10.1016/j.socec.2012.06.002

Altunışık, R., Torlak, Ö., & Özdemir, Ş. (2003). Ekonomik kriz ve değişen alişveriş alışkanliklari üzerine bir araştirma. *Ulusal Pazarlama Kongresi Bildiri Kitabı*, 16-19.

Altuntaş, C. (2010). Çalışan destek programları[Employee assistance programs]. *Dokuz Eylül Üniversitesi Sosyal Bilimler Enstitüsü Dergisi*, *12*(1), 57–75.

American Association for Marriage and Family Therapy. (2014). *Financial Stress & the Family* Retrieved May 22, 2014 from http://www.aamft.org/imis15 /Content/ Consumer_ Updates/ Financial_Distress.aspx

Anonymous. (2013). *Ekonomik kriz dönemleri; stagflasyon, enflasyon, durgunluk ve kitlik*. Retrieved from http:// www.ekodialog.com/Konular/ekonomik-kriz-donemleri.html

Anthes, W. L. (2004). Financial Illiteracy in America: A Perfect Storm, A Perfect Opportunity. *Journal of Financial Service Professionals*, *58*(6), 49–56.

Antonczyk, R. C., & Salzmann, A. J. (2014). Overconfidence and optimism: The effect of national culture on capital structure. *Research in International Business and Finance*, *31*, 132–151. doi:10.1016/j.ribaf.2013.06.005

Antonides, G. (1996). *Psychology in economics and business: an introduction to economic psychology*. Springer. doi:10.1007/978-94-009-1710-1

Araújo, L., & Gava, R. (2012). *Proactive Companies How to Anticipate Market Changes*. U.K.: Palgrave Macmillan. doi:10.1057/9780230363014

Arıcıoğlu, A. M. (2002). Yönetsel başarının değerlendirilmesinde duygusal zekânın kullanımı: Öğrenci yurdu yöneticileri bağlamında bir araştırma. *Akdeniz University Economics and Administrative Sciences Faculty Journal*, (4).

Arıkan, G. (1997). Ataerkillik kavramıyla ilgili sosyolojik tartışmalar [Sociological debates on the concept of patriarchy]. *H.Ü. Edebiyat Fakültesi Dergisi*, *14*(1-2), 1–24.

Arkes, H. R., Faust, D., Guilmette, T. J., & Hart, K. (1988). Eliminating the hindsight bias. *The Journal of Applied Psychology*, *73*(2), 305–307. doi:10.1037/0021-9010.73.2.305

Arlı, E. (2012). Effect of relationship marketing applications on re-purchasing intention, advising intention and satisfaction in marina management. *Anadolu University Journal of Social Sciences*, *13*(1), 61–76.

Arrow, K. J., & Debreu, G. (1954). The existence of an equilibrium for a competitive economy. *Econometrica*, *23*(3), 265–290. doi:10.2307/1907353

Arslan, A. (2008, July25). Boosting relationship marketing. *Electronic Journal of Social Sciences*, *7*(25), 139–156.

Arslantaş, C. C., & Dursun, M. (2008). Etik liderlik davranışının yöneticiye duyulan güven ve psikolojik güçlendirme üzerindeki etkisinde etkileşim adaletinin dolaylı rolü. *Anadolu Üniversity Social Sciences Journal*, *8*, 1.

Ashby, K. J., & Burgoyne, C. B. (2008). Separate financial entities? Beyond categories of money management. *Journal of Socio-Economics*, *37*(2), 458–480. doi:10.1016/j.socec.2006.12.035

Atkinson, A., & Messy, F. (2012). Measuring Financial Literacy: Results of the OECD / International Network on Financial Education (INFE) Pilot Study. In OECD (Ed.), *OECD Working Papers on Finance, Insurance and Private Pensions* (Vol. 15). OECD Publishing.

ATO. (2005). *Ankara Ticaret Odası, ATO'DAN Krizler Tarihi Raporu, Ankara 17/04/2005*. Retrieved from http:// www.atonet. org.tr/yeni/index. php? p=276&l=1

Ay, Ü.,& Karadal, H. (2003). Yönetici yaşam biçimleri ile yöneticinin etkinliği ve iş tatmini arasındaki ilişki: Tekstil, çimento, sigorta ve gıda sektöründe bir araştırma. *Erciyes Üniversity Economics and Administrative Sciences Faculty Journal*, *20*.

Aydınonat, N. E. (2012). *Değerlendirme Notu*. TEPAV.

Aykın, S., & Mehter, A. (2014). Türkiye ve üye ülkelerin AB-2020 stratejisi göstergeleri açisindan kümelenmesi. *Eskişehir Osmangazi Üniversitesi İİBF Dergisi*, *9*(1), 7–20.

Bachman, J. G. (1983). Affluence: Do High Schools Students Earn Too Much? *Economic Outlook USA*, *10*(3), 25–60.

Baek, E., & DeVane, S. A. (2010). How do families manage their economic hardship? *Family Relations*, *59*(4), 358–368. doi:10.1111/j.1741-3729.2010.00608.x

Baier, S. L., Dwyer, J. G. P. Jr, & Tamura, R. (2004). Does Opening a Stock Exchange Increase Economic Growth? *Journal of International Money and Finance*, *23*(3), 311–331. doi:10.1016/j.jimonfin.2004.01.001

Bailey, A. W. (1987). Social and economic factors affecting the financial welfare of families. *Journal of Home Economics*, *79*(2), 4–18.

Bailey, J. J., & Kinerson, C. (2005). Regret avoidance and risk tolerance. *Financial Counseling and Planning*, *16*(1), 23–28.

Bakan, İ. (2008). Örgüt kültürü ve liderlik türlerine ilişkin algılamalar ile yöneticilerin demografik özellikleri arasındaki ilişki: Bir alan araştırması. *KMU Economics and Administrative Sciences Faculty Journal*, *10*(14).

Baker, M., Ruback, R. S., & Wurgler, J. (2006). Behavioral corporate finance: A survey. In E. Eckbo (Eds.), The Handbook of Corporate Finance: Empirical Corporate Finance (pp. 146-178). New York: Elsevier/North Holland.

Baker, H. K., & Nofsinger, J. R. (2002). Psychological biases of investors. *Financial Services Review*, *11*(2), 97–116.

Baker, M., & Stein, J. (2004). Market liquidity as a sentiment indicator. *Journal of Financial Markets*, *7*(3), 271–299. doi:10.1016/j.finmar.2003.11.005

Baker, M., & Wurgler, J. (2006). Investor sentiment and the cross section of stock returns. *The Journal of Finance*, *61*(4), 1645–1680. doi:10.1111/j.1540-6261.2006.00885.x

Baker, M., & Wurgler, J. (2007). Investor sentiment in the stock market. *The Journal of Economic Perspectives*, *21*(2), 129–151. doi:10.1257/jep.21.2.129

Baker, M., Wurgler, J., & Yuan, Y. (2012). Global, local, and contagious investor sentiment. *Journal of Financial Economics*, *104*(2), 272–287. doi:10.1016/j.jfineco.2011.11.002

Bakken, M. R. (1967). Money Management Understandings of Tenth Grade Students. *National Business Education Quarterly*, *36*, 6.

Baltacı, H. Ş., & Selvitopu, A. (2012). Teacher's view about retirement and pre-retirement training. *Elementary Education Online*, *11*(3), 800–812.

Baltaş, A. (2013). *Ekip liderinin el notları*. Retrieved from http://www.baltas-baltas.com/web/makaleler/l_1.htm

Baltaş, A. (2001). *Değişimin içinden geleceğe doğru*. İstanbul: Remzi Publishing.

Baltussen, G. (2009). *Behavioral finance: An introduction*. Retrieved from http://ssrn.com/abstract=1488110

Baltzer, M., Stolper, O., & Walter, A. (2014, in press). Home-field advantage or a matter of ambiguity aversion? Local bias among German individual investors. *The European Journal of Finance*, 1-21.

Bandura, A. (1989). Human agency in social cognitive theory. *The American Psychologist*, *44*(9), 1175–1184. doi:10.1037/0003-066X.44.9.1175 PMID:2782727

Banerjee, A. (1992). A Simple Model of Herd Behaviour. *The Quarterly Journal of Economics*, *107*(3), 797–817. doi:10.2307/2118364

Bank, A. N. Z. (2008). *ANZ survey of adult financial literacy in Australia*. Retrieved May 25, 2014 from http://www.anz.com/Documents/AU/Aboutanz/AN_5654_Adult_Fin_Lit_Report_08_Web_Report_full.pdf

Barber, B. M., & Odean, T. (1999). The courage of misguided convictions. *Financial Analysts*, *55*(6), 41–55. doi:10.2469/faj.v55.n6.2313

Barber, B., & Odean, T. (2000). Trading is hazardous to your wealth: The common stock investment performance of individual investors. *The Journal of Finance*, *55*(2), 773–806. doi:10.1111/0022-1082.00226

Barber, B., & Odean, T. (2001). Boys will be boys: Gender, overconfidence and common stock investment. *The Quarterly Journal of Economics*, *116*(1), 261–292. doi:10.1162/003355301556400

Barber, B., Odean, T., & Zhu, N. (2009). Systematic noise. *Journal of Financial Markets*, *12*(4), 547–569. doi:10.1016/j.finmar.2009.03.003

Barberis, N. C., & Huang, M. (2006, July). *The loss aversion/narrow framing approach to the equity premium puzzle* (NBER Working Paper No. 12378).

Barberis, N. C., & Thaler, R. H. (2003). A Survey of Behavioral Finance. In Handbook of the Economics of Finance (pp. 1053-1128). North Holland: Elsevier Science.

Barberis, N., & Thaler, R. (2003).A survey of behavioral finance. In Handbook of the Economics of Finance, 1 (pp. 1053-1128).

Barberis, N. C., & Huang, M. (2001). Mental Accounting, Loss Aversion and Individual Stock Returns. *The Journal of Finance*, *56*(4), 1247–1292. doi:10.1111/0022-1082.00367

Barberis, N., Shleifer, A., & Vishny, R. (1998). A model of investor sentiment. *Journal of Financial Economics*, *49*(3), 307–343. doi:10.1016/S0304-405X(98)00027-0

Barberis, N., & Thaler, R. (2003). A survey of behavioral finance. In G. M. Constantinides, M. Harris, & R. Stulz (Eds.), *Handbook of the economics of finance* (pp. 1051–1121). Amsterdam, The Netherlands: Elsevier.

Barca M., (2009). Stratejik yönetim düşüncesinin gelişimi [History of strategic management development]. *Ankara Sanayi Odası Dergisi*, Nisan, Mayıs, Haziran, 35-51.

Bareika, G. (2010). Customer Equity in Airline Industry. Master's Thesis, Universiteit van Amsterdam.

Barney, M. (2010). *Leadership @ Infosys*. Penguin Group.

Barone-Adesi, G., Mancini, L., & Shefrin, H. (2012, 12 June). *A Tale of two investors: Estimating risk aversion, optimism and overconfidence* (Working Paper).

Barone-Adesi, G., Bourgoin, F., & Giannopoulos, K. (1998). Don't look back. *Risk (Concord, NH)*, *11*, 100–104.

Barone-Adesi, G., Giannopoulos, K., & Vosper, L. (1999). VaR without correlations for non-linear portfolios. *Journal of Futures Markets*, *19*, 583–602. doi:10.1002/(SICI)1096-9934(199908)19:5<583::AID-FUT5>3.0.CO;2-S

Bar-On, R., & Parker, J. D. A. (2000). *The handbook of emotional intelligence*. New York: Jossey-Bass Company.

Barry, B. W. (1986). *Strategic Planning Workbook for Public and Nonprofit Organizations* (p. 10). St. Paul: Amherst Wilder Foundation.

Barsky, R. B., Juster, F. T., Kimball, M. S., & Shapiro, M. D. (1997). Preference parameters and behavioral heterogeneity: An experimental approach in the Health and Retirement Study. *The Quarterly Journal of Economics*, *112*(2), 537–579. doi:10.1162/003355397555280

Bathia, D., & Bredin, D. (2013). An examination of investor sentiment effect on G7 stock market returns. *European Journal of Finance*, *19*(9), 909–937. doi:10.1080/1351847X.2011.636834

Baz, M., Kaya, S., & Savaş, K. (2011). *İşveren ve işgören ilişkileri* (Vol. 1). Academic Social Sciences Journal.

Beaulier, S., & Caplan, B. (2007). Behavioral economics and perverse effects of the welfare state. *Kyklos*, *60*(4), 485–507. doi:10.1111/j.1467-6435.2007.00382.x

Beceren, E. (2013). *Lider dediğin*. Retrieved from http://www.egedesonsoz.com/yazar/Lider-dedigin-/6243

Becker, G. S. (1988). Family economics and macro behavior. *The American Economic Review*, *78*(1), 1–13.

Behbahani, A. A. (2011). A comparative study of the relation between emotional intelligence and employee's performance. *Procedia: Social and Behavioral Sciences*, *30*, 386–389. doi:10.1016/j.sbspro.2011.10.076

Bektaş, M., & Erkal, P. (2007). Kamu ve özel sektörde çalışan büro elemanlarının etik olaylara bakış açısı üzerine bir araştırma: Balıkesir ve Burdur illeri çalışması. *VI.National Bureau Management and Secretarial Congress*, Ankara.

Bell, D. (1982). Regret in decision making under uncertainty. *Operations Research*, *30*(5), 961–981. doi:10.1287/opre.30.5.961

Bell, D. E., Raiffa, H., & Tversky, A. (1988). Descriptive, normative, and prescriptive interactions in decision making. In D. E. Bell, H. Raiffa, & A. Tversky (Eds.), *Decision making: Descriptive, normative, and prescriptive interactions* (pp. 9–30). Cambridge, UK: Cambridge University Press. doi:10.1017/CBO9780511598951.003

Belloumi, M. (2009). Energy Consumption and GDP in Tunisia: Cointegration and Causality Analysis. *Energy Policy*, *37*(7), 2745–2753. doi:10.1016/j.enpol.2009.03.027

Belobaba, P., Odoni, A., & Barnhart, C. (2009). *The Global Airline Industry*. West Sussex: John Wiley & Sons. doi:10.1002/9780470744734

Benartzi, S., & Thaler, R. (2001). Naı¨ve diversification strategies in defined contribution savings plans. *The American Economic Review*, *91*(1), 79–98. doi:10.1257/aer.91.1.79

Ben-David, I., Graham, J. R., & Harvey, C. R. (2007). *Managerial overconfidence and corporate policies* (NBER Working Paper No. 13711).

Ben-Rephael, A., Kandel, S., & Wohl, A. (2012). Measuring investor sentiment with mutual fund flows. *Journal of Financial Economics*, *104*(2), 363–382. doi:10.1016/j.jfineco.2010.08.018

Bentham, J. (1789). *An Introduction to the Principles of Morals and Legislations*. Oxford: Clarendon Press.

Berger, A. N., Kashyap, A. K., Scalise, J. M., Gertler, M., & Friedman, B. M. (1995). The Transformation of the U.S. banking industry: What a long, strange trip it's been. *Brookings Papers on Economic Activity*, *2*(2), 55–218. doi:10.2307/2534612

Berkelaar, A., & Kouwenberg, R. (2008, 29 October). *From boom till bust: How loss aversion affects asset prices* (Working Paper).

Berk, L. E. (2003). *Child development*. Boston: Allyn and Bacon.

Bernheim, B. D., Garrett, D. M., & Maki, D. M. (2001). Education and saving: The long-term effects of high school financial curriculum mandates. *Journal of Public Economics*, *80*(3), 435–465. doi:10.1016/S0047-2727(00)00120-1

Bernoulli, D. (1954). *Exposition of a new theory on the measurement of risk*.[Originally published in 1738]. *Econometrica*, *22*(1), 23–36. doi:10.2307/1909829

Berry, L. L. (1995). Relationship marketing of services: Growing interest, emerging perspectives. *Journal of the Academy of Marketing Science*, *23*(4), 236–245. doi:10.1177/009207039502300402

Berry, L. L. (2002). Relationship marketing of services: Perspectives from 1983 and 2000. *Journal of Relationship Marketing*, *1*(1), 59–77. doi:10.1300/J366v01n01_05

Berry, L. L., Parasuraman, A., & Zeithaml, V. A. (1983). Service firms need marketing skills. *Business Horizons*, 28–31.

Bertrand, M., Mullainathan, S., & Shafir, E. (2004). A behavioral-economics view of poverty. *The American Economic Review*, *94*(2), 419–423. doi:10.1257/0002828041302019

Bertrand, M., & Schoar, A. (2003). Managing with style: The effect of managers on firm policies. *Quantitative Journal of Economics*, *118*(4), 1169–1208. doi:10.1162/003355303322552775

Bhallaand, A. S., & Frederic, L. (2004). *Poverty and exclusion in a global world* (2nd ed.). Palgrave Macmillan. doi:10.1057/9780230005624

Bianco, C., & Bosco, S. (2001, October). Financial Illiteracy of College Students. Presentation at the Financial Management Association Conference, Toronto, Canada.

Bikas, E., Jureviciene, D., Dubinskas, P., & Novickyte, L. (2014). Behavioural finance: The emergence and development trends. *Procedia: Social and Behavioral Sciences*, *82*, 870–876. doi:10.1016/j.sbspro.2013.06.363

Bildirici, Z. (2011). *Avrupa Birliği'nde yoksullukla mücadele ve Türkiye'nin uyum sürecindeki yeni uygulamalar.* unpublished master thesis, University of Istanbul, Institute of Social Sciences, Istanbul.

Bilge, O. (2009). Ekonomik krizlerin yoksulluk üzerine etkileri. Sosyal yardım uzmanlık tezi Başbakanlık Sosyal Yardımlaşma ve Dayanışma Genel Müdürlüğü, Ankara.

Bird, K. (2007). *The intergenerational transmission of poverty: An overview* (Working Paper 99) Manchester, IDPM/Chronic Poverty Research Centre (CPRC). Retrieved from www.chronicpoverty.org/resources/cp99.htm

Black, F. (1986). Noise. *The Journal of Finance*, *41*(3), 529–543. doi:10.1111/j.1540-6261.1986.tb04513.x

Blaug, M. (1962). *Economic theory in Retrospect*. Cambridge, Illinois: Cambridge University Press.

Blumstein, P. W., & Schwartz, P. (1983). *American couples: money, work, sex*. New York: William Morrow.

Bodie, Z., Kane, A., Marcus, A. J., & Mohanty, P. (2009). *Investments* (8th ed.). New York: Mc Graw Hill.

Bollen, K. A., & Long, J. S. (Eds.). (1993). *Testing structural equation models*. Newbury Park, CA: Sage.

Bora, A. (2007). *Dosya: Yoksulluk ve sosyal dışlanma*. Retrieved from http://www.tes-is.org.tr/TR/tesis_dergi/2007

Borokhovich, K. A., Parrino, R., & Trapani, T. (1996). Outside directors and CEO selection. *Journal of Financial and Quantitative Analysis*, *31*(3), 337–355. doi:10.2307/2331395

Bowen, C. F., Laux, S. C., Ratcliffe, J., Staten, M. E., Walstad, W. B., & Willis, L. E. (2008, October). Financial Education and Program Evaluation. *National Research Priorities for Financial Literacy and Education Results of the National Research Symposium on Financial Literacy and Education*, Washington DC (pp.10).

Bowen, C. F. (2002). Financial Knowledge of Teens and Their Parents. *Financial Counseling and Planning*, *13*(2), 93–102.

Bozoklu, S., & Yilanci, V. (2013). Energy Consumption and Economic Growth for Selected OECD Countries: Further Evidence from the Granger Causality Test in the Frequency Domain. *Energy Policy*, *63*(C), 877–881. doi:10.1016/j.enpol.2013.09.037

Brabazon, T. (2000). *Behavioural Finance: A new sunrise or a false dawn*? Retrieved from http://introduction.behaviouralfinance.net/Brab00.pdf

Brahmana, R. K., Hooy, W. W., & Ahmad, Z. (2012). Psychological factors on irrational financial decision making: Case of day-of-the week anomaly. *Humanomics*, *28*(4), 236–257. doi:10.1108/08288661211277317

Bram, J., & Ludvigson, S. (1998). Does consumer confidence forecast household expenditure? A sentiment index horse race. *FRBNY Economic Policy Review*, *4*, 59–78.

Brandão, L., Dyer, J., & Hahn, W. (2005). Using binomial trees to solve real-option valuation problems. *Decision Analysis*, *2*(2), 69–88. doi:10.1287/deca.1050.0040

Branden, N. (1971). *The psychology of self-esteem: A new concept of man's psychological nature*. Bantam Books.

Brandt, M. W., & Wang, K. Q. (2003). Time-varying risk aversion and unexpected inflation. *Journal of Monetary Economics*, *50*(7), 1457–1498. doi:10.1016/j.jmoneco.2003.08.001

Brennan, K. A., Clark, C. L., & Shaver, P. R. (1998). Self-report measurement of adult attachment. *Attachment theory and close relationships*, 46-76.

Breuer, W., Rieger, M. O., & Soypak, K. C. (2014). The behavioral foundations of corporate dividend policy a cross-country analysis. *Journal of Banking & Finance*, *42*, 247–265. doi:10.1016/j.jbankfin.2014.02.001

Brines, J., & Joyner, K. (1999). The ties that bind: Principles of cohesion in cohabitation and marriage. *American Sociological Review*, *64*(3), 333–355. doi:10.2307/2657490

Brockbank, W. (1999). If HR were really strategically proactive: Present and future directions in HR's contribution to competitive advantage. *Human Resource Management*, *38*(4), 337–352. doi:10.1002/(SICI)1099-050X(199924)38:4<337::AID-HRM8>3.0.CO;2-5

Brock, W., Lakonishock, J., & LeBaron, B. (1992). Simple technical trading rules and the stochastic properties of stock returns. *The Journal of Finance*, *47*(5), 1731–1764. doi:10.1111/j.1540-6261.1992.tb04681.x

Brown, S. J., Goetzmann, W. N., Hiraki, T., Shiraishi, N., & Watanabe, M. (2003). *Investor sentiment in Japanese and U.S. daily mutual fund flows* (NBER Working Paper, No. 9470).

Brown, A. L., & Kagel, J. H. (2009). Behavior in a simplified stock market: The status quo bias, the disposition effect and the ostrich effect. *Annals of Finance*, *5*(1), 1–14. doi:10.1007/s10436-007-0092-0

Brown, G. W., & Cliff, M. T. (2004). Investor sentiment and the near-term stock market. *Journal of Empirical Finance*, *11*(1), 1–27. doi:10.1016/j.jempfin.2002.12.001

Brown, R. (1828). A brief account of microscopical observations made in the months of June, July and August 1827 on the particles contained in the pollen of plants. *Philosophical Magazine Series 2*, *4*(21), 161–173. doi:10.1080/14786442808674769

Brown, R. L., Durbin, J., & Evans, J. M. (1975). Techniques for Testing the Constancy of Regression Relations over Time. *Journal of the Royal Statistical Society. Series B. Methodological*, *37*, 149–163.

Bruton, G. D., Keels, J. K., & Scrifes, E. L. (1999). The ethics of the complete management buyout cycle: A multi perspective analysis. *Journal of Business Ethics*, *19*(4), 403–413. doi:10.1023/A:1005987208869

Budescu, D. V., & Bruderman, M. (1995). The relationship between the illusion of control and the desirability bias. *Journal of Behavioral Decision Making*, *8*(2), 109–125. doi:10.1002/bdm.3960080204

Buehler, R., Griffin, D., & Ross, M. (1994). Exploring the planning fallacy: Why people underestimate their task completion times. *Journal of Personality and Social Psychology*, *67*(3), 366–381. doi:10.1037/0022-3514.67.3.366

Buğra, A. (2007). Yoksulluk ve sosyal haklar. *TES-İŞ Dergisi,* June.

Buğra, A., Keyder, Ç., Balaban, U., & Yakut, B. (2003). *New poverty and changing welfare regime of Turkey.* UNDP.

Buhalis, D. (2003, November 13). *eAirlines: Strategic and tactical use of ICTs in the airline industry.* Guildford, England, UK.

Bureau of Labor Statistics, United States Department of Labor. (2014). *Consumer Price Index.* Last modified October 13, 2013. http://www.bls.gov/cpi/

Bureau of Labor Statistics, United States Department of Labor. (2014). *Local Area Unemployment Statistics.* Last modified October 13, 2013. http://www.bls.gov/lau/#tables

Burns, P. (1985). Experience in decision making: A comparison of students and businessmen in a simulated progressive auction. In V. L. Smith (Ed.), *Research in experimental economics* (pp. 1–43). Greenwich, CT: JAI Press.

Büyüköztürk, Ş. (2008). Sosyal bilimleriçinverianaliz el kitabı [Handbook for the Social Sciences Data Analysis]. Ankara: Pegem Akademi Yayıncılık.

Çağlar, E., & Acar, O. (2013). *Değerlendirme notu.* TEPAV.

Çakar, B. Y. (2007). Yoksulluk ve sosyal dişlanmaya genel bakiş: Leaken göstergeleri ile Avrupa Birliği'nde durum. *TES-İŞ Dergisi,* June.

Çakmak, Z., & Kara, H. (2011). Yöneticilerde benlik algılamalarının belirlenmesi: Sanayi örgütlerinde bir araştırma. *Dumlupınar Üniversity Social Sciences Journal, 30*, 301–310.

Caman Karadağ & Cilingiroğlu. (2009). Ekonomik krizler ve sağlığa etkisi. *Toplum Hekimliği Bülteni, 28*(2), 1–11.

Camerer, C. (2005). Three cheers—psychological, theoretical, empirical—for loss aversion. *JMR, Journal of Marketing Research*, *42*(2), 129–133. doi:10.1509/jmkr.42.2.129.62286

Camerer, C., & Hogarth, R. (1999). The effects of financial incentives in experiments: A review and capital-labor production framework. *Journal of Risk and Uncertainty*, *19*(1-3), 7–42. doi:10.1023/A:1007850605129

Campbell, S., & Sharpe, S. (2007). *Anchoring Bias in Consensus Forecasts and its Effect on Market Prices* (Staff Working Paper). Finance and Economic Discussion Series. Washington, DC: Federal Reserve Board.

Campbell, J. Y. (2006). Household finance. *The Journal of Finance*, *61*(4), 1553–1604. doi:10.1111/j.1540-6261.2006.00883.x

Campbell, J. Y., Lo, A. W., & MacKinlay, A. C. (1997). *The Econometrics of Financial Markets.* Princeton: Princeton University Press.

Campos-Vazquez, R. M., & Cuilty, E. (2014). The role of emotions on risk aversion: A prospect theory experiment. *Journal of Behavioral and Experimental Economics*, *50*, 1–9. doi:10.1016/j.socec.2014.01.001

Canbas, S., & Kandir, S. Y. (2009). Investor sentiment and stock returns: Evidence from Turkey. *Emerging Markets Finance & Trade*, *45*(4), 36–52. doi:10.2753/REE1540-496X450403

Cao, J. X. (2007). *Do Buyout Sponsors Time RLBO to Exit?* (Working paper, pp. 1-20). Singapore Management University.

Caplan, G. (1981). Mastery of stress: Psychological aspects. *The American Journal of Psychiatry*, *138*(4), 413–420. doi:10.1176/ajp.138.4.413 PMID:7212098

Carroll, C. D., Fuhrer, J. C., & Wilcox, D. W. (1994). Does consumer sentiment forecast household spending? If so, why? *The American Economic Review*, *84*(5), 1397–1408.

Castanier, C., Le Scanff, C., & Woodman, T. (2010). Beyond sensation seeking: Affect regulation as a framework for predicting risk-taking behaviors in high-risk sport. *Journal of Sport & Exercise Psychology*, *32*, 731–738. PMID:20980713

Cavazotte, F., Moreno, V., & Hickmann, M. (2012). Effects of leader intelligence, personality and emotional intelligence on transformational leadership and managerial performance. *The Leadership Quarterly*, *23*(3), 443–455. doi:10.1016/j.leaqua.2011.10.003

Çelik, C., & Sünbül, Ö. (2008). Liderlik algılamalarında eğitim ve cinsiyet faktörü: Mersin ilinde bir alan araştırması. *Süleyman Demirel Üniversity Economics and Administrative Sciences Faculty Journal*, *13*(3), 49–66.

Çelikten, M., & Çelikten, Y. (2007). Televizyon programlarında çizilen öğrenci, öğretmen ve yönetici profilleri. *Social Sciences Institute Journal*, *23*(2), 369–378.

Çelik, Y. (2011). *Sağlık Ekonomisi*. Ankara: Siyasal Bookstore.

Cengiz, E., Acuner, T., & Baki, B. (2006). Liderlerin sahip oldukları duygusal zekânın örgütsel yaratıcılık üzerine etkileri: Bir model önerisi. *Atatürk Üniversity Social Sciences Institute Journal*, *7*(1), 421–433.

Center for Financial Inclusion. (2008). *Financial inclusion glossary*. Retrieved May 22, 2014, from http://www.centerforfinancialinclusion.org/publications-a-resources/financial-inclusion-glossary

Çetin, C. (2009). *Liderlik stilleri, değişim yönetimi ve ekip çalışması*. İstanbul: İTO Publishing.

Çetinkaya, Ö., & Alparslan, A. M. (2011). Duygusal zekânın iletişim becerileri üzerine etkisi: Üniversite öğrencileri üzerinde bir araştırma. *Süleyman Demirel Üniversity Economics and Administrative Sciences Faculty Journal*, *16*(1), 363–377.

Chaffey, D., Ellis-Chadwick, F., Johnston, K., & Mayer, R. (2006). *Internet Marketing: Strategy, Implementation and Practice* (3rd ed.). Essex: Prentice Hall.

Chan, W. S. (2001). Stock price reaction to news and no-news: Drift and reversal after headlines. *NBER Working Paper Series*. Retrieved August 23, 2014, from http://www.nber.org/~confer/2001/bfs01/chan.pdf

Chandler, A. D. (1962). *Strategy and Structure*. Cambridge, MA: MIT Press.

Charness, G., & Gneezy, U. (2003) '*Portfolio Choice and Risk Attitudes: An Experiment*' (February 20, 2003). Retrieved from http://ssrn.com/abstract=397300 or doi:10.2139/ssrn.397300

Charoenrook, A. (2005). *Does sentiment matter?* (Working Paper, No: 3301937). Vanderbilt University. Retrived from http://apps.olin.wustl.edu/workingpapers/pdf/2008-12-003.pdf

Chaudhuri, K., & Wu, Y. (2003). Random-walk versus breaking trend in stock prices: Evidence from emerging markets. *Journal of Banking & Finance*, *27*(4), 575–589. doi:10.1016/S0378-4266(01)00252-7

Chen, G., Kim, K. A., Nofsinger, J. R., & Rui, O. M. (2007). Trading performance, disposition effect, overconfidence, representativeness bias, and experience of emerging market investors. *Journal of Behavioral Decision Making*, *20*(4), 425–451. doi:10.1002/bdm.561

Chen, H., & Volpe, R. P. (1998). An analysis of personal financial literacy among college students. *Financial Services Review*, *7*(2), 107–128. doi:10.1016/S1057-0810(99)80006-7

Chen, H., & Volpe, R. P. (2002). Gender differences in personal financial literacy among college students. *Financial Services Review*, *11*(3), 289–307.

Chen, M., Chen, P., & Lee, C. (2013). Asymmetric effects of investor sentiment on industry stock returns: Panel data evidence. *Emerging Markets Review*, *14*, 35–54. doi:10.1016/j.ememar.2012.11.001

Chen, S. (2011a). Consumer confidence and stock returns over market fluctuations. *Quantitative Finance*, *12*(10), 1–13.

Chen, S. (2011b). Lack of consumer confidence and stock returns. *Journal of Empirical Finance*, *18*(2), 225–236. doi:10.1016/j.jempfin.2010.12.004

Cherchye, L., De Rock, B., & Vermeulen, F. (2008). *Economic well-being and poverty among the elderly: an analysis based on a collective consumption model* (Discussion Paper, IZA DP No. 3349) Bonn, Germany: Institute for the Study of Labor.

Chew, S. (1983). A generalization of the quasilinear mean with applications to the measurement of income inequality and decision theory resolving the Allais Paradox. *Econometrica*, *51*(4), 1065–1092. doi:10.2307/1912052

Chew, S. (1989). Axiomatic utility theories with the betweenness property. *Annals of Operations Research*, *19*(1-4), 273–298. doi:10.1007/BF02283525

Chew, S. H., Ebstein, R. P., & Zhong, S. (2012). Ambiguity aversion and familiarity bias: Evidence from behavioral and gene association studies. *Journal of Risk and Uncertainty*, *44*(1), 1–18. doi:10.1007/s11166-011-9134-0

Chi, L., Zhuang, X., & Song, D. (2012). Investor sentiment in the Chinese stock market: An empirical analysis. *Applied Economics Letters*, *19*(4), 345–348. doi:10.1080/13504851.2011.577003

Child & Youth Finance International. (2012). Child and youth finance education. In *An Introduction to Child and Youth Finance Education* (pp. 19–24). Developing Quality Financial Social and Livelihoods Education for Children and Youth.

Child & Youth Finance International. (2013). *Global Money Week Report 2013*, (pp.4-10). Retrieved June 2, 2014, from http://globalmoneyweek.org/resources/2014-GlobalMoneyWeek-Toolkit-sm.pdf

Child & Youth Finance International. (2014). *I Can Manage My Money (Habitat)*. Retrieved May 22, 2014, from http://childfinanceinternational.org/world-programs/europe/turkey-programs/i-can-manage-my-money-harnessing-financial-awareness-among-young-men-and-women

Chong, T. T., & Ng, W. (2008). Technical analysis and the London stock exchange: Testing the MACD and RSI rules using the FT30. *Applied Economics Letters*, *15*(14), 1111–1114. doi:10.1080/13504850600993598

Chopra, N., Lakonishok, J., & Ritter, J. (1992). Measuring abnormal performance: Do stocks overreact? *Journal of Financial Economics*, *31*(2), 235–268. doi:10.1016/0304-405X(92)90005-I

Chow, G. (1960). Test of Equality between Sets of Coefficients in two Linear Regressions. *Econometrica*, *28*(3), 591–605. doi:10.2307/1910133

Christensen-Szalanski, J. J., & Beach, L. R. (1984). The citation bias: Fad and fashion in the judgment and decision literature. *The American Psychologist*, *39*(1), 75–78. doi:10.1037/0003-066X.39.1.75

Christie, W. G., & Huang, R. D. (1995). Following the Pied Piper: Do individual returns herd around the market? *Financial Analysts Journal*, *51*(4), 31–37. doi:10.2469/faj.v51.n4.1918

Çırpan, H., & Koyuncu, M. (1998). İşletme kültürünün alt kademe yöneticileri üzerindeki etkisi: Bir örnek olay çalışması. *Kırıkkale Üniversity Economics and Administrative Sciences Faculty Journal*, *2*(9), 223–230.

Clark, A. E., Frijters, P., & Shields, M. A. (2006). *Income and happiness: Evidence, explanations and economic implications*.

Clarke, S. (2002). Budgetary management in Russian households. *Sociology*, *36*(3), 539–557. doi:10.1177/0038038502036003003

Coban, S., & Topcu, M. (2013). The Nexus between Financial Development and Energy Consumption in the EU: A Dynamic Panel Data Analysis. *Energy Economics*, *39*, 81–88. doi:10.1016/j.eneco.2013.04.001

Cohen, E. S., & Fromme, K. (2002). Differential determinants of young adult substance use and high-risk sexual behavior. *Journal of Applied Social Psychology*, *32*(6), 1124–1150. doi:10.1111/j.1559-1816.2002.tb01429.x

Coleman, L. (2014). Why finance theory fails to survive contact with the real world: A fund manager perspective. *Critical Perspectives on Accounting*, *25*(3), 226–236. doi:10.1016/j.cpa.2013.02.001

Coleman, S. (2003). Risk tolerance and the investment behavior of Black and Hispanic heads of household. *Financial Counseling and Planning*, *14*(2), 43–52.

Colledge, M. (1982). Economic cycles and health: Towards a sociological understanding of the impact of the recession on health and illness. *Social Science & Medicine*, *16*(22), 1919–1927. doi:10.1016/0277-9536(82)90391-4 PMID:7157025

Commission on Higher Education. (2009). *Statistics index*. Retrieved from http://www.ched.gov.ph/index.html

Conger, R., Conger, K., Elder, G., Lorenz, F., Simons, R., & Whitbeck, L. (1993). Family economic status and adjustment of early adolescent girls. *Developmental Psychology*, *29*(2), 206–219. doi:10.1037/0012-1649.29.2.206

Connolly, T., & Zeelenberg, M. (2002). 'Regret in Decision Making'. *Current Directions in Psychological Science*, *11*(6), 212–216. doi:10.1111/1467-8721.00203

Consumer Federation of America and American Express Company (CFAJAMEX). (1991). Student Consumer Knowledge: Results of a National Test. Washington, D.C.

Consumer Federation of America/American Express. (1991). *Report of Findings: High School Competency Test*. Washington, D.C.: Consumer Federation of America.

Consumer Research and Resource Centre. (2012).Report on the Survey of Financial Behaviours and Financial Habits of Young Workers. Accessed from http://www.crrc.org.my/crrc/A-report-on-the-survey-of-financial-behaviours-and-financial-habits-of-young-workers/pdf

Cook, S., Macaulay, S., & Coldicott, H. (2004). *Change Management Excellence Using the Four intelligences for Successful Organizational Change*. Kogan Page Limited.

Cooper, M. J., Dimitrov, O., & Rau, P. R. (2001). A rose.com by any other name. *The Journal of Finance*, *56*(6), 2371–2388. doi:10.1111/0022-1082.00408

Copulsky, J. R., & Wolf, M. J. (1990). Relationship marketing: Positioning for the future. *The Journal of Business Strategy*, *11*(4), 16–20. doi:10.1108/eb060069 PMID:10106864

Copur, Z., Gutter, S. M., & Erkal, S. (2014). Behavioral approach to financial distress and health: Globalization of financial institutions. In Dinçer, H., Hacioğlu (Ed.), A Competitive Approach of Finance and Banking, (pp: 217-233). Switzerland: Springer International Publishing. doi:10.1007/978-3-319-01125-7_16

Çopur, Z., & Şafak, Ş. (2000). Ailede gelirin kullanımına ilişkin karşılaşılan problemlerin incelenmesi [Examine the problems on using of the income in the families]. *Aile ve Toplum*, *2*(6), 7–14.

Çopur, Z., Şafak, Ş., Terzioğlu, G. R., & Dodder, R. A. (2009). Perception of adequacy of resources with a Turkish sample. *Journal of Family Issues*, *30*(12), 1624–1650. doi:10.1177/0192513X09334915

Coricelli, G., Dolan, R. J., & Sirigu, A. (2007). Brain, emotion and decision making: The paradigmatic example of regret. *Trends in Cognitive Sciences*, *11*(6), 258–265. doi:10.1016/j.tics.2007.04.003 PMID:17475537

Corredor, P., Ferrer, E., & Santamaria, R. (2013). Investor sentiment effect in stock markets: Stock characteristics or country-specific factors? *International Review of Economics & Finance*, *27*, 572–591. doi:10.1016/j.iref.2013.02.001

Council of Europe. (1996). *European Social Charter*.

Council of the European Union. (2004). *Joint report by the commission and the council on social inclusion*. Brussels.

Coval, J. D., & Shumway, T. (2005). Do behavioral biases affect prices? *The Journal of Finance*, *60*(1), 1–34. doi:10.1111/j.1540-6261.2005.00723.x

Coval, J., & Moskowitz, T. (1999). 'Home Bias at home: Local equity preference in domestic portfolios'. *The Journal of Finance*, *54*(6), 2045–2073. doi:10.1111/0022-1082.00181

Crant, J. M., & Bateman, T. S. (2000). Charismatic leadership viewed from above: The impact of proactive personality. *Journal of Organizational Behavior*, *21*(1), 63–75. doi:10.1002/(SICI)1099-1379(200002)21:1<63::AID-JOB8>3.0.CO;2-J

Çulcuoğlu, C. (2009). *Kriz Dönemlerinde Tüketim Alışkanlıklarındaki Değişim Üzerine Bir Araştırma. Sakarya üniversitesi Sosyal Bilimler Enstitüsü Yayınlanmamış Yüksek Lisans Tezi*. Sakarya.

Cummins, R. A., & Nistico, H. (2002). Maintaining life satisfaction: The role of positive cognitive bias. *Journal of Happiness Studies*, *3*(1), 37–69. doi:10.1023/A:1015678915305

Curtin, R. (2007). Consumer sentiment surveys: World review and assessment. *Journal of Business Cycle Measurement and Analysis*, *1*(1), 7–42. doi:10.1787/jbcma-v2007-art2-en

Daly, M. (1992). Europe's poor women? Gender in research on poverty. *European Sociological Review*, *8*(1), 1–12.

Danes, S. M., & Haberman, H. R. (2007). Teen financial knowledge, self-efficacy, and behavior: A gendered view. *Financial Counseling and Planning*, *18*(2), 48–60.

Danes, S. M., & Hira, T. K. (1987). Money management knowledge of college students. *Journal of Student Financial Aid*, *17*(1), 4–16.

Danes, S. M., Huddleston Casas, C., & Boyce, L. (1999). Financial planning curriculum for teens: Impact evaluation. *Financial Counseling and Planning*, *10*(1), 26–39.

Daniel, K., Hirshleifer, D., & Subrahmanyam, A. (1998). Investor psychology and security market under-and overreactions. *The Journal of Finance*, *53*(5), 1839–1886. doi:10.1111/0022-1082.00077

Daniel, K., Hirshleifer, D., & Teoh, S. H. (2002). Investor psychology in capital markets: Evidence and policy implications. *Journal of Monetary Economics*, *49*(1), 139–209. doi:10.1016/S0304-3932(01)00091-5

Dash, M. (2001). *Tulipomania: The story of world's most coveted flower and the extraordinary passions it aroused* (2nd ed.). New York: Three Rivers Press.

Davis, E. P., & Helmick, S. A. (1985). Family financial satisfaction: The impact of reference points. *Home Economics Research Journal*, *14*(1), 123–131. doi:10.1177/1077727X8501400112

De Bondt, W., Muradoglu, G., Shefrin, H., & Staikouras, S. K. (2008). Behavioral finance: Quo vadis? *Journal of Applied Finance (JAF)*, (Fall/Winter): 1–15.

de Haan, A. (2000). Social exclusion: enriching the understanding of deprivation, Retrieved March 11, 2014, from http://www.socialinclusion.org.np/userfiles/file/Arjan_de_Haan.pdf

De Laurentis, G. (Ed.). (2005). *Strategy and Organization of Corporate Banking, Springer Theoretical Drivers of Divisionalization*. Springer. doi:10.1007/b138020

De Long, J. B., Shleifer, A., Summers, L. H., & Waldmann, R. J. (1990). Noise trader risk in financial markets. *Journal of Political Economy*, *98*(4), 703–738. doi:10.1086/261703

Deacon, R. E., & Firebaugh, F. M. (1988). *Family research management* (2nd ed.). Boston: Allyn and Bacon Inc.

Deaton, A., & Paxson, C. (1998). *Inquiries in the Economics of Aging* (D. Wise, Ed.). Chicago: Chicago University Press.

DeBondt, W. F. M. (1998). A portrait of the individual investor. *European Economic Review*, *42*(3), 831–844. doi:10.1016/S0014-2921(98)00009-9

DeBondt, W., Forbes, W., Hamalainen, P., & Muragoglu, Y. G. (2010). What can behavioural finance teach us about finance? *Qualitative Research in Financial Markets*, *2*(1), 29–36. doi:10.1108/17554171011042371

DeBondt, W., Muradoglu, G., Shefrin, H., & Staikouras, S. K. (2008). Behavioural finance: Quo vadis? *Journal of Applied Finance (JAF)*, *18*(2), 7–21.

DeFond, M. L., & Park, C. W. (1999). The Effect of competition on CEO turnover. *Journal of Accounting and Economics*, *27*(1), 35–56. doi:10.1016/S0165-4101(98)00044-5

Degeorge, F., & Zeckhauser, R. (1993). The reverse LBO decision and firm performance: Theory and evidence. *The Journal of Finance*, *48*(4), 1323–1348. doi:10.1111/j.1540-6261.1993.tb04756.x

Dekel, E. (1986). An axiomatic characterization of preferences under uncertainty: Weakening the independence axiom. *Journal of Economic Theory*, *40*(2), 304–318. doi:10.1016/0022-0531(86)90076-1

DeLamater, J. D., & Myers, D. J. (2011). Social Psychology (7th ed.). Belmont, CA: Wadsworth.

Demir, C., Yılmaz, M.K., & Çevirgen, A. (2010). Liderlik yaklaşımları ve liderlik tarzlarına ilişkin bir araştırma. *Alanya Management Faculty Journal*, *2*(1).

Denis, D. J., & Denis, D. K. (1995). Performance changes following top management dismissals. *The Journal of Finance*, *50*(4), 1029–1057. doi:10.1111/j.1540-6261.1995.tb04049.x

Department Of Health. (2009a). *Health indicators*. Retrieved from http://www.doh.gov.ph/research_statistics.html

Department Of Health. (2012). *National objectives for health 2011-2016*. Retrieved from http://www.doh.gov.ph/content/national-objectives-health-2011-2016.html

Department of Health. (2012). *Philippine health system at a glance*. Retrieved from http://www.doh.gov.ph/sites/default/files/3%20chapter1.pdf

Department of Human Settlements. (2004). "Breaking New Ground": A Comprehensive Plan for the Development of Sustainable Human Settlements. Pretoria.

Department of Human Settlements. (2005). Social Housing Policy for South Africa: Towards an Enabling Environment for Social Housing Development. Pretoria.

Department of Human Settlements. (2011). Annual Report 2011/13. Pretoria.

Deshmukh, S., Goel, A. M., & Howe, K. M. (2013). CEO overconfidence and dividend policy. *Journal of Financial Intermediation*, *22*(3), 440–463. doi:10.1016/j.jfi.2013.02.003

Devaney, S. A. (1995). Retirement preparation of older and younger Baby Boomers. *Financial Counseling and Planning*, *6*, 25–33.

Devicienti, F., & Poggi, A. (2007). *Poverty and social exclusion: Two sides of the same coin or dynamically interrelated processes?* Laboratorio R. Revelli: Collegio Carlo Alberto.

Dew, J., & Xiao, J. J. (2011). The financial management behavior scale: Development and validation. *Journal of Financial Counseling and Planning*, *22*(1), 43–59.

Dhar, R., & Kumar, A. (2001, December). *A non-random walk down the main street: Impact of price trends on trading decisions of individual investors* (Working Paper). Yale School of Management.

Di Tella, R., & MacCulloch, R. (2006). Some uses of happiness data in economics. *The Journal of Economic Perspectives*, *20*(1), 25–46. doi:10.1257/089533006776526111

Diaz-Serrano, L., & O'Neill, D. (2004). *The relationship between unemployment and risk-aversion* (IZA Discussion Paper No. 1214).

Diaz-Serrano, L. (2005). On the negative relationship between labor income uncertainty and homeownership: Risk aversion vs. credit constraints. *Journal of Housing Economics*, *14*(2), 109–126. doi:10.1016/j.jhe.2005.06.002

DiCicco-Bloom, B., & Gibson, D. R. (2010). More than a game: Sociological theory from the theories of games. *Sociological Theory*, *28*(3), 247–271. doi:10.1111/j.1467-9558.2010.01377.x

Dickey, D. A., & Fuller, W. A. (1979). Distribution of the estimators for autoregressive time series with a unit root. *Journal of the American Statistical Association*, *74*(366), 427–431. doi:10.2307/2286348

Diener, E., & Oishi, S. (2000). Money and happiness: Income and subjectivewell-being across nations. In E. Diener & E. M. Suh (Eds.), *Culture and Subjective Well-being* (pp. 185–218). Cambridge: MIT Press.

Dinçer, H., Gencer, G., Orhan, N., & Şahinbaş, K. (2011). The significance of emotional intelligence on the innovative work behavior of managers as strategic decision-makers. *Procedia: Social and Behavioral Sciences*, *24*, 909–919. doi:10.1016/j.sbspro.2011.09.052

Dodds, W. B., Monroe, K. B., & Grewal, D. (1991, August). Effects of price, brand, and store information on buyers' product evaluations. *JMR, Journal of Marketing Research*, *28*(3), 307–319. doi:10.2307/3172866

Doganis, R. (2005). *Flying off Course, The Economics of International Airlines*. New York: Routledge.

Doganis, R. (2006). *The Airline Business*. New York: Routledge.

Doğan, S., & Demiral, Ö. (2007). Kurumların başarısında duygusal zekânın rolü ve önemi. *Management and Economics Journal*, *14*(1), 209–230.

Doğan, Y., & Özdevecioğlu, M. (2009). Pozitif ve negatif duygusallığın çalışanların performansları üzerindeki etkisi. *Selçuk Üniversity Economics and Administrative Sciences Faculty Social and Economical Researches Journal*, *12*(18), 165–190.

Dorn, D. (2009). Does sentiment drive the retail demand for IPOs? *Journal of Financial and Quantitative Analysis*, *44*(1), 85–108. doi:10.1017/S0022109009090024

Doukas, J. A., & Milonas, N. T. (2004). Investor sentiment and the closed-end fund puzzle: Out-of-sample evidence. *European Financial Management, 10*(2), 235–266. doi:10.1111/j.1354-7798.2004.00249.x

Doukas, J. A., & Petmezas, D. (2007). Acquisitions, overconfident managers and self-attribution bias. *European Financial Management, 13*(3), 531–577. doi:10.1111/j.1468-036X.2007.00371.x

DPT (Devler Planlama Teşkilatı). (2002). Sayılarla Türkiye Ekonomisi Gelişmeler (1980-2001) Tahminler (2002-2005).

DPT. (2006). *Ninth Five Year Development Plan*

Dremen, D., & Lufkin, E. (2000). Investor overreaction: Evidence that its basis is psychological. *The Journal of Psychology and Financial Markets, 1*(1), 61–75. doi:10.1207/S15327760JPFM0101_06

Drentea, P., & Lavrakas, P. J. (2000). Over the limit: The association among health status, race and debt. *Social Science & Medicine, 50*(4), 517–529. doi:10.1016/S0277-9536(99)00298-1 PMID:10641804

Drucker, P. (2000). *Yüzyıl Için Yönetim Tartışmaları* [Management Discussions for the 21st Century, 2nd edition]. Baskı, İstanbul, Çev. İrfan Bahçıvangil, Gülenay Gorbon, Epsilon Yayınları.

Dunn, E. W., Aknin, L. B., & Norton, M. I. (2008). Spending money on others promotes happiness. *Science, 319*(5870), 1687–1688. doi:10.1126/science.1150952 PMID:18356530

Dursun, Y., & Nakip, M. (1997). 1994 Ekonomik Krizinin İşletmelerin Pazarlama Faaliyetleri ve Tüketiciler Üzerindeki Etkileri. Üniversite-Sanayi Araştırma Birliği Vakfı Yayın No:1, Kayseri.

EAPN.(2009). *Poverty and inequality in the EU.*

Earleywine, M., & Finn, P. R. (1991). Sensation seeking explains the relation between behavioral disinhibition and alcohol consumption. *Addictive Behaviors, 16*(3–4), 123–128. doi:10.1016/0306-4603(91)90004-2 PMID:2063699

Eberlein, E., Frey, R., Kalkbrener, M., & Overbeck, L. (2007). Mathematics in Financial Risk Management. *Jahresbericht der Deutschen Mathematiker Vereinigung, 109*, 165–193.

Economou, F., Kostakis, A., & Philippas, N. (2011). Cross-country effects in herding behaviour: Evidence from four south European markets. *Journal of International Financial Markets, Institutions and Money, 21*(3), 443–460. doi:10.1016/j.intfin.2011.01.005

Edizler, G. (2010). Karizmatik liderlikte duygusal zekâ boyutuyla cinsiyet faktörüne ilişkin literatürsel bir çalışma. *Selçuk Communication Journal, 6*(2).

Edwards, W. (1968). Conservatism in human information processing. In B. Kleinmutz (Ed.), *Formal representation of human judgment* (pp. 17–52). New York, NY: John Wiley & Sons.

Egan, J. (2011). *Relationship Markering: Exploring relational strategies in marketing*. Essex: Pearson.

Einstein, A. (1905). Uber die von der molekularkinetischen Theorie der Wärme geforderte Bewegung von in ruhenden Flüssigkeiten suspendierten Teilchen. *Annalen der Physik, 322*(8), 549–560. doi:10.1002/andp.19053220806

El-Sehity, T., Haumer, H., Helmenstein, C., Kirchler, E., & Maciejovsky, B. (2002). Hindsight bias and individual risk attitude within the context of experimental asset markets. *The Journal of Psychology and Financial Markets, 3*(4), 227–235. doi:10.1207/S15327760JPFM0304_04

Elton, E. J., Gruber, M. J., & Busse, J. A. (1998). Do investors care about sentiment? *The Journal of Business, 71*(4), 477–500. doi:10.1086/209754

Enç, E. (1993). ENFLASYON: Tanımı, Ölçümü ve Sorumluları. *Ekonomik Yaklaşım, 4*(8), 1–8. doi:10.5455/ey.10801

Engelhardt, G., & Gruber, J. (2004). *Social security and the evolution of elderly poverty* (NBER Working Paper, WP 10466). National Bureau of Economic Research.

Engle, R. F., & Granger, C. W. J. (1987). Cointegration and Error Correction Representation: Estimation and Testing. *Econometrica*, *55*(2), 251–276. doi:10.2307/1913236

Englmaier, F. (2004). *A strategic rationale for having overconfident managers* (Unpublished results). Harvard University, Cambridge, MA.

Epel, E. S., Blackburn, E. H., Lin, J., Dhabhar, F. S., Adler, N. E., Morrow, J. D., & Cawthon, R. M. (2004). Accelerated telomere shortening in response to life stress. *Proceedings of the National Academy of Sciences of the United States of America*, *101*(49), 17312–17315. www.pnas.org/cgi/doi/10.1073/pnas.0407162101 Retrieved January 27, 2005

Erbil, N., & Pasinlioğlu, T. (2004). Kadının ailede karar vermeye etkisi [The efffect of the woman in decision making within the family]. *Journal of Anatolia Nursing and Health Sciences*, *7*(2), 1–11.

Erçetin, Ş. (2000). *Lider sarmalında vizyon*. Ankara: Nobel Yayın Dağıtım.

Er, D. (2009). Psikososyal açıdan yaşlılık[Elderly from a psychosocial respect]. *Fırat Sağlık Hizmetleri Dergisi*, *4*(11), 131–144.

Erdem, T. (2003).*Ankara kent yoksulları* [The urban poor in Ankara]. Unpublished doctoral dissertation, Hacettepe University, Ankara.

Erdem, A. R. (1997). İçerik kuramları ve eğitim yönetimine katkıları. *Pamukkale University Education Faculty Journal*, *3*(1), 68–77.

Erdoğan, N. (2011a). Garibanların dünyası: Türkiye'de yoksulların kültürel temsilleri üzerine ilk notlar. [The world of the wretched poor: First notes on the cultural representations of the poor in Turkey] In N. Erdoğan (Ed.), *Yoksulluk halleri: Türkiye'de kent yoksulluğunun toplumsal görünümleri* [Cases of poverty: Social aspects of urban poverty in Turkey]. (pp. 29–46). İstanbul: İletişim Yayınları.

Erdoğan, N. (Ed.). (2011b). *Yoksulluk halleri: Türkiye'de kent yoksulluğunun toplumsal görünümleri* [Cases of poverty: Social aspects of urban poverty in Turkey]. İstanbul: İletişim Yayınları.

Eren, E. (2010). *Örgütsel davranış ve yönetim psikolojisi*. İstanbul: Beta Publishing.

Eriotis, N., Vasiliou, D., & Papathanasiou, S. (2006). Testing Technical Anomalies in Athens Stock Exchange (ASE). *European Research Studies Journal*, *9*(3-4), 75–90.

Eroğluer, K. (2011). Örgütsel iletişim ile iş tatmini unsurları arasındaki ilişkiler: Kuramsal bir inceleme. *Ege Academic View Journal*, *11*(1), 121–136.

European Commission website on Employment, Social Affairs & Inclusion (n.d.) Retrieved March 12, 2014, from http://ec.europa.eu/social/main.jsp?catId=961&langId=en

European Commission. (2010a). *Special Eurobarometer poverty and social exclusion report*. Belgium.

European Commission. (2010b). *Lisbon strategy evaluation document*. Brussels.

European Commission. (2010c). *The European platform against poverty and social exclusion: A European framework for social and territorial cohesion*. Brussels.

European Commission. (2012). *The 2012 Ageing Report: Economic and Budgetary Projections for The EU 27 Member States (2010-2060)*.European Commission, Brussels. Retrieved from http://ec.europa.eu/economy_finance/publications/european_economy/2012/pdf/ee-2012-2_en.pdf

European Commission. (2013). *Employment and social affairs*. Brussels.

European Commission. (2013). Report on Public Finances in European Monetary Union European Economy (No.4/2013). Brussels: Directorate General for Economic and Financial Affairs.

European Commission. (2014). *Taking stock of the Europe 2020 strategy of smart, sustainable and inclusive growth*. Brussels.

European Commission. *Economic and Financial Affairs, AMECO database*. Retrieved from: http://eu.spindices.com/indices/real-estate/sp-case-shiller-20-city-composite-home-price-index

European Communities. (1975). *Pilot schemes and studies to combat poverty approved*. Brussels.

European Communities. (1982). *Europe against poverty*. Brussels.

Faff, R., Mulino, D., & Chai, D. (2008). On the linkage between financial risk tolerance and risk aversion. *Journal of Financial Research*, *31*(1), 1–23. doi:10.1111/j.1475-6803.2008.00229.x

Fama, E. (1965). The Behavior of Stock-Market Prices. *The Journal of Business*, *38*(1), 34–105.

Fama, E. (1970). Efficient capital markets: A review of theory and empirical work. *The Journal of Finance*, *25*(2), 383–417. doi:10.2307/2325486

Fama, E., & Blume, E. (1966). Filter rules and stock market trading. *The Journal of Business*, *39*(S1), 226–241. doi:10.1086/294849

Fama, E., & French, K. (1992). The cross-section of expected stock returns. *The Journal of Finance*, *47*(2), 427–465. doi:10.1111/j.1540-6261.1992.tb04398.x

Fan, J. X., & Xiao, J. J. (2006). Cross-cultural differences in risk tolerance: A comparison between Americans and Chinese. *Journal of Personal Finance*, *5*(3), 54–75.

Federation of Malaysian Consumers Associations. (2011). Accessed from http://www.fomca.org.my/kewangan/images/stories/pub/FLM2011(ENG).pdf

Fee, C. E., & Hadlock, C. J. (2000). Management turnover and product market competition: Empirical evidence from the U.S. newspaper industry. *The Journal of Business*, *73*(2), 205–243. doi:10.1086/209640

Fenton-O'Creevy, M., Nicholson, N., Soane, E., & Willman, P. (2003). Trading on illusions: Unrealistic perceptions of control and trading performance. *Journal of Occupational and Organizational Psychology*, *76*(1), 53–68. doi:10.1348/096317903321208880

Fernandes, D., Lynch, J. G. Jr, & Netemeyer, R. G. (2014). Financial literacy, financial education, and downstream financial behaviors. *Management Science*, 60.

Fernandez, R., & Rodrik, D. (1991). 'Resistance to Reform: Status Quo Bias in the Presence of Individual-Specific Uncertainty', American *Economic Review*[December]. *American Economic Association*, *81*(5), 1146–1155.

Ferreira, V. R. D. M. (2011, December). Can Economic Psychology and Behavioural Economics Help Improve Financial Education? In *Improvıng Fınancıal Educatıon Effıcıency: OECD-Bank of Italy Symposium on Financial Literacy.* (pp. 104-118).

Ferron, J. M., & Hess, M. R. (2007). Estimation in SEM: A concrete example. *Journal of Educational and Behavioral Statistics*, *32*(1), 110–120. doi:10.3102/1076998606298025

Festinger, L., Riecken, H. W., & Schachter, S. (1956). *When prophecy fails: A social and psychological study of a modern group that predicted the destruction of the world* (1st ed.). Minneapolis: University Of Minnesota Press. doi:10.1037/10030-000

Finke, M. S., & Huston, S. J. (2003). The brighter side of financial risk: Financial risk tolerance and wealth. *Journal of Family and Economic Issues*, *24*(3), 233–256. doi:10.1023/A:1025443204681

Finney, M. I. (2008). *Building High-Performance People and Organizations* (Volume 1 the New Employer-Employee Relationship). Praeger Perspectives.

FINRA Investor Education Foundation. (2009). *Financial Capability in the United States: National survey executive summary.* Washington, DC. Retrieved from www.finrafoundation.org/capability

FINRA. (2003). *NASD Investor Literacy Research: Executive Summary.* Retrieved May 22, 2014, from,http://www.finrafoundation.org/web/groups/foundation/@foundation/documents/foundation/p118411.pdf

Fischhoff, B., Slovic, P., & Lichtenstein, S. (1977). Knowing with certainty: The appropriateness of extreme confidence. *Journal of Experimental Psychology. Human Perception and Performance*, *3*(4), 552–564. doi:10.1037/0096-1523.3.4.552

Fischoff, B. (1975). 'Hindsight =/ Foresight:The Effect of Outcome Knowledge on Judgment Under Uncertainty'. *Journal of Experimental Psychology. Human Perception and Performance*, *1*(3), 288–299. doi:10.1037/0096-1523.1.3.288

Fisher, K. L., & Statman, M. (2000). Investor sentiment and stock returns. *Financial Analysts Journal*, *56*(2), 16–23. doi:10.2469/faj.v56.n2.2340

Fisher, K. L., & Statman, M. (2003). Consumer confidence and stock returns. *Journal of Portfolio Management*, *30*(1), 115–127. doi:10.3905/jpm.2003.319925

Fletcher, C. N., Beebout, G., & Mendenhall, S. (1997). Developing and evaluating personal finance education at the worksite: A case study. *Personal Finances and Worker Productivity*, *1*(1), 54–59.

Flores, S. A. M., & Vieira, K. M. (2014). Propensity toward indebtedness: An analysis using behavioral factors. *Journal of Behavioral and Experimental Finance*, *3*, 1–10. doi:10.1016/j.jbef.2014.05.001

Foad, H. (2010). Familiarity Bias. In *Behavioral finance: Investors, corporations, and markets*. Wiley.

Folkman, S., & Lazarus, R. S. (1980). An analysis of coping in a middle- aged community sample. *Journal of Personality and Social Psychology*, *21*, 219–239. PMID:7410799

Fox, J., Bartholomae, S., & Lee, J. (2005). Building the case for financial education. *The Journal of Consumer Affairs*, *39*(1), 195–214. doi:10.1111/j.1745-6606.2005.00009.x

Frederick, D., & Libby, R. (1986). Expertise and auditor's judgments of conjunctive events. *Journal of Accounting Research*, *24*(3), 270–290. doi:10.2307/2491134

Freiberg, K., & Freiberg, J. (1996). *Nuts! Southwest Airlines' Crazy Recipe for Business and Personal Success*. Austin, Texas: Bard Press.

French, K., & Poterba, J. (1991). Investor Diversification and International Equity Markets. *The American Economic Review*, *81*(2), 222–226.

Friedman, H. (2007). Does Overconfidence Affect Entrepreneurial Investment? *Wharton Research Scholars Journal. University of Pennsylvania.* Retrieved from http://repository.upenn.edu/wharton research scholars/42

Fromlet, H. (2001). Behavioral finance-theory and practical application. *Business Economics (Cleveland, Ohio)*, *7*(1), 63–69.

Fuchs, G. (2013). Low versus high sensation-seeking tourists: A survey of backpackers' experience risk perception. *International Journal of Tourism Research*, *15*(1), 81–92. doi:10.1002/jtr.878

Fukuda-Parr, S. (1999). What does feminization of poverty mean? It isn't just lack of income. *Feminist Economics*, *5*(2), 99–103. doi:10.1080/135457099337996

Fünfgeld, B., & Wang, M. (2008). Attitudes and behavior in everyday finance: Evidence from Switzerland. *International Journal of Bank Marketing*, *27*(9), 108–127.

Furnham, A. (1986). Economic Lotus of Control. *Human Relations*, *39*(1), 29–43. doi:10.1177/001872678603900102

Garling, T., Kirchler, E., Lewis, A., & Van Raaij, F. (2009). Psychology, financial decision making, and financial crises. *Psychological Science in the Public Interest*, *10*(1), 1–47. doi:10.1177/1529100610378437

Garman, E. T., Junk, V. W., Kim, J., O'Neill, B. J., Prochaska-Cue, K., Prawitz, A. D., ... (2005). *Financial stress among American workers, Final report*. Retrieved March, 23, 2005, from http://www.personalfinancefoundation.org/features/Financial-Distress-Among-American-Workers-Final-Report-full.html

Garman, E. T., Kim, J., Kratzer, C. Y., Brunson, B. H., & Joo, S. H. (1999). Workplace financial education improves personal financial wellness. *Financial Counseling and Planning*, *10*(1), 79–88.

Garman, E. T., Sorhaindo, B., Bailey, W., Kim, J., & Xiao, J. J. (2004a). Financially Distressed Credit Counseling Clients and the InCharge Financial Distress Scale, *Proceedings of the Eastern Regional Family Economics and Resource Management Association* (pp.71-81).

Garman, E. T., Sorhaindo, B., Kim, J., Xiao, J. J., Bailey, W., & Prawitz, A. (2004b). The evaluation of the beta version of the ıncharge financial distress scale. *Consumer Interests Annual*, *50*, 134–144.

Gazete Vatan. (2014, Ocak 13). *Türkiye'nin alışveriş istatistiği*. Retrieved Mayıs 17, 2014, from http://haber.gazetevatan.com/turkiyenin-alisveris-istatistigi/600264/184/haber

General Directorate on the Status of Women. (2008). *Kadın ve Yoksulluk* (pp. 1–20). Ankara.

Germain, L., Rosseau, F., & Vanhems, A. (2005, July). Optimistic and pessimistic trading in financial markets (Working Paper).

Gerrans, P., Faff, R. W., & Hartnett, N. (2012, February). Individual financial risk tolerance and the global financial crisis. In *25th Australasian Finance and Banking Conference*. doi:10.2139/ssrn.1990811

Gervais, S., Heaton, J. B., & Odean, T. (2011). Overconfidence, compensation contracts, and capital budgeting. *The Journal of Finance*, *66*(5), 1735–1777. doi:10.1111/j.1540-6261.2011.01686.x

Gervais, S., & Odean, T. (2001). Learning to be overconfident. *Review of Financial Studies*, *14*(1), 1–27. doi:10.1093/rfs/14.1.1

Ghani, G. M. (2013). Does Trade Liberalization Effect Energy Consumption? *Energy Policy*, *43*, 285–290. doi:10.1016/j.enpol.2012.01.005

Gibbons, R. S. (1997, Winter). An introduction to applicable game theory. *The Journal of Economic Perspectives*, *11*(1), 127–149. doi:10.1257/jep.11.1.127

Gibson, J. L., Ivancevich, J. M., Donnelly, J. H., & Konopaske, R. (2009). *Organizations: Behavior, Structure, Processes* (14th ed.). McGraw-Hill.

Gilbert, D. C. (1996). Relationship marketing and airline loyalty schemes. *Tourism Management*, *17*(8), 575–582. doi:10.1016/S0261-5177(96)00078-7

Gilovich, T., Griffin, D., & Kahneman, D. (2002). *Heuristics and biases: The psychology of intuitive judgment*. Cambridge, UK: Cambridge University Press. doi:10.1017/CBO9780511808098

Gilovich, T., Vallone, R., & Tversky, A. (1985). The hot hand in basketball: On the misperception of random sequences. *Cognitive Psychology*, *17*(3), 295–314. doi:10.1016/0010-0285(85)90010-6

Gittell, J. H. (2003). *The Southwest Airlines Way*. New York: McGraw-Hill.

Glaser, M., Noth, M., & Weber, M. (2004). Behavioral finance. In D. J. Koehler & N. Harvey (Eds.), *Blackwell handbook of judgment and decision making* (pp. 527–546). Oxford, UK: Blackwell. doi:10.1002/9780470752937.ch26

Glass, J. C. Jr, & Kilpatrick, B. B. (1998). Gender comparisons of baby boomers and financial preparation for retirement. *Educational Gerontology*, *24*(8), 719–745. doi:10.1080/0360127980240802

Godfrey, N. S. (2006). Making our students smart about money. *Education Digest*, *71*(7), 21–26.

Godoi, C. K., Marcon, R., & Barbosa da Silva, A. (2005). Loss Aversion: A Qualitative Study In Behavioural Finance. *Managerial Finance*, *31*(4), 46–56. doi:10.1108/03074350510769613

Godwin, D. D. (1990). Family financial management. *Family Relations*, *39*(2), 221–228. doi:10.2307/585728

Goel, A. M., & Thakor, A. V. (2008). Overconfidence, CEO selection, and corporate governance. *The Journal of Finance*, *63*(6), 2737–2784. doi:10.1111/j.1540-6261.2008.01412.x

Goetzmann, W. N., & Kumar, A. (2005). *Why Do Individual Investors Hold Under-Diversified Portfolios?* Yale School of Management.

Goldberg, J., & Von Nitzsch, R. (1999). *Behavioural finance*. John Willey & Sons.

Goldsmith, E. B. (2000). *Resource management for individuals and families* (2nd ed.). Florida: Florida State University Wadsworth Thomson Learning.

Goldsmith, R. (1969). *Financial structure and development*. New York: Yale University Press.

Goleman, D. (2012). *Duygusal zeka neden IQ' dan daha önemlidir?* (B. S. Yüksel, Trans.). İstanbul: Varlık Publishing.

Gönen, E., Hablemitoğlu, Ş., & Özmete, E. (1997). *Değişen Türkiye'de İnsan Hakları Açısından Sosyal Hizmetler* (K. Karataş, Ed.). Ankara: Sosyal Hizmet Uzmanları Derneği Genel Merkezi.

Gonzalez, C., Dana, J., Koshino, H., & Just, M. (2005). The framing effect and risky decisions: Examining cognitive functions with fMRI. *Journal of Economic Psychology*, *26*(1), 1–20. doi:10.1016/j.joep.2004.08.004

Goodman, A., & Oldfield, Z. (2004). *Permanent differences? Income and expenditure inequality in the 1990s and 2000s* (Report Series No 66). Retrieved April 13, 2013, from www.ifs.org.uk/comms/r66.pdf

Gottesman, A., & Morey, M. (2010). CEO educational background and firm financial performance. *Journal of Applied Finance (JAF)*, *20*(2), 70–82.

Gottschalk, P. (2008). The rising instability of US earnings. *The Journal of Economic Perspectives*, 3–24.

Grable, J. E. (2000). Financial risk tolerance and additional factors which affect risk taking in everyday money matters. *Journal of Business and Psychology*, *14*(4), 625–630. doi:10.1023/A:1022994314982

Grable, J. E. (2008). Risk tolerance. In J. J. Xiao (Ed.), *Handbook of Consumer Finance Research*. New York, NY: Springer. doi:10.1007/978-0-387-75734-6_1

Grable, J. E., & Joo, S. (1999). Financial help-seeking behavior: Theory and implications. *Financial Counseling and Planning*, *10*(1), 25–38.

Grable, J. E., & Joo, S.-H. (2004). Environmental and biopsychosocial factors associated with financial risk tolerance. *Financial Counseling and Planning*, *15*(1), 73–88.

Grable, J. E., & Lytton, R. H. (1999). Financial risk tolerance revisited: The development of a risk assessment instrument. *Financial Services Review*, *8*(3), 163–181. doi:10.1016/S1057-0810(99)00041-4

Grable, J. E., & Lytton, R. H. (2001). Assessing the concurrent validity of the SCF risk tolerance question. *Financial Counseling and Planning*, *12*(2), 43–53.

Graham, J. R., & Harvey, C. R. (2001). The theory and practice of corporate finance: Evidence from the field. *Journal of Financial Economics*, *60*(2-3), 187–243. doi:10.1016/S0304-405X(01)00044-7

Granger, C. W. J. (1969). Investigating causal relations by econometric models and cross-spectral methods. *Econometrica*, *37*(3), 424–438. doi:10.2307/1912791

Granger, C. W. J. (1988). Some recent development in a concept of causality. *Journal of Econometrics*, *39*(1-2), 199–211. doi:10.1016/0304-4076(88)90045-0

Gratton, B. (1996). The poverty of impoverishment theory: The economic well-being of the elderly. *The Journal of Economic History*, *56*(1), 39–61. doi:10.1017/S0022050700016016

Grigoli, F., & Kapsoli, J. (2013), *Waste Not, Want Not: The Efficiency of Health Expenditure in Emerging and Developing Countries* (IMF Working Paper 13/87). Washington.

Grinblatt, M., & Hahn, B. (2005). Prospect theory, mental accounting, and momentum. *Journal of Financial Economics*, *78*(2), 311–339. doi:10.1016/j.jfineco.2004.10.006

Grinblatt, M., & Keloharju, M. (2001). How distance, language, and culture influence stockholdings and trades. *The Journal of Finance*, *56*(3), 1053–1073. doi:10.1111/0022-1082.00355

Grinblatt, M., & Keloharju, M. (2001). What makes investors trade? *The Journal of Finance*, *56*(2), 589–616. doi:10.1111/0022-1082.00338

Grönroos, C. (1994). From marketing mix to relationship marketing: Towards a paradigm shift in marketing. *Management Decision*, *32*(2), 4–20. doi:10.1108/00251749410054774

Grönroos, C. (1999). Relationship marketing: Challenges for the organization. *Journal of Business Research*, *46*(3), 327–335. doi:10.1016/S0148-2963(98)00030-7

Grönroos, C. (2004). The relationship marketing process: Communication, interaction, dialogue, value. *Journal of Business and Industrial Marketing*, *19*(2), 99–113. doi:10.1108/08858620410523981

Gruen, T. W. (1995). The outcome set of relationship marketing in consumer markets. *International Business Review*, *4*(4), 447–469. doi:10.1016/0969-5931(95)00026-7

Güçlü, N. (2001). Stres yönetimi. *G.Ü. Gazi Eğitim Fakültesi Dergisi*, *21*(1), 91–109.

Guermat, C., & Harris, R. (2002). Robust conditional variance estimation and value-at-risk. *Journal of Risk*, *4*, 25–41.

Gujarati, D. (2004). *Basic Econometrics*. Tata: McGraw Hill.

Güleç, M., & Tekbaş, Ö. F. (1997). Sağlık perspektifinden yaşlılık[The health of elderly]. *Türkiye Klinikleri Tıp Bilimleri Dergisi, 17*(6), 369–377.

Gul, F. (1991). A theory of disappointment in decision making under uncertainty. *Econometrica, 59*(3), 667–686. doi:10.2307/2938223

Gummesson, E. (1994). Making relationship operational. *International Journal of Service Industry Management, 5*(5), 5–20. doi:10.1108/09564239410074349

Gummesson, E. (1997). Relationship marketing as a paradigm shift: Some conclusions from the 30R approach. *Management Decision, 35*(4), 267–272. doi:10.1108/00251749710169648

Gummesson, E. (1998). Implementation requires a relationship marketing paradigm. *Journal of the Academy of Marketing Science, 26*(3), 242–249. doi:10.1177/0092070398263006

Gummesson, E. (2002). Relationship marketing in the new economy. *Journal of Relationship Marketing, 1*(1), 37–57. doi:10.1300/J366v01n01_04

Gummesson, E. (2002). *Total Relationship Marketing*. Oxford: Butterworth-Heinemann.

Günay, G. (2006). *Bireylerin kişi ve aile olarak emekliliğe hazırlanmalarına ilişkin plan* [individuals' planning in preparation for retirement as an individual and a family]. Published doctoral thesis, Hacettepe University, Turkey.

Günay, G. (2013). Emekliliği planlama süreci ölçeğinin Türkçe geçerlilik ve güvenirlilik çalışması: Karabük Üniversitesi örneği.[Turkish reliability and validity study of the process of the retirement planning scale: The Example of Karabük University]. *Türk Geriatri Dergisi, 16*(1), 84–94.

Gündoğan, N. (2008). Türkiye'de yoksulluk ve yoksullukla mücadele. [Poverty and the struggle against poverty in Turkey]. *Ankara Sanayi Odası. Asodosya.* Ocak-Şubat. 42-56.

Gundogan, N. (2008). Türkiye'de yoksullukla mücadele, Ankara. *Sanayi Odası Dergisi,* January/February.

Gunnarsson, J., & Wahlund, R. (1997). Household financial strategies in Sweden: An exploratory study. *Journal of Economic Psychology, 18*(2-3), 201–233. doi:10.1016/S0167-4870(97)00005-6

Gupta, S., Hanssens, D., Hardie, B., Kahn, W., Kumar, V., Lin, N., & Sriram, S. (2006, November). Modeling customer lifetime value. *Journal of Service Research, 9*(2), 139–155. doi:10.1177/1094670506293810

Gutter, M. S., Copur, Z., & Blanco, A. (2014). Racial differences in financial socialization and financial behaviors of U.S. college students. In H. Dinçer & Ü. Hacioğlu (Eds.), *Global Strategies in Banking and Finance* (pp. 272–292). Hershey, PA: Business Science Reference; doi:10.4018/978-1-4666-4635-3.ch018

Gutter, M. S., Fox, J., & Montalto, C. P. (1999). Racial differences in investor decision making. *Financial Services Review, 8*(3), 149–162. doi:10.1016/S1057-0810(99)00040-2

Gutter, M., & Copur, Z. (2011). Financial behaviors and financial well-being of college students: Evidence from a national survey. *Journal of Family and Economic Issues, 32*(4), 699–714. doi:10.1007/s10834-011-9255-2

Habisch, A., Jonker, J., Wegner, M., & Schmidpeter, R. (2005). *Corporate Social Responsibilities across Europe*. Springer Germany. doi:10.1007/b138371

Hablemitoğlu, Ş., & Özmete, E. (2010). *Yaşlı refahı: Yaşlılar için sosyal hizmet.* Ankara: Kilit Yayınları.

Habschick, M., Seidl, B., & Evers, J. (2007). Survey of financial literacy schemes in the EU27, Hamburg. (pp.24-30).

Hair, J. F., Black, W. C., Babin, B. J., & Anderson, R. E. (2010). *Multivariate data analysis: a global perspective*. Upper Saddle River, N.J.: Pearson.

Hall, B. J., & Murphy, K. J. (2002). Stock options for undiversified executives. *Journal of Accounting and Economics, 33*(1), 3–42. doi:10.1016/S0165-4101(01)00050-7

Hallowell, R. (1996). The relationships of customer satisfaction, customer loyalty, and profitability:an empirical study. *International Journal of Service Industry Management, 7*(4), 27–42. doi:10.1108/09564239610129931

Halpern, P. (1999). On the heterogeneity of leveraged going private transactions. *Review of Financial Studies*, *12*(2), 281–309. doi:10.1093/rfs/12.2.281

Hanna, S. D., & Lindamood, S. (2005). Risk tolerance of married couples. In the *Proceedings of the Academy of Financial Services*, G2 (pp. 1-28).

Hanna, S. D., Gutter, M. S., & Fan, J. X. (2001). A measure of risk tolerance based on economic theory. *Financial Counseling and Planning*, *12*(2), 53–60.

Hanna, Sh., Fan, J. X., & Chang, R. Y. (1995). Optimal life cycle savings. *Financial Counseling and Planning*, *6*, 1–15.

Hansen, B. E. (1992). Tests for Parameter Instability in Regressions with I(1) Processes. *Journal of Business & Economic Statistics*, *10*, 321–335.

Hanssens, D. M., & Dekimpe, M. G. (2008). Models for the Financial-Performance Effects. In B. Wieranga (Ed.), *Handbook of Marketing Decision Models* (pp. 501–523). Los Angeles: Springer ScienceþBusiness Media. doi:10.1007/978-0-387-78213-3_15

Harker, P. T., & Zenios, S. A. (1998). *What Drives the Performance of Financial Institutions*, Working Paper, the Wharton School, University of Pennsylvania.

Harrington, B. (2010). *On the limitations of behavioral finance*. Retrieved December 12, 2013, from http://thesocietypages.org/economicsociology/2010/10/31/on-the-limitations-of-behavioral-finanance/

Harris Scholastic Research (HSR). (1993). *Liberty financial young investor survey*. New York, NY.

Harvey, N., & Bolger, F. (1996). Graphs versus tables: Effects of data presentation format on judgmental forecasting. *International Journal of Forecasting*, *12*(1), 119–137. doi:10.1016/0169-2070(95)00634-6

Harvey, N., & Reimers, S. (2013). Trend damping: Under-adjustment, experimental artifact, or adaptation to features of the natural environment? *Journal of Experimental Psychology. Learning, Memory, and Cognition*, *39*(2), 589–607. doi:10.1037/a0029179 PMID:22774857

Harveys, B. (1994). *Combating exclusion 1989-1994 lessons from the third EU poverty programme in Ireland.* Retrieved March 18, 2014, fromhttp://www.combatpoverty.ie/publications/CombatingExclusion_1994.pdf

Haselton, M. G., & Buss, D. M. (2003). Design Flaws or Design Features? *Social judgments: Implicit and explicit processes, 5*, 23.

Haselton, M. G., Nettle, D., & Andrews, P. W. (2005). The evolution of cognitive bias. The handbook of evolutionary psychology, 724-746.

Haselton, M. G., & Buss, D. M. (2000). Error management theory: A new perspective on biases in cross-sex mind reading. *Journal of Personality and Social Psychology*, *78*(1), 81–91. doi:10.1037/0022-3514.78.1.81 PMID:10653507

Haselton, M. G., & Nettle, D. (2006). The paranoid optimist: An integrative evolutionary model of cognitive biases. *Personality and Social Psychology Review*, *10*(1), 47–66. doi:10.1207/s15327957pspr1001_3 PMID:16430328

Hatch, M. J., & Cunliffe, A. L. (2013). *Organization Theory Modern, Symbolic, and Postmodern Perspectives* (3rd ed.). UK: Oxford University Press.

Haveman, R., & Wolff, E. N. (2005). Who are the asset poor? Levels, trends, and composition, 1983-1998. *Inclusion in the American dream: Assets, poverty, and public policy* (pp. 61-86).

Heath, C., & Tversky, A. (1991). Preference and belief: Ambiguity and competence in choice under uncertainty. *Journal of Risk and Uncertainty*, *4*(1), 5–28. doi:10.1007/BF00057884

Heider, F. (1958). *The psychology of interpersonal relations*. New York, NY: John Wiley & Sons. doi:10.1037/10628-000

Heifetz, A., & Siegel, Y. (2001, October). *The evolution of biased perceptions* (Working Paper).

Heimdal, K. R., & Houseknecht, S. K. (2003). Cohabiting and married couples income organization: Approaches in Sweden and the United States. *Journal of Marriage and the Family*, *65*(3), 525–538. doi:10.1111/j.1741-3737.2003.00525.x

Henderson, P., & Peterson, P. (1992). Mental accounting and categorization. *Organizational Behavior and Human Decision Processes*, *51*(1), 92–117. doi:10.1016/0749-5978(92)90006-S

Hennig-Thurau, T., Gwinner, K. P., & Gremler, D. D. (2002). Understanding relationship marketing outcomes. *Journal of Service Research*, *4*(3), 230–247. doi:10.1177/1094670502004003006

Henry, R. A., Weber, J. G., & Yarbrough, D. (2001). Money Management Practices Of College Students. *College Student Journal*, *35*(2).

Heo, W., Grable, J. E., & Chatterjee, S. (2013). Life insurance consumption as a function of wealth change. *Financial Services Review*, *22*(4), 389–404.

Hilgert, M., Hogarth, J., & Beverley, S. (2003). *Household financial management: The connection between knowledge and behavior*. (Technical Report #309-322). Federal Reserve Bulletin.

Hill, R. P., & Gaines, J. (2007). The consumer culture of poverty: Behavioral research findings and their implications in an ethnographic context. *Journal of American Culture*, *30*(1), 81–95. doi:10.1111/j.1542-734X.2007.00466.x

Hilton, D. J. (2001). The psychology of financial decision-making: Applications to trading, dealing, and investment analysis. *The Journal of Psychology and Financial Markets*, *2*(1), 37–53. doi:10.1207/S15327760JPFM0201_4

Hira, T. K. (1987). Satisfaction with money management practices among dual-earner households. *Journal of Home Economics*, *79*(2), 19–22.

Hira, T. K., & Mueller, M. J. (1987). The application of managerial systems to money management practices. *Iowa State Journal of Research*, *62*(2), 219–233.

Hira, T. K., & Mugenda, O. (1998). Predictors of financial satisfaction: Differences between retirees and non-retirees. *Financial Counseling and Planning*, *9*(2), 75–83.

Hira, T. K., & Mugenda, O. M. (2000). Gender Differences in Financial Perceptions, Behaviors and Satisfaction. *Journal of Financial Counseling and Planning*, *13*(2), 86–92.

Hirshleifer, D. (2001). Investor psychology and asset pricing. *The Journal of Finance*, *56*(4), 1533–1597. doi:10.1111/0022-1082.00379

Hirshleifer, D., Low, A., & Toeh, S. H. (2012). Are overconfident CEOs better innovators? *The Journal of Finance*, *67*(4), 1457–1498. doi:10.1111/j.1540-6261.2012.01753.x

Hoffmann, A., & Post, T. (2012, 22 November). *What makes investors optimistic, what makes them afraid*. (Netspar Working Paper Series No. 44).

Hoffmann, A. O. I., & Post, T. (2014). Self-attribution bias in consumer financial decision-making: How investment returns affect individuals' belief in skill. *Journal of Behavioral and Experimental*, *52*, 23–28. doi:10.1016/j.socec.2014.05.005

Hogan, K. M., Olson, G. T., & Kish, R. J. (2001). A comparison of reverse leveraged buyouts and original initial public offers: Factors impacting their issuance in IPO market. *Financial Review*, *38*(3), 1–18. doi:10.1111/j.1540-6288.2001.tb00017.x

Hogarth, J. M. (1991). Assest management and retired households: Savers, dissavers and alternators. *Financial Counseling and Planning*, *2*, 97–122.

Hogarth, J. M. (2002). Financial literacy and family and consumer sciences. *Journal of Family and Consumer Sciences*, *94*(1), 14–28.

Hollensen, S. (2010). *Marketing Management, A Relationship Approach* (2nd ed.). Essex: Prentice Hall.

Holloway, S. (2008). *Straight and Level: Practical Airline Economics* (3rd ed.). Aldershot, Hampshire: Ashgate.

Holthausen, R. W., & Larcker, D. F. (1996). The financial performance of reverse leveraged buyouts. *Journal of Financial Economics*, *42*(3), 293–332. doi:10.1016/0304-405X(96)00884-7

Hooley, G., Piercy, N. F., & Nicoulaud, B. (2008). *Marketing Strategy and Competetive Positioning* (4th ed.). Essex: Prentice Hall.

Horvath, P., & Zuckerman, M. (1993). Sensation seeking, risk appraisal and behavior. *Personality and Individual Differences*, *14*(1), 41–52. doi:10.1016/0191-8869(93)90173-Z

Hougaard, S., & Bjerre, M. (2002). *Strategic Relationship Marketing*. Heidelberg: Springer. doi:10.1007/978-3-540-24813-2

Huberman, G. (2001). Familiarity breeds investment. *Review of Financial Studies*, *14*(3), 659–680. doi:10.1093/rfs/14.3.659

Hugo, P. (2004). Dutch Housing Allowances: Social Housing at Risk. *International Journal of Urban and Regional Research*, *28*(3), 706–712. doi:10.1111/j.0309-1317.2004.00545.x

Hu, L. T., & Bentler, P. (1995). Evaluating model fit. In R. H. Hoyle (Ed.), *Structural Equation Modeling. Concepts, Issues, and Applications* (pp. 76–99). London: Sage.

Hull, J., & White, A. (1998). Incorporating volatility updating into the historical simulation method forvalue-at-risk. *The Journal of Risk*, *1*, 5–19.

Human Development Report. (2009). *Community-based care*. Retrieved from http://hdr.undp.org/en/content/human-development-report-2009

Hung, A., Parker, A. M., & Yoong, J. K. (2009). *Defining and measuring financial literacy* (Working Paper, WR-708) Rand Corparation.

Hüsnüoğlu, N., & Güler, A. (2010). Krizin tüketim harcamalari üzerine etkisi: Giresun ili uygulamasi. *Marmara Üniversitesi İİBF Dergisi*, *29*(2), 197–226.

Huson, M. R., Malatesta, P. H., & Parrino, R. (2004). Managerial succession and firm performance. *Journal of Financial Economics*, *74*(2), 237–275. doi:10.1016/j.jfineco.2003.08.002

Huston, S. J. (2010). Measuring financial literacy. *The Journal of Consumer Affairs*, *44*(2), 296–316. doi:10.1111/j.1745-6606.2010.01170.x

Hwang, S., & Satchell, S. E. (2010, 19 February). *How loss averse are investors in financial markets*? (Working Paper).

IATA. (2010). *Annual Report 2010*. Berlin: June.

IATA. (2011). *The Impact of September 11 2001 on Aviation*. IATA.

İbicioğlu, H., Özmen, H. İ., & Taş, S. (2009). Liderlik davranışı ve toplumsal norm ilişkisi: Ampirik bir çalışma. *Süleyman Demirel Üniversity Economics and Administrative Sciences Faculty Journal*, *14*(2).

İçağasıoğlu, Ç. A. (2006).Yoksulluğun aile sistemi üzerindeki etkileri ve yoksul ailelere ilişkin sosyal hizmet müdahalesi. [The effects of poverty on the family system and social work intervention in poor families].In Ü. Onat (Ed.), *Sosyal Hizmet Sempozyumu 2003: Yoksullukve Sosyal Hizmetler [Social Work Symposium 2003: Poverty and Social Work]*. (196-204). Vol.1. Antalya, 9-11 Ekim 2003, Ankara: Hacettepe Üniversitesi Sosyal Hizmetler Yüksekokuluve Sosyal Hizmet Uygulama, Araştırmave Geliştirme Derneği.

Içli, G. (2008). Yaşlılar ve yetişkin çocuklar[Elderly people and adults]. *Yaşlı Sorunları ve Araştırma Dergisi*, *1*, 29–38.

İlban, M. O., & Kaşlı, M. (2013). A model of commitment for Generation Y: A survey on airline companies. *Istanbul University Journal of the School of Business*, *42*(1), 133–152.

IMF (2010). *Macro-Fiscal Implications of Health Care Reform in Advanced and Emerging Economies*.

IMF (2014). *Fiscal Monitor*. April 2014.

Indro, D. C. (2004). Does mutual fund flow reflect investor sentiment? *Journal of Behavioral Finance*, *5*(2), 105–115. doi:10.1207/s15427579jpfm0502_4

Ingstad, B., & Eide, A. H. (2011). *Disability and poverty: a global challenge*. USA: The Policy Press.

Insider Mortgage Finance (2010). In *The Mortgage Market Statistical Annual* (Vol. 1). Bethesda, MD: Insider Mortgage Finance Publishing.

International Labour Organization (ILO). (2011). *Financial education for youth*. Retrieved May 22, 2014, from http:// www.ilo.org/publns

International Monetary Fund. (2012, October). World Economic Outlook, Coping with High Debt and Sluggish Growth (p. 190).

International Organization for Standardization (ISO). (2009a). *ISO Guide 73:2009 Risk Management Vocabulary*. Retrieved from http://www.iso.org/iso/iso_catalogue/catalogue_tc/catalogue_detail.htm?csnumber=44651

International Organization for Standardization. (2005). *ISO 22222:2005 Personal financial planning: Requirements for personal financial planners.*

Irwin, C. E. (1993). Adolescence and risk taking: How are they related? In N. J. Bell & R. W. Bell (Eds.), *Adolescent risk taking*. Newbury Park, CA: Sage.

Irwin, C. E., & Millstein, S. G. (1986). Biopsychosocial correlates of risk-taking behaviors during adolescence: Can the physician intervene? *Journal of Adolescent Health Care*, *7*(Suppl), 82S–96S. PMID:3536822

Işık, S., Duman, K., & Korkmaz, A. (2004). Türkiye ekonomisinde finansal krizler: Bir faktör analizi uygulaması. *D.E.Ü. İ.İ.B.F. Dergisi*, *19*(1), 45–69.

Islam, F., Shahbaz, M., Ahmed, A. U., & Alam, M. M. (2013). Financial Development and Energy Consumption Nexus in Malaysia: A Multivariate Time Series Analysis. *Economic Modelling*, *30*, 435–441. doi:10.1016/j.econmod.2012.09.033

Islam, F., Shahbaz, M., & Alam, M. (2011). *Financial Development and Energy Consumption Nexus in Malaysia: A Multivariate Time-Series Analysis. MPRA Paper 28403*. Germany: University Library of Munich.

ISO. (2014). *Kadın sanayiciler platformu*. Retrieved March 18, 2014, from file:///C:/Users/davuthang%C3%BCnayd%C4%B1n/Downloads/8_MART_MANIFEST OSU-ek-363%20(1).pdf

Iversen, R. R., Napolitano, L., & Furstenberg, F. F. (2011). Middle-income families in the economic downturn: Challenges and management strategies over Time. *Longitudinal and Life Course Studies: International Journal*, *2*(3), 286–300.

Jansen, W. J., & Nahuis, N. J. (2003). The stock market and consumer confidence: European evidence. *Economics Letters*, *79*(1), 89–98. doi:10.1016/S0165-1765(02)00292-6

Jegadeesh, N., & Titman, S. (1993). Returns to buying winners and selling losers. *Implications for Stock Market Efficiency*, *48*, 65–91.

Jehoel-Gijsbers, G., & Vrooman, C. (2007). *Explaining social exclusion: A theoretical model tested in the Netherlands*. The Hague: The Netherlands Institute for Social Research.

Jensen, M. (1978). Some anomalous evidence regarding market efficiency. *Journal of Financial Economics*, *6*(2-3), 95–101. doi:10.1016/0304-405X(78)90025-9

Jensen, M. (1989). Takeovers: Their causes and Consequences. *The Journal of Economic Perspectives*, *2*(1), 21–48. doi:10.1257/jep.2.1.21

Jensen, M. C. (1989). Eclipse of public corporations. *Harvard Business Review*, *67*, 61–75.

Jiang, L., & Gao, L. (2013). Investor sentiment and IPO pricing during pre-market and aftermarket periods: Evidence from Hong Kong. *Pacific-Basin Finance Journal*, *23*, 65–82. doi:10.1016/j.pacfin.2013.01.006

Jing, G., Hao, C., & Xian, Z. (2013). Influence of psychological and emotional factors on the venture enterprise value and the investment decision-making. *Procedia Computer Science*, *17*, 919–929. doi:10.1016/j.procs.2013.05.117

Johansen, S. (1988). Statistical analysis of cointegration vector. *Journal of Economic Dynamics & Control*, *12*(2/3), 231–254. doi:10.1016/0165-1889(88)90041-3

Johansen, S. (1991). Estimation and hypothesis testing of cointegration vectors in gaussian vector autoregressive models. *Econometrica*, *59*(6), 1551–1580. doi:10.2307/2938278

Johansen, S., & Juselies, K. (1990). Maximum Likelihood Estimation and Inferences on Cointegration. *Oxford Bulletin of Economics and Statistics*, *52*, 169–210. doi:10.1111/j.1468-0084.1990.mp52002003.x

Johar, S. S., Shah, I. M., & Bakar, Z. A. (2012). The impact of emotional intelligence towards relationship of personality and self-esteem at work place. *Procedia: Social and Behavioral Sciences*, *65*(3), 150–155. doi:10.1016/j.sbspro.2012.11.104

Johnson, E., & Sherraden, M. S. (2007). From financial literacy to financial capability among youth. *Journal of Sociology and Social Welfare*, *34*(3), 119–146.

Jones, T. O., & Sasser, W. E. (1995, November-December). Why Satisfied Customers Defect. *Harvard Business Review*, 88-99.

Joo, S. H., & Pauwels, V. W. (2002). Factors affecting workers' retirement confidence: A gender perspective. *Financial Counseling and Planning*, *13*(2), 1–10.

Joo, S., & Grable, J. E. (2004). An exploratory framework of the determinants of financial satisfaction. *Journal of Family and Economic Issues*, *25*(1), 25–50. doi:10.1023/B:JEEI.0000016722.37994.9f

Jordan, B., & Miller, T. (2008). *Fundamentals of investments*. New York, NY: McGraw-Hill.

Joumard, I., Andre, C., & Nicq, C. (2010), *Health Care Systems: Efficiency and Institutions* (Working Paper No. 769). Paris: Economics Department, Organisation for Economic Co-operation and Development.

Jureviciene, D., Bikas, E., & Gausiene, E. (2012). Behavioural finance during economic downturn in Lithuania. In *The 7th International Scientific Conference Business and Management 2012* (pp. 75-83). Selected Papers. May 10-11, 2012. Vilnius Gediminas Technical University.

Kabaklı Çimen, L. (2012). Bir faktör olarak eğitimin kadının aile içi kararlara katılımı üzerine etkisi (The effect of education, as a factor, on the participation of women in domestic decisions). *International Journal of New Trends in Arts. Sports and Science Education*, *1*(2), 78–90.

Kaestner, M. (2005, March). *Anomalous price behavior following earnings surprises: Does representativeness cause overreaction*? (Working Paper). Université Montpellier II.

Kahler, R. (2007). 'Beyond the Numbers'. *Financial Planning*. May

Kahneman, D. (2003). A psychological perspective on economics. *The American Economic Review*, *93*(2), 162–168. doi:10.1257/000282803321946985

Kahneman, D., & Riepe, M. W. (1998). Aspects of investor psychology. *Journal of Portfolio Management*, *24*(1), 52–65. doi:10.3905/jpm.1998.409643

Kahneman, D., Slovic, P., & Tversky, A. (1982). *Judgment under uncertainty: Heuristics and biases*. Cambridge, UK: Cambridge University Press. doi:10.1017/CBO9780511809477

Kahneman, D., & Tversky, A. (1979). *Prospect theory: An analysis of decision under risk. Econometrica*, *47*(2), 263–292. doi:10.2307/1914185

Kahneman, D., & Tversky, A. (2000). *Choices, values and frames*. Cambridge, UK: Cambridge University Press.

Kahneman, D., & Tversky, A. (Eds.). (2000). *Choices, values, and frames*. Cambridge, U.K.: Cambridge University Press.

Kaliski, B. S. (2007). *Encyclopedia of Business and Finance* (2nd ed., Vol. 2). J–Z, Thomson Gale.

Kanagal, N. (2005). Role of Relationship Marketing in Competitive Marketing Strategy. *Journal of Management and Marketing Research*, 1-17.

Kaplan, S. N., & Stein, J. D. (1991). *The evolution of buyout pricing and financial structure in the 1980s* (Discussion Paper). University of Chicago

Kaplan, S. N. (1989). The effects of management buyouts on operating performance and value. *Journal of Financial Economics*, *24*(2), 217–254. doi:10.1016/0304-405X(89)90047-0

Kaplan, S. N. (1991). The staying power of leverage buyouts. *Journal of Financial Economics*, *29*(2), 287–314. doi:10.1016/0304-405X(91)90004-4

Kaplan, S. N. (1997). The evaluation of US corporate governance: We are all Henry Kravis now. *Journal of Private Equity*, *1*, 7–14. doi:10.3905/jpe.1997.409664

Karabıçak, M. (2002). Küreselleşme sürecinde Gelişmekte Olan Ülke Ekonomilerinde Ortaya Çıkan Yönelim ve Tepkiler. *Süleyman Demirel Üniversitesi İktisadi İdari Bilimler Fakültesi Dergisi*, *7*(1), 115–131.

Karabıçak, M. (2010). Küresel Krizleri Tetikleyen Nedenler ve Küresel Krizin Türkiye Boyutu. *Süleyman Demirel Üniversitesi İktisadi ve İdari Bilimler Fakültesi Dergisi*, *15*(3), 251–270.

Karaca, Ş. (2010). Hizmet Sektöründe İlişki Pazarlaması. *Selçuk ÜNiversitesi İİBF Sosyal ve Ekonomik Araştırmalar Dergisi*, *13*(9), 440–455.

Karluk, R. (2009). Cumhuriyet'in İlanından Günümüze Türkiye Ekonomisi'nde Yapısal Dönüşüm. Beta yayıncılık. İstanbul.

Kasser, T., & Ahuvia, A. (2002). Materialistic values and well-being in business students. *European Journal of Social Psychology*, *32*(1), 137–146. doi:10.1002/ejsp.85

Katarachia, A., & Konstantinidis, A. (2014). Financial education and decision making processes. *Procedia Economics and Finance*, *9*, 142–152. doi:10.1016/S2212-5671(14)00015-X

Katz, M. L. (1991). Game-playing agents: Unobservable contracts as precommitments. *The Rand Journal of Economics*, *22*(3), 307–328. doi:10.2307/2601049

Kaya, E. (2009). *Yoksullukla mücadelede Avrupa'nın ve Türkiye'nin sosyal modeli*. Directorate of Social Assistance and Solidarity.

Kaya, İ., & Kozak, M. A. (2006). *Kariyer uygulamaları ve duygusal zekâ: Beş yıldızlı otel işletmesinde bir araştırma. III.* Postgraduate Tourism Students Research Congress National Free Proceedings.

Kayamandi Development Services. (2011). *Economic Impact and Expenditure of Housing Delivery Programmes from 1994 to 2010.National Department of Human Settlements*. Pretoria: NDHS.

Kaynak, T. (1975). Beşeri ilişkiler açısından yönetim ve verimlilik. *İstanbul University Management Faculty Management Economics Institute Journal, 1*(2).

Keçecioğlu, T., & Çiçek, A. (2012). Örgüt DNA'sına Yerleşen Yeni Bir Kavram ve Marka: Örgütsel ve Stratejik Çeviklik (Örgütsel Bağışıklık Sistemini Güçlendirmek). *Marmara Üniversitesi İ.İ.B. Fakültesi Dergisi*, *33*(2), 295–308.

Keil, M., Depledge, G., & Rai, A. (2007). Escalation: The role of problem recognition and cognitive bias. *Decision Sciences*, *38*(3), 391–421. doi:10.1111/j.1540-5915.2007.00164.x

Kelley, H. H. (1967). Attribution theory in social psychology. *Nebraska Symposium on Motivation*, *15*, 192–238.

Kelley, H. H., & Michela, J. L. (1980). Attribution theory and research. *Annual Review of Psychology*, *31*(1), 457–501. doi:10.1146/annurev.ps.31.020180.002325 PMID:20809783

Kempf, A., & Ruenzi, S. (2006). Status Quo Bias and the Number of Alternatives: An Empirical Illustration from the Mutual Fund Industry. *Journal of Behavioral Finance*, *7*(4), 204–213. doi:10.1207/s15427579jpfm0704_3

Kempson, E. (2011,December). A framework for developing international financial literacy surveys. In *Improving Financial Education Efficiency: OECD-Bank Of Italy Symposium on Financial Literacy* (pp.13-41).

Kenny, D. A. (2014). Measuring model fit [reference website]. Retrieved from http://davidakenny.net/cm/fit.htm

Keren, G., & Teigen, K. H. (2004). Yet another look at the heuristics and biases approach. Blackwell handbook of judgment and decision making, 89.

Kerkmann, B. C., Lee, T. R., Lown, J. M., & Allgood, S. M. (2000). Financial management, financial problems and marital satisfaction among recently married university students. *Financial Counseling and Planning Education*, *11*(2), 55–64.

Keynes, J. M. (1967). *The General Theory of Employment, Interest, and Money*. London: McMillan. (Originally published 1936)

Khan, M. A., Khan, M. Z., Zaman, K., Khan, M. M., & Zahoor, H. (2013). (in press). Growth Factors Determining Financial Development Impact on SAARC's Energy Demand: Energy-starved or Energy-efficient Region? *Energy Policy*. doi:10.1016/j.enpol.2013.07.135

Kibritçioğlu, A. (2001). Türkiye'de Ekonomik Krizler ve Hükümetler, 1969-2001.*Yeni Türkiye Dergisi, Ekonomik Kriz Özel Sayısı*, 1, *7*(41) (Eylül-Ekim),174-182.

Kim, J., Garman, E. T., & Sorhaindo, B. (2003). Relationship among credit counseling clients' financial wellbeing, financial behaviors, financial stressor events, and health. *Financial Counseling and Planning*, *14*, 75–87.

Kim, J., Garman, T., & Sorhaindo, B. (2003). Relationship among credit counseling clients' financial well-being, financial behaviors, financial stressor events, and health. *Financial Counseling and Planning*, *14*(2), 75–87.

Kinney, A. (2000). Positive Illusions of Well-Being and Irrationality: Implications for Rational-Emotive Behaviour Therapy. *Journal of Contemporary Psychotherapy*, *30*(4), 401–415. doi:10.1023/A:1010235620775

Kishore, R. (2006). *Theory of behavioural finance and its application to property market: A change in paradigm*. Paper presented at the Twelfth Annual Pacific Rim Real Estate Society Conference, Auckland, New Zealand.

Klein, C., & Gotti, R. (1992). *Overcoming Regret: Lessons from the Roads Not Taken*. Bantam Books.

Klein, J. T. (1990). *Interdisciplinarity: History, theory, and practice*. Detroit, MI: Wayne State University Press.

Kliger, D., & Kudryavtsev, A. (2010). The availability heuristic and investors' reaction to company specific events. *Journal of Behavioral Finance*, *11*(1), 50–65. doi:10.1080/15427561003591116

Kline, R. B. (2011). *Principles and Practice of Structural Equation Modeling* (3rd ed.). New York, NY: The Gulford Press.

Kling, G., & Gao, L. (2008). Chinese institutional investors' sentiment. *International Financial Markets. Institutions and Money*, *18*(4), 374–387. doi:10.1016/j.intfin.2007.04.002

Kloman, H. (1999). Does risk matter? EARTH Matters, Special Edition on Risk Management, Lamont-Doherty Earth Observatory, Columbia University.

Kobliner, B. (2010). *Money as You Grow: 20 Things Kids Need to Know to Live Financially Smart Lives*. Retrieved May 24, 2014, from http://moneyasyougrow.org

Koesten, J. (2005). Reducing stress and burnout for financial planners. *Journal of Financial Planning*, *18*(10), 64–74.

kokpit.aero. (2013, Ağustos 21). *Kokpit.aero*. Retrieved Haziran 21, 2014, from http://kokpit.aero/index.php?route=content/flight_fear&flight_fear_id=55

Kosedag, A., Mehran, J., & Qian, J. (2009). Reverse-LBOs, re-LBOs and informational asymmetry hypothesis of LBO transactions. *Managerial Finance*, *35*, 716–728.

Kotler, P. (2000). *Marketing Management, Milennium Edition*. Upper Saddle River, New Jersey: Prentice-Hall, Inc.

Kotler, P., & Keller, K. L. (2009). *Marketing Management*. New Jersey: Prentice Hall.

Krause, N., Jay, G., & Liang, J. (1991). Financial strain and psychological wellbeing among the American and Japanese elderly. *Psychology and Aging*, *6*(2), 170–181. doi:10.1037/0882-7974.6.2.170 PMID:1863386

Krohne, H. W. (2002). *Stress and coping theories*. Retrieved March 10, 2014, from http://userpage.fu-berlin.de/schuez/folien/Krohne_Stress.pdf

Kruythoff, H. (2008). *Tenant Participation in the Netherlands: The role of Laws, Covenants and (power) Positions*. Housing Studies.

Küçükkancabaş, S., Akyol, A., & Ataman, B. M. (2007, August 15). *Examination of the effects of the relationship marketing orientation on the company performance*. Springer Science+Business Media.

Kuhnen, C. M., & Knutson, B. (2005). The neural basis of financial risk taking. *Neuron*, *47*(5), 763–770. doi:10.1016/j.neuron.2005.08.008 PMID:16129404

Kumar, A. (2009). Hard-to-value stocks, behavioral biases, and informed trading. *Journal of Financial and Quantitative Analysis*, *44*(6), 1375–1401. doi:10.1017/S0022109009990342

Kumar, N., Scheer, L., & Kotler, P. (2000). From Market Driven to Market Driving. *European Management Journal*, *18*(22), 129–142.

Kumar, V., Pozza, I. D., Peterson, J. A., & Shah, D. (2009). Reversing the Logic: The Path to Profitability through Relationship Marketing. *Journal of Interactive Marketing*, 147–156.

Kwiatkowski, D., Phillips, P. C. B., Schmidt, P., & Shin, Y. (1992). Testing the Null Hypothesis of Stationarity against the Alternative of a Unit Root. *Journal of Econometrics*, *54*(1-3), 159–178. doi:10.1016/0304-4076(92)90104-Y

Kwon, K., & Kish, R. (2002). Technical trading strategies and return predictability: NYSE. *Applied Financial Economics*, *12*(9), 639–653. doi:10.1080/09603100010016139

Lakonishok, J., Shleifer, A., & Vishny, R. W. (1991). *Do institutional investors destabilize stock prices- evidence on herding and feedback trading* (NBER Working paper, no. 3846).

Lange, C., & Byrd, M. (1998). The relationship between perception of financial distress and feelings of psychological well-being in New Zeland university students. *International Journal of Adolescence and Youth*, *7*(3), 193–209. doi:10.1080/02673843.1998.9747824

Langer, E. J. (1975). The illusion of control. *Journal of Personality and Social Psychology*, *32*(2), 311–328. doi:10.1037/0022-3514.32.2.311

Lang, L. H. P., & Stulz, R. M. (1992). Contagion and competitive intra-industry effects ofbankruptcy announcements: An empirical analysis. *Journal of Financial Economics*, *32*, 45–60. doi:10.1016/0304-405X(92)90024-R

Langrehr, F. W. (1979). Consumer education: Does it change students' competencies and attitudes? *The Journal of Consumer Affairs*, *13*(1), 41–53. doi:10.1111/j.1745-6606.1979.tb00126.x

Laux, P., Starks, L. T., & Yoon, P. S. (1998). The relative importance of competition and contagion in intra-industry information transfers: An investigation of dividend announcements. *Financial Management*, *27*(3), 5–16. doi:10.2307/3666270

Lawrence, P. R., & Lorsch, J. W. (1967). *Organization and Environment: Managing Differentiation and Integration*. Boston: Harvard Business School Press.

Lazarus, R. S. (1966). *Psychological Stress and the coping process*. New York: McGraw-Hill.

Lea, S. E. G., Tarpy, R. M., & Webiey, P. (1987). *The individual in the economy*. Cambridge: Cambridge University Press.

Lee, C., Shleifer, A., & Thaler, R. H. (1991). Investor sentiment and the closed-end fund puzzle. *The Journal of Finance*, *46*(1), 75–109. doi:10.1111/j.1540-6261.1991.tb03746.x

Lee, D. (2007). *The Economics of Airline Institutions, Operations and Marketing*. Cambridge, USA: Elsevier.

Lee, W. K. M. (2003). Women and retirement planning: Towards the "feminization of poverty" in an aging Hong Kong. *Journal of Women & Aging*, *15*(1), 31–53. doi:10.1300/J074v15n01_04 PMID:12678184

Leick, R. (2007, October). *Building Airline Passenger Loyalty through an Understanding of Customer Value: A Relationship Segmentation of Airline Passengers*. PhD Thesis, Cranfield University.

Lemmon, M., & Portniaguina, E. (2006). Consumer confidence and asset prices: Some empirical evidence. *Review of Financial Studies*, *19*(4), 1499–1529. doi:10.1093/rfs/hhj038

Leonard, D. C., & Shull, D. M. (1996). Investor sentiment and the closed-end fund evidence: Impact of the January effect. *The Quarterly Review of Economics and Finance*, *36*(1), 117–126. doi:10.1016/S1062-9769(96)90032-0

Lettau, M., & Ludvigson, S. (2001). Consumption, aggregate wealth, and expected stock returns. *The Journal of Finance*, *56*(3), 815–849. doi:10.1111/0022-1082.00347

Levine, R. (1997). Financial Development and Economic Growth: Views and Agenda. *Journal of Economic Literature*, *35*(2), 688–726.

Li, B., Shang, W., Li, H., Huo, L., & Xu, S. (2014). Disposition effect in an agent-based financial market model. *Procedia Computer Science*, *31*, 680–690. doi:10.1016/j.procs.2014.05.316

Li, J., Ren, G., Ma, Q., & Liu, L. (2009). An experimental study on investors' status quo bias and its determinants. *Frontiers of Business Research in China*, *3*(4), 543–565. doi:10.1007/s11782-009-0026-y

Lin, J. Y., & Treichel, V. (2012, January). *The Unexpected Global Financial Crisis, Researching Its Root Cause* (Policy Research WP: 5937). The World Bank.

Lindgreen, A., & Crawford, I. (1999). Implementing, Monitoring and Measuring Programme of Relationship Marketing. *Marketing Intelligence & Planning*, 231–239.

Lintner, J. (1965). The valuation of risk assets and the selection of risky investments in stock portfolios and capital budgets. *The Review of Economics and Statistics*, *73*(1), 13–37. doi:10.2307/1924119

Lisbon European Council. (2000). Retrieved February 20, 2014, from http://www.europarl.europa.eu/summits/lis1_en.htm

Liston-Heyes, C. (2002). Pie in the sky? Real versus perceived values of air miles. *Journal of Consumer Policy*, *25*(1), 1–26. doi:10.1023/A:1014594718701

Liu, J., & Wang, M. C. (2010). Narrow framing: Professions, sophistication and experience. *Journal of Futures Markets*, *30*(3), 203–244.

Li, Y., & Yang, L. (2013). Prospect theory, the disposition effect, and asset prices. *Journal of Financial Economics*, *107*(3), 715–739. doi:10.1016/j.jfineco.2012.11.002

Lo, A. W., & MacKinlay, C. (1988). Stock Market Prices Do Not Follow Random Walks: Evidence from a Simple Specification Test. *Review of Financial Studies*, *1*(1), 41–66. doi:10.1093/rfs/1.1.41

Lo, H. Y., & Harvey, N. (2012). Effects of shopping addiction on consumer decision making: Web-based studies in real time. *Journal of Behavioral Addictions*, *1*(4), 162–170. doi:10.1556/JBA.1.2012.006

Long, W. F., & Ravenscraft, D. J. (1993). LBOs, Debt and R&D Intensity. *Strategic Management Journal, 14 (summer),* 119-135.

Loomes, G., & Sugden, R. (1982). Regret theory: An alternative theory of rational choice under uncertainty. *The Economic Journal*, *92*(368), 805–824. doi:10.2307/2232669

Lord, C., Ross, L., & Lepper, M. (1979). Biased assimilation and attitude polarization: The effects of prior theories on subsequently considered evidence. *Journal of Personality and Social Psychology*, *37*(11), 2098–2109. doi:10.1037/0022-3514.37.11.2098

Lovric, M., Kaymak, U., & Spronk, J. (2008). *A Conceptual Model of Investor Behaviour* (ERIM Report Series Reference No. ERS-2008-030-F&A). Retrieved from http://ssrn.com/abstract=1144293

Luce, M. F. (1998). Choosing to Avoid: Coping with Negatively. Emotion-Laden Consumer Decisions. *The Journal of Consumer Research*, *24*(4), 409–433. doi:10.1086/209518

Lusardi, A. (2008). *The importance of being financially literate*.

Lusardi, A. (2008a). *Household saving behavior: The role of financial literacy, information, and financial education programs* (NBER Working Paper 13824).

Lusardi, A. (2008b). Financial literacy: An essential tool for informed consumer choice? (Dartmouth College Working Paper).

Lusardi, A., & Tufano, P. (2008). *Debt literacy, financial experiences, and over in debtedness* (Dartmouth Working Paper).

Lusardi, A., Mitchell, O. S., & Curto, V. (2010). *Financial literacy among the young: Evidence and implications for consumer policy* (NBER Working Paper Series, Working Paper No. 15352, pp. 3-30). Center for Financial Studies (CFS).

Lusardi, A., & Mitchell, O. S. (2007). Financial literacy and retirement preparedness: Evidence and implications for financial education. *Business Economics*, *42*(January), 35–44. doi:10.2145/20070104

Lyons, A. C., & Yılmazer, T. (2005). Health and financial strain: Evidence from the survey of consumer finances. *Southern Economic Journal*, *71*(4), 873–890. doi:10.2307/20062085

Maastricht Treaty. (1992). Retrieved April 1, 2014, from http://www.eurotreaties.com/maastrichtprotocols.pdf

MacCallum, R. C., Browne, M. W., & Sugawara, H. M. (1996). Power analysis and determination of sample size for covariance structure modeling. *Psychological Methods*, *1*(2), 130–149. doi:10.1037/1082-989X.1.2.130

Mackay, C. (2003). *Memoirs of extraordinary popular delusions and the madness of crowds. original.* Minneapolis, New York: Dover Publication Inc.(Originally published 1841)

Macroeconomic Outlook Report. (2012). Republic of Turkey Ministry of Finance Strategy Development Unit, May-June, Vol. 19, 1-15. Retrieved from http://www.maliye.gov.tr/Lists/TabMenuIcerik/ Attachments/107/ Macroeconomic%20Outlook%20Report%20may-june%202012.pdf

Mahajan, J. (1992). The overconfidence effect in marketing management predictions. *JMR, Journal of Marketing Research*, *29*(3), 329–342. doi:10.2307/3172743

Malmendier, U., & Tate, G. (2005). CEO overconfidence and corporate investment. *The Journal of Finance*, *60*(6), 2661–2700. doi:10.1111/j.1540-6261.2005.00813.x

Malmendier, U., & Tate, G. (2008). Who makes acquisitions? CEO overconfidence and the market's reaction. *Journal of Financial Economics*, *89*(1), 20–43. doi:10.1016/j.jfineco.2007.07.002

Mandelbrot, B. B. (1963). The variation of certain speculative prices. *The Journal of Business*, *XXXVI*, 392–417.

Mandell, L. (2008). Background the 1997-98 Baseline Survey of High School Seniors. The Financial Literacy of Young American Adults Result of the 2008 National Jump$Tart Coalition Survey of High School Seniors and College Students (pp.7-8). Washington, DC: The Jump$Tart Coalition for Personal Financial Literacy.

Mandell, L. (1997). *Personal Financial Survey of High School Seniors. Jump Start Coalition for Personal Financial Literacy* (p. 7). Washington, D.C.: March/April.

Mandell, L. (2007). Financial Literacy of High School Students. In J. J. Xiao (Ed.), *Handbook of Consumer Finance Research* (pp. 163–183). New York, NY: Springer.

Mandell, L., & Klein, L. S. (2009). The impact of financial literacy education on subsequent financial behavior. *Journal of Financial Counseling and Planning*, *20*(1), 15–24.

Man, L. W. (1998). *Relationship marketing: the case of Cathay Pacific*. Hong Kong: The University of Hong Kong.

Manring, S. L. (2003). How Do You Create Lasting Organizational Change? You must first slay Grendel's Mother. *Research in Organizational Change and Development*, *14*, 195–224. doi:10.1016/S0897-3016(03)14083-9

Manusov, V., & Spitzberg, B. H. (2008). Attributes of attribution theory: Finding good cause in the search for theory. In D. O. Braithwaite & L. A. Baxter (Eds.), *Engaging Theories in Interpersonal Communication* (pp. 37–49). Thousand Oaks, CA: Sage. doi:10.4135/9781483329529.n3

Marangoz, M., & Uluyol, O. (2010). Küresel Ekonomik Krizin Tüketicilerin Harcama ve Tasarruf Eğilimleri Üzerine Etkilerinin Belirlenmesine Yönelik Bir Araştırma. *Muhasebe ve Finansman Dergisi*, *45*, 82–98.

Marjanovic, Z., Greenglass, E. R., Fiksenbaum, L., & Bell, C. M. (2013). Psychometric evaluation of the Financial Threat Scale (FTS) in the context of the great recession. *Journal of Economic Psychology*, *36*, 1–10. doi:10.1016/j.joep.2013.02.005

Markowitz, H. M. (1952). Portfolio selection. *The Journal of Finance*, *7*(1), 77–91.

Marlowe, J., & Godwin, D. (1988). The relationship of income and human capital to debt/asset ratio of farm families. *Home Economics Research Journal*, *17*(1), 93–109. doi:10.1177/1077727X8801700110

Marshall, J. A., Trimmer, P. C., Houston, A. I., & McNamara, J. M. (2013). On evolutionary explanations of cognitive biases. *Trends in Ecology & Evolution*, *28*(8), 469–473. doi:10.1016/j.tree.2013.05.013 PMID:23790393

Martin, E. (1998). Behind the rhetoric: The institutional basis of social exclusion and poverty. *IDS Bulletin*, *29*(1), 42–49. doi:10.1111/j.1759-5436.1998.mp29001005.x

Mason, C., & Wilson, R. (2000). Conceptualizing Financial Literacy (Research Series Paper 2000:7, pp. 4–34). London: Business School, Laughborough University.

Massa, M., & Simonov, A. (2005). Behavioral biases and investment. *Review of Finance*, *9*(4), 483–507. doi:10.1007/s10679-005-4998-y

Masud, J. (2007, July). *Testing of Malaysia's Financial Well-Being Scale*. Paper presented in the Seventh Biennial Conference 2007 ACFEA, Purajaya, Malaysia.

Matheson, T. (2013). *The Global Financial Crisis: An Anatomy of Global Growth.* IMF WP: 13/76, March.

Maxim, A. (2009). Relationship Marketing: A New Paradigm in Marketing Theory and Practice. University of Iasi, 287-300.

Maxwell, S. (1999). The meaning and measurement of poverty (Poverty briefing: 3). Overseas Development Institute.

Mayer, J. D., & Salovey, P. (1993). The intelligence of emotional intelligence. *Intelligence*, *17*(4), 433–442. doi:10.1016/0160-2896(93)90010-3

Mazzeo, M. A., & Yilmaz, N. (2014). The effect of CEO overconfidence on turnover abnormal returns. *Journal of Behavioral and Experimental Finance*, *3*, 11–21. doi:10.1016/j.jbef.2014.07.001

McGarry, K., & Schoeni, R. (2005). Widow(er) poverty and out-of-pocket medical expenditures near the end of the life. *Journal of Gerontology*, *60*(3), 160–168. doi:10.1093/geronb/60.3.S160 PMID:15860793

McInish, T. (1982). Individual investors and risk-taking. *Journal of Economic Psychology*, *2*(2), 125–136. doi:10.1016/0167-4870(82)90030-7

McIntyre, J. R., Ivanaj, S., & Ivanaj, V. (2009). *Multinational Enterprises and the Challenge of Sustainable Development*. Cheltenham, UK: Edward Elgar.

Mckenna, F. P. (1993). It won't happen to me-unrealistic optimism or illusion of control. *British Journal of Psychology*, *84*(1), 39–50. doi:10.1111/j.2044-8295.1993.tb02461.x

McKensey and Company. (2011, October). Sales 2.0 For Airlines. *Cost Analyse*. McKensey and Company.

McKinnon, R. (1973). *Money and capital in economic development*. Washington, DC: Brookings Institution.

McKinsey Global Survey Results. (2009). April retrieved from http://www.mckinsey.com/

McNeil, A., & Frey, R. (2000). Estimation of tail-related risk measures for heteroscedastic financial time series: An extreme value approach. *Journal of Empirical Finance*, *7*(3-4), 271–300. doi:10.1016/S0927-5398(00)00012-8

Mendel, B., & Shleifer, A. (2012). Chasing noise. *Journal of Financial Economics*, *104*(2), 303–320. doi:10.1016/j.jfineco.2011.02.018

Merikas, A. A., Merikas, A. G., Vozikis, G. S., & Prasad, D. (2004). Economic factors and individual investor behaviour: The case of the Greek stock exchange. *Journal of Applied Business Research*, *20*(4), 93–98.

Merton, R. C. (1969). Lifetime portfolio selection under uncertainty: The continuous-time case. *The Review of Economics and Statistics*, *51*(3), 247–257. doi:10.2307/1926560

Mian, S., & Rosenfeld, J. (1993). Takeover activity and the long run performance of reverse leverage buyouts. *Financial Management*, *22*(Winter), 46–57. doi:10.2307/3665576

Michael, H., & Morris, J. B. (1998). Relationship marketing in practice. *Industrial Marketing Management*, *27*, 360–361.

Miller, N., & Pazgal, A. (2002). Relative performance as a strategic commitment mechanism. *Managerial and Decision Economics*, *23*(2), 51–68. doi:10.1002/mde.1045

Mill, J. S. (1968). *Essays on Some Unsettled Questions of Political Economy*. New York: Augustus M. Kelley. (Original work published 1844)

Mills, R. J., Grasmick, H. G., Morgan, C. S., & Wenk, D. (1992). The effects of gender, family satisfaction, and economic strain on psychological well-being. *Family Relations*, *41*(4), 440–446. doi:10.2307/585588

Ministry of Family and Social Policies. (n.d.). *Mevzuat*. Retrieved from http://www.aile.gov.tr/mevzuat/mevzuat

Mintzberg, H. (1987). Crafting Strategy. *Harvard Business Review*, *87*(4), 67.

Mirowsky, J., & Ross, C. (2003). *Social causes of psychological distress* (2nd ed.). New York: Aldine de Gruyter.

Mishkin, F. S. (2004). *The Economics of Money, Banking and Financial Markets* (7th ed.). New York: Pearson Addison Wesley.

Mishra, A., Mishra, V., & Smyth, R. (2014). *The random-walk hypothesis on the Indian stock market* (Discussion Paper: 07/14). Monash University, Department of Economics.

Mitchell, W. J. T. (1995). Interdisciplinary and visual culture. *The Art Bulletin*, *77*(4), 540–544.

Monti, M., & Legrenzi, P. (2009). *Investment Decision-Making and Hindsight Bias*. Retrieved on 15th September 2009 from http://141.14.165.6/CogSci09/papers/135/paper135.pdf

Montier, J. (2002). *Darwin's Mind: The Evolutionary Foundations of Heuristics and Biases*. Retrieved from http://papers.ssrn.com/sol3/papers.cfm?abstract_id=373321

Montier, J. (2002). *Behavioural finance: Insights into irrational minds and markets*. Hoboken, NJ: John Wiley & Sons.

Moore, D. (2003). Survey of financial literacy in Washington State: Knowledge, behavior, attitudes, and experiences. (Technical Report Num: 03-39), Social and Economic Sciences Research Center, Washington State University.

Morel-Guimaraes, L., Khalil, T. M., & Hosni, Y. A. (2005). Management of Technology Key Success Factors for Innovation and Sustainable Development. Selected Papers from the *Twelfth International Conference on Management of Technology*. Elsevier.

Morgan, R. M., & Hunt, S. D. (1994). The commitment-trust theory of relationship marketing. *Journal of Marketing, 58*(3), 20–38.

Morris, M. H., Brunyee, J., & Page, M. (1998). Relationship marketing in practice: Myths and realities. *Industrial Marketing Management, 27*, 359–371.

Mossin, J. (1966). Equilibrium in a capital asset market. *Econometrica, 34*(4), 768–783. doi:10.2307/1910098

Mudakkar, S. R., Zaman, K., Shakir, H., Arif, M., Naseen, I., & Naz, L. (2013). Determinants of energy consumption function in SAARC countries: Balancing the odds. *Renewable & Sustainable Energy Reviews, 28*, 566–574. doi:10.1016/j.rser.2013.08.006

Mugenda, O. M., Hira, T. K., & Fanslow, A. M. (1990). Assessing the causal relationship among communication, money management practices, satisfaction with financial status, and satisfaction with quality of life. *Lifestyles: Family and Economic Issues, 11*(4), 343–360. doi:10.1007/BF00987345

Mukhopadyay, S., & Shambhu, S. (2011). *Analyzing linkages between gender and poverty: A methodological note*. Retrieved from http://www.isst-india.org/PDF/Gender%20and%20Poverty-Methodological%20Note%20GN%20II.pdf

Mullainathan, S. (2009). How behavioral economics can help change the fight against poverty. Retrieved December 9, 2013, fromhttp://seedmagazine.com/content/article/poor_decision_making/

Muradoglu, G., Altay-Salih, A., & Mercan, M. (2005). A behavioral approach to efficient portfolio formation. *Journal of Behavioral Finance, 6*(5), 202–212. doi:10.1207/s15427579jpfm0604_4

Muscarella, C. J., & Vetsuypens, M. R. (1989). The under pricing of 'second' initial public offerings. *Journal of Financial Research, 12*(3), 183–192. doi:10.1111/j.1475-6803.1989.tb00512.x

Muscarella, C. J., & Vetsuypens, M. R. (1990). Efficiency and organizational structure: A study of reverse LBOs. *The Journal of Finance, 45*(5), 1389–1413. doi:10.1111/j.1540-6261.1990.tb03720.x

Mynatt, J. (2009). *Encyclopedia of Management* (6th ed.). Gale, Cengage Learning.

National Assessment of Educational Progress (NAEP). (1979). *Teenage Consumers: A Profile*. Denver, CO.

National Council for Economic Education (NCEE). (2005). *What American Teens & Adults Know About Economics*. Retrieved May 22, 2014, from http://www.ncee.net/cel/WhatAmericansKnowAboutEconomics_042605-3.pdf

National Housing Finance Corporation, (2013). *Report of Tenant Audit Survey for Housing Association.*

National Statistical Coordination Board. (2010). *National statistical coordination board*. Retrieved from http://nscb.gov.ph/

National Statistical Coordination Board. (2013). *Philippine indicators for 2013*. Retrieved from http://www.nscb.gov.ph/stats/pnha/#sthash.CQmpSwVK_dpuf

National Treasury. (2014). *Finance Minister's Budget Policy Statement, 2014/15*. Cape Town: Parliament.

Nawrocki, D., & Viole, F. (2014). Behavioral finance in financial market theory, utility theory, portfolio theory and the necessary statistics: A review. *Journal of Behavioral and Experimental Finance*, *2*, 10–17. doi:10.1016/j.jbef.2014.02.005

Neal, R., & Wheatley, S. M. (1998). Do measures of investor sentiment predict returns? *Journal of Financial and Quantitative Analysis*, *33*(4), 523–547. doi:10.2307/2331130

Neftci, S. (1991). Naive trading rules in financial markets and Wiener-Kolmogorov prediction theory: A study of "technical analysis.". *The Journal of Business*, *24*(4), 549–571. doi:10.1086/296551

Nelson, D. L., & Quick, J. C. (2008). *Understanding Organizational Behaviour* (3rd ed.). Canada: Thompson South Western.

Neupane, S., Paudyal, K., & Thapa, C. (2014). Firm quality or market sentiment: What matters more for IPO investors? *Journal of Banking & Finance*, *44*, 207–218. doi:10.1016/j.jbankfin.2014.04.010

Nevins, D. (2004). Goals-based investing integrating traditional and behavioral finance. *The Journal of Wealth Management*, *6*(4), 8–23. doi:10.3905/jwm.2004.391053

Nga, J. K. H., & Yien, L. K. (2013). The influence of personality trait and demographics on financial decision making among Generation Y. *Young Consumers*, *14*(3), 230–243. doi:10.1108/YC-11-2012-00325

Nicholson, W., & Snyder, C. M. (2008). *Microeconomic theory: Basic principles and extensions*. Stamford, CT: Thomson Publishing.

Nickerson, C., Schwarz, N., & Diener, E. (2007). Financial aspirations, financial success, and overall life satisfaction: Who? and how? *Journal of Happiness Studies*, *8*(4), 467–515. doi:10.1007/s10902-006-9026-1

Nielsen (2013a). *Q1 2013 Global Consumer Confidence Report*. Retrieved from https://docs.google.com/file/d/0B05V_TqPz0euN09KMGdBb2hieTQ/edit?usp=sharing

Nielsen (2013b). *Q2 2013 Global Consumer Confidence Report*. Retrieved from https://docs.google.com/file/d/0B05V_TqPz0euX050VF9wUHQ5dHM/edit?usp=sharing

Nofsinger, J. R. (2001). *Investment Madness: How Psychology Affects Your Investing--and what to Do about it*. Financial Times Prentice Hall.

Noone, J. H. (2010). *Psychological and socioeconomic factors influencing men and women's planning for retirement*. Published doctoral dissertation, Massey University, New Zealand.

Nosic, A., & Weber, M. (2007). *Determinants of Risk Taking Behavior: The role of Risk Attitudes, Risk Perceptions and Beliefs*. Sonderforschungsbereich 504, Universität Mannheim & Sonderforschungsbereich 504, University of Mannheim. No 07-56. Retrieved from http://www.sfb504.uni-mannheim.de/publications/dp07-56.pdf

O'Connell, J. F. (2011). The rise of the Arabian Gulf carriers: An insight into the business model of Emirates Airline. *Journal of Air Transport Management*, 339–346.

O'Neil, B. (1992). National Survey, The Status of Consumer Education. In *U.S. Schools K-12*. Chatham, NJ: National Coalition for Consumer Education, Inc.

O'Neill, B., Sorhaindo, B., Xiao, J. J., & Garman, E. T. (2005b). Negative health effects of financial stress. *Consumer Interests Annual*, *51*(3). Retrieved from URL: www.consumerinterests.org/i4a/pages/Index.cfm?pageid=4077

O'Neill, B., Prawitz, A. D., Sorhaindo, B., Kim, J., & Garman, E. T. (2006a). Financial distress: Definition, effects and measurement. *Consumer Interests Annual*, *52*, 458–465.

O'Neill, B., Prawitz, A. D., Sorhaindo, B., Kim, J., & Garman, E. T. (2006b). Changes in health, negative financial events, and financial distress/financial well-being for debt management program clients. *Financial Counseling and Planning*, *17*(2), 46–63.

O'Neill, B., Sorhaindo, B., Prawitz, A. D., Kim, J., & Garman, E. T. (2006). Financial distress: Definition, effects, and measurement. *Consumer Interest Annual*, *52*, 1–8.

O'Neill, B., Xiao, J. J., Sorhaindo, B., & Garman, E. T. (2005a). Financially distressed consumers: Their financial practices, financial well-being, and health. *Financial Counseling and Planning*, *16*(1), 71–85.

Oakeshott, M. (1991). On being conservative. *Rationalism in politics and other essays*, 168-96.

Obradovic, V., Jovanovic, P., Petrovic, D., Mihic, M., & Mitrovic, Z. (2013). Project managers' emotional intelligence-A ticket to success. *Procedia: Social and Behavioral Sciences*, *74*, 274–284. doi:10.1016/j.sbspro.2013.03.034

Odabaşı, Y. (2009). Küresel Kriz ve Pazarlamanın Yeni Dünyası: Paradigmadan Enigmaya. *Pazarlama ve İletişim (Pİ) Kültürü Dergisi, 8*(28).

Odabaşı, Y. (2010). Küresel kriz ortamında tüketici davranışları. In M. Babaoğul & A. Şener (Eds.), *Tüketici Yazıları-II, Hacettepe Üniversitesi Tüketici - Pazar - Araştırma - Danışma Test ve Eğitim Merkezi. TÜPADEM Yayınları*. Ankara: Comart Kurumsal İletişim Hizmetleri Ltd. Şti.

Odabaşı, Y., & Barış, G. (2002). *Tüketici davranışı*. İstanbul: Mediacat Kitapları.

Odean, T. (1998a). Volume, volatility, price and profit when all traders are above average. *The Journal of Finance*, *53*(6), 1887–1934. doi:10.1111/0022-1082.00078

Odean, T. (1998b). Are investors reluctant to realize losses? *The Journal of Finance*, *53*(5), 1775–1798. doi:10.1111/0022-1082.00072

Odean, T. (1999). Do investors trade too much? *The American Economic Review*, *89*(5), 1279–1298. doi:10.1257/aer.89.5.1279

OECD. (2005a). Improving financial literacy: Analysis of issues and policies. *Financial Market Trends*, *2*, 111–115.

OECD. (2005b). *Recommendation on Principles and Good Practices for Financial Education and Awareness*. Recommendation of the Council, Directorate for Financial and Enterprise Affairs. Retrieved June 2, 2014, from http://www.oecd.org/daf/fin/financial-education/35108560.pdf

OECD. (2010). *Health Care Systems: Efficiency and Policy Settings*. OECD Publishing.

OECD. (2011, November), *OECD Health Data*. Retrieved from www.oecd.org

OECD. (2013). *Health at a Glance, OECD Indicators*. Retrieved from http://www.oecd-ilibrary.org/social-issues-migration-health/health-at-a-glance-2013_health_glance-2013-en

OECD. (2013). OECD. *Economic Outlook*, *2013*(1).

Oktik, N. (2008). *Türkiye'de yoksulluk çalışmaları*. İzmir: Yakın Kitabevi.

Olsen, R., A. (2007). Investors' Predisposition for Annuities: A Psychological Perspective. *Journal of Financial Service Professionals*. September

Olsen, R. A. (2010). Toward a theory of behavioural finance: Implications from the natural sciences. *Qualitative Research in Financial Markets*, *2*(2), 100–128. doi:10.1108/17554171080000383

Olsson, H. (2014). Measuring overconfidence: Methodological problems and statistical artifacts. *Journal of Business Research*, *67*(8), 1766–1770. doi:10.1016/j.jbusres.2014.03.002

O'Malley, L., & Tynan, C. (2000). Relationship marketing in consumer markets: Rhetoric or reality? *European Journal of Marketing*, *34*(7), 797–815.

Onkal, D., & Muradoglu, G. (1996). Effects of task format on probabilistic forecasting of stock prices. *International Journal of Forecasting*, *12*(1), 9–24. doi:10.1016/0169-2070(95)00633-8

Onur, B. (1995). *Gelişim Psikolojisi: Yetişkinlik Yaşlılık Ölüm* [Developmental Psychology, Older Age, Death]. Ankara: İmge Yayınevi.

Organization for Economic Cooperation Development (OECD). (2005). Improving financial literacy: Analysis of issues and policies. Paris: OECD. *Psychology (Savannah, Ga.)*, *56*(3), 218.

Ormsby, P., & Fairchild, T. G. (1987). Perceived income adequacy and selected financial management practices among families in Chile and Mexico. *Social Indicators Research*, *19*(3), 317–327. doi:10.1007/BF00300364

Ottoo, M. W. (1999). *Consumer sentiment and the stock market* (Finance and Economics Discussion Paper, No. 60). Federal Reserve Board. Retrieved from http://www.federal-reserve.gov/pubs/feds/1999/199960/199960abs.html

Özer, İ. Ç. (2010). *Duygusal zeka ile liderlik tarzları arasındaki ilişki*. MA thesis. Marmara University.

Özgül, E., & Özgüven, N. (2011). Ekonomik durgunluk dönemlerinde tüketicilerin satin alma davranişinda yaşanan değişimlerin analizi. *ZKÜ Sosyal Bilimler Dergisi*, *7*(13), 239–263.

Özmete, E. (2004). Ailelerin öznel refah düzeylerine ilişkin bir değerlendirme (Evaluating the subjective well-being of families). *Aile ve Toplum Dergisi*, *2*(6), 23–31.

Özmete, E. (2011). *Sosyal dışlanma ve aile: Sosyal hizmet müdahalelerinde güçlendirme yaklaşımı*. Ankara: Maya Akademi Yayını.

Öznacar, M. D. (2011). Küreselleşmenin yarattığı etkiler performans görevi. Retrieved from http://websites.ekampus.orav.org.tr/mehmetduranoznacar/2011/3/1/16883/page.aspx

PACFL. (2008). Enhancing youth financial education. 2008 Annual Report to the President (pp. 11-19)

Palmatier, R. W. (2008). *Relationship Marketing*. Cambridge, MA: Marketing Science Institute.

Palmatier, R. W., Gopalakrishna, S., & Houston, M. B. (2006). Returns on business-to-business relationship marketing investments strategies for leveraging profits. *Marketing Science*, *25*(5), 477–493.

Palmatier, R. W., Scheer, L. K., Houston, M. B., Kenneth, R. E., & Gopalakrishna, S. (2007). Use of relationship marketing programs in building customer-salesperson and customer-firm relationships: Differential influences on financial outcomes. *International Journal of Research in Marketing*, 210–223.

Palmer, A. J. (1995). Relationship Marketing:Local Implementation of a Universal Concept. *International Business Review*, *4*(4), 471–481.

Pan, C., & Statman, M. (2010). *Beyond risk tolerance: Regret, overconfidence, and other investor propensities* (Research Paper 10-05). SCU Leavey School of Business. Retrieved from http://papers.ssrn.com/sol3/papers.cfm?abstract_id=1549912

Pankow, D. & Brotherson, S. (2009). *Talking to children about money* (NDSU Extension Service, FS-1441).

Panopoulou, E., & Pittis, N. (2004). A Comparison of Autoregressive Distributed Lag and Dynamic OLS Cointegration Estimators in the Case of a Serially Correlated Cointegration Error. *The Econometrics Journal*, *7*(2), 585–617. doi:10.1111/j.1368-423X.2004.00145.x

Papatya, G. (1997). İşletmelerin örgütsel verimliliğine ulaşmada yetki devri sorunu ve yönetici engeli –motivasyon kuramları bağlamında. *Süleyman Demirel University Economics and Administrative Sciences Faculty Journal*, *2*, 127–146.

Paramı Yönetebiliyorum. (2014). *2013 Etki Analizi Sonuçları: Haberler*. Retrieved May 2, 2014, from http://www.paramiyonetebiliyorum.net/bizden-haberler.aspx

Parlak, Z., & Aykaç, M. (2004). *AB sosyal politikasi: refah devletinden Avrupa sosyal modeline*. Retrieved March 15, 2014, from http://web.sakarya.edu.tr/~kaymakci/makale/absosyal.pdf

Parrino, R. (1997). CEO turnover and outside succession a cross-sectional analysis. *Journal of Financial Economics*, *46*(2), 165–197. doi:10.1016/S0304-405X(97)00028-7

Parrotta, J. L., & Johnson, P. J. (1998). The impact of financial attitudes and knowledge on financial management and satisfaction of recently married individuals. *Financial Counseling and Planning*, *9*(2), 59–75.

Parsa, B. (2008). *Financial status among the Malaysian elderly*. Unpublished Master's Dissertation, University Putra Malaysia, Malaysia.

Pavot, W., & Diener, E. (1993). Review of the satisfaction with life scale. *Psychological Assessment*, *5*(2), 164–172. doi:10.1037/1040-3590.5.2.164

Payne, A., Christopher, M., Clark, M., & Peck, H. (1999). *Relationship marketing for competetive advantage*. Oxford: Butterworth-Heinemann.

Payne, J. E. (2010). On Biomass Energy Consumption and Real Output in the US. Energy Sources. *Economics. Planning and Policy*, *6*, 47–52.

Pehlivan, İ. (1995). *Yönetimde stres kaynakları*. Ankara: Pegem Yayınları.

Peirce, R. S., Frone, M. R., Russell, M., & Cooper, M. L. (1996). Financial stress, social support, and alcohol involvement: A longitudinal test of the buffering hypothesis in a general population survey. *Health Psychology*, *15*(1), 38–47.

Perry, V. G. (2000). Antecedents of consumer financing decisions: A mental accounting model of revolving credit usage (Ph.D. dissertation, The University of North Carolina at Chapel Hill). *ABI/INFORM Global Publication No. AAT 9979480.*

Pesaran, M. H., & Shin, Y. (1999). An autoregressive distributed lag modeling approach to cointegration analysis. Econometrics and Economic Theory in 20th century: The Ragnar Frisch Centennial Symposium, eds. S. Strom, Cambridge University Press, Cambridge. doi:10.1017/CCOL521633230.011

Pesaran, M. H., Shin, Y., & Smith, R. (2001). Bounds Testing Approaches to the Analysis of Level Relationships. *Journal of Applied Econometrics*, *16*(3), 289–326. doi:10.1002/jae.616

Peter, M. S. (2007). *Airline Finance*. Hampshire: Ashgate.

Pfeffer, J., & Salancik, G. R. (1977). Organization context and the characteristics and tenure of hospital administrators. *Academy of Management Journal*, *20*(1), 74–88. doi:10.2307/255463 PMID:10305921

Pfeiffer, J. W. (1996). *Theories and Models in Applied Behavioural Science: Individual* (Vol. 1). New Delhi: Pfeiffer & Company.

Phau, I., & Woo, C. (2008). Understanding compulsive buying tendencies among young Australians: The roles of money attitude and credit card usage. *Marketing Intelligence & Planning*, *26*(5), 441–458. doi:10.1108/02634500810894307

Philippine Health Insurance Corporation. (2008). *PhilHealth annual report 2008*. Retrieved from http://www.philHealth.gov.ph/about_us/annual_report/ar2008.pdf

Philippine Health Insurance Corporation. (2009a). *Lifetime members*. Retrieved from http://www.PhilHealth.gov.ph/members/lifetime/index.htm

Philippine Overseas Employment Association. (2009). *Number of deployed nurses by top 10 destinations, New Hires, 2003-2009*. Retrieved from http://www.poea.gov.ph/stats/2009_OFW%20Statistics.pdf

Phillips, P. C. B., & Perron, P. (1988). Testing for Unit Roots in Time Series Regression. *Biometrika*, *75*(2), 335–346. doi:10.1093/biomet/75.2.335

Phua, V., & Mcnally, J. W. (2008). Men planning for retirement: Changing meanings of preretirement planning. *Journal of Applied Gerontology*, *27*(5), 588–608. doi:10.1177/0733464808321885

Pilarski, A. M. (2007). *Why Can't We Make Money in Aviation?* New York: Ashgate.

Pillai, K. R., Carlo, R., & D'souza, R. (2010). *Financial Prudence among Youth* (MPRA Paper No. 22450, pp. 2-22). Retrieved June 2, 2014, from, http://mpra.ub.uni-muenchen.de/22450/1/MPRA_paper_22450.pdf

Pines, H. A. (1996). The Psychology of Investor Decision Making. In S. Lofthouse (Ed.), *Readings in Investments*. Wiley Publishers.

Pittman, J. F., & Lloyd, S. A. (1988). Quality of family life, social support, and stress. *Journal of Marriage and the Family*, *50*(1), 53–67. doi:10.2307/352427

Plagnol, A. C. (2011). Financial satisfaction over the life course: The influence of assets and liabilities. *Journal of Economic Psychology*, *32*(1), 45–64. doi:10.1016/j.joep.2010.10.006

Plous, S. (1993). *The psychology of judgment and decision making*. Mcgraw-Hill Book Company.

Pompian, M. (2011). *Behavioral Finance and Wealth Management: How to Build Optimal Portfolios That Account for Investor Biases* (2nd ed.). New Jersey: Wiley Finance Publications.

Pompian, M. M. (2006). *Behavioral finance and wealth management: How to build optimal portfolios that account for investor biases*. New York, NY: John Wiley & Sons.

Pompian, M. M. (2008). Using behavioral investor types to build better relationships with your clients. *Journal of Financial Planning*, *21*(10), 64–76.

Popham, L. E., Kennison, S. M., & Bradley, K. I. (2011). Ageism, sensation-seeking, and risk-taking behavior in young adults. *Current Psychology (New Brunswick, N.J.)*, *10*(3), 184–193. doi:10.1007/s12144-011-9107-0

Population Institute. (2011). *From 6 Billion to 7 Billion: How Population Growth is Changing and Challenging Our World.* Retrieved from https://www.populationinstitute.org/external/files/reports/from-6b-to-7b.pdf

Prast, H. (2004). Investor Psychology: A Behavioural Explanation of Six Financial Puzzles. *Research Series of De nederlandsche Bank*

Pratt, J. W. (1964). Risk aversion in the small and in the large. *Econometrica*, *32*(1/2), 122–136. doi:10.2307/1913738

Prawitz, A. D., Garman, E. T., Sorhaindo, B., O'Neill, B., Kim, J., & Drentea, P. (2006). InCharge financial distress/financial well-being scale: Development, administration, and score interpretation. *Financial Counseling and Planning*, *17*(1), 34–50.

Priemus, H. (2003). Dutch Housing Associations: Current Developments and Debates. *Housing Studies*, *18*(3), 327–351. doi:10.1080/02673030304237

Priemus, H., & Dieleman, F. (1997). Social Rented Housing: Recent Changes in Wester Europe-introduction. *Housing Studies*, *12*(4), 421–425. doi:10.1080/02673039708720907

Qiu, L. X., & Welch, I. (2006). *Investor sentiment measures*. (SSRN Working Paper, No: 589641).

Quiggin, J. (1982). A theory of anticipated utility. *Journal of Economic Behavior & Organization*, *3*(4), 323–343. doi:10.1016/0167-2681(82)90008-7

Rabin, M. (1998). Psychology and economics. *Journal of Economic Literature*, *36*(1), 11–46.

Rabin, M. (2002). Inference by believers in the law of small numbers. *The Quarterly Journal of Economics*, *117*(3), 775–816. doi:10.1162/003355302760193896

Rahim, M. A., & Psenicka, C. (2002). A model of emotional intelligence and conflict management strategies: A study in seven countries. *The International Journal of Organizational Analysis*, *10*(4), 302–326. doi:10.1108/eb028955

Raiffa, H. (1968). *Decision Analysis: Introductory Lectures on Choices under Uncertainty*. Reading, MA: Addison-Wesley.

Raijas, A. (2011). Money management in blended and nuclear families. *Journal of Economic Psychology*, *32*(4), 556–563. doi:10.1016/j.joep.2011.02.006

Ramli, Z., Sum, S. M., Manaf, A. A., Saad, S., Hussain, M. Y., & Lyndon, N. (2012). Kualitihidupdankesejahteraanbelia: Kajiankeataspekerjasektorawam Malaysia. *Geografia: Malaysian Journal of Society and Space*, *8*(6), 150–156.

Rapp, R. (2000). Customer Relationship Marketing in the Airline Industry. In U. Hansen & T. Hennig-Thurau (Eds.), *Relationship Marketing* (pp. 317–330). Berlin, Heidelberg: Springer-Verlag.

Ravald, A., & Grönroos, C. (1996). The value concept and relationship marketing. *European Journal of Marketing*, *30*(2), 19–30.

Reichheld, F. F., & Sasser, W. E. (1990). Zero Defections: Quality Comes to Services. *Harvard Business Review*, 3-8.

Reimers, S., & Harvey, N. (2011). Sensitivity to autocorrelation in judgmental time series forecasting. *International Journal of Forecasting*, *27*(4), 1196–1214. doi:10.1016/j.ijforecast.2010.08.004

Reinchheld, F. F., Markey, R. G., & Hopton, C. (2000). The Loyalty Effect: The Relationship Between Loyalty and Profits. *European Business Journal*, 134-139.

Reinsch, M. (2012). Youth financial inclusion: Promising examples for achieving youth economic empowerment. Europan Dialouge, 5, 5-7.

Renneboog, L., & Simons, T. (2005).*Public-to-Private Transactions: LBOs, MBOs, MBIs and IBOs* (Discussion paper 2005-23). Tilburg University, Tilburg Law and Economic Center

Rettig, K. D., Leichtentritt, R. D., & Danes, S. M. (1999). The effects of resources, decision making, and decision implementing on perceived family welfare in adjusting to an economic stressor. *Journal of Family and Economic Issues*, *20*(1), 5–34. doi:10.1023/A:1022163729635

Retting, K., & Schultz, C. (1991). Cognitive style preferences and financial management. *Financial Counseling and Planning*, *2*, 55–78.

Ricciardi, V., & Simon, H. K. (2000). What is behavioral finance? *Business, Education and Technology Journal*, Fall, 1-9.

Ricciardi, V., & Simon, H. (2000). What is behavioral finance? *The Business. Education and Technology Journal, 2*(1), 26–34.

Ritter, J. R. (2003). Behavioral finance. *Pacific-Basin Finance Journal, 11*(4), 429–437. doi:10.1016/S0927-538X(03)00048-9

Roberti, J. W. (2004). A review of behavioral and biological correlates of sensation seeking. *Journal of Research in Personality, 38*(3), 256–279. doi:10.1016/S0092-6566(03)00067-9

Roberts, J. A., & Jones, E. (2001). Money attitudes, credit card use, and compulsive buying among american college students. *The Journal of Consumer Affairs, 35*(2), 213–240. doi:10.1111/j.1745-6606.2001.tb00111.x

Robila, M. (2006). Economic pressure and social exclusion in Europe. *The Social Science Journal, 43*(1), 85–97. doi:10.1016/j.soscij.2005.12.009

Roese, N. J., & Vohs, K. D. (2012). Hindsight bias. *Perspectives on Psychological Science, 7*(5), 411–426. doi:10.1177/1745691612454303

Rogers, J., Viding, E., & Chamorro-Premuzic, T. (2013). Instrumental and disinhibited financial risk taking: Personality and behavioural correlates. *Personality and Individual Differences, 55*(6), 645–649. doi:10.1016/j.paid.2013.05.011

Ross, C., & Huber, J. (1985). Hardship and depression. *Journal of Health and Social Behavior, 26*(4), 312–327. doi:10.2307/2136655 PMID:4086755

Roszkowski, M. J., & Grable, J. (2007). How are income and net worth related to happiness? *Journal of Financial Service Professionals, 61*(1).

Roszkowski, M. J., Snelbecker, G. E., & Leimberg, S. R. (1993). Risk-tolerance and risk aversion. In S. Leimberg, M. Satinsky, R. LeClair, & R. Doyle (Eds.), *The Tools and Techniques of Financial Planning* (4th ed., pp. 213–225). Cincinnati, OH: National Underwriter.

Roszkowski, M., & Cordell, D. (2009). A longitudinal perspective on financial risk tolerance: Rank-order and mean level stability. *International Journal of Behavioural Accounting and Finance, 1*(2), 111–134. doi:10.1504/IJBAF.2009.027448

Roszkowski, M., Delaney, M., & Cordell, D. (2009). Intraperson consistency in financial risk tolerance assessment: Temporal stability, relationship to total score, and effect on criterionrelated validity. *Journal of Business and Psychology, 24*(4), 455–467. doi:10.1007/s10869-009-9115-3

Rotter, J. B. (1954). *Social learning and clinical psychology*. New York: Prentice-Hall. doi:10.1037/10788-000

Rowe, W. G., & Barnes, J. J. (1998). Relationship Marketing and Sustained Competitive Advantage. *Journal of Market Focused Management, 2*, 281–297.

Rubaltelli, E., Rubichi, S., Savadori, L., Tedeschi, M., & Ferretti, R. (2005). Numerical information format and investment decisions: Implications for the disposition effect and the status quo bias. *Journal of Behavioral Finance, 6*(1), 19–26. doi:10.1207/s15427579jpfm0601_4

Rud, O. P. (2009). *Business Intelligence Success Factors Tools for Aligning Your Business in the Global Economy*. Wiley.

Ruiz-Menjivar, J., Blanco, A., Çopur, Z., Gutter, M. S., & Gillen, M. (2014). A cross-cultural comparison of three risk tolerance measures: Turkey and The United States case. *International Journal of Research in Business and Social Science, 3*(1), 1–14.

Rumelt, R. P. (1974). *Strategy, Structure and Economic Performance*. Boston, MA: Division of Research, Harvard Business School.

Sabri, M. F., Masud, J., & Paim, L. (2006). *Financial Literacy, Attitude and Practice among Malaysian IPTs Students*. Serdang: UPM.

Sadorsky, P. (2010a). The Impact of Financial Development on Energy Consumption in Emerging Economies. *Energy Policy, 38*(5), 2528–2535. doi:10.1016/j.enpol.2009.12.048

Sadorsky, P. (2010b). Trade and Energy Consumption in the Middle East. *Energy Economics*, *33*(5), 739–749. doi:10.1016/j.eneco.2010.12.012

Sadorsky, P. (2011). Financial Development and Energy Consumption in Central and Eastern European Frontier Economies. *Energy Policy*, *39*(2), 999–1006. doi:10.1016/j.enpol.2010.11.034

Sadorsky, P. (2012). Energy Consumption, Output and Trade in South America. *Energy Economics*, *34*(2), 476–488. doi:10.1016/j.eneco.2011.12.008

Şahin, J. (2006). *Emekliler ve sorunları üzerine sosyolojik bir araştırma: Şanlıurfa örneği* [A sociological research on the retired and their problems: Sample of Şanlıurfa]. Published master's thesis, Fırat University, Turkey.

Şahinkaya, B. (2006). *Yöneticilik ve liderlikte duygusal zekâ*. MSc Thesis, Balıkesir Universitesi Natural Sciences Institute.

Şahin, T. (2010). Sosyal dışlanma ve yoksulluk ilişkisi. *Yardım ve Dayanışma*, *2*(1), 71–80.

Sahi, S. K. (2012). Neurofinance and investment behaviour. *Studies in Economics and Finance*, *29*(4), 246–267. doi:10.1108/10867371211266900

Sahm, C. (2007). How much does risk tolerance change? Finance and Economics Discussion Series 2007-66. Washington: Board of Governors of the Federal Reserve System; Available https://federalreserve.gov/Pubs/FEDS/2007/200766/200766abs.html

Salman, S. (2005). *Öğretmenlerin emeklilik dönemine uyumları ve yaşam tatminleri* [Adjustment to retirement and life satisfaction of teacher]. Published doctoral dissertation, Ankara University, Turkey.

Samanez-Larkin, G. R., Hollon, N. G., Carstensen, L. L., & Knutson, B. (2008). Individual differences in insular sensitivity during loss anticipation predict avoidance learning. *Psychological Science*, *19*(4), 320–323. doi:10.1111/j.1467-9280.2008.02087.x PMID:18399882

Samuelson, W., & Zeckhauser, R. (1988). Status quo bias in decision making. *Journal of Risk and Uncertainty*, *1*(1), 7–59. doi:10.1007/BF00055564

Santacruz, L. (2009). Effect of general economic mood on investor risk tolerance – implications for financial planning. *JASSA*, *1*, 35–42.

Sapancalı, F. (2005). Avrupa Birliği'nde sosyal dışlanma sorunu ve mücadele yöntemleri. *Çalışma ve Toplum*, 2005/3.

Sarım, S. (1996). *Emeklilerin zamanlarını değerlendirme durumlarının incelenmesi* [Analysis on how the retired spend their time]. Unpublished master's thesis, Istanbul University, Turkey.

Savage, L. (1964). *The foundations of statistics*. New York, NY: John Wiley & Sons.

Schacter, S., Oulette, R., Whittle, B., & Gerin, W. (1987). Effects of trend and of profit or loss on the tendency to sell stock. *Basic and Applied Social Psychology*, *8*(4), 259–271. doi:10.1207/s15324834basp0804_1

Scharfstein, D. S., & Stein, J. C. (1990). Herd behavior and investment. *The American Economic Review*, *80*, 465–479.

Scheinkman, J. A., & Xiong, W. (2003). Overconfidence and speculative bubbles. *Journal of Political Economy*, *111*(6), 1183–1219. doi:10.1086/378531

Schmeling, M. (2009). Investor sentiment and stock returns: Some international evidence. *Journal of Empirical Finance*, *16*(3), 394–408. doi:10.1016/j.jempfin.2009.01.002

Schultz, D. E., Tannenbaum, S. I., & Robert, F. L. (1993). *Integrated Marketing Communications*. Lincolnwood: NTC Business Books.

Schwartz, R. M., Burkhart, B. R., & Green, S. B. (1978). Turning on or turning off: Sensation seeking or tension reduction as motivational determinants of alcohol use. *Journal of Consulting and Clinical Psychology*, *46*(5), 1144–1145. doi:10.1037/0022-006X.46.5.1144 PMID:701550

Schwarz, G. (1978). Estimating the dimension of a model. *Annals of Statistics*, *6*(2), 41–464. doi:10.1214/aos/1176344136

Scott, E. (2011). *Financial stress: How it affects you and what you can do*. Retrieved May, 16, 2011, from http://stress.about.com/od/financialstress/a/financialstress.htm

Sefil, S. & Çilingiroğlu, H. K. (2011, Bahar). Davranışsal finansın temelleri: Karar vermenin bilişsel ve duygusal eğilimleri. [The basics of behavioral finance: cognitive and emotional biases in decision making]. *İstanbul Ticaret Üniversitesi Sosyal Bilimler Dergisi*. *10*(19), 247-268.

Segal, U. (1989). Anticipated utility: A measure representation approach. *Annals of Operations Research, 19*(1-4), 359–373. doi:10.1007/BF02283529

Selden, G. C. (1912). *Psychology of the stock market: Human impulses lead to speculative disasters*. New York: Ticker Publishing.

Selvi, M. S. (2007). *İlişkisel Pazarlama*. Ankara: Detay Yayıncılık.

Şendur, F. (2009). The Importance of Creating customer Value in Relational context of Marketing: A Research on Bank Sector. *Master Thesis*, 25-29. Balıkesir, turkey: Balıkesir University.

Şener, A., & Terzioğlu, G. R. (2005). Determining the expenditure, investment and saving patterns in respect of family life cycles. *Aile ve Toplum Dergisi, 2*(8), 53–59.

Şenses, F. (2013). *Küreselleşmenin öteki yüzü yoksulluk: Kavramlar, nedenler, politikalar ve temel eğilimler* [Poverty, the other face of globalization: Concepts, causes, policies and basic trends]. İstanbul: İletişimYayınları.

Sentana, E., & Sushil W. (. (1991). Feedback traders and stock returns autocorrelations: Evidence from a century of daily data. *The Review of Economic Studies, 58*, 547–563. doi:10.2307/2298011

Seo, M., & Barrett, L. F. (2007). Being emotional during decision making—Good or bad? An empirical investigation. *Academy of Management Journal, 50*(4), 923–940. doi:10.5465/AMJ.2007.26279217 PMID:18449361

Serpen, E. (2013, November 21). Airline Business and Financial Planning. *Aviation Economics and Financial Analysis*. Istanbul: Istanbul Technical University.

Sevim, Y., & Şahin, J. (2007). Toplumun yeni yoksulları: Emekliler (Şanlıurfa İli Örneği)[The New Poor Persons of The Society: The Retirements (A Case Study of Şanlıurfa Province)]. *Sosyoloji Araştırma Dergisi, 10*(1), 195–207.

Sewell, M. (2010, April). *Behavioral Finance* (Revised). University of Cambridge

Shaari, N. A., Hasan, N. A., Mohammed, R. K. M. H., & Sabri, M. A. J. M. (2013). Financial literacy: A study among the university students. *Interdıscıplınary Journal of Contemporary Research in Business, 5*(2), 279–299.

Shahbaz, M., Nasreen, S., Ling, C.H., & Sbia, R. (2013a). *Causality between Trade Openness and Energy Consumption: What Causes What in High, Middle and Low Income Countries*. (MPRA No. 50382, pp. 1-47).

Shahbaz, M. (2012). Does Trade Openness Affects Long Run Growth? Cointegration, Causality and Forecast Error Variance Decomposition Tests for Pakistan. *Economic Modelling, 29*(6), 2325–2339. doi:10.1016/j.econmod.2012.07.015

Shahbaz, M., Islam, F., & Islam, M. M. (2010). The Impact of Financial Development on Energy Consumption in Pakistan: Evidence from ARDL Bounds Testing Approach to Cointegration. In: *Proceedings of the Second International Conference on the Role of Social Sciences and Humanities in Engineering (ICoHSE)*, 12-14 November 2010, Penang, Malaysia.

Shahbaz, M., Khan, S., & Tahir, M. I. (2013b). The Dynamic Link between Energy Consumption, Economic Growth, Financial Development and Trade in China: Fresh Evidence from Multivariate Framework Analysis. *Energy Economics, 40*, 8–21. doi:10.1016/j.eneco.2013.06.006

Shahbaz, M., & Lean, H. H. (2012). Does Financial Development Increase Energy Consumption? The Role of Industrialization and Urbanization in Tunisia. *Energy Policy, 40*, 473–479. doi:10.1016/j.enpol.2011.10.050

Shahbaz, M., Zeshan, M., & Afza, T. (2012). Is Energy Consumption Effective to Spur Economic Growth in Pakistan? New Evidence from Bounds Test to Level Relationships and Granger Causality Tests. *Economic Modelling, 29*(6), 2310–2319. doi:10.1016/j.econmod.2012.06.027

Shama, A. (1981). Coping with Stagflation: Voluntary Simplicity. *Journal of Marketing, 45*(Summer), 120–134. doi:10.2307/1251547

Sharma, A., Tzokas, N., Saren, M., & Kyziridis, P. (1999). Antecedents and Consequences of Relationship Marketing. *Industrial Marketing Management*, 601–611.

Sharpe, W. (1964). Capital asset prices: A theory of market equilibrium under conditions of risk. *The Journal of Finance, 19*(3), 425–442.

Shaw, E. (1973). *Financial deepening in economic development*. New York: Oxford University Press.

Shaw, S. (2007). *Airline Marketing and Management*. Hampshire, England: Ashgate Publishing Company.

Shefrin, H. (2001). *Behavioural corporate finance*. Retrieved August 23, 2014, from http://bbs.cenet.org.cn/UploadImages/20055612105669608.pdf

Shefrin, H., & Statman, M. (2011, November). *Behavioral finance in the financial crisis: Market efficiency, Minsky, and Keynes* (Working Paper). Santa Clara University.

Shefrin, H. (2000). *Beyond Greed and Fear: Understanding Behavioral Finance and Psychology of Investing*. New York: Oxford University Press.

Shefrin, H. (2001). Behavioural corporate finance. *Journal of Applied Corporate Finance*, *14*(3), 113–126. doi:10.1111/j.1745-6622.2001.tb00443.x

Shefrin, H., & Statman, M. (1985). The disposition to sell winners too early and ride losers too long: Theory and evidence. *The Journal of Finance*, *40*(3), 777–779. doi:10.1111/j.1540-6261.1985.tb05002.x

Shefrin, H., & Statman, M. (1994). Behavioral capital asset pricing theory. *Journal of Financial and Quantitative Analysis*, *29*(3), 323–349. doi:10.2307/2331334

Shefrin, H., & Thaler, R. H. (1988). The behavioral life-cycle hypothesis. *Economic Inquiry*, *26*(4), 609–643. doi:10.1111/j.1465-7295.1988.tb01520.x

Shelbecker, G., & Roszkowski, M. (1993). Risk tolerance and risk aversion. In S. R. Leimberg, M. J. Satinsky, R. T. LeClair, & R. J. Doyle (Eds.), *The tools and techniques of financial planning* (4th ed., pp. 213–225). Cincinnati, OH: National Underwriter.

Shiller, R. (1998). Human behavior and the efficiency of the financial system. *NBER Working Paper Series*. Retrieved August 23, 2014, from: http://www.nber.org/papers/w6375

Shiller, R. (1995). Conversation, information and herd behaviour. *The American Economic Review*, *85*(2), 181–185.

Shiller, R. J. (1981). Do stock prices move too much to be justified by subsequent changes in dividend. *The American Economic Review*, *71*, 457–498.

Shiller, R. J. (2000). *Irrational Exuberance*. Princeton: Princeton University Press.

Shim, S., Barber, B. L., Card, N. A., Xiao, J. J., & Serido, J. (2010). Financial socialization of first-year college students: The roles of parents, work, and education. *Journal of Youth and Adolescence*, *39*(12), 1457–1470. doi:10.1007/s10964-009-9432-x PMID:20938727

Shim, S., Xiao, J. J., Barber, B. L., & Lyons, A. (2009). Pathways to life success: A conceptual model of financial well-being for young adults. *Journal of Applied Developmental Psychology*, *30*(6), 708–723. doi:10.1016/j.appdev.2009.02.003

Shleifer, A. (2000). *Inefficient Markets: An Introduction to Behavioral Finance* (1st ed.). New York: Oxford University Press Inc. doi:10.1093/0198292279.001.0001

Shleifer, A., & Summers, L. H. (1990). The Noise trader approach to finance. *The Journal of Economic Perspectives*, *4*(2), 19–33. doi:10.1257/jep.4.2.19

Shumway, T., & Wu, G. (2006, May). *Does disposition drive momentum?* (Working paper).

Siegling, A. B., Nielsen, C., & Petrides, K. V. (2014). Trait emotional intelligence and leadership in a European multinational company. *Personality and Individual Differences*, *65*, 65–68. doi:10.1016/j.paid.2014.01.049

Siegling, A. B., Sfeir, M., & Smyth, H. J. (2014). Measured and self-estimated trait emotional intelligence in a UK sample of managers. *Personality and Individual Differences*, *65*, 59–64. doi:10.1016/j.paid.2014.01.027

Sighieri, C., Desantis, G., & Tanturri, M. L. (2006). The richer, the happier? An empirical investigation in selected European Countries. *Social Indicators Research*, *79*(3), 455–476. doi:10.1007/s11205-005-5394-x

Simon, H. (1957). A Behavioural Model of Rational Choice. In *Models of Man, Social and Rational: Mathematical Essays on Rational Human Behaviour in a Social Setting*. New York: Wiley.

Simon, H. A. (1955). A behavioral model of rational choice. *The Quarterly Journal of Economics*, *69*(1), 99–118. doi:10.2307/1884852

Simon, H. A. (1956). Rational Choice and the Structure of Environments. *Psychological Review*, *6*(2), 129–138. doi:10.1037/h0042769 PMID:13310708

Şimşek, Ş. (2010). Yönetim ve organizasyon (12th Edition). Konya: Eğitim Akademi Publishing.

Sindell, K. (2000). *Loyalty Marketing for the Internet Age: How to Identify, Attract, Serve, and Retain Customers in an E-Commerce Environment: Search Results*. Chicago: Dearborn Trade Pub.

Sin, L. Y., Tse, A. C., Yau, O. H., Chow, R. P., Lee, J. S., & Lorett, L. B. (2005). Relationship marketing orientation: Scale development. *Journal of Business Research*, (58): 185–194.

Skala, D. (2008). *Overconfidence in Psychology and Finance - An Interdisciplinary Literature Review (September 1, 2008). Bank i Kredyt, No. 4* (pp. 33–50). Available at SSRN; http://ssrn.com/abstract=1261907

Skinner, M. A., Zautra, A. J., & Reich, J. W. (2004). Financial stress predictors and the emotional and physical health of chronic pain patients. *Cognitive Therapy and Research*, *28*(5), 695–713.

Slovic, P. (1972). Psychological study of human judgment: Implications for investment decision making. *The Journal of Finance*, *27*(4), 779–799. doi:10.1111/j.1540-6261.1972.tb01311.x

Smith, A. (1759). *The theory of moral sentiments*. London: A. Millar.

Smith, N. (2011). *Herding and speculation in experimental asset market*. Unpublished dissertation, University of Michigan, Michigan.

Smith, A. (1776). *The Wealth of Nations*. London, W.: Strahan and T. Cadell.

Smith, A. J. (1990). Corporate ownership structure and performance: The case of management buyouts. *Journal of Financial Economics*, *27*(1), 143–164. doi:10.1016/0304-405X(90)90024-T

Smith, V. L. (1991). Rational choice: The contrast between economics and psychology. *Journal of Political Economy*, *99*(4), 877–897. doi:10.1086/261782

Smith, V. L. (1998). The two faces of Adam Smith. *Southern Economic Journal*, *65*(1), 1–19. doi:10.2307/1061349

Social Bakers. (2013, April 01). *Havadaki Rekabet Sosyal Medya'da Nasıl?* Retrieved June 18, 2014, from http://www.pazarlamasyon.com/2013/02/havadaki-rekabet-sosyal-medyada-nasil/

Social Housing Foundation (Social Housing Regulatory Authority). (2003). *Social Housing Toolkit for Housing Associations*. Retrieved from wwww.shra.org.za

SocialBakers. (2014). *Statistics*. Retrieved April 27, 2014, from Social Bakers: http://www.socialbakers.com/twitter/group/brands/tag/airlines/

Sorce, P. (2002). *Marketing Strategies that Build Customer Commitment and Loyalty*. Rochester, New York: Printing Industry Center.

Sosik, J. J., & Megerian, L. E. (1999). Understanding leader emotional intelligence and performance. *Group & Organization Management*, *24*(3), 367–390. doi:10.1177/1059601199243006

South African Reserve Bank (SARB). (2013). *Quarterly Report, December*. Pretoria: Government Publishers.

Soyak, A. (2004). Yapısal uyum programları ve yoksulluk ilişkisi üzerine bir değerlendirme. *Bilim ve Ütopya Dergisi*, *125*, 36–45.

Squalli, J. (2007). Electricity Consumption and Economic Growth: Bounds and Causality Analyses of OPEC Countries. *Energy Economics*, *29*(6), 1192–1205. doi:10.1016/j.eneco.2006.10.001

Stambaugh, R. F., Yu, J., & Yuan, Y. (2012). The Short of it: Investor sentiment and anomalies. *Journal of Financial Economics*, *104*(2), 288–302. doi:10.1016/j.jfineco.2011.12.001

Statistics South Africa. (2014). *Economic Overview: Practice Forex Trading*. Pretoria: Statistics South Africa Publishers.

Statman, M. (2008). Countries and culture in behavioral finance. *Wealth Management Conference*, 8-9 April, Atlanta. CFA Institute, cfapubs.org p.38-44.

Statman, M. (1999). Behavioral Finance: Past Battles and Future Engagements. *Financial Analysts Journal*, *55*(6), 18–27. doi:10.2469/faj.v55.n6.2311

Statman, M. (2008). What is behavioral finance? In *Handbook of Finance* (Vol. II). New Jersey: John Wiley & Sons, Inc.

Statman, M. (2014). Behavioral finance: Finance with normal people. *Borsa Istanbul Review*, *14*(2), 65–73. doi:10.1016/j.bir.2014.03.001

Stern, D. I. (2010). *The Role of Energy in Economic Growth* (USAEE-IAEE Working Paper, No. 10-055, pp. 1-55).

Stracca, L. (2004). Behavioral finance and asset prices: Where do we stand? *Journal of Economic Psychology*, *25*(3), 373–405. doi:10.1016/S0167-4870(03)00055-2

Straub, A. (2002). Strategic Technical Management of Housing Stock: Lessons from Dutch Housing Associations. *Building Research and Information*.

Sumarwan, U., & Hira, T. K. (1992). Credit, saving and insurance practices influencing satisfaction with preparation for financial emergencies among rural households. *Home Economics Research Journal*, *21*(2), 206–227. doi:10.1177/1077727X9202100205

Sumarwan, U., & Hira, T. K. (1993). The effects of perceived locus of control and perceived income adequacy on satisfaction with financial status of rural households. *Journal of Family and Economic Issues*, *14*(4), 343–364. doi:10.1007/BF01013984

Sun, R. (2010). *How pre-retirement education in the work place helps workers to plan for retirement*. Master's thesis, North Carolina State University, United State of America.

Sung, J., & Hanna, S. (1996). Factors Related to Risk Tolerance. *Financial Counseling and Planning*, *7*, 11–20.

Suwanaphan, S. (2013, June). Personal Financial Literacy of Academic Support-Employee in Chiang Mai University. In *Proceedings of the Management, Knowledge and Learning International Conference*. (pp.1061-1065). Zadar, Croatia. ToKnowPress.

Swedberg, R. (2001). Sociology and game theory: Contemporary and historical perspectives. *Theory and Society*, *30*(3), 301–335. doi:10.1023/A:1017532512350

Sweeney, R. (1988). Some filter rule tests: Methods and results. *Journal of Financial and Quantitative Analysis*, *23*(3), 285–300. doi:10.2307/2331068

Szinovacz, M., & Washo, C. (1992). Gender differences in exposure to life events and adaptation to retirement. *The Journals of Gerontology. Series B, Psychological Sciences and Social Sciences*, *47*(4), 191–196. PMID:1624714

Szyszka, A. (2013). *Behavioral Finance and Capital Markets: How Psychology Influences Investors and Corporations*. Palgrave Macmillan. doi:10.1057/9781137366290

Taffler, R. J.(2010). The Representativeness Heuristic. *Behavioral Finance: Investors, Corporations, and Markets*, 259-276.

Takayasu, M., Mizuno, T., Ohnishi, T., & Takayasu, H. (2005). *Practical Fruits of Econophysics*. Tokyo: Springer.

Talpsepp, T., Vlcek, M., & Wang, M. (2014). Speculating in gains, waiting in losses: A closer look at the disposition effect. *Journal of Behavioral and Experimental Finance*, *2*, 31–43. doi:10.1016/j.jbef.2014.04.001

Taneja, N. K. (2010). *Looking Beyond the Runway*. Farnham: Ashgate.

Tang, C. F., & Tan, B. W. (2014). The Linkages among Energy Consumption, Economic Growth, Relative Price, Foreign Direct Investment, and Financial Development in Malaysia. *Quality & Quantity*, *48*(2), 781–797. doi:10.1007/s11135-012-9802-4

Tangri, R. (2003). *Stress costs stress-cures: How to recover productivity lost to stress*. Retrieved January 22, 2013, from www.Stress-Cures.com

Taş, A., & Önder, E. (2010). Yöneticilerin liderlik davranışlarının personel iş doyumuna etkisi. *Electronic Social Sciences Journal*, *9*, 17–30.

Tavşancıl, E. (2006). *Tutumların ölçülmesi ve SPSS ileveri analizi (Measurement of attititudes and data analysis with SPSS)*. Ankara: Nobel Yayın Dağıtım.

Tawatnuntachai, O., & D'Mello, R. (2002). Intra-industry reactions to stock split announcements. *Journal of Financial Research*, *25*(1), 39–57. doi:10.1111/1475-6803.00003

Taylor, S. E., & Brown, J. D. (1988). Illusion and well-being: A social psychological perspective on mental health. *Psychological Bulletin*, *103*(2), 193–210. doi:10.1037/0033-2909.103.2.193 PMID:3283814

TC Başbakanlık Aile ve Sosyal Araştırmalar Genel Müdürlüğü. (2010). *Sosyal yardım algısı ve yoksulluk kültürü. Türkiye'de kamusal sosyal yardım alanların yardım algısı ve yoksulluk kültürü araştırması* [The perception of social welfare and the culture of poverty.The perception of aid by recipients of public social aid and the study of the culture of poverty in Turkey]. Ankara: Ermat Matbaacılık. [Republic of Turkey, Prime Minister's Office General Directorate of Family and Social Studies]

Teichert, T., Shehu, E., & von Wartburg, I. (2008). Customer segmentation revisited: The case of the airline industry. *Transportation Research*, 227–242.

Tennen, H., & Sharp, J. P. (1983). Control orientation and the illusion of control. *Journal of Personality Assessment*, *47*(4), 369–374. doi:10.1207/s15327752jpa4704_6 PMID:16367577

Terzioğlu, G. R. (1990). Ailenin Ekonomik Faaliyetleri [Economic Activities of Families] (Pub. No: 10). Türkiye Aile Yıllığı. Ankara: Başbakanlık Aile Araştırma Kurumu Yayınları.

Thaler, R. (1980). Toward a positive theory of consumer choice. *Journal of Economic Behavior & Organization*, *1*(1), 39–60. doi:10.1016/0167-2681(80)90051-7

Thaler, R. (1999). Mental accounting matters. *Journal of Behavioral Decision Making*, *12*(3), 183–206. doi:10.1002/(SICI)1099-0771(199909)12:3<183::AID-BDM318>3.0.CO;2-F

Thaler, R. H. (1999). The end of behavioral finance. *Financial Analysts Journal*, *55*(6), 12–17. doi:10.2469/faj.v55.n6.2310

The European Anti-poverty Network. (n.d.) Retrieved March 13, 2014, from http://www.eapn.eu/news-publications/events?view=events&lang=en

Theories of Poverty. The culture of poverty (n.d.). Retrieved January 14, 2014, from http:// www. blacksacademy.net/ content/ 3253.html

Tirole, J. (2002). Rational irrationality: Some economics of self-management. *European Economic Review*, *46*(4-5), 633–655. doi:10.1016/S0014-2921(01)00206-9

Tom, S. M., Fox, C. R., Trepel, C., & Poldrack, R. A. (2007). The neural basis of loss aversion in decision-making under risk. *Science*, *315*(5811), 515–518. doi:10.1126/science.1134239 PMID:17255512

Töremen, F. (2008). Yönetimde etkili bir yaklaşım: Duygu yönetimi. *Kuramsal Eğitimbilim*, *1*(1).

Toshino, M., & Suto, M. (2004, 25 October). *Cognitive biases of Japanese institutional investors: Consistency with behavioral finance*. (Working Paper Series No. WNIF-04-05). Waseda University Institute of Finance, Japan.

Tosun, K. (1992). İşletme yönetimi (6th Edition). Ankara: Savaş Publishing.

Treaty of Amsterdam. (1997). Retrieved March 12, 2014, from http://www.eurotreaties.com/amsterdamtreaty.pdf

Trueman, B. (1988). A theory of noise trading in securities markets. *The Journal of Finance*, *43*(1), 83–95. doi:10.1111/j.1540-6261.1988.tb02590.x

TUIK, (2012). 2010 yoksulluk çalışması sonuçları. *TUIK Haber Bülteni*, 58.

TÜİK. (2008). Tüketim harcamaları, yoksulluk ve gelir dağılımı. *Sorularla Resmi İstatistikler Dizisi*– 6.

TUIK. (2011a). *2009 yoksulluk çalışması sonuçları*. Ankara: T.C. Başbakanlık Türkiye İstatistik Kurumu. Retrieved from: http:www.tuik.gov.tr

TUIK. (2011b). *Adrese dayalı nüfus kayıt sistemi (ADNKS)*. Ankara: Türkiye İstatistik Kurumu Matbaası.

Tuna, Y. (2008). *Örgütsel iletişim sürecinde yöneticilerin duygusal zekâ yeterlilikleri*. PhD. Thesis, Eskişehir Anadolu University.

Tuna, Y. (2009). Örgütsel iletişim sürecinde yöneticilerin duygularını yönetebilme yeterlilikleri. *Selçuk Communication Journal*, *5*(4).

Turaman, C. (2007). Yaşlı sağlığı hizmetlerinin birinci basamakta planlanması. *Geriatri*, *4*(1), 22–27.

Turan, Z. (2011). Dünyadaki ve Türkiye'deki Krizlerin Ortaya Çıkış Nedenleri ve Ekonomik Kalkınmaya Etkisi. *Niğde Üniversitesi İİBF Dergisi*, *4*(1), 56–80.

Türk Dil Kurumu (TDK). (2013a). *Kriz*. Retrieved from http://www.tdk.gov.tr/index.php?option=com_gts&arama=gts&guid=TDK.GTS.5294a709bac895.50212827

Türk Dil Kurumu (TDK). (2013b). *Kıtlık*http://www.tdk.gov.tr/index.php?option=com_bts&arama=kelime&guid=TDK.GTS.529dd39ad6b7f7.63149192

Turkey Statistics Institution (2012, April), *Türkiye İstatistik Yıllığı 2011*. Ankara: Turkey Statistics Institution Printing.

Turkey Statistics Institution News Bulletin (2011, February). *Sağlık Harcama İstatistikleri 2008*. Ankara.

Turkey Statistics Institution News Bulletin (2013, October). *Sağlık Harcama İstatistikleri 2009 2010 2011, 2012*. Ankara.

Turkey Statistics Institution News Bulletin. (2010, February). *Sağlık Harcama İstatistikleri 2007*. Ankara: World Bank Statics. Retrieved from, www.worldbank.org

Turkey Statistics Institution News Bulletin. (2014, November). *Sağlık Harcama İstatistikleri 2013*. Retrieved from http://www.tuik.gov.tr/PreHaberBultenleri.do?id=16161

Turkish Airlines. (2014, March.). *Turkish Airlines 2013 Annual Financial Statement*. Istanbul: Turkish Airlines.

Turkish Ministry of Development. (2013). Tenth Five Year Development Plan 2014-2018.

Turkish Statistical Institute (TUIK). (2013a). *Tüketici Güven Endeksi Tüketici, EİSBEV Kapsam, Dönem ve Zamanlılık*. Retrieved from http://www.tuik.gov.tr/PreTablo.do?alt_id=1010

Turkish Statistical Institute (TUİK). (2014b). Tüketici Güven Endeksi, Ocak 2014. Türkiye İstatistik Kurumu Haber Bülteni. Sayı: 16093,28 Ocak 2014, Retrieved from http://www.tuik.gov.tr/PreHaberBultenleri.do?id=16093

Türkiye İstatistik Kurumu (TÜİK). [Turkish Statistical Institute]. (2011). *Hanehalkı bütçe araştırması tüketim harcamaları 2009. [Household Budget Survey Consumption Expenditures 2009]*. Ankara: TürkiyeİstatistikKuru muMatbaası.

TurkStat Poverty Study. (2010). Retrieved fromhttp://www.turkstat.gov.tr/PreHaberBultenleri.do?id=8642

Tversky, A., & Kahneman, D. (1973). Availability: A heuristic for judging frequency and probability. *Cognitive Psychology*, *5*(2), 207–232. doi:10.1016/0010-0285(73)90033-9

Tversky, A., & Kahneman, D. (1974). Judgment under uncertainty: Heuristics and biases. *Science*, *185*(4157), 1124–1131. doi:10.1126/science.185.4157.1124 PMID:17835457

Tversky, A., & Kahneman, D. (1986). Rational choice and the framing of decisions. *The Journal of Business*, *59*(4), 251–278. doi:10.1086/296365

Tversky, A., & Kahneman, D. (1992). Advances in prospect theory: Cumulative representation of uncertainty. *Journal of Risk and Uncertainty*, *5*(4), 297–323. doi:10.1007/BF00122574

Uğurluoğlu, Ö.,& Çelik,Y. (2009). Örgütlerde stratejik liderlik ve özellikleri. *Hacettepe Health Management Journal, 12*(2).

Ulas, H., & Kaya, B. (2009). Ekonomik krizin ruh sağlığına etkileri ve çözüm önerileri. *TPD Bülteni*, *12*(1), 59–62.

Ülker, H. İ. (2008). Kurumsal liderlikte duygusal yeterlilik. *Economic and Social Researches Journal*, *4*(2), 74–84.

Ülkü, N., & Prodan, E. (2013). Drivers of technical trend-following rules' profitability in world stock markets. *International Review of Financial Analysis*, *30*, 214–229. doi:10.1016/j.irfa.2013.08.005

UNDP. (1997). Human Development Report. Retrieved March 25, 2014, from http://hdr.undp.org/sites/default/files/reports/258/hdr_1997_en_complete_nostats.pdf

UNDP. (2007). *Human Development Report 2007/2008. Fighting climate change: Human solidarity in a divided world*. New York: Palgrave Macmillan.

UNDP. (2010). *Human development report 2010: The real wealth of nations: pathways to human development (20th ed.)*. Retrieved fromhttp://hdr.undp.org/sites/default/files/reports/270/hdr_2010_en_complete_reprint.pdf

UNDP. (2011). 2010 *Human development report: 40-year trends analysis shows poor countries making faster development gains*. Retrieved from http: www.undp.org

UNDP. (2014a). *I Can Manage My Money*. Retrieved May 22, 2014, from http://jobs.undp.org/cj_view_job.cfm?cur_job_id=44330

UNDP. (2014b). *Global Money Week Celebrated in Turkey with Financial Literacy Events*. Retrieved May 22, 2014, from http://www.tr.undp.org/content/turkey/en/home/presscenter/news-from-new-horizons/2014/04/_global-money-week-celebrated-in-turkey-with-financial-literacy-/

UNICEF. (2012). Child social and financial education. A Companion to the Child Friendly Schools Manual Unit for Children, (pp. 38-41).

US Energy Information Administration. (2013). Turkey Report 2013. Retrieved from http://www.eia.gov/countries /analysisbriefs/Turkey/turkey.pdf

Uslu, A., Durmuş, B., & Kolivar, B. K. (2013). Analyzing the Brand Equity of Turkish Airlines Services: Comparing the Japanese and Turkish Perspectives. *9th International Strategic Management Conference* (pp. 446-454). Istanbul: Procedia - Social and Behavioral Sciences.

Van der Sar, N. L. (2004). Behavioral finance: How matters stand. *Journal of Economic Psychology*, *25*(3), 425–444. doi:10.1016/j.joep.2004.02.001

van Wezel, W., Jorna, R., & Meystel, A. (2006). Planning. In *Intelligent Systems Aspects, Motivations, and Methods*. Hoboken, NJ: John Wiley & Sons, Inc.

Van Zyl, J. D., Cronjé, E. M., & Payze, C. (2006). Low Self-Esteem of Psychotherapy Patients: A Qualitative Inquiry. *Qualitative Report*, 182–208.

Varcoe, K. P., Martin, A., Devitto, Z., & Go, C. (2005). Using a financial education curriculum for teens. *Financial Counseling and Planning*, *16*(1), 63–71.

Varcoe, K., Peterson, S., Go, C., Johns, M., Rene Fitch, P., Powell, C., & Costello, C. (2002). Teen financial literacy evaluated to develop outreach materials. *California Agriculture*, *56*(2), 65–68.

Vasileiou, E. (2014a). *Long Live Day of the Week Patterns and the Financial Trends' Role: Evidence from the Greek Stock Market during the Euro Era (2002-12)*. Retrieved from; doi:10.2139/ssrn.2338430

Vasileiou, E. (2014b). Turn Of the Month Effect and Financial Crisis: A new explanation from the Greek Stock Market (2002-2012). *Theoretical and Applied Economics*, *10*, 33–58.

Vasileiou, E., & Samitas, A. (2014). *Does the Financial Crisis Influence the Month and the Trading Month Effects?* Evidence from the Athens Stock Exchange. Retrieved from; doi:10.2139/ssrn.2345450

Vasiliou, D., Eriotis, N., & Papathanasiou, S. (2008). Technical Trading Profitability in Greek Stock Market. *The Empirical Economics Letters*, *7*(7), 749–756.

Vaydonoff, P., & Donnely, B. W. (1989). Economic distress and mental health: The role of family coping resources and behaviors. *Lifestyles*, *10*(2), 139–162. doi:10.1007/BF00988534

Venter, J., & Jongh, P. D. (2002). Risk estimation using the normal inverse Gaussian distribution. *Journal of Risk*, *4*, 1–23.

Vera-Toscano, E., Ateca-Amestoy, V., & Serrano-Del-Rosal, R. (2006). Building financial satisfaction. *Social Indicators Research*, *77*(2), 211–243. doi:10.1007/s11205-005-2614-3

Verhoef, P. C. (2003). Understanding the effect of customer relationship management efforts on customer retention and customer share development. *Journal of Marketing*, *67*, 30–45.

VISA. (2011). *Financial Awareness* (pp.5-6) Retrieved May 22, 2014, fromhttp://www.fo-der.org/wp-content/uploads/2013/09/Visa-Turkey-Financial-Literacy-Conference-2011-Whitepaper-ENG.pdf

Vitt, L. A., Anderson, C., Kent, J., Lyter, D. M., Siegenthaler, J. K., & Ward, J. (2000). *Personal finance and the rush to competence: Personal financial literacy in the US*. Retrieved May 22, 2014, fromhttp://content.knowledgeplex.org/kp2/kp/report/report/relfiles/ht_pfrc_execsumm.pdf

Voinea, L., & Filip, A. (2011). Analyzing the Main Changes in New Consumer Buying Behavior during Economic Crisis. *International Journal of Economic Practices and Theories*, *1*(1), 14–19.

Volpe, R. P., Chen, H., & Pavlicko, J. J. (1996). Personal investment literacy among college students: A survey. *Financial Practice and Education*, *6*(2), 86–94.

Von Neumann, J., & Morgenstern, O. (1944). *Theory of games and economic behavior*. Princeton, NJ: Princeton University Press.

von Neumann, J., & Morgenstern, O. (1944). *Theory of Games and Economic Behavior*. Princeton: Princeton University Press.

Voss, G. B., & Voss, Z. G. (1997). Implementing a relationship marketing program: A case study and managerial implications. *Journal of Services Marketing*, *11*(4), 278–298.

Wachter, J. A. (2002). Comment on: Are behavioral asset pricing models structural? *Journal of Monetary Economics*, *49*(1), 229–233. doi:10.1016/S0304-3932(01)00102-7

Wandji, Y. D. F. (2013). Energy Consumption and Economic Growth: Evidence from Cameroon. *Energy Policy*, *61*, 1295–1304. doi:10.1016/j.enpol.2013.05.115

Wang, P. (1993). Helping your kids become financially independent. *Money*, *22*, 72–78.

Waters, L. K., & Kirk, W. E. (1968). Stimulus-seeking motivation and risk taking behavior in a gambling situation. *Educational and Psychological Measurement*, *28*(2), 549–550. doi:10.1177/001316446802800242

WB. (2011). *Poverty and social exclusion in India*. Washington.

Weber, M. (1999). *Behavioral finance. Research for Practitioners* (Vol. 0-8). University of Mannheim.

Weijermars, R. (2011). *Building Corporate IQ: Moving the Energy Business from Smart to Genius Executive Guide to Preventing Costly Crises*. Springer.

Weinstein, N. (1980). Unrealistic optimism about future life events. *Journal of Personality and Social Psychology*, *39*(5), 806–820. doi:10.1037/0022-3514.39.5.806

Weir, D., Willis, R., & Sevak, P. (2004). The economic consequences of a husband' death: Evidence from the HRS and AHEAD. *Social Security Bulletin*, *65*, 31–44.

Weisman, R. (2002). Personal financial stress, depression, and workplace performance. In E. T. Garman, F. Williams, R. Weisman, H. Fried, W. A. Kelly, & W. W. Sayles (Eds.), *Financial stress and workplace performance: Developing employer-credit union partnerships*. Madison, WI: Center for Credit Union Innovation and Filene Research Institute.

Wessels, D. (2006). *Consumer Loyalty in the Airline Industry*. Philadelphia: University of Pennsylvania.

Weston, R., & Gore, P. A. (2006). A brief guide to structural equation modeling. *The Counseling Psychologist*, *34*(5), 719–751. doi:10.1177/0011000006286345

Wiener, N. (1923). Differential space. *Journal of Mathematics and Physics*, *58*, 131–174.

Wiggins, S. D., & Henderson, C. M. (1996). Preretirement planning of female registered nurses. *Western Journal of Nursing Research*, *18*(5), 580–594. doi:10.1177/019394599601800508 PMID:8918209

Williams, N. (2001). *The Work We Were Born to Do*. London: Element Books.

Wilson, K. N., & Aggrey, M. E. A. (2012). Retirement planning and counseling: Issues and challenges for teachers in public schools in the Sekondi Circuit. *United States-China Education Review A*, *8*, 755–767.

Wolman, B. B. (1973). *Dictionary of Behavioural Science*. Van Nostrand Reinhold Company.

Wong, A., & Carducci, B. J. (1991). Sensation seeking and financial risk taking in everyday money matters. *Journal of Business and Psychology*, *5*(4), 525–530. doi:10.1007/BF01014500

World Bank World Development Indicators Database. (2013). Retrieved from http://data.worldbank.org/data-catalog/world-development-indicators

World Bank. (1990). *World Development Report 1990*. Oxford University Press.

World Bank. (2000). *World Development Report 2000/2001: Attacking poverty*. New York: Oxford University Press. Retrieved from http://www.worldbank.org/poverty/wdrpoverty/report/index

World Bank. (2005). *World Bank/WB, Turkey joint poverty assessment report*. Human Development Sector Unit, Europe and Central Asia Region, State Institute of Statistics Turkey. Volume 1: Main Report, Report No: 296-19-TU. World Summit for Social Development Programme of Action, UN. Chapter 2: Eradication of Poverty. Retrieved from: http://www.un.org/esa/socdev/wssd/text-version/agreements/poach2.htm

World Health Organization (WHO). (2009). *The financial crisis and global health, report on a high-level consultation* (pp. 1–6). Geneva: WHO.

World Health Organization. (2007). *Philippine health information system: Review & Assessment*. Retrieved from http://www.who.int/healthmetrics/library/countries/HMN_PHL_Assess_Final_2007_07_en.pdf

World Health Organization. (2009b). *National health accounts: Country information*. Retrieved from http://www.who.int/nha/country/en/index.html

World Health Organization. (2012). *Health service delivery profile Philippines*. Retrieved from http://www.wpro.who.int/health_service_service_delivery_profile_philippines.pdf

World Health Organization. (n.d.). Retrieved from, www.who.org

Wunder, S., Engel, S., & Pagiola, S. (2008). Taking stock: A comparative analysis of payments for environmental services programs in developed and developing countries. *Ecological Economics*, *65*(4), 834–852. doi:10.1016/j.ecolecon.2008.03.010

www.new-milesandsmiles.com. (2014, april 28). *Miles and Smiles*. Retrieved May 21, 2014, from Turkish Airlines: http://www.turkishairlines.com/tr-tr/kurumsal/haberler/miles-smiles/pek-yakinda-miles-smilesta-yeni-bir-donem-yeniliklerle-basliyor

Xiao, J. J., Sorhaindo, B., & Garman, E. T. (2006). Financial behavior of consumers in credit counseling. *International Journal of Consumer Studies*, *30*(2), 108–121. doi:10.1111/j.1470-6431.2005.00455.x

Xiao, J. J., Tang, C., & Shim, S. (2009). Acting for happiness: Financial behavior and life satisfaction of college students. *Social Indicators Research*, *92*(1), 53–68. doi:10.1007/s11205-008-9288-6

Yaari, M. (1987). The dual theory of choice under risk. *Econometrica*, *55*(1), 95–115. doi:10.2307/1911158

Yadollahi, M., Paim, L. H., Othman, M., & Suandi, T. (2009). Factors affecting economic status. *European Journal of Scientific Research*, *37*, 99–109.

Yao, R., Gutter, M. S., & Hanna, S. D. (2005). The financial risk tolerance of Blacks, Hispanics, and Whites. *Journal of Financial Counseling and Planning*, *16*(1), 51–62.

Yao, R., Hanna, S. D., & Lindamood, S. (2004). Changes in financial risk tolerance, 1983-2001. *Financial Services Review*, *13*(4), 249–266.

Yazıcıoğlu, A. (2006). *Emekliliğin kadının sosyal yaşamında meydana getirdiği değişmeler üzerine bir grounded theory denemesi* [A grounded theory essay on the changes in woman's social life affected by retirement]. Unpublished master's thesis, Hacettepe University, Turkey.

Yılmaz, S. (1996). *Türkiye'de emeklilik yaşantısı* [The experience of retirement in Turkey]. Unpublished master's thesis, Dokuz Eylül University, Turkey.

Yılmaz, B. E. (2013). Reflections of the Global Economic Crisis on the Countries of PIIGS and Turkey's Macroeconomic Variables. *Marmara Üniversitesi İktisadi ve İdari Bilimler Dergisi*, *34*(1), 231.

Yoong, J. (2011, December). Can behavioural economics be used to make financial education more effective? *Improving Financial Education Efficiency: OECD-Bank of Italy Symposium on Financial Literacy* (pp.66-89).

Yu, J., & Yuan, Y. (n.d.). *BIST Second National Index data from Borsa Istanbul*. Retrieved from http://borsaistanbul.com/en/data

Yu, J., & Yuan, Y. *Consumer Confidence Index data from Turkish Statistical Institute*. Retrieved from http://www.turkstat.gov.tr/Start.do

Yu, J., & Yuan, Y. (2011). Investor sentiment and the mean–variance relation. *Journal of Financial Economics*, *100*(2), 367–381. doi:10.1016/j.jfineco.2010.10.011

Yunus, M. (1999). *Yoksulluğun bulunmadığı bir dünyaya doğru (Çev:G. Şen)*. Doğan Kitap Yayınevi.

Zaidi, A., Makovec, M., Fuchs, M., Lipszyc, B., Lelkes, O., Rummel, M., & De Vos, K. (2006). *Poverty of elderly people in EU25 Report*. European Centre for Social Welfare Policy and Research.

Zaleskiewicz, T. (2006). Behavioural Finance. In M. Altman (Ed.), *Handbook of Contemporary Behavioural Economics* (pp. 706–728). New York: M.E. Sharpe.

Zastrow, C. (2008). *Introduction to social work and social welfare: empowering people*. United States: Thomson Brooks Cole.

Zastrow, C. (2013). *Sosyal hizmete giriş* [Introduction to social work]. Ankara: Nika Yayınevi.

Zengingönül, O. (2005). Nedir Bu Küreselleşme? Kaçabilir miyiz? Kullanabilir miyiz? *Siyasal*, *1*(1), 85–106.

Zhang, Y., Fan, J., & Chang, H. (2011). Impact of China's Stock Market Development on Energy Consumption: An Empirical Analysis. *Energy Procedia*, *5*, 1927–1931. doi:10.1016/j.egypro.2011.03.331

Zhao, J., & Zhang, P. (n.d.).Game analysis on coordinated development in Beijing and Tianjin and poverty-stricken around Beijing and Tianjin. Retrieved December 23, 2013, from http://www.rrojasdatabank.info/zhaojunyan2008.pdf

Zhou, W.-X., & Sornette, D. (2006). Is there a real-estate bubble in the U.S.? *Physica A*, *361*(1), 297–308. doi:10.1016/j.physa.2005.06.098

Zineldin, M. (2000). Total relationship management (TRM) and total quality management (TQM). *Managerial Auditing Journal*, *2*, 20–28.

Zineldin, M., & Philipson, S. (2007). Kotler and Borden are not dead: Myth of relationship marketing and truth of the 4Ps. *Journal of Consumer Marketing*, 229–241.

Zuckerman, M. (1987). Is sensation seeking a predisposing trait for alcoholism? In E. Gottheil, K. A. Druley, S. Pashkey. & S. P. Weinstein (Eds.), Stress and Addiction (pp. 283-301). New York, NY: Bruner/Mazel.

Zuckerman, M. (2010). Sensation Seeking. Corsini Encyclopedia of Psychology. 1–4.

Zuckerman, M. (1969). Theories of sensory deprivation. In I. J. P. Zubek (Ed.), *Sensory deprivation: Fifteen years of research* (pp. 407–432). New York, NY: Appleton-Century-Crofts.

Zuckerman, M. (1974). The sensation seeking motive. In B. Maher (Ed.), *Progress in experimental personality research*. New York, NY: Academic Press.

Zuckerman, M. (1976). Sensation seeking and anxiety, traits and states, as determinants of behavior in novel situations. In I. G. Sarason & C. D. Spielberger (Eds.), *Stress and anxiety*. Washington, DC: Hemisphere.

Zuckerman, M. (1979a). *Sensation Seeking: Beyond the Optimal Level of Arousal*. Hillsdale, NJ: Erlbaum.

Zuckerman, M. (1979b). Sensation seeking and risk taking. In C. E. Izard (Ed.), *Emotions in Personality and Psychopathology* (pp. 163–197). New York, NY: Plenum Press. doi:10.1007/978-1-4613-2892-6_7

Zuckerman, M. (1994). *Behavioural Expressions and Biosocial Bases of Sensation-Seeking*. Cambridge: Cambridge University Press.

Zuckerman, M. (2007). *Sensation Seeking and Risky Behavior*. Washington, DC: American Psychological Association. doi:10.1037/11555-000

Zuckerman, M., Bone, R. N., Neary, R., Mangelsdorff, D., & Brustman, B. (1972). What is the sensation seeker? Personality trait and experience correlates of the Sensation Seeking Scales. *Journal of Consulting and Clinical Psychology*, *39*, 308–321.

Zuckerman, M., Buchsbaum, M. S., & Murphy, D. L. (1980). Sensation seeking and its biological correlates. *Psychological Bulletin*, *88*(1), 87–214. doi:10.1037/0033-2909.88.1.187

Zuckerman, M., & Kuhlman, D. M. (2000). Personality and risk-taking: Common biosocial factors. *Journal of Personality*, *68*(6), 999–1029. doi:10.1111/1467-6494.00124 PMID:11130742

Zurlo, K. A. (2009). Personal attributes and the financial well-being of older adults: the effects of control beliefs (PARC Working Papers, 27).

About the Contributors

Zeynep Copur, Ph.D. is a Professor in the Department of Family and Consumer Sciences, Faculty of Economics and Administrative Sciences at the Hacettepe University in Ankara, Turkey. Currently, she serves Associate Dean Position at same faculty. She had been a visiting scholar in the Department of Family, Youth and Community Sciences and the Department of Sociology and Criminology & Law at the University of Florida. Her research and teaching specialties include family resource management, family economics, consumer economics, family financial management, family relations, and family issues. As a visiting scholar at the University of Florida, she had been actively working on several research projects with Dr. Michael S. Gutter and Dr. Tanya Koropeckyj-Cox, includes a co-authored publication on the financial management practices of college students, using data drawn from college students in the United States and comparing Turkish and American university students' attitudes and preferences regarding gender, childbearing, and family issues. She also worked as a co-investigator on a funded extension project at the University of Florida on the Economic Impact of Earned Income Tax Credit in Florida, funded by Real Sense Prosperity Campaign, SPA agreement. She has published in a variety of social science journals, including Journal of Family Issues, Journal of Comparative Family Studies, Family and Consumer Sciences Research Journal, Social Behavior and Personality: An International Journal, The Indian Journal of Social Work, Journal of Family and Economic Issues. Some of her works title are; Perception of the Adequacy of Resources with a Turkish Sample, Social Learning Opportunities and the Financial Behaviors of College Students, Exploring the Relationship between Financial Behaviors and Financial Well-Being of College Students.

***

Yaşar Akdağ received his master's degree in Institute of Social Sciences from the University of Pamukkale in 2012. In 2010 he was hired as Research Assistant by the Faculty of Economics and Administrative Sciences at the University of Hakkari and is currently conducting his PhD in Institue of Social Sciences at the University of Marmara. His research focuses on issues of Public Financing on Renewable Energy, Green Economy and Health Economics (2014, Hakkari).

Veli Akel is an Associate Professor of Finance at Faculty of Economics and Administrative Sciences in Erciyes University, Kayseri, Turkey. Assoc. Prof. Akel teaches Capital Markets, International Finance, Portfolio Management, Corporate Finance and related courses. He received the B.S. degree in Business Administration, Erciyes University, 1998, M.S. degree in Finance, Anadolu University, 2001, and PhD degree in Finance, Erciyes University, 2006. His main research areas focus on financial contagion, neural networks, institutional investor and capital markets.

Nuray Akpolat graduated from Nevsehir Ataturk Vocational School of Health, Department of Nursing in 1997. She also graduated from Anadolu University, Faculty of Economics, Department of Public Administration in 2009. She received her master's degree from Ankara University (Turkey), Institute of Health Sciences, Department of Social Work in 2014. She has been working as school nurse in Nevşehir.

Aybala Demirci Aksoy graduated from the Department of Family and Consumer Sciences, Hacettepe University in 1999 and started to do her master's at the Educational Sciences Institute of Gazi University, Home Economics and Nutrition Education in the same year. Accomplishing her education, she got a master degree, and she started to do her PhD at the Department Home Economics and Nutrition Education in the same year DEMİRCİ AKSOY, completing her thesis titled "Consumer Education Model via Internet", is proficient in English. She became assistant professor in 2009 and associate professor in 2013. She has various publications in the realm of consumer education, consumer behavior, consumer protection, consumer rights, and disabled consumer groups.

Korhan Arun received a BA in mathematics from Hacettepe University (Turkey) and an M.B.A in Total Quality Management from Dokuz Eylul University in 2003 and a Ph.D. in Organization and Management from Ataturk University (Turkey) in 2008. He is an assistant Professor of Organization and Management at the University at Namik Kemal University (Tekirdag/Turkey). His current research and teaching interests include: leadership, power and influence, organization and management development. Dr. Arun worked at the government agencies for 15 years. Also, he had an advisor position for NATO (KFOR/ Kosovo Force) in 2012. He has been involved in several projects to improve leadership in the Turkish Army.

Sinan Ataer, graduated from the Department of Public Finance in Istanbul University at 2010. He is now MS student of two different program in Social Sciences Institute of Istanbul University. Both of them predicted to be end at the year of 2014. He is a research assistant at Public Finance Department since 2011. Now he is assisting the Public Debts, Public Finance classes in the Faculty of Economy, Istanbul University. His MS subject is about railway investments and infrastructure investments in Turkey.

Ayfer Aydıner Boylu received her MS and PhD in Family and Consumer Sciences from the Hacettepe University Ankara in 2001/2007. In 2012 she was hired as Associate Professor and is currently the vice chair for the Department of Family and Consumer Sciences of the Hacettepe University. She writes and presents widely on issues of family quality of life, family crisis, economical activities of families, financial distress, and she had been actively working on several research projects. Some of her published articles are; the impact of the economic crisis on lifestyles of families, an examination of factors affecting economic status and finances satisfaction of families, an assessment of economic costs and contributions of children to the family, investigating the effect of working wives on family expenditure, analyses of debt related behaviors of families, and examination of socio-economic variables having effect on functions of single parent families.

Hakan Cavlak is an assistant professor of international relations at Namık Kemal University, Faculty of Economics and Administrative Sciences, Tekirdağ-Turkey. Dr. Cavlak has BAs in International Relations at Istanbul University (2000). He received PhD in EU Politics and International Relations with his thesis entitled as "Europeanization of Environmental Policy in Turkey". European Policies, Integration Theories, Enlargement of the EU, EU – Turkey Relations are his main research areas. He is the editor in chief of Balkan Journal of Social Sciences (BJSS).

Neslihan Cavlak is a lecturer of tourism and marketing at Namık Kemal University, Malkara School of Higher Education, Tekirdağ-Turkey. Cavlak has BA in Tourism and Hotel Management at Bilkent University (1999). She is a PhD candidate in Business Administration. Marketing, tourism, tourism management, tourism marketing, are her main research areas.

Seher Cesur-Kılıçaslan received her Ph.D. in 2006 from Hacettepe University. She also received her M.Sc. (2001), and B.Sc. (1997) from Hacettepe University. Dr. Cesur-Kılıçaslan is head of department of Social Work at Istanbul Arel University. Her areas of expertise include: immigrant families, refugee families, refugee women, immigration and emigration, family structure, gender studies, honor killings, poverty and consumption. She has published in a variety of social science journals, including *The International Journal of the Humanities, Ethnologia Balkanica, International Journal of Arts & Sciences* and *The International Journal of Interdisciplinary Cultural Studies.* Some of her works' titles are: "The Family Structure of the Bulgarian Immigrants and the Local Residents Living in Inegöl Region," "The Problems of Refugee Women," "The Effects of Immigration and Emigration on the Family Structure in Turkey" and "Families Immigrating from Bulgaria to Turkey since 1878."

Murat Cetin is an Associate Professor of Economic Development at Faculty of Economics and Administrative Sciences in Namik Kemal University, Tekirdag, Turkey. Assoc. Prof. Cetin teaches Economic Growth and Development, Macroeconomics, Monetary Policy related courses. He received the B.S. degree in Economics Karadeniz Teknik University, 1994, M.S. degree in Economics, Karadeniz Teknik University, 1996, and PhD degree in Economics Karadeniz Teknik University, 2000. His main research areas focus on growth economics, energy economics, time-series and panel data analyses.

Hasan Dinçer is an associate professor of finance at Istanbul Medipol University, Faculty of Economics and Administrative Sciences, Istanbul- Turkey. Dr. Dinçer has BAs in Financial Markets and Investment Management at Marmara University. He received PhD in Finance and Banking with his thesis entitled as "The Effect of Changes on the Competitive Strategies of New Service Development in the Banking Sector". He has a work experience in Finance sector as portfolio specialist and his major academic studies focusing on financial instruments, performance evaluation, and economics. He is the executive editor of International Journal of Finance and Banking Studies (IJFBS) and the founder member of the Society for the Study of Business and Finance (SSBF).

Eyyup Ecevit is an Assistant Professor of Economic Development at Faculty of Economics and Administrative Sciences in Erciyes University, Kayseri, Turkey. Assistant Prof. Ecevit teaches Macroeconomics, Microeconomics courses. He received the B.S. degree in Economics, Erciyes University, 1999; M.S. degree in Economics, Niğde University, 2002 and PhD degree in Economics Erciyes University, 2007. His main research areas focus on health economics, growth, time-series.

Sibel Erkal is a Professor at the Hacettepe University, Family and Consumer Sciences Department. Her BS (1992) and her PhD (1997) is in Family and Consumer Sciences from the Hacettepe University. She teaches in the undergraduate and graduate programs in the areas of Family and Consumer Sciences. Dr. Erkal's research interests include Hygiene in home and institutions, home accidents, housing and health, housekeeping. She has published in a variety of social science journals. She worked as a Visiting Associate Professor at Minnesota University, School of Public Health, Department of Environmental Health Sciences on 9th August-19th December 2006.

John E. Grable, holds an Athletic Association Endowed Professorship at the University of Georgia. Dr. Grable served as the founding editor for the *Journal of Personal Finance* and the co-editor of the *Journal of Financial Therapy*. His research interests include financial risk-tolerance assessment, financial planning help-seeking behavior, and psychophysiological economics. Dr. Grable received his Ph.D. degree from Virginia Tech.

Sevilay Gumus has double BS in Economics and International Relations from Gazi University (Ankara,TURKEY). She received her MS in Finance from the Drexel University LeBow College of Business in 2010 and in the same year she was hired as a Research and Teaching Assistant at Usak University. She was transferred to Hacettepe University in 2011.She is currently studying two doctoral program simultaneously at Hacettepe University Public Finbance Department and Police Academy International Security. "A Comparison of European Union and Turkey Concerning Social Parafiscal Burden between 1995 and 2008" and "Analysis of Protective Economic Policies and Trade Defense Measures in Market Economy" are some of her works. Recently she won the best presentation award with "Socio-demographic and Socio-economic Profiles of Satisfaction with Local Public Services in Turkey: An Analysis on Turkey between 2004 and 2012" in Singapore.

Gülay Günay received her MS in Family and Consumers Sciences from the University of Hacettepe University in 1992. She was a Research Assistant of Family and Consumer Sciences at Hacettepe University Faculty of Economics and Administrative Sciences (1996 – 2006). She works in Karabuk University as an As Prof. (2009 - 2012). Now she is working as Associated Prof. (since 2012). She writes and presents widely on issues of preretirement planning, post retirement life, consumer problems, consumer behavior, consumer education, ageing and family. She has published in a variety of social science journals. She is married and has two children.

Davuthan Günaydin is an Assistant Professor of Labor Economics at Faculty of Economics and Administrative Sciences in Namık Kemal University, Tekirdag, Turkey. Assist. Prof. GÜNAYDIN teaches Social Policy, Sociology of Work and regional development related courses. He received the B.S. degree in Economics Anadolu University, 2003, M.S. degree in Operations research, Marmara University, 2006, and PhD degree in Labor Economics Marmara University, 2011. His main research areas focus on health policies regional development policies and social policies.

Abdulhamid Mauyag Gunda, was born in Philippine. He completed undergraduate degree from Nursing High School in Philippine. He earned his bachelor's degree in nursing from the Mindanao State University in 2010 and has passed the Nursing Licensure Examinations given by the Philippine's Professional Regulation Commission in the same year. He has worked as a community nurse under the

Department of Health in 2011. He has lived in Turkey for about three years as a Turkish Government's scholar for master's degree in health management. He is a post graduate student at Health Care Management, Institute of Social Sciences, Namık Kemal University, Tekirdag-Turkey. He continues to writing his thesis on Philippine Health Care System in Namık Kemal University. His main research fields focus on health care management, health care systems, Philippine health care system, health care system analyses, health care economics and Philippine economy.

Burcu Bozkurt Hacioglu, following her graduate study of Business and Economics at Bilgi University, has pursued her educational life as a postgraduate student of Management and Organization at Kadir Has University. She has teaching experience as a lecturer of Business, Marketing and Logistics between 2004 and 2011 at Beykent University.

Ümit Hacıoğlu is an associate professor of finance at Istanbul Medipol University, Faculty of Economics and Administrative Sciences, Istanbul-Turkey. Dr. Hacıoğlu has BAs in Business Administration and International Relations (2002). He received PhD in Finance and Banking with his thesis entitled as "Effects of Conflict on Equity Performance". Finance and Banking, Strategic Management and International Political economy are the main pillars of his interdisciplinary studies. He is the executive editor of International Journal of Research in Business and Social Science (IJRBS) and the founder member of the Society for the Study of Business and Finance (SSBF).

Wookjae Heo is a Ph.D. candidate in the Department of Financial Planning, Housing, and Consumer Economics at the University of Georgia. Prior to enrolling the University of Georgia, he worked for a marketing consulting firm as a Strategic Marketing Planner and Consumer Research Specialist in Korea. Before working at the consulting firm, he received a Masters of Arts Degree in Consumer Sciences from Seoul National University, South Korea. His main research interest is broadly about consumer welfare including financial stress on consumer behavior, demand of life insurance, and marketing impact on financial behaviors. In terms of financial planning, his research interest is to explore financial stress on financial planning and to find proper education for financial planning.

Abdülkadir Işık was born in 1972 Ahlat-Bitlis/ Turkey. He is a professor at Namık Kemal University, Faculty of Economics and Administrative Sciences, Tekirdag-Turkey. He completed undergraduate degree from Anadolu University, Faculty of Economics and Administrative Sciences, Department of Public Finance. He completed master's degree (MA) in Public Finance at Marmara University and he holds a Ph.D in Public Finance from Marmara University. He was a visiting researcher at Sussex University/ UK, and a post doctoral researcher at New York State University/ USA. His main research fields focus on public finance, public sector economics, taxation and health care economics.

Hayriye Işik, was born in Karacabey Bursa/Turkey. She completed undergraduate degree from Anadolu University, Faculty of Economics and Administrative Sciences, Public Finance. She completed master's degree (MA) in public finance and she holds a Ph.D in Public Finance from Celal Bayar University. Her main research fields focus on tax law, Turkish tax system, health and education spending, and public finance. She works as the faculty members at Namik Kemal University, Faculty of Economics and Administrative Sciences, Public Finance.

Toprak Işık (Erdal Kılıçaslan): Toprak Işık was born in 1973 in Elazığ in Eastern Turkey. His childhood and youth were spent in Inegöl in Western Turkey. After he studied electric engineering in Bilkent University, he moved to New York and lived there for two years. In 2008 he settled in Istanbul and since then he does "just a bit of engineering" and mostly devoting himself to writing. He has seven published fiction books for children and five books for adults. Three of his plays are in the Repertory of Turkish State Theatre. Beside fiction writing, he also academically interested in the areas of women, gender studies, family structure, honor killings, poverty and consumption.

Serkan Yılmaz Kandır is an Associate Professor of Finance at Faculty of Economics and Administrative Sciences in Çukurova University, Adana, Turkey. Assoc. Prof. Kandır teaches Capital Markets, Portfolio Management, Behavioral Finance, Corporate Finance and similar courses in finance. He received the B.S. degree in Business Administration, Çukurova University, 1999; M.S. degree in Finance, Çukurova University, 2001; PhD degree in Finance, Çukurova University, 2006. His main research areas focus on behavioral finance, event study and capital markets.

Sujata Kapoor has been working as faculty in the area of Finance with reputed business schools for around 10 years. She is an MBA (Finance) and has earned her B.Com (Hons) degree from Delhi University. She completed her PhD in the area of Corporate Finance in the year 2010. She also holds certification in financial markets. Currently, she works as an Assistant Professor in Jaypee Business School Noida, a premier B school and is also serving as an Area chair (Finance). She has contributed numerous of publications in the area of Corporate finance and behavior finance. She has also presented various research papers in prestigious international conferences like FMA annual meet.

Kijpokin Kasemsap received his BEng degree in Mechanical Engineering from King Mongkut's University of Technology Thonburi, his MBA degree from Ramkhamhaeng University, and his DBA degree in Human Resource Management from Suan Sunandha Rajabhat University. He is a Special Lecturer at Faculty of Management Sciences, Suan Sunandha Rajabhat University based in Bangkok, Thailand. He is a Member of International Association of Engineers (IAENG), International Association of Engineers and Scientists (IAEST), International Economics Development and Research Center (IEDRC), International Association of Computer Science and Information Technology (IACSIT), International Foundation for Research and Development (IFRD), and International Innovative Scientific and Research Organization (IISRO). He also serves on the International Advisory Committee (IAC) for International Association of Academicians and Researchers (INAAR). He has numerous original research articles in top international journals, conference proceedings, and book chapters on business management, human resource management, and knowledge management published internationally.

Jorge Ruiz-Menjivar is a doctoral student and research assistant in the department of Financial Planning, Housing and Consumer Economics at the University of Georgia. His research interests include financial risk-tolerance measurement, personal and family finance, and international and Latin American economics. Mr. Ruiz-Menjivar holds a Master's Degree in Personal and Family Financial Planning from the University of Florida.

Vuyisani Moss is an experienced and trained development economist with a Masters' Degree in Policy and Development Economics (cum-laude); a PhD degree-Engineering (property finance) thesis-'measuring the correlation between the lack of borrower education and the risk of mortgage default in low income homeowners in South Africa'. Has fifteen years of housing finance work experience and operational research both retail and wholesale. Dr Moss worked for the National Housing Finance Corporation and as a Consultant for the UN- Habitat based in Nairobi. He is currently a Director of Planning and Strategy at the National Department of Human Settlements in SA and gives occasional lectures on micro-credit, development finance and property finance at Wits University.

Ahmet Oğuz received his MS in Economics from Dumlupınar University in 1999. He was a Research Assistant of Economics at Dumlupınar University Institute of Social Sciences (1999 – 2002) and Dokuz Eylul University Faculty of Economics and Administrative Sciences (2002 – 2010). Now he is working in Karabuk University as an As Prof. (since 2010). He writes and presents widely on issues of international economics, economic policy, development and growth analysis, economics and strategic planning. He has published in a variety of social science journals. He is married and has a child.

Aydın Özdemir is a marketing professional at Turkish Airlines, Istanbul, Turkey. He has BA at Middle East Technical University, Ankara, Turkey and MBA at Polytechnic University on Marketing Management and Business Administration at Beykent University. He has work experience in Airline Marketing and Flight Training. He has studies focusing on airline marketing and specifically on pricing strategies.

Gamze Özel received her PhD., Master of Science in 2009, and Bachelor of Science in 2005 from Department of Statistics, Hacettepe University. Her research interests include stochastic processes, risk management, probability theory, survival analysis, and applied statistics. She is an associate professor in the Department of Statistics at Hacettepe University.

Emine Özmete is professor at Ankara University, at the Department of Social Work. She is the head of the Center on Aging Studies Implementation and Research at Ankara University. She is conducting her studies about quality of life, well-being, social capital, life skill education, financial behavior- financial planning and resource management in the family. Prof. Dr. Emine Ozmete received her MS in Family and Consumer Sciences from the University of Ankara in 1997 about quality of life and values. In 2002 she received her doctorate degree fromthe University of Ankara. She visited to USA Iowa State University, Department of Family Studies and Human Development as scholar. She carried out her studies about financial behavior there in 2008.

Jaya M. Prosad is a resident of NOIDA, U.P., India. She is a graduate from Delhi University (Year 2009) and completed her MBA degree in finance from Jaypee Institute of Information and Technology University, NOIDA (Year 2011). Her major area of interest is behavioral finance. She is currently working as a PhD. Scholar with Jaypee Business School, NOIDA. She has publications in various national and international journals in the area of behavioral finance. She has also presented papers in reputed conferences like India Finance Conference by IIM A, B, C. Ms. Prosad is presently a member of International Economics Development and Research Center (IEDRC).

Mohamad Fazli Sabri is the Head Department (Senior Lecture) at the Department of Resource Management and Consumer Studies, Faculty of Human Ecology, University Putra Malaysia. He was graduated with Master of Science (Consumer Science) from University Putra Malaysia and holds a Doctorate in the field of Consumer Finance from Iowa State University, USA. He is actively engaged in research in the field of consumer finance and financial education from childhood through to the elderly. He has presented papers at national and international level. Moreover, he also participated as a speaker and trainer, and related consumer financial education. He is also the one of the executive council Consumer and Family Economics Association Malaysia (MACFEA) for the session 2012-2014. In addition, he is also a member (board members) in research and education committee, Malaysian Financial Planning Council. Currently, he is Editor- in-Chief of the Journal of Wealth Management & Financial Planning and engaged in "research working group committee" in Child & Youth Finance International.

Shalini Kalra Sahi is an Assistant Professor in the area of Finance at Management Development Institute, Gurgaon, India. She received her Masters in Business Economics (MBE) and M.Phil. (Business Economics), both from University of Delhi, New Delhi, India. She is also a Fellow(FPM-doctoral programme) of Management Development Institute (MDI), Gurgaon, India. She has around 7 years of teaching experience and has published a number of articles in the area of Behavioural Finance and Investor Psychology.

Hande Sahin, PhD is an Assoc. Prof. in the Department of Social Work at the Kırıkkale University in Kırıkkale, Turkey. Her research and teaching specialties include disabled and elderly, home accidents, quality of life of elderly, environmental problems. Some of her published articles are; Comparison of Environmental Attitudes of University Students Determined Via the New Environmental Paradigm Scale According to the Students' Personal Characteristics, Behaviors of Students Towards Safety Measures to Prevent School Accidents, Home Accidents and Assistance in Daily Activities of Older Women in Turkey, Analysis of Disabled Individuals' Level of Satisfaction with Accommodation Facilities.

Fahri Seker is an Assistant Professor of Economic Development at Faculty of Economics and Administrative Sciences in Bozok University, Yozgat, Turkey. Ass. Prof. Seker teaches Economic Growth and Development, Macroeconomics, Monetary Policy related courses. He received the B.S. degree in Economics Marmara University, 1997, M.S. degree in Economics, Marmara University, 2001, and PhD degree in Economics Erciyes University, 2007. His main research areas focus on development economics, environmental economics, applied time-series econometrics.

Jhumur Sengupta is a PhD in Political Economy from University of Calcutta, is an Assistant Professor at Dinabandhu Andrews College, Calcutta University. West Bengal, India. She has more than nine years of teaching experience in various reputed Universities in India. She has to her credit a number of research articles in the field of Economics and Political Economy.

Ferda Yerdelen Tatoğlu, received her MS degree in Econometrics from Istanbul University Social Sciences Institute at 2001. She received her PhD degree on Econometrics at 2005, from the same institute. She was selected as a research assistant for Econometrics of Faculty of Economy in Istanbul University when she was a MS student. In 2007, she was awarded young researcher prize. She became an associate professor at 2011 in Econometrics. The areas which are she is interested in and tutoring are theoretical and applied econometrics and panel data econometrics. She has had numerous articles and she is the author of seven books two of which have been published in expanded second editions. Her latest two books are Panel Data Econometrics and Advanced Panel Data Analysis.

Zeynep Tezel, graduated from Gazi University of Industrial Arts Education Faculty. In 1993 she was hired as the Assistant Professor by the Family and Consumer Sciences Education Department at the Gazi University. She is currently as Assoc. Prof. Dr. for Social Services Department in Health Sciences Faculty at University of Kırıkkale. She writes and presents on issues about young consumers for social services.

Birol Topcu is an Assistant Professor of Biostatistics at Faculty of Medicine in Namik Kemal University, Tekirdag, Turkey. Assist. Prof. Topcu teaches Statistics, Biostatistics, Mathematical Statistics related courses. He received the B.S. degree in Mathematics Ankara University, 1995, M.S. degree in Mathematics, Afyon Kocatepe University, 1997, and PhD degree in Statistics Ankara University, 2003. His main research areas focus on dependence, statistics, biostatistics and mathematical statistics.

Türker Tuğsal is a doctorate student of management at Istanbul Commerce University, Institute of Social Sciences, Istanbul-Turkey and researcher of capital markets and portfolio management department at Beykent University, Faculty of Applied Sciences. He has BAs in Business Administration at Süleyman Demirel University (2003) and Capital Markets and Finance masters degree from Bahçeşehir University (2006). Management and Organization Theories, Strategic Management, Organizational Behavior, Leadership, Organizational Economics and Financial Crisis are the main pillars of his academic studies.

Evangelos Vasileiou is a certified Financial Analyst (Hellenic Republic Capital Market Commission) with extensive banking and finance professional experience in Greek financial institutions. He holds a bachelors' degree in Economics (University of Piraeus, Greece) and MSc degree in Banking and Finance (University of Piraeus, Greece). Since 2011, Evangelos is a Phd Candidate in Banking and Finance at the Department of Business Administrator of the University of the Aegean, Greece. His major fields of interest are: Economics, Financial Analysis, Banking, Financial Risk and Forecasting. His papers has been presented in international conferences and published in international refereed journals such as Journal of Financial Regulation and Compliance, International Journal of Finance & Banking Studies, International Journal of Research in Business and Social Science, Journal of Money, Investment and Banking and others.

Pelin Şahin Yarbağ is an assistant professor of entreprenuership at Beykent University, Faculty of Economics and Administrative Sciences, Istanbul- Turkey. Dr. Yarbağ has BAs in Business Administration at Beykent University (2001). She received PhD in International Economics with her thesis entitled as "After the 2008 Global Crisis, The Comparative Efficiency Analysis of Banks in Turkey, European Union and United States". Her major academic studies focusing on entrepreneurship, international economics, strategic management, efficiency analysis and emotional intelligence.

Tekin Yenigün was born in Agrı/Turkey. He completed undergraduate degree from Afyon Kocatepe University, Faculty of Economics and Administrative Sciences, Public Finance. He completed master's degree (MA) in business and he holds a Ph.D in Accounting and Finance from Afyon Kocatepe University. His main research fields focus on Accounting, Finance, Accounting Management and Control, Taxation and Business discipline. He works as the General Secretary at Namik Kemal University.

Filiz Yıldırım is an assistant professor at Ankara University (Turkey), Faculty of Health Sciences, Department of Social Work. She received her master's and doctorate degrees from the Department of Family and Consumer Sciences. She was awarded a "Doctorate Research Scholarship" from TUBITAK to carry out a part of her doctorate research at the Department of Sociology, Criminology & Law at the University of Florida, the USA in 2011. She received the "International Young Scholar Award" from the Society for Research on Adolescence in Canada in 2012. She worked as a "Visiting Research Associate" at London University, Institute of Education, Department of Childhood, Families & Health in 2014. Her main research interests include aging & youth sociology, love, early (child) marriage, social justice and health literacy. She is also a post-doctoral fellow at Hacettepe University (Turkey), Department of Sociology.

Binhan Elif Yılmaz, received her MS degree in Theory of Public Finance from Istanbul University Social Sciences Institute at 1994. She received her Phd degree on Public Finance at 2001, from the same institute. She was selected as a research assistant for Public Finance Department of Faculty of Economy in Istanbul University when she was a MS student. She became an associate professor at 2008 and professor at 2014 in Public Finance. The areas which are she is interested in and tutoring are Public Debts, Public Economy and Fiscal Sociology. She is the author of two books which are named as, *The Debt Predicament from Ottomans to Our Today* (2008) and *The Transformation of Global Crisis into the Debt Predicament in Europe* (2013). Beside the several administrative duties, she is the vice president of the Department of Public Finance.

Neslihan Yilmaz earned her PhD degree from Michigan State University and is an Assistant Professor of Finance at the Department of Management at Bogazici University. Neslihan Yilmaz's research mainly focuses on behavioral finance. She presented her work on CEO overconfidence and investor behavioral biases in different conferences including the Financial Management Association Annual Meeting, 2013 and Fifth Annual Meeting of the Academy of Behavioral Finance and Economics. She also has a paper on market microstructure focusing on price discovery between New York Stock Exchange and Istanbul Stock Exchange. She serves as ad-hoc referee for Journal of International Financial Markets, Institutions & Money, Boğaziçi Journal, Review of Social, Economic and Administrative Studies and Istanbul Stock Exchange Review.

Nurul Farhana Zakaria is a Research Assistant at the Department of Resource Management and Consumer Studies, Faculty of Human Ecology, University Putra Malaysia. She was graduated with Master of Science (Family Economics and Management) from University Putra Malaysia. She has presented papers at national level and actively participated in conducting research funded by Fundamental Research Grant Scheme from Ministry of Higher Education and Ministry of Domestic Trade, Co-operative and Consumerism, Malaysia.

Index

G

H

I

K

L

M

N

O

P

Q

R

S

T

V

W

www.ingramcontent.com/pod-product-compliance
Lightning Source LLC
LaVergne TN
LVHW080620300926
849162LV00005B/1218
* 9 7 8 1 4 6 6 6 7 4 8 4 4 *